23 PRACTICE SETS *for*
IBPS RRB
OFFICER SCALE 1
PRELIMINARY & MAINS EXAM
with 4 ONLINE TESTS

- **Corporate Office :** 45, 2nd Floor, Maharishi Dayanand Marg, Corner Market,
  Malviya Nagar, New Delhi-110017
  Tel. : 011-49842349 / 49842350

Typeset by Disha DTP Team

Compiled and Edited by Disha Expert Term

Get free access to Online Test(s)?
INSTRUCTIONS

1. You can access your test on any Window based Desktop, android tablets or ipads and mobile phones absolutely free.

2. Visit the link below or scan the QR code:

4 Mock Tests - 2 Prelims & 2 Mains

http://bit.ly/os-prelim　　**http://bit.ly/os-main**

3. Click on **"Attempt Free Mock Tests"**, a Registration window pops up, enter all the details in the form & click "Sign UP".

4. User is now logged in the account & all the Mock Tests appears in the grid. User can attempt the Free Mock Test(s) by clicking the **"Start"** button.

5. Contact us at support@mylearninggraph.com for any support.

DISHA PUBLICATION
ALL RIGHTS RESERVED

For further information about the books from DISHA,

Log on to **www.dishapublication.com** or email to **info@dishapublication.com**

CONTENTS

4 (2 FOR MAINS & 2 FOR PRELIMS) ONLINE PRACTICE SETS WITH SOLUTIONS

PRACTICE SET 1

Time : 45 Min. **Max. Marks : 80**

QUANTITATIVE APTITUDE

DIRECTIONS (Qs. 1-5): Find out the approximate value which should come in place of the question mark in the following questions. (You are not expected to find the exact value.)

1. $13379.75 \div 9.75 + (45.95 \times \sqrt{398.95}) = ?$
   - (a) 2580
   - (b) 2260
   - (c) 2600
   - (d) 2570
   - (e) 2250

2. $\dfrac{(10008.99)^2}{10009.001} \times \sqrt{3589} \times 0.4987 = ?$
   - (a) 3000
   - (b) 300000
   - (c) 3000000
   - (d) 5000
   - (e) 9000000

3. $399.9 + 206 \times 11.009 = ?$
   - (a) 2800
   - (b) 6666
   - (c) 4666
   - (d) 2400
   - (e) 2670

4. $\dfrac{2}{5} + \dfrac{7}{8} \times \dfrac{17}{19} \div \dfrac{6}{5} = ?$
   - (a) 1
   - (b) $\dfrac{1}{2}$
   - (c) $2\dfrac{1}{2}$
   - (d) $\dfrac{3}{4}$
   - (e) $\dfrac{9}{11}$

5. $\sqrt{330} + \sqrt{8200} + 125.25 - 1264.95 = ?$
   - (a) -1560
   - (b) -1030
   - (c) 1030
   - (d) -1254
   - (e) -1155

DIRECTIONS (Qs. 6-10) : Study the following table carefully and answer the given questions. Data related to number of candidates appeared and qualified in a competitive exam from two states during five years.

Years	State-A		State-B	
	Number of appeared candidates	Percentage of appeared candidates who qualified	Number of appeared candidates	Percentage of appeared candidates who qualified
2013	900	60%	-	30%
2014	1200	43%	-	45%
2015	-	60%	560	60%
2016	960	70%	1100	50%
2017	760	-	800	-

Note : Few value are missing in the table (indicated by A candidate is expected to calculate the missing value, if it is required to answer the given questions on the basis of given data and information.)

6. Out of the number of qualified candidates from state A in 2015, the respective ratio of male and female candidates is 11 : 7. If the number of female qualified candidates from state A is 252, then what is the number of appeared candidates (both male and female) from state A in 2015 ?
   - (a) 930
   - (b) 1010
   - (c) 1570
   - (d) 1690
   - (e) 1080

7. The number of appeared candidates from state B is increased by 100% from 2013 to 2014. If the total number of qualified candidates from state B in 2013 and 2014 together is 816, then what is number of appeared candidates from state B in 2013?

   (a) 780   (b) 560

   (c) 680   (d) 640

   (e) 800

8. What is the difference between the number of qualified candidates from state A in 2013 and 2014 ?

   (a) 24   (b) 22

   (c) 34   (d) 28

   (e) 36

9. If the average number of qualified candidates from state B in 2015, 2016 and 2017 is 420, then what is the number of qualified candidates from state B in 2017?

   (a) 384   (b) 395

   (c) 483   (d) 374

   (e) 479

10. If the respective ratio between the number of qualified candidates from state A in 2016 and 2017 is 14 : 9, then what is the number of qualified candidates from state A in 2017?

   (a) 352   (b) 407

   (c) 432   (d) 534

   (e) 598

DIRECTIONS (Qs. 11-15) : Identify which number is wrong in the given series.

11. 2, 3, 4, 4, 6, 8, 9, 12, 16.

   (a) 3   (b) 9

   (c) 6   (d) 12

   (e) None of these

12. 3, 4, 10, 32, 136, 685, 4116

   (a) 136   (b) 10

   (c) 4116   (d) 32

   (e) None of these

13. 69, 55, 26, 13, 5

   (a) 26   (b) 13

   (c) 5   (d) 55

   (e) None of these

14. 24576, 6144, 1536, 386, 96, 24

   (a) 386   (b) 6144

   (c) 96   (d) 1536

   (e) None of these

15. 11, 5, 20, 12, 40, 26, 74, 54

   (a) 5   (b) 20

   (c) 40   (d) 26

   (e) None of these

DIRECTIONS (Qs. 16-20) : Study the following chart to answer the questions given below.

Villages	% population below poverty line
A	45
B	52
C	38
D	58
E	46
F	49
G	51

Proportion of population of seven villages in 2014

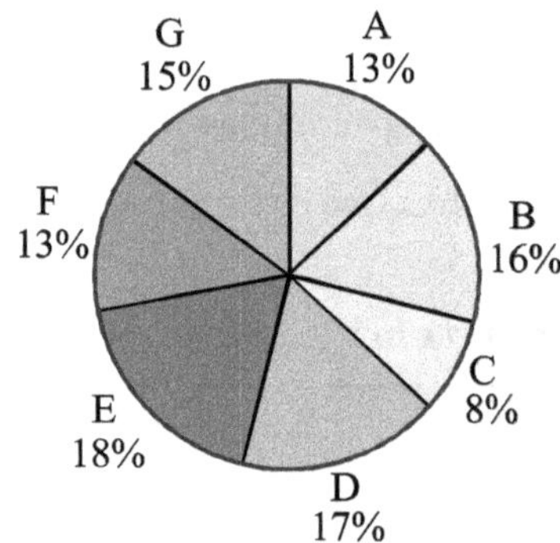

16. In 2015, the population of villages A as well as B is increased by 10% from the year 2014. If the population of village A in 2014 was 5000 and the percentage of population below poverty line in 2015 remains same as in 2014, find approximately the population of village B below poverty line in 2015.

   (a) 4000   (b) 45000

   (c) 2500   (d) 3500

   (e) None of these

17. If in 2016 the population of village D is increased by 10% and the population of village G is reduced by 5% from 2014 and the population of village G in 2014 was 9000, what is the total population of villages D and G in 2016?

   (a) 19770   (b) 19200

   (c) 18770   (d) 19870

   (e) None of these

18. If in 2014 the total population of the seven villages together was 55,000 approximately, what will be population of village F in that year below poverty line ?

   (a) 3000   (b) 2500

   (c) 4000   (d) 3500

   (e) None of these

19. If the population of village C below poverty line in 2014 was 1520, what was the population of village F in 2014?

   (a) 4000   (b) 6000

   (c) 6500   (d) 4800

   (e) None of these

20. The population of village C is 2000 in 2014. What will be the ratio of population of village C below poverty line to that of the village E below poverty line in that year ?

   (a) 207 : 76   (b) 76 : 207

   (c) 152 : 207   (d) Data inadequate

   (e) None of these

DIRECTIONS (Qs. 21-25): These questions are based on the table and information given below.

There are 6 refineries, 7 depots and 9 districts. The refineries are BB, BC, BD, BE, BF and BG. The depots are AA, AB, AC, AD, AE, AF and AG. The districts are AAA, AAB, AAC, AAD, AAE, AAF, AAG, AAH ad AAI. Table A gives the cost of transporting one unit from refinery to depot. Table B gives the cost of transporting one unit from depot to a district.

Table A

	BB	BC	BD	BE	BF	BG
AA	928.2	537.2	567.8	589.9	589.9	800.1
AB	311.1	596.7	885.7	759.9	759.9	793.9
AC	451.1	0	320.1	780.1	720.7	1000
AD	371.1	150.1	350.1	750.1	650.4	980.1
AE	1137.3	314.5	0	1158	1158	1023
AF	617.1	516.8	756.5	1066	1066	406.3
AG	644.3	299.2	537.2	1093	1093	623.9

Table B

	AA	AB	AC	AD	AE	AF	AG
AAA	562.7	843.2	314.5	889.1	0	754.8	537.2
AAB	532.7	803.2	284.5	790.5	95.2	659.6	442
AAC	500.7	780.2	0	457.3	205.7	549.1	331.5
AAD	232.9	362.1	286.2	275.4	523.6	525.3	673.2
AAE	345.1	268.6	316.2	163.2	555.9	413.1	227.8
AAF	450.1	644.3	346.2	372.3	933.3	402.9	379.1
AAG	654.5	0	596.7	222.7	885.7	387.6	348.5
AAH	804.1	149.6	627.2	360.4	1035.3	537.2	498.1
AAI	646	255	433.5	137.7	698.7	112.2	161.5

21. What is the least cost of sending one unit from any refinery to any district?
(a) 95.2
(b) 0
(c) 205.7
(d) 284.5
(e) None of these

22. What is the least cost of sending one unit from any refinery to the district AAB?
(a) 0
(b) 284.5
(c) 95.2
(d) 294.8
(e) None of these

23. What is the least cost of sending one unit from refinery BB to any district?
(a) 284.5
(b) 311.1
(c) 451.1
(d) 297.5
(e) None of these

24. What is the least cost of sending petrol from refinery BB to district AAA?
(a) 765.6
(b) 1137.3
(c) 1154.3
(d) 1174.8
(e) None of these

25. How many possible ways are there for sending petrol from any refinery to any district?
(a) 63
(b) 42
(c) 54
(d) 378
(e) None of these

DIRECTIONS (Qs. 26-30) : In the following questions, two equations I and II are given. You have to solve both the equations and give answer.

Give answer (a) if $x > y$
Give answer (b) if $x \geq y$
Give answer (c) if $x < y$
Give answer (d) if $x \leq y$
Give answer (e) if $x = y$ or the relationship cannot be established

26. I. $\sqrt{289x} + \sqrt{25} = 0$

    II. $\sqrt{676y} + 10 = 0$

27. I. $8x^2 - 78x + 169 = 0$

    II. $20y^2 - 117y + 169 = 0$

28. I. $\dfrac{15}{\sqrt{x}} + \dfrac{9}{\sqrt{x}} = 11\sqrt{x}$

    II. $\dfrac{\sqrt{y}}{4} + \dfrac{5\sqrt{y}}{12} = \dfrac{1}{\sqrt{y}}$

29. I. $\dfrac{8}{\sqrt{x}} + \dfrac{6}{\sqrt{x}} = \sqrt{x}$

    II. $y^3 - \dfrac{(14)^2}{\sqrt{y}} = 0$

30. I. $x^2 + 208 = 233$

    II. $y^2 - 47 + 371 = 0$

31. Neeraj's age is 1/5 of his father's age. Neeraj's father's age will be twice Vinod's age after 10 years. If Vinod's eighth birthday was celebrated two years ago, then what is Neeraj's present age ?
(a) 14 years
(b) 6 years
(c) 30 years
(d) 10 years
(e) None of these

32. Mrs. X spends ₹ 535 in purchasing some shirts and ties for her husband. If shirts cost ₹ 43 each and the ties cost ₹ 21 each, then what is the ratio of the shirts to the ties, that are purchased ?
(a) 1 : 2
(b) 2 : 1
(c) 2 : 3
(d) 3 : 4
(e) None of these

33. The percentage marks obtained by Suman in History and Maths is 60. If she got 180 marks out of 250 in Maths, then out of 200 the marks obtained by Suman in History is
(a) 140
(b) 120
(c) 50
(d) 90
(e) None of these

34. $\dfrac{2}{5}$ th of Anil's salary is equal to Bhuvan's salary and seven-ninth of Bhuvan's salary is equal to Chandra's salary. If the sum of the salary of all of them is ₹ 77,000, then, how much is Bhuvan's salary?
(a) ₹ 45,000
(b) ₹ 18,000
(c) ₹ 15,000
(d) ₹ 28,000
(e) None of these

35. A tap can fill an empty tank in 12 hours and a leakage can empty the whole tank in 20 hours. If the tap and the leakage are working simultaneously, how long will it take to fill the whole tank?

(a) 25 hours   (b) 40 hours

(c) 30 hours   (d) 35 hours

(e) None of these

36. A train is moving at a speed of 132 km/h. If the length of the train is 110 metres, how long will it take to cross a railway platform, 165 metres long ?

(a) 5 s   (b) 7.5 s

(c) 10 s   (d) 15 s

(e) None of these

37. If 15 women or 10 men can complete a project in 55 days, in how many days will 5 women and 4 men working together complete the same project ?

(a) 75   (b) 8

(c) 9   (d) 85

(e) None of these

38. Ashu's mother was three times as old as Ashu, 5 years ago. After 5 years, she will be twice as old as Ashu. How old is Ashu at present?

(a) 15   (b) 20

(c) 10   (d) 5

(e) None of these

39. A conical flask has base radius 'a' cm and height 'h' cm. It is completely filled with milk. The milk is poured into a cylindrical thermos flask whose base radius is 'p' cm. What will be the height of the solution level in the flask ?

(a) $\dfrac{a^2h}{3p^2}$ cm   (b) $\dfrac{3hp^2}{a^2}$ cm   (c) $\dfrac{p^2}{3h^2}$ cm   (d) $\dfrac{3a^2}{hp^2}$ cm

(e) None of these

40. A sum was put at simple interest at a certain rate for 2 years. Had it been put at 3% higher rate, it would have fetched ₹ 300 more. Find the sum.

(a) ₹ 6000   (b) ₹ 8230

(c) ₹ 5000   (d) ₹ 4600

(e) None of these

REASONING

DIRECTIONS (Q. 41-45): Study the following information to answer the given questions.

Eight friends L, M, N, O, P, Q, R and S are sitting around a circle facing the centre. There are equal number of males and females in the group. No two females are immediate neighbours of each other. N is a male and N sits third to the right of R. O is a female and O is not an immediate neighbor of N. P sits second to the left of O. S sits fourth to the right of L and S is not an immediate neighbour of R. Q is a female.

41. What is Q's position with respect to O?

(a) Immediate right   (b) Third to the right

(c) Third to the left   (d) Fourth to the left

(e) Fifth to the right

42. Four of the following five are a like in a certain way based on their seating positions in the above arrangement and so form a group. Which is the one that **does not** belong to the group?

(a) LO   (b) NL

(c) OP   (d) PQ

(e) MS

43. If all the eight friends are made to sit alphabetically in the clockwise direction starting from L, positions of how many will remain unchanged (excluding L)?

(a) None   (b) One

(c) Two   (d) Three

(e) Four

44. Which of the following is true about M ?

(a) M sits third to the right of Q.

(b) M sits second to the right of L.

(c) M is a male.

(d) M sits on the immediate left of O.

(e) None of these

45. Which of the following groups represents the females in the group?

(a) O, P, Q, S   (b) Q, R, P, O

(c) Q, L, M, O   (d) O, M, Q, R

(e) None of these

DIRECTIONS (Q. 46-48): Study the following information to answer the given questions.

In a certain code, 'weapons hidden in town' is written as 'white black yellow red', 'ready weapons for attack' is written as 'grey indigo red green', 'hidden for own safety' is written as 'silver grey violet white' and 'own town under attack' is written as 'violet blue indigo black'.

46. What is the code for 'ready'?

(a) red   (b) indigo

(c) green   (d) grey

(e) Cannot be determined

47. What does 'silver' stand for?

(a) safety   (b) own

(c) hidden   (d) for

(e) Either 'own' or 'for'

48. 'black pink yellow' could be a code for which of the following?

(a) town under attack

(b) hidden for safety

(c) attack in town

(d) my own town

(e) risk in town

DIRECTIONS (Qs. 49-50): Read the following information carefully and answer the questions which follow.

Sudha weighs more than Bharat and Abhishek.

Rahul weighs less than only Karan.

Parul weighs as much as Sudha but less than Dana.

Abhishek does not weigh the minimum.

49. Who among the following is the third heaviest?

   (a) Karan   (b) Rahul

   (c) Bharat   (d) Dana

   (e) Cannot be determined

50. Which of the following is true?

   (a) Only four people are heavier than Rahul.

   (b) Bharat weighs more than Parul.

   (c) No one weighs less than Bharat.

   (d) Only two people are heavier than Karan.

   (e) All are true

DIRECTIONS (Qs. 51-55): Study the following information to answer the given questions.

In a certain code 'support the other group' is written as 'ja pe la no' 'the mission gains support' is written as' ke ja zi la', 'gains other than money' is written as 'fu no ho zi' and 'more support and money' is written as ' re qi fu ja'.

51. What is the code for 'group' ?

   (a) ja   (b) pe

   (c) la   (d) no

   (e) Cannot be determined

52. What does 'zi' stand for ?

   (a) mission   (b) than

   (c) other   (d) the

   (e) gains

53. Which of the following may represent 'more than the group'?

   (a) la qi ho pe   (b) re la qi ho

   (c) re no la pe   (d) pe ke qi la

   (e) qi ho la fu

54. What is the code for 'mission'?

   (a) la   (b) zi

   (c) ke   (d) ja

   (e) ke or la

55. Which of the following may represent 'money matters more'?

   (a) fu bu re   (b) re bu qi

   (c) zi qi yo   (d) yo fu no

   (e) la fu bu

DIRECTIONS (Qs. 56-60): In each question below are three statements followed by three conclusions numbered I, II and III. You have to take the three given statements to be true even if they seem to be at variance from commonly known facts and then decide which of the answers (a), (b), (c), (d) and (e) is the correct answer and indicate it on the answer sheet.

56. **Statements:**   Some chairs are tables.

                  Some tables are drawers.

                  All drawers are shelves.

Conclusions: **I.** Some shelves are tables.

                  II. Some drawers are chairs.

                  III. Some shelves are drawers.

   (a) Only I and III follow

   (b) Only I and either II or III follow

   (c) Only II and either I or III follow

   (d) All I, II and III follow

   (e) None of the above

57. **Statements:**   All trees are flowers.

                  Some flowers are leaves.

                  No leaf is bud.

Conclusions: **I.** No bud is a flower.

                  II. Some buds are flowers.

                  III. Some leaves are trees.

   (a) Only II and III follow

   (b) Only III follows

   (c) Only either I or II follows

   (d) Either I or II and III follow

   (e) None of the above

58. **Statements:**   All stones are rocks.

                  Some rocks are bricks.

                  Some bricks are cement.

Conclusions: **I.** Some cements are rocks.

                  II. Some bricks are stone

                  III. Some stones are cement.

   (a) Only I and either II or III follow

   (b) Only either II or III follows

   (c) Only I and II follow

   (d) All follow

   (e) None of the above

59. **Statements:**   All teachers are lawyers.

                  No doctor is a teacher.

                  No engineer is a lawyer.

Conclusions: **I.** No teacher is a engineer.

                  II. No teacher is a doctor.

                  III. At least some lawyers are not doctors.

   (a) Only II and III follow

   (b) Only III doesn't follow

   (c) All I, II and III follow

   (d) None follows

   (e) None of these

60. **Statements:**   Some dogs are cats.

                  No rat is a dog.

                  All cats are bats.

Conclusions: **I.** At least some dogs are definitely bats.

                  II. At least some cats are not rats.

                  III. No bat is a cat.

   (a) Only I doesn't follows

   (b) Only III doesn't follows

   (c) Only I and II follow

   (d) None follows

   (e) both (b) and (c)

DIRECTIONS (Qs. 61-65): Study the following information and answer the questions given below it.

Seven people—A, B, C, D, E, F and G are sitting in a circle. Five of them are facing the centre while two of them are facing opposite to the centre. C sits third to the left of D and both are facing the centre. E is neither on immediate neighbour of D nor of C. The one sitting exactly between D and F is facing opposite to centre. G sits third to the right of A and G is facing the centre. One of B's neighbour is facing opposite to the centre.

61. Which of the following pairs represents persons facing opposite to the centre?

(a) A and F
(b) E and F
(c) A and E
(d) Cannot be determined
(e) None of these

62. Who is sitting second to the left of A?

(a) C
(b) G
(c) E
(d) B
(e) None of these

63. Who is sitting to the immediate left of E?

(a) C
(b) G
(c) B
(d) A
(e) None of these

64. What is the position of F with respect to B?

(a) Fourth to the left
(b) Second to the right
(c) Third to the right
(d) Second to the left
(e) None of these

65. If all the persons are asked to sit in a clockwise direction in an alphabetical order starting from A, the position of how many will remain unchanged, excluding A?

(a) Three
(b) One
(c) Two
(d) None
(e) Four

DIRECTIONS (Qs. 66-70): In the questions given below, certain symbols are used with the following meanings.

A @ B means A is greater than B.

A * B means A is either greater than or equal to B.

A # B means A is equal to B.

A $ B means A is either smaller than or equal to B.

A + B means A is smaller than B.

Now in each of the following questions, assuming the given statements to be true, find which of the two conclusions I and II given below them is/are definitely true?

(a) If only conclusion I is true
(b) If only conclusion II is true
(c) If either conclusion I or II is true
(d) If neither conclusion I nor II is true
(e) If both conclusions I and II are true

66. Statements : B + D; E$T; T * P; P@B

Conclusions : I. P$D
II. P@D

67. Statements : E*F; G$H; H#E; G@K

Conclusions : I. H@K
II. H*F

68. Statements : P$Q; N#M; M@R; R*P

Conclusions : I. P+N
II. Q$M

69. Statements : D+T; E $V; F *T; E@D

Conclusions : I. D$V
II. D+F

70. Statements : T*U; U$W; V @L; W+V

Conclusions : I. V@T
II. L#W

DIRECTIONS (Qs. 71-75) : In each question below, is given a group of letters followed by found combinations of digits/symbols numbered (a), (b), (c) and (d). You have to find out which of the four combinations correctly represents combination as your answer. If none of the combinations correctly represents the group of letters, mark (e) 'None of these', as your answer.

Letter	R	E	A	U	M	D	F	P	Q	I	O	H	N	W	Z	B
Digit/Symbol code	7	#	$	6	%	8	5	★	4	9	@	©	3	D	1	2

(i) If the first letter is a consonant and the third letter is a vowel, their codes are to be interchanged.

(ii) If the first letter is a vowel and the fourth letter is a consonant, both are to be coded as the code for the vowel.

(iii) If the second and the third letters are consonants, both are to be coded as the code for the third letter.

71. NABAQE

(a) 263$4#
(b) 326$4#
(c) 362$4#
(d) 362$3#
(e) None of these

72. FWZERA

(a) 5D #7$
(b) 5DD #7$
(c) D17#$
(d) 511#7$
(e) None of these

73. HUBDIN

(a) © 62893
(b) © 2689%
(c) © 6289 ©
(d) © 62 © 9%
(e) None of these

74. EMIRDP

(a) #%978★
(b) #%9#8★
(c) 7%9#8★
(d) #9%78★
(e) None of these

75. OREDHM

(a) @7#8©%
(b) #7#8©%
(c) @78# ©%
(d) @7#@©%
(e) None of these

DIRECTIONS (Qs. 76-80) : Study the following information carefully and answer the given quesions following it.

(i)   Eleven students A, B, C, D, E, F, G, H, I, J and K are sitting in the first row of a class facing the teacher.

(ii)   D, who is on the immediate left of F, is second to the right of C.

(iii)   A is second to the right of E, who is at one of the ends.

(iv)   J is the immediate neighbour of A and B and third to the left of G.

(v)   H is on the immediate left of D and third to the right of I.

76. Who is sitting midway between E and H?

(a)   J   (b)   B

(c)   I   (d)   G

(e)   None of these

77. Which of the following statements is not ture in the context of the above sitting arrangement?

(a)   There are seven students sitting between K and D

(b)   G is the immediate neighbour of I and C

(c)   H is the immediate neighbour of D and F

(d)   K is between E and A

(e)   F is third to the right of C

78. To obtain the respective seats of all the persons which statement given above is not required?

(a)   I   (b)   II

(c)   III   (d)   IV

(e)   None of these

79. Besides 'E', who among the following is at the extreme end?

(a)   K   (b)   F

(c)   B   (d)   Can't say

(e)   None of these

80. Which of the following groups is at the left of I?

(a)   AJB   (b)   GCH

(c)   HDF   (d)   CHD

(e)   None of these

HINTS & EXPLANATIONS

1. (b) $13379.75 \div 9.75 + (45.95 \times \sqrt{398.95}) = ?$
   $\Rightarrow 1338 + (46 \times 20) = 2258$

2. (b) $? = \dfrac{(10008.99)^2}{10009.001} \times \sqrt{3589} \times 0.4987$

   $= \dfrac{(10009)^2 \times \sqrt{3600}}{10009} \times 0.50 = 10009 \times 60 \times 0.50 \approx 300000$

3. (e) $? = 399.9 + 206 \times 11.009$
   $= 400 + (200 + 6) \times 11 = 400 + 2200 + 66 \approx 2670$

4. (a) $? = \dfrac{2}{5} + \dfrac{7}{8} \times \dfrac{17}{19} \div \dfrac{6}{5} = \dfrac{2}{5} + \dfrac{7}{8} \times \dfrac{17}{19} \times \dfrac{5}{6}$

   $= \dfrac{2}{5} + \dfrac{595}{912} = 0.40 + 0.65 \approx 1.05 \approx 1$

5. (b) $\sqrt{330} + \sqrt{8200} + 125.25 - 1264.95 = ?$
   $\Rightarrow 18 + 90 + 125 - 1265$
   $\Rightarrow -1032$

6. (e) Required number of appeared candidates who qualified from state A in 2015
   $= (252/7) \times (11+7) = 648$
   So Total number of appeared candidate from state A in 2015
   $= (648/60 \times 100) = 1080$

7. (c) Let the number of appeared candidate from state B in $2013 = 100$
   So number of appeared candidate in 2014 from state B in $2014 = 200$
   So Required number of appeared candidate from B in 2013
   $= 816/(30+90) \times 100 = 680$

8. (a) Required difference
   $= 900 \times 60/100 - 1200 \times 43/100$
   $= 540 - 516 = 24$

9. (d) Required number of qualified candidate from state B in
   $2017 = (3 \times 420) - (560 \times 60/100 + 1100 \times 50/100)$
   $= 1260 - (336 + 550)$
   $= 1260 - 886$
   $= 374$

10. (c) Number of qualified candidate from state P in
    $2016 = 960 \times 70/100 = 672$
    So Required number of qualified candidate from state A in 2017
    $= 672/14 \times 9 = 432$

11. (b)
    $$\begin{array}{cccccccc} 2 & 3 & 4 & 4 & 6 & 8 & \boxed{8} & 12 \ 16 \end{array}$$
    $\times 2 \quad \times 2 \quad \times 2 \quad \times 2 \quad \times 2 \quad \times 2$

12. (d)
    $$3 \quad 4 \quad 10 \quad \boxed{33} \quad 136 \quad 685 \quad 4116$$
    $\times 1 + 1 \quad \times 2 + 2 \quad \times 3 + 3 \quad \times 4 + 4 \quad \times 5 + 5 \quad \times 6 \times 6$
    Thus, 32 is out of place and must be replaced by 33.

13. (c)
    $$69 \quad 55 \quad 26 \quad 13 \quad \boxed{4}$$
    $6 \times 9 + 1 \quad 5 \times 5 + 1 \quad 2 \times 6 + 1 \quad 1 \times 3 + 1$
    Thus, 5 does not fit in the series and should be replaced by 4.

14. (a) The succeeding numbers are obtained by dividing the preceding numbers by 4. Therefore, the number 386 does not fit in the series and must be replaced by 384.

15. (c) There are two series in the given series :
    I. $\quad 5 \quad 12 \quad 26 \quad 54$
    $\quad \times 2 + 2 \quad \times 2 + 2 \quad \times 2 + 2$
    II. $\quad 11 \quad 20 \quad \boxed{40} \quad 74$
    $\quad \times 2 - 2 \quad \times 2 - 2 \quad \times 2 - 2$
    Hence the wrong term is 40.

16. (d) Population of village B in 2014 $= 5000 \times \dfrac{16}{13} \approx 6150$

    Population of village B in 2015 $= 6150 \times \dfrac{110}{100} \approx 6750$

    Population below poverty line $= 52\%$ of $6750 \approx 3500$

17. (a) Population of village D in 2014 $= 9{,}000 \times \dfrac{17}{15} = 10{,}200$

    Population of village D in 2016 $= 10{,}200 \times \dfrac{110}{100}$

    $\qquad\qquad = 11{,}220$

    Population of village G in 2016 $= 9{,}000 \times \dfrac{95}{100} = 8{,}550$

    $\therefore$ Total population of village D and G in 2016
    $= 11{,}220 + 8{,}550 = 19{,}770$

18. (d) Population of village F below poverty line

    $= 55000 \times \dfrac{13}{100} \times \dfrac{49}{100} \approx 3500$

19. (c) Population of village F in 2014

    $= 1520 \times \dfrac{100}{38} \times \dfrac{13}{8} = 6500$

20. (b) Population of village C below poverty line

    $= 2000 \times \dfrac{38}{100} = 760$

Population of village E below poverty line

$$= \frac{2000}{8} \times 18 \times \left(\frac{46}{100}\right) = 2070$$

$\therefore$ Required ratio $= \dfrac{760}{2070} = 76 : 207$

21. (b) The least cost of sending one unit is 0 as it is obvious from table A & B that

$$BC \xrightarrow[\text{cost}=0]{} AC \xrightarrow[\text{cost}=0]{} AAC$$

or $BD \xrightarrow[\text{cost}=0]{} AE \xrightarrow[\text{cost}=0]{} AAA$

22. (c) From table A & table B

$BC \to AC$, Cost $= 0$ which is minimum &

$AC \to AAB$, Cost $= 284.5$

$BC \to AAB$, Cost $= 0 + 284.5 = 284.5$

Also we have

$BD \to AE$, Cost $= 0$ which is minimum

$AE \to AAB$, Cost $= 95.2$ which is least

$BD \to AAB$, Cost $= 0 + 95.2 = 95.2$

Hence least cost from any refinery to AAB $= 95.2$

23. (b) Cost from $BB \to AB = 311.1$ which is least

Cost from $AB \to AAG = 0$ which is also least

so least cost from $BB \to AAG = 311.1 + 0 = 311.1$

24. (a) Least cost from BB to AAA would be on the route BB $\to AC \to AAA = 451.1 + 314.5 = 765.6$

25. (d) There are 6 refineries, 7 depot, 9 districts. So total ways from refinery to district $= 6 \times 7 \times 9 = 378$

26. (c) I. $\sqrt{289x} + \sqrt{25} = 0$

or, $\sqrt{289x} = -\sqrt{25}$

Squaring both sides, we get

$289x = 25$

$x = \dfrac{25}{289}$

II. $\sqrt{676y} + 10 = 0$

or, $\sqrt{676y} = -10$

Squaring both sides, we get

$676y = 100$

$y = \dfrac{100}{676}$ $\therefore$ $y > x$

27. (b) I. $8x^2 - 78x + 169 = 0$

$8x^2 - 52x - 26x + 169 = 0$

$4x(2x - 13) - 13(2x - 13) = 0$

$(2x - 13)(4x - 13) = 0$

$\therefore$ $x = \dfrac{13}{2}$ or $\dfrac{13}{4} = 6.5$ or 3.25

II. $20y^2 - 117y + 169 = 0$

$\Rightarrow 20y^2 - 52y - 65y + 169 = 0$

$\Rightarrow 4y(5y - 13) - 13(5y - 13) = 0$

$\Rightarrow (5y - 13)(4y - 13) = 0$

$\therefore$ $y = \dfrac{13}{5}$ or $\dfrac{13}{4} = 2.6$ or 3.25 $\therefore$ $x \geq y$

28. (a) I. $\dfrac{15}{\sqrt{x}} + \dfrac{9}{\sqrt{x}} = 11\sqrt{x}$

$\dfrac{15 + 9}{\sqrt{x}} = 11\sqrt{x}$

$24 = 11x$

$\therefore$ $x = \dfrac{24}{11}$

$= 2.18$

II. $\dfrac{\sqrt{y}}{4} + \dfrac{5\sqrt{y}}{12} = \dfrac{1}{\sqrt{y}}$

$\dfrac{3\sqrt{y} + 5\sqrt{y}}{12} = \dfrac{1}{\sqrt{y}}$

or, $8y = 12$

$y = 1.5 \therefore$ $x > y$

29. (a) I. $\dfrac{8}{\sqrt{x}} + \dfrac{6}{\sqrt{x}} = \sqrt{x}$

$\dfrac{14}{\sqrt{x}} = \sqrt{x}$

$x = 14$

II. $y^3 - \dfrac{(14)^2}{\sqrt{y}} = 0$

or, $y^3 = \dfrac{(14)^2}{\sqrt{y}}$

$y^{3 + \frac{1}{2}} = (14)^2$

$y^{7/2} = (14)^2$ $\therefore$ $x > y$

30. (e) I. $x^2 + 208 = 233$

$x^2 = 233 - 208$

$x = \sqrt{25}$

$= \pm 5$

II. $y^2 - 47 + 371 = 0$

$y^2 + 324 = 0$

$y^2 = -324$

$y = \sqrt{-324}$

Relationship cannot be established.

31. (b) Vinod's present age $= 8 + 2 = 10$ years

$F + 10 = 2(V + 10)$

or, $F + 10 = 2(10 + 10) = 40$

or, $F = 30$;

So Neeraj's present age $= 1/5 \times 30 = 6$ years

32. (b) Mrs. X spends $= ₹ 535$

$\therefore$ Total cost $= 43$ shirt $+ 21$ ties $= 535$

By hit and trial, S $= 10$, T $= 5$

$\Rightarrow$ Total cost $= 43 \times 10 + 21 \times 5 = 535$

Hence, Ratio of shirts to ties $= 10 : 5 = 2 : 1$

33. (d) Total marks $= 250 + 200 = 450$

Sushma obtained $= 60\%$ of $450 = 270$

Therefore, she got $270 - 180 = 90$ marks in History.

34. (b) Let Anil's salary be ₹ x.

$\therefore$ Bhuvan's salary = ₹ $\dfrac{2x}{5}$

Chandra's salary = ₹ $\dfrac{2x}{5} \times \dfrac{7}{9} = \dfrac{14x}{45}$

$\therefore$ Anil : Bhuvan : Chandra = $x : \dfrac{2x}{5} : \dfrac{14x}{45} = 45 : 18 : 14$

$\therefore$ Bhuvan's salary

$= ₹ \left[\dfrac{18}{(45+18+14)} \times 77000 \right] = ₹\ 18000$

35. (c) Part of the tank filled in an hour

$= \dfrac{1}{12} - \dfrac{1}{20} = \dfrac{5-3}{60} = \dfrac{1}{30}$

Hence, the tank will be filled in 30 hours

36. (b) Speed of the train $= 132$ km/h $= \dfrac{132 \times 5}{18}$ m/s

Distance $= (110 + 165) = 275$ m

Time required to cross the railway platform

$= \dfrac{275 \times 18}{132 \times 5} = 7.5$ s

37. (a) $15\,W = 10\,M$

Now, $5W + 4M = 5W + \dfrac{4 \times 15}{10}\,W = 5W + 6W = 11\,W$

Now, 15 women can complete the project in 55 days, then 11 women can complete the same project in

$\dfrac{55 \times 15}{11} = 75$ days

38. (a) Let the present ages of Ashu's mother and that of Ashu be x and y, respectively.

Then, $(x-5) = 3(y-5)$ or $x - 5 = 3y - 15$

or $x - 3y = -10$ ...(i)

and $(x+5) = 2(y+5)$

And $x + 5 = 2y + 10$ or $x - 2y = 5$ ...(ii)

From (i) and (ii), we have $x = 35$ and $y = 15$

Hence, the present age of Ashu = 15 years

39. (a) Volume of the conical flask = Volume of the cylindrical flask upto the required height (x) cm

$\dfrac{1}{3}\pi a^2 h = \pi p^2 \times x \Rightarrow x = \dfrac{ha^2}{3p^2}$ cm

40. (c) Let the sum = Rs. x and original rate $= y$ % per annum then, New rate $= (y + 3)$% per annum

$\therefore \dfrac{x \times (y+3) \times 2}{100} - \dfrac{x \times y \times 2}{100} = 300$

$xy + 3x - xy = 15000$

$\therefore x = 5000$ Thus, the sum = ₹ 5000

Solution (41-45) :

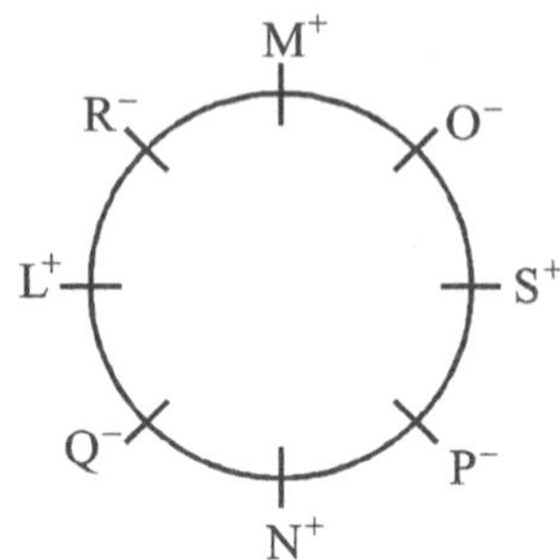

41. (d)   **42.** (a)   **43.** (b)   **44.** (c)   **45.** (b)

Solution (46-48):

weapons hidden in town → white black yellow red ... (a)
ready weapons for attack → grey indigo red green ... (b)
hidden for own safety → silver grey violet white ... (c)
own town under attack → violet blue indigo black ... (d)
Using (a) and (b), weapons → red
Using (a) and (c), hidden → white
Using the just found codes and equations,
(a) and (d), town → black   in → yellow
(b) and (d), attack → indigo
(c) and (d), own → violet
(b) and (c), for → grey
From (b), ready → green
From (c), safety → silver
From (d), under → blue

46. (c)

47. (a)

48. (e) 'black' and 'yellow' means 'town' and 'in' respectively. Pink is a new colour, so new word for 'pink' is 'risk'.

Solution (49-50):

The information can be reproduced as follows:

Karan > Rahul > Dana > Sudha = Parul > Abhishek > Bharat

49. (d)

50. (c)

(51-55) :

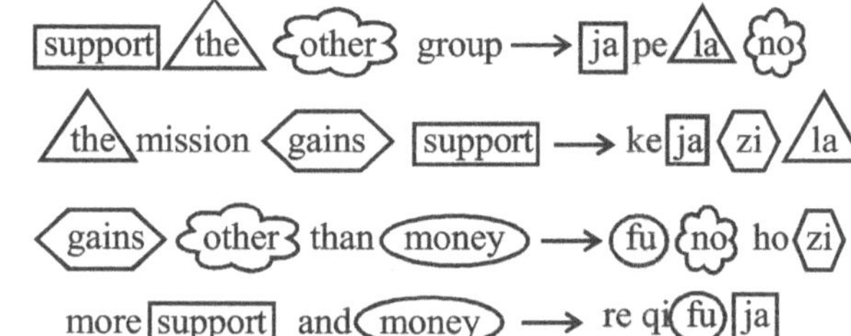

51. (b) The code for 'group' is 'pe'.

52. (e) 'zi' stands for 'gains'.

53. (a) more ⇒ re or qi
than ⇒ ho
the ⇒ la
group ⇒ pe

54. (c) The code for 'mission' is 'ke'.

55. (a) money ⇒ fu
more ⇒ re or qi
The code for 'matters' may be 'bu'.

56. (a)
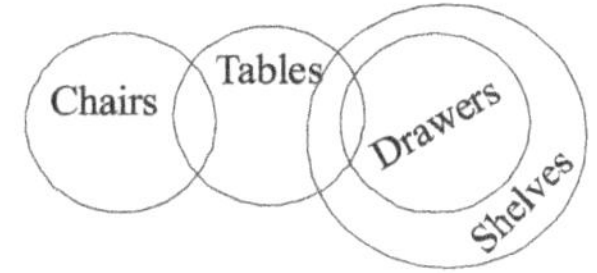

Hence, conclusions   I. ✓   II. ✗   III. ✓

57. (c)
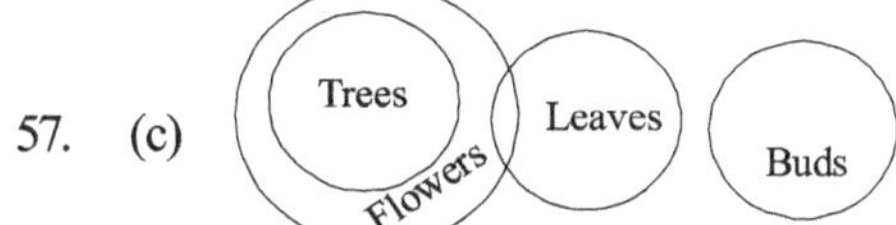

Hence, conclusions I. ✗ II. ✗ III. ✗

But I and II are complementary pairs.

58. (e)
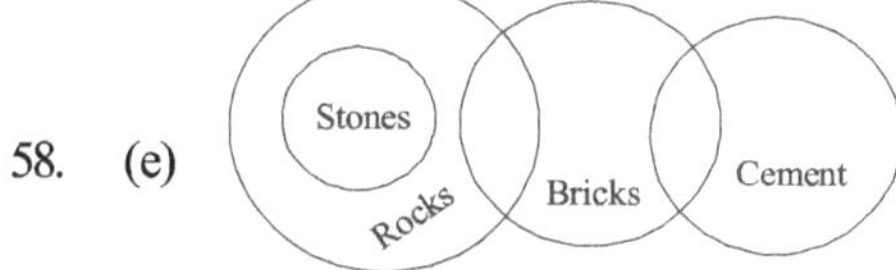

Hence, conclusions   I. ✗   II. ✗   III. ✗

59. (c)   All I, II and III follow.

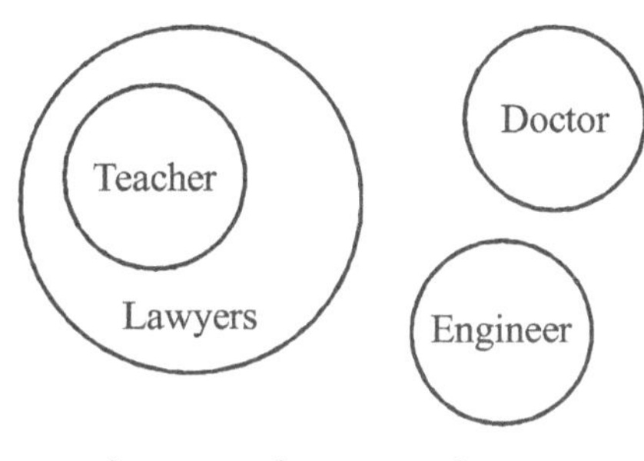

I. ✓   II. ✓   III. ✓

60. (e)   Both (b) and (c)

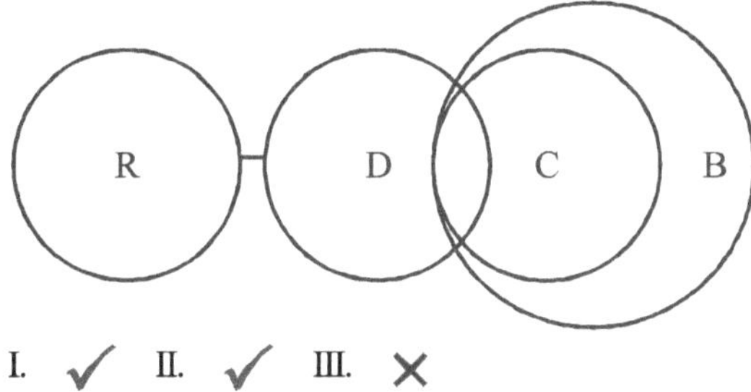

I. ✓   II. ✓   III. ✗

Solutions : (Qs. 61-65)

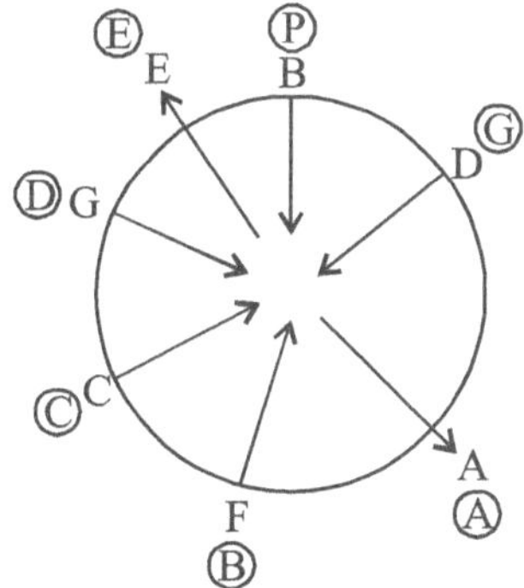

A and E is not facing centre. Rest of all facing centre.

61. (c)   A and E person facing opposite to centre.
62. (d)   B, because A is facing opposite to centre.
63. (b)   G, because E is facing opposite to centre.
64. (e)   It is either third to left or fourth to right.
65. (c)   Two (C and E) will remain unchanged.
66. (c) $B < D$ ...(i), $E \leq T$ ...(ii), $T \geq P$ ....(iii), $P > B$...(iv) From (i) and (iv), we get, $P > B < D \Rightarrow$ no conclusion. But the exhaustive possibilities are $P > D, P = D$ and $P < D$. Hence either I or II is true.
67. (e) $E \geq F$ ...(i), $G \leq H$ ...(ii), $H = E$ ...(iii), $G > K$ ...(iv) From (ii) and (iv), we get, $H \geq G > K \Rightarrow H > K$. Hence I is true.

From (i) and (iii), we get, $H = E \geq F \Rightarrow H \geq F$. Hence, II is true.
68. (a) $P \leq Q$ ...(i), $N = M$ ....(ii), $M > R$ ...(iii), $R \geq P$ ...(iv) From (ii), (iii) and (iv), we get, $N = M > R \geq P$

$\Rightarrow N > P$ or $P < N$. Hence I is true.

From (ii), (iv) and (i), we get, $M > R \geq P \leq Q \Rightarrow$ No conclusion about the relationship between M and Q can be established.
69. (b) $D < T$ ...(i), $E \leq V$ ...(ii), $F \geq T$ ... (iii), $E < D$ ...(iv)
Therefore, $V \geq E < D < T \leq F$
From conclusion I. $D \leq V$ ... (False)
From conclusion II. $D < F$ ... (True)
Hence, only conclusion II is true.
70. (d) $T \geq U$ ...(i), $U \leq W$ ...(ii), $V < L$ ...(iii), $W < V$ ...(iv)
Therefore, $T \geq U \leq W < V > L$
From conclusion I. $V > T$ ...(False)
From conclusion II. $L = W$ ... (False)
Hence, neither conclusion I nor II is true.
71. (e)   Here, none of the condition is applied, so the coding is done as follows

N   A   B   A   Q   E
↓   ↓   ↓   ↓   ↓   ↓
3   \$ 2   \$ 4   #

∴ Code for NABAQE ⟹ 3\$2\$4#
72. (d)   When no condition is applied, the coding is done as follows

F   W   Z   E   R   A
↓   ↓   ↓   ↓   ↓   ↓
5   D   1   #   7   \$

But here the second and third letters are consonants, therefore condition (iii) is applied here. As condition (iii) is applied here, both the seond and third letters are to be coded as the code for the third letter.

F   W   Z   E   R   A
↓   ↓   ↓   ↓   ↓   ↓
5   1   1   #   7   \$

∴ Code for FWZERA ⟹ 511#7\$

73. (a) Here, none of the condition is applied, so the coding is done as follows.

H U B D I N
↓ ↓ ↓ ↓ ↓ ↓
© 6 2 8 9 3

74. (b) When no condition is applied, the coding is done as follows.

E M I R D P
↓ ↓ ↓ ↓ ↓ ↓
% 9 7 8 ★

But here the first letter is a vowel and the fourth letter is a consonant, therefore condition (ii) is applied. As condition (ii) is applied here, both the first and the fourth letters are to be coded as the code for the vowel.

E M I R D P
↓ ↓ ↓ ↓ ↓ ↓
% 9 # 8 ★

∴ Code for EMIRDP ⇒ #%9#8 ★

75. (d) When no condition is applied, the coding is done as follows.

O R E D H M
↓ ↓ ↓ ↓ ↓ ↓
@ 7 # 8 © %

But here the first letter is a vowel and the fourth letter is a consonant, therefore condition (ii) is applied. As condition (ii) is applied here, both the first and fourth letters as to be coded as the code for the vowel.

O R E D H M
↓ ↓ ↓ ↓ ↓ ↓
@ 7 # @ © %

∴ Code for OREDHM ⇒ @7#@©%

(Qs. 76-80) : According to the given information, the sitting arrangement of eleven students in a row of a class facing the teacher is as following :

76. (b) There are seven person which are sitting between E and H. B is in the midway of them.

77. (c) H is not the immediate neighbour of D and F.

78. (e) To get the final arrangement, we require all the statements.

79. (b) F is at the extreme end.

80. (a) A, J and B are at the left of I.

PRACTICE SET 2

Time : 45 Min. **Max. Marks : 80**

QUANTITATIVE APTITUDE

DIRECTIONS (Qs. 1-5): What will come in place of question mark (?) in the following questions?

1. $\left[\left(5\sqrt{7}+\sqrt{7}\right)+\left(4\sqrt{7}+8\sqrt{7}\right)\right]-(19)^2 = ?$

   (a) 143   (b) $72\sqrt{7}$

   (c) 134   (d) $70\sqrt{7}$

   (e) None of these

2. $(4444 \div 40) + (645 \div 25) + (3991 \div 26) = ?$

   (a) 280.4   (b) 290.4

   (c) 295.4   (d) 285.4

   (e) None of these

3. $\sqrt{33124} \times \sqrt{2601} - (83)^2 = (?)^2 + (37)^2$

   (a) 37   (b) 33

   (c) 34   (d) 28

   (e) None of these

4. $5\dfrac{17}{37} \times 4\dfrac{51}{52} \times 11\dfrac{1}{7} + 2\dfrac{3}{4} = ?$

   (a) 303.75   (b) 305.75

   (c) $303\dfrac{3}{4}$ (d) $305\dfrac{1}{4}$

   (e) None of these

5. $(39260 + 27980 + 22050) + 96048 \div 48 = ?$

   (a) 91177   (b) 91291

   (c) 81324   (d) 71262

   (e) None of these

DIRECTIONS (Qs. 6-10) : Find out the wrong number in the following given series.

6. 9 5 8 10.5 23 60 183

   (a) 8   (b) 5

   (c) 23   (d) 10.5

   (e) 183

7. 14 21 48 105 315 1102.5 4410

   (a) 315   (b) 48

   (c) 21   (d) 4410

   (e) 105

8. 13 14 33 48 97 178 299

   (a) 48   (b) 33

   (c) 178   (d) 14

   (e) 299

9. 24 25 49 148 492 2956 17735

   (a) 25   (b) 49

   (c) 492   (d) 148

   (e) 2956

10. 12 26 56 118 276 498 1008

    (a) 26   (b) 56

    (c) 498   (d) 1008

    (e) 276

DIRECTIONS (Qs. 11-15) : In each of the following questions two equations are given. Solve these equations and give answer:

(a) if $x \geq y$, i.e., x is greater than or equal to y.

(b) if $x > y$, i.e., x is greater than y.

(c) if $x \leq y$, i.e., x is less than or equal to y.

(d) if $x < y$, i.e., x is less than y.

(e) x = y or no relation can be established between x and y

11. I. $x^2 + 5x + 6 = 0$

 II. $y^2 + 7y + 12 = 0$

12. I. $x^2 + 20 = 9x$

 II. $y^2 + 42 = 13y$

13. I. $2x + 3y = 14$

 II. $4x + 2y = 16$

14. I. $x = \sqrt{625}$

 II. $y = \sqrt{676}$

15. I. $x^2 + 4x + 4 = 0$

 II. $y^2 - 8y + 16 = 0$

DIRECTION (Qs. 16-20) : Study the following graph carefully to answer the question given below it.

Production of paper (in lakh tonnes) by 3 different companies A, B & C over the years

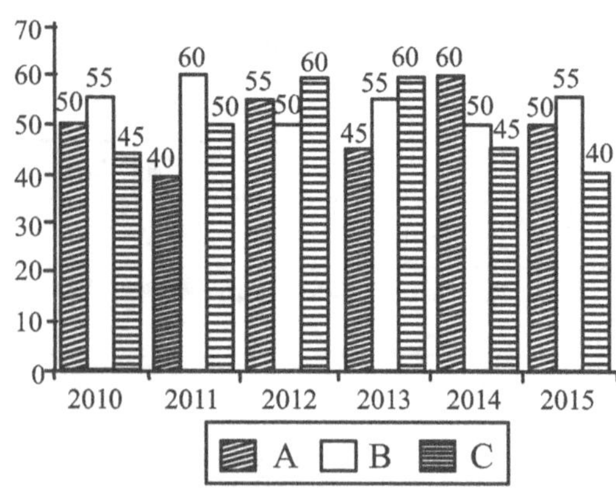

16. What is the difference between the production of company C in 2010 and the production of Company A in 2015?

(a) 50,000 tonnes (b) 5,00,00,000 tonnes

(c) 50,00,000 tonnes (d) 5,00,000 tonnes

(e) None of these

17. What is the percentage increase in production of Company A from 2011 to 2012?

(a) 37.5 (b) 38.25

(c) 35 (d) 36

(e) None of these

18. For which of the following years the percentage of rise/fall in production from the previous year the **maximum** for Company B?

(a) 2011 (b) 2012

(c) 2013 (d) 2014

(e) 2015

19. The total production of Company C in 2012 and 2013 is what percentage of the total production of Company A in 2010 and 2011?

(a) 95 (b) 90

(c) 110 (d) 115

(e) None of these

20. What is the difference between the average production per year of the company with highest average production and that of the company with lowest average production in lakh tonnes?

(a) 3.17 (b) 4.33

(c) 4.17 (d) 3.33

(e) None of these

DIRECTIONS (Qs. 21-25) : Study the given pie-chart and table and answer the following questions.

Percentage distribution of total TV viewers (in prime time) among different TV channels.

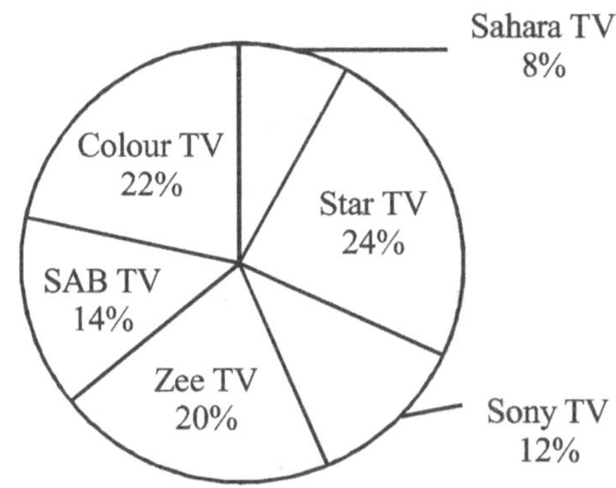

Percentage of urban TV viewers of these channels (Total number of TV viewers is 12 lakh)

Channel	% Urban Viewers
Star TV	70%
Sony TV	65%
Zee TV	68%
SAB TV	75%
Colors TV	60%
Sahara TV	72%

21. What is the total number of TV viewers from urban areas for all the channels?

(a) 721780 (b) 786486

(c) 8119208 (d) 824864

(e) None of these

22. What is the average number of TV viewers from rural areas for all the channels?

(a) 62178 (b) 64680

(c) 66370 (d) 68484

(e) None of these

23. Total number of rural viewers of Sony TV is what percentage of the total number of urban viewers of the same channel?

(a) 51.68% (b) 52278%

(c) 53.846% (d) 54.272%

(e) None of these

24. Total number of Sahara TV viewers from urban areas is what percentage more than the total number of rural viewers of SAB TV?

(a) 61.24% (b) 62.83%

(c) 63.58% (d) 64.57%

(e) None of these

25. What is the ratio of the total number of rural viewers of Zee TV to the total number of urban viewers of Star TV?

(a) 7:23 (b) 8:21
(c) 9:25 (d) 11:32
(e) None of these

DIRECTIONS (Qs. 26-30) : Study the following table carefully to answer the given questions.

Maximum and Minimum temperature (in degree Celsius) recorded on 1st day of each month of five different states

Months	Temperature									
	Bihar		Delhi		Punjab		Goa		Rajasthan	
	Max	Min	Max	Min	Max	Min	Max	Min	Max	Min
1st Oct	28	18	24	20	32	25	32	28	42	32
1st Nov	36	24	16	14	24	18	18	12	28	20
1st Dec	24	16	14	12	22	14	16	10	18	16
1st Jan	16	10	12	10	18	12	14	8	16	14
1st Feb	12	8	10	6	16	10	24	18	24	18

26. What is the difference between the maximum temperature of Rajasthan on 1st November and the minimum temperature of Bihar on 1st January ?

(a) 13°C (b) 14°C
(c) 15°C (d) 19°C
(e) 18°C

27. In which month respectively is the maximum temperature of Delhi the second highest and the minimum temperature of Punjab the highest ?

(a) 1st November and 1st February
(b) 1st October and 1st November
(c) 1st December and 1st January
(d) 1st October and 1st January
(e) 1st December and 1st October

28. In which month (on 1st day) is the difference between maximum temperature and minimum temperature of Bihar the second highest?

(a) 1st February (b) 1st October
(c) 1st November (d) 1st December
(e) 1st January

29. What is the average maximum temperature of Goa over all the months together?

(a) 18.4°C (b) 19.6°C
(c) 17.6°C (d) 19.2°C
(e) 20.8°C

30. What is the ratio of the minimum temperature of Goa on 1st October to the maximum temperature of Punjab on 1st November?

(a) 3 : 4 (b) 7 : 6
(c) 4 : 5 (d) 7 : 5
(e) 3 : 4

31. Average age of 36 children of the class is 15 years. 12 more children joined whose average age is 16 years. What is the average age of all the 48 children together ?

(a) 15.25 years (b) 15.5 years
(c) 15.3 years (d) 15.4 years
(e) None of these

32. Madhu bought some toys at 20% discount on the original price. The original price of each toy was ₹ 80. If she made a total savings of ₹ 480, how many toys did she buy?

(a) 30 (b) 8
(c) 12 (d) 24
(e) None of these

33. If the compound interest on a certain sum of money for 3 years at 10% p.a. be ₹ 993, what would be the simple interest ?

(a) ₹ 800 (b) ₹ 950
(c) ₹ 900 (d) ₹ 1000
(e) None of these

34. Saket has deposited a certain amount in the bank to earn compound interest at the rate of 10% per annum. The difference in the interests on the amounts in the third and in the second year is ₹ 24,200. What amount has Saket deposited ?

(a) ₹ 2.10 lakhs (b) ₹ 219,000
(c) ₹ 2 lakhs (d) ₹ 190,000
(e) None of these

35. How much water must be added to 100 cc of 80% solution of boric acid to reduce it to a 50% solution ?

(a) 20 cc (b) 40 cc
(c) 80 cc (d) 60 cc
(e) None of these

36. Sanjay earned a profit of ₹ 600 by selling 100 kg of a mixture of A and B types of rice at total price of ₹ 2200. What was the proportion of A and B types of rice in the mixture if the cost prices of A and B types of rice are ₹ 20 and ₹ 10 per kg respectively?

(a) 4 : 1 (b) 2 : 5
(c) 3 : 2 (d) 5 : 2
(e) 2 : 3

37. Two cars start together in the same direction from the same place. The first goes with a uniform speed of 10 km/h. The second goes at a speed of 8 km/h in the first hour and increases its speed by $\dfrac{1}{2}$ km with each succeeding hour. After how many hours will the second car overtake the first one, if both go non-stop?

(a) 9 hours (b) 5 hours
(c) 7 hours (d) 8 hours
(e) None of these

38. 24 men working 8 hours a day can finish a work in 10 days. Working at the rate of 10 hours a day, the number of men required to finish the same work in 6 days is

(a) 30 (b) 32
(c) 34 (d) 36
(e) None of these

39. The sum of digits of a two digit number is 15. If 9 be added to the number, then the digits are reversed. The number is

(a) 96. (b) 87
(c) 78 (d) 69
(e) None of these

40. Three cubes of a metal are of edges 3 cm, 4 cm and 5 cm. These are melted together and from the melted material another cube is formed. The edge of this cube is :

(a) 8 cm   (b) 10 cm

(c) 9 cm   (d) 6 cm

(e) None of these

REASONING ABILITY

41. Read the following information carefully and answer the question which follows.

A is the brother of B. B is the sister of T. T is the mother of P. If it is provided that R is the grandfather of P, how would T be related to R?

(a) Daughter   (b) Granddaughter

(c) Sister   (d) Wife

(e) Either Daughter or Daughter-in-law

42. Saroj is mother-in-law of Vani who is sister-in-law of Deepak. Rajesh is father of Ramesh, the only brother of Deepak. How is Saroj related to Deepak?

(a) Mother-in-law   (b) Wife

(c) Aunt   (d) Mother

(e) None of these

43. A directional post is erected on a crossing. In an accident, it was turned in such a way that the arrow which was first showing east is now showing south. A passerby went in a wrong direction thinking it is west. In which direction is he actually travelling now ?

(a) North   (b) South

(c) East   (d) West

(e) None of these

DIRECTIONS (Qs. 44-48) : In each question below, there are three statements followed by two conclusions numbered I and II. You have to take the three given statements to be true even if they seem to be at variance from commonly known facts and then decide which of the given conclusions logically follows from the three statements disregarding commonly known facts.

Give answer (a) if only conclusion I follows.

Give answer (b) if only conclusion II follows.

Give answer (c) if either I or II follows.

Give answer (d) if neither I nor II follows.

Give answer (e) if both I and II follow.

44. **Statements:** All shoes are pens.

Some pens are razors.

Some razors are desks.

Conclusions :

I.   Some desks are shoes.

II.   Some razors are shoes.

45. **Statements:**

Some benches are windows.

Some windows are walls.

Some walls are trains.

Conclusions:

I.   Some trains are benches.

II.   No train is bench.

46. **Statements :**

All brushes are chocolates.

All chocolates are mirrors.

All mirrors are tables.

Conclusions:

I.   Some tables are brushes

II.   Some mirrors are chocolates.

47. **Statements :**

All dogs are cats,

No cat is Pig.

All Pigs are Monkeys.

Conclusions :

I.   All dogs being monkeys is a possibility.

II.   All monkeys being cat is a possibility.

48. **Statements :**

Some books are bags.

All books are notes.

No note is a paper.

Conclusions :

I.   All notes are books.

II.   All papers being book is a possibility.

DIRECTIONS (Qs. 49-53) : Study the following information to answer the given questions.

P, Q, R, S, T, V, X and Y are seated in a straight line facing North, P sits fourth to the left of V. V sits either sixth from the left end of the line or fourth from the right end of the line. S sits second to right of R. R is not an immediate neighbour of V. T and Q are immediate neighbours of each other but neither T nor Q sits at extreme ends of the line. Only one person sits between T and X. X does not sit at the extreme end of the line.

49. What is the position of Q with respect to P?

(a) Fifth to the right

(b) Immediate neighbour

(c) Second to right

(d) Third to left

(e) None of the above

50. Which of the following represents persons seated at the two extreme ends of the line?

(a) P, V   (b) Y, S

(b) R, V   (d) Y, P

(e) R, Y

51. How many persons are seated between R and T ?

(a) One   (b) Two

(c) Three   (d) Four

(e) None of these

52. If P is related to Q and S is related to T in a certain way, to which of the following would V be related to following the same pattern ?

(a) Y   (b) P

(c) R   (d) S

(e) X

53. Who amongst the following sits exactly in the middle of the persons who sit second from the left and the person who sits fifth from the right?

   (a) V   (b) Q

   (c) T   (d) S

   (e) P

DIRECTIONS (Q. 54-60): Study the following information to answer the given questions.

Eight people, viz A, B, C, D, E, F, G and H are sitting in a straight line facing North. Each of them has passed a recruitment exam and must join the office in different months, viz January, February, March, April, May, June, July and August but not necessarily in the same order.

G sits third to the right of the person who joins in May. The person who joins in August sits second to the right of G. A and E are immediate neighbours of each other. Neither A nor E has joining dates in either May or August. Neither A nor E is an immediate neighbour of G.

H sits third to the right of the person whose joining date is in January. Neither A nor E has joining dates in January.

H's joining date is not in August.

Only two people sit between E and the person whose joining date is in July. The person whose joining date is in February sits on the immediate left of D.

Only one person sits between E and B. C joins before July. E joins after April. G joins after A.

54. In which of the following months does H join the office?

   (a) April   (b) June

   (c) July   (d) February

   (e) March

55. Who among the following sits exactly between E and B?

   (a) The person whose joining date is in May

   (b) The person whose joining date is in January

   (c) D

   (d) A

   (e) The person whose joining date is in August

56. 'H' is related to 'July' in a certain way based on the above arrangement. 'B' is related to 'June' following the same pattern. '___' is related to 'May' following the same pattern.

   (a) F   (b) G

   (c) A   (d) D

   (e) C

57. Which of the following is true regarding D?

   (a) Only two people sit to the left of D.

   (b) D is sitting second to the right of the person whose joining date is in July.

   (c) E and B are immediate neighbours of D.

   (d) D's joining date is in May.

   (e) None is true

58. Who among the following has joining date in June?

   (a) F   (b) E

   (c) G   (d) D

   (e) C

59. How many people sit between C and the person whose joining date is in April?

   (a) None   (b) One

   (c) Two   (d) Three

   (e) Four

60. Who among the following are sitting at extreme ends of the line?

   (a) A and the person whose joining date is in August

   (b) The person whose joining date is in May and E

   (c) C and G

   (d) The persons whose joining dates are in March and June

   (e) None of these

DIRECTIONS (Qs. 61-65) : In these questions, relationship between different elements is shown in the statements.

These statements are followed by two conclusions.

Given answer

(a) if only Conclusion I follows

(b) if only Conclusion II follows

(c) if either Conclusion I or II follows

(d) if neither Conclusion I nor II follows

(e) if both Conclusion I and II follow

61. **Statements**   L > M, M > N, N > P

   Conclusions I. L > P   **II.** M > P

62. **Statements**   A > B, B = H, H > G

   Conclusions I. A > G   **II.** A > H

63. **Statements**   H < J, F < H, I ≤ J = K

   Conclusions I. H > I   **II.** I ≥ F

64. **Statements**   A < B < C ≤ D = E

   Conclusions I. B ≤ E   **II.** B < E

65. **Statements**   P > M > Q, Q > Z > N

   Conclusions I. M ≥ Z   **II.** N < P

DIRECTIONS (Qs. 66-70): Study the following sequence carefully and answer the questions given below:

M E 5 P B 2 A 7 K N 9 T R U 4 6 I J D F 1 Q 3 W 8 V I S Z

66. How many such numbers are there in the above sequence, each of which is both immediately preceded by and immediately followed by a consonant ?

   (a) None   (b) One

   (c) Two   (d) Three

   (e) More than three

67. If the order of the first twenty letters/numbrs in the above sequence is reversed and the remaining letters/numbers are kept unchanged, which of the following will be the fourteenth letter/number from the right end after the rearrangement?

   (a) B   (b) 6

   (c) 2   (d) 1

   (e) None of these

68. Which of the follwing letter/number is the eighth to the left of the nineteenth letter/number from the left end?

(a) N
(b) T
(c) 1
(d) D
(e) None of these

69. Four of the following five are alike in a certain way with regard to their position in the above sequence and so form a group. Which is the one that **does not** belong to that group?

(a) WIQ
(b) PAE
(c) NR7
(d) 4JR
(e) D16

70. How many such vowels are there in the above sequence, each of which is immediately preceded by a consonant and immediately followed by a vowel?

(a) None
(b) One
(c) Two
(d) Three
(e) More than three

DIRECTIONS (Qs. 71-75) : Study the following information to answer the given questions.

Eight friends, A, B, C, D, E, F, G and H are sitting in a circle facing the centre, not necessarily in the same order. D sits third to the left of A. E sits to the immediate right of A. B is third to the left of D. G is second to the right of B. C is an immediate neighbour of B. C is third to the left of H.

71. Who amongst the following is sitting exactly between F and D ?

(a) C
(b) E
(c) H
(d) A
(e) None of these

72. Three of the following four are alike in a certain way based on the information given above and so from a group. Which is the one that does not belong to that group ?

(a) D C
(b) AH
(c) EF
(d) CB
(e) None of these

73. Who amongst the following is sitting second to the left of H?

(a) E
(b) B
(c) A
(d) Data inadequate
(e) None of these

74. Who amongst the following are immediate neighbours of G?

(a) CA
(b) AF
(c) D C
(d) DF
(e) None of these

75. Who amongst the following is sitting third to the right of A?

(a) F
(b) B
(c) B
(d) C
(e) None of these

DIRECTIONS (Qs. 76-80): Study the following information to answer the given questions.

In a certain code, 'always create new ideas' is written as 'ba ri sha gi', 'ideas and new thoughts' is written as 'fa gi ma ri', 'create thoughts and insights' is written as 'ma jo ba fa', and 'new and better solutions' is written as 'ki ri to fa'.

76. What is the code for 'ideas'?

(a) sha
(b) ba
(c) gi
(d) ma
(e) Cannot be determined

77. What does 'fa' stand for?

(a) thoughts
(b) insights
(c) new
(d) and
(e) solutions

78. 'fa lo ba' could be a code for which of the following?

(a) thoughts and action
(b) create and innovate
(c) ideas and thoughts
(d) create new solutions
(e) always better ideas

79. What is the code for 'new'?

(a) ki
(b) ri
(c) to
(d) fa
(e) ba

80. Which of the following may represent 'insights always better'?

(a) jo ki to
(b) ki to ri
(c) sha jo ri
(d) to sha jo
(e) sha to ba

HINTS & EXPLANATIONS

1. (a) $\left[\left(5\sqrt{7}+\sqrt{7}\right)\times\left(4\sqrt{7}+8\sqrt{7}\right)\right]-(19)^2=?$

$\Rightarrow (6\sqrt{7}\times12\sqrt{7})-(361)=?$

$\Rightarrow 72\times\sqrt{7}\times\sqrt{7}-361=?$

$\therefore ?=504-361=143$

2. (b) $(4444\div40)+(645\div25)+(3991\div26)=?$

$\Rightarrow ?=(111.1)+(25.8)+(153.5)\Rightarrow ?=290.4$

3. (e) $\sqrt{33124}\times\sqrt{2601}-(83)^2=(?)^2+(37)^2$

$\Rightarrow (?)^2=\sqrt{33124}\times\sqrt{2601}-(83)^2-(37)^2$

$\Rightarrow (?)^2=182\times51-6889-1369$

$\Rightarrow (?)^2=9282-6889-1369$

$\Rightarrow (?)^2=1024$

$\therefore ?=\sqrt{1024}=32$

4. (b) $5\frac{17}{37}\times4\frac{51}{52}\times11\frac{1}{7}+2\frac{3}{4}=?$

$\Rightarrow\left(\frac{202}{37}\times\frac{259}{52}\times\frac{78}{7}\right)+\left(\frac{11}{4}\right)=?$

$\Rightarrow 303+\frac{11}{4}=?$

$\therefore ?=\frac{1223}{4}=305.75$

5. (b) $(39260+27980+22050)+96048\div48=?$

$\Rightarrow 89290+96048\div48=91291$

6. (a) The given number series is based on the following pattern

$9\times0.5+0.5=5$

$5\times1+1=6$

$6\times1.5+1.5=10.5$

$10.5\times2+2=23$

$23\times2.5+2.5=60$

$60\times3+3=183$

Hence the wrong number is 8.

7. (b) The given number series is based on the following pattern :

$14\times1.5=21$

$21\times2=42$

$42\times2.5=105$

$105\times3=315$

$315\times3.5=1102.5$

$1102.5\times4=4410$

Hence, the wrong number is 48.

8. (b) The given number series is based on the following pattern:

$14-13=1^2$

$23-14=3^2$

$48-23=25=5^2$

$97-48=49=7^2\ ......$

So, the wrong number is 33.

9. (c) The number series follows the rule as mentioned below:

$24\times1+1=25$

$25\times2-1=49$

$49\times3+1=148$

$148\times4-1=591$

$591\times5+1=2956$

$2956\times6-1=17735$

Hence 492 is the wrong number.

10. (e) The followed pattern is :

$12\times2+2=26$

$26\times2+4=56$

$56\times2+6=118$

$118\times2+8=244$

$244\times2+10=498$

$498\times2+12=1008$

Hence, the wrong number is 276.

11. (a) I. $x^2+5x+6=0$

$\Rightarrow x^2+2x+3x+6=0$

$\Rightarrow x(x+2)+3(x+2)=0$

$\Rightarrow (x+3)(x+2)=0$

$\Rightarrow x=-3\text{ or }-2$

II. $y^2+7y+12=0$

$\Rightarrow y^2+4y+3y+12=0$

$\Rightarrow y(y+4)+3(y+4)=0$

$\Rightarrow (y+3)(y+4)=0$

$\Rightarrow y=-3\text{ or }-4$

On comparing the value of equ. (i) and equ. (ii)

$x\geq y$

12. (d) I. $x^2-9x+20=0$

$\Rightarrow x^2-5x-4x+20=0$

$\Rightarrow x(x-5)-4(x-5)=0$

$= (x-4)(x-5)=0$

$x=4\text{ or }5$

II. $y^2-13y+42=0$

$\Rightarrow y^2-7y-6y+42=0$

$\Rightarrow y(y-7)-6(y-7)=0$

$\Rightarrow (y-6)(y-7)=0$

$\Rightarrow y=6\text{ or }7$

Here, $y>x$

13. (d) $2x+3y=14$ ...(I)

$4x+2y=16$ ...(II)

By equation (I) × 2 – equation II.

$4x+6y-4x-2y=28-16$

$\Rightarrow 4y=12\Rightarrow y=3$

From equation I,
$2x + 3 \times 3 = 14$

$\Rightarrow 2x = 14 - 9 = 5 \Rightarrow x = \dfrac{5}{2}$

Here, $y > x$

14. (d) I. $x = \sqrt{625} = 25$

II. $y = \sqrt{676} = 26$

$\therefore y > x$

15. (d) I. $x^2 + 4x + 4 = 0$

$(x + 2)^2 = 0 \Rightarrow x = -2$

II. $y^2 - 8y + 16 = 0$

$\Rightarrow (y - 4)^2 = 0$

$\Rightarrow y = 4$

Here, $y > x$

16. (d) Difference of production of C in 2010 and A in 2015 = 5,00,000 tonnes

17. (a) Percentage increase of A from 2011 to 2012

$\dfrac{55 - 40}{40} \times 100 = 37.5\%$

18. (b) Percentage rise/fall in production for B

2011	2012	2013	2014	2015
9%	−16.6%	10%	− 9%	10%

Here, the maximum difference is from 2011 to 2012, which is 10. And the second nearest to it is fall or rise of 5. So, undoubtedly the answer is 2012.

19. (e) Percentage production = $\dfrac{120}{90} \times 100 = 133.3\%$

20. (c) Average production of A = 50

Average production of B = 54.17

Average production of C = 50

Difference of production = 54.17 − 50 = 4.17

21. (e)

22. (b) Total no. of rural viewers = 388080

$\therefore$ Avg = $\dfrac{388080}{6} = 64680$

23. (c) Rural viewers$_{sony}$ = $1200000 \times \dfrac{12}{100} \times \dfrac{35}{100} = 50400$

Urban viewer$_{sony}$ = $1200000 \times \dfrac{12}{100} \times \dfrac{65}{100} = 93600$

Reqd% = $\dfrac{50400}{93600} \times 100 = 53.846\%$

24. (d) Urban$_{sahara}$

$= 1200000 \times \dfrac{8}{100} \times \dfrac{72}{100} = 69120$

Rural$_{SAB}$ = $1200000 \times \dfrac{14}{100} \times \dfrac{25}{100} = 42000$

$\therefore$ Reqd% = $\dfrac{69120 - 42000}{42000} \times 100 = 64.57\%$

25. (b) Ratio = $\dfrac{1200000 \times \dfrac{20}{100} \times \dfrac{32}{100}}{1200000 \times \dfrac{24}{100} \times \dfrac{70}{100}} = \dfrac{20 \times 32}{24 \times 70} = \dfrac{8}{21}$

26. (e) Maximum temperature of Rajasthan on 1st November = 28°C

Minimum temperature of Bihar on 1st January = 10°C

So Difference = 28 − 10 = 18°C

27. (a) There is second highest temperature of Delhi on 1st November = 16°C

The minimum temperature of Punjab is on 1st February (10°C)

28. (b) Diff of temp in Bihar on 1st October
$= 28 - 18 = 10°C$

Diff of temp in Bihar on 1st November
$= 36 - 24 = 12°C$

Diff of temp in Bihar on 1st December
$= 24 - 16 = 8°C$

Diff of temp in Bihar on 1st January
$= 16 - 10 = 6°C$

Diff of temp in Bihar on 1st February
$= 12 + 8 = 4°C.$

Hence, the second highest difference in temperature is on 1st October.

29. (e) Average = (32 + 18 + 16 + 14 + 24)/5 = 104/5 = 20.8°C

30. (b) Required ratio = 28:24 = 7 : 6

31. (a) Required average age

$= \left(\dfrac{15 \times 36 + 12 \times 16}{36 + 12}\right) \text{years} = \left(\dfrac{540 + 192}{48}\right) \text{years}$

$= 15.25$ years.

32. (a) Madhu saves 20% of 80 = ₹16 on each toy.
So she bought = 480/16 = 30 toys

33. (c) Let Principal = ₹ P

$P\left(1 + \dfrac{10}{100}\right)^3 - P = 993 \Rightarrow \left(\dfrac{11}{10} \times \dfrac{11}{10} \times \dfrac{11}{10} - 1\right)P = 993$

$\Rightarrow \left(\dfrac{1331 - 1000}{1000}\right)P = 993$ or,

$P = \dfrac{993 \times 1000}{331} = 3000$

$\therefore$ Simple interest = ₹$\left(\dfrac{3000 \times 3 \times 10}{100}\right) = ₹900$

34. (c) Interest for 2 yrs = 10 + 10 + (10 ×10)/100
$= 21\%$

Interest for 3 yrs = 21 + 10 + (21×10)/100 = 33.1%

Now, (33.1 - 21)% of P = 24200

or, 12. 1% of P = 14200

or, P = (14200 ×100)/12.1 = 2 lakh

35. (d) Concentration of boric acid = 80% = 80 cc
Quantity of water = 20 cc

Let x cc of water be added to get the concentration of 50%.

$$\Rightarrow \frac{80}{100+x} = \frac{50}{100} \text{ or } \frac{80}{100+x} = \frac{1}{2} \text{ or } x = 60 \text{ cc}$$

36. (c) CP of 100 kg of mixture $= 2200 - 600 = ₹1600$
CP of 1 kg of mixture $= 1600/100 = 16$
By the Method of Alligation:

A   B
20   10
$\diagdown$ 16 $\diagup$
6   4

Required ratio $= 3 : 2$

37. (a) Let the second car overtakes the first car after t hours.
Distance covered by the first car = Distance covered by the second car.

$$\Rightarrow 10\,t = 8 + \left(8 + \frac{1}{2}\right) + \left(8 + \frac{2}{2}\right) + \ldots\ldots + \left(8 + \frac{t-1}{2}\right)$$

$$\text{or } 10t = 8t + \frac{1}{2}[1 + 2 + \ldots + (t-1)]$$

$$\text{or } 10t = 8t + \frac{1}{2}\frac{t(t-1)}{2} \text{ or } 2t = \frac{1}{4}(t^2 - t)$$

$$\Rightarrow t = 9 \text{ hrs. } [t \neq 0]$$

38. (b) $m_1 \times d_1 \times t_1 \times w_2 = m_2 \times d_2 \times t_2 \times w_1$
$24 \times 10 \times 8 \times 1 = m_2 \times 6 \times 10 \times 1$

$$\Rightarrow m_2 = \frac{24 \times 10 \times 8}{6 \times 10} = 32 \text{ men}$$

39. (c) Let the two digit number be $10x + y$
We have $x + y = 15$ ...(i)
and $(10x + y) + 9 = (10y + x)$ or $9x - 9y = -9$
or $x - y = -1$ ...(ii)
From (i) and (ii) $x = 7$ and $y = 8$
The number is $10 \times 7 + 8 = 78$

40. (d) Let edge of the new cube $= x$ cm.
Volume of the newly formed figure (cube)
= Sum of volume of smaller cubes.
i.e. $(x)^3 = (3)^3 + (4)^3 + (5)^3 = 27 + 64 + 125 = 216 \Rightarrow x = 6 \text{ cm}$

41. (e)

R (+)
|
A (+) — B(–) — T(–) $\Leftrightarrow$
|
P

T is daughter-in-law of R.
or
R (+)
|
A (+) — B(–) — T(–)
|
P

T is daughter of R.

42. (d) 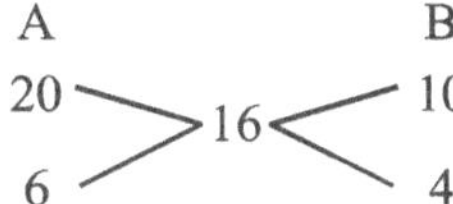

So, it is clear from the above family tree that Saroj is Mother to Deepak.

43. (b)

When the arrow turns, East becomes South, North becomes East, West becomes North and South becomes West.

So, the traveller must be actually travelling in the South thinking it is West.

44. (d) All shoes are pens. (A-type)

Some pens are razors. (I-type)
$A + I \Rightarrow$ No Conclusion

45. (c) All the three Premises are Particular Affirmative (I-type).
No Conclusion follows from Particular Premises.
Conclusion I and II from Complementary Pair.
Therefore, either I or II follows

46. (e) All brushes are chocolates. (A-type)

All chocolates are mirrors. (A-type)
$A + A \Rightarrow$ A-type Conclusion
"All brushes are mirrors"
All brushes are mirrors. (A-type)

All mirrors are tables. (A-type)
"All brushes are tables"
Conclusion I is converse of this Conclusion.
Conclusion II is converse of the second Premise.

47. (a) Only conclusion I follows
Explanation: I. ✓ II. ✗

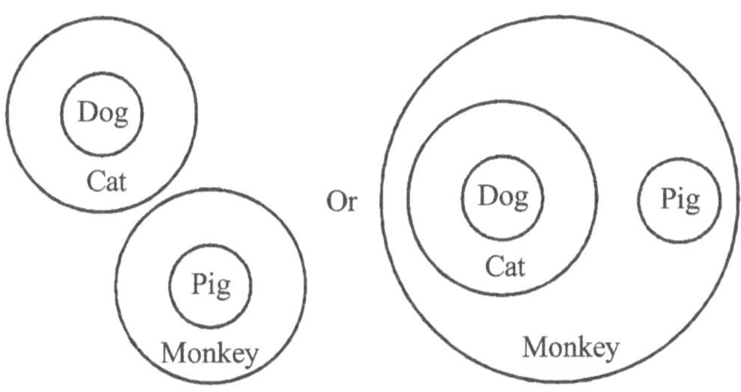

48. (d) Neither conclusion I nor II follows

Explanation : I. ✗ II. ✗

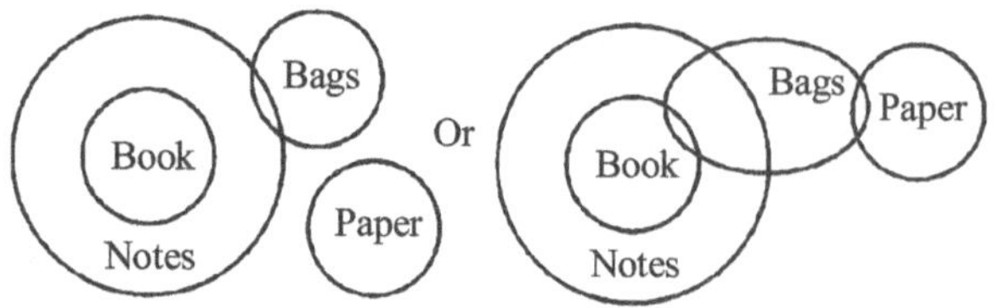

(Q. No. 49-53): On the basis of given information, the final sitting arrangment of eight persons in a straight line facing North is as following

| R | P | S | Q | T | V | X | Y |

↑ Facing North

49. (c) Q is second to the right of P.
50. (e) R and Y are sitting at the two extreme ends of the line.
51. (c) Three persons P, S and Q are seated between R and T.
52. (a) In the given pairs, second person is seated second to the right of first person.

So, V be related to Y as Y is sitting second to the right of V.

53. (d) Second from the left is P and fifth from the right is Q. S is sitting between P and Q.

Solution (54- 60)

March	June	May	Jan	July	April	Feb	Aug
A	E	C	B	F	G	H	D

54. (d) 55. (a) 56. (a) 57. (e)
58. (b) 59. (c) 60. (a)

61. (e) Given that, $L > M$ ...(i)

$M > N$ ...(ii)

$N > P$ ...(iii)

On combining all the three statements, we get

$L > M > N > P$

Conclusions I. $L > P$ ...(true)

II. $M > P$ ...(true)

So, it is clear that both Conclusions I and II follow from that given statements.

62. (e) Given that, $A > B$ ...(i)

$B = H$ ...(ii)

$H > G$ ...(iii)

On combining the statements (i), (ii) and (iii), we get

$A > B = H > G$

Conclusions I. $A > G$ ...(true)

II. $A > H$ ...(true)

So, it is clear that both Conclusions I and II follow from the given statements.

63. (d) Given that, $H < J$ ...(i)

$F < H$ ...(ii)

$I \leq J = K$ ...(iii)

On combining that statements (i), (ii) and (iii), we get

$F < H < J = K \geq I$

Conclusions I. $H > I$ ...(false)

II. $I \geq F$ ...(false)

So, it is clear that neither conclusion I nor II follows.

64. (b) Given that, $A < B < C \leq D = E$

Here, statements are already combined.

Conclusions I. $B \leq E$ ...(false)

II. $B < E$ ...(true)

So, it is clear that only Conclusions II follows from the given statements.

65. (b) Given that, $P > M > Q$ ...(i)

$Q > Z > N$ ...(ii)

On combining that statements (i), and (ii) we get

$P > M > Q > Z > N$

Conclusions I. $M \geq Z$ ...(false)

II. $N < P$ ...(true)

So, it is clear that only Conclusions II follows from the given statements.

66. (e) Four numbers in the sequence.

M E 5 P B 2 A 7 K N**9**T R U 4 6 I J D F**1 Q** 3 W **8** V I S Z

i.e. N9T, F1Q, Q3W, W8V

67. (a) F D J I 6 4 U R T 9 N K 7 A 2 B P 5 E M 1 Q 3 W 8 V I S Z

B 14th from right end.

68. (e) Eighth to the left of the nineteenth letter/number from the left $\Rightarrow (19 - 8 =)$ 11th letter/number from left. Hence, required element is 9.

69. (e) Except D16, second element in each group is third to the right of first element while third element of each group is second to the left of first element of the respective group.

70. (a) There are no such vowels.

(Q. Nos. 71-75) Arrangement according to the question is as follows:

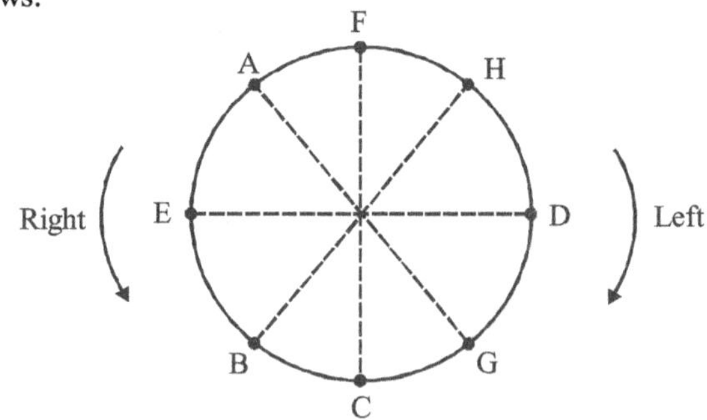

71. (c) Clearly, H is sitting exactly between F and D.

72. (d) DGC AFH EAF C None B

↑ ↑ ↑ ↑

Skipped Skipped Skipped No Member

is skipped in between

So, CB does not belong to the group.

73. (e) Clearly, G is sitting second to the left of H.
74. (c) Clearly, D and C are immediate neighbours of G.
75. (d) Clearly, C is sitting third to the right of A.

(76-80) : 'always create new ideas' → 'ba ri sha gi' ... (1)

'ideas and new thoughts' → 'fa gi ma ri' ... (2)

'create thoughts and insights' → 'ma jo ba fa' ... (3)

'new and better solutions' → 'ki ri to fa' ... (4)

Using (1) and (4),

new → ri

Using (1), (2) and (4),

ideas → gi

and → fa

thoughts → ma

Using (1) and (3),

create → ba

always → sha

insights → jo

better solutions → ki to

76. (c) 77. (d) 78. (b) 79. (b) 80. (d)

PRACTICE SET 3

Time : 45 Min.

Max. Marks : 80

QUANTITATIVE APTITUDE

DIRECTION (Qs. 1-5): Study the following graphs and table carefully and answer accordingly;

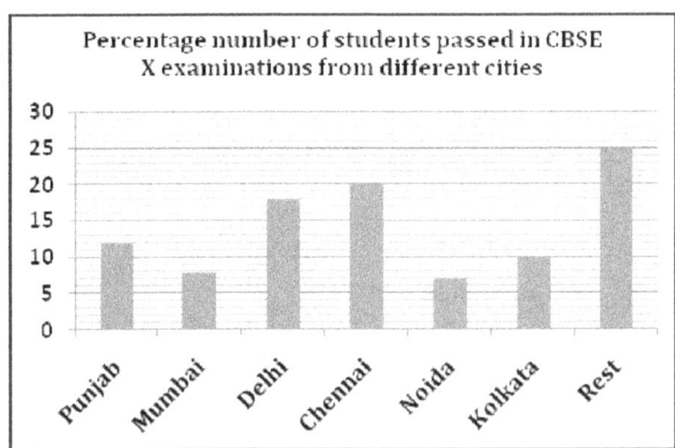

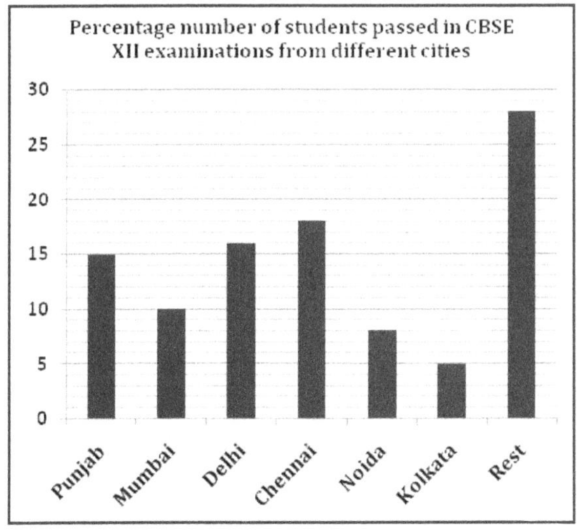

The following table shows the ratio of the number of boys and girls passing from different cities.

City	X		XII	
	Boys	**Girls**	**Boys**	**Girls**
Punjab	2	3	3	5
Mumbai	7	5	7	8
Delhi	5	7	3	5
Chennai	13	12	9	6
Noida	3	5	4	6
Kolkata	12	13	7	8
Rest	4	6	7	3

1. In X exam, if there are 2000 girls passing from Mumbai then find the approx number of boys passing from Chennai in the same exam.
   - (a) 6250
   - (b) 6430
   - (c) 6750
   - (d) Data inadequate
   - (e) 6240

2. If 18000 students passed in XII exam from Mumbai, then find the number of girls passing from Delhi in the same exam.
   - (a) 19600
   - (b) 15760
   - (c) 18000
   - (d) Data inadequate
   - (e) None of these

3. Which of the following cities shows the maximum percentage of girls passing (with respect to total students passing in that city) in X examination?
   - (a) Delhi
   - (b) Mumbai
   - (c) Chennai
   - (d) Rest
   - (e) Noida

4. If the difference between the number of boys passing from Chennai and that from Delhi in XII exam is 7260, find the total number of students passed in XII exam in 2013.
   - (a) 172000
   - (b) 151250
   - (c) 150000
   - (d) Can't say
   - (e) None of these

5. In X exam, if 2.40 lakh students pass, then what will be the approx number of boys passing in the remaining part of the country?
   - (a) 24600
   - (b) 24000
   - (c) 30740
   - (d) 28680
   - (e) 20760

DIRECTIONS (Qs. 6-10): Following pie-charts show the distribution of annual expenditure of two persons P and Q. Answer the following question based on these charts. Total expenditure of P and Q is Rs. 9 and 10.5 lakhs respectively.

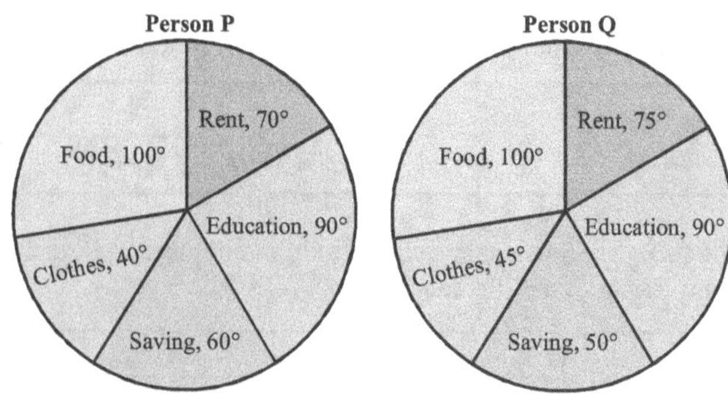

6. What is the amount person P and person Q save yearly?
   - (a) 3.25 lakhs
   - (b) 2.95 lakhs
   - (c) 2.15 lakhs
   - (d) 3.10 lakhs
   - (e) 2.5 lakhs

7. What is the difference between amount spent on clothe by person P to that of person Q?
   - (a) 42500
   - (b) 31500
   - (c) 31000
   - (d) 36500
   - (e) None of these

8. Money spent by person Q on food is what percentage of the money spent by person P on education?
   - (a) 80%
   - (b) 95%
   - (c) 120%
   - (d) 140%
   - (e) 130%

9. What is the average of the amount spent for house rent by person P and person Q?
   - (a) 1.75 lakhs
   - (b) 1.84 lakhs
   - (c) 1.96 lakhs
   - (d) 1.28 lakhs
   - (e) 2.25 lakhs

10. Money spent by Person Q on education is how much percentage more than that of money spent by Person P on education?
   - (a) 20.25%
   - (b) 12.5%
   - (c) 25.25%
   - (d) 16.66%
   - (e) 32.12%

DIRECTIONS (Qs. 11-15): What approximate value will come in place of the question mark (?) in the following questions ? (You are not required to find the exact value).

11. $2371 \div 6 + (43 \times 4.35) = ?$
   - (a) 582
   - (b) 590
   - (c) 600
   - (d) 570
   - (e) 595

12. $(4.989)^2 + (21.012)^3 + \sqrt{1090} = ?$
   - (a) 9219
   - (b) 9391
   - (c) 9319
   - (d) 9129
   - (e) None of these

13. 24.99% of $5001 - 65.01\%$ of $2999 = ?$
   - (a) 840
   - (b) 500
   - (c) 700
   - (d) −500
   - (e) −700

14. $(81)^{-\frac{1}{2}} - (64)^{-\frac{2}{3}} = ?$
   - (a) $\dfrac{3}{19}$
   - (b) $\dfrac{1}{16}$
   - (c) $\dfrac{7}{144}$
   - (d) $\dfrac{1}{9}$
   - (e) None of these

15. $\dfrac{\sqrt{29241}}{\sqrt{361}} \times 5\dfrac{2}{9} = ?$
   - (a) 47
   - (b) 49
   - (c) 46
   - (d) 45
   - (e) 61

DIRECTIONS (Qs. 16-20): What should come in place of question mark (?) in the following number series ?

16. 121 117 108 92 67 ?
   - (a) 31
   - (b) 29
   - (c) 41
   - (d) 37
   - (e) None of these

17. 50 26 14 ? 5 3.5
   - (a) 6
   - (b) 8
   - (c) 10
   - (d) 12
   - (e) None of these

18. 3 23 43 ? 83 103
   - (a) 33
   - (b) 53
   - (c) 63
   - (d) 73
   - (e) None of these

19. 748 737 715 682 638 ?
   - (a) 594
   - (b) 572
   - (c) 581
   - (d) 563
   - (e) None of these

20. 1 9 25 49 81 ? 169
   - (a) 100
   - (b) 64
   - (c) 81
   - (d) 121
   - (e) None of these

21. The number of employees in Companies A, B and C are in a ratio of 4 : 5 : 6 respectively. If the number of employees in the Companies is increased by 25%, 30% and 50% respectively, what will be the new ratio of employees working in Companies A, B and C respectively ?

   (a) $13:10:18$ (b) $10:13:17$
   (c) $13:15:18$ (d) Cannot be determined
   (e) None of these

22. The average of five positive numbers is 213. The average of the first two numbers is 233.5 and the average of last two numbers is 271. What is the third number ?
   (a) 64   (b) 56
   (c) 106   (d) Cannot be determined
   (e) None of these

23. Sonali invests 15% of her monthly salary in insurance policies. She spends 55% of her monthly salary in shopping and on household expenes. She saves the remaining amount of ₹ 12,750. What is Sonali's monthly income ?
   (a) ₹42,500   (b) ₹38,800
   (c) ₹40,000   (d) ₹35,500
   (e) None of these

24. What **approximate** amount of compound interest can be obtained on an amount of ₹ 9, 650 at the rate of 6% p.a. at the end of 3 years ?
   (a) ₹1,737   (b) ₹1,920
   (c) ₹1,720   (d) ₹1,860
   (e) ₹1,843

25. A milkman sells 120 litres of milk for ₹ 3,360 and he sells 240 litres of milk for Rs. 6,120. How much concession does the trader give per litre of milk, when he sells 240 litres of milk ?
   (a) ₹2   (b) ₹3.5
   (c) ₹2.5   (d) ₹1.5
   (e) None of these

26. When 3,626 is divided by the square of a number and the answer so obtained is multiplied by 32, the final answer obtained is 2,368. What is the number ?
   (a) 7   (b) 36
   (c) 49   (d) 6
   (e) None of these

27. The sum of the digits of a two digit number is 14. The difference between the first digit and the second digit of the two digit number is 2. What is the product of the two digits of the two digit number ?
   (a) 56   (b) 48
   (c) 45   (d) Cannot be determined
   (e) None of these

28. A car runs at the speed of 50 kmph when not serviced and runs at 60 kmph, when serviced. After servicing the car covers a certain distance in 6 hours. How much time will the car take to cover the same distance when not serviced ?
   (a) 8.2 hours   (b) 6.5 hours
   (c) 8 hours   (d) 7.2 hours
   (e) None of these

29. The sum of the two digits of a two digit number is 13. The difference between the two digits of the number is 3. What is the two digit number?
   (a) 85   (b) 49
   (c) 57   (d) Cannot be determined
   (e) None of these

30. The profit earned after selling a pair of shoes for ₹ 2,033 is the same as loss incurred after selling the same pair of shoes for ₹ 1,063. What is the cost of the shoes?
   (a) ₹1,650   (b) ₹1,548
   (c) ₹1,532   (d) Cannot be determined
   (e) None of these

DIRECTIONS (Q. 31-35) : In each of these questions, two equations are given. You have to solve these equations and find out the values of x and y and

---

Given answer If
   (a) $x < y$
   (b) $x > y$
   (c) $x \le y$
   (d) $x \ge y$
   (e) $x = y$

31.   I. $16x^2 + 20x + 6 = 0$
    II. $10y^2 + 38y + 24 = 0$

32.   I. $18x^2 + 18x + 4 = 0$
    II. $12y^2 + 29y + 14 = 0$

33.   I. $8x^2 + 6x = 5$
    II. $12y^2 - 22y + 8 = 0$

34.   I. $17x^2 + 48x = 9$
    II. $13y^2 = 32y - 21$

35.   I. $4x^2 + 7y = 209$
    II. $12x - 14y = -38$

DIRECTIONS (Qs. 36-40) : Study the following graph carefully and answer the questions that follow.

The graph given below represents the number of users of two broadband services A and B across 5 cities P, Q, R, S and T.

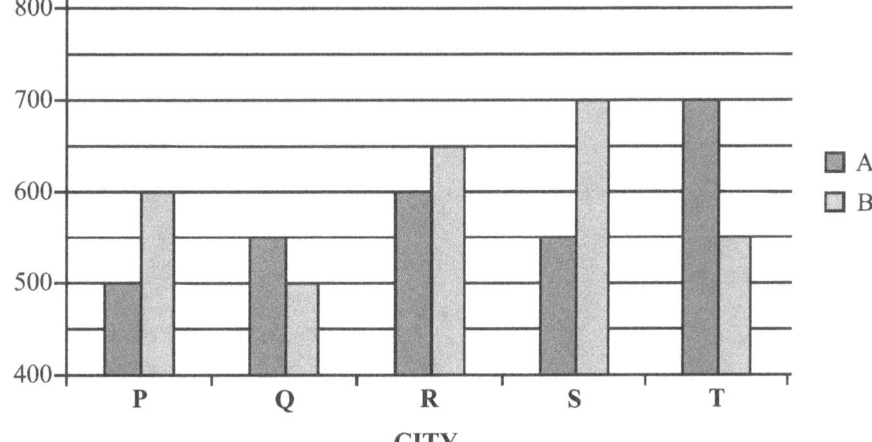

36. What is the total number of users of brand B across all five cities together ?
 (a) 2700   (b) 3000
 (c) 3100   (d) 2900
 (e) 3200

37. The number of users of brand A in city T is what percent of the number of users of brand B in City Q ?
 (a) 150   (b) 110
 (c) 140   (d) 160
 (e) 120

38. What is the average number of users of brand A across all five cities together ?
 (a) 560   (b) 570
 (c) 580   (d) 590
 (e) 550

39. What is the difference between the total number of users of Brand A and B together in city R and the total number of users of brand A and B together in city P ?
 (a) 170   (b) 140
 (c) 130   (d) 150
 (e) 160

40. What is the respective ratio of the number of users of brand A in city P to the number of users of brand B in city S ?
 (a) 5 : 7   (b) 4 : 7
 (c) 2 : 5   (d) 3 : 4
 (e) 5 : 6

REASONING ABILITY

DIRECTIONS (Qs. 41-45) : In each of the questions below are given three statements followed by four conclusions numbered I, II, III and IV. You have to take the given statements to be true even if they seem to be at variance with commonly known facts. Read all the conclusions and then decide which of the given conclusions logically follows from the given statements disregarding commonly known facts.

41. **Statements :** All books are notes.
             Some notes are pencils.
             No pencil is paper.
 Conclusions : I. Some notes are books.
             II. Some pencils are books.
             III. Some books are papers.
             IV. No book is a paper.
 (a) Only I and either III or IV follow
 (b) Either III or IV follows
 (c) Only I and III follow
 (d) Neither II nor III follows
 (e) None of these

42. **Statements :** Some fruits are seeds.
             All seeds are trees.
             All plants are trees.
 Conclusions : I. Some plants are seeds.
             II. Some plants are fruits.
             III. Some trees are fruits.
             IV. No plant is a seed.
 (a) Only III follow
 (b) III and either I or IV follow
 (c) II and either I or IV follow
 (d) Either I or IV follow
 (e) None of these

43. **Statements :** Some motors are books.
             Some scooters are motors.
             All girls are scooters.
 Conclusions : I. Some girls are motors.
             II. Some girls are books.
             III. Some scooters are girls.
             IV. No girl is a book
 (a) I and III follow   (b) II and III follow
 (c) I and II follow   (d) I, II and III follow
 (e) Either II or IV and III follow

44. **Statements :**
Some Oranges are Apples
All apples are grapes
No grapes is Banana
Conclusions:
I.   All Bananas are grapes
II.   Some Oranges being Banana is a possibility
III.   All grapes are apples
IV.   Some grapes are definitely Banana
 (a) Only I follows
 (b) Only II follows
 (c) Only III and IV follow
 (d) All follow
 (e) None follows

45. **Statements :**
All monkeys are Donkeys
No Donkey is elephant
All elephants are Tigers
Conclusions :
I.   No elephant is a monkey
II.   All Donkeys being Tigers is a possibility
III.   All Monkeys being Tigers is a possibility
IV.   Some Donkeys are elephants
 (a) Only I follows
 (b) Only II follows
 (c) Only I, II and III follow
 (d) All follow
 (e) None follows

DIRECTIONS (Qs. 46-50) : In the following questions, the symbols %, *, @, $ and # are used with the following meaning as illustrated below :

'P @ Q' means 'P is not smaller than Q'.
'P # Q' means 'P is not greater than Q'.
'P % Q' means 'P is neither greater than nor equal to Q'.
'P * Q' means 'P is neither smaller than nor greater than Q'.
'P $ Q' means 'P is neither smaller than nor equal to Q'.

46. **Statements :** T$K, K#R, R*M
 Conclusions : I. M*K
             II . M % T
             III. M$K
 (a) All follows
 (b) Only either I or III follows
 (c) Only either I or II follows
 (d) Only either II or III follows
 (e) None of the above

47. Statements : M%R, R#T, T*N
Conclusions : I. N*R
          II . N$R
          III .N$M
(a) All follows
(b) Either I or II follows
(c) Either I or II and III follows
(d) Either I or III and II follows
(e) None of the above

48. Statements : V@M, A$M, R#V
Conclusions : I. R#A
          II . V@A
          III. R$M
(a) Only I follows   (b) Only II follows
(c) Only III follows   (d) None follows
(e) All follow

49. Statements : B*D, D@H, H%F
Conclusions : I. B*F
          II . B$F
          III. D$F
(a) None follows
(b) Only either I or II follows
(c) Only either I or II and III follows
(d) Only III follows
(e) All follow

50. Statements : J#N, K@N, T$K
Conclusions : I. J%T
          II. T$N
          III .N@J
(a) None follows
(b) Only I or II follow
(c) Only I and III follow
(d) Only II and III follow
(e) All follow

DIRECTIONS (Qs. 51-55) : Read the following information carefully and answer the questions based on it.

Ten students– A, B, C, D, E, F, G, H, I and J are sitting in a row facing West.
I. B and F are not sitting on either of the edges.
II. G is sitting to the left of D and H is sitting to the right of J.
III. There are four persons between E and A.
IV. I is to the North of B and F is to the South of D.
V. J is in between A and D and G is in between E and F.
VI. There are two persons between H and C.

51. Who is sitting at the seventh place counting from left?
(a) H   (b) C
(c) J   (d) Either H or C
(e) None of these

52. Who among the following is definitely sitting at one of the ends?
(a) C   (b) H
(c) E   (d) Cannot be determined
(e) None of these

53. Who are immediate neighbours of I?
(a) BC   (b) BH
(c) AH   (d) Cannot be determined
(e) None of these

54. Who is sitting second left of D?
(a) G   (b) F
(c) E   (d) J
(e) None of these

55. If G and A interchange their positions, then who become the immediate neighbours of E?
(a) G and F   (b) Only F
(c) Only A   (d) J and H
(e) None of these

DIRECTIONS (Qs. 56-60): Answer these questions referring to the symbol-letter-number sequence given below:

E G 4 B H 7 5 @ K 8 D N £ Q Z $ W 3 C 1 9 * 1 B 2 S 6

56. How many such consonants are there in the above sequence which are immediately preceded by a symbol and immediately followed by a digit ?
(a) One   (b) Two
(c) None   (d) Three
(e) More than three

57. What should come in place of the question mark (?) in the following sequence ?
4H@, KDQ, ?, 9IS
(a) ZW1   (b) NQ$
(c) @8N   (d) $W9
(e) None of these

58. Which of the following is exactly in the midway between the ninth from left end and the seventh from right end ?
(a) Q   (b) Z
(c) $ (d) W
(e) None of these

59. If the first fifteen elements are written in the reverse order then which of the following will be seventh to the left of twelfth element from right end ?
(a) 7   (b) @
(c) 5   (d) K
(e) None of these

60. How many such digits are there in the above sequence which are immediately preceded as well as followed by digits ?
(a) None   (b) One
(c) Two   (d) Three
(e) None of these

DIRECTIONS (Qs. 61-65) : Read the following information carefully to answer the given questions.

A university organised exams for six different subjects, viz Maths, Physics, Chemistry, Electronics, Statistics and English on six days of a week, not necessarily in the same order. The exams start from Monday, with a holiday on any day of the week. Only full day is devoted to one exam.

The exam of Maths is scheduled immediately after the exam of Physics. The exam of Electronics is scheduled on Wednesday but not after the exam of English. The exam of Chemistry is scheduled on Friday. There is only one exam between the exams of Statistics and Maths. There is only one day when no paper is scheduled but that is not Saturday. The exam of English is scheduled just before the holiday.

61. On which of the following days is the exam of Statistics scheduled?
  - (a) Tuesday
  - (b) Wednesday
  - (c) Friday
  - (d) Saturday
  - (e) None of these

62. On which day is a holiday?
  - (a) Sunday
  - (b) Monday
  - (c) Tuesday
  - (d) Wednesday
  - (e) None of these

63. How many exams is/are scheduled between the exams of Maths and Electronics?
  - (a) One
  - (b) Two
  - (c) Three
  - (d) Four
  - (e) None

64. Which two exams are scheduled on the first and last day?
  - (a) Electronics, English
  - (b) Maths, English
  - (c) Physics, Chemistry
  - (d) Physics, English
  - (e) None of these

65. Which of the following combinations is correct?
  - (a) English - Thursday
  - (b) Maths-Monday
  - (c) Statistics- Saturday
  - (d) Physics-Monday
  - (e) None of these

DIRECTIONS (Q. 66-71): Study the following information to answer the given questions:

In a certain code, 'always create new ideas' is written as 'ba ri sha gi', 'ideas and new thoughts' is written as 'fa gi ma ri', 'create thoughts and insights' is written as 'ma jo ba fa', and 'new and better solutions' is written as 'ki ri to fa'.

66. What is the code for 'ideas'?
  - (a) sha
  - (b) ba
  - (c) gi
  - (d) ma
  - (e) Cannot be determined

67. What does 'fa' stand for?
  - (a) thoughts
  - (b) insights
  - (c) new
  - (d) and
  - (e) solutions

68. 'fa lo ba' could be a code for which of the following?
  - (a) thoughts and action
  - (b) create and innovate
  - (c) ideas and thoughts
  - (d) create new solutions
  - (e) always better ideas

69. What is the code for 'new'?
  - (a) ki
  - (b) ri
  - (c) to
  - (d) fa
  - (e) ba

70. Which of the following may represent 'insights always better'?
  - (a) jo ki to
  - (b) ki to ri
  - (c) sha jo ri
  - (d) to sha jo
  - (e) sha to ba

71. What is the code for 'thoughts'?
  - (a) ma
  - (b) fa
  - (c) ba
  - (d) jo
  - (e) Either jo or fa

DIRECTIONS (72-74) : Study the given information carefully and answer the given questions:

A is father of P. B has three children. C is sister-in-law of D. P and Q are brother and sister but not necessarily in the same order. P is niece of F. E is grandfather of Q. D is sister of F. There are two married couple in the family.

72. How is F related to B ?
  - (a) Son
  - (b) Daughter
  - (c) Sister
  - (d) Can't be determined
  - (e) None of these

73. How is C related to F ?
  - (a) Mother
  - (b) Brother
  - (c) Sister-in-law
  - (d) Can't be determined
  - (e) None of these

74. Who among the following is grandmother of P?
  - (a) B
  - (b) E
  - (c) C
  - (d) D
  - (e) None of these

DIRECTIONS (Qs. 75-80) : Study the following information carefully to answer the given questions.

Eight friends A, B, C, D, E, F, G and H are sitting around a circle facing the centre but not necessarily in the same order. G sits third to left of D. Only one person sits between D and F. B sits second to right of H. H is not an immediate neighbour of D. C is not an immediate neighbour of D. E is an immediate neighbour of H.

75. What is the position of E with respect to the position of C?
  - (a) Third to the left
  - (b) Second to the left
  - (c) Immediate right
  - (d) Third to the right
  - (e) Second to the right

76. Who amongst the following sits exactly between A and G?
  - (a) B
  - (b) C
  - (c) E
  - (d) F
  - (e) D

77. Four of the following five are alike in a certain way and thus form a group. Which is the one that does not belong to that group?
  - (a) CG
  - (b) AE
  - (c) HD
  - (d) BC
  - (e) None of these

78. Which of the following is true with respect to given seating arrangement ?
  - (a) Both A and D are immediate neighbours of E
  - (b) C sits exactly between H and F
  - (c) Only three people sit between C and E
  - (d) H is to the immediate left of B
  - (e) None of these

79. Who amongst the following sits third to the left of F?
  - (a) A
  - (b) B
  - (c) C
  - (d) G
  - (e) H

80. What is the position of A with respect to H?
  - (a) Second to the left
  - (b) Fourth to the left
  - (c) Third to the right
  - (d) Third to the left
  - (e) Second to the right

HINTS & EXPLANATIONS

1. (e) Total girls passing from Mumbai = 2000
So Total students passing from Mumbai
$$= \frac{2000}{5} \times 12 = 4800$$
So Total students $= \frac{4800}{8} \times 100 = 60000$
So Total students passing from Chennai
$= 60000 \times 20/100 = 12000$
Total number of boys passing from Chennai
$= 12000 \times 13/25 = 6240$

2. (c) Total students passed in XII from Mumbai = 18000
So Total students passed in XII from Delhi = 28800
Total number of girls passing from Delhi
$= 28800 \times 5/8 = 18000$

3. (d) According to graph, Answer will be rest.

4. (b) Let the total no of passing students be 'x'
18% of x × 9/15 – 16% of x × 3/8 = 7260
x = 151250

5. (b) 25% of 2,40,000 × 4/10 = 24000

6. (b) Saving of P = 60/360 × 9 = 1.5
Saving of Q = 50/360 × 10.5 = 1.45
Total = 1.5 + 1.45 = 2.95 lakh

7. (c) Required difference
$= 45/360 \times 10.5 - 40/360 \times 9$
$= 1.31 - 1 = 31000$

8. (e) Food of Q = 100/360 × 10.5 = 2.91
Education of P = 90/360 × 9 = 2.25
Req.% = (2.91 × 100)/2.25 = 130%

9. (c) Rent of P = 70/360 × 9 = 1.75
Rent of Q = 75/360 × 10.5 = 2.18
Average = (1.75 + 2.18)/2 = 1.96 lakh

10. (d) Education of Q = 262500
Education of P = 225000
Red.% = (262500 – 225000)/225000 × 100
$= 16.66\%$

11. (a) $? \approx 395 + 187 = 582$

12. (c) $? \approx (5)^2 + (21)^3 + \sqrt{1089}$
$\approx 25 + 9261 + 33 \approx 9319$

13. (e) $? \approx \dfrac{5000 \times 25}{100} - \dfrac{3000 \times 65}{100}$
$\approx 1250 - 1950 \approx -700$

14. (c) $? = (81)^{-1/2} - (64)^{-2/3}$
$$= \left(\frac{1}{81}\right)^{\frac{1}{2}} - \left(\frac{1}{64}\right)^{\frac{2}{3}} = \frac{1}{9} - \frac{1}{16} = \frac{16-9}{144} = \frac{7}{144}$$

15. (a) $? = \dfrac{\sqrt{29241}}{\sqrt{361}} \times \dfrac{47}{9} = \dfrac{171}{19} \times \dfrac{47}{9} = 47$

16. (a) 121   117   108   92   67 $\boxed{31}$
$-2^2 \quad -3^2 \quad -4^2 \quad -5^2 \quad -6^2$

17. (b) 50   26   14 $\boxed{8}$ 5   3.5
$\div 2 + 1 \quad \div 2 + 1 \quad \div 2 + 1 \quad \div 2 + 1 \quad \div 2 + 1$

18. (c) 3   23   43 $\boxed{63}$ 83   103
$+20 \quad +20 \quad +20 \quad +20 \quad +20$

19. (e) 748   737   715   682   638 $\boxed{583}$
$-11 \quad -22 \quad -33 \quad -44 \quad -55$

20. (d) 1   9   25   49   81 $\boxed{121}$ 169
$1^2 \quad 3^2 \quad 5^2 \quad 7^2 \quad 9^2 \quad 11^2 \quad 13^2$

21. (e) The number of employees in companies A, B and C be 4x, 5x and 6x respectively
After increase in the number of employees, required ratio will be
$$= 4x \times \frac{125}{100} : 5x \times \frac{130}{100} : 6x \times \frac{150}{100}$$
$= 4 \times 25 : 5 \times 26 : 6 \times 30$
$= 10 : 13 : 18$

22. (b) According to the questions, third number will be
$= 5 \times 213 - 2 \times 233.5 - 2 \times 271$
$= 1065 - 467 - 542 = 56$

23. (a) Let Sonali's monthly income $= ₹\, x$
Sonali's percentage monthly spendings
$= (55 + 15)\% = 70\%$
Percentage savings $= 100 - 70 = 30\%$
ATQ,
∴ 30% of x = 12750
$$\Rightarrow x = \frac{12750 \times 100}{30} = ₹\, 42500$$

24. (e) $C.I. = P\left[\left(1 + \dfrac{r}{100}\right)^t - 1\right] = 9650\left[\left(1 + \dfrac{6}{100}\right)^3 - 1\right]$
$= 9650\,(1.191016 - 1)$
$= 9650 \times 0.191016 \approx ₹\, 1843$

25. (c) The rate of milk when milkman sells 120 litres of milk for ₹ 3360
$$\therefore \quad SP = \left(\frac{3360}{120}\right) = ₹\, 28$$

The rate of milk when milkman sells 240 litres of milk for ₹ 6120.

$$\therefore \quad SP = \left(\frac{6120}{240}\right) = ₹\, 25.5$$

$\therefore$ Required discount $= (28 - 25.5) = ₹\, 2.5$

26. (a) Let the number be x.

ATQ, $\dfrac{3626}{x^2} \times 32 = 2368$

$$\Rightarrow x^2 = \frac{3626 \times 32}{2368} = 49$$

$$\therefore \quad x = \sqrt{49} = 7$$

27. (b) Let the two digits number be $10n + m$ and $n > m$.

As given,

$n + m = 14$

$n - m = 2$

On solving the equation,

$n = 8, m = 6$

$\therefore$ Product of digits $= 8 \times 6 = 48$

28. (d) After servicing, speed of car $= 60$ km/h

$\therefore$ Distance covered in 6 hours

$= (60 \times 6)$km $= 360$ km

Before servicing, time taken to cover 360 km

$$\therefore \text{ Time taken } = \frac{360\,\text{km}}{50\,\text{km/h}} = 7.2\,\text{hours}$$

29. (a) $x + y = 13$ ...(i)

$x - y = 3$ ...(ii)

On adding,

$2x = 16$

$\Rightarrow x = 8$

$\therefore y = 5$

$\therefore$ Numbers are 85 and 58.

30. (b) Le the CP of the shoes be ₹ x.

$\therefore 2033 - x = x - 1063$

$\Rightarrow 2x = 2033 + 1063 = 3096$

$$\Rightarrow x = \frac{3096}{2} = ₹\,1548$$

31. (b) $x = \dfrac{-3}{4}, \dfrac{-1}{2}$; $y = -3, \dfrac{-4}{5}$ $\therefore$ $x > y$

32. (d) $x = \dfrac{-2}{3}, \dfrac{-1}{3}$; $y = \dfrac{-7}{4}, \dfrac{-2}{3}$ $\therefore$ $x \geq y$

33. (c) $x = \dfrac{-5}{4}, \dfrac{1}{2}$; $y = \dfrac{4}{3}, \dfrac{1}{2}$ $\therefore$ $x \leq y$

34. (a)

35. (e) $x = 19, y = 19$

36. (b) Total number of users of brand B across all Five cities

$= 600 + 500 + 650 + 700 + 550 = 3000$

37. (c) $700 = x\%$ of 500

$$700 = \frac{x \times 500}{100} \Rightarrow x = \frac{700}{5} = 140\,\%$$

38. (c) Required average $= \dfrac{500 + 550 + 600 + 550 + 700}{5}$

$$= 580$$

39. (d) Required difference $= 1250 - 1100 = 150$

40. (a) Required Ratio $= \dfrac{500}{700} = 5{:}7$

41. (a)

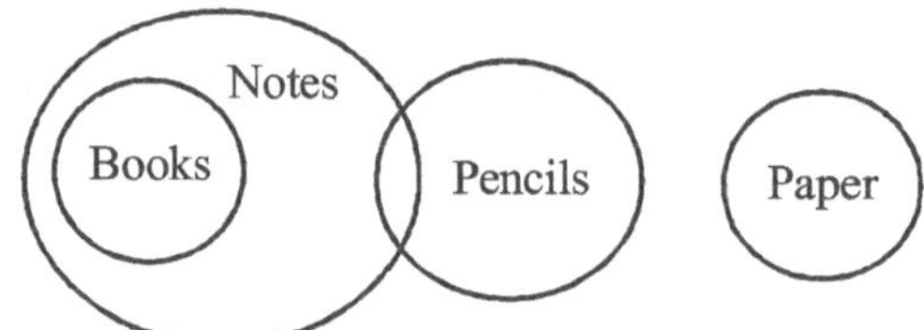

Conclusions: I √ II. × III. ￤ IV. ↑
                      Complementary pair

So, only I and either III and IV follow.

42. (d)

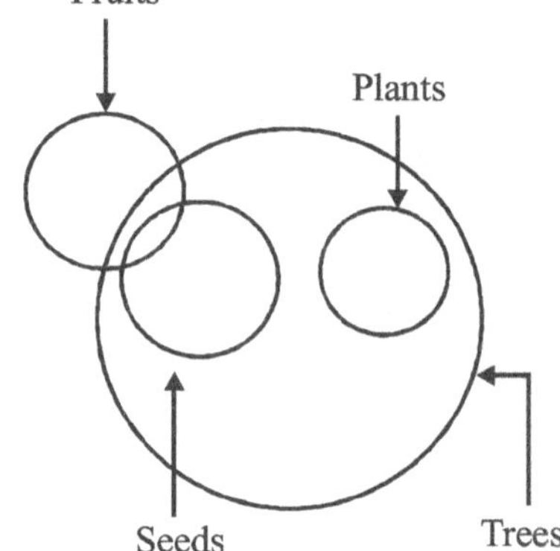

Conclusions

I. Some plants are seeds.

II. Some plants are fruits. (×)   Complementary

III. Some trees are fruits. (×)   pair (I-E)

IV. No plant is a seed.

So, either I or IV follow.

43. (e)

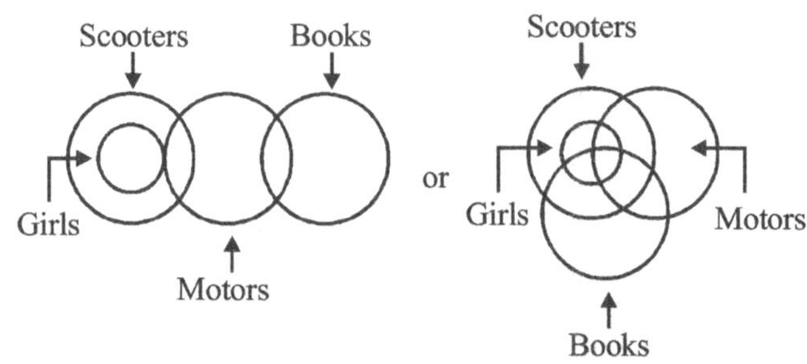

Conclusions

  I.   Some girls are motors. (×)

  II. Some girls are books. (×)

  III. Some scooters are girls. (√)

  IV. No girl is a book. (×)

Complementary pair (I-E)

So, either II or IV and III follow.

44. (b) Only II follows

    Explanation :

    I. ✗ II. ✓ III. ✗ IV. ✗

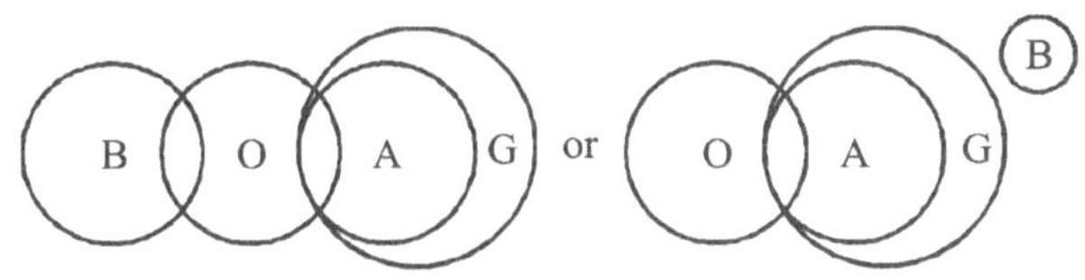

45. (c) Only I, II and III follow

    Explanation :

    I. ✓ II. ✓ III. ✓ IV. ✗

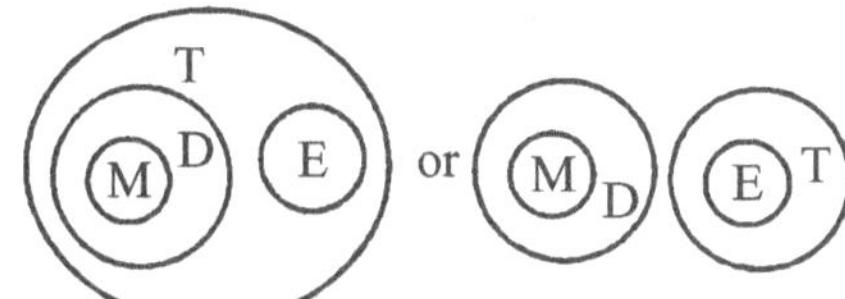

46. (b) Here, $T > K$ ...(i)

    $K \leq R$ ...(ii)

    $R = M$ ...(iii)

    From (ii) and (iii), we get

    $R = M \geq K$ ...(iv)

    Now, from (iv) we get $M > K$ (conclusion III) for $M = K$ (conclusion I). Hence, either conclusion I or conclusion III follows. Again, from (i) and (iv) we can't get any specific relationship between 'M' and 'T'. Hence, conclusion II does not follow.

47. (c) Here, $M < R$ ...(i)

    $R \leq T$ ...(ii)

    $T = N$ ...(iii)

    From (i), (ii) and (iii), we get

    $T = N \geq R > M$ ...(iv)

    Hence, from (iv) we get $N = R$ (conclusion I) or $N > R$ (conclusion II). Hence, either conclusion I or conclusion II follows. Also, from (iv) we get $N > M$ (conclusion III). Hence, conclusion III follows.

48. (d) Here, $V \geq M$ ...(i)

    $A > M$ ...(ii)

    $R \leq V$ ...(iii)

    Therefore, $R \leq V \geq M < A$

    Conclusions I. $R < A$ ...(false)

            II. $V \geq A$ ...(false)

            III. $R > M$ ...(false)

    So, none follows.

49. (a) Here, $B = D$ ...(i)

    $D \geq H$ ...(ii)

    $H < F$ ...(iii)

    Therefore; $B = D \geq H < F$

    Conclusions: I. $B = F$ ...(false)

              II. $B > F$ ...(false)

              III. $D > F$ ...(false)

    So, none follows.

50. (e) Here, $J \leq N$ ...(i)

    $K \geq N$ ...(ii)

    $T > K$ ...(iii)

    From (i), (ii) and (iii), we get

    $T > K \geq N \geq J$ ...(iv)

    Conclusions: I. $J < T$ ...(True)

              II. $T > N$ ...(True)

              III. $N \geq J$ ...(True)

    Thus, all follow.

51. (d) Either H or C will occupy seventh position from the left.

52. (c) Clearly, E is definitely sitting at one of the ends.

53. (d) The immediate neighbours of I cannot be determined because the position of H and C are not fixed.

54. (a) G is sitting to the second left of D.

55. (c) A will become the immediate neighbour of E after interchanging position.

56. (b) E G 4 B H 7 5 @ <u>K</u> 8 D N £ Q Z $ <u>W</u> 3 C 1 9 * 1 B 2 S 6

57. (a) The first, second and third element of each group is sixth element to the right of the respective element of previous group as given in all in the sequence.

58. (b) There are 27 elements in all in the sequence.

    So, $(27 - 9 - 7 =)$ 11 elements are between the 9th from left and 7th from right.

    Hence, $(9 + 6 =)$ 15th element from the left and will be the required answer.

59. (c) 7th to the left of 12th from right

    $= (12 + 7 =)$ 19th from right

    $= (27 - 19 + 1 =)$ 9th from left

    But the first 15 elements are reversed.

    $= (15 - 9 + 1 =)$ 7th from left in the original sequence $= 5$.

60. (a) For the condition to be fulfilled, three digits should be together but it is not so in the given sequence.

Sol. (Qs. 61-65) : From the given information we can draw the following table :-

Monday	Physics
Tuesday	Maths
Wednesday	Electronics
Thursday	Statistics
Friday	Chemistry
Saturday	English
Sunday	Holiday

61. (e)   62. (a)   63. (e)   64. (d)   65. (d)

(66-71) :

'always create new ideas' → 'ba ri sha gi' ....(a)

'ideas and new thoughts' → 'fa gi ma ri' ....(b)

'create thoughts and insights' → 'ma jo ba fa' ....(c)

'new and better solutions' → 'ki ri to fa' ....(d)

Using (a) and (d),

  new → ri

Using (a), (b) and (d),

  ideas → gi

  and → fa

  thoughts → ma

Using (a) and (c),

  create → ba

  always → sha

  insights → jo

  better solution → ki to

66.   (c)   67.   (d)   68.   (b)   69.   (b)   70.   (d)

71.   (a)

Solution (72-74)

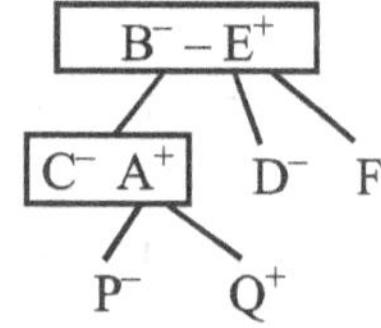

72.   (d)   73.   (c)   74.   (a)

(75-80): On the basis of given information the final sitting arrangement of eight person in a circle failing centre is as following :

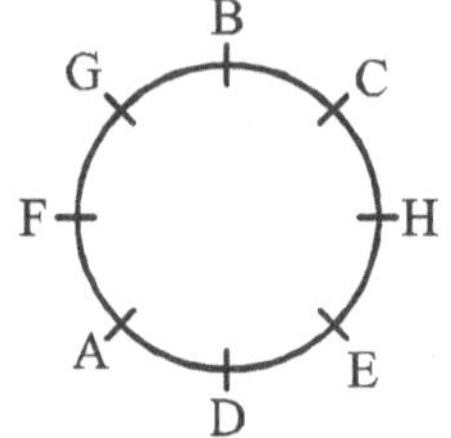

75.   (b)   Clearly, E is second to the left of C.

76.   (d)   F sits exactly between A and G.

77.   (c)   Except HD, in all other pairs, first member is present on the clockwise side of other.

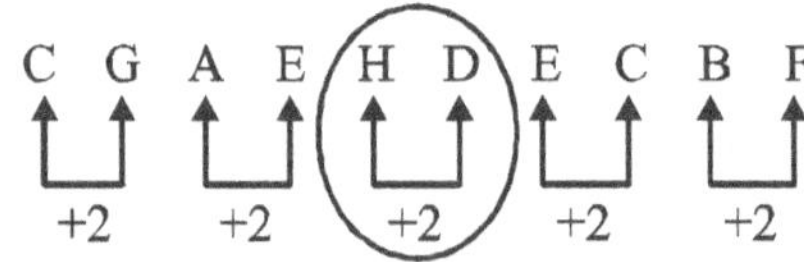

78.   (e)   It is clear from the figure that none of the options (a) - (d) is true.

79.   (d)   Clearly, C is third to the left of F.

80.   (d)   A is third to the left of H.

PRACTICE SET 4

Time : 45 Min.　　　　**Max. Marks : 80**

QUANTITATIVE APTITUDE

DIRECTIONS (Qs. 1-5) : What should come in place of question mark (?) in the following number series?

1. 36 20 ? 8 6 5
   - (a) 10
   - (b) 12
   - (c) 14
   - (d) 16
   - (e) None of these

2. 668 656 632 584 ? 296
   - (a) 392
   - (b) 438
   - (c) 488
   - (d) 536
   - (e) None of these

3. 1   121   441   961   1681   ?
   - (a) 2701
   - (b) 2511
   - (c) 2611
   - (d) 2801
   - (e) None of these

4. 9 49 201 1009 ? 20209 80841
   - (a) 4054
   - (b) 4049
   - (c) 4050
   - (d) 4041
   - (e) None of these

5. 31   35   44   60   85   ?
   - (a) 121
   - (b) 111
   - (c) 109
   - (d) 97
   - (e) None of these

6. The average of five positive numbers is 308. The average of first two numbers is 482.5 and the average of last two numbers is 258.5. What is the third number?
   - (a) 224
   - (b) 58
   - (c) 121
   - (d) Cannot be determined
   - (e) None of these

7. Sophia invests 25% of her monthly salary in insurance policies. She spends 15% of her monthly salary in shopping and 35% of her salary on household expenses. She saves the remaining amount of ₹ 9,050. What is Sophia's annual income?
   - (a) ₹84,500
   - (b) ₹5,30,000
   - (c) ₹3,25,200
   - (d) ₹4,34,400
   - (e) None of these

8. The number of employees in companies A, B and C are in a ratio of 3 : 2 : 4 respectively. If the number of employees in the three companies is increased by 20%, 30% and 15% respectively, what will be the new ratio of employees working in companies A, B and C respectively ?
   - (a) 18 : 13 : 24
   - (b) 13 : 18 : 23
   - (c) 17 : 3 : 23
   - (d) 18 : 11 : 23
   - (e) None of these

9. The ages of Vaibhav and Jagat are in the ratio of 12 : 7 respectively, After 6 years the ratio of their ages will be 3 : 2. What is the difference in their ages?
   - (a) 8 years
   - (b) 12 years
   - (c) 9 years
   - (d) 10 years
   - (e) None of these

10. The owner of a book shop charges his customer 28% more than the cost price. If a customer paid ₹ 1,408 for some books, then what was the cost price of the books ?
    - (a) ₹1,100
    - (b) ₹1,111
    - (c) ₹1,110
    - (d) ₹1,000
    - (e) None of these

DIRECTIONS (Q. 11-15): Study the following table carefully to answer the questions that follow.

Monthly Rent (in ₹ thousand) at five different places in six different years

Years	Place				
	Churchgate	Dadar	Kandivali	Borivali	Virar
2005	5.3	3.8	1.5	2.7	1.1
2006	12.5	8.3	3.4	4.8	2.1
2007	16.7	11.7	5.5	6.6	1.8
2008	20.9	13.6	9.8	12.7	3.6
2009	25.8	14.5	11.5	14.1	5.5
2010	30.3	20.9	15.6	15.9	7.8

11. In which place did the monthly rent not increase consistently from year 2005 to 2010?
   (a) Churchgate   (b) Dadar
   (c) Kandivali   (d) Borivali
   (e) Virar

12. In which year at Churchagate, the monthly rent increased more than 100 per cent from the previous year?
   (a) 2006   (b) 2007
   (c) 2008   (d) 2009
   (e) 2010

13. What was the difference between the monthly rent at Dadar in the year 2009 and Borivali in the year 2007?
   (a) ₹ 7,600   (b) ₹ 7,900
   (c) ₹ 8,100   (d) ₹ 8,600
   (e) None of these

14. Monthly rent at Kandivali in the year 2008 was approximately what per cent of the total monthly rent at Virar over all the years together?
   (a) 30   (b) 33
   (c) 38   (d) 42
   (e) 45

15. Which city was most expensive in terms of rent?
   (a) Churchgate   (b) Dadar
   (c) Kandivali   (d) Borivali
   (e) Virar

DIRECTIONS (Q. 16-20): Study the following pie-chart carefully to answer these questions.

Total number of passengers = 8500
Percentage of Passengers

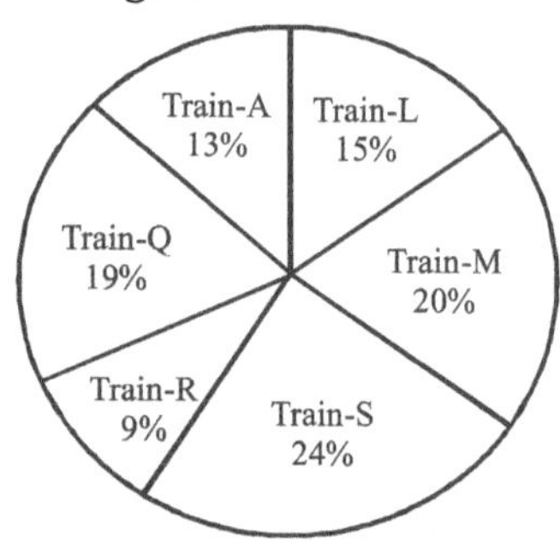

16. What was the **approximate** average number of passenger in Train-S, Train-M and Train-L together?
   (a) 1521   (b) 1641
   (c) 1651   (d) 1671
   (e) 1691

17. If in Train-R 34 per cent of the passengers are females and 26 per cent are children, what is the number of males in that train?
   (a) 306   (b) 316
   (c) 308   (d) 318
   (e) None of these

18. The number of passengers in Train-Q is approximately what percentage of the total number of passengers in Train-A and Train-R?
   (a) 90   (b) 70
   (c) 75   (d) 80
   (e) 86

19. Which train has the second highest number of passengers?
   (a) A   (b) Q
   (c) S   (d) M
   (e) L

20. How many more per cent (approximately) number of passengers are there in Train-M as compared to the number of passengers in Train-L?
   (a) 29   (b) 49
   (c) 43   (d) 33
   (e) 39

DIRECTIONS (Qs. 21-25) : In the following questions, two equations numbered I and II are given. You have to solve both the equations and give answers.

(a) if $x > y$
(b) if $x \geq y$
(c) if $x < y$
(d) if $x \leq y$
(e) if $x = y$ or the relationship cannot be established

21. I. $12x^2 + 11x + 12 = 10x^2 + 22x$
    II. $13y^2 - 18y + 3 = 9y^2 - 10y$

22. I. $\dfrac{18}{x^2} + \dfrac{6}{x} - \dfrac{12}{x^2} = \dfrac{8}{x^2}$
    II. $y^3 + 9.68 + 5.64 = 16.95$

23. I. $\sqrt{1225x} + \sqrt{4900} = 0$
    II. $(81)^{1/4} y + (343)^{1/3} = 0$

24. I. I. $\dfrac{(2)^5 + (11)^3}{6} = x^3$
    II. $4y^3 = -(589 \div 4) + 5y^3$

25. I. $(x^{7/5} \div 9) = 169 \div x^{3/5}$
    II. $y^{1/4} \times y^{1/4} \times 7 = 273 \div y^{1/2}$

DIRECTIONS (Qs. 26-30) : What should come in place of the question mark (?) in the following questions?

26. $(84)^2 - (67)^2 + \sqrt{?} = 2588$

    (a) 361   (b) 529
    (c) 441   (d) 625
    (e) None of these

27. $668 \div 167 \times 284 = ?$

    (a) 1156   (b) 1136
    (c) 1096   (d) 1116
    (e) None of these

28. $\sqrt[3]{10648} \times \sqrt[3]{5832} = ?$

    (a) 396   (b) 216
    (c) 432   (d) 576
    (e) None of these

29. 60% of 25% of $\dfrac{5}{6}$ th of $? = 630$

    (a) 5060   (b) 5200
    (c) 4880   (d) 4500
    (e) None of these

30. $(85410 + 36885 + 24705) \div 1600 = ?$

    (a) 90.25   (b) 94.386
    (c) 95.50   (d) 91.875
    (e) None of these

31. What amount of compound interest can be obtained on an amount of ₹ 8, 840 at the rate of 5% p.a at the end of 3 years?

    (a) ₹1,393.405   (b) ₹1,326
    (c) ₹1,384.50   (d) ₹1340
    (e) None of these

32. A trader sells 150 metres of cloth for ₹ 6, 600 and he sells 300 metres of cloth for ₹ 12, 750. How much concession does the trader give per metre of cloth, when he sells 300 metres of cloth?

    (a) ₹ 3   (b) ₹ 2.5
    (c) ₹ 1.5   (d) ₹ 2
    (e) None of these

33. When 3888 is divided by the square of a number and the answer so obtained is multiplied by 21, the final answer so obtained is 252. What is the number?

    (a) 324   (b) 16
    (c) 256   (d) 144
    (e) None of these

34. The sum of the digits of a two digit number is 14. The difference between the first digit and the second digit of the two digit number is 4. What is the two digit number ?

    (a) 86   (b) 95
    (c) 68   (d) 77
    (e) None of these

35. A car runs at the speed of 40 kmph when not serviced and runs at 65 kmph. when serviced. After servicing, the car covers a certain distance in 5 hours. How much **approximate** time will the car take to cover the same distance when not serviced?

    (a) 10   (b) 7
    (c) 12   (d) 8
    (e) 6

DIRECTIONS (Qs. 36-40) : Study the following table carefully and answer the questions given below.

Number of literates in various cities over the years
M = Males, F = Females

Year	2012		2013		2014		2015		2016	
City	M	F	M	F	M	F	M	F	M	F
U	15000	25000	18550	20000	18590	25000	25000	25500	28000	28800
V	12500	9200	14680	10520	16000	11000	16850	13680	16920	14360
W	18660	17380	18950	18000	18980	19000	19500	19500	19250	19600
X	14200	14350	14820	14500	15250	15000	15390	15250	16000	16200
Y	9700	8320	9990	8540	9870	8820	10200	10000	10520	10300

36. What is the total number of male literates in City W over the years?

    (a) 97650   (b) 95670
    (c) 99280   (d) 96570
    (e) None of these

37. What is the total number of literates across the cities in the year 2016 ?

    (a) 180280   (b) 182000
    (c) 188050   (d) 180500
    (e) None of these

38. What is the difference between the total number of female literates across the cities in the year 2013 and the year 2015 ?

    (a) 11850   (b) 12000
    (c) 11500   (d) 12800
    (e) None of these

39. What is the ratio of literates of City X in the year 2012 to the literates of the same city in the year 2014 ?

    (a) 581 : 624   (b) 64 : 75
    (c) 571 : 605   (d) 84 : 131
    (e) None of these

40. What is the average number of female literates across the cities in the year 2016 ?

    (a) 18725   (b) 15872
    (c) 17582   (d) 17852
    (e) None of these

REASONING ABILITY

41. In a certain code language 'money makes profit' is written as 've jo qi', 'makes is expected' is written as 'qi lo mn', and 'profit expected number' is written as 'lo ve pr' ,then what is code for "money" ?

    (a) lo   (b) pr
    (c) qi   (d) ve
    (e) jo

42. If 1 is subtracted from each odd digit in the number 8756432 and 1 is added to each even digit in number then which of the following digit is repeated in the digits so obtained ?
    (a) 9
    (b) 6
    (c) 5
    (d) 4
    (e) None of these

43. If a boy moves from his house to his school that is 20m from his home towards south. He goes in the north direction thinking it south direction and walks for 20, until he realizes his mistake. How much more distance and in which direction he must walk in order to reach the actual destination?
    (a) 40 m in Southeast direction
    (b) 20 m in South direction
    (c) 40 m in South direction
    (d) 60 m in North direction
    (e) None of these

DIRECTIONS (Qs. 44-49) : Study the following information and answer the questions.

S, T, U, V, W, X, Y and Z live on eight different floors of a building but not necessarily in the same order. The lowermost floor of the building is numbered one, the one above that is numbered two and so on till the topmost floor is numbered eight. Each of them also works at a different banks namely IDBI, SBI, HDFC, BOI, PNB, TJSB, Axis Bank and SVC, but not necessarily in the same order.

- Z lives on an even numbered floor. Only three people live between Z and the one who works at BOI. W lives immediately below the one who works at BOI.
- Only three people live between W and the one who works at Axis Bank.
- V lives immediately above T. V lives on an odd numbered floor. T does not work at BOI.
- Only two people live between T and the one who works at SBI. The one who works at SBI does not live on the lowermost floor.
- The one who works at SVC lives immediately above the one who works at PNB. The one who works at SVC lives on an even numbered floor but not on floor numbered two.
- Only one person lives between the one who works at SVC and the one who works at IDBI.
- X lives immediately above S. X lives on an even numbered floor. X does not work at TJSB.
- U does not work at PNB and does not live on floor numbered four.

44. Four of the following five are alike in a certain way based on the given arrangement and hence form a group. Which of the following does not belong to that group ?
    (a) S-Floor numbered two
    (b) T-Floor numbered eight
    (c) W-Floor numbered six
    (d) Z-Floor numbered one
    (e) U-Floor numbered seven

45. V works at which of the following banks ?
    (a) Axis Bank
    (b) SVC
    (c) IDBI
    (d) SBI
    (e) Other than those given as options

46. Which of the following pair represent those who live immediately above and immediately below Z ?
    (a) S, T
    (b) S, V
    (c) Other than those given as options
    (d) T, V
    (e) X, Y

47. W works at which of the following banks ?
    (a) Other than those given as options
    (b) PNB
    (c) Axis Bank
    (d) BOI
    (e) SBI

48. U lives on which of the following floor numbers ?
    (a) One
    (b) Two
    (c) None of these
    (d) Five
    (e) Seven

49. As per the given arrangement, U is related to PNB and S is related to HDFC in a certain way. To which of the following is V related to in the same way ?
    (a) SVC
    (b) SBI
    (c) IDBI
    (d) TJSB
    (e) Axis Bank

DIRECTIONS (Qs. 50-51) : Study the following information and answer the given questions.

- K is the brother of J. J is the mother of Y.
- Y is the sister of T. T is married to Q. S is the father of J.
- S has only one daughter. S is married to R.
- K is the brother of D. U is the father-in-law of D.

50. How is D related to Y ?
    (a) Cannot be determined
    (b) Mother
    (c) Uncle
    (d) Father
    (e) Aunt

51. If Y is married to P, then how is S related to P ?
    (a) None of these
    (b) Sister
    (c) Brother-in-law
    (d) Sister-in-law
    (e) Brother

**DIRECTIONS (Qs. 52-56) : In each of the questions below are given three statements followed by three conclusions numbered I, II and III. You have to take the given statements to be true even, if they seems to be at variance with commonly known facts. Read all the conclusions and then decide which of the given conclusions logically follows from the given statements disregarding commonly known facts.

52. Statements　　Some carrots are brinjals.
　　　　　　　　　　Some brinjals are apples.
　　　　　　　　　　All apples are bananas.

　　Conclusions　I.　Some apples are carrots.
　　　　　　　　　　II.　Some bananas are brinjals.
　　　　　　　　　　III.　Some bananas are carrots.

(a)　Only I follows　　　　(b)　Only II follows
(c)　Only III follows　　　(d)　Either II or III follows
(e)　None of these

53. Statements　　All keys are locks.
　　　　　　　　　　All locks are bangles.
　　　　　　　　　　All bangles are cars.

　　Conclusions　I.　Some cars are locks.
　　　　　　　　　　II.　Some bangles are keys.
　　　　　　　　　　III.　Some cars are keys.

(a)　Only I follows　　　　(b)　I and II follow
(c)　I and III follow　　　(d)　II and III follow
(e)　All I, II and III follow

54. Statements　　All fruits are leaves.
　　　　　　　　　　Some leaves are trees.
　　　　　　　　　　No tree is house.

　　Conclusions　I.　Some houses are fruits.
　　　　　　　　　　II.　Some trees are fruits.
　　　　　　　　　　III.　No house is a fruit.

(a)　Only follows　　　　(b)　Only II follows
(c)　Only III follows　　(d)　Either I or III follows
(e)　None follows

55. Statements :　　All drivers are swimmers,
　　　　　　　　　　Some athletes are swimmers,
　　　　　　　　　　No banker is a driver

　　Conclusions:　I.　Some drivers are definitely not athletes
　　　　　　　　　　II.　At least some swimmers are athletes
　　　　　　　　　　III.　Some bankers are swimmers.

(a)　Only I doesn't follow
(b)　Both I and II doesn't follows
(c)　Only II follows
(d)　Both I and III follows
(e)　None follows

56. Statements :　　Some light are sound.
　　　　　　　　　　All sounds are air.
　　　　　　　　　　No air is dust.

　　Conclusions :　I.　All dust being light is a possibility.
　　　　　　　　　　II.　All light being air is a possibility.
　　　　　　　　　　III.　All sound being light is a possibility.

(a)　Only conclusion I does not follow.
(b)　Only conclusion II does not follow.
(c)　Only conclusion III does not follow.
(d)　Both conclusions I and II does not follow.
(e)　None of these

DIRECTIONS (Qs. 57-61) : Read the following information and answer the questions given below.

I.　　A, B, C, D, E, F, G and H are sitting in a row facing North
II.　　A is fourth to the right of E.
III.　H is fourth to the left of D.
IV.　C and F, who are not at the ends, are neighbours of B and E, respectively.
V.　　H is next to the left of A and A is the neighbour of B.

57. What is the position of F?
(a)　Next to the right of E　　(b)　Next to the right of G
(c)　Sixth to the right of D　　(d)　Between G and H
(e)　None of these

58. Which of the following statements is not true?
(a)　G is the neighbour of H and F
(b)　B is next to the right of A
(c)　E is at left end
(d)　D is next to the right of B
(e)　None of the above

59. Who is/are the neighbour/(s) of D?
(a)　F alone　　　　　　(b)　C alone
(c)　B and C　　　　　　(d)　Cannot be determined
(e)　None of these

60. Which of the following statements is not true?
(a)　H is second to the right of F
(b)　E is fourth to the left of A
(c)　D is fourth to the right of H
(d)　All are true
(e)　None of the above

61. Who are sitting at the ends?
(a)　E and C　　　　　　(b)　F and D.
(c)　G and B　　　　　　(d)　Data inadequate
(e)　None of the above

DIRECTIONS (Qs. 62-67) : In each of the questions given below a group of digits is given followed by four combinations of letters/symbols. You have to find out which of the four combinations correctly represents the group of digits based on the letter/symbol codes and the conditions given below. If none of the four combinations represents the group of digits correctly, give (e) i.e. "None of these" as the answer.

Digit:	3	9	6	2	8	7	5	4	1
Symbol :	K	T	$	F	H	#	%	D	M

Conditions for the coding the group of digits:

1.　If the first digit is odd and last digit is even, the codes for the first and the last digits are to be interchanged.
2.　If the first as well as the last digit is even, both are to be coded by the code for last digit.
3.　If the first as well as the last digit is odd, both are to be coded as 'X'.

62. 564923
(a)　%$DTFK　　　　　(b)　K$DTFK
(c)　X$DTFX　　　　　(d)　K$DTF%
(e)　None of these

63. 658247
- (a) $%HFD#
- (b) #%HFD$
- (c) %$HFD#
- (d) %#HFD$
- (e) None of these

64. 436958
- (a) DK$T%D
- (b) DK$T%H
- (c) HK$T%H
- (d) #%$HK#
- (e) None of these

65. 756834
- (a) #%$HKD
- (b) D%$HK#
- (c) D%$HKD
- (d) #%$HK#
- (e) None of these

66. 291378
- (a) FTMK#H
- (b) XTMK#X
- (c) HTMK#F
- (d) FTMK#F
- (e) None of these

67. 128547
- (a) XFH%DX
- (b) XFH#DX
- (c) MFH%DX
- (d) XFH%D#
- (e) None of these

DIRECTIONS (Qs. 68-71) : In each of these questions, relationship between different elements is shown in the statements. The statements are followed by two conclusions.

Give answer
- (a) if only Conclusion I is true
- (b) if only Conclusion II is true
- (c) if either Conclusion I or II is true
- (d) if neither Conclusion I nor II is true
- (e) if both the Conclusions I and II are true

68. Statements $P > R, R < S \leq X, Y = X$

     Conclusions   I. $P < S$ II. $Y > R$

69. Statements $Z = C, B < A = N, C < B$

     Conclusions   I. $Z < B$ II. $N > Z$

70. Statements $T < V = W, X \geq Y, W > X$

     Conclusions   I. $V > Y$ II. $V < X$

71. Statements $J \geq K > P = R < N = S$

     Conclusions   I. $S \geq P$ II. $J < R$

DIRECTIONS (Qs. 72-76) : Study the following information carefully to answer the questions given below.

P, T, V, R, M, D, K and W are sitting around a circular table facing the centre. V is second to the left of T. T is fourth to the right of M. D and P are not immediate neighbours of T. D is third to the right of P. W is not an immediate neighbour of P. P is to the immediate left K.

72. Who is second to the left of K?
- (a) P
- (b) R
- (c) M
- (d) W
- (e) Data inadequate

73. Who is to the immediate left of V?
- (a) D
- (b) M
- (c) W
- (d) Data inadequate
- (e) None of these

74. Who is the third to the right of V?
- (a) T
- (b) K
- (c) P
- (d) M
- (e) None of these

75. What is R's position with respect to V?
- (a) Third to the right
- (b) Fifth to the right
- (c) Third to the left
- (d) Second to the left
- (e) Fourth to the left

76. Four of the following five are alike in a certain way based on their positions in the above sitting arrangement and so form a group. Which of the following does not belong to that group?
- (a) DW
- (b) TP
- (c) VM
- (d) RD
- (e) KR

DIRECTIONS (Qs. 77-80): Read the following information carefully to answer the question:

$P \times Q$ means "P is sister of Q"

$P \div Q$ means " P is mother of Q"

$P + Q$ means " P is brother of Q"

$P - Q$ means " P is father of Q"

77. Which of the following represent W is grandfather of H?
- (a) $W + T - H$
- (b) $W \div T - H$
- (c) $W \times T + H$
- (d) $W \div T + H$
- (e) None of these

78. Which of the following represent "M is nephew of R"?
- (a) $M \div T - R$
- (b) $R \div T - M$
- (c) $R \times T \div M \times J$
- (d) $R \div T - M + J$
- (e) None of these

79. How T is related to S "$W \div T - H + V - S$"?
- (a) sister
- (b) mother
- (c) aunt
- (d) uncle
- (e) None of these

80. The expression means "$S \div T - H \times V - N$"?
- (a) S is grandmother of N
- (b) S is great grandmother of N
- (c) S is mother of V
- (d) N is grandson of S
- (e) None of these

HINTS & EXPLANATIONS

1. (b) $36 \quad 20 \quad \boxed{12} \quad 8 \quad 6 \quad 5$
with $\div 2 + 2$ between each term.

2. (c) $668 \quad 656 \quad 632 \quad 584 \quad \boxed{488} \quad 296$
differences $-12, -24, -48, -96, -192$ (each $\times 2$).

3. (e) $1 \quad 121 \quad 441 \quad 961 \quad 1681 \quad \boxed{2601}$
$= 1^2, \ 11^2, \ 21^2, \ 31^2, \ 41^2, \ 51^2$

4. (d) $9 \quad 49 \quad 201 \quad 1009 \quad \boxed{4041} \quad 20209 \quad 80841$
pattern $\times 5 + 4, \ \times 4 + 5, \ \times 5 + 4, \ \times 4 + 5, \ \times 5 + 4, \ \times 4 + 5$

5. (a) $31 \quad 35 \quad 44 \quad 60 \quad 85 \quad \boxed{121}$
adding $+2^2, +3^2, +4^2, +5^2, +6^2$

6. (b) Third number
$= 5 \times 308 - 2 \times 482.5 - 2 \times 258.5$
$= 1540 - 965 - 517 = 58$

7. (d) Let Sophia's monthly salary $= ₹. \ x$.
ATQ,
Sophia's % monthly expenditure
$= (25 + 15 + 35)\% = 75\%$
Saving $\% = 100 - 75 = 25\%$
$\therefore \quad 25\%$ of $x = 9050$
$\Rightarrow \quad x = 9050 \times 4 = ₹ 36200$
$\therefore \quad$ Sophia's annual income
$= ₹ (12 \times 36200) = ₹ 434400$

8. (e) Let the number of employees in the companies A, B and C be $3x$, $2x$ and $4x$ respectively.
Required ratio
$$= \frac{3x \times 120}{100} : \frac{2x \times 130}{100} : \frac{4x \times 115}{100}$$
$= 18 : 13 : 23$

9. (d) Let the present ages of Vaibhav and Jagat be $12x$ and $7x$ years respectively.
According to the question,
$$\frac{12x + 6}{7x + 6} = \frac{3}{2}$$
$\Rightarrow 24x + 12 = 21x + 18$
$\Rightarrow 24x - 21x$
$= 18 - 12$
$\Rightarrow 3x = 6$
$$\Rightarrow x = \frac{6}{3} = 2$$
$\therefore$ Required difference $= 12x - 7x = 5x = 5 \times 2$
$= 10$ years

10. (a) CP of the books
$$= ₹ \left(\frac{100}{128} \times 1408 \right)$$
$= ₹ 1100$

(11-15):

11. (e) It is clear from the table.

12. (a) Per cent increase in 2006 $= \dfrac{12.5 - 5.3}{5.3} \times 100 \approx 136$

13. (b) Required difference $= (14.5 - 6.6) \times 1000 = ₹ 7900$

14. (e) Total monthly rent at Virar over all the years together
$= (1.1 + 2.1 + 1.8 + 3.6 + 5.5 + 7.8) \times 1000 = 21900$
$$\therefore \text{ Required per cent } = \frac{9800}{21900} \times 100 \approx 45$$

15. (a) It is clear from the table.

16. (d) Required average number of passengers
$$= \frac{1}{3}[(24 + 20 + 15)\% \text{ of } 8500]$$
$$= \frac{1}{3} \times \frac{8500 \times 59}{100} \approx 1671$$

17. (a) Number of passengers in Train R $= \dfrac{8500 \times 9}{100} = 765$
$\therefore$ Number of males $= (100 - 34 - 26)\%$ of 765
$$= \frac{765 \times 40}{100} = 306$$

18. (e) Required per cent $= \dfrac{19}{(13 + 9)} \times 100 \approx 86$

19. (d) It is clear from the pie-chart.

20. (d) Required per cent $= \dfrac{20 - 15}{15} \times 100 \approx 33$

21. (b) I. $\quad 12x^2 + 11x + 12 = 10x^2 + 22x$
$2x^2 - 11x + 12 = 0$
$2x^2 - 8x - 3x + 12 = 0$
$(x - 4)(2x - 3) = 0$
$x = 4, \ x = 3/2$
II. $\quad 13y^2 - 18y + 3 = 9y^2 - 10y$
$4y^2 - 8y + 3 = 0$
$4y^2 - 6y - 2y + 3 = 0$
$(2y - 3)(2y - 1) = 0$
$$y = \frac{3}{2}, \frac{1}{2}$$
$\therefore x \geq y$

22. (c) $\dfrac{18}{x^2} + \dfrac{6}{x} - \dfrac{12}{x^2} = \dfrac{8}{x^2}$
$$\Rightarrow \frac{18 + 6x - 12}{x^2} = \frac{8}{x^2} \Rightarrow 6x + 6 = 8$$

$$\therefore \quad x = \frac{2}{6} = 0.33$$

II. $\quad y^3 + 9.68 + 5.64 = 16.95$

$\Rightarrow \quad y^3 = 16.95 - 15.32$

$\Rightarrow \quad y^3 = 1.63 = y = \sqrt[3]{1.63} \quad \therefore y > x$

23. (a) I. $35x + 70 = 0$

$$\therefore \quad x = \frac{-70}{35} = -2$$

II. $(81)^{1/4}\, y + (343)^{1/3} = 0$

$\Rightarrow \quad 3y + 7 = 0 \Rightarrow 3y = -7$

$$\therefore \quad y = -\frac{7}{3} = -2.33$$

$$\therefore \quad x > y$$

24. (a) I. $\dfrac{(2)^5 + (11)^3}{6} = x^3$

$$\Rightarrow \quad \frac{32 + 1331}{6} = x^3 \Rightarrow \frac{1363}{6} = x^3$$

$$\therefore \quad x^3 = 227.167$$

II. $4y^3 = \dfrac{-589}{4} + 5y^3 \Rightarrow \dfrac{589}{4} = y^3$

$$\therefore \quad y^3 = 147.25 \quad \therefore x > y$$

25. (d) I. $\quad x^{7/5} \div 9 = 169 \div x^{3/5}$

$$\frac{x^{7/5}}{9} = \frac{169}{x^{3/5}}$$

$$\Rightarrow \quad x^{10/5} = 9 \times 169 \Rightarrow x^2 = 9 \times 169$$

$$x = \pm(3 \times 13) = \pm 39$$

II. $y^{1/4} \times y^{1/4} \times 7 = \dfrac{273}{y^{1/2}}$

$$y = \frac{273}{7} = 39$$

$$\therefore \quad x \le y$$

26. (c) $\Rightarrow (84 + 67)(84 - 67) + \sqrt{?} = 2588$

$\Rightarrow \quad 151 \times 17 + \sqrt{?} = 2588$

$\Rightarrow \quad \sqrt{?} = 2588 - 2567 = 21$

$\therefore \quad ? = 21 \times 21 = 441$

27. (b) $? = 4 \times 284 = 1136$

28. (a) $? = \sqrt[3]{10648} \times \sqrt[3]{5832} = 22 \times 18 = 396$

29. (e) $\dfrac{60}{100} \times \dfrac{25}{100} \times \dfrac{5}{6} \times ? = 630$

$\therefore \quad ? = 8 \times 630 = 5040$

30. (d) $? = 147000 \div 1600 = 91.875$

31. (a) $\text{C.I.} = P\left[\left(1 + \dfrac{r}{100}\right)^t - 1\right]$

$$= 8840\left[\left(1 + \frac{5}{100}\right)^3 - 1\right] = 8840\left[\left(\frac{21}{20}\right)^3 - 1\right]$$

$$= 8840\left[\frac{9261}{8000} - 1\right] = \frac{8840 \times 1261}{8000} = ₹\,1393.405$$

32. (c) SP of 150 metres of clothes $= ₹\,6600$

$$\therefore \quad \text{SP of 1 m cloth} = ₹\left[\frac{6600}{150}\right] = ₹\,44$$

SP of 300 metres of cloth $= ₹\,12750$

$$\therefore \quad \text{SP of 1 m cloth} = ₹\left[\frac{12750}{300}\right] = ₹\,42.5$$

$$\therefore \quad \text{Concession} = ₹\,(44 - 42.5) = ₹\,1.5$$

33. (e) Let the number $= x$.

ATQ,

$$\frac{3888}{x^2} \times 21 = 252$$

$$\Rightarrow \quad x^2 = \frac{3888}{252} \times 21 = 324$$

$$\therefore \quad x = \sqrt{324} = 18$$

34. (b) Let two digit number $= 10x + y$

ATQ,

$$x + y = 14 \qquad \qquad \text{..... (i)}$$
$$x - y = 4 \qquad \qquad \text{..... (ii)}$$

From equation (i) & (ii), we get

$$y = 5$$

Now, $x + y = 14$

$$\therefore \qquad x = 14 - 5 = 9$$

Thus, required two-digit number

$$= 10x + y = 10 \times 9 + 5$$
$$= 90 + 5 = 95$$

35. (d) After servicing, the distance covered in 5 hours
$= 65 \times 5 = 325$ km.

Without servicing, speed $= 40$ km/h

$$\therefore \quad \text{Time} = \frac{\text{Distance}}{\text{Speed}} = \frac{325}{40} \approx 8 \text{ hours}$$

36. (e)   37. (e)

38. (e) Female literates in 2013 $= 71560$

Female literates in 2015 $= 83930$

Required difference

$$= 83930 - 71560 = 12370$$

39. (c) No. of literates of city X in 2012

$$= 14200 + 14350 = 28550$$

No. of literates of city X in 2014

$$= 15250 + 15000 = 30250$$

$\therefore$ Required ratio $= 28550 : 30250$

$$= 571 : 605$$

40. (d) Required average

$$= \frac{28800 + 14360 + 19600 + 16200 + 10300}{5}$$

$$= \frac{89260}{5} = 17852$$

41. (e) Money = jo

42. (e) The given number is = 8756432
    Number after operation = 9647523
    Thus there is no repeated digit.

43. (c)

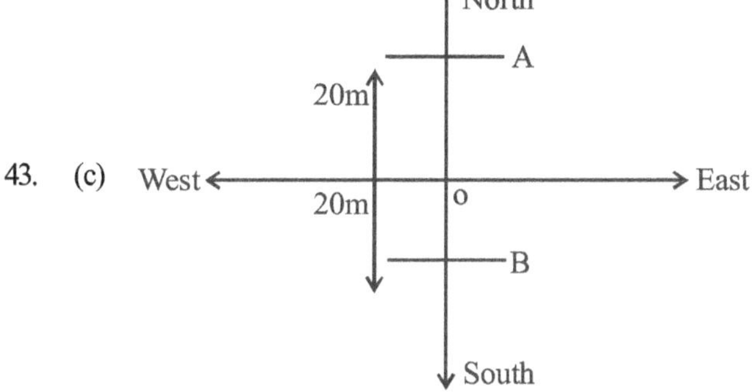

The boy started from Point O and he walked 20 m in the north direction and reached at point A he thought that Point A is his actual destination. However, his actual destination is Point B. So he must walk 40 m in south direction to reach his actual destination.

(44-49): **The given information can be written as follows :-**

Floor	Person	Bank
8	X	HDFC
7	S	SBI
6	Z	IDBI
5	V	AXIS
4	T	SVC
3	Y	PNB
2	U	BOI
1	W	TJBS

44. (b) 45. (a) 46. (b) 47. (a) 48. (b)

49. (c)

(50-51):

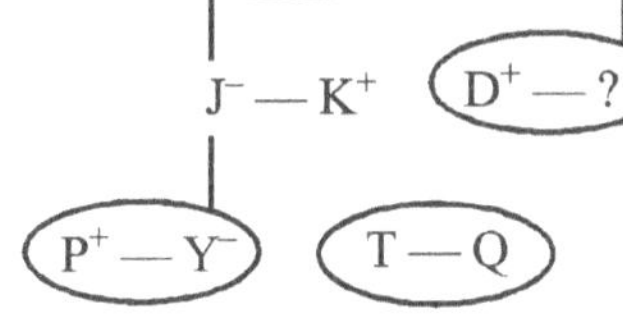

50. (c) Maternal uncle

51. (a) Maternal Grand father

52. (b)

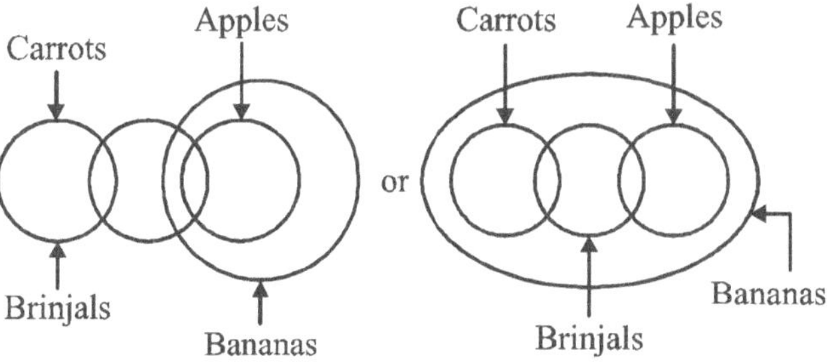

Conclusions I. Some apples are carrots. (×)
II. Some bananas are brinjals (√)
III. Some bananas are carrots (×)

53. (e)

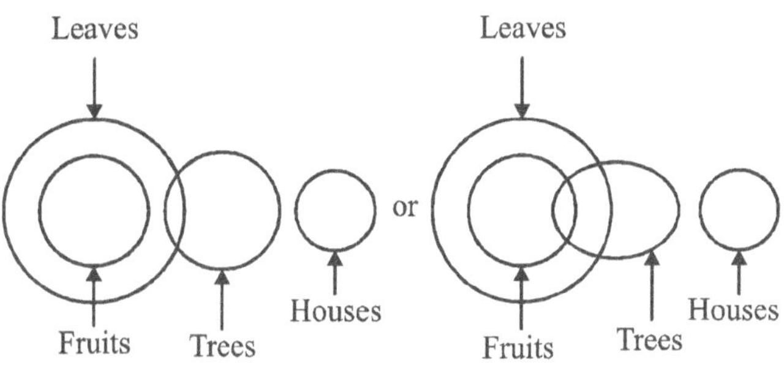

Conclusions I. Some cars are locks. (√)
II. Some bangles are keys. (√)
III. Some cars are keys. (√)

54. (d)

Conclusions I. Some houses are fruits. (×)
II. Some trees are fruits. (×)
III. No house is a fruit. (×)
Complementary pair (I-III)

55. (c) Only II follows
Explanation: I. ✗ II. ✓ III. ✗

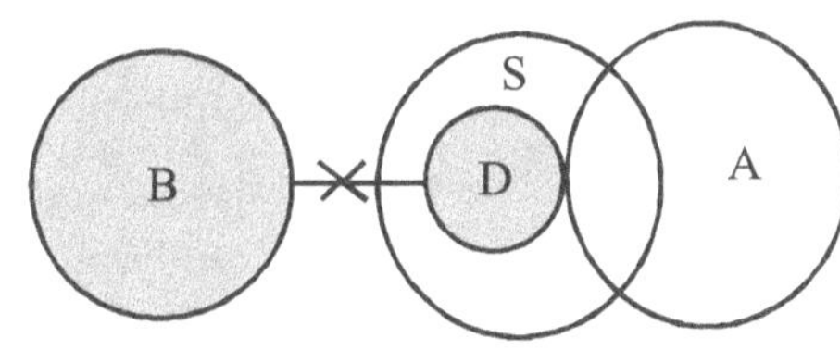

Or,

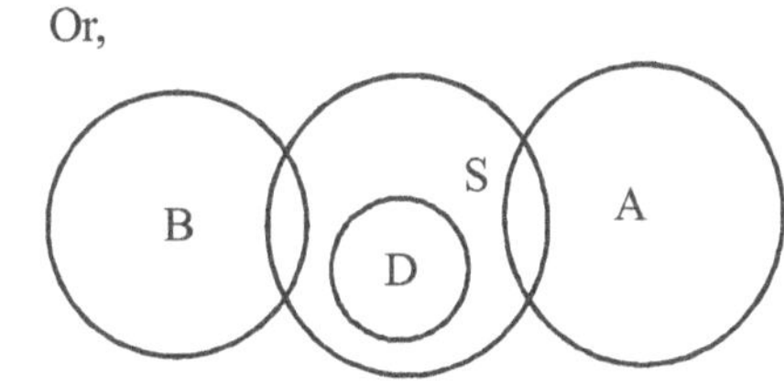

56. (e) None of these
   Possibility Diagram :
   Conclusion - (I)

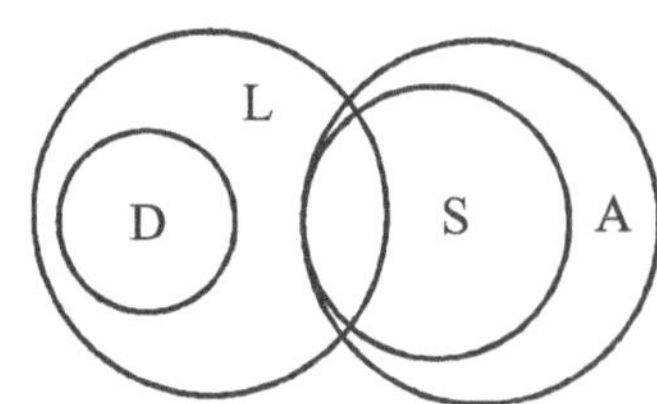

   Explanation :
   Possibility Diagram :
   Conclusion - (II)

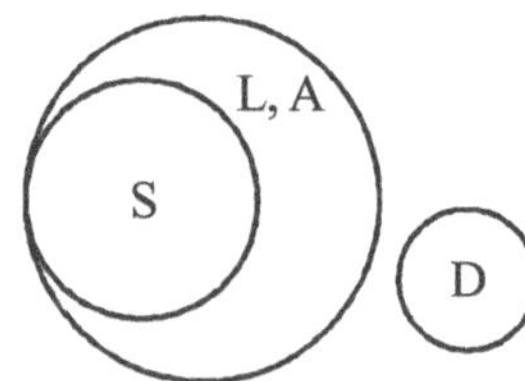

   Possibility Diagram :
   Conclusion - (III)

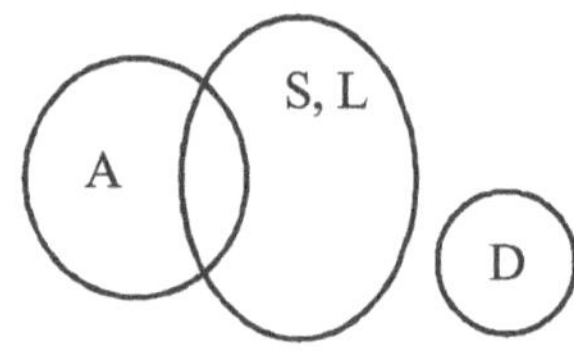

   Some + all = some → some + no → some not → I follow
   Some + all → some → possibility exist → II follow
   Conversion of I → III → III follows

(57-61) :

```
     E   F   G   H   A   B   C   D
     |---•---•---•---•---•---•---•---|
   Left                          Right
```

57. (a) F is next to the right of E.
58. (d) D is 2nd to the right of B. Hence, statement (d) is not true.
59. (b) C alone is the neighbour of D.
60. (d) All the given statements are correct.
61. (e) E and D are sitting at the ends.

For (62-66): Simply follow the rules of the codes and do these sums.

62. (c) X$DTFX (Because 1st and last digits are odd.)
63. (a) $%HFD# (No any condition.)
64. (c) HK$T%H (Because 1st and the last digits are even.)
65. (b) D%$HK# (Because 1st digit is odd and the last digit is even.)
66. (e) HTMK#H (Because Ist and the last digits are even.)
67. (a) XFH% D X (Because Ist and last digits are odd)
68. (b) According to the question,
   $$P > R \qquad ...(i)$$

$$R < S \leq X \qquad ...(ii)$$
$$Y = X \qquad ...(iii)$$

On the combining statements (i), (ii) and (iii), we get

$$P > R < S \leq X = Y$$

Conclusions   I. $P < S$ (false)
               II. $Y > R$ (true)

So, it is clear that only Conclusion II is true.

69. (e) According to the question,
   $$Z = C \qquad ...(i)$$
   $$B < A = N \qquad ...(ii)$$
   $$C = B \qquad ...(iii)$$

On combining the statements (i), (ii) and (iii), we get

$$Z = C < B < A = N$$

Conclusions   I. $Z < B$ (true)
               II. $N > Z$ (true)

So, it is clear that both Conclusion I and II are true.

70. (a) According to the question,
   $$T < V = W \qquad ...(i)$$
   $$X \geq Y \qquad ...(ii)$$
   $$W = X \qquad ...(iii)$$

On combining statements (i), (ii) and (iii), we get

$$T < V = W > X \geq Y$$

Conclusions   I. $V > Y$ (true)
               II. $V < X$ (false)

So, it is clear that only Conclusion I is true.

71. (b) According to the question,

$$J \geq K > P = R < N = S$$

Conclusions   I. $S \geq P$ (false)
               II. $J > R$ (true)

So, it is clear that only Conclusion I is true.

(72-76) : Arrangement according to the question is as follows:-

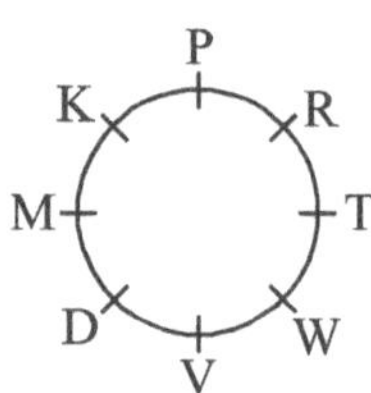

72. (b) Clearly, R is second to the left of K.
73. (a) Clearly, D is to the immediate left of V.
74. (e) Clearly, R is third to the right of V. So, none of the given options is correct.
75. (a) Clearly, R is the third to the right of V.
76. (d) In all the others, there is only one individual between the two. But, R and D are opposite to each other.
77. (e) 78. (e)
79. (e) T is grandfather.
80. (b)

PRACTICE SET 5

Time : 45 Min. **Max. Marks : 80**

QUANTITATIVE APTITUDE

DIRECTIONS (Qs. 1-5) : What will come in place of question mark (?) in the following questions ?

1. 48% of $525 + ?\%$ of $350 = 399$
- (a) 42
- (b) 46
- (c) 28
- (d) 26
- (e) None of these

2. $2\dfrac{5}{9} \times 3\dfrac{4}{5} + ? = 12\dfrac{1}{5}$
- (a) $2\dfrac{13}{45}$
- (b) $2\dfrac{4}{5}$
- (c) $3\dfrac{22}{45}$
- (d) $3\dfrac{5}{9}$
- (e) None of these

3. $\dfrac{3}{7}$ of $455 + \dfrac{5}{8}$ of $456 = ?$
- (a) 448
- (b) 476
- (c) 480
- (d) 464
- (e) None of these

4. 1.05% of $2500 + 2.5\%$ of $440 = ?$
- (a) 37.50
- (b) 37.25
- (c) 370.25
- (d) 372.50
- (e) None of these

5. $4900 \div 28 \times 444 \div 12 = ?$
- (a) 6575
- (b) 6475
- (c) 6455
- (d) 6745
- (e) None of these

DIRECTIONS (Qs. 6-10) : In the following questions two equations numbered I and II are given. You have to solve both the equations and give answer.

If
- (a) $x > y$
- (b) $x \geq y$
- (c) $x < y$
- (d) $x \leq y$
- (e) $x = y$ or the relationship cannot be established.

6. I. $x^2 - 11x + 24 = 0$ II. $2y^2 - 9y + 9 = 0$

7. I. $x^3 \times 13 = x^2 \times 247$ II. $y^{1/3} \times 14 = 249 \div y^{2/3}$

8. I. $\dfrac{12 \times 4}{x^{4/7}} - \dfrac{3 \times 4}{x^{4/7}} = x^{10/7}$ II. $y^3 + 783 = 999$

9. I. $\sqrt{500x} + \sqrt{402} = 0$ II. $\sqrt{360y} + (200)^{1/2} = 0$

10. I. $(17)^2 + 144 \div 18 = x$ II. $(26)^2 - 18 \times 21 = y$

DIRECTIONS (Qs. 11-15): Study the following graph carefully and answer the questions that follow:

Percentage of employees in different departments of a company Total No. of employees = 4500

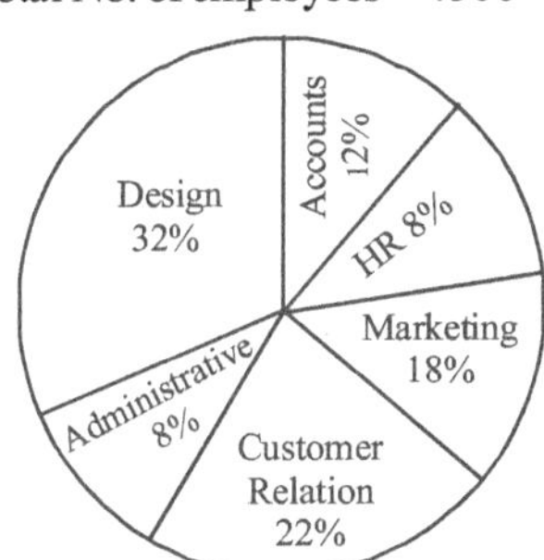

Percentage of females in each department in the same company Total No. of females in the organisation = 2000

11. What is the total number of males from Design, Customer Relation and HR departments together ?

(a) 1550   (b) 1510

(c) 1540   (d) 1580

(e) None of these

12. What is the ratio of number of males in HR department to the number of males in Accounts department respectively ?

(a) 3 : 17   (b) 4 : 15

(c) 2 : 15   (d) 2 : 13

(e) None of these

13. The number of females in the Marketing department are approximately what per cent of the total employees in Marketing and Customer Relation Departments together?

(a) 26   (b) 36

(c) 6   (d) 46

(e) 16

14. What is the respective ratio of number of employees in Administrative department to the number of males in the same department ?

(a) 9 : 4   (b) 8 : 3

(c) 7 : 2   (d) 8 : 5

(e) None of these

15. The total number of females are what per cent of the total number of males in the organisation ?

(a) 90   (b) 70

(c) 80   (d) 60

(e) None of these

DIRECTIONS (Qs. 16-20) : What will come in place of the question mark (?) in the following number series?

---

16. 7 9 12 16 ?

(a) 2 2   (b) 19

(c) 20   (d) 21

(e) None of these

17. 384 192 96 48 ?

(a) 36   (b) 28

(c) 24   (d) 32

(e) None of these

18. 5 6 14 45 ?

(a) 183   (b) 185

(c) 138   (d) 139

(e) None of these

19. 8 9 13 22 ?

(a) 30   (b) 31

(c) 34   (d) 36

(e) None of these

20. 6 11 21 41 ?

(a) 81   (b) 61

(c) 71   (d) 91

(e) None of these

21. Number of students studying in colleges A and B are in the ratio of 3 : 4 respectively. If 50 more students join college A and there is no change in the number of students in college B, the respective ratio becomes 5 : 6. What is the number of students in college B ?

(a) 450   (b) 500

(c) 400   (d) 600

(e) None of these

22. What is the compound interest accrued on an amount of ₹ 8500 in two years @ interest 10% per annum?

(a) ₹ 1875   (b) ₹ 1885

(c) ₹ 1775   (d) ₹ 1765

(e) None of these

23. A train running at the speed of 60 kmph crosses a 200 m long platform in 27 s. What is the length of the train ?

(a) 250 m   (b) 200 m

(c) 240 m   (d) 450 m

(e) None of these

24. Sum of the digits of a two digit number is 8 and the digit in the ten's place is three times the digit in the unit's place. What is the number?

(a) 26   (b) 36

(c) 71   (d) 62

(e) None of these

25. 10 men can complete a piece of work in 8 days. In how many days can 16 men complete that work?

(a) 4 days   (b) 5 days

(c) 6 days   (d) 3 days

(e) None of these

26. Average of five consecutive odd numbers is 95. What is the fourth number in descending order?

(a) 91   (b) 95

(c) 99   (d) 97

(e) None of these

27. Latika spends 45% of her monthly income on food and 30% of the monthly income on transport. Remaining amount of ₹4500 she saves. What is her monthly income?

(a) ₹16000   (b) ₹18000

(c) ₹16500   (d) ₹18500

(e) None of these

28. Amount of simple interest accrued on an amount of Rs 28500 in seven years is Rs 23940 what is the rate of interest % per annum?

(a) 10.5   (b) 12.5

(c) 11   (d) 12

(e) None of these

29. *A* and *B* started a business investing amounts of ₹150000 and ₹250000 respectively. What will be *B*'s share in the profit of ₹160000 ?

(a) ₹100000   (b) ₹60000

(c) ₹80000   (d) ₹110000

(e) None of these

30. The average age of 60 boys in a class was calculated as 12 years. It was later realised that the actual age of one of the boys in the class was 12.5 years but it was calculated as 14 years. What is the actual average age of the boys in the class?

(a) 11 years   (b) 11.275 years

(c) 11.50 years   (d) 11.975 years

(e) None of these

DIRECTIONS (Qs. 31-35) : Study the table carefully to answer the questions that follow:

Number of girls and boys (in hundreds) in six different years in five different schools

School →	A		B		C		D		E	
Years ↓	Boys	Girls	Boys	Girls	Boys	Girls	Boys	Girls	Boys	Girls
2005	3.3	3.6	5.2	3.1	5.5	4.5	2.4	1.4	6.5	6.6
2006	6.6	4.2	4.9	2.2	6.9	3.3	4.4	2.3	5.5	3.6
2007	9.3	6.9	4.7	4.2	5.8	4.9	6.4	3.3	2.7	2.4
2008	5.4	9.6	6.3	5.4	6.6	5.2	5.3	5.4	5.4	5.7
2009	8.4	12.9	7.5	5.9	8.7	6.6	12.1	5.2	6.8	6.5
2010	12.3	14.4	9.8	4.4	11.7	4.2	12.2	9.4	10.8	12.7

31. What is the **approximate** percentage decrease in the number of boys in school D in the year 2008 as compared to that in the previous year ?

(a) 17   (b) 12

(c) 9   (d) 5

(e) None of these

32. The number of girls in school B in the year 2009 is **approximately** what percent of the total number of students (both boys and girls) in school E in the year 2006 ?

(a) 46   (b) 52

(c) 65   (d) 58

(e) None of these

33. What is the average number of girls in school A in all the years taken together ?

(a) 760   (b) 800

(c) 860   (d) 600

(e) None of these

34. What is the ratio of the number of boys in school C in the year 2009 to the number of girls in school A in the year 2009?

(a) 29 : 41   (b) 36 : 11

(c) 29 : 43   (d) 36 : 13

(e) None of these

35. In which year is the total number of students (both girls and boys together) the third highest in school E ?

(a) 2006   (b) 2007

(c) 2008   (d) 2005

(e) None of these

DIRECTIONS (Qs. 36-40) : Study the following pie chart and bar-graph and answer the following question.

Percentage wise distribution of teachers in six different districts Total number of Teachers = 4500

Percentage of Teachers

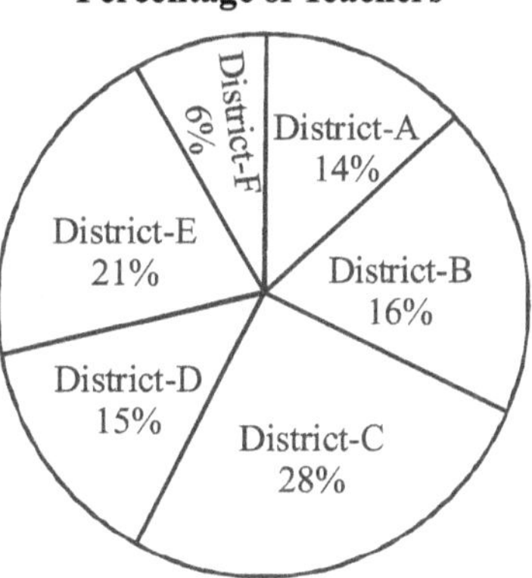

Number of males out of 4500 teachers is each district separately

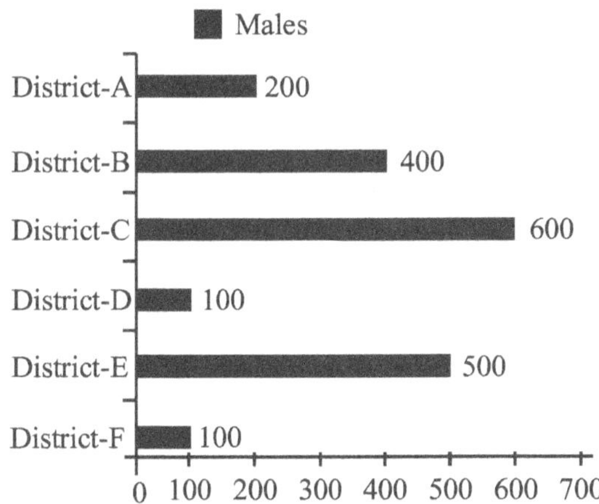

36. What is the total number of male teachers in District F, female teachers in District C and female teachers in District B together?

(a) 1080   (b) 1120

(c) 1180   (d) 1020

(e) None of these

37. The number of female teachers in District D is approximately what percent of the total number of teachers (both male and female) in District A ?

(a) 70   (b) 75

(c) 80   (d) 90

(e) None of these

38. In which district is the number of male teachers more than the number of female teachers ?

(a) B only   (b) D only

(c) Both B and E   (d) Both E and F

(e) None of these

39. What is the difference between the number of female teachers in District F and the total number of teacher (both male and female) in District E ?

    (a) 625   (b) 775

    (c) 675   (d) 725

    (e) None of these

40. What is the ratio of the number of male teachers in District C to the number of female teachers in District B ?

    (a) 11 : 15   (b) 15 : 11

    (c) 15 : 8   (d) 30 : 13

    (e) None of these

REASONING ABILITY

41. B is the father of Q. B has only two children. Q is the brother of R. R is the daughter of P. A is the granddaughter of P and S is the father of A. How is S related to Q?

    (a) Son   (b) Son-in-law

    (c) Brother   (d) Brother-in-law

    (e) None of these

42. Pritampur town is located bank of river 'Ganga'. It has another town 'Amroha' to its west. Tivura is to the east of Amroha but to the west of town 'Pritampur', 'Kasari' is east of 'Basra' but west of 'Tivura' and 'Amroha'. If these are all in the same area which town furthest towards west?

    (a) Pritampur   (b) Amroha

    (c) Tivura   (d) Kasari

    (e) Basra

43. Pointing to a boy, Radhika says, "He is the son of my grandfather's only son." How is the boy's mother related to Radhika?

    (a) Mother   (b) Aunt

    (c) Sister   (d) Cousin

    (e) Data inadequate

44. Six boys are standing that they form a circle each facing the centre. Alok is to the left of Prabhat, Sunil is between Alok and Ashok. Who is to the left of Vikash?

    (a) Prabhat   (b) Hari

    (c) Ashok   (d) Sunil

    (e) Alok

45. City D is to the West of city M. City R is to the South of City D. If city K is to the East of city R, then in which direction is city K located in respect of city D?

    (a) North   (b) East

    (c) North-East   (d) South-East

    (e) None of these

DIRECTIONS (Qs. 46- 50) : In each of the questions below are given three statements followed by two conclusions numbered I and II. You have to take the given statements to be true even if they seem to be at variance from commonly known facts and decide which of the given conclusion(s) logically follow(s) from the three given statements.

Give answer

(a) if only Conclusion I follows

(b) if only Conclusion II follows

(c) if either Conclusion I or II follows

(d) if neither Conclusion I nor II follows

(e) if both Conclusions I and II follow

46. **Statements:** All pens are papers.

            Some papers are blades.

            All blades are knives.

     Conclusions: I. Some knives are papers.

                II. Some blades are pens.

47. **Statements:** All fans are televisions.

            Some televisions are channels.

            Some channels are radios.

     Conclusions: I. Some fans are channels.

                II. Some radios are televisions.

48. **Statements:** Some roots are stems.

            All stems are branches.

            All branches are leaves.

     Conclusions: I. Some leaves are roots.

                II. Some branches are stems.

49. **Statements :** All doctors are teachers.

            All teachers are students.

            No Student is a lawyer.

     Conclusions :

         I. No teacher is a lawyer.

         II. Some doctors being lawyer is a possibility

50. **Statements :** All books are tables,

            Some tables are not Chairs.

            Some chairs are benches.

     Conclusions :

         I. All books being chairs is a possibility.

         II. Atleast some banches are tables.

DIRECTIONS (Qs. 51-55) : Read the following information carefully to answer the given questions.

V, U and T are sitting around a circle. A, B and C are also sitting around the same circle but two of them are not facing centre (they are facing the direction opposite to centre). V is second to the left of C. U is second to the right of A. B is third to the left of T. C is second to the right of T. A is seated next to V.

51. Which of the following are not facing centre?

    (a) BA   (b) CA

    (c) BC   (c) Cannot be determined

    (e) None of these

52. Which of the following is the position of T in respect of B?

    (a) Third to the right   (b) Second to the right

    (c) Third to the left   (d) Third to the left or right

    (e) None of these

53. What is the position of V in respect of C?

(a) Second to the right   (b) Third to the left

(c) Fourth to the right   (d) Fourth to the left

(e) Cannot be determined

54. Which of the following statement is correct?

(a) A, B and C are sitting together.

(b) V, U and T are sitting together

(c) Sitting arrangement of two persons cannot be determined

(d) Those who are not facing centre are sitting together

(e) Only two people are sitting between V and T

55. What is the position of A in respect of U?

(a) Second to the left   (b) Second to the right

(c) Third to the right   (b) Cannot be determined

(e) None of these

DIRECTIONS (Qs. 56-60) : Study the following information carefully to answer the given questions.

A, B, C, D, E, F, G, and H are seated in straight line facing North. C sits fourth to left of G. D sits second to right of G. Only two people sit between D and A. B and F are immediate neighbours of each other. B is not an immediate neighbour of A. H is not an immediate neighbour of D.

56. Who amongst the following sits exactly in the middle of the persons who sit fifth from the left and the person who sits sixth from the right?

(a) C   (b) H

(c) E   (d) F

57. Who amongst the following sits third to the right of C?

(a) B   (b) F

(c) A   (d) E

58. Which of the following represents persons seated at the two extreme ends of the line?

(a) C, D   (b) A, B

(c) B, G   (d) D, H

59. What is the position of H with respect to F?

(a) Third to the left   (b) Immediate right

(c) Second to right   (d) Fourth to left

60. How many persons are seated between A and E?

(a) One   (b) Two

(c) Three   (d) Four

DIRECTIONS (Qs. 61- 65) : In these questions symbols #, @, $, *, % are to be used with different meanings as follows:

'A # B' means 'A is neither smaller than nor equal to B'.

'A @ B' means 'A is neither greater than nor equal than to B'.

'A $ B' means 'A is not greater than B'

'A * B' means 'A is not smaller than B'.

'A % B' means 'A is neither smaller than nor greater than B'.

In each question, three statements showing relationships have

been given, which are followed by two conclusions I & II. Assuming that the given statements are true, find out which conclusion(s) is/are definitely true. Mark answer

(a) if only conclusion I is true;

(b) if only conclusion II is true;

(c) if either conclusion I or II is true;

(d) if neither conclusion I nor II is true and

(e) if both conculsions I and II are true.

61. **Statements:**   T @ J, J * M, M $ B

Conclusions: I.   T # M

II.   J $ B

62. **Statements:**   R# F, F @ K, K $ V

Conclusions : I.   R # V

II.   V # F

63. **Statements:**   E @ A, A % F, F $ Q

Conclusions : I.   E @ Q

II.   Q * A

64. **Statements:**   L # M, M % D, D * Q

Conclusions: I.   M # Q

II.   Q @ L

65. **Statements:**   W $ F, F @ H, H # R

Conclusions: I.   W # R

II.   W $ R

DIRECTIONS (Qs. 66-72) : Study the following information carefully and answer the given questions.

Seven friends A, B, C, D, E, F and G studied in colleges X, Y and Z and are currently in different professions, namely Medicines, Fashion Designing, Engineering, Business, Acting, Teaching and Architecture (not necessarily in the same order). At least two and not more than three friends had studied in the same college.

C is an architect and studied in college Y. E is not a businessman. Only G amongst the seven friends studied in college X along with E. F is an engineer and did not study in college Y. B is an actor and did not study in the same college as F. A did not study in college Z. Those who studied in college X are neither Fashion Designers nor teachers. None of those who studied in college Y is a teacher.

66. Who amongst the following have studied in college Z?

(a) B, A   (b) C, F

(c) B, D, F   (d) A, D

(e) D, F

67. Which of the following groups represents the students of college Y ?

(a) C, E, G   (b) A, C, D

(c) A, B, C   (d) D, B, C

(e) None of these

68. What is the profession of F ?
- (a) Engineering
- (b) Business
- (c) Medicines
- (d) Acting
- (e) None of these

69. Who amongst the following is in the profession of Medicine?
- (a) E
- (b) G
- (c) A
- (d) D
- (e) None of these

70. What is the profession of A?
- (a) Teaching
- (b) Medicine
- (c) Business
- (d) Fashion Designing
- (e) None of these

71. Which of the following combinations of person, college and profession is definitely correct ?
- (a) E-X-Fashion Designing
- (b) F-X-Engineering
- (c) A-Y-Businessman
- (d) D-Z-Teaching
- (e) None of these

72. Who amongst the following is a businessman?
- (a) A
- (b) D
- (c) E
- (d) G
- (e) None of these

DIRECTIONS (Qs. 73-77): Answer these questions referring to the letter sequence given below:

N O P Q Y B Z A R S H I J K I L M T U V G E F W X D C

73. If letters of the above given series are written in reverse order then which letter will be third to the left of eighteenth letter from your right?
- (a) Z
- (b) G
- (c) I
- (d) L
- (e) None of these

74. What will come in place of question mark (?) in the following series ?

NDP, QWB, ZER, ?
- (a) SVJ
- (b) AFS
- (c) IVS
- (d) SFA
- (e) None of these

75. Which of the following is the fifth to the right of thirteenth letter from you left ?
- (a) T
- (b) J
- (c) S
- (d) Z
- (e) None of these

76. If every alternate letter starting from O is replaced with odd numbers starting from 1, which letter or number will be third to the left of tenth letter from your right ?
- (a) 15
- (b) L
- (c) K
- (d) I
- (e) None of these

77. If it is possible to make a meaningful word from the eighth, sixteenth, seventeenth and twenty-second letters from your left in the given series, which will be th first letter of that word? If no such word can be formed, your answer would be *X*, and if more than one such word can be formed, answer is *P*.
- (a) M
- (b) T
- (c) X
- (d) E
- (e) P

DIRECTIONS (Qs. 78-80) : In each of the questions below, a group of numerals is given followed by four groups of symbols/ letter combinations lettered (a), (b), (c) and (d). Numerals are to be coded as per the codes and conditions given below. You have to find out which of the combinations (a), (b), (c) and (d) is correct and indicate your answer accordingly. If none of the four combinations represents the correct code, mark (e) as your answer.

Numerals	3	5	7	4	2	6	8	1	0	9
Letter/Symbol Code	★	B	E	A	@	F	K	%	R	M

Following conditions apply

(i) if the first digit as well as the last digits is odd, both are to be coded as 'x'.

(ii) if the first digit as well as the last digit is even, both are to be coded as $.

(iii) if the last digit is 'zero', it is to be coded as #.

78. 487692
- (a) $KEFM@
- (b) AKEFM@
- (c) AKEFM$
- (d) $KEFM$
- (e) None of these

79. 713540
- (a) X%★BA
- (b) E%★BA#
- (c) E%★BAR
- (d) X%★BAR
- (e) None of these

80. 765082
- (a) EFB#K@
- (b) XFBRK@
- (c) EFBRK@
- (d) EFBR#K
- (e) None of these

HINTS & EXPLANATIONS

1. (a) 48% of $525 + ?\%$ of $350 = 399$

$\Rightarrow \quad \dfrac{48}{100} \times 525 + \dfrac{?}{100} \times 350 = 399$

$\Rightarrow \quad 25200 + ? \times 350 = 399 \times 100$

$\Rightarrow \quad ? \times 350 = 39900 - 25200 = 14700$

$\Rightarrow \quad ? = \dfrac{14700}{350} = 42$

2. (e) $2\dfrac{5}{9} \times 3\dfrac{4}{5} + ? = 12\dfrac{1}{5}$

$\Rightarrow \quad \dfrac{23}{9} \times \dfrac{19}{5} + ? = \dfrac{61}{5}$

$\Rightarrow \quad ? = \dfrac{61}{5} - \dfrac{437}{45}$

$\Rightarrow \quad ? = \dfrac{549 - 437}{45}$

$\Rightarrow \quad ? = \dfrac{112}{45} = 2\dfrac{22}{45}$

3. (c) $? = \dfrac{3}{7}$ of $455 + \dfrac{5}{8}$ of 456

$\Rightarrow \quad ? = \dfrac{3}{7} \times 455 + \dfrac{5}{8} \times 456$

$\Rightarrow \quad ? = 195 + 285 \quad \Rightarrow \ ? = 480$

4. (b) $? = 1.05\%$ of $2500 + 2.5\%$ of 440

$\Rightarrow \quad ? = \dfrac{1.05}{100} \times 2500 + \dfrac{2.5}{100} \times 440$

$\Rightarrow \quad ? = \dfrac{2625}{100} + \dfrac{1100}{100}$

$\Rightarrow \quad ? = \dfrac{3725}{100} = 37.25$

5. (b) $? = 4900 \div 28 \times 444 \div 12$

$\Rightarrow \quad ? = 175 \times 37$

$\Rightarrow \quad ? = 6475$

6. (b) I. $x^2 - 11x + 24 = 0$
$\Rightarrow x^2 - 8x - 3x + 24 = 0$
$\Rightarrow x(x-8) - 3(x-8) = 0$
$\Rightarrow (x-3)(x-8) = 0$
$\therefore x = 3$ or 8

II. $2y^2 - 9y + 9 = 0$
$2y^2 - 3y - 6y + 9 = 0$
$(2y-3)(y-3) = 0$
$\therefore y = \dfrac{3}{2}$ or 3
Clearly, $x \geq y$

7. (c) I. $x^3 \times 13 = x^2 \times 247$
$\Rightarrow \dfrac{x^3}{x^2} = \dfrac{247}{13}$
$\therefore x = 19$

II. $y^{1/3} \times 14 = 249 \div y^{2/3}$
$\Rightarrow y^{\frac{1}{3}} \times y^{\frac{2}{3}} = \dfrac{294}{14}$
$\Rightarrow y^{\frac{1}{3}} \times y^{\frac{2}{3}} = 21$
$\therefore y = 21$
Clearly, $x < y$

8. (d) I. $\dfrac{12 \times 4}{x^{\frac{4}{7}}} - \dfrac{3 \times 4}{x^{\frac{4}{7}}} = x^{\frac{10}{7}}$

$\Rightarrow \dfrac{48}{x^{\frac{4}{7}}} - \dfrac{12}{x^{\frac{4}{7}}} = x^{\frac{10}{7}}$

$\Rightarrow \dfrac{48 - 12}{x^{\frac{4}{7}}} = x^{\frac{10}{7}}$

$\Rightarrow 36 = x^{\frac{10}{7} + \frac{4}{7}} \Leftrightarrow 36 = x^2$
$\therefore x = \sqrt{36} = \pm 6$

II. $y^3 + 783 = 999$
$\Rightarrow y^3 = 999 - 793 \Leftrightarrow y^3 = 216$
$\therefore y = \sqrt[3]{216} = 6$
Clearly, $x \leq y$

9. (c) I. $\sqrt{500}x + \sqrt{402} = 0$
$\Rightarrow \sqrt{500}x = -\sqrt{402}$
$\therefore x = -\sqrt{\dfrac{402}{500}} = -\sqrt{\dfrac{400}{500}} = -0.9$

II. $\sqrt{360}y + (200)^{1/2} = 0$
$\Rightarrow \sqrt{360}y = -\sqrt{200}$
$\therefore y = -\sqrt{\dfrac{200}{360}} = -0.74$
Clearly, $x < y$

10. (c) I. $(17)^2 + 144 \div 18 = x$
$\Rightarrow x = 17^2 + 144 \times \dfrac{1}{18}$
$\therefore x = 289 + 8 = 297$

II. $(26)^2 - 18 \times 21 = y$
$\Rightarrow y = 26^2 - 18 \times 21$
$\therefore y = 676 - 378 = 298$
Clearly, $x < y$

11. (b) Number of employees in design, customer relation and HR departments together
$4500 \times (32 + 22 + 8)\%$

$= \dfrac{4500 \times 62}{100} = 2790$

Number of women employees in these departments
$= 2000 \times (28 + 20 + 16)\%$

$= \dfrac{2000 \times 64}{100} = 1280$

$\therefore$ Required number of males
$= 2790 - 1280 = 1510$

12. (c) Number of employees in HR department

$= \dfrac{4500 \times 8}{100} = 360$

$\therefore$ Number of males

$= 360 - \dfrac{2000 \times 16}{100}$

$= 360 - 320 = 40$

Number of employeess in Accounts department

$= \dfrac{4500 \times 12}{100} = 540$

$\therefore$ Number of males

$= 540 - \dfrac{2000 \times 12}{100}$

$= 540 - 240 = 300$

$\therefore$ Required ratio $= 40 : 300 = 2 : 15$

13. (e) Number of employees in marketing and customer relation departments

$= \dfrac{4500 \times 40}{100} = 1800$

Number of females in the marketing department

$= \dfrac{2000 \times 14}{100} = 280$

$\therefore$ Required percentage $= \dfrac{280}{1800} \times 100 \approx 16\%$

14. (a) Total number of employees in administrative department

$= \dfrac{4500 \times 8}{100} = 360$

Number of males in the same department
$= 360 - 200 = 160$
$\therefore$ Required ratio
$= 360 : 160 = 9 : 4$

15. (c) Required percentage

$= \dfrac{2000}{2500} \times 100 = 80\%$

16. (d) Pattern of the series would be as follows

7   9   12   16   21
$+2$ $+3$ $+4$ $+5$

17. (c) Pattern of the series would be as follows

384   192   96   48   24
$\div 2$ $\div 2$ $\div 2$ $\div 2$

18. (e) Pattern of the series would be as follows
$5 \times 1 + 1 = 6$
$6 \times 2 + 2 = 14$
$14 \times 3 + 3 = 45$
$\therefore \quad 45 \times 4 + 4 = 184$

19. (e) Pattern of the series would be as follows

8   9   13   22   38
$+(1)^2$ $+(2)^2$ $+(3)^2$ $+(4)^2$

20. (a) Pattern of the series would be as follows

6   11   21   41   81
$+5$ $+10$ $+20$ $+40$

21. (d) Let total number of students in college $A = 3x$
and total number of students in college $B = 4x$
After 50 more students join college A

New Ratio $= \dfrac{3x + 50}{4x} = \dfrac{5}{6}$

$\Rightarrow \quad 18x + 300 = 20x$
$\Rightarrow \quad 2x = 300$

$\Rightarrow \quad x = \dfrac{300}{2} = 150$

Total number of students in college
$B = 4x = 4 \times 150 = 600$

22. (e) Compound Interest after two years

$= 8500\left(1 + \dfrac{10}{100}\right)^2 - 8500$

$= 8500 \times \dfrac{11}{10} \times \dfrac{11}{10} - 8500$

$= 10285 - 8500 = ₹\, 1785$

23. (a) Let length of the train be x m

Speed of the train be 60 km/h $= 60 \times \dfrac{5}{18} = \dfrac{50}{3}$ m/s

Then, $\dfrac{x + 200}{\frac{50}{3}} = 27$

$\Rightarrow \quad \dfrac{3(x + 200)}{50} = 27$

$\Rightarrow \quad 3x + 600 = 1350$
$\Rightarrow \quad 3x = 1350 - 600$
$\Rightarrow \quad 3x = 750$

$\Rightarrow \quad x = \dfrac{750}{3} = 250$ m

24. (d) Let ten's digit be x and unit's digit be $8 - x$
Then, $x = 3(8 - x)$
$\Rightarrow \quad x = 24 - 3x$,
$\Rightarrow \quad 4x = 24$

$\Rightarrow \quad x = \dfrac{24}{4} = 6$

$\therefore$ unit's digit $= 8 - x = 8 - 6 = 2$
So, required number $= 62$

25. (b) Suppose 16 men can complete the same work in x days
Then,   Men   days
        10   8
        16   x

$16 : 10 :: 8 : x$
$\Rightarrow \quad 16 \times x = 10 \times 8$

$\Rightarrow \quad x = \dfrac{10 \times 8}{16} = 5$ days

26. (e)   27. (b)   28. (d)   29. (a)   30. (d)

31. (a)   Percentage decrease $= \dfrac{(6.4-5.3)}{6.4} \times 100$
$= 17.18$

32. (c)   Girls in school B in 2009 = 590
Boys and girls in school E in 2006 = 550 + 360 = 910
Percentage $= \dfrac{590}{910} \times 100 = 64.83\%$ (approx)

33. (c)   Average number of girls is school A over the years
$= \dfrac{360+420+690+960+1290+1440}{6}$
$= \dfrac{5160}{6} = 860$

34. (c)   Required ratio $= \dfrac{\text{Boys in school C in 2009}}{\text{Girls in school A in 2009}}$
$= \dfrac{870}{1290} = 29 : 43$

35. (d)

Year	Total number of students
2005	1310
2006	910
2007	510
2008	1110
2009	1330
2010	2350

36. (a)   Male teachers in District F = 100
Female teachers in District C
$= \dfrac{28}{100} \times 4500 - 600$
$= 1260 - 600 = 660$
Female teachers in District B
$= \dfrac{16}{100} \times 4500 - 400 = 720 - 400 = 320$
Total = 100 + 660 + 320 = 1080

37. (d)   Female teachers in District D
$= \dfrac{15}{100} \times 4500 - 100 = 675 - 100 = 575$
Total number of teachers in District A
$= \dfrac{14}{100} \times 4500 = 630$
Percentage $= \dfrac{575}{630} \times 100 = 91.2\% \gg 90\%$

38. (c)

39. (b)   Female teacher in District F
$= \dfrac{6}{100} \times 4500 - 100 = 270 - 100 = 170$
Total number of teachers in District E
$= \dfrac{21}{100} \times 4500 = 945$
Difference = 945 − 170 = 775

40. (c) $\dfrac{\text{Male teachers in District C}}{\text{Female teachers in District B}} = \dfrac{600}{320} = \dfrac{15}{8}$

41. (d)   Let us draw the family diagram

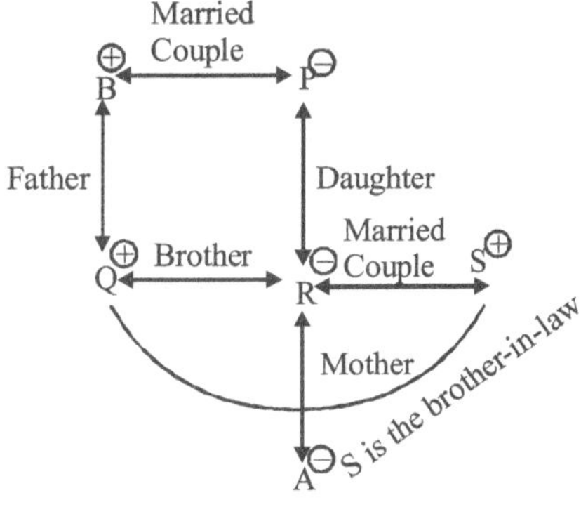

Hence, S is the brother-in-law of Q.

42. (e)   First draw direction arrows →

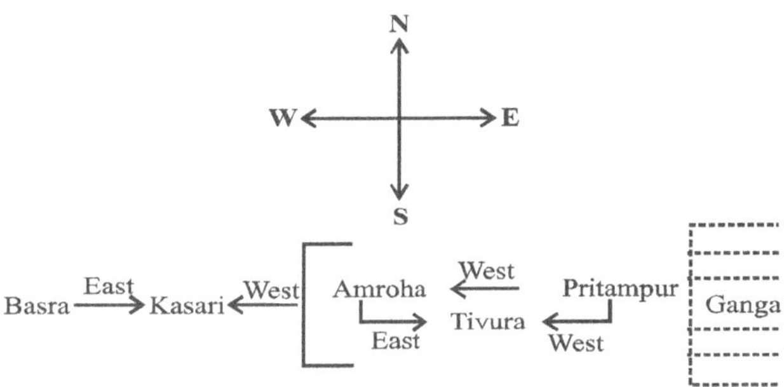

Clearly, Basra is the town to the farthest west.

43. (a)   My grandfather's only son- my father
My father's only son- my brother -his mother-my mother

44. (a)

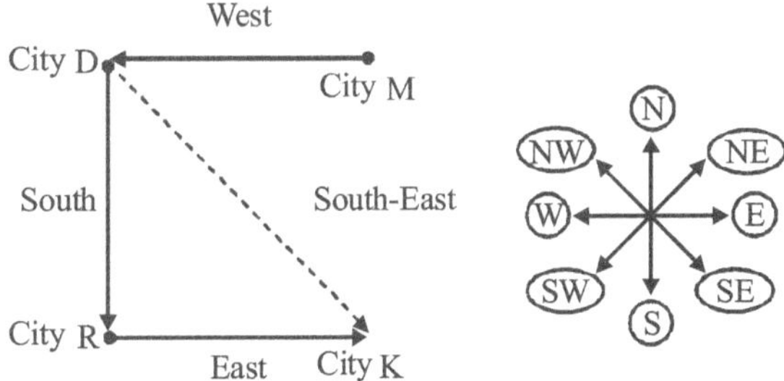

45. (d)   According to the question, the direction diagram is as follows

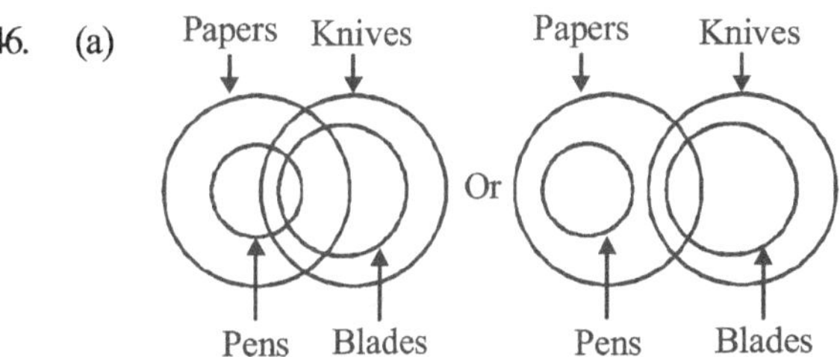

Hence, city K is located in the South-East direction.

46. (a)

Conclusions I.   Some knives are papers $(\sqrt{})$
II.   Some blades are pens $(\times)$

47. (d) 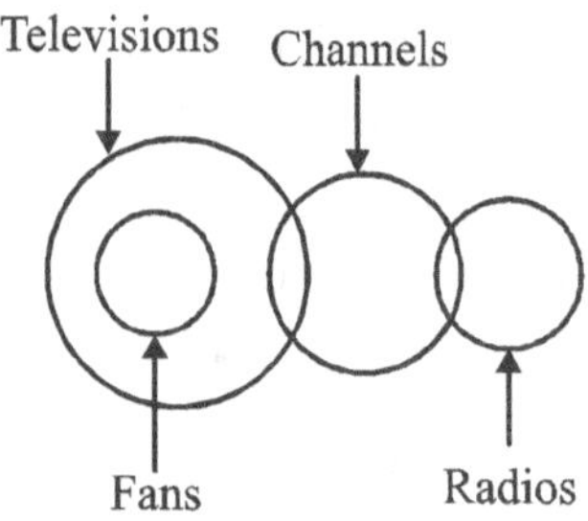

Conclusions I.   Some fans are channels. (×)
           II.   Some radios are televisions (×)

48. (e) 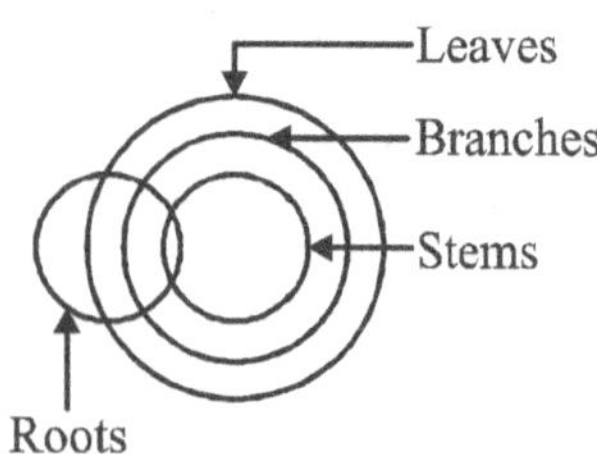

Conclusions I.   Some leaves are roots (√)
           II.   Some branches are stems (√)

49. (a) Only conclusion I follows

    Explanation : I. ✓   II. ✗

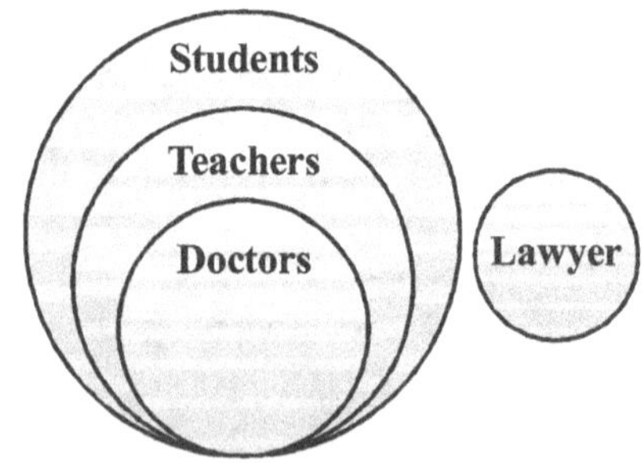

50. (a) Only conclusion I follows

    Explanation : I. ✓   II. ✗

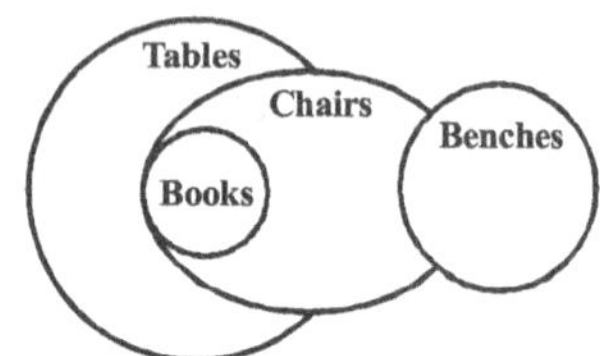

(Qs. 51-55):
    Sitting Arrangement:

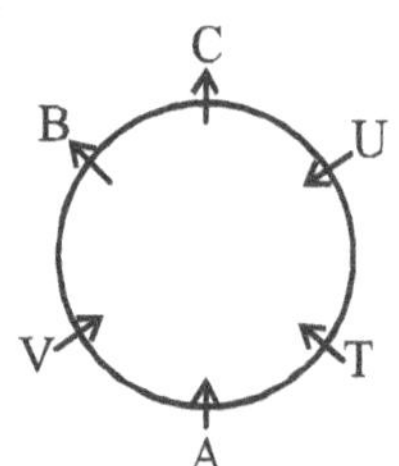

51. (c) B and C are not facing centre.
52. (d) The position of T in respect of B is third to the left or right.
53. (c) The position of V in respect of C is fourth to the right.
54. (d) B and C are not facing centre are sitting together.

55. (a) The position of A in respect of U is second to the left.

(Qs. 56-60):
    Sitting Arrangement:

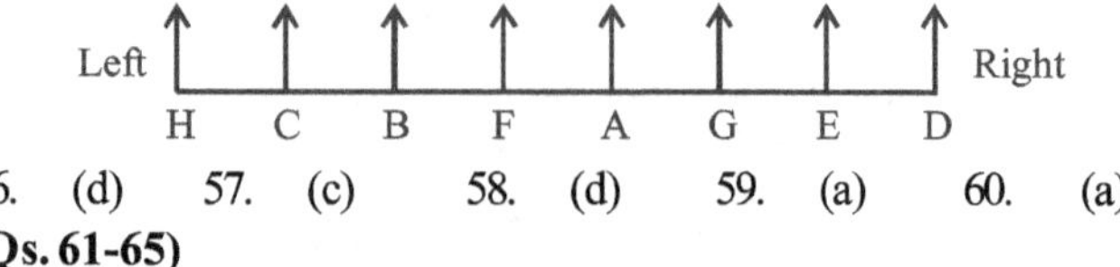

56. (d)   57. (c)   58. (d)   59. (a)   60. (a)

(Qs. 61-65)

$\# \Rightarrow >$	$@ \Rightarrow <$	$\$ \Rightarrow \leq$
$* \Rightarrow \geq$	$\% \Rightarrow =$	

61. (d) $T < J$, $J \geq M$, $M \leq B$
    No relation between T and M, and J and B.
    So neither I nor II is true.

62. (b) $R > F$, $F < K$, $K \leq V$
    No relation between R and V. So conclusion I is not true.
    But $V \geq K > F$ or $V > F$
    So, conclusion II is true.

63. (e) $E < A$, $A = F$, $F \leq Q$
    Combining all, $Q \geq F = A > E$ or $E < Q$ and $Q \geq A$
    So, both conclusions I and II are true.

64. (b) $L > M$, $M = D$, $D \geq Q$
    Combining all, $L > M = D \geq Q$ or $M \geq Q$ and $Q < L$.
    So, only conclusion II is true.

65. (c) $W \leq F$, $F < H$, $H > R$
    Although no direct relation between W and R but I and II together show all three probable relations. Hence, either I or II is true.

(66-72): From the given information we can draw the following table:-

Friend	College	Subject
A	Y	Fashion
B	Y	Acting
C	Y	Architecture
D	Z	Teaching
E	X	Medicine
F	Z	Engineering
G	X	Business

66. (e) 67. (c) 68. (a) 69. (a) 70. (d)
71. (d) 72. (d)
73. (b) $18 + 3 = 21$st letter from the right in the reverse series or, 21st letter from the left in the original series.
74. (e) $N + 3 = Q$, $Q + 3 = Z$, $Z + 3 = S$
    $D - 2 = W$, $W - 2 = E$, $E - 2 = V$
    $P + 3 = B$, $B + 3 = R$, $R + 3 = I$ Hence, ? = SVI
75. (a) $13 + 5 = 18$th from you left
76. (d) $10 + 3 = 13$th from the right
77. (e) Given A, L, M, E
    MALE, LAME, MEAL
78. (d) Condition II apply
79. (b) Condition III apply
80. (c) No Condition apply

PRACTICE SET   ⑥

INSTRUCTIONS

- This practice set consists of two sections. Quantitative Aptitude (Qs. 1-40) & Reasoning Ability (Qs. 41-80).
- All the questions are compulsory.
- Each question has five options, of which only one is correct. The candidates are advised to read all the options thoroughly.
- There is negative marking equivalent to $1/4^{th}$ of the mark allotted to the specific question for wrong answer.

Time : 45 Min.   **Max. Marks : 80**

QUANTITATIVE APTITUDE

DIRECTIONS (Qs. 1-5) : What will come in place of question mark (?) in the following questions?

1. $72.42 + 385.66 + 4976.38 = ?$
    (a) 5234.46   (b) 5434.46
    (c) 5434.66   (d) 5244.66
    (e) None of these

2. 16% of $250 + 115\%$ of $480 = ?$
    (a) 522   (b) 588
    (c) 582   (d) 498
    (e) None of these

3. 55% of $860 + ?\%$ of $450 = 581$
    (a) 24   (b) 28
    (c) 32   (d) 36
    (e) None of these

4. $\dfrac{5}{9}$ of $504 + \dfrac{3}{8}$ of $640 = ?$
    (a) 520   (b) 480
    (c) 460   (d) 540
    (e) None of these

5. 3.2% of $250 + 1.8\%$ of $400 = ?$
    (a) 14.8   (b) 15.75
    (c) 14.75   (d) 15.2
    (e) None of these

6. Difference between the digits of a two digit number is 5 and the digit in the unit's place is six times the digit in the ten's place. What is the number?
    (a) 27   (b) 72
    (c) 16   (d) 61
    (e) None of these

7. Populations of two villages X and Y are in the ratio of $5 : 7$ respectively. If the population of village Y increases by 25000 and the population of village X remains unchanged the respective ratio of their populations becomes 25:36. What is the population of village X?
    (a) 625000   (b) 675000
    (c) 875000   (d) 900000
    (e) None of these

8. Ajay spends 25 per cent of his salary on house rent, 5 per cent on food, 15 per cent on travel, 10 per cent on clothes and the remaining amount of ₹ 27,000 is saved. What is Ajay's income?
    (a) ₹ 60,000   (b) ₹ 80,500
    (c) ₹ 60,700   (d) ₹ 70,500
    (e) None of these

9. The length of a rectangular field is thrice its breadth. If the cost of cultivating the field at ₹ 367.20 per square metre is ₹ 27,540, then what is the perimeter of the rectangle?
    (a) 47 m   (b) 39 m
    (c) 52 m   (d) 40 m
    (e) None of these

DIRECTIONS (Qs. 10-14): In each of these questions, a number series is given. In each series, only one number is wrong. Find out the wrong number.

10. 3601 3602 1803 604 154 36 12
    (a) 3602   (b) 1803
    (c) 604   (d) 154
    (e) 36

11. 4 12 42 196 1005 6066 42511
    (a) 12   (b) 42
    (c) 1005   (d) 196
    (e) 6066

12. 2 8 12 20 30 42 56
    (a) 8   (b) 42
    (c) 30   (d) 20
    (e) 12

13. 32 16 24 65 210 945 5197.5
    (a) 945   (b) 16
    (c) 24   (d) 210
    (e) 65

14. 7 13 25 49 97 194 385
    (a) 13   (b) 49
    (c) 97   (d) 194
    (e) 25

DIRECTIONS (Qs. 15-19): Study the following table carefully and answer the given questions.

Table show the data released to eight offices across eight different state of XYZ Institute.

State	Offices	Total Employees	Ratio between male and female	% of Teacher
Delhi	16	2568	5:07	75
UP	18	2880	11:05	65
Haryana	14	2310	10:11	40
Bihar	22	3575	3:02	60
Bengal	13	2054	7:06	50
MP	17	2788	20:21	75
Mumbai	24	3720	8:07	55
Bangalore	21	3360	8:06	80

15. The number of male teacher in Banglore is 1800. If the number of female teacher is increased by 50% in the next year, then the number of female teacher are what percentage of total number of female employees in that state?
    (a) 76.8%   (b) 74%
    (c) 92.5%   (d) 90%
    (e) None of these

16. In which state, is the percentage of female employees to total number of employees (both male and female) is ranked third lowest?
    (a) Bengal   (b) UP
    (c) Banglore   (d) MP
    (e) Delhi

17. What is the ratio between the total number of male employees in UP and Banglore together and the total number of teachers in same states?
    (a) 76 : 65   (b) 86 : 85
    (c) 75 : 76   (d) 65 : 76
    (e) None of these

18. What is the difference between the average number of teacher in Delhi, UP and Bihar together and the average number of teacher in teacher MP, Mumbai and Banglore together?
    (a) 294   (b) 282
    (c) 284   (d) 280
    (e) None of these

19. Which state has the second highest number of average employees per office?
    (a) Bihar   (b) Banglore
    (c) Mumbai   (d) Delhi
    (e) MP

20. Mr. Sharma invested an amount of ₹25000 in fixed deposit @ compound interest 8% per annum for two years. What amount Mr. Sharma will get on maturity?
    (a) ₹28540   (b) ₹29160
    (c) ₹29240   (d) ₹28240
    (e) None of these

21. Nandkishore gives 35% of the money he had to his wife and gave 50% of the money he had to his sons. Remaining amount of ₹11250 he kept for himself. What was the total amount of money Nandkishore had ?
    (a) ₹63750   (b) ₹75000
    (c) ₹73650   (d) ₹72450
    (e) None of these

22. A shopkeeper purchased 200 bulbs for ₹ 10 each. However, 5 bulbs were fused and had to be thrown away. The remaining were sold at ₹ 12 each. What will be the percentage profit?
    (a) 25   (b) 15
    (c) 13   (d) 17
    (e) None of these

23. The average monthly income of a family of four earning members was ₹15,130. One of the daughter in the family got married and left home, so the average monthly income of the family came down to ₹ 14,660. What is the monthly income of the married daughter?
    (a) ₹15,350   (b) ₹12,000
    (c) ₹16,540   (d) Cannot be determined
    (e) None of these

24. On a test consisting of 250 questions, Jassi answered 40% of the first 125 questions correctly. What percent of the other 125 question does she need to answer correctly for her grade on the entire exam to be 60%?
    (a) 75   (b) 80
    (c) 60   (d) Cannot be determined
    (e) None of these

25. Swapnil, Aakash and Vinay begin to jog around a circular stadium. They complete their revolutions in 36 seconds, 48 seconds and 42 seconds respectively. After how many seconds will they be together at the starting point.
    (a) 504 seconds   (b) 940 seconds
    (c) 1008 seconds   (d) 470 seconds
    (e) None of these

DIRECTIONS (Qs. 26-30): In the following questions two equations numbered I and II are given. You have to solve both the equations and Give answer :

    (a) If $x > y$ (b) if $x \geq y$
    (c) if $x < y$ (d) if $x \leq y$
    (e) If $x = y$ or the relationship cannot be established.

26. I. $14x - 25 = 59 - 7x$
    II. $\sqrt{y + 222} - \sqrt{36} = \sqrt{81}$

27. I. $144x^2 - 16 = 9$
    II. $12y + \sqrt{4} = \sqrt{49}$

28. I. $x^2 - 9x + 20 = 0$
    II. $y^2 - 13x + 42 = 0$

29. I. $\dfrac{\sqrt{x}}{5}+\dfrac{3\sqrt{x}}{10}=\dfrac{1}{\sqrt{x}}$

    II. $\dfrac{10}{\sqrt{y}}-\dfrac{2}{\sqrt{y}}=4\sqrt{y}$

30. I. $x^2-19x+84=0$

    II. $y^2-25y+156=0$

DIRECTIONS (Qs. 31-35): Study the table carefully to answer the questions that follow:

Total number of employees in different departments of an organization and (of these) percentage of females and males

Department	Total Number of Employees	Percentage of Females	Percentage of Males
IT	840	45	55
Accounts	220	35	65
Production	900	23	77
HR	360	65	35
Marketing	450	44	56
Customer Service	540	40	60

31. What is the total number of employees in all the departments together?

(a) 3260   (b) 3310

(c) 3140   (d) 3020

(e) None of these

32. The total number of employees in the HR department forms approximately what percent of the total number of employees in the Accounts department?

(a) 149   (b) 178   (c) 157   (d) 164   (e) 137

33. What is the total number of males in the IT and Customer Service departments together?

(a) 687   (b) 678

(c) 768   (d) 876

(e) None of these

34. What is the total number of females in the HR, Marketing and Production departments together?

(a) 639   (b) 729

(c) 712   (d) 648

(e) None of these

35. What is the difference between total no. of males employees in HR and IT to the total no. of males employees in Accounts and Marketing departments.

(a) 212   (b) 187

(c) 193   (d) 178

(e) None of these

DIRECTIONS (Qs. 36 & 40) : Seven companies A, B, C, D, E, F and G are engaged in production of two items I and II. The comparative data about production of these items by the seven companies is given in the following pie-chart and the table. Study them carefully and answer the questions given below.

Percentage of the total production produced by the seven companies

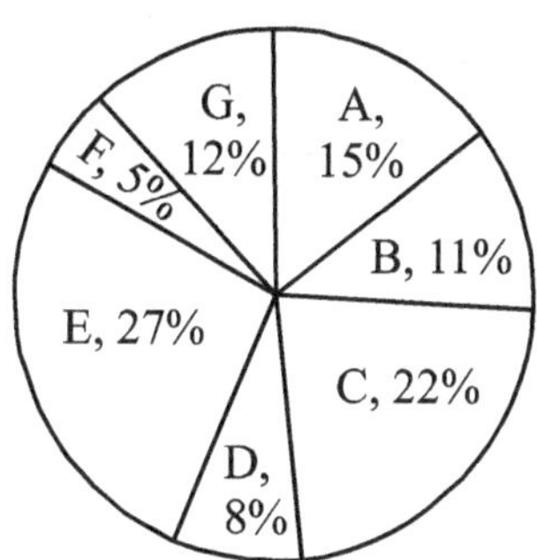

Cost of the total production (both items together) by seven companies. = ₹ 25 crores

Ratio of production between items I and II and the per cent profit earned for the two items.

Company	Ratio of Production		Per cent profit earned	
	Item I	Item II	Item I	Item II
A	2	3	25	20
B	3	2	32	35
C	4	1	20	22
D	3	5	15	25
E	5	3	28	30
F	1	4	35	25
G	1	2	30	24

36. What is the total cost of the production of item 'I' by companies A and C together in ₹ crore?

(a) 9.25   (b) 5.9

(c) 4.1625   (d) 4.9

(e) None of these

37. What is the amount of profit eared by company 'D' on item 'II'?

(a) ₹ 3.125 crores   (b) ₹ 31.25 crores

(c) ₹ 3.125 lakhs   (d) ₹ 31.25 lakhs

(e) None of these

38. What is the difference between cost of the total production by companies G and C to the cost of the total production by companies A and B together.

(a) 2.85 crores   (b) 3.2 crores

(c) 1.95 crores   (d) 2 crores

(e) None of these

39. What is the total cost of the production of item '11' by companies G, A and B together in ₹ crore?

(a) 13.15   (b) 12.85

(c) 16.25   (d) 14.65

(e) None of these

40. What is the amount of profit earned by companies 'E' and 'G' on items 'II' together in ₹ crore?

(a) 5.25   (b) 4.75

(c) 3.25   (d) 8.15

(e) None of these

REASONING ABILITY

DIRECTIONS (Qs. 41-43) : In each of the questions below are given three statements followed by four conclusions numbered I, II, III and IV. You have to take the given statements to be true even if they seem to be at variance with commonly know facts. Read all the conclusions and then decide which of the given conclusions logically follows from the given statements disregarding commonly known facts.

41. Statements :

A. Some boys are rains.
B. All rains are clouds.
C. Some clouds are cars.

Conclusions :

I. Some clouds are boys.
II. Some cars are boys.
III. Some cars are rains.
IV. Some rains are boys.

(a) Only II follows
(b) Only IV follows
(c) Only I follows
(d) Both I and IV follow
(e) None of these

42. Statements :

A. All bricks are flowers.
B. Some houses are flowers.
C. All pens are houses.

Conclusions :

I. Some houses are bricks.
II. Some pens are flowers.
III. Some flowers are bricks.
IV. No pen is flower.

(a) Only either II or IV and III follow
(b) Only either II or IV and I follow
(c) Only either I or II and IV follow
(d) Either II or IV follow
(e) None of these

43. Statements :

A. All lions are ducks.
B. No duck is a horse.
C. All horses are fruits.

Conclusions :

I. No lion is a horse.
II. Some fruits are horses.
III. Some ducks are lions.
IV. Some lions are horses.

(a) I, II and III follow
(b) Only either I or II and both III and IV follow
(c) Only either I or IV and both II and III follow
(d) Neither I nor II follow
(e) None of these

DIRECTIONS (Qs. 44-45) : Some statements are given followed by some conclusions. You have to consider the statements to be true even if they seem to be at variance from commonly known facts. You have to decide which of the following conclusions if any, follow from the given statements:

44. Statements:

Some psycho are sinners.
All sinners are killers.
No ruthless are sinners.
Some ruthless are psycho.

Conclusion:

I. Some ruthless can possibly be killers.
II. Some psycho are not ruthless.
III. Some killers are ruthless.

(a) Only I and III follow
(b) Only III follow
(c) Only I and II follow
(d) All follow
(e) None of these

45. Statements:

All boys are pens
Some toys are pens
All pots are toys.

Conclusion:

I. All pens are pots.
II. Some boys are toys.
III. Some pots are boys.
IV. Some pots are toys.

(a) Only II and III follow
(b) Only III follow
(c) Only IV and II follow
(d) All follow
(e) None of these

DIRECTIONS (Qs. 46-50) : Study the following information carefully to answer the questions that follow.

(I) M, N, P, Q, S and T are six members of a group in which there are three female members. Females work in three departments – Accounts, Administration and Personnel and sit in three different floors – 1st, 2nd and 3rd. Persons working in the same department are not on the same floor. On each floor, two persons work.

(II) No two ladies, work in the same department or on the same floor. N and S work in the same department but not in personnel. Q works in Administration. S and M are on the 1st and 3rd floors respectively and work in the same department. Q, a lady, does not work on 2nd floor. P, a man, works on the Ist floor.

46. Which of the following groups of persons is females ?
(a) SQT
(b) QMT
(c) QPT
(d) Data inadequate
(e) None of these

47. T works in which department ?
(a) Accounts
(b) Administration
(c) Personnel
(d) Accounts or Personnel
(e) None of these

48. Which of the following pairs of persons work on IInd floor?
(a) PT
(b) SM
(c) QN
(d) Data inadequate
(e) None of these

49. If T is transferred to Accounts and S is transferred to Administration, who is to be transferred to Personnel to maintain the original distribution of females on each floor ?
(a) P
(b) N
(c) Q
(d) Data inadequate
(e) None of these

50. Which of the following pairs of persons works in Administration ?
(a) QP
(b) QN
(c) SP
(d) Data inadequate
(e) None of these

DIRECTIONS (Qs. 51-55) : In each of these questions a group of letters is given followed by four combinations of numbers codes lettered (a), (b), (c) and (d). The group of letters is to be coded with the numbers codes and the condition given below. The 'serial number of the number combination'. Which correctly represents the letter group, is your answer.

Letters	D	J	K	Q	H	V	N	E	B	A
Numbers Codes	3	9	7	6	4	8	2	1	5	0

Conditions : If the first or the last letter or both in the letter group is /are a vowel then the same is/are to be coded by symbol #.

51. EHNDJV
- (a) #42389
- (b) 142398
- (c) #42398
- (d) 14239#
- (e) None of these

52. KQDJNH
- (a) 763942
- (b) 736924
- (c) #36924
- (d) #63924
- (e) None of these

53. AJNVQE
- (a) #9286#
- (b) 09286#
- (c) #92861
- (d) 092861
- (e) None of these

54. QHJVND
- (a) 648923
- (b) 649823
- (c) #49823
- (d) 64892#
- (e) None of these

55. JKEDHA
- (a) 97#34#
- (b) 971340
- (c) 971430
- (d) 97134#
- (e) None of these

DIRECTIONS : (Qs. 56-60): In the questions given below, certain symbols are used with the following meaning:

A @ B means A is greater than B.

A + B means A is either greater than or equal to B.

A † B means A is smaller than B

A ⊗ B means A is either smaller than or equal to B.

A $ B means A is equal to B

Now in each of the following questions assuming the given statements to be true find which of the two conclusions I and II given below them is /are definitely **true.** Give answer
- (a) if only conclusion I is true.
- (b) if only conclusion II is true.
- (c) if either I or II is true.
- (d) if neither I nor II are true.
- (e) if both I and II are true.

56. **Statements :** T $ G, K @ P, M † T, P + M

   Conclusions: I. K @ M **II.** G$P

57. **Statements :** R + N, S ⊗ B, A @ N, B$A

   Conclusions: I. S $ N   **II.** A @N

58. **Statements :** G $ K, F @ J. K + Q, Q + F

   Conclusions: I. K $ F   **II.** F †K

59. **Statements :** W @ S, K ⊗ Z, U + W, S $ K

   Conclusions: I. U @ K **II.** Z @ S

60. **Statements :** G $ E, D † K, E † S, K ⊗ G

   Conclusions: I. S @ D   **II.** D † E

DIRECTIONS (Qs. 61-65) : Study the following information carefully and answer the given questions :

Eight friends P, Q, R, S, T, V, W and Y are sitting around a square table in such a way that four of them sit at four corners of the square while four sit in the middle of each of the four sides. The ones who sit at the four corners face the centre while those who sit in the middle of the sides face outside.

P, who faces the centre, sits third to the right of V. T, who faces the centre, is not an immediate neighbour of V. Only one person sits between V and W. S sits second to right of Q. Q faces the centre. R is not an immediate neighbour of P.

61. Who sits second to the left of Q?
- (a) V
- (b) P
- (c) T
- (d) Y
- (e) Cannot be determined

62. What is the position of T with respect to V ?
- (a) Fourth to the left
- (b) Second to the left
- (c) Third to the left
- (d) Third to the right
- (e) Second to the right

63. Four of the following five are alike in a certain way and so form a group. Which is the one that does not belong to the group?
- (a) R
- (b) W
- (c) V
- (d) S
- (e) Y

64. Which of the following will come in place of the question mark based upon the given seating arrangement ?
   WP TR QW RS   ?
- (a) YT
- (b) VY
- (c) VQ
- (d) PY
- (e) QV

65. Which of the following is true regarding R ?
- (a) R is an immediate neighbour of V
- (b) R faces the centre
- (c) R sits exactly between T and S
- (d) Q sits third to left of R
- (e) None of these

DIRECTIONS (Qs. 66-68) : Study the following information carefully and answer the questions given below:

In a family there are three fathers, two brothers, two sisters, one husband, one wife, two brothers-in-law, two daughters, three sons, three cousins, two nephews, one grandfather and a niece.

66. What is the minimum possible number of persons In the family?
- (a) 22
- (b) 7
- (c) 9
- (d) 30
- (e) None of these

67. How many female members are there in the family ?
- (a) Two
- (b) Three
- (c) Four
- (d) One
- (e) None of these

68. Deepak drove 15km towards north from his home and took a left turn. He covered 5km and turned towards south. After driving for 15km. he stopped. What should have been Deepak's choice of direction with respect to his home in order to reach his destination earlier?
- (a) North
- (b) South
- (c) East
- (d) West
- (e) None of these

DIRECTIONS (Qs. 69-70) : Study the following information carefully and answer the questions given below:

The distance between the pole X and Y is 2 km. Pole Y is 9 km to the south of Pole E. Pole M is 1 km to the west of Pole Q, which is 5 km to the north of Pole X. Pole M is not to the east of Pole E. Pole X is to the west of Pole Y.

69. What is the distance between Pole M and Pole E ?
- (a) 2km
- (b) 5km
- (c) 8km
- (d) 7km
- (e) None of these

70. In which direction is Pole Q with respect to Pole Y ?

    (a) South - west   (b) North-east

    (c) South-east   (d) North-west

    (e) None of these

DIRECTIONS (Qs. 71-75) : Study the following information carefully and answer the given questions.

P, Q, R, S, T, V, W and X are captains of eight different cricket teams, namely Australia, New Zealand, India, Pakistan, Sri Lanka, England, West Indies and South Africa, but not necessarily in the same order. All of them are seated around a circular table and are facing the centre.

P sits third to the left of the Sri Lankan captain. Only two people sit between T and W. Neither T nor W is an immediate neighbour of P. Neither T and W is the captain of Sri lanka. The captain of South Africa sits second to the right of S. S is not an immediate neighbour of P.S. is not the Sri Lankan captain and P is not the captain of South Africa. The Australian captain sits third to the left of V. The Australian and Sri Lankan captains are not immediate neighbours. Only one person sits between S and the Indian captain. Captains of Pakistan and New Zealand are immediate neighbours. S is not the captain of New Zealand's team. Only one person sits between Q and the captain of England. The captain of England is an immediate neighbour of X. W and Q are not immediate neighbours.

71. How many people sit between T and the captain of England when counted in clockwise direction from T?

    (a) None   (b) One

    (c) Two   (d) Four

    (e) Five

72. Who is the captain of the Australian team?

    (a) P   (b) V

    (c) W   (d) T

    (e) Q

73. Which of the following would come in place of question mark based upon the given seating arrangement?

VS   XR TV RP ?

    (a) SW   (b) WX

    (c) QW   (d) QX

    (e) VR

74. Which of the following is **true** with respect to the given arrangement?

    (a) R is the captain of South Africa

    (b) W is an immediate neighbour of V.

    (c) The captain of Australia and England are immediate neighbours.

    (d) Four people sit between W and Q.

    (e) X sits second to the left of S.

75. Who is the Indian captain?

    (a) Q   (b) V

    (c) X   (d) T

    (e) Cannot be determined

DIRECTIONS (Qs. 76-78) : Study the given information carefully and answer the given questions.

Among six people - A, B, C, D, E and F each of a different age, A is younger than only D. Only three people are younger than C. F is younger than E. F is not the youngest.

76. Who amongst the following is the youngest?

    (a) B   (b) A

    (c) E   (d) C

    (e) None of these

77. If E's age 16 years, then which of the following may be B's age?

    (a) 19 years   (b) 22 years

    (c) 18 years   (d) 17 years

    (e) 12 years

78. How many people are younger than E?

    (a) One   (b) Two

    (c) Three   (d) Four

    (e) More than four

DIRECTIONS (Qs. 79 & 80): Study the given information carefully and answer the given questions.

Twenty students are standing in a straight line facing north. Rina is standing sixth from the left end. There are only three students between Rina and Shweta. Radha is standing exactly between Shweta and Rina. Tina is standing sixth to the right of Radha. Anita is standing fourth from the right end of the line. There are more than four students between Rina and Tina.

79. How many people are standing between Anita and Tina.

    (a) One   (b) Two

    (c) Three   (d) None

    (e) More than three

80. What is Shweta's position with respect to Anita?

    (a) Sixth to the left   (b) Eighth to the left

    (c) Seventh to the left   (d) Ninth to the left

    (e) None of these

HINTS & EXPLANATIONS

1. (b) $? = 72.42 + 385.66 + 4976.38$

$\Rightarrow ? = 5434.46$

2. (e) $? = 16\%$ of $250 + 115\%$ of 480

$\Rightarrow ? = \dfrac{16}{100} \times 250 + \dfrac{115}{100} \times 480$

$\Rightarrow ? = \dfrac{4000}{100} + \dfrac{55200}{100}$

$\Rightarrow ? = 40 + 552 = 592$

3. (a) 55% of $860 + ?\%$ of $450 = 581$

$\Rightarrow \dfrac{55}{100} \times 860 + \dfrac{?}{100} \times 450 = 581$

$\Rightarrow 473 + \dfrac{?}{100} \times 450 = 581$

$\Rightarrow \dfrac{?}{100} \times 450 = 581 - 473 = 108$

$\Rightarrow ? = \dfrac{108 \times 100}{450} = 24$

4. (a) $? = \dfrac{5}{9}$ of $504 + \dfrac{3}{8}$ of 640

$\Rightarrow ? = \dfrac{5}{9} \times 504 + \dfrac{3}{8} \times 640$

$\Rightarrow ? = 280 + 240$

$\Rightarrow ? = 520$

5. (d) $? = 3.2\%$ of $250 + 1.8\%$ of 400

$\Rightarrow ? = \dfrac{3.2}{100} \times 250 + \dfrac{1.8}{100} \times 400$

$\Rightarrow ? = \dfrac{800}{100} + \dfrac{720}{100}$

$\Rightarrow ? = 8 + 7.2 = 15.2$

6. (c) Let ten's digit $= x$ and units digit $= x + 5$

Then, $x + 5 = 6x$

$x = 1$

$\therefore$ units digit $= x + 5 = 1 + 5 = 6$

So required number $= 16$

7. (a) Let the population of village X and Y be $5p$ and $7p$ respectively.

If population of village Y, increases by 25000

the new ratios $\rightarrow \dfrac{5p}{7p + 25000} = \dfrac{25}{36}$

$\Rightarrow 180p = 175p + 625000$

$\Rightarrow 5p = 625000$

$\therefore$ population of village x $= 625000$.

8. (a) Saving percentage $= (100 - 55)\% = 45\%$

If the income of Ajay be ₹ x, then,

$\dfrac{45 \times x}{100} = 27000$

$\Rightarrow x = \dfrac{27000 \times 100}{45} = ₹\, 60000$

9. (d) Let the breadth of the rectangle be x metre.

$\therefore$ Length $= 3x$ metre

$\therefore 3x \times x = \dfrac{27540}{367.20} = 75$

$\Rightarrow x^2 = 25$

$\Rightarrow x = 5$

$\therefore$ Perimeter of the rectangle

$= 2(3x + x) = 8x$

$= 8 \times 5 = 40$ metre

10. (d)

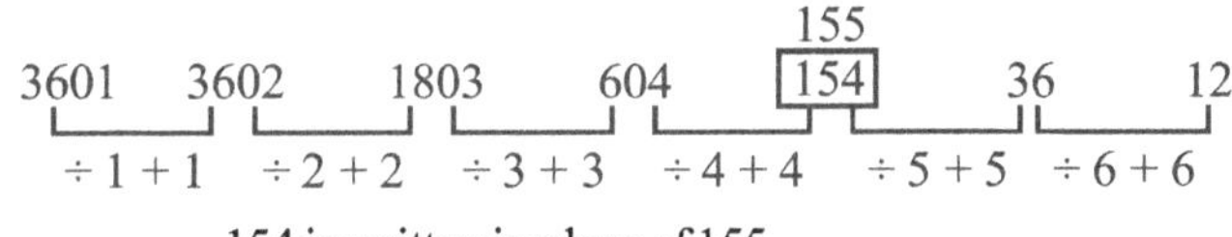

154 is written in place of 155.

11. (b)

42 is written in place of 45.

12. (a)

8 is written in place of 6.

13. (e)

65 is written in place of 60.

14. (d)

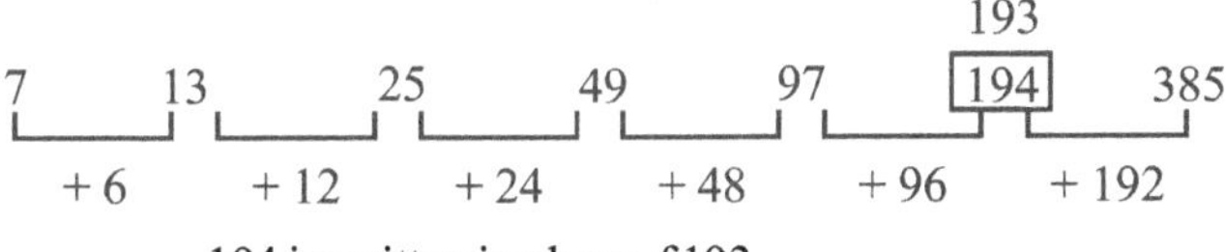

194 is written in place of 193

15. (c) Total no. of teachers in Banglore

$$= 3360 \times \frac{80}{100} = 2688$$

$\therefore$ No. of female teachers

$= 2688 - 1800 = 888$

No. of female teachers in the next year

$$= 888 \times \frac{150}{100} = 1332$$

and the no. of female exployees in

$$\text{Banglore} = \frac{3360}{14} \times 6 = 1440$$

$\therefore$ Required % $= \left(\frac{1332}{1440} \times 100 \right)\%$

$= 92.5\%$

16. (a) No. of female employees in Bengal

$$= \frac{2054}{13} \times 6 = 948$$

$\therefore$ Required % $\left(\frac{948}{2054} \times 100 \right)\% = 46.15\%$

No. of female employees in UP

$$= \frac{2880}{16} \times 5 = 900$$

$\therefore$ Required % $= \left(\frac{900}{2880} \times 100 \right)\% = 31.25\%$

No. of female employees in Banglore

$$= \frac{3360}{14} \times 6 = 1440$$

$\therefore$ Required % $= \left(\frac{1440}{3360} \times 100 \right)\% = 42.85\%$

No. of female employees in MP

$$= \frac{2788}{41} \times 21 = 1428$$

$\therefore$ Required % $= \left(\frac{1428}{2788} \times 100 \right)\% = 51.21\%$

No. of female employees in Delhi

$$= \left(\frac{2568}{12} \right) \times 7 = 1498$$

$\therefore$ Required % $= \left(\frac{1498}{2568} \times 100 \right)\% = 58.33\%$

$\therefore$ Required answer is Bengal.

17. (d) Total no. of male employees in UP and Banglore together

$$= \frac{2880}{16} \times 11 + \frac{3360}{14} \times 8$$

$= 1980 + 1920 = 3900$

Total no. of teachers in UP and Banglore together

$$= 2880 \times \frac{65}{100} + 3360 \times \frac{80}{100}$$

$= 1872 + 2688 = 4560$

$\therefore$ Required ratio $= 3900 : 4560 = 65 : 76$

18. (a) Average no. of teachers in Delhi, UP and Bihar together

$$= \frac{2568 \times \frac{75}{100} + 2880 \times \frac{65}{100} + 3575 \times \frac{60}{100}}{3}$$

$$= \frac{1926 + 1872 + 2145}{3} = 1981$$

Average no. of teachers in MP, Mumbai and Bangalore together

$$= \frac{2788 \times \frac{75}{100} + 3720 \times \frac{55}{100} + 3360 \times \frac{80}{100}}{3}$$

$$= \frac{2091 + 2046 + 2688}{3} = 2275$$

$\therefore$ Required difference $= 2275 - 1981 = 294$

19. (a) Average no. of employees per office in

$$\text{Bihar} = \frac{3575}{22} = 162.5$$

$$\text{Bangalore} = \frac{3360}{21} = 160$$

$$\text{Mumbai} = \frac{3720}{24} = 155$$

$$\text{Delhi} = \frac{2568}{16} = 160.5$$

$$\text{MP} = \frac{2788}{17} = 164$$

$\therefore$ Required answer is Bihar.

20. (b) Required amount $= 25000 \left(1 + \frac{8}{100} \right)^2$

$$= 25000 \times \frac{27}{25} \times \frac{27}{25} = ₹29160$$

21. (b) Let Nand Kishore's total money was $= ₹\, x$

After giving some amount to his wife and his sons, remaining amount

$$= x - \left(x \times \frac{35}{100} + x \times \frac{50}{100} \right) = x - \frac{85x}{100} = ₹\frac{15x}{100}$$

Then, $\dfrac{15x}{100} = ₹11250$

$\Rightarrow \quad x = \dfrac{11250 \times 100}{15} = ₹75000$

22. (d) Total cost price $= 200 \times 10 = ₹2000$

Total selling price $= 12 \times 195 = ₹2340$

$\therefore$ Profit per cent $= \dfrac{2340 - 2000}{2000} \times 100 = 17\%$

23. (c) $\Rightarrow$ Total income of the four-membered family

$= 4 \times 15130 = ₹60520$

$\Rightarrow$ Total income of three family members

$= 3 \times 14660 = ₹43980$

$\Rightarrow$ Monthly income of the married daughter

$= 60520 - 43980 = ₹16540$

24. (b) Total correct questions for getting 60% grade

$= 250 \times \dfrac{60}{100} = 150$

40% of 125 = 50 questions

$\therefore$ x% of 125 = 150 – 50 = 100 questions

$\Rightarrow x = \dfrac{100 \times 100}{125} = 80$

Required percentage = 80%

Note: This can be solved by alligation method quickly. Try it.

25. (c) LCM of 36 sec, 48 sec and 42 sec = 1008 sec

$\therefore$ After 1008 seconds, they will be together at the starting point.

26. (a) I. $14x + 7x = 59 + 25$

$\Rightarrow 21x = 84$

$\Rightarrow x = \dfrac{84}{21} = 4$

II. $\sqrt{y + 222} = \sqrt{36} + \sqrt{81}$

$\Rightarrow \sqrt{y + 222} = 6 + 9 = 15$

$\therefore y + 222 = 225$

$\Rightarrow y = 225 - 222 = 3$

clearly, x > y

27. (d) I. $144x^2 = 16 + 9 = 25$

$\Rightarrow x^2 = \dfrac{25}{144}$

$\Rightarrow x = \pm \dfrac{5}{12}$

II. $12y = \sqrt{49} - \sqrt{4} = +5$

$\Rightarrow y = \dfrac{5}{12}$

$\quad x \le y$

28. (c) I. $x^2 - 9x + 20 = 0$

$\Rightarrow x^2 - 5x - 4x + 20 = 0$

$\Rightarrow x(x - 5) - 4(x - 5) = 0$

$\Rightarrow (x - 5)(x - 4) = 0$

$\therefore x = 5$ or 4

II. $y^2 - 7y - 6y + 42 = 0$

$\Rightarrow y(y - 7) - 6(y - 7) = 0$

$\Rightarrow (y - 6)(y - 7) = 0$

$\therefore y = 6$ or 7

clearly, x < y

29. (e) I. $\dfrac{2\sqrt{x} + 3\sqrt{x}}{10} = \dfrac{1}{\sqrt{x}}$

$\Rightarrow 5\sqrt{x} \times \sqrt{x} = 10$

$\Rightarrow 5x = 10$

$\Rightarrow x = 2$

II. $\dfrac{10 - 2}{\sqrt{y}} = 4\sqrt{y}$

$\Rightarrow 4y = 8$

$\Rightarrow y = \dfrac{8}{4} = 2$

clearly, x = y

30. (d) I. $x^2 - 19x + 84 = 0$

$\Rightarrow x^2 - 7x - 12x + 84 = 0$

$\Rightarrow (x - 7)(x - 12) = 0$

$\Rightarrow x = 7, 12$

II. $y^2 - 25y + 156 = 0$

$\Rightarrow y^2 - 13y - 12y + 156 = 0$

$\Rightarrow (y - 13)(y - 12) = 0$

$\Rightarrow x = 12, 13$

$\therefore x \le y$

31. (b) Total no. of employees

$= (840 + 220 + 900 + 360 + 450 + 540) = 3310$

32. (d) Required % $= \dfrac{360}{220} \times 100 \approx 164\%$

33. (e) Total no. of male employees in IT and Customer Service

$= 840 \times \dfrac{55}{100} + 540 \times \dfrac{60}{100} = 462 + 324 = 786$

34. (a) Total no. of females employees in HR, Marketing and Production

$= 360 \times \dfrac{65}{100} + 450 \times \dfrac{44}{100} + 900 \times \dfrac{23}{100}$

$= 234 + 198 + 207 = 639$

35. (c) Required difference =

$\Rightarrow \left(360 \times \dfrac{35}{100} + 840 \times \dfrac{55}{100}\right) - \left(220 \times \dfrac{65}{100} + 450 \times \dfrac{56}{100}\right)$

$\Rightarrow 588 - 395 = 193$

36. (b) Cost of production of both items for

Company $A = \dfrac{15}{100} \times 25 = 3.75$ crores

Company $C = \dfrac{22}{100} \times 25 = ₹\,5.5$ crores

These costs will be divided in the ratio of production of items I and II.

Cost of production of item I for

Company $A = \dfrac{2}{2+3} \times 3.75 = ₹\,1.5$ crores

Company $C = \dfrac{4}{4+1} \times 5.5 = ₹\,4.4$ crores

∴ Total cost of production of item 1 by companies A and C together

$= ₹\,(1.5 + 4.4)$ crores $= ₹\,5.9$ crores

37. (d) Cost of production of both items for company D

$= \dfrac{8}{100} \times 25 = ₹\,2$ crores

Cost of production of item II for company D

$= \dfrac{5}{3+5} \times 2 = ₹\,\dfrac{5}{4}$ crores

% profit earned by company D on item II = 25%

∴ Amount of profit earned by company D on item II.

$= \dfrac{25}{100} \times \dfrac{5}{4} = ₹\,\dfrac{5}{16}$ crores

$= ₹\,\dfrac{5}{16} \times 100$ lakhs $= ₹\,31.25$ lakhs

38. (d) Required difference =

$= \left[25 \times \left(\dfrac{12}{100} + \dfrac{22}{100} \right) - 25 \times \left(\dfrac{15}{100} + \dfrac{11}{100} \right) \right]$

$= 8.5 - 6.5$

$\Rightarrow 2$ crores

39. (e) **40.** (e)

41. (d) 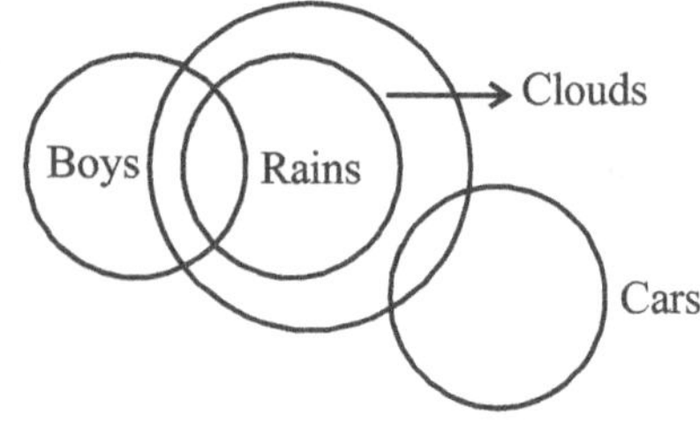

OR

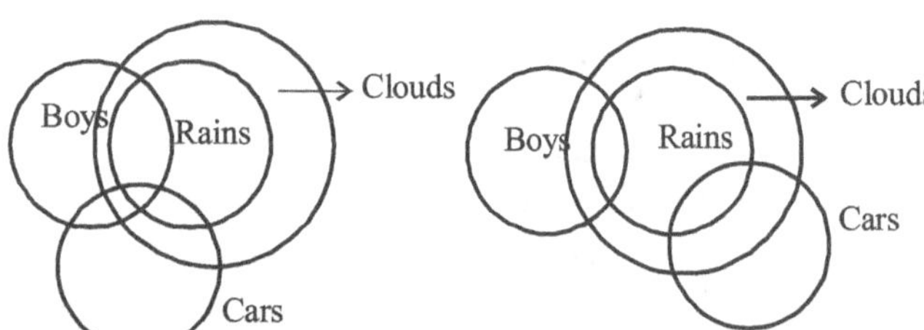

OR

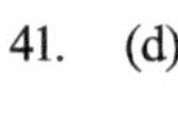

Conclusion - I. ✔

II. can't say

III. can't say

IV. ✔ (Conversion of I Statement)

or

42. (a) 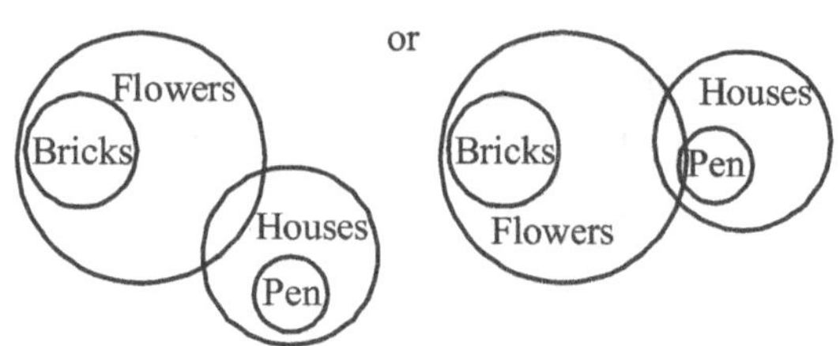

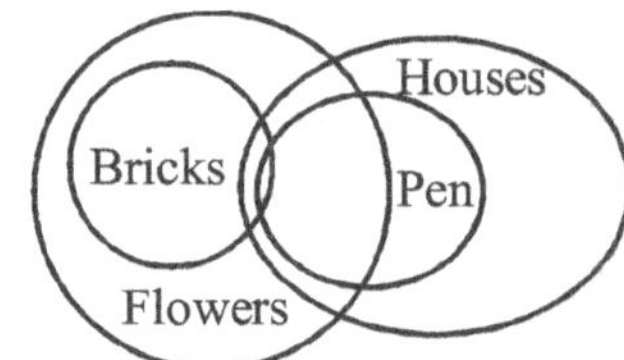

Conclusion - I. ✘ (can't say)

II. ✘ (can't say)

III. ✔

IV. ✘ (can't say)

Option (a)

43. (a) 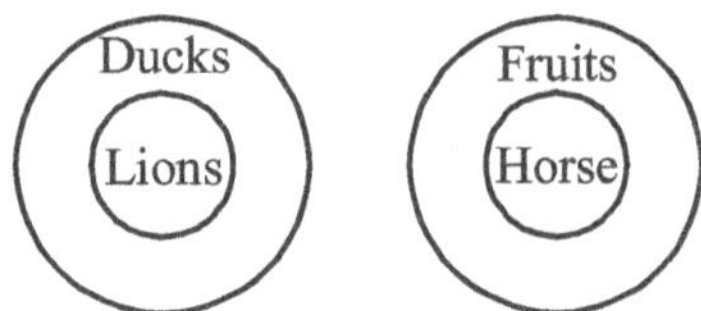

Conclusion - I. ✔
II. ✔
III. ✔ } Either
IV. ✘

44. (c) 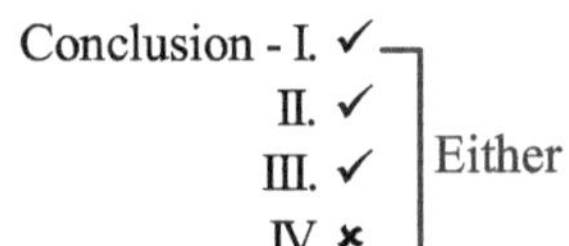

I. ✔
II. ✔
III. ✘

45. (e) 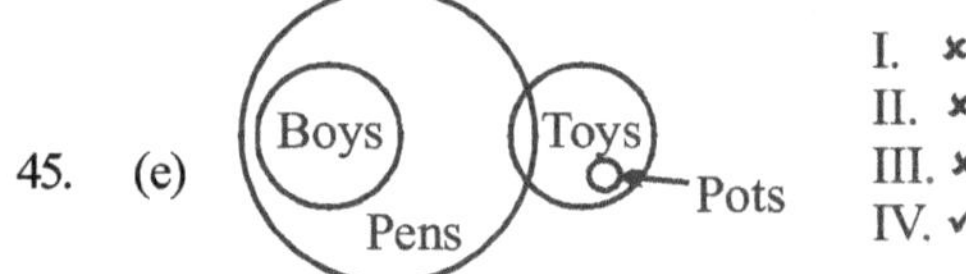

I. ✘
II. ✘
III. ✘
IV. ✔

For (Qs. 46-50) :

The given information can be summarized as follows.

Member	Floors					
	I		II		III	
Member	P	S	N	T	M	Q
Department	Not clear	Acc	Acc	Per-sonnel	Acct.	Adm.
Sex	M	F	M	F	M	F

46. (a) From the analysis of table constructed above, SQT is the group of females.

47. (c) Clearly, T works in personnel.

48. (e) N and T work on the second floor.

49. (c) To maintain the original distribution of females on each floor, Q must be transferred to personnel.

50. (d) Data is inadequate to determine the department of P. From the information provided only we can say that Q works in administration.

51. (c)

Letter	E	H	N	D	J	V
Code	#	4	2	3	9	8

Condition is applied.

52. (e)

Letter	K	Q	D	J	N	H
Code	7	6	3	9	2	4

53. (a)

Letter	A	J	N	V	Q	E
Code	#	9	2	8	6	#

Condition is applied.

54. (b)

Letter	Q	H	J	V	N	D
Code	6	4	9	8	2	3

55. (d)

Letter	J	K	E	D	H	A
Code	9	7	1	3	4	#

Condition is applied.

56. (a) $T = G$, $K > P$, $M < T$, $P \geq M$

$K > P \geq M < T = G$

Conclusions: I. $K > M$ (✓)
II. $G = P$ (×)

Hence, only conclusion I is true.

57. (b) $R \geq N$, $S \leq B$, $A > N$, $B = A$

$S \leq B = A > N \leq R$

Conclusions : I. $S = N$ (×)
II. $A > N$ (✓)

Hence, only conclusion II is true.

58. (c) $G = K$, $F > J$, $K \geq Q$, $Q \leq F$

$G = K \geq Q \geq F > J$

Conclusions : I. $K = K$ (✓)
II. $F < K$ (✓) Either

Hence, either I or II is true.

59. (e) $W > S$, $K \leq Z$, $U \geq W$, $S = K$

$U \geq W > S = K \leq Z$

Conclusions : I. $U > K$ (✓)
II. $Z > S$ (✓)

60. (e) $G = E$ ....(i), $D < K$ ...(ii), $E < S$ .....(iii), $K \leq G = E < S$.
Clearly, both conclusions I and II follow.

(61-65): Arrangement according to the questions :

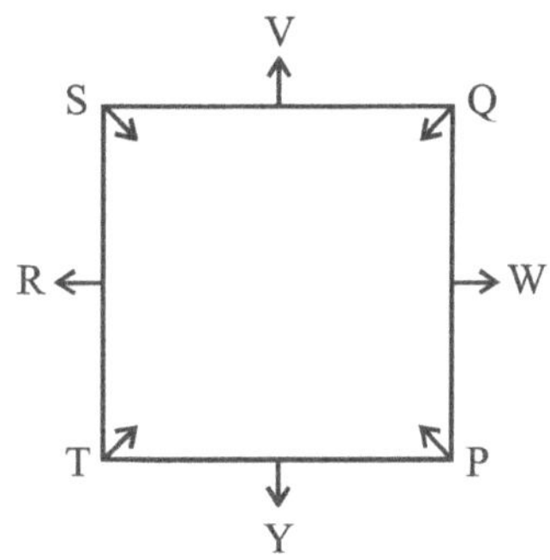

61. (b) 62. (c)

63. (d) Others sit at the middle of the sides.

64. (a) Move $1\frac{1}{2}$, 2, $2\frac{1}{2}$, 3...... sides clockwise on the square.

65. (c)

(66-67)

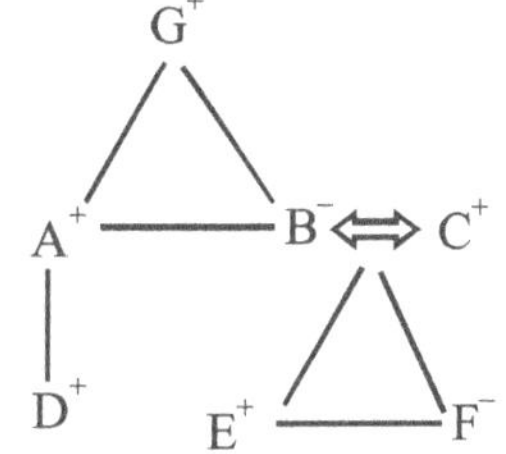

Three fathers (G, A, C) two brothers (A and B), two sisters (B and F), one husband (c), one wife (b), two brothers-in-law (A and C), two daughters (B and F), three sons (A, D and E), three cousins (D, E and F), two nephews (D and E), one grandfather (G) and one niece (F)

66. (b)

67. (a)

68. (d) The path taken by Deepak is shown below

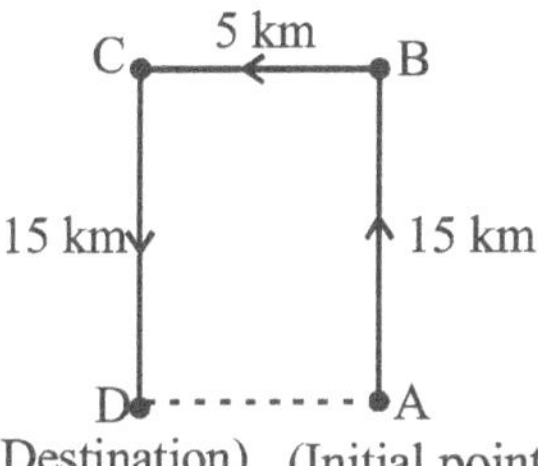

It is evident that if Deepak had driven along AD, then he would have reached earlier because length of AD is only 5km which is much smaller as compared to length of path taken by him

Since AD points along west direction therefore Deepak's right choice should have been west direction.

(69-70):

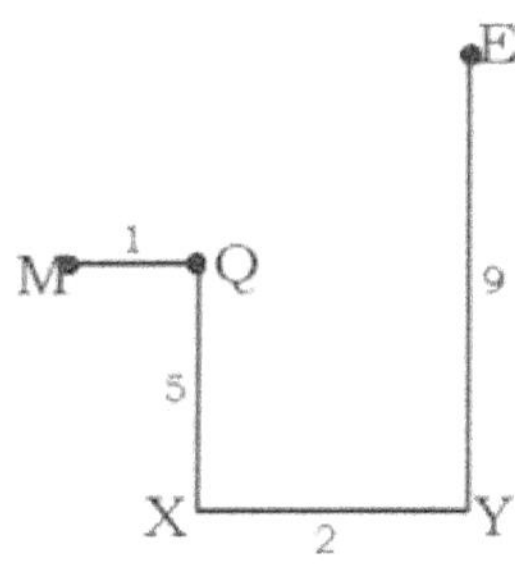

69. (b) $\sqrt{3^2 + 4^2} = 5$
70. (d)

(71-75) : Arrangement according to the question is as follows :

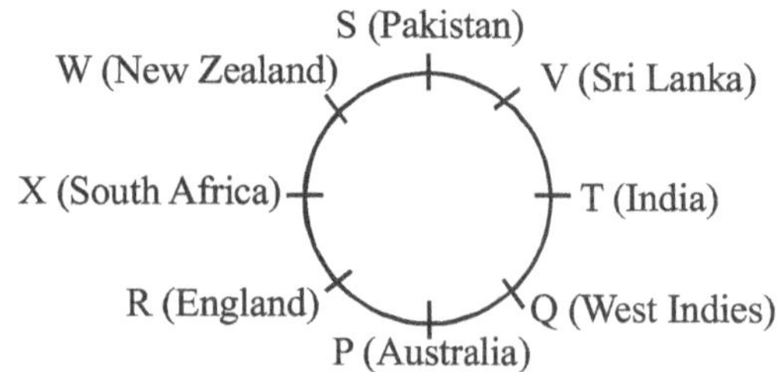

71. (c)
72. (a)
73. (b) There is pattern of going from second member of a pair to the first member of the next pair: +2, +3, +4 ... CW.
74. (c)
75. (d)

(Qs. 76-78). According to given information

D > A > — > — > — > —   A is younger than only D
⇓
D > A > C > — > — > — > — Only three are younger than C
⇓
D > A > C > E > F > B
F is younger than E, F is not the youngest

76. (a)
77. (e) (B is younger than E)
78. (b) (Only two F and B)

(Qs. 79-80).

According to information given
Final arrangement is as follows
1 2 3 4 5 Rina 7 Radha 9 Shweta 11 12 13 Tina 15 16 Anita 18 19 20.

79. (b) Two person are between Anita and Tina.
80. (c) Anita is at 17th position and Shweta at 10th position.

PRACTICE SET 

Time : 45 min.   **Max. Marks : 80**

QUANTITATIVE APTITUDE

DIRECTIONS (Qs. 1-5): What will come in place of the question mark (?) in the following questions.

1. $\dfrac{5}{11}$ of $\dfrac{4}{5}$ of $\dfrac{11}{6}$ of 848 = ?
   - (a) 216
   - (b) 222
   - (c) 208
   - (d) 212
   - (e) None of these

2. 1.4% of 750 + 2.2% of 480 = ?
   - (a) 21.06
   - (b) 21.16
   - (c) 20.88
   - (d) 21.18
   - (e) None of these

3. $6.96 \div 1.2 - 18.24 \div 7.6 = ?$
   - (a) 3.4
   - (b) 3.14
   - (c) 3.04
   - (d) 3.24
   - (e) None of these

4. 136% of 250 + ? % of 550 = 670
   - (a) 64
   - (b) 55
   - (c) 56
   - (d) 65
   - (e) None of these

5. 45% of 660 + 28% of 450 = ?
   - (a) 413
   - (b) 428
   - (c) 423
   - (d) 418
   - (e) None of these

DIRECTIONS (Qs. 6-10): What will come in place of the question mark (?) in the following number series.

6. 12   16   24   40   ?
   - (a) 76
   - (b) 72
   - (c) 84
   - (d) 88
   - (e) None of these

7. 9   19   39   79   ?
   - (a) 139
   - (b) 129
   - (c) 159
   - (d) 149
   - (e) None of these

8. 8   17   42   91   ?
   - (a) 170
   - (b) 142
   - (c) 140
   - (d) 172
   - (e) None of these

9. 7   8   18   57   ?
   - (a) 244
   - (b) 174
   - (c) 186
   - (d) 226
   - (e) None of these

10. 3840   960   240   60   ?
    - (a) 20
    - (b) 18
    - (c) 12
    - (d) 22
    - (e) None of these

11. Simple interest accrued on an amount in 8 years at the rate of 12 p.c.p.a. is ₹ 5,520. What is the principal?
    - (a) ₹ 5,750
    - (b) ₹ 8,500
    - (c) ₹ 5,650
    - (d) ₹ 8,250
    - (e) None of these

12. Srikant and Vividh started a business investing amounts of ₹ 1,85,000 and ₹ 2,25,000 respectively, If Vividh's share in the profit earned by them is ₹ 9,000, what is the total profit earned by them together?
    - (a) ₹ 17,400
    - (b) ₹ 16,400
    - (c) ₹ 16,800
    - (d) ₹ 17,800
    - (e) None of these

13. Present ages of father and son are in the ratio of 6 : 1 respectively. Four years after the ratio of their ages will become 4 : 1 respectively. What is the son's present age?
    - (a) 10 years
    - (b) 6 years
    - (c) 4 years
    - (d) 8 years
    - (e) None of these

14. Number obtained by interchanging the digit of a two digit number is more than the original number by 27 and the sum of the digits is 13. What is the original number?
    (a) 58   (b) 67
    (c) 76   (d) 85
    (e) None of these

15. 22 men can complete a job in 16 days. In how many days will 32 men complete that job?
    (a) 14   (b) 12
    (c) 16   (d) 9
    (e) None of these

16. Mr. Davar spends 38% of his monthly income on food, 25% on children's education and 12% on transport and the remaining amount of ₹ 5,800 he saves. What is Mr. Davar's monthly income?
    (a) ₹ 23,200   (b) ₹ 24,200
    (c) ₹ 23,800   (d) ₹ 24,400
    (e) None of these

17. The salary of a man increases by 20% every year in the month of January. His salary was ₹ 5,000 in the month of February in year 2009. What will be his salary in the month of February in the year 2011 ?
    (a) ₹ 7,200   (b) ₹ 6,200
    (c) ₹ 7,800   (d) ₹ 6,800
    (e) None of these

18. The simple interest on a certain principal in 5 years at the rate of 12 p.c. p.a. is ₹ 1,536. What amount of the simple interest would one get if one invests ₹ 1,000 more than the previous principal for 2 years and at the same rate p.c.p.a.?
    (a) ₹ 845.40   (b) ₹ 614.40
    (c) ₹ 2,136   (d) ₹ 1,536
    (e) None of these

19. If 3 men or 9 boys can finish a piece of work in 21 days. In how many days can 5 men and 6 boys together do the same piece of work?
    (a) 12 days   (b) 8 days
    (c) 14 days   (d) Cannot be determined
    (e) None of these

20. In a test, Rajesh got 112 marks which is 32 more than the passing marks. Sonal got 75% marks which is 70 more than the passing marks. What is the minimum passing percentage of the test?
    (a) 35   (b) 45
    (c) 40   (d) 30
    (e) None of these

DIRECTIONS (Qs. 21-25): In each of these questions, two equations I and II are given. You have to solve these equations and give answer.

If
(a) $x > y$ (b) $x < y$
(c) $x \geq y$ (d) $x \leq y$
(e) $x = y$ or no relation can be established

21. I. $5x^2 - 87x - 378 = 0$
    II. $3y^2 - 49y + 200 = 0$

22. I. $(x + 1)(x + 18) = -66$
    II. $\sqrt{(y - 3)(y - 27)} = 9$

23. I. $\dfrac{15}{x} + \dfrac{16}{y} = 1$
    II. $\dfrac{3}{x} - \dfrac{7}{y} = 5$

24. I. $17x^2 + 48x = 9$
    II. $13y^2 + 12 = 32y$

25. I. $4x + 7y = 209$
    II. $12x - 14y = -38$

DIRECTIONS (Qs. 26-30) : Study the following table carefully and answer the given questions. Table shows the data related to different types of laptop.

Laptop	Cost Price	Selling Price	% of Profit	Profit
HP	₹ 35, 000	—	—	₹ 3,500
Acer	₹ 53, 000	—	14%	—
Dell	—	₹ 22, 000	—	—
Lenovo	₹ 28, 000	—	—	—
Apple	—	₹ 33, 000	10%	—
HCL	₹ 32, 000	—	—	₹ 4, 000

26. What is the selling price and profit percentage of HCL Laptop?
    (a) ₹ 36, 000 and 12.5%   (b) ₹ 36,00 and 15%
    (c) ₹ 36,000 and 18%   (d) ₹ 36,000 and 20%
    (e) None of these

27. What is the profit percentage of Dell Laptop, if cost price of Dell Laptop is $\dfrac{3}{5}$ of cost price of Apple Laptop?
    (a) $33\dfrac{1}{3}\%$ (b) $26\dfrac{4}{9}\%$
    (c) $22\dfrac{2}{9}\%$ (d) $24\dfrac{5}{9}\%$
    (e) None of these

28. What is the selling price and profit percentage of Lenovo Laptop, if the profit is ₹ 500 more than the profit of HP Laptop?
    (a) ₹ 32, 000 and $14\dfrac{1}{7}\%$ (b) ₹ 34, 000 and $14\dfrac{4}{7}\%$
    (c) ₹ 32, 000 and $15\dfrac{2}{7}\%$ (d) ₹ 34, 000 and $17\dfrac{5}{7}\%$
    (e) None of these

29. What is the profit earned on Acer Laptop?
(a) ₹7360   (b) ₹7450
(c) ₹7420   (d) ₹7560
(e) None of these

30. What is the ratio between the cost price and selling price of HP Laptop ?
(a) 14 : 15   (b) 10 : 11
(c) 10 : 14   (d) 14 : 15
(e) None of these

DIRECTIONS (Qs. 31-35) : Study the following bar-graph carefully and answer the given questions.

Bar graph show the total population of six different villages and percentage of males among them.

Total Population of villages

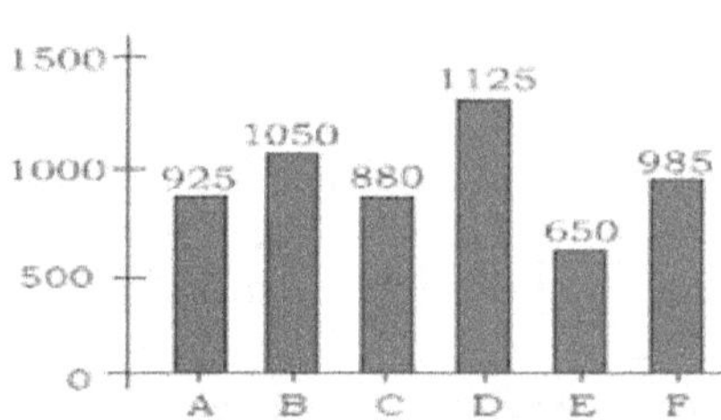

Percentage of Males

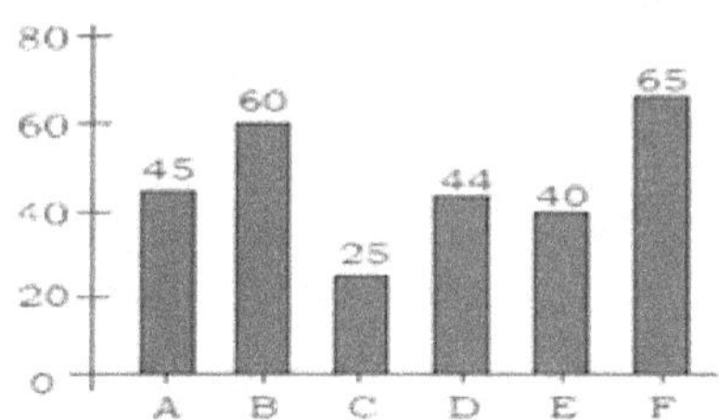

31. What is the respective ratio between the total number of males in village A and the total number of female in village E?
(a) 115 : 104   (b) 111 : 104
(c) 104 : 111   (d) 104 : 115
(e) None of these

32. What are total number of males in village C and the total number of females in village D and E together?
(a) 1420   (b) 1240
(c) 1140   (d) 1000
(e) None of these

33. The total number of females in village B is approximately what percent of the total population of in village D?
(a) 73%   (b) 37%
(c) 47%   (d) 65%
(e) None of these

34. What is the approx total number of females in the entire village together? (approximately)
(a) 2513   (b) 2400
(c) 1585   (d) 2325
(e) None of these

35. What is the approx average number of males in all the village together?
(a) 430   (b) 625
(c) 492   (d) 410
(e) None of these

DIRECTIONS (Qs. 36–40) : Study the following graph carefully to answer the questions that follows :

Number of units produced (in crores) and exported (in crores) by a Company over the years.

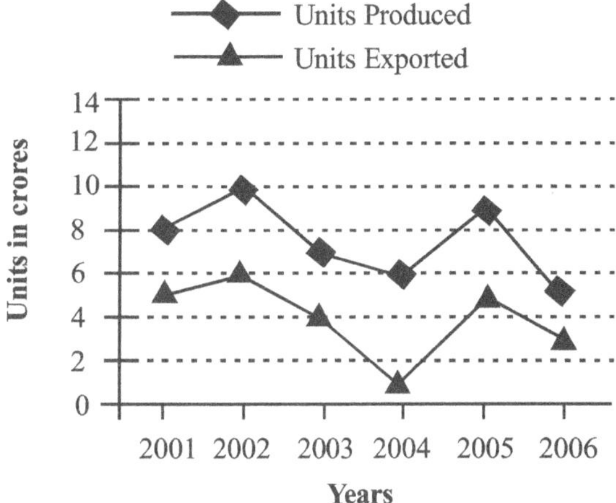

36. What is the average number of units exported over the years?
(a) 40000000   (b) 38333333
(c) 36666666   (d) 20000000
(e) None of these

37. In which year is the percent of units exported with respect to the units produced the **minimum** ?
(a) 2001   (b) 2002
(c) 2003   (d) 2004
(e) None of these

38. In which year is the percent of units exported with respect to the units produced the **maximum** ?
(a) 2003   (b) 2004
(c) 2005   (d) 2006
(e) None of these

39. In which year is the difference between the units produced and exported the **maximum** ?
(a) 2002   (b) 2003
(c) 2004   (d) 2005
(e) None of these

40. What is the difference between the number of units exported in 2002 and 2005 ?
(a) 100000000   (b) 1000000
(c) 10000000   (d) 100000
(e) None of these

REASONING ABILITY

DIRECTIONS (Qs. 41-45): Study the given information carefully to answer the given question:

Seven persons, namely L, M, N, O, P, Q and R will appear for a different exam but not necessarily in the same order, in seven different months (of the same year) namely January, February, April, May, July, September and December. Each of them also like colours viz. Red, White, Blue, Pink, Purple, Black and Green but not necessarily in the same order. O will appear for an exam in a month which has only 30 days. Only one person will appear between the one who likes Purple colours and O. the one who likes White colour will appear for an exam immediately before the one who likes Purple Colour. The one who likes Green colour will appear for an exam neither in the month which has 31 days nor in the month which has 30 days. Only two persons will appear for an exam between the one who likes Green colour and Q. M will appear for an exam immediately after Q and does not likes White Colour. R will appear for an exam immediately before N. P likes Black colour and appear for exam in December. The one who likes Red colour will appear for an exam in a month which has 31 days. O does not like Blue colour.

41. Which of the following colour does O like?
   (a) Black   (b) Green
   (c) Red   (d) White
   (e) Pink

42. How many persons will appear for an exam between the months on which N and L will appear for an exam?
   (a) One   (b) None
   (c) Three   (d) Two
   (e) More than three

43. As per the given arrangement, January is related to Pink colour and February is related to White colour following a certain pattern, with which of the following is July related to following the same pattern?
   (a) Red colours   (b) Green colours
   (c) Blue colours   (d) Black colours
   (e) Purple colours

44. Which of the following represents the month in which L will appear for an exam?
   (a) December   (b) May
   (c) July   (d) September
   (e) cannot be determined

45. Which of the following represents the persons who will appear for an exam in January and December respectively?
   (a) N, P   (b) N, M
   (c) R, P   (d) R, M
   (e) M, P

DIRECTIONS (Qs. 46-50): In this question, relationship between different elements is shown in the statements. The statements are followed by conclusions. Study the conclusions based on the given statement and select the appropriate answer. Mark answer as:

   (a) Only conclusion I is true
   (b) Only conclusion II is true
   (c) Either conclusion I or II is true
   (d) Neither conclusion I nor II is true
   (e) Both conclusion I and II are true

46. Statements : $L = P \le W < V \le K \ge Q; B < L; K = M$
   Conclusions : I. $B < V$ II. $M > P$

47. Statements : $L = P \le W < V \le K \ge Q; B < L; K = M$
   Conclusions : I. $L \ge Q$ II. $W = M$

48. Statements : $R \le U = B < S; B \le X$
   Conclusions : I. $X > R$ II. $X = R$

49. Statements : $C > U \le S < T = O > D \ge Y; Z = O \le P$
   Conclusions : I. $U > D$ II. $S < P$

50. Statements : $C > U \le S < T = O > D \ge Y; Z = O \le P$
   Conclusions : I. $Z > Y$ II. $C < O$

DIRECTIONS (Qs. 51 -55): Study the following information carefully and answer the given questions.

Eight friends, Meenal, Rumia, Shikha, Ali, Peter, Harleen, Ketan and Bharat, are sitting around a square table in such a way that four of them sit at four corners of the square while four sit in the middle of each of the four sides. The ones who sit at the four corners face the centre while those who sit in the middle of the sides face outside.

Bharat sits second to the right of Shikha. Bharat does not sit at any of the corners. Meenal sits third to the right of Peter. Peter is not an immediate neighbour of Shikha. Rumia and Ketan are immediate neighbours of each other but Rumia does not sit at any of the corners of the table. Harleen is an immediate neighbour of neither Peter nor Shikha.

51. Four of the following five are alike in a certain way and so form a group. Which is the one that does not belong to that group?
   (a) Peter   (b) Rumia
   (c) Harleen   (d) Shikha
   (e) Bharat

52. Who sits third to the left of Ali?
   (a) Bharat   (b) Rumia
   (c) Shikha   (d) Peter
   (e) Cannot be determined

53. What is the position of Peter with respect to Meenal?
   (a) Immediate to the left
   (b) Second to the left
   (c) Third to the left
   (d) Third to the right
   (e) Second to the right

54. Who amongst the following sits second to the right of Ketan?
   (a) Shikha   (b) Ali
   (c) Bharat   (d) Harleen
   (e) Meenal

55. Who amongst the following represent the immediate neighbours of Harleen?
   (a) Meenal, Ketan   (b) Bharat, Rumia
   (c) Bharat, Meenal   (d) Ali, Rumia
   (e) Ali, Ketan

DIRECTIONS (Qs. 56-60) : In each of the questions below are given three statements followed by two conclusions numbered I and II. You have to take the given statements to be true even if they seem to be at variance from commonly known facts. Read both of the conclusions and then decide which of the given conclusions logically follows from the given statements disregarding commonly known facts.

Read the statements and the conclusions which follow it and give answer

(a) If only conclusion I is true.

(b) If only conclusion II is true.

(c) If either conclusion I or conclusion II is true.

(d) If neither conclusion I nor conclusion II is true.

(e) If both conclusions I and II are true.

56. Statements :

All stars are suns.

Some suns are planets.

All planets are satellites.

Conclusions :

I. Some satellites are stars.

II. No star is a satellite.

57. Statements :

All curtains are rods.

Some rods are sheets.

Some sheets are pillows.

Conclusions:

I. Some pillows are rods.

II. Some rods are curtains.

58. Statements :

Some walls are windows.

Some windows are doors.

All doors are roofs.

Conclusions :

I. Some doors are walls.

II. No roof is a window.

(59-60) Statements:

All roses are flowers

Some trees are roses

Some flowers are seeds

59. Conclusion :

I. All trees being seeds is a possibility

II. Some roses are definitely not seeds.

60. Conclusion:

I. Some flowers which are trees are also a part of seeds.

II. All seeds if they are trees then they must be a part of roses.

DIRECTIONS (Qs. 61-63) : Read the following information carefully and answer the questions, which follow :

'A - B' means 'A is father of B'.

'A + B' means 'A is daughter of B'.

'A ÷ B' means 'A is son of B'.

'A × B' means 'A is wife of B'.

61. How is P related to T in the expression 'P + S – T' ?

(a) Sister   (b) Wife

(c) Son   (d) Daughter

(e) None of these

62. In the expression 'P × Q – T' how is T related to P ?

(a) Daughter   (b) Sister

(c) Mother   (d) Can't be determined

(e) None of these

63. Which of the following means T is wife of P ?

(a) P × S ÷ T   (b) P ÷ S × T

(c) P – S ÷ T   (d) P + T ÷ S

(e) None of these

DIRECTIONS (Qs. 64-65): Study the given information carefully and answer the given questions.

A is the mother of B. B is the sister of C. D is the son of C. E is the brother of D. F is the mother of E. G is the granddaughter of A. H has only two children-B and C.

64. How is C related to E?

(a) Father   (b) Son

(c) Mother   (d) Cousin Brother

(e) Cannot be determined

65. Who is mother of G?

(a) C   (b) B

(c) F   (d) Either B or F

(e) Either C or F

DIRECTIONS (Qs. 66-70) : In each question a group of letters is given followed by four combinations of number/symbol numbered (a), (b), (c) and (d). Letters are to be coded as per the scheme and conditions given below. You have to find out the serial number of the combination, which represents the letter group. Serial number of that combination is your answer. If none of the combinations is correct, your answer is (e) i.e. None of these.

Letters	Q	M	S	I	N	G	D	K	A	L	P	R	B	J	E
Number/ Symbol	7	@	4	#	%	$	6	1	2	£	5	*	9	8	3

Conditions :

(i) If the first letter is a consonant and the last a vowel, both are to be coded as the code of the vowel.

(ii) If the first letter is vowel and the last a consonant, the codes for the first and the last are to be interchanged.

(iii) If no vowel is present in the group of letters, the second and the fifth letters are to be coded as ©.

66. BARNIS

(a) 9 2 * % # 4   (b) 9 2 4 # * %

(c) 9 2 * # % 9   (d) 4 2 * # % 4

(e) None of these

67. DMBNIA

(a) 6 @ 9 % # 2   (b) 2 @ 9 % # 6

(c) 2 @ 9 % # 6   (d) 2 @ 9 % # 2

(e) None of these

68.   IJBRLG
(a) # 8 9 * £ $ (b) # 8 9 * £ #
(c) $ 8 9 * £ #   (d) $ 8 9 * £ $
(e) None of these

69.   BKGQJN
(a) 9 © $ 7 © %   (b) © 9 $ 7 % ©
(c) 9 1 $ 7 8 %   (d) % 1 $ 7 8 9
(e) None of these

70.   EGAKRL
(a) # £ $ 2 1 *   (b) £ $ 2 1 * 3
(c) £ $ 2 1 * #   (d) # £ $ 2 1 #
(e) None of these

DIRECTIONS (Qs. 71-75) : Study the following information carefully to answer these questions.

Eight persons A, B, C, D, E, F, G and H work for three different companies namely X, Y and Z. Not more than three persons work for a company. There are only two ladies in the group who have different specialisations and work for different companies. Of the group of friends, two have specialisation in each HR, Finance and Marketing. One member is an engineer and one is a doctor. H is an HR specialist and works with a Marketing specialist B who does not work for company Y. C is an engineer and his sister works in company Z. D is a specialist in HR working in company X while her friend G is a finance specialist and works for company Z. No two persons having the same specialisation work together. Marketing specialist F work for company Y and his friend A who is a Finance expert works for company X in which only two specialists work. No lady is a marketing specialist or a doctor.

71.   Which of the following combinations is correct ?
(a) C - Z - Engineer   (b) E - X - Doctor
(c) H – X – HR   (d) C – Y – Engineer
(e) None of these

72.   For which of the following companies does C work?
(a) Y   (b) X
(c) Z   (d) Data inadequate
(e) None of these

73.   Which of the following pairs represents the two ladies in the group ?
(a) A and D   (b) B and D
(c) D and G   (d) Data inadequate
(e) None of these

74.   Which of the following represents the pair working in the same company ?
(a) D and C   (b) A and B
(c) A and E   (d) H and F
(e) None of these

75.   Who amongst the friends is a doctor ?
(a) H   (b) E
(c) C   (d) Either E or C
(e) None of these

DIRECTIONS (Qs. 76-80) : Study the given information carefully to answer the given questions :

In a certain code language, 'festival for women only' is written as 'pa ge bo xu' 'Provide peace to women' is written as 'wr dl nj ge' 'Women like to celebrate' is written as 'ge ct fx wr' 'Celebrate peace in festival' is written as 'dl bo sv ct' (All codes are two letter codes only)

76.   What may be the possible code for 'provide idea' in the given code language?
(a) fx hy   (b) xu bo
(c) hy nj   (d) nj xu
(e) wr fx

77.   What is the code for 'celebrate' in the given code language?
(a) ct   (b) wr
(c) s v   (d) dl
(e) fx

78.   In the given code language what does the code 'pa' stand for?
(a) peace
(b) either 'for' or 'only'
(c) either 'women' or 'to'
(d) celebrate
(e) festival

79.   What is the code for 'women' in the given code language?
(a) bo
(b) xu
(c) ct
(d) Other than those given as options
(e) ge

80.   If 'peace to mind' is coded as 'zg wr dl' in the given code language, then what is the code for 'mind in festival'?
(a) zg bo dl   (b) dl zg sv
(c) zg nj wr   (d) bo sv zg
(e) sv wr bo

HINTS & EXPLANATIONS

1. (d) $? = 848 \times \dfrac{11}{16} \times \dfrac{4}{5} \times \dfrac{5}{11} = 212$

2. (a) $? = \dfrac{750 \times 1.4}{100} + \dfrac{480 \times 2.2}{100}$

   $= 10.50 + 10.56 = 21.06$

3. (a) $? = \dfrac{6.96}{1.2} - \dfrac{18.24}{7.6}$

   $= 5.8 - 2.4 = 3.4$

4. (e) $\dfrac{250 \times 136}{100} + \dfrac{550 \times ?}{100} = 670$

   $\Rightarrow 340 + 5.5 \times ? = 670$

   $\Rightarrow 5.5 \times ? = 670 - 340 = 330$

   $\Rightarrow ? = \dfrac{330}{5.5} = 60$

5. (c) $? = \dfrac{660 \times 45}{100} + \dfrac{450 \times 28}{100}$

   $= 297 + 126 = 423$

6. (b) The pattern of the number series is:

   $12 + 2^2 = 16$

   $16 + 2^3 = 24$

   $24 + 2^4 = 40$

   $40 + 2^5 = \boxed{72}$

7. (c) The patern of the number series is :

   $9 + 10 = 19$

   $19 + 20 = 39$

   $39 + 40 = 79$

   $79 + 80 = \boxed{159}$

8. (d) The pattern of the number series is:

   $8 + 3^2 = 17$

   $17 + 5^2 = 42$

   $42 + 7^2 = 91$

   $91 + 9^2 = \boxed{172}$

9. (e) The pattern of the number series is:

   $7 \times 1 + 1 = 8$

   $8 \times 2 + 2 = 18$

   $18 \times 3 + 3 = 57$

   $57 \times 4 + 4 = \boxed{232}$

10. (e) The pattern of the number series is:

    $3840 \div 4 = 960$

    $960 \div 4 = 240$

    $240 \div 4 = 60$

    $60 \div 4 = \boxed{15}$

11. (a) $\text{Principal} = \dfrac{SI \times 100}{\text{Time} \times \text{Rate}} = \dfrac{5520 \times 100}{8 \times 12} = ₹\,5750$

12. (b) Ratio of the profit of Srikant and Vividh

    $= 185000 : 225000 = 37 : 45$

    Sum of the ratios $= 37 + 45 = 82$

    ∴ Total profit earned

    $= \dfrac{82}{45} \times 9000$

    $= ₹\,16400$

13. (b) Father's present age $= 6x$ years

    Son's present age $= x$ years

    After four years

    $\therefore \dfrac{6x + 4}{x + 4} = \dfrac{4}{1}$

    $\Rightarrow 6x + 4 = 4x + 16$

    $\Rightarrow 2x = 12 \Rightarrow x = \dfrac{12}{2} = 6$

    ∴ Son's present age $= 6$ years

14. (a) Let the original number be $10x + y$ where $y > x$.

    $\therefore \quad 10y + x - 10x - y = 27$

    $\Rightarrow \quad 9(y - x) = 27$

    $\Rightarrow \quad y - x = 3 \qquad ....(i)$

    and $x + y = 13 \qquad ....(ii)$

    From equations (i) and (ii),

    $y = 8$ and $x = 5$

    ∴ Original number $= 58$

15. (e) $M_1 D_1 = M_2 D_2$

    $\Rightarrow 22 \times 16 = 32 \times D_2$

    $\Rightarrow D_2 = \dfrac{22 \times 16}{32} = 11$ days

16. (a) Davar's total expenditure percentage

    $= (38 + 25 + 12)\,\% = 75\,\%$

    Savings percentage $= 25\%$

    If this monthly salary be $₹\,x$, then

    $\dfrac{x \times 25}{100} = 5800$

    $\Rightarrow x = ₹\,(4 \times 5800) = ₹\,23200$

17. (a) $\boxed{\text{Tricky Approach}}$

    Man's salary in the month of February, 2011

    $= 5000\left(1 + \dfrac{20}{100}\right)^2 = 5000 \times \dfrac{6}{5} \times \dfrac{6}{5}$

    $= ₹\,7200$

18. (e) **Case I**

    $\text{Principal} = \dfrac{S.I. \times 100}{\text{Time} \times \text{Rate}}$

$$= \frac{1536 \times 100}{5 \times 12} = ₹\,2560$$

Case II

$$\text{S.I.} = \frac{\text{Principal} \times \text{Time} \times \text{Rate}}{100}$$

$$= \frac{3560 \times 2 \times 12}{100} = ₹\,854.40$$

19. (e) $\because$ 3 men $\equiv$ 9 boys

$\therefore$ 1 man $\equiv$ 3 boys

$\therefore$ 5 man + 6 boys

$\therefore$ $(5 \times 3 + 6)$ boys = 21 boys

$\therefore$ $M_1 D_1 = M_2 D_2 \Rightarrow 9 \times 21 = 21 \times D_2$

$$\Rightarrow D_2 = \frac{9 \times 21}{21} = 9\,\text{days}$$

20. (c) Let the total marks of the exam be x.

Passing marks $= 112 - 32 = 80$

$$\therefore \frac{x \times 75}{100} = 80 + 70 = 150$$

$$\Rightarrow x = \frac{150 \times 100}{75} = 200$$

If the minimum Pass percentage is y, then

$\therefore$ y% of 200 = 80 $\Rightarrow$ y = 40

Solution (21-25):

21. (e) I. $5x^2 - 87x - 378 = 0$

$\Rightarrow 5x^2 - 105x + 18x - 378 = 0$

$\Rightarrow 5x(x - 21) + 18(x - 21) = 0$

$\Rightarrow (5x + 18)(x - 21) = 0$

$$\Rightarrow x = -\frac{18}{5}, 21$$

II. $3y^2 - 49y + 200 = 0$

$\Rightarrow 3x^2 - 24y - 25y + 200 = 0$

$\Rightarrow 3y(y - 8) - 25(y - 8) = 0$

$\Rightarrow (3y - 25)(y - 8) = 0$

$$\Rightarrow y = \frac{25}{3}, 8$$

Clearly, x = y or no relation

22. (b) I. $(x + 1)(x + 18) = -66$

$\Rightarrow x^2 + 18x + x + 18 + 66 = 0$

$\Rightarrow x^2 + 19x + 84 = 0$

$\Rightarrow x^2 + 12x + 7x + 84 = 0$

$\Rightarrow x(x + 12) + 7(x + 12) = 0$

$\Rightarrow (x + 7)(x + 12) = 0$

$\Rightarrow x = -7, -12$

II. $\sqrt{(y - 3)(y - 27)} = 9$

$\Rightarrow (y - 3)(y - 27) = 81$

$\Rightarrow y^2 - 27y - 3y + 81 - 81 = 0$

$\Rightarrow y^2 - 30y = 0$

$\Rightarrow y(y - 30) = 0$

$\Rightarrow y = 0, 30$

Clearly, $x < y$

23. (a) I. $\dfrac{15}{x} + \dfrac{16}{y} = 1$ ...(i)

II. $\dfrac{3}{x} - \dfrac{7}{y} = 5$ ...(ii)

equation (i) $-$ (ii) $\times$ 5, we get

$$\frac{15}{x} + \frac{16}{y} - \frac{15}{x} + \frac{35}{y} = 1 - 25$$

$$\Rightarrow \frac{51}{y} = -24 \Rightarrow y = \frac{-51}{24}$$

Put the value of y in equation (i), we get

$$\frac{15}{x} + \frac{16}{-51} \times 24 = 1$$

$$\Rightarrow \frac{15}{x} = 1 + \frac{128}{17} \Rightarrow \frac{15}{x} = \frac{145}{17}$$

$$\Rightarrow x = \frac{15 \times 17}{145} = \frac{255}{145}$$

Clearly, $x > y$

24. (b) I. $17x^2 + 48x = 9$

$\Rightarrow 17x^2 + 48x - 9 = 0$

$\Rightarrow 17x^2 + 51x - 3x - 9 = 0$

$\Rightarrow 17x(x + 3) - 3(x + 3) = 0$

$\Rightarrow (17x - 3)(x + 3) = 0$

$$\Rightarrow x = \frac{3}{17}, -3$$

II. $13y^2 + 12 = 32y$

$\Rightarrow 13y^2 - 32y + 12 = 0$

$\Rightarrow 13y^2 - 26y - 6y + 12 = 0$

$\Rightarrow 13y(y - 2) - 6(y - 2) = 0$

$\Rightarrow (13y - 6)(y - 2) = 0$

$$\Rightarrow y = \frac{6}{13}, 2$$

Clearly, $x < y$

25. (e) I. $4x + 7y = 209$ ...(i)

II. $12x - 14y = -38$ ...(ii)

equation (i) $\times$ 2 + (ii), we get

$8x + 14y + 12x - 14y = 418 - 38$

$\Rightarrow 20x = 380 \Rightarrow x = 19$

Now, put the value of x in equation (ii)

$12 \times 19 - 14y = -38$

$\Rightarrow 14y = 228 + 38$

$\Rightarrow 14y = 266 \Rightarrow y = \dfrac{266}{14} = 19$

$\therefore$ Clearly, $x = y$

(26-30) :

26. (a) S.P of HCL Laptops
$= 32000 + 4000 = ₹36000$

and profit % $= \left(\dfrac{4000}{32000} \times 100\right)\%$

$= 12.5\%$

27. (c) C.P of Apple Laptop

$= \dfrac{33000}{110} \times 100 = ₹30,000$

$\therefore$ C.P of Dell Laptop

$= 30000 \times \dfrac{3}{5} = ₹18,000$

Now, Profit $= 22000 - 18000 = ₹4,000$

$\therefore$ Profit % $= \left(\dfrac{4000}{18000} \times 100\right)\% = 22\dfrac{2}{9}\%$

28. (e) Profit of Lenovo Laptop
$= 3500 + 500 = ₹4,000$

$\therefore$ Profit % $= \left(\dfrac{4000}{28000} \times 100\right)\% = 14\dfrac{2}{7}\%$

and SP $= 28000 + 4000 = ₹32,000$

29. (c) Profit earned on Acer Laptop

$= 53000 \times \dfrac{14}{100} = ₹7,420$

30. (b) S.P of HP Laptop
$= 35000 + 3500 = ₹38,500$

$\therefore$ Required ratio $= 35000 : 38500$

$= 10 : 11$

Solution (31-35) :

31. (b) Required Ratio $= \dfrac{(45 \times 925)}{(60 \times 650)} = \dfrac{111}{104}$

$= 111 : 104$

32. (b) Required sum $= 25\%$ of $880 + 56\%$ of $1125 + 60\% + 60\%$ of 650

$= \dfrac{25}{100} \times 880 + \dfrac{56}{100} \times 1125 + \dfrac{60}{100} \times 650$

$= 220 + 630 + 390 = 1240$

33. (b) Number of females of village B $= 40\%$ of $1050 = 420$

Required percentage $= \left(\dfrac{420}{1125} \times 100\right)\%$

$= 37.33\% \approx 37\%$

34. (e) Sum of total number of female in entire village $= 55\%$ of $925 + 40\%$ of $1050 + 75\%$ of $880 + 56\%$ of $1125 + 60\%$ of $650 + 35\%$ of 985

$= 508.75 + 420 + 660 + 630 + 390 + 344.75$

$= 2953.5 \approx 2954$

35. (e) Total no. of males in entire village $= 45\%$ of $925 + 60\%$ of $1050 + 25\%$ of $880 + 44\%$ of $1125 + 40\%$ of $650 + 65\%$ of 985

$= 416.25 + 630 + 220 + 495 + 260 + 640.25$

$= 2661.5$

$\therefore$ Required Average $= \dfrac{2661.5}{6}$

$= 443.58 \approx 444$

36. (a) Required average

$= \dfrac{5 + 6 + 4 + 1 + 5 + 3}{6} = \dfrac{24}{6} = 4$ crores

37. (d) It is clear from graph. The % value for 2004 is $\dfrac{1}{6} \times 100$

$= 16.67$, which is the lowest.

38. (e) % of units exported with respect to units produced is the maximum for year 2001.

It is equal to $\dfrac{5}{8} \times 100 = 62.5\%$

39. (c) The maximum difference is in 2004.
It is equal to $6 - 1 = 5$ crore units.

40. (c) The required difference
$= 1$ cr $= 10000000$ units.

Solution (41-45) :

Persons	Months	Colours
R	January	Red
N	February	Green
O	April	Pink
L	May	White
Q	July	Purple
M	September	Blue
P	December	Black

41. (e)   42. (a)   43. (d)   44. (b)   45. (c)

Solution (46-50) :

46. (e) I. $B < L = P \leq W < V$ (TRUE)
II. $M = K \geq V > W \geq P$ (TRUE)

47. (d) I. $L = P \leq W < V \leq K \geq Q$ (FALSE)
II. $W < V \leq K = M$ (FALSE)

48. (c) I. $X \geq B = U \geq R$ (FALSE)
II. $X \geq B = U \geq R$ (FALSE)

49. (b) I. $U \leq S < T = O > D$ (FALSE)
II. $S < T = O \leq P$ (TRUE)

50. (a) I. $Z = O > D \geq Y$ (TRUE)
II. $C > U \leq S < T = O$ (FALSE)

Solutions (51-55):

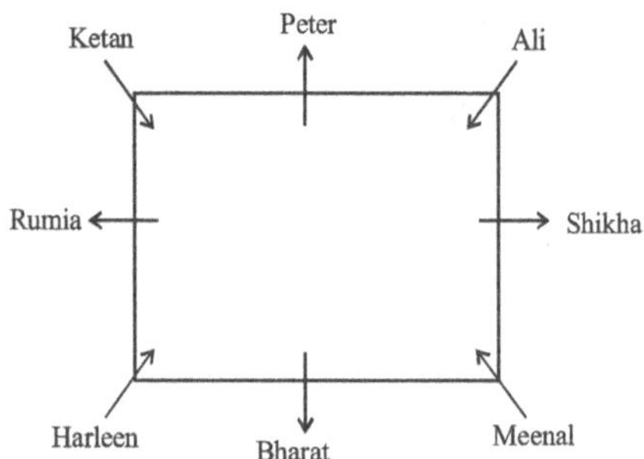

51. (c) All others sit in the middle of the sides.
52. (a) 53. (d) 54. (d) 55. (b)
56. (c) Some suns are planets.

All planets are satellites.
(I + A ⇒ I-type)
"Some suns are satellites".
Conclusions I and II form Complementary Pair.
Therefore, either I or II follows.
57. (b) All curtains are rods.

Some rods are sheets.
(A + I ⇒ No Conclusion)
58. (d) Some windows are doors.

All doors are roofs.
(I + A ⇒ I-type)
"Some windows are roots".

Solution (59-60):

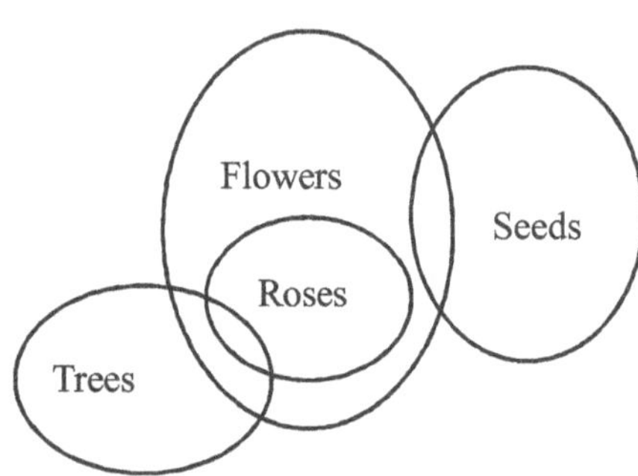

59. (a)
60. (d)
61. (a) P + S → P is daughter of S.
S – T → S is father of T.
Therefore, P is sister of T.
62. (d) P × Q → P is wife of Q.
Q – T → Q is father of T.
T is child of P and Q.
The gender of T is not known.
T is either son or daughter of P.
63. (e) P × S → P is wife of S.
S ÷ T → S is son of T.

T is either father-in-law or mother-in-law of P.
P ÷ S → P is son of S.
S × T → S is daughter of T
Therefore, T is father of P.
P – S → P is father of T.
P + T → P is daughter of T
T ÷ S → T is son of S.
Therefore, T is father of P.

Solution (64-65):

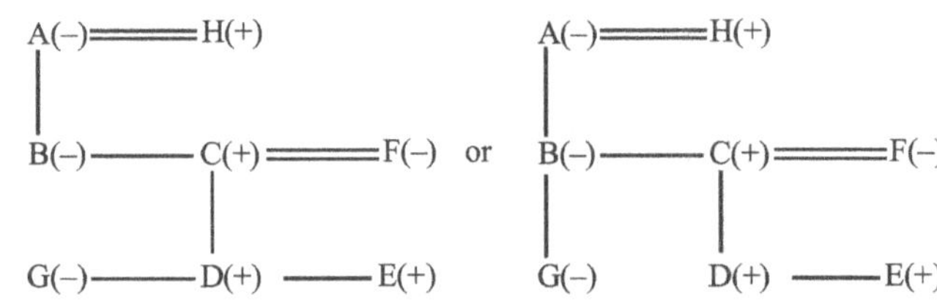

64. (a)
65. (d)
66. (a) B → 9; A → 2; R → *; N → %; I → #; S → 4
67. (d) D → 2; M → @; B → 9; N → %; I → #; A → 6
Condition (i) is applied.
68. (c) I → $; J → 8; B → 9; R → *; L → £; G → #
Condition (ii) is applied.
69. (a) B → 9; K → ©; G → $; Q → 7; J → ©; N → %
Condition (iii) is applied.
70. (b) E → £; G → $; A → 2; K → 1; R → *; L → 3
Condition (ii) is applied.

For (Qs. 71-75): Given information can be tabulated as follows

Person	Sex	Company	Specialisation
A	Male	X	Finance
B	Male	Z	Marketing
C	Male	Y	Engineer
D	Female	X	HR
E	Male	Y	Doctor
F	Male	Y	Marketing
G	Female	Z	Finance
H	Male	Z	HR

Thus, 'G' is a sister of 'C'.

71. (d) 72. (a) 73. (c) 74. (e) 75. (b)

Solution (76-80):

Festival	Bo
Women	Ge
For	Pa/xu
Only	Pa/xu
To	Wr
Celebrate	Ct
Peace	Dl
Provide	Nj
Like	Fx
In	Sv

76. (c) 77. (a) 78. (b) 79. (e) 80. (d)

PRACTICE SET 8

Time : 45 Min.   **Max. Marks : 80**

QUANTITATIVE APTITUDE

DIRECTIONS (Qs. 1-5): What will come in place of question mark (?) in the following questions?

1. $\dfrac{3}{5}$ of $\dfrac{4}{7}$ of $\dfrac{5}{12}$ of $1015 = ?$

  (a) 220   (b) 340
  (c) 240   (d) 145
  (e) None of these

2. 125% of $260 + ?\%$ of $700 = 500$

  (a) 32   (b) 56
  (c) 23   (d) 46
  (e) None of these

3. 45% of $750 - 25\%$ of $480 = ?$

  (a) 216   (b) 217.50
  (c) 245   (d) 236.50
  (e) None of these

4. $75^{8.5} \div 75^{3.8} = 75^{?}$

  (a) 4.9   (b) 3.6
  (c) 3.3   (d) 4.7
  (e) None of these

5. $5431 + 10500 - 4371 - 1357 = ?$

  (a) 9203   (b) 10003
  (c) 10203   (d) 11203
  (e) None of these

DIRECTIONS (Qs. 6-10): In the following questions two equations numbered I and II are given. Solve both the equations and give answer.

If

  (a) $x > y$ (b) $x \geq y$
  (c) $x < y$ (d) $x \leq y$
  (e) $x = y$ or no relationship can be established

6. I. $3x + 4y = (1681)^{1/2}$
    II. $3x + 2y = (961)^{1/2}$

7. I. $3x^2 - (6 + \sqrt{17})x + 2\sqrt{17} = 0$
    II. $10y^2 - (15 + \sqrt{17})y - 3\sqrt{17} = 0$

8. I. $x^2 - 16x + 63 = 0$
    II. $y^2 - 2y - 35 = 0$

9. I. $(289)^{1/2}x - \sqrt{324} = 203$
    II. $(484)^{1/2}y + \sqrt{225} = 183$

10. I. $679x^2 - 168x^2 = 3066$
    II. $\sqrt{144}\, y^3 - 9y^3 = 1536$

11. The number zero (0) is surrounded by the same 2-digit number on both (left and right) the sides; for example, 25025, 67067, etc. The largest number that always divides such a number is

  (a) 7   (b) 11
  (c) 13   (d) 1001
  (e) None of these

12. If a certain sum of money becomes double at simple interest in 12 years, what would be the rate of interest per annum ?

  (a) $8\dfrac{1}{3}$ (b) 10
  (c) 12   (d) 14
  (e) None of these

13. Three successive discounts of 10%, 12% and 15% amount to a single discount of
    (a) 36.28 % (b) 34.68%
    (c) 37% (d) 32.68%
    (e) None of these

14. The ratio of the prices of two houses A and B was 4 : 5 last year. This year, the price of A is increased by 25% and that of B by ₹ 50000. If their prices are now in the ratio 9 : 10, the price of A last year was
    (a) ₹ 3,60,000 (b) ₹ 4,50,000
    (c) ₹ 4,80,000 (d) ₹ 5,00,000
    (e) None of these

15. The number of 3-digit number exactly divisible by 5 is
    (a) 181 (b) 180
    (c) 179 (d) 199
    (e) None of these

DIRECTIONS (Qs. 16-20) : Find the *next term* in the given series in each of the questions below.

16. 198, 194, 185, 169, (?)
    (a) 136 (b) 144
    (c) 9 (d) 92
    (e) None of these

17. 6, 9, 7, 10, 8, 11, (?)
    (a) 12 (b) 13
    (c) 9 (d) 14
    (e) None of these

18. 7, 11, 19, 35, 67, (?)
    (a) 121 (b) 153
    (c) 141 (d) 133
    (e) None of these

19. 5, 6, 10, 19, 35, (?)
    (a) 55 (b) 65
    (c) 60 (d) 70
    (e) None of these

20. 1, 3, 8, 18, 35, (?)
    (a) 61 (b) 72
    (c) 67 (d) 52
    (e) 71

21. The average age of A, B and C is 26 years. If the average age of A and C is 29 years, what is the age of B in years ?
    (a) 26 (b) 20
    (c) 29 (d) 23
    (e) None of these

22. A man walks at the speed of 5 km/hr and runs at the speed of 10 km/hr. How much time will the man require to cover the distance of 28 km, if he covers half (first 14 km) of his journey walking and half of his journey running ?
    (a) 8.4 hrs (b) 6 hrs
    (c) 5 hrs (d) 4.2 hrs
    (e) None of these

23. a, b, c and d are four consecutive numbers. If the sum of a and d is 103, what is the product of b and c ?
    (a) 2652 (b) 2562
    (c) 2970 (d) 2550
    (e) None of these

24. The letters of the word SOCIETY are placed at random in a row. The probability that the three vowels come together is
    (a) $\dfrac{1}{6}$ (b) $\dfrac{1}{7}$
    (c) $\dfrac{2}{7}$ (d) $\dfrac{5}{6}$
    (e) None of these

25. A man can swim 72 km upstream and 54 km downstream in 9 hours. Also, he can swim 84 km upstream and 90 km downstream in 12 hours. What is the speed of the man in still water?
    (a) 9 kmph (b) 12 kmph
    (c) 15 kmph (d) 18 kmph
    (e) 21 kmph

DIRECTIONS (Qs. 26-30) : Study the following bar-graph and pie-chart carefully and answer the given questions.

Bar graph shows the population of male and female in six different cities and bar graph shows the percentage distribution of total income of six different cities.

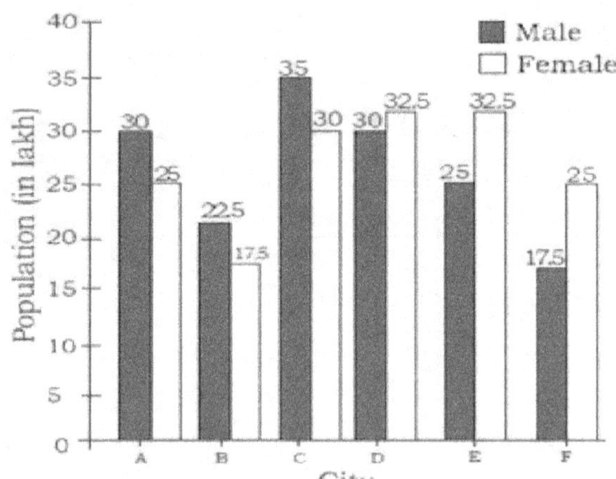

Total income = ₹ 200 Crore

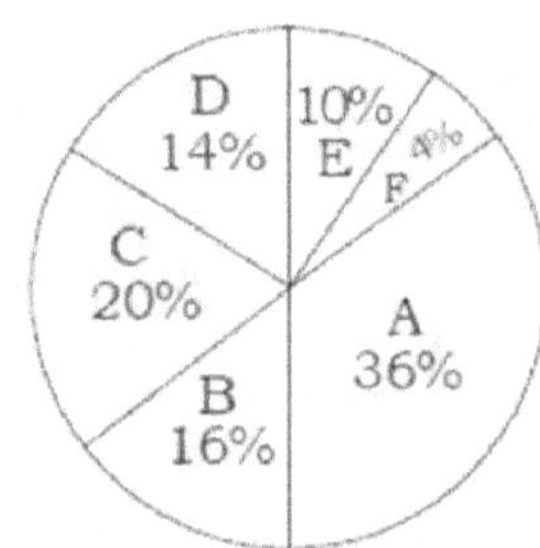

26. What is the difference between the number of females in City E and the number of males in City B?
    (a) 10 lakh (b) 11 lakh
    (c) 9 lakh (d) 12 lakh
    (e) None of these

27. In which city is the income per person the minimum?
    (a) A (b) F
    (c) E (d) B
    (e) C

28. What is the approximate sum of the average male and average female population of the six Cities?
    (a) 63 lakh (b) 50 lakh
    (c) 42 lakh (d) 54 lakh
    (e) None of these

29. What is the difference between the income of males and females in city A? [Assume each person (male/female) has equal income.
    (a) ₹ 6.545 Crore (b) ₹ 5.055 Crore
    (c) ₹ 2.935 Crore (d) ₹ 3.455 Crore
    (e) None of these

30. The number of females in city C is what percent of the number of males in city E?
    (a) 95% (b) 110%
    (c) 120% (d) 132%
    (e) None of these

DIRECTIONS (Qs. 31-35) : Study the following line graphs carefully and answer the given questions.

Line graph shows the profit percent earned by two companies A and B over the given years.

$$\text{Profit \%} = \frac{\text{Income} - \text{Expenditure}}{\text{Expenditure}} \times 100$$

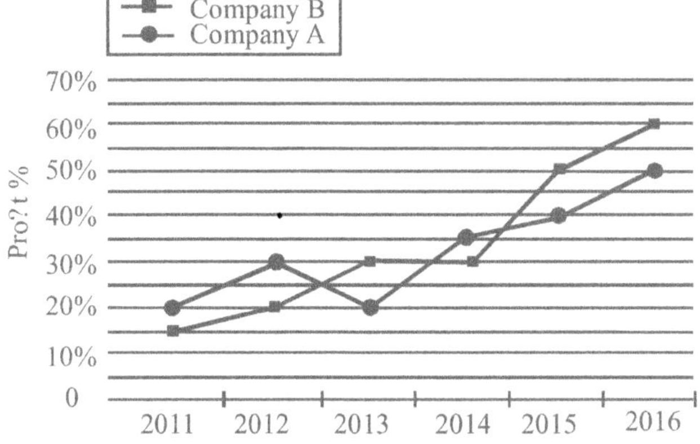

31. If the income of Company A in the year 2012 was equal to the expenditure of Company B in the year 2015, then what was the ratio of their respective profits?
    (a) 13 : 15 (b) 15 : 26
    (c) 13 : 26 (d) Cannot be determined
    (e) None of these

32. If the income of Company A in the year 2015 was equal to its expenditure in the year 2016, then what was the ratio of its respective incomes in these two years?
    (a) 4 : 5 (b) 3 : 4
    (c) 2 : 3 (d) Cannot be determined
    (e) None of these

33. For Company B, in which year is the percent of increase in percent profit over that of previous year the highest?
    (a) 2016 (b) 2013
    (c) 2015 (d) Cannot be determined
    (e) None of these

34. If the expenditure of Company A in the year 2011 was ₹ 40 crores, then what was its income in that year?
    (a) ₹ 50 crore (b) ₹ 48 crore
    (c) ₹ 46 crore (d) Cannot be determined
    (e) None of these

35. What was the difference in the expenditures of these two Companies in the year 2013?
    (a) 10 (b) 100
    (c) 1000 (d) Cannot be determined
    (e) None of these

DIRECTIONS (Qs. 36-40) : Study the following graph and table carefully and answer the questions given below :

TIME TAKEN TO TRAVEL (IN HOURS) BY SIX VEHICLES ON TWO DIFFERENT DAYS

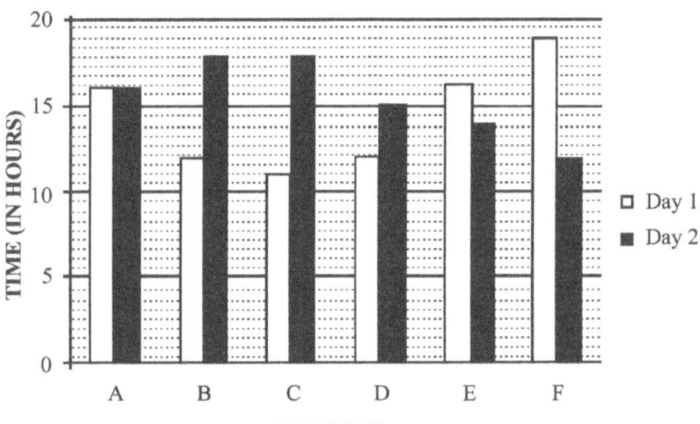

DISTANCE COVERED (IN KILOMETERS) BY SIX VEHICLES ON EACH DAY

Vehicle	Day 1	Day 2
A	832	864
B	516	774
C	693	810
D	552	765
E	935	546
F	703	636

36. Which of the following vehicles travelled at the same speed on both the days ?
    (a) Vehicle A (b) Vehicle C
    (c) Vehicle F (d) Vehicle B
    (e) None of these

37. What was the difference between the speed of vehicle A on day 1 and the speed of vehicle C on the same day ?
    (a) 7 km/hr. (b) 12 km/hr.
    (c) 11 km/hr. (d) 8 km/hr.
    (e) None of these

38. What was the speed of vehicle C on day 2 in terms of meters per second ?
    (a) 15.3 (b) 12.8
    (c) 11.5 (d) 13.8
    (e) None of these

39. The distance travelled by vehicle F on day 2 was approximately what percent of the distance travelled by it on day 1 ?

(a) 80   (b) 65
(c) 85   (d) 95
(e) 90

40. What is the respective ratio between the speeds of vehicle D and vehicle E on day 2 ?

(a) 15:13   (b) 17:13
(c) 13:11   (d) 17:14
(e) None of these

REASONING ABILITY

DIRECTIONS (Qs. 41-45) : In the following questions, the symbols #, %, @, © and δ are used with the following meanings illustrated.

'P % Q' means 'P is not greater than Q'.

'P δ Q' means 'P is not smaller than Q'.

'P # Q' means 'P is neither equal to nor smaller than Q'.

'P © Q' means 'P is neither equal to nor greater than Q'.

'P @ Q' means 'P is neither smaller than nor greater than Q'.

In each question, three statements showing relationships have been given, which are followed by three conclusions I, II and III. Assuming that the given statements are true, find out which conclusion(s) is/are **definitely true**.

41. Statements : M © K, K δ T, T © J

Conclusions :

I. J # K   II. T # M

III. M # J

(a) None is true   (b) Only I is true
(c) Only II is true   (d) Only III is true
(e) II and III are true

42. Statements : F @ T, T % M, M # R

Conclusions :

I. R © T   II. F @ M

III. F © M

(a) Only I is true   (b) Only II is true
(c) Only III is true   (d) either II or III is true
(e) II and III are true

43. Statements : J δ H, H @ B, B % N

Conclusions :

I. N δ H   II. N @ J

III. J δ B

(a) I and II are true   (b) II and III are true
(c) I and III are true   (d) All I, II and III are true
(e) None of the above

44. Statements : B # T, T © K, K % M

Conclusions :

I. K # B   II. M # T

III. B # M

(a) Only I is true   (b) Only II is true
(c) Only III is true   (d) II and III are true
(e) None of the above

45. Statements : D % F, F δ K, K @ R

Conclusions :

I. R % F   II. R % D

III. R @ D

(a) Only I is true   (b) Only II is true
(c) Only III is true   (d) I and II are true
(e) None of the above

DIRECTIONS (Q. 46-50) : Study the following arrangement carefully and answer the questions given below

D 5 δ R @ A K © 3 9 B J E   F $ M P I 4 H 1 W 6 2 # U Q 8 T N

46. How many such numbers are there in the above arrangement each of which is immediately preceded by a symbol and immediately followed by a letter?

(a) None   (b) One
(c) Two   (d) Three
(e) More than three

47. Which of the following is the ninth to the right of the twenty second from the right end of the above arrangement ?

(a) E   (b) I
(c) D   (d) N
(e) None of these

48. How many such symbols are there in the above arrangement each of which is immediately preceded by a number and immediately followed by a letter?

(a) None   (b) One
(c) Two   (d) Three
(e) More than three

49. If all the numbers are dropped from the above arrangement, which of the following will be the eleventh from the left end ?

(a) B   (b) H
(c) $ (d)
(e) None of these

50. How many such consonants are there in the above arrangement each of which is immediately preceded by a number and immediately followed by another consonant ?

(a) None   (b) One
(c) Two   (d) Three
(e) More than three

DIRECTIONS (Q. 51-56) : Study the following information carefully and answer the questions given below:

Eight friends - E, F, G, H, J, K, L and M are sitting around a circular table facing the centre. Each of them is wearing dress of different cartoon characters i.e. Nobita, Osward, Popeye, Yogi, Simpon, Minion, Scrooge and Dexter but not necessarily in the same order. F is sitting second to the left of K. The one who is wearing dress of Dexter is an immediate neighbour of K. There are only three people sits between the one who is wearing dress of Dexter and E. Only one person sits between the one who is wearing dress of Yogi and E. The one who is wearing dress of Osward is to the immediate right of the one who is wearing dress of Yogi. M is second to the right of K. H is wearing dress of Dexter. G and J are immediate neighbours of each other. Neither G nor J is wearing dress of Yogi. The one who is wearing dress of Simpon is to the immediate left of F. The one who is wearing dress of Minion is second to the right of the one who is wearing dress of Osward. The one who is wearing dress of Scrooge is an immediate neighbour of the one who is wearing dress of Yogi. G is second to the right of the one who is wearing dress of Nobita.

51. Who is sitting second to the right of E?

(a) The one who wearing dress of Minion

(b) G

(c) The one who wearing dress of Yogi

(d) F

(e) K

52. Who amongst the following is wearing dress of Scrooge?
(a) F
(b) L
(c) M
(d) K
(e) None of these

53. Four of the following five are alike in a certain way based on the given arrangement and hence form a group. Which of the following does not belong to group?
(a) Nobita - H
(b) M-Popeye
(c) J - Yogi
(d) Simpon - L
(e) Minion- K

54. What is the position of L with respect to the one who is wearing dress of Dexter?
(a) Third to the left
(b) Second to the right
(c) Second to the left
(d) Third to the right
(e) Immediate right

55. Which of the following statements is true accordingly the given sitting arrangement?
(a) The one who is wearing dress of Minion sits second to the left of the one who is wearing dress of Popeye
(b) E is an immediate neighbour of the one who is wearing dress of Simpon
(c) H sits exactly between F and the one who is wearing dress of Simpon
(d) Only four people sit between the one who is wearing dress of Osward and F
(e) All of the given statements are true

56. Who amongst the following is wearing dress of Nobita?
(a) E
(b) L
(c) M
(d) K
(e) None of these

DIRECTIONS (Qs. 57-61) : Study the following information to answer the given questions

Seven persons S, T, U, V, W, X, and Z are sitting in a straight line equidistant from each other (but not necessarily in the same order). Some of them are facing south while some are facing north.

(Note: Facing the same direction means, if one is facing north then the other also faces north and vice-versa. Facing the opposite directions means, if one is facing north then the other faces south and vice-versa)

S faces north. Only two people sit to the right of S. T sits third to the left of S. Only one person sits between T and X. X sits to the immediate right of W. Only one person sits between W and Z. Both the immediate neighbors of T face the same direction. U sits third to the left of X. T faces the opposite direction as S. V faces the same direction as W. Both Z and U face the opposite direction.

57. How many persons in the given arrangement are facing North?
(a) More than four
(b) Four
(c) One
(d) Three
(e) Two

58. Four of the following five are alike in a certain way, and so form a group. Which of the following does not belong to the group?
(a) W, X
(b) Z, U
(c) T, S
(d) T, U
(e) V, U

59. What is the position of X with respect to Z?
(a) Second to the left
(b) Third to the right
(c) Third to the left
(d) Fifth to the right
(e) Second to the right

60. Who amongst the following sits exactly between Z and W?
(a) T
(b) V
(c) X
(d) W
(e) U

61. Who is sitting 2nd to the right of T?
(a) Z
(b) V
(c) X
(d) W
(e) None of these

DIRECTIONS (Qs. 62-66) : Study the following information carefully and answer the given questions :

In a certain code language :
"only in serial order" is written as "ve pu na to".
"order in the state" is written as "li ve su pu".
"the logical idea only" is written as "su na ri jo".
"in idea or theory" is written as "zt jo bk pu".

62. Which of the following is code of 'theory' ?
(a) zt
(b) bk
(c) jo
(d) pu
(e) Either 'zt' or 'bk'

63. The code 'li ri to ve' may represent
(a) serial order theory only
(b) only idea state order
(c) state logical serial order
(d) serial theory state the
(e) only the idea logical

64. Which of the following represent "logical idea is only order"?
(a) jo na ri ge ve
(b) ve na ri jo pu
(c) ri ve na zt bk
(d) bk to pu jo ve
(e) na ve su li pu

65. Which of the following is code of "logical" ?
(a) su
(b) jo
(c) na
(d) ri
(e) None of these

66. Which of the following is code of "serial" ?
(a) pu
(b) to
(c) ve
(d) su
(e) Cannot be determined

DIRECTIONS (Q. 67-69) : In each question below are three statements followed by three conclusions numbered I, II and III. You have to take the three given statements to be true even if they seem to be at variance from commonly known facts and then decide which of the given conclusions logically follows from the three given statements disregarding commonly known facts. Then decide which of the answers (a), (b), (c), (d) and (e) is the correct answer and indicate it on the answer sheet.

67. **Statements :** Some desks are chairs. All chairs are tables. Some tables are mats.
Conclusions : I. Some mats are desks.
II. Some tables are desks.
III. Some mats are chairs.
(a) Only I follows
(b) Only II follows
(c) Only III follows
(d) II and III follow
(e) None of the above

68. **Statements :** All sweets are fruits. No fruit is pencil. Some pencils are glasses.

    Conclusions : I. Some glasses are sweets.

                   II. Some pencils are sweets.

                   III.No glass is sweet.

(a) Only I follows   (b) Only II follows

(c) Only III follows   (d) either I or III follows

(e) None of the above

69. **Statements :** Some books are flowers. Some flowers are chains. Some chains are hammers.

    Conclusions : I. Some hammers are flowers.

                   II. Some chairs are books.

                   III.Some hammers are books.

(a) None follows   (b) Only I follows

(c) Only II follows   (d) Only III follows

(e) II and III follow

DIRECTIONS (Qs. 70-72) : Each question consists of two/three or four statements followed by two conclusions numbered I and II. Consider the given statements to be true even if they seem to be at variance with commonly known facts. Read all the conclusions and then decide which of the given conclusions logically follow from the given statements using all statements together.

Mark your answer as,

(a) If only conclusions I follows

(b) If only conclusions II follows

(c) If either conclusion I or conclusion II follows

(d) If neither conclusion I nor conclusions II follows

(e) If both conclusion I and conclusion II follow

70. **Statements:** All cake are biscuit

    Some pastries are cake Some biscuits are chips

    Conclusions: I. All pastries being chips is a possibility

    II. Some cake are definitely not chips.

71. Statements: Some blues are greens

    Some reds are blues All greens are whites

    Conclusions: I. Some reds are neither blues nor whites is a possibility

    II. All greens are reds is a possibility

72. Statements: All floor are roof

    No window is roof All windows are wall

    Conclusions: I. Some roof which are wall are also floor.

    II. No wall is floor

DIRECTIONS (Qs. 73-74) : Study the following information carefully to answer these questions.

Rahul starts running from point P and run 10 km towards North. he takes a right turn and runs 15 km. he now runs 6 km after taking a left turn. finally he takes a left turn, runs 15 km and stops at point Q.

73. How far is point Q with respect to point P?

(a) 16 km   (b) 25 km

(c) 4 km   (d) 0 km

(e) None of these

74. Towards which direction was the Rahul moving before it stopped at point Q?

(a) North   (b) East

(c) South   (d) West

(e) North - West

75. If it is possible to make only one meaningful word with the first, the third, the fifth and the eight letters of the word SHAREHOLDING, which of the following will be the second letter of the word ? If no such word can be made, give 'X' as the answer and if more than one such word can be made, give 'Y' as the answer.

(a) L   (b) E

(c) S   (d) X

(e) Y

DIRECTIONS (Qs. 76-80): Study the given information carefully and answer the given questions:

Auditions for a show were held in seven different cities of India Chennai, Bangalore, Cochin, Mumbai, Delhi, Bhopal and Kolkata, not necessarily in the same order, during the first seven months of the year 2011 (starting in January and ending" in July). The auditions were held only in one city during a month. Auditions in only four cities were held between the Kolkata audition and the Cochin audition. The Kolkata audition was not held in June. Only one audition was held between the Kolkata audition and the Bangalore audition. The Chennai audition was held immediately after the Kolkata audition. The Delhi audition was held immediately before the Bhopal audition. The Bhopal audition was not held in May.

76. How many auditions were held between the Mumbai audition and the Chennai audition?

(a) One   (b) Two

(c) Three   (d) None

(e) More than three

77. Which of the following statements is **true** according to the given sequence?

(a) Mumbai audition was held in July

(b) Delhi audition was held in April

(c) Cochin audition was held before May

(d) Kolkata audition was held in January

(e) None is true

78. Four of the following five are alike in a certain way based on the given sequence and hence form a group.

    Which one does **not** belong to the group?

(a) January-Kolkata   (b) March-Bangalore

(c) June-Cochin   (d) May-Delhi

(e) February-Chennai

79. During March, the audition was held in which of the following cities?

(a) Bangalore   (b) Kolkata

(c) Mumbai   (d) Chennai

(e) None of these

80. The audition in Mumbai was held in which of the following months?

(a) July   (b) May

(c) February   (d) March

(e) None of these

HINTS & EXPLANATIONS

1. (d) $\dfrac{3}{5}$ of $\dfrac{4}{7}$ of $\dfrac{5}{12}$ of $1015 = \dfrac{3}{5} \times \dfrac{4}{7} \times \dfrac{5}{12} \times 1015 = \dfrac{1015}{7} = 145$

2. (e) 125% of $260 + ?\%$ of $700 = 500$
   $\Rightarrow ?\%$ of $700 = 500 - 125\%$ of 260
   $\Rightarrow ?\%$ of $700 = 175$
   $\therefore ? = \dfrac{175 \times 100}{700} = 25$

3. (b) 45% of $750 - 25\%$ of 480
   $= \dfrac{45 \times 750}{100} - \dfrac{25 \times 480}{100} = 337.5 - 120 = 217.5$

4. (d) $75^{8.5} \div 75^{3.8} = 75^{(8.5-3.8)} = 75^{4.7}$

5. (c)

6. (a) I. $3x + 4y = (1681)^{1/2}$
   $3x + 4y = 41$ ...(i)
   II. $3x + 2y = (961)^{1/2}$
   $3x + 2y = 31$ ..(ii)
   Subtracting (i) and (ii)

   $3x + 4y = 41$
   $3x + 2y = 31$
   ———————
   $2y = 10$ ...(iii)
   $y = 5$

   From (ii)
   $3x + 2y = 31$
   $\Rightarrow 3x + 2 \times 5 = 31$
   $\Rightarrow 3x = 21,$
   $\therefore x = 7$
   Hence, $x > y$

7. (e) I. $3x^2 - 6x - \sqrt{17}x + 2\sqrt{17} = 0$ ...(i)
   $\Rightarrow 3x(x{-}2) - \sqrt{17}\,(x{-}2) = 0$
   $\Rightarrow x = 2, \dfrac{\sqrt{17}}{3}$

   II. $10y^2 - (15 + \sqrt{17})y - 3\sqrt{17} = 0$ ...(ii)
   $\Rightarrow y = \dfrac{-b \pm \sqrt{b^2 - 4ac}}{2a}$

   $y = \dfrac{\left(15 + \sqrt{17}\right) \pm \sqrt{\left(15 + \sqrt{17}\right)^2 + 4 \times 10 \times 3\sqrt{17}}}{20}$

   $\Rightarrow y = -0.51, 2.42$
   $\therefore x = y$ or no relation.

8. (b) I. $x^2 - 16x + 63 = 0$
   $\Rightarrow x^2 - 9x - 7x + 63 = 0$
   $\Rightarrow x(x - 9) - 7(x - 9) = 0$
   $\Rightarrow x = 7, 9$
   II. $y^2 - 2y - 35 = 0$
   $\Rightarrow y^2 + 5y - 7 - 35 = 0$
   $\Rightarrow y(y + 5) - 7(y + 5) = 0$
   $\Rightarrow y = -5, 7$
   $\therefore$ Hence $x \geq y$

9. (a) I. $(289)^{\frac{1}{2}} x - \sqrt{324} = 203$
   $\Rightarrow 17x - 18 = 203$
   $\Rightarrow 17x = 221$
   $\Rightarrow x = 13$
   II. $(484)^{1/2}y - \sqrt{225} = 183$
   $\Rightarrow 22y - 15 = 183$
   $\Rightarrow 22y = 198$
   $\Rightarrow y = 9$
   $\therefore$ Hence $x > y$

10. (c) I. $679x^2 - 168x^2 = 3066$
    $\Rightarrow 511x^2 = 3066$
    $\Rightarrow x^2 = +6$
    $\Rightarrow x = -\sqrt{6}, +\sqrt{6}$
    II. $\sqrt{144}y^3 - 9y^3 = 1536$
    $\Rightarrow 12y^3 - 9y^3 = 1536$
    $\Rightarrow 3y^3 = 1536$
    $\Rightarrow y^3 = 512$
    $\Rightarrow y = 8$
    $\therefore$ Hence $y > x$

11. (d) First start with the option (d).
    $1001 \times 25 = 25025$
    $1001 \times 67 = 67067$ etc.
    Thus 1001 is the largest number which divides the numbers of the type 25025, 67067 etc.

12. (a) Let the principal be P, then amount after 12 years $= 2P$
    $\Rightarrow SI = (2P - P) = P$
    Now, $I = \dfrac{P \times r \times t}{100} \Rightarrow P = \dfrac{P \times r \times 12}{100}$
    or $r = \dfrac{100}{12} = \dfrac{25}{3} = 8\dfrac{1}{3}\%$

13. (d) Applying successive discounts of 10%, 12% and 15% on 100, we get $100 \times 0.9 \times 0.88 \times 0.85 = 67.32$
    $\Rightarrow$ Single discount $= 100 - 67.32 = 32.68$

14. (a) Let the prices of two houses A and B be Rs $4x$ and Rs $5x$, respectively for the last year.
    Then, the prices of A this year $=$ Rs $(1.25 \times 4x)$ and that of B $=$ Rs $(5x + 50,000)$
    This year, Ratio of their prices $= 9 : 10$
    $\therefore \dfrac{1.25 \times 4x}{5x + 50,000} = \dfrac{9}{10}$
    $\Rightarrow 50x - 45x = 450000 \Rightarrow 5x = 4,50,000$
    $\Rightarrow x = 90,000$
    Hence, the price of A last year was
    $4x =$ Rs $3,60,000$

15. (b) A three digit number to be exactly divisible by 5 must have either 0 or 5 at its units place.
    Such numbers will be 100, 105, 110, ..., 995.
    First term $= 100$, last term $= 995$
    Let the required number be n.
    To find the value of n, we may use the following formula of arithmetic progression,

$T_n = a + (n-1)d$ .... (1)
Where d = common difference = 5
$T_n = 995$
a = 100
Hence from (1)
$995 = 100 + (n-1)5$
$\Rightarrow 5n = 900$
n = 180
Digits to be used = 0, 1, 2, 3, 4, 5, 6, 7, 8, 9.

16. (b)

$$\underbrace{198 \quad\quad 194}_{-2^2} \underbrace{\quad 185}_{-3^2} \underbrace{\quad 169}_{-4^2} \underbrace{\quad \boxed{144}}_{-5^2}$$

17. (c)   The first, third, fifth .... and second, fourth .... terms are groups of consecutive natural numbers.

18. (e)   The pattern of the number series is:
$7 \times 2 - 3 = 11$
$11 \times 2 - 3 = 19$
$19 \times 2 - 3 = 35$
$35 \times 2 - 3 = 67$
$67 \times 2 - 3 = 134 - 3 = \boxed{131}$

19. (c)   The pattern of the number series is:
$5 + 1^2 = 6$
$6 + 2^2 = 10$
$10 + 3^2 = 19$
$19 + 4^2 = 35$
$35 + 5^2 = 35 + 25 = \boxed{60}$

20. (a)   The pattern of the number series is:
$1 + 2 = 3$
$3 + (2+3) = 8$
$8 + (2+3+5) = 18$
$18 + (2+3+5+7) = 35$
$35 + (2+3+5+7+9) = 61$

21. (b)   Age of B = Age of (A + B + C) − Age of (A + C) = $26 \times 3 - 29 \times 2 = 78 - 58 = 20$ years.

22. (d)   Total time required $= \dfrac{14}{5} + \dfrac{14}{10}$

$= \dfrac{28+14}{10} = 4.2 \text{ hrs}$

23. (a)   Here d = a + 3
$a + a + 3 = 103$
$2a = 100$
$a = 50$
So, numbers are 50, 51, 52 and 53
$\therefore b \times c = 51 \times 52 = 2652$

24. (b)   The word 'SOCIETY' contains seven distinct letters and they can be arranged at random in a row in $^7P_7$ ways, i.e. in 7! = 5040 ways.

Let us now consider those arrangements in which all the three vowels come together. So in this case we have to arrange four letters. S, C, T, Y and a pack of three vowels in a row which can be done in $^5P_5$ i.e. 5! = 120 ways.

Also, the three vowels in their pack can be arranged in $^3P_3$ i.e. 3! = 6 ways.

Hence, the number of arrangements in which the three vowels come together is $120 \times 6 = 720$

$\therefore$ The probability that the vowels come together

$= \dfrac{720}{5040} = \dfrac{1}{7}$

25. (c)   Let the speed of the man upstream be x kmph and that downstream be y kmph.

$\therefore \dfrac{72}{x} + \dfrac{54}{y} = 9 \quad \therefore \dfrac{8}{x} + \dfrac{6}{y} = 1$

$\therefore 8u + 6v = 1 \quad\quad\quad ...(i)$

where $u = \dfrac{1}{x}$ and $v = \dfrac{1}{y}$

$\dfrac{84}{x} + \dfrac{90}{y} = 12 \quad\quad \therefore \dfrac{14}{x} + \dfrac{15}{y} = 2$

$\therefore 14u + 15v = 2 \quad\quad ...(ii)$
From equations (i) and (ii),

$u = \dfrac{1}{12}$ and $v = \dfrac{1}{18} \therefore x = 12, y = 18$

$\therefore$ speed of the man in still water

$= \dfrac{12+18}{2} \text{kmph} = 15 \text{kmph}$

(26-30) :

26. (a)   Required difference = (32.5 − 22.5) lakh = 10 lakh

27. (b)   Income per person in

$\text{City A} = \dfrac{200 \times \dfrac{36}{100}}{55} = 1.30 \text{ crore}$

$\text{City B} = \dfrac{200 \times \dfrac{16}{100}}{40} = 0.8 \text{ crore}$

$\text{City C} = \dfrac{200 \times \dfrac{20}{100}}{65} = 0.61 \text{ crore}$

$\text{City E} = \dfrac{32}{243} = 0.34 \text{ crore}$

$\text{City F} = \dfrac{200 \times \dfrac{4}{100}}{42.5} = 0.18 \text{ crore}$

$\therefore$ Required answer is city F.

28. (d)   Required sum

$= \dfrac{30 + 22.5 + 35 + 30 + 25 + 17.5}{6}$

$+ \dfrac{25 + 17.5 + 30 + 32.5 + 32.5 + 25}{6}$

$= 26.66 + 27.08 = 53.74 \approx 54 \text{ lakh}$

29. (a)   Required difference

$= \dfrac{200 \times \dfrac{36}{100}}{55} \times 5 = 6.545 \text{ crore}$

30. (c)   Required % $= \left(\dfrac{30}{25} \times 100 \right)\% = 120\%$

(31-35) :

31. (e)   Let expenditure of Company A in the year 2012 = ₹ 100

$\therefore$ Income = $100 \times \dfrac{130}{100}$ ₹ 130

and expenditure of Company B in the year 2015 = ₹ 130

$$\therefore \text{ Required ratio} = 100 \times \frac{130}{100} : 130 \times \frac{50}{100}$$

$$= 30 : 65 = 6 : 13$$

32. (c) Let expenditure of Company A in the year 2015 = ₹ 100

$$\therefore \text{ Income} = 100 \times \frac{140}{100} = ₹\,140$$

and expenditure of company A in the year 2016 = ₹ 140

$$\therefore \text{ Income} = 140 \times \frac{150}{100} = ₹\,210$$

$$\therefore \text{ Required ratio} = 140 : 210 = 2 : 3$$

33. (c) Percentage profit increased over the previous year is as follows :

$$2012 = \left[\frac{20-15}{15} \times 100\right]\% = 33.33\%$$

$$2013 = \left[\frac{30-20}{20} \times 100\right]\% = 50\%$$

$$2014 = 0\%$$

$$2015 = \left[\frac{50-30}{30} \times 100\right]\% = 66.66\%$$

$$2016 = \left[\frac{60-50}{50} \times 100\right]\% = 20\%$$

$$\therefore \text{ Required answer is 2015.}$$

34. (b) Expenditure of company A in the year 2011 = ₹ 40 crore

$$\therefore \text{ Income} = 40 \times \frac{120}{100} = ₹\,48 \text{ crore}$$

35. (d)

36-40.

	Day 1			**Day 2**		
Vehicle	**Time in hr**	**Distance in km**	**Speed in km / hr**	**Time in hr**	**Distance in km**	**Speed in km/hr**
A	16	832	52	16	864	54
B	12	516	43	18	774	43
C	11	693	63	18	810	45
D	12	552	46	15	765	51
E	16	935	58.4	14	546	39
F	19	703	37	12	636	53

36. (d) Vehicle B.
37. (c) Speed of vehicle A on day 1 = 52 km/hr
Speed of vehicle C on day 1 = 63 km/hr
Difference = 63 − 52 = 11 km / hr

38. (e) Speed of vehicle C on day 2 = 45 km/hr

$$\Rightarrow \left(45 \times \frac{5}{18}\right) \text{m/sec} = 12.5 \,\text{m/sec}$$

39. (e) Percentage

$$= \frac{\text{Distance travelled by vehicle F on day 2}}{\text{Distance travelled by vehicle F on day 1}} \times 100$$

$$= \frac{636}{703} \times 100 \approx \frac{630}{700} \times 100 \approx 90\%$$

40. (b) Speed of vehicle D on day 2 = 51
Speed of vehicle E on day 2 = 39

$$\text{Required ratio} = \frac{51}{39} = \frac{17}{13} \text{ or } 17:13$$

41. (a) 42. (d) 43. (a) 44. (a) 45. (b) 46. (a)
47. (b) 48. (c) 49. (d) 50. (c)

Solution (51 -56):

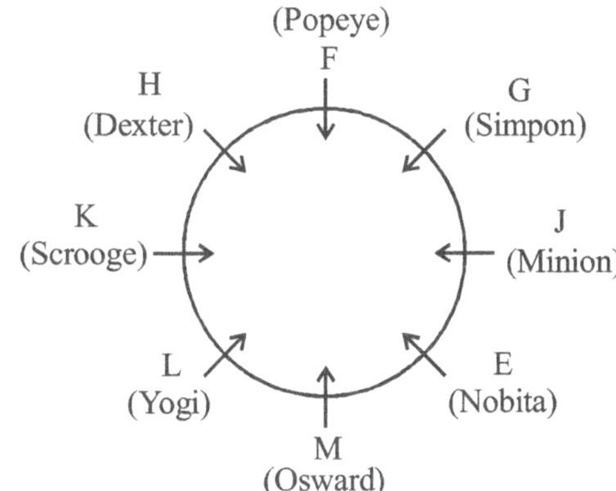

51. (b) 52. (d) 53. (c) 54. (b) 55. (a) 56. (a)

Solution (57 -61):

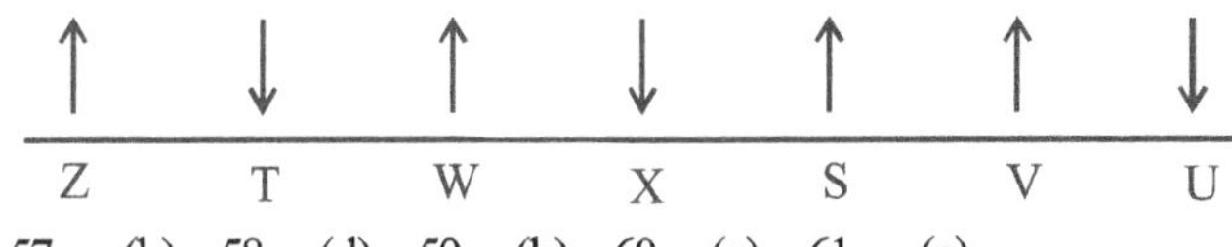

57. (b) 58. (d) 59. (b) 60. (a) 61. (e)

Soultion (62-66):

only [in] serial [order] → [ve] [pu] [na] to

[order] [in] the [state] → [li] [ve] su [pu]

the logical [idea] only → su [na] ri [jo]

[in] [idea] or theory → zt [jo] bk [pu]

Codes are :

only ⇒ na	the ⇒ su	or ⇒ zt or bk	
in ⇒ pu	state ⇒ li	theory ⇒ zt or bk	
serial ⇒ to	logical ⇒ ri		
order ⇒ ve	idea ⇒ jo		

62. (e) The code of 'theory' is either 'zt' or 'bk',
63. (c) li ⇒ state
ri ⇒ logical
to ⇒ serial
ve ⇒ order

64. (a) logical ⇒ ri
         idea   ⇒ jo
         only   ⇒ na
         order   ⇒ ve
         The code for 'is' may be 'ge'
65. (d) logical ⇒ ri
66. (b) serial ⇒ to
67. (b)

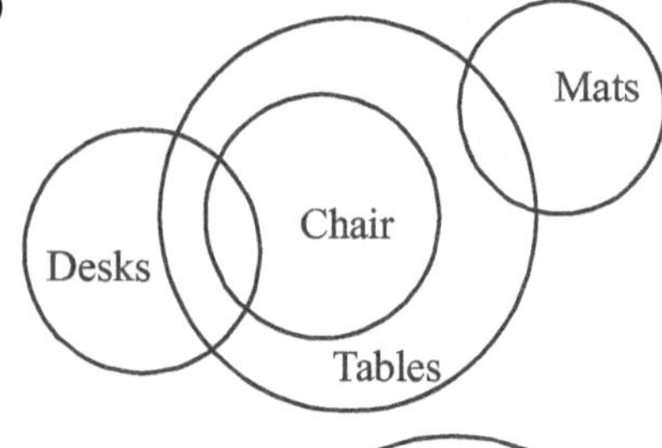

or

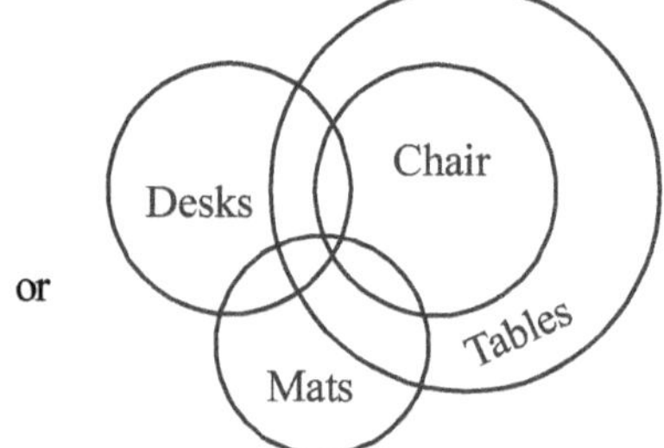

I. False   II. True   III. False

68. (e)

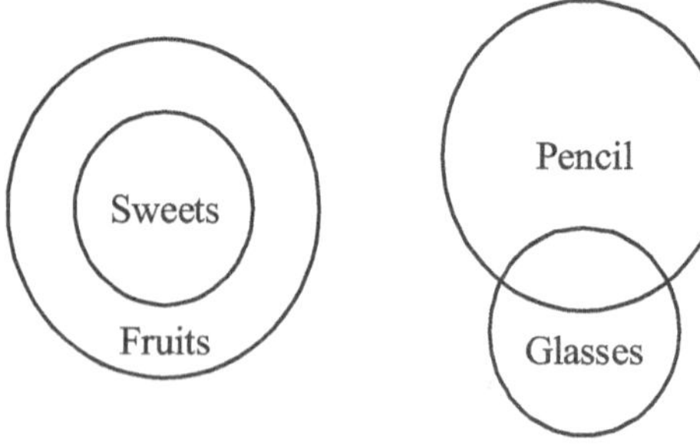

or

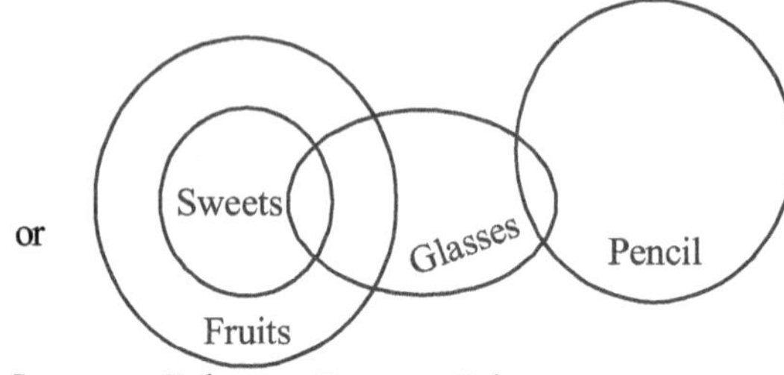

I.   False   II.   False   II.   False

69. (a)

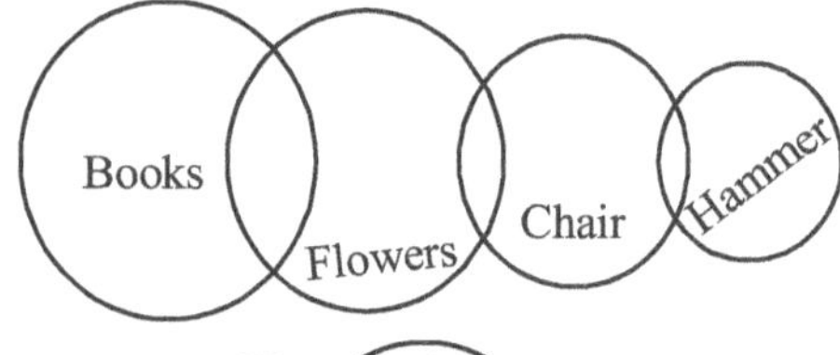

or

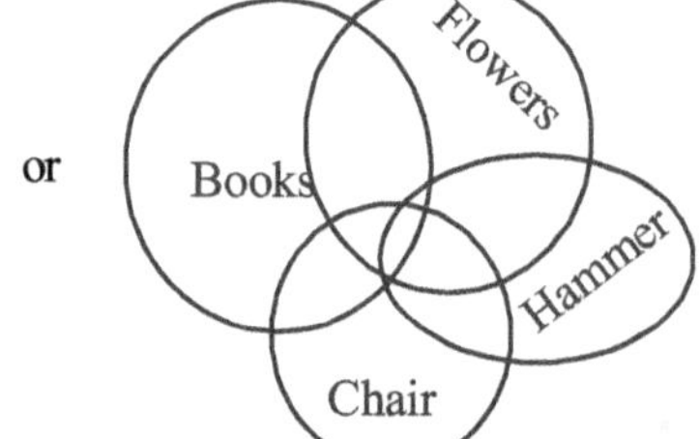

I. False   II. False   III. False

Solution (70 -72):

70. (a)

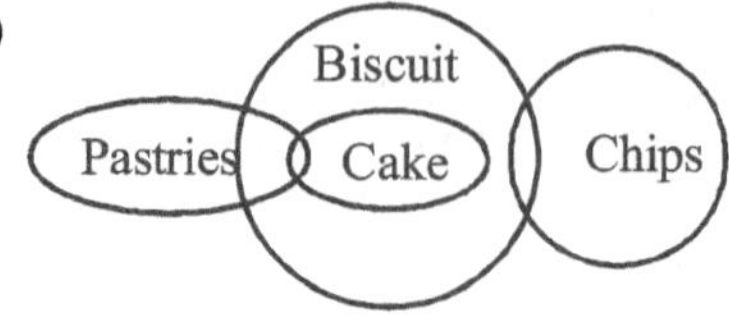

I. follow   II. not follow

71. (e)

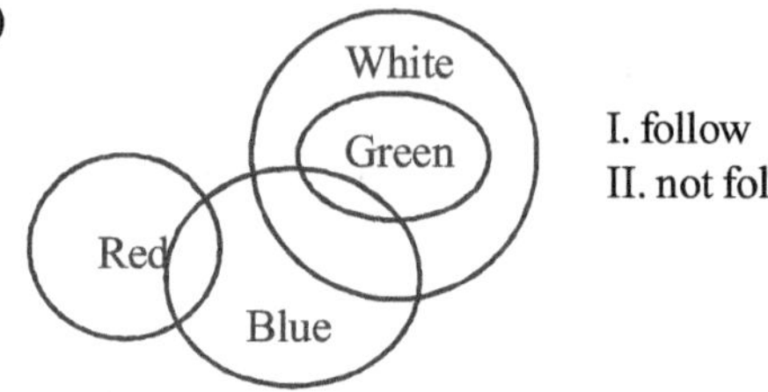

I. follow
II. not follow

I. follow   II. not follow

72. (d)

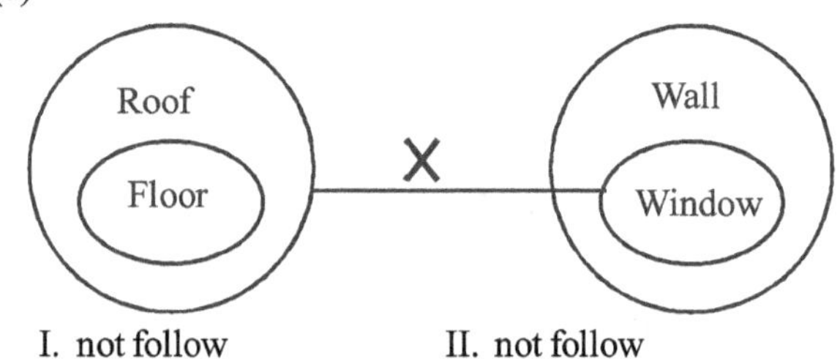

I. not follow   II. not follow

Solution (73-75) :

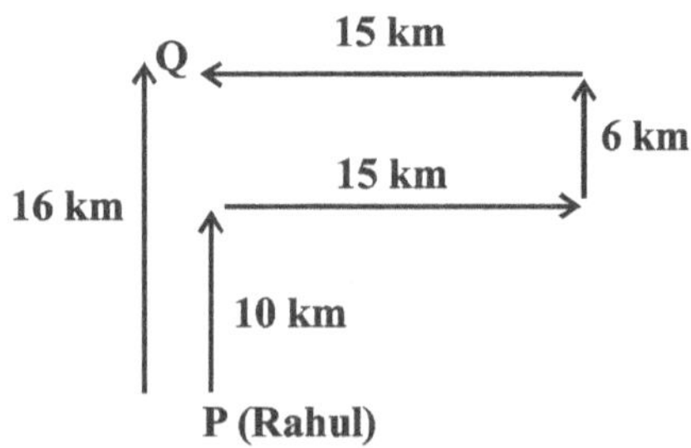

73. (a)
74. (d)
75. (e)   SALE, SEAL
(Qs. 76-80).
From the information given we can draw the following table

S.No.	Month	City
1.	January	Mumbai
2.	February	Kolkata
3.	March	Channai
4.	April	Bangalore
5.	May	Delhi
6.	June	Bhopal
7.	July	Cochin

76. (a) Only one audition held in Kolkata.

77. (e)

78. (d) (May-Delhi) is correct sequence rest are in Month
         (+ 1) city manner.

79. (d) In March audition held in Channai.

80. (e) Audition in Mumbai held in January.

PRACTICE SET 9

Time : 45 Min. **Max. Marks : 80**

QUANTITATIVE APTITUDE

DIRECTIONS (Q. 1-5) : What should come in place of the question mark (?) in the following questions?

1. $4\dfrac{1}{2} + 6\dfrac{2}{3} + 5\dfrac{1}{3} = ?$

   (a) $15\dfrac{1}{2}$ (b) $16\dfrac{2}{3}$

   (c) $16\dfrac{1}{2}$ (d) 17

   (e) None of these

2. $792.02 + 101.32 - 306.76 = ?$

   (a) 893.34 (b) 1200.10
   (c) 997.11 (d) 586.58
   (e) None of these

3. 300% of $150 = ?$% of 600
   (a) 75 (b) 45

   (c) 450 (d) $133\dfrac{1}{2}$

   (e) None of these

4. $34.95 + 240.016 + 23.9800 = ?$
   (a) 299.09 (b) 298.0946
   (c) 298.111 (d) 298.946
   (e) None of these

5. $3889 + 12.952 - ? = 3854.002$
   (a) 47.95 (b) 47.752
   (c) 47.095 (d) 47.932
   (e) None of these

DIRECTIONS (Q. 6-10) : In the following questions two equations numbered I and II are given. You have to solve both the equations and give answer.

If
(a) $x > y$ (b) $x \geq y$
(c) $x < y$ (d) $x \leq y$
(e) $x = y$ or the relationship cannot be established

6. I. $5x^2 - 87x + 378 = 0$
   II. $3y^3 - 49y + 200 = 0$
7. I. $14x^2 - 37x + 24 = 0$
   II. $28y^2 - 53y + 24 = 0$
8. I. $2x^2 - 3x - 35 = 0$
   II. $y^2 - 7y + 6 = 0$
9. I. $6x^2 - 29x + 35 = 0$
   II. $2y^2 - 19y + 35 = 0$
10. I. $12x^2 - 47x + 40 = 0$
    II. $4y^2 + 3y - 10 = 0$

11. A machine is sold at a profit of 10%. Had it been sold for ₹ 80 less, there would have been a loss of 10%. The cost price of the machine is
    (a) ₹ 350 (b) ₹ 400
    (c) ₹ 450 (d) ₹ 520
    (e) None of these

12. During a journey of 80 km a train covers first 60km with a speed of 40 km/h and completes the remaining distance with a speed of 20 km/h. What is the average speed of the train during the whole journey?
    (a) 30 km/h (b) 32 km/h
    (c) 36 km/h (d) 40 km/h
    (e) None of these

13. An aeroplane takes off 30 minutes later than the scheduled time and in order to reach its destination 1500 km away in time, it has to increase its speed by 250 km/h from its usual speed. Find its usual speed.
    (a) 1000 km/h   (b) 750 km/h
    (c) 850 km/h   (d) 650 km/h
    (e) None of these

14. In an examination 35% of the candidates failed in one subject and 42% failed in another subject. While 15% failed in both the subjects. If 2500 candidates appeared at the examination, how many students passed in either subject but not in both?
    (a) 325   (b) 1175   (c) 2125   (d) 1230
    (e) None of these

15. If the length of a certain rectangle is decreased by 4 cm and the width is increased by 3 cm, a square with the same area as the original rectangle would result. The perimeter of the original rectangle (in centimetres) is :
    (a) 44   (b) 46   (c) 48   (d) 50
    (e) None of these

16. Raju decided to marry 3 years after he gets a job. He was 17 years old when he passed class 12th. After passing class 12th', he had completed his graduation course in 3 years and PG Course in 2 years. He got the job exactly 1 year after completing his PG Course. At what age will he get married?
    (a) 27 years   (b) 26 years
    (c) 28 years   (d) 23 years
    (e) None of these

DIRECTIONS (Qs. 17-21): Study the following table and bar graph carefully and answer the given question.

Table and bar graph shows the percentange of appeared and qualified candidates in a RRB PO examination from six different institutes respectively.

Appeared candidates = 36000

Institute	% of appeared candidates
P	12%
Q	18%
R	20%
S	15%
T	10%
U	25%

Qualified candidates = 8000

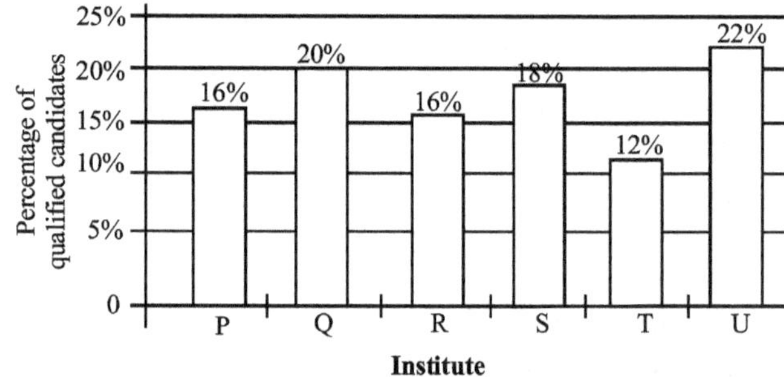

17. What is the ratio between the qualified candidates from institutes P, Q and R together and the appeared candidates from institutes S, T and U together?
    (a) 52 : 225   (b) 26 : 125
    (c) 125 : 26   (d) 13 : 200
    (e) None of these

18. What percent of the candidates from institute T has been declared qualified out of the total candidates appeared from this institute?
    (a) 16%   (b) 26%
    (c) 16.66%   (d) 18%
    (e) None of these

19. What is the approximate percentage of students qualified with respect to those appeared from the institutes Q and R together?
    (a) 20%   (b) 21%
    (c) 22%   (d) 23%
    (e) None of these

20. Which institute has the highest percentage of candidates qualified with respect to those appeared?
    (a) P   (b) Q
    (c) R   (d) S
    (e) None of these

21. What is the average number of appeared candidates from the institutes P, Q and U together?
    (a) 19800   (b) 2200
    (c) 6600   (d) 8600
    (e) None of these

DIRECTIONS (Qs. 22-26): Study the following line graph carefully and answer the given questions.

The line graph shows the number of printers sold by two companies HP and Canon over the years

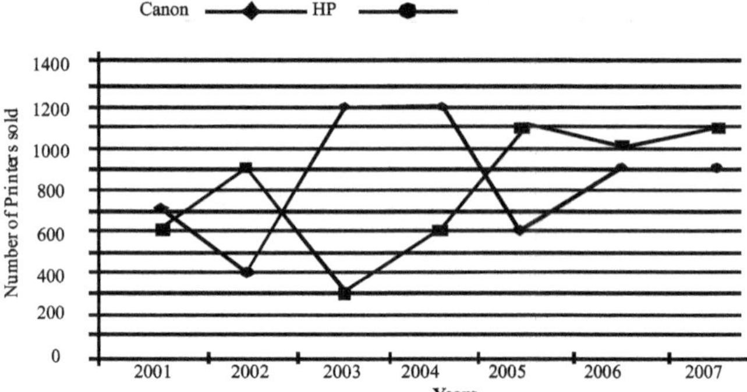

22. The sales of HP printer in the year 2005 is approximately what per cent of total sales of HP printer in all the years together?
    (a) 20%   (b) 18%
    (c) 11%   (d) 24%
    (e) None of these

23. Which of the following combinations of year and percentage rise in sales from the previous year for HP printer is correct?
    (a) 2004 - 99.85%   (b) 2005 - 83.33%
    (c) 2002 - 43.21%   (d) 2007 - 7.68%
    (e) None of these

24. Total sales of Canon printer in the years 2001, 2002 and 2005 together is approximately what per cent of the total sales of Canon printer in all the years together?
    (a) 24%   (b) 46%
    (c) 29%   (d) 37%
    (e) None of these

25. What is the ratio between the total sales of HP printer and the total sales of Canon printer over the given years?
(a) 26 : 29   (b) 27 : 31
(c) 53 : 51   (d) 56 : 59
(e) None of these

26. In which year was percentage rise/fall in sales from the previous year the highest for HP printer?
(a) 2003   (b) 2005
(c) 2002   (d) 2004
(e) None of these

DIRECTIONS (Qs. 27-31): What will come in place of the question mark (?) in the following number series?

27. 2 9 30 105 ? 2195
(a) 432   (b) 426
(c) 440   (d) 436
(e) None of these

28. 3 4 12 45 ? 1005
(a) 152   (b) 198
(c) 144   (d) 192
(e) None of these

29. 1 3 9 31 ? 651
(a) 97   (b) 127
(c) 129   (d) 109
(e) None of these

30. 5 ? 4 7.5 17 45
(a) 3.5   (b) 3
(c) 2.5   (d) 2
(e) None of these

31. 15 30 ? 720, 5760
(a) 100   (b) 120
(c) 118   (d) 128
(e) None of these

32. Mr Duggal invested ₹20,000 with rate of interest @ 20 pcpa. The interest was compounded half-yearly for the first one year and in the next year it was compounded yearly. What will be the total interest earned at the end of two years?
(a) ₹8,800   (b) ₹9,040
(c) ₹8,040   (d) ₹9,800
(e) None of these

33. In how many different ways can the letters of the word DESIGN be arranged so that the vowels are at the two ends?
(a) 48   (b) 72
(c) 36   (d) 24
(e) None of these

34. 4 men can complete a piece of work in 2 days. 4 women can complete the same piece of work in 4 days whereas 5 children can complete the same piece of work in 4 days. If, 2 men, 4 women and 10 children work together, in how many days can the work be completed ?
(a) 1 day   (b) 3 days
(c) 2 days   (d) 4 days
(e) None of these

35. A boat takes 6 hours to travel from place M to N downstream and back from N to M upstream. If the speed of the boat in still water is 4 km./hr., what is the distance between the two places?
(a) 8 kms.   (b) 12 kms.
(c) 6 kms.   (d) Data inadeqate
(e) None of these

DIRECTIONS (Qs. 36-40): Study the following information carefully and answer the given questions.

Cost of three different fruits (in rupees per kg. in five different cities)

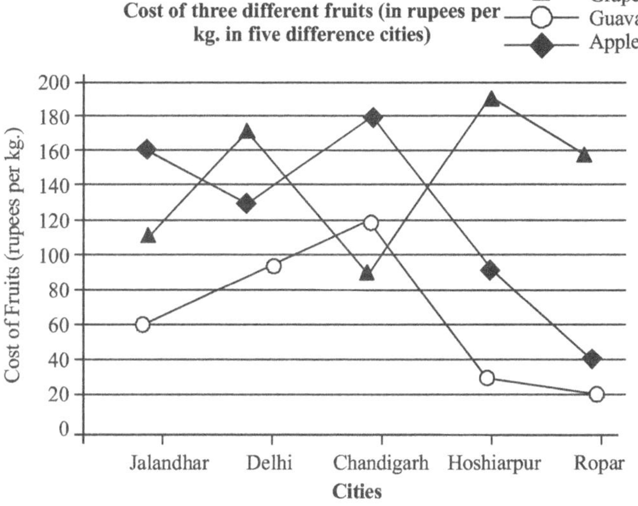

36. In which city is the difference between the cost of one kg of apple and cost of one kg of guava second lowest?
(a) Jalandhar   (b) Delhi
(c) Chandigarh   (d) Hoshiarpur
(e) Ropar

37. Cost of one kg of guava in Jalandhar is approximately what percent of the cost of two kgs of grapes in Chandigarh?
(a) 66   (b) 24
(c) 28   (d) 34
(e) 58

38. What total amount will Ram pay to the shopkeeper for purchasing 3 kgs of apples and 2 kgs of guavas in Delhi?
(a) ₹ 530/-   (b) ₹ 450/-
(c) ₹ 570/-   (b) ₹ 620/-
(e) ₹ 490/-

39. Ravinder had to purchase 45 kgs of grapes from Hoshiarpur. Shopkeeper gave him discount of 4% per kg. What amount did he pay to the shopkeeper after the discount?
(a) ₹ 8,208/-   (b) ₹ 8,104/-
(c) ₹ 8,340/-   (b) ₹ 8,550/-
(e) ₹ 8,410/-

40. What is the respective ratio between the cost of one kg of apples from Ropar and the cost of one kg of grapes from Chandigarh?
(a) 3 : 2   (b) 12 : 32
(c) $2^2 : 3^2$ (d) $4^2 : 9^2$
(e) $9^2 : 4^2$

REASONING ABILITY

DIRECTIONS (Qs. 41-45): In these questions, relationships between different elements is shown in the statements. These statements are followed by two conclusion.

Give answer (a) if **only** conclusion **I** follows
Give answer (b) if **only** conclusion **II** follows
Give answer (c) if **either** conclusion **I** or conlcusion **II** follows
Give answer (d) if **neither** conclusions **I** nor conlcusion **II** follows
Give answer (e) if **both** conclusions **I and II** follow

41. **Statement:** $R \geq S \geq T > U > X; T < V < W$
    Conclusions: I. $R > X$
    II. $X < W$
42. **Statement:** $E = F < G < H; G \geq I$
    Conclusions: I. $H > I$
    II. $E \geq I$
43. **Statement:** $A > B > F > C; D > E > C$
    Conclusions: I. $C < A$
    II. $B > D$
44. **Statement:** $K \leq L \leq M = N; P \geq O \geq N$
    Conclusions: I. $K < P$
    II. $K = P$
45. **Statement:** $D < E < F < G; K > F$
    Conclusions: I. $K \leq G$
    II. $K > D$

DIRECTIONS (Qs. 46-51): Study the following information carefully and answer the given questions.

Eight Persons, A, B, C, D, E, F, G and H are sitting around a circular table facing the centre but not necessarily in the same order. Each one of them likes different Subjects viz. English, Civics, Biology, History, Geography, Mathematics, Chemistry and Hindi.

A sits third to right of the person who likes Hindi. Only two people sit between the person who likes Hindi and H. The persons who like the Geography and the Civics are immediate neighbours of each other. Neither A nor H likes Geography or Civics. The one who likes Geography is not an immediate neighbour of the person who likes Hindi. The person who likes English sits second to left of E. E is not an immediate neighbour of H. The person who likes English is an immediate neighbour of both the persons who like Mathematics and Chemistry. The person who likes Chemistry sits third to right of B. B does not likes Geography. C sits to the immediate right of the person who likes Biology. A does not likes Biology. F is not an immediate neighbour of A. G is not an immediate neighbour of the person who likes English.

46. Who amongst the following sits third to the left of E?
    (a) The one who likes English
    (b) G
    (c) A
    (d) The person who likes Chemistry
    (e) B
47. Four of the following five are alike in a certain way based on the given arrangement and thus form a group. Which is the one that does not belong to that group?
    (a) F-Biology (b) G-History
    (c) D-English (d) A-Chemistry
    (e) B-Hindi
48. Who amongst the following is the person who likes History?
    (a) A (b) C
    (c) H (d) G
    (e) D
49. Which of the following is TRUE with respect to the given seating arrangement?
    (a) The person who likes Mathematics is an immediate neighbour of the Geography
    (b) G sits second to right of D
    (c) The one who likes Mathematics and the Civics are immediate neighbours of each other

(d) The person who likes Biology sits to the immediate left of the person who likes Hindi
(e) The one who likes Mathematics sits second to the left of D

50. Which of the following Subjects does B likes?
    (a) Biology (b) English
    (c) Civics (d) Geography
    (e) Chemistry
51. A girl walks 3.5 km to the west and then turns the south and walks 4 km. Again, she turns to the west and walks 6.5 km. Next, she turns and walks 4 km in north direction. How far is she now from her starting point?
    (a) 18 km (b) 6.5 km
    (c) 10 km (d) 12 km
    (e) 9 km

DIRECTIONS (Qs. 52-54): Study the following information carefully and answer the given questions.

If A + B means A is the father of B
If A × B means A is the sister of B
If A $ B means A is the wife of B
If A % B means A is the mother of B
If A ÷ B means A is the son of B

52. What should come in place of the question mark, to establish that J is the brother of T in the expression?
    J ÷ P % H ? T % L
    (a) × (b) ÷
    (c) $ (d) Either ÷ or ×
    (e) Either + or ÷
53. Which among the given expressions indicate that M is the daughter of D?
    (a) L % R $ D + T × M (b) L + R $ D + M × T
    (c) L % R % D + T ÷ M (d) D + L $ R + M × T
    (e) L $ D ÷ R % M ÷ T
54. Which among the following options is true if the expresssion 'I + T % J × L ÷ K' is **definitely true**?
    (a) L is the daughter of T (b) K is the son-in-law of I
    (c) I is the grandmother of L (d) T is the father of L
    (e) J is the brother of L

DIRECTIONS (Qs. 55-59) : Study the following information to answer the given questions.

In a certain code language, 'growth of Indian economy' is written as `ga mo ti su', 'heavy trade growth depends on', is written as 'ki zo mo ye na', 'economy trade this year' is written as `zo ra ti da' and 'this condition of depends' is written as `da ga nic ki'.

55. What is the code, for 'on'?
    (a) ye (b) na
    (c) zo (d) Either na or zo
    (e) Either ye or na
56. What does `su' stand for?
    (a) economy (b) growth
    (c) of (d) Indian
    (e) None of these
57. What is the code for 'year growth condition'?
    (a) nic ye ti (b) mo ra nic
    (c) ra ga mo (d) da ra nic
    (e) None of these

58. Which of the following does `ki ti na' stand for?
    - (a) depends of growth
    - (b) heavy growth depends
    - (c) economy depends heavy
    - (d) economy depends on
    - (e) Either (c) or (d)

59. Which of the following may represent 'record rate of growth'?
    - (a) ga zo ti da
    - (b) ga ba mo nee
    - (c) ga ba nic ki
    - (d) mo ba ti ra
    - (e) None of these

DIRECTIONS (Qs. 60-64): Study the given information carefully and answer the given questions.

Eight people - J, K, L, M, N, O, P and Q are sitting around a circular table facing the centre, not necessarily in the same order. O is sitting third to the right of M. There is only one person sitting between M and J. There are only three people between J and K. P is an immediate neighbour of J. There are only three people between P and L. N is second to the right of P.

60. Which of the following is **true** regarding the given arrangement?
    - (a) M is an immediate neighbour of K
    - (b) N is an immediate neighbour of J
    - (c) P is second to the left of O
    - (d) There are four people between N and O.
    - (e) None is true

61. Who is sitting second to the left of the one who is sitting second to the left of Q?
    - (a) M
    - (b) K
    - (c) N
    - (d) L
    - (e) J

62. 'Four of the following five are alike in a certain way based on their seating positions in the above arrangement and so form a group. Which one does **not** belong to the group?
    - (a) PQ
    - (b) KL
    - (c) MN
    - (d) QO
    - (e) KO

63. What is N's position with respect to K?
    - (a) Second to the left
    - (b) Second to the right
    - (c) Third to the left
    - (d) Third to the right
    - (e) Fourth to the left

64. How many people are sitting between K and P when counted from the right side of K?
    - (a) One
    - (b) Two
    - (c) Three
    - (d) None
    - (e) More than three

DIRECTIONS (Qs. 65-69): In each of the questions below, two statements are given followed by two conclusions numbered I and II. You have to take the two statements to be true even if they seem to be at variance from the commonly known facts and then decide which of the given conclusions logically follows from the given statement disregarding the commonly known facts.

Give answer (a) if **only** concluion **I** follows
Give answer (b) if **only** concluion **II** follows
Give answer (c) if **either** concluion **I** or conclusion **II** follows
Give answer (d) if **neither** conclusion **I** nor conclusion **II** follows
Give answer (e) if **both** conclusions **I and II** follow

65. **Statements :** Some rings are circles.
             No circle is a square.
    Conclusions : I. No ring is a square.
                II. All rings are squares.

66. **Statements :** All rows are lines.
             All lines are queues.
    Conclusions: I. All rows are queues.
                II. Atleast some queues are lines.

67. **Statements :** All laptops are computers.
             Some laptops are notebooks.
    Conclusions: I. Some notebooks are computers
                II. All notebooks are computers.

68. **Statements :** Some participants are students.
             Some students are boys.
    Conclusions: I. No boy is a participant.
                II. All boys are participants.

69. **Statements :** All sparrows are birds.
             No birds is a reptile.
    Conclusions: I. No sparrow is a reptile.
                II. Some reptiles are sparrows.

DIRECTIONS (Qs. 70-75) : Study they following information carefully to answer the questions given below it.

Seven professionals A, B, C, D, E, F and G are practising their professions in different cities Chennai, Bangalore, Hyderabad, Mumbai, Ahmedabad, Jaipur and Bhubaneshwar, not necessarily in the same order. Each has a different profession-Doctor, Engineer, Pharmacist, Lawyer, Counsellor, Professor and Artist, not necessarily in the same order.

A is a Pharmacist and practises in Bhubaneshwar. D practises in Bangalore but is not a Doctor or an Artist. The one who practises in Hyderabad is a Professor. G is a Counsellor and does not practise in Mumbai or Chennai. E is a Lawyer and practises in Ahmedabad. F practises in Chennai but is not an artist. C practises in Mumbai.

70. What is D's profession?
    - (a) Doctor
    - (b) Professor
    - (c) Engineer
    - (d) Cannot be determined
    - (e) None of these

71. Who is the Professor?
    - (a) B
    - (b) C
    - (c) D
    - (d) E
    - (e) None of these

72. Which of the following combinations of profession and place is **correct**?
    - (a) Pharmacist-Jaipur
    - (b) Engineer-Chennai
    - (c) Doctor-Bangalore
    - (d) Artist-Mumbai
    - (e) None of these

73. Which of the following persons works in Jaipur?
    - (a) B
    - (b) G
    - (c) C
    - (d) B or G
    - (e) None of these

74. Who is the Doctor?
    - (a) D
    - (b) B
    - (c) C
    - (d) B or C
    - (e) None of these

75. A man walks 5 km toward south and then turns to the right. After walking 3 km he turns to the left and walks 5 km. Now in which direction is he from the starting place?
- (a) West
- (b) South
- (c) North-East
- (d) South-West
- (e) None of these

DIRECTIONS (Qs. 76-80) : Following questions are based on five words given below :

WIT   BAR   URN   ELF   TOP

(The new words formed after performing the mentioned operations may or may not necessarily be meaningful English words)

76. If in each of the words, all the alphabets are arranged in English alphabetical order within the word, how many words will NOT begin with a vowel ?
- (a) None
- (b) One
- (c) Two
- (d) Three
- (e) More than three

77. How many letters are there in the English alphabetical series between second letter of the word which is second from the right and the third letter of the word which is third from the left of the given words?
- (a) One
- (b) Two
- (c) Three
- (d) Four
- (e) Five

78. If in each of the given words, each of the consonants is changed to previous letter and each vowel is changed to next letter in the English alphabetical series, in how many words thus formed will no vowels appear ?
- (a) None
- (b) One
- (c) Two
- (d) Three
- (e) More than three

79. If the each alphabet in each of the words is changed to the next alphabet in the English alphabetical order, how many words having two vowels (same or different vowels) will be formed ?
- (a) None
- (b) One
- (c) Two
- (d) Three
- (e) Four

80. If the given words are arranged in the order as they would appear in a dictionary from left to right, which of the following will be fourth from the left ?
- (a) WIT
- (b) BAR
- (c) URN
- (d) ELF
- (e) TOP

HINTS & EXPLANATIONS

1. **(c)** $? = 4\dfrac{1}{2} + 6\dfrac{2}{3} + 5\dfrac{1}{3}$

$= (4+6+5) + \dfrac{3+4+2}{6} = 15 + \dfrac{9}{6} = 16\dfrac{1}{2}$

2. **(d)** $? = 792.02 + 101.32 - 306.76 = 586.58$

3. **(a)** 300% of $150 = ?$ % of 600

or , ? of $600 = 45000$ or, $? = 75$

4. **(d)** $34.95 + 240.016 + 23.9800 = 298.946$

5. **(a)** $3889 + 12.952 - ? = 3854.002$

or $? = 3889 + 12.952 - 3854.002 = 47.95$

Solution (6-10)

6. **(a)** I. $5x^2 - 87x + 378 = 0$

$\Rightarrow 5x^2 - 45x - 42x + 378 = 0$

$\Rightarrow 5x(x-9) - 42(x-9) = 0$

$\Rightarrow (5x - 42)(x - 9) = 0$

$\Rightarrow x = \dfrac{42}{5}, 9$

II. $3y^2 - 49y + 200 = 0$

$\Rightarrow 3y^2 - 24y - 25y + 200 = 0$

$\Rightarrow 3y(y-8) - 25(y-8) = 0$

$\Rightarrow (3y - 25)(y - 8) = 0$

$\Rightarrow y = \dfrac{25}{3}, 8$

Cleary, $x > y$

7. **(b)** I. $14x^2 - 37x + 24 = 0$

$\Rightarrow 14x^2 - 21x - 16x + 24 = 0$

$\Rightarrow 7x(2x-3) - 8(2x-3) = 0$

$\Rightarrow (7x - 8)(2x - 3) = 0$

$\Rightarrow x = \dfrac{8}{7}, \dfrac{3}{2}$

II. $28y^2 - 53y + 24 = 0$

$\Rightarrow 28y^2 - 21y - 32y + 24 = 0$

$\Rightarrow 7y(4y-3) - 8(4y-3) = 0$

$\Rightarrow (7y - 8)(4y - 3) = 0$

$\Rightarrow y = \dfrac{8}{7}, \dfrac{3}{4}$

Clearly, $x \geq y$

8. **(e)** I. $2x^2 - 3x - 35 = 0$

$\Rightarrow 2x^2 - 10x + 7x - 35 = 0$

$\Rightarrow 2x(x-5) + 7(x-5) = 0$

$\Rightarrow (2x + 7)(x - 5) = 0$

$\Rightarrow x = -\dfrac{7}{2}, 5$

II. $y^2 - 7y + 6 = 0$

$\Rightarrow y^2 - 6y - y + 6 = 0$

$\Rightarrow y(y-6) - 1(y-6) = 0$

$\Rightarrow (y - 1)(y - 6) = 0$

$\Rightarrow y = 1, 6$

9. **(d)** I. $6x^2 - 29x + 35 = 0$

$\Rightarrow 6x^2 - 15x - 14x + 35 = 0$

$\Rightarrow \quad 3x(2x-5)-7(2x-5)=0$

$\Rightarrow \quad (3x-7)(2x-5)=0$

$\Rightarrow \quad x=\dfrac{7}{3}, \dfrac{5}{2}$

II. $\quad 2y^2-19y+35=0$

$\Rightarrow \quad 2y^2-14y-5y+35=0$

$\Rightarrow \quad 2y(y-7)-5(y-7)=0$

$\Rightarrow \quad (2y-5)(y-7)=0$

$\Rightarrow \quad y=\dfrac{5}{2}, 7$

Clearly, $x \leq y$

10. (b) I. $\quad 12x^2-47x+40=0$

$\Rightarrow \quad 12x^2-15x-32x+40=0$

$\Rightarrow \quad 3x(4x-5)-8(4x-5)=0$

$\Rightarrow \quad (3x-8)(4x-5)=0$

$\Rightarrow \quad x=\dfrac{8}{3}, \dfrac{5}{4}$

II. $\quad 4y^2+3y-10=0$

$\Rightarrow \quad 4y^2+8y-5y-10=0$

$\Rightarrow \quad 4y(y+2)-5(y+2)=0$

$\Rightarrow \quad (4y-5)(y+2)=0$

$\Rightarrow \quad y=\dfrac{5}{4}, -2$

Clearly, $x \geq y$

11. (b) Let the cost price of the machine be ₹ x.

Then, selling price at a profit of 10% = ₹ $\dfrac{11x}{10}$

And the selling price at a loss of 10% = ₹ $\dfrac{9x}{10}$

Consequently, we find that

$\left(\dfrac{11x}{10}-\dfrac{9x}{10}\right)=80$

$\Rightarrow \dfrac{x}{5}=80 \Rightarrow x=$ ₹ 400

12. (b) Average speed = $\dfrac{\text{Total distance}}{\text{Total time}}$

$= \dfrac{80}{\dfrac{60}{40}+\dfrac{20}{20}}=\dfrac{80}{2.5}=32 \,\text{km/h}$

13. (b) Let the usual speed of the aeroplane be x km/h.

Then, $\dfrac{1500}{x}-\dfrac{1}{2}=\dfrac{1500}{(x+250)}$

Solving, we get $x=750 \,\text{km/h}$

14. (b) Using Venn Diagram

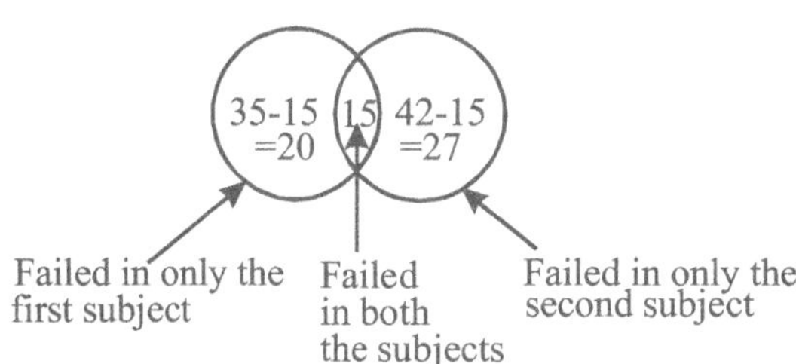

Thus, percentage of students who passed in both subjects

$= 100-[(35-15)+(42-15)+15]=100-(35+42-15)$

$= 100-(62)=38\%$

and percentage of students who failed in both subject

$= 15\%$

Therefore, the percentage of students who passed in either subject $= 100-(38+15)=100-53=47\%$

Hence, required no. of students who passed in either

subject but not in both $= 2500 \times \dfrac{47}{100}=1175$

15. (d) Let the length and breadth of the rectangle be x and y cm, respectively.

Then, $(x-4)(y+3)=xy \Rightarrow 3x-4y=12$ ... (i)

Also, $(x-4)=(y+3)$ [sides of square]

$\Rightarrow x-y=7$ ...(ii)

From (i) and (ii),

$x=16$ and $y=9$

Perimeter of the original rectangle $= 2(x+y)=50 \,\text{cm}$

16. (b) Raju's age at the time of marriage

$= 17+3+2+1+3=26 \,\text{years}$

17. (a) Total no. of qualified candidate from institute P, Q and R together

$= 8000 \times \left(\dfrac{16+20+16}{100}\right)$

$= 8000 \times \dfrac{52}{100}=4160$

Total no. of appeared candidates from institute S, T, and U together

$= 36000 \times \left(\dfrac{15+10+25}{100}\right)$

$= 36000 \times \dfrac{50}{100}=18000$

∴ Required ratio $= 4160 : 18000 = 52 : 225$

18. (e) No. of qualifed candidates from institute

$T=8000 \times \dfrac{12}{100}=960$

No. of appeared candidate from institute

$T=36000 \times \dfrac{10}{100}=3600$

∴ Required% $= \left(\dfrac{960}{3600} \times 100\right)\% = 26.66\%$

19. (b) Total of qualified candidates from institute Q and R together

$8000 \times \left(\dfrac{20+16}{100}\right)=8000 \times \dfrac{36}{100}=2880$

Total no. of appeared candidates from institute Q and R together

$= 36000 \times \left(\dfrac{18+20}{100}\right)$

$= 36000 \times \dfrac{38}{100}=13680$

$$\therefore \quad \text{Required\%} = \left(\frac{2880}{13680} \times 100\right)\%$$

$$= 21.05\% \approx 21\%$$

20. (a)

21. (c) Total no. of appeared candidates from institute P, Q and U together

$$36000 \times \left(\frac{12+18+25}{100}\right)$$

$$= 36000 \times \frac{55}{100} = 19800$$

$$\therefore \quad \text{Required average} = \frac{19800}{3} = 6600$$

Solution (22-26)

22. (c) Required %

$$= \left[\frac{600}{700+400+1200+1200+600+900+900} \times 100\right]\%$$

$$= \left(\frac{600}{5900} \times 100\right)\% = 10.16\% \approx 11\%$$

23. (e) In $2004 = 0\%$
In $2005 = $ No increase
In $2002 = $ No increase
In $2007 = 0\%$

24. (b) Total sales of Cannon printer in the year 2001, 2002 and 2005
$= 600 + 900 + 1100 = 2600$
Total sales of Cannon printer in all the years
$= 600 + 900 + 300 + 600 + 1100 + 1000 + 1100 = 5600$

$$\therefore \quad \text{Required \%} = \left(\frac{2600}{5600} \times 100\right)\%$$

$$= 46.42\% \approx 46\%$$

25. (e) Total sales of HP printer in all the years
$= 700 + 400 + 1200 + 1200 + 600 + 900 + 900 = 5900$
and total sales of Canon printer in all the year $= 5600$
$\therefore \quad$ Required % $= 5900 : 5600 = 59 : 56$

26. (a) The sale of HP Printer from the Previous year in

$$2003 = \left(\frac{1200-400}{400} \times 100\right)\%$$

$$= 200\% \text{ more}$$

$$2005 = \left(\frac{1200-600}{1200} \times 100\right)\%$$

$$= 50\% \text{ less}$$

$$2002 = \left(\frac{700-400}{700} \times 100\right)\%$$

$$= 42.85\% \text{ less}$$

$$2004 = \left(\frac{1200-1200}{1200} \times 100\right)\% = 0\%$$

$$\therefore \quad \text{Required answer is } 2003.$$

27. (d) The series is $\times 1 + 1 \times 7, \times 2 + 2 \times 6, \times 3 + 3 \times 5...$

28. (e) The series is $\times 1 + 1^2, \times 2 + 2^2, \times 3 + 3^2.., ...$

29. (c) The series is $\times 1 + 2, \times 2 + 3, \times 3 + 4, ...$

30. (b) The series is $\times 0.5 + 0.5, \times 1 + 1, + 1.5 + 1.5, ...$

31. (b) The series is $\times 2, \times 4, \times 6, ...$

32. (b) Interest earned in 1st half of a year

$$= 20,000 \times \frac{1}{2} \times \frac{20}{100} = 2000$$

Similarly,
During second half, interest earned $= 2200$
During second year, interest earned $= 4840$
(**Note :** Interest is calculated as compound)

33. (a) Required no. of ways $= {}^2P_2 \times {}^4P_4 = 48$

34. (a) 4×2 men $= 4 \times 4$ women $= 5 \times 4$ children
$\Rightarrow 2$ men $= 4$ women $= 5$ children
$\therefore 2$ men $+ 4$ women $+ 10$ children
$= 20$ children
$\therefore M_1 D_1 = M_2 D_2$
$\Rightarrow 5 \times 4 = 20 \times D_2 \Rightarrow D_2 = 1$ day

35. (d) Total Time $= 6$ hours
Speed of the boat in still water $= 4$ km/hr.
Let the distance between M and N be D.
and the speed of the stream be x.

$$D\left[\frac{1}{4+x} + \frac{1}{4-x}\right] = 6 \quad \text{or} \quad D\left[\frac{4-x+4+x}{(4+x)(4-x)}\right] = 6$$

$$D\left[\frac{8}{4^2-x^2}\right] = 6 \quad \text{or} \quad \frac{8D}{16-x^2} = 6$$

$$D = \frac{6}{8}\left(16-x^2\right) = \frac{3}{4}\left(16-x^2\right)$$

Since the speed of the stream (x) is not given, the distance D cannot be determined.

36. (b) Difference between cost of 1 kg apple and cost of 1 kg guava in 5 cities.
J $160 - 60 = 100$
D $130 - 90 = 40$
C $180 - 120 = 60$
H $90 - 30 = 60$
R $40 - 20 = 20$
$\therefore$ Cost is second lowest in Delhi.

37. (d) Cost of 1 kg guava in Jalandhar $= ₹ 60$
Cost of 2 kg grapes in chandigarh $= ₹ 90 \times 2 = ₹ 180$

$$\% = \frac{60}{180} \times 100 = 33.3 \approx 34\%$$

38. (c) Cost of 3 kgs apples for Ram $= 3 \times 130 = ₹ 390$
Cost of 2 kgs guavas for Ram $= 2 \times 90 = ₹ 180$
Total cost that Ram pay $= 390 + 180 = ₹ 570$

39. (a) Total cost of 45 kgs grapes from Hoshiarpur $= 45 \times 190$
$= ₹ 8550$

$$\text{After discount 4\% Ravinder paid} = 8550 - \frac{8550 \times 4}{100}$$

$$= ₹ 8208$$

40. (c) Cost of 1 kg apples from Ropar :
Cost of 1kg grapes from chandigarh
$40 : 90$
$4 : 9$ or $2^2 : 3^2$

41. (e) As (i) U > X (ii) T > U
         Hence T > X
         As R > T So R > X Ist follows
         As (i) W > T (ii) T > X
         Combining, we get W > X IInd follows.
42. (a) As (i) H > G (ii) G ≥ I
         Combining, we get H > I Ist follows.
         As (i) G ≥ I (ii) G > E
         Combining, we get E = I but E > I not possible.
43. (a) As (i) A > F (ii) F > C
         So A > C Ist follows
44. (c) As (i) P ≥ O (ii) O ≥ N
         So (i) P = N or (ii) P > N
         (i) P = N
         As (a) N = M (b) M ≥ L (c) L ≥ K
         Combining, we get
         (i) N = K   (ii) N > K
         If N = K then P = K IInd follow
         If N > K then P > K Ist follow
         (ii) Similarly if P > N
         then also both conclusion can be establish.
45. (b) As (i) K > F (ii) F > D
         So K > D IInd follow
         As (i) K > F (ii) G > F
         So K ≤ G can't be establish.

Solution (46 - 50)

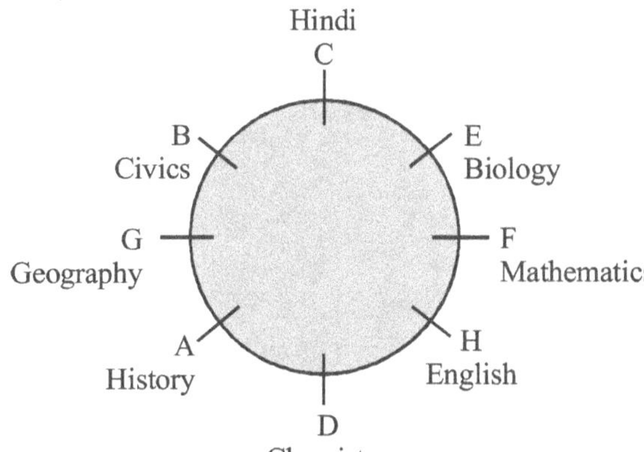

46. (d)   47. (e)   48. (a)   49. (d)   50. (c)

51. (c) Final position

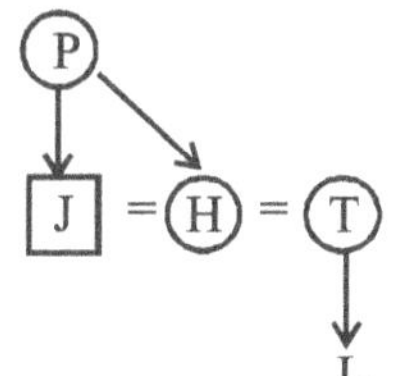

Distance between Starting and Final Positions = 3.5 + 6.5 = 10 km.

52. (a) J ÷ P % H × T % L can be represented in diagram. As follows.

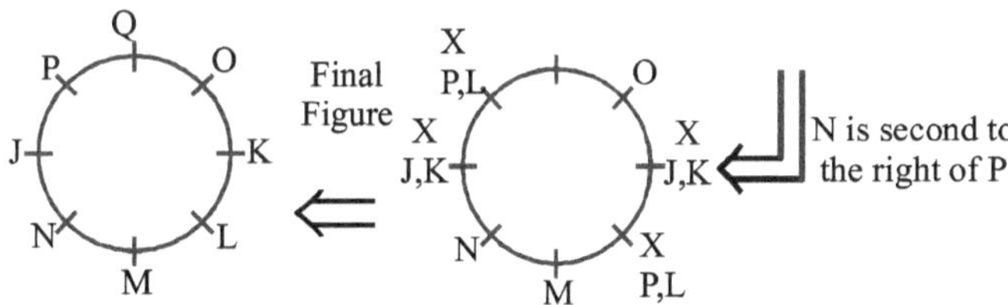

53. (b) L + R $ D + M × T

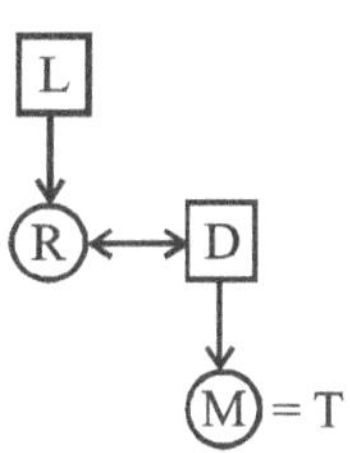

54. (b) I + T % J × L ÷ K

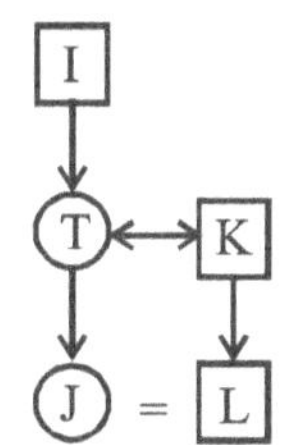

Solution (55-59)

Growth	→	mo
Ecomnoy	→	ti
of	→	ga
Indian	→	su
Trade	→	zo
Depends	→	ki
Heavy/on	→	ye/na
This	→	da
Year	→	ra
Condition	→	nic

55. (e)   56. (d)   57. (b)   58. (e)   59. (b)

Solution (60-64)

Formation of fig according to information given

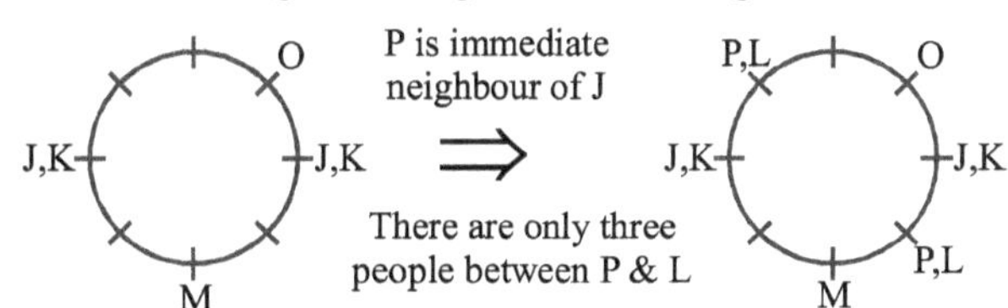

60. (b) N is immediate neighbour of J.
61. (a) 'K' is second to the left of 'Q' and 'M' is second to the left of 'K'.
62. (e) PQ, KL, MN, QO are in clockwise way and KO in anticlockwise way.
63. (c) Third to the left.
64. (b) Only two persons are sitting i.e. 'O' and 'Q'.

65. (d) 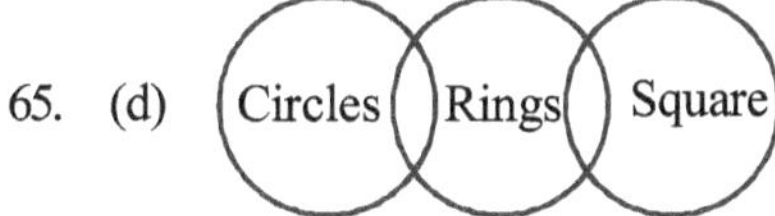

OR

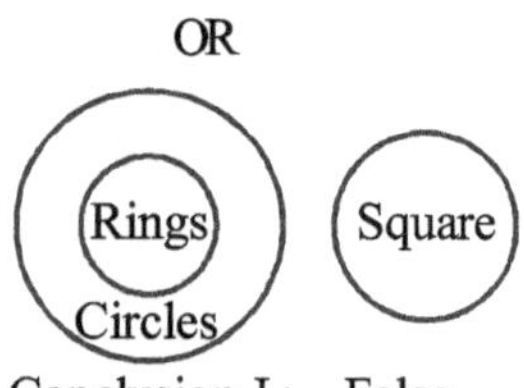

Conclusion-I :   False
Conclusion-II :   False

66. (e)

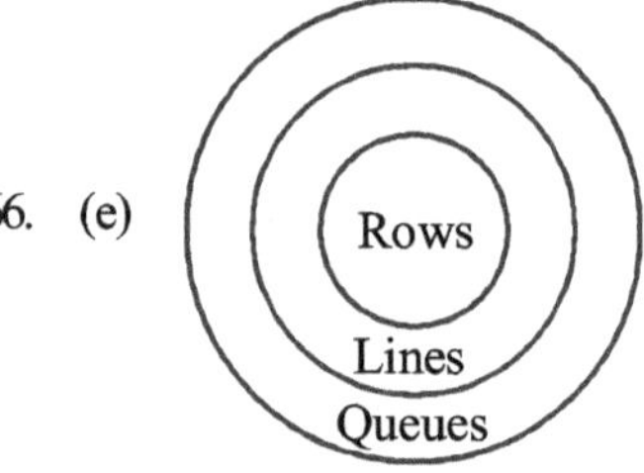

Conclusion-I :   True
Conclusion-II :   True

67. (a)

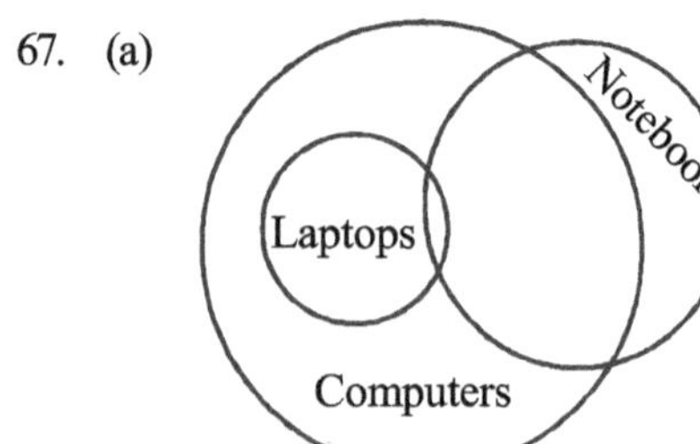

OR

Conclusion-I :   True
Conclusion-II :   False

68. (d)

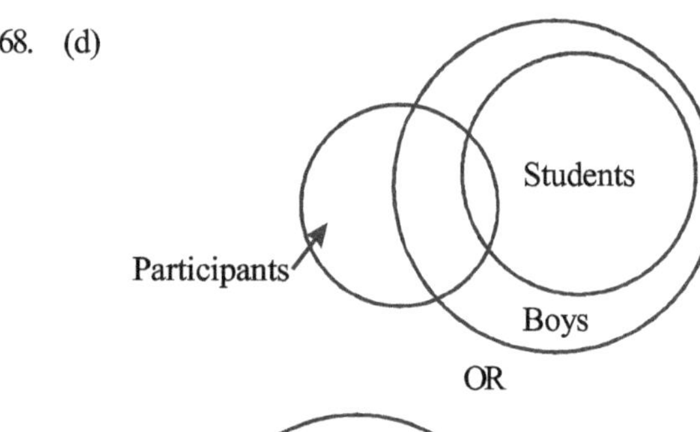

OR

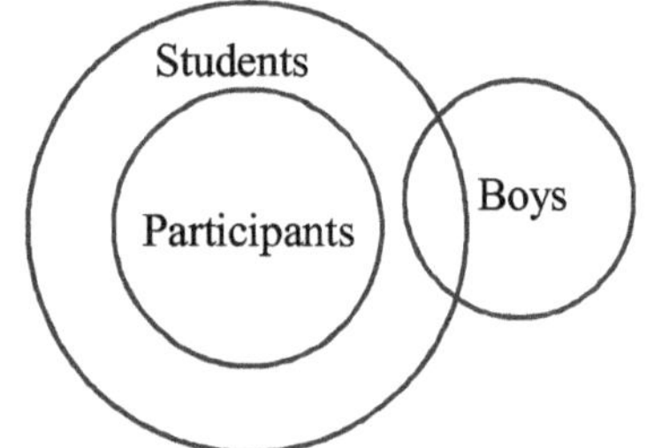

Conclusion-I   False
Conclusion-II   False

69. (a)

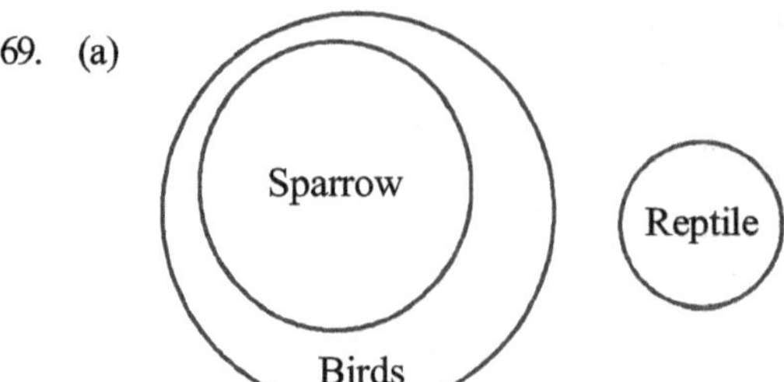

Conclusion-I   True
Conclusion-II   False

Solution : (70-74)

Professional	City	Profession
A	Bhubaneshwar	Pharmacist
B	Hyderabad	Professor
C	Mumbai	Artist
D	Bangalore	Engineer
E	Ahmedabad	Lawyer
F	Chennai	Doctor
G	Jaipur	Counsellor

70. (c)   71. (a)   72. (d)   73. (b)   74. (e)

75. (d)

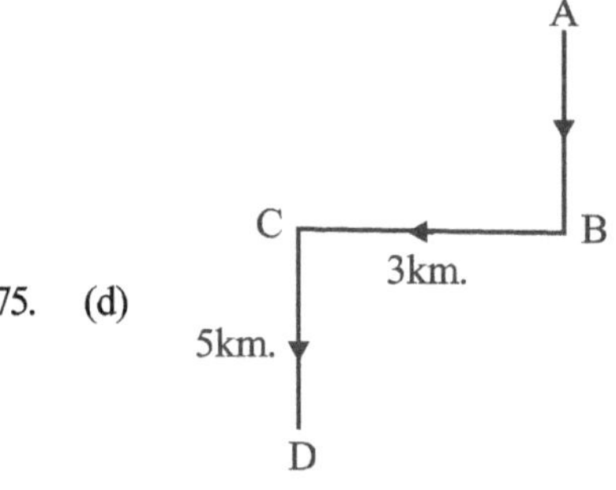

76. (b)   After arranging –

ITW, ABR ‖NRU‖ EFL OPT

77. (e) 78. (c)

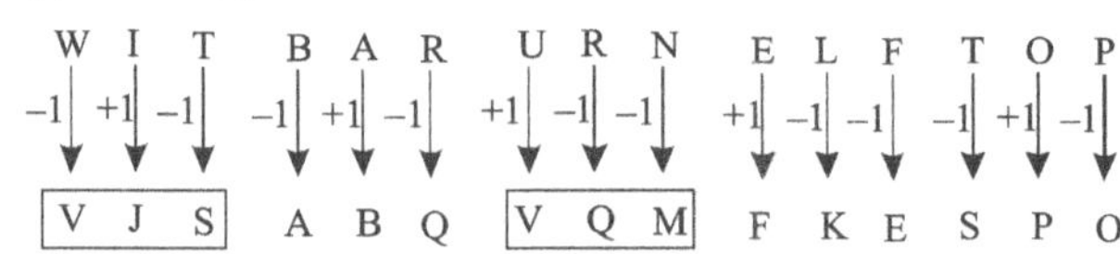

79. (a)

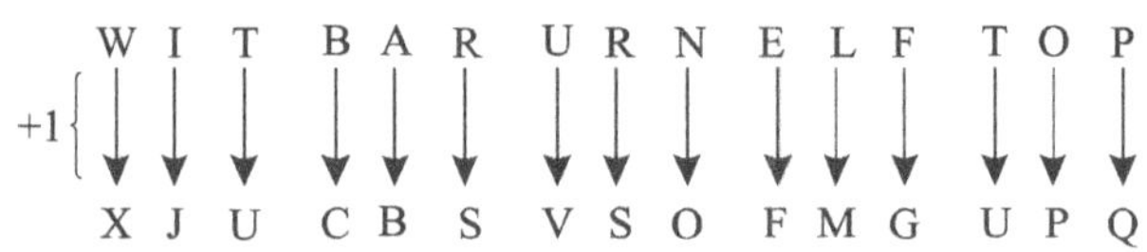

80. (c)   Dictionary oder is–

    1   2   3   4   5

BAR ELF TOP ‖URN‖ WIT

PRACTICE SET ⬤ 10

Time : 45 Min. **Max. Marks : 80**

QUANTITATIVE APTITUDE

DIRECTIONS (Qs. 1-5): What will come in place of the question mark (?) in the following questions ?

1. $40.83 \times 1.02 \times 1.2 = ?$
   - (a) 49.97592
   - (b) 41.64660
   - (c) 58.7952
   - (d) 42.479532
   - (e) None of these

2. $3\dfrac{1}{3} + 6\dfrac{3}{7} \times 1\dfrac{1}{2} \times \dfrac{22}{7} = ?$
   - (a) 4.4
   - (b) $\dfrac{22}{7}$
   - (c) $\dfrac{5}{22}$
   - (d) 40.5
   - (e) None of these

3. $3978 + 112 \times 2 = ? \div 2$
   - (a) 8400
   - (b) 8406
   - (c) 8600
   - (d) 8404
   - (e) None of these

4. $\left(10^{3.7} \times 10^{1.3}\right)^{2} = 10^{?}$
   - (a) 6
   - (b) 7
   - (c) 5
   - (d) 3
   - (e) None of these

5. $25.05 \times 123.95 + 388.999 \times 15.001 = ?$
   - (a) 900
   - (b) 8950
   - (c) 8935
   - (d) 8975
   - (e) 8995

DIRECTIONS (Qs. 6-10): In the following questions two equations numbered I and II are given. You have to solve both the equations and give answers.

If
- (a) $x > y$
- (b) $x \geq y$
- (c) $x < y$
- (d) $x \leq y$
- (e) $x = y$ or the relationship cannot be established

6.   I. $8x^2 - 3y = 38$
       II. $6y^2 + 34 = 39y$

7.   I. $7x^2 + 15x - 18 = 0$
       II. $2y^2 - 13y + 21 = 0$

8.   I. $3x^2 - 15x + 18 = 0$
       II. $y^2 + 13y = -42$

9.   I. $2x + 3y = 13$
       II. $4x + y = 6$

10. I. $x^2 = 529$
       II. $y^2 + 241 = 770$

DIRECTIONS (Qs. 11-15): Read the following pie-charts carefully and answer the given questions. Pie charts show the percentage of the total sales and expenses of five companies A, B, C, D and E.

Percentage of sales   Percentage of expenses

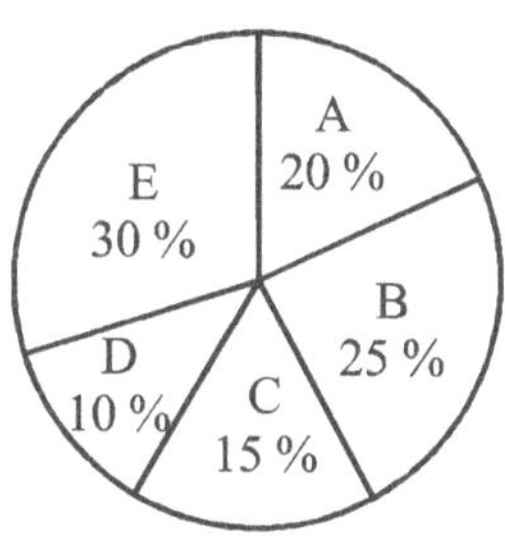

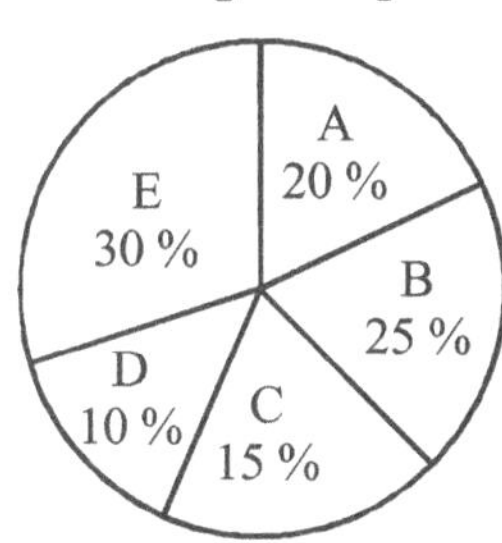

Note :-
(i) Profit = Sales - Expenses
(ii) Profit Percentage = (Profit/Expenses) × 100
(iii) No company made a loss

11. The ratio between expenses and profit is the heighest for which of the following company?
(a) A
(b) B
(c) C
(d) D
(e) None of these

12. If the overall profit percentage of all the five companies put together was 50% then how many company/companies had a profit percentage greater than 60%?
(a) None
(b) Two
(c) Four
(d) Three
(e) None of these

13. If the total sales were ₹ 800 lakh and the overall percentage of profit of all the five companies put together was 100%, then what was the expenses of company C?
(a) ₹ 60 lakh
(b) ₹ 68 lakh
(c) ₹ 80 lakh
(d) ₹ 88 lakh
(e) None of these

14. What is the **approx** least profit percentage of company D?
(a) 22%
(b) 33%
(c) 44%
(d) 25%
(e) None of these

15. If the total expenses were 594 lakh and overall percentage profit of all the five companies put together was 50%, then what was the sales of Company B?
(a) ₹ 222.75 lakh
(b) ₹ 230.75 lakh
(c) ₹ 323.5 lakh
(d) Can't be determined
(e) None of these

16. A boy was asked to write $2^5 \times 9^2$ but he wrote 2592. The numerical difference between the two is:
(a) 0
(b) 3
(c) 2
(d) 9
(e) None of these

17. A, B and C enter into a partnership with investments of ₹ 3500, ₹ 4500 and ₹ 5500, respectively. In the first six months, profit is ₹ 405. What is A's share in the profit ?
(a) ₹ 200
(b) ₹ 105
(c) ₹ 250
(d) ₹ 151
(e) None of these

18. Pipes A and B can fill a tank in 5 and 6 hours, respectively. Pipe C can empty it in 12 hours. The tank is half full. All the three pipes are in operation simultaneously. After how much time, the tank will be full ?

(a) $3\dfrac{9}{17}$ h
(b) 11 h

(c) $2\dfrac{8}{11}$ h
(d) $1\dfrac{13}{17}$ h

(e) None of these

19. A water tank in the form of a cuboid has its base 20 m long, 7 m wide and 10 m deep. Initially, the tank is full but later when water is taken out of it, the level of water in the tank reduces by 2 m. The volume of water left in the tank is :
(a) $1120 \, m^3$
(b) $400 \, m^3$
(c) $280 \, m^3$
(d) $140 \, m^3$
(e) None of these

20. The area of a circular plot is twice the area of a rectangular plot. If the area of the rectangular plot is 11088 sq. metres., what is the perimeter of the circular plot?
(a) 484 metres
(b) 572 metres
(c) 528 metres
(d) 440 metres
(e) None of these

21. The sum of the two digits of a two-digit number and the difference between the two digits of the two-digit number is 8. What is the two digit number?
(a) 80
(b) 88
(3) 44
(d) Cannot be determined
(e) None of these

22. The total number of students studying in a college is 4220. If the number of girls studying in the college is 2420, what is the respective ratio of the number of boys to the number of girls studying in the college?
(a) 90 : 131
(b) 90 : 121
(c) 121 : 70
(d) 121 : 80
(e) None of these

23. The cost of 14 kgs. of rice is ₹ 672, the cost of 12 kgs. of wheat is ₹ 432 and the cost of 18 kgs. of sugar is ₹ 504. What is the total cost of 20 kgs. of rice, 15 kgs. of wheat and 16 kgs. of sugar?
(a) ₹ 1,898
(b) ₹ 1,948
(c) ₹ 2,020
(d) ₹1,964
(e) None of these

24. If the length of a rectangular field is increased by 20% and the breadth is reduced by 20%, the area of the rectangle will be 192 m^2. What is the area of the original rectangle?
(a) $184 \, m^2$
(b) $196 \, m^2$
(c) $204 \, m^2$
(d) $225 \, m^2$
(e) None of these

25. Inside a square plot, a circular garden is developed which exactly fits in the square plot and the diameter of the garden is equal to the side of the square plot which is 28 metres. What is the area of the space left out in the square plot after developing the garden?
(a) $98 \, m^2$
(b) $146 \, m^2$
(c) $84 \, m^2$
(d) $168 \, m^2$
(e) None of these

DIRECTIONS (Qs. 26-30) : Find the next term in the given series in each of the questions below.

26. 41, 31, ?, 17, 11, 5
(a) 19
(b) 21
(c) 23
(d) 27
(e) None of these

27. 8, 15, 28, 53, ?
(a) 106
(b) 98
(c) 100
(d) 102
(e) None of these

28. 3, 732, 1244, 1587, 1803, 1928 ?
(a) 2144
(b) 1992
(c) 1955
(d) 2053
(e) None of these

29. 16, 24, ?, 210, 945, 5197.5, 33783.75
    (a) 40
    (b) 36
    (c) 58
    (d) 60
    (e) None of these
30. 2, 3, 10, 15, 26, ?, 55
    (a) 32
    (b) 33
    (c) 34
    (d) 35
    (e) None of these

DIRECTIONS (Qs. 31-35) : Study the following table carefully and answer the given questions.

Company	% of employees who like tea	Ratio of employees who like coffee Male : Female	Ratio of employees who like tea Male : Female
A	78	3 : 2	2 : 3
B	90	11 : 7	3 : 5
C	92	12 : 11	13 : 10
D	80	13 : 7	1 : 3
E	85	8 : 7	2 : 3
F	98	4 : 3	3 : 1

31. If the total number of female in company B who like coffee is 11,900, then what is the total employee in company B?
    (a) 3,10,900
    (b) 3,06,000
    (c) 2,06,000
    (d) 3,07,000
    (e) None of these
32. If the total number of employees in company C is 9200, then what is the difference between the total number of males who like coffee in company C and the total number of females who like tea in company C?
    (a) 4400
    (b) 3696
    (c) 3936
    (d) 3600
    (e) None of these
33. The total number of females who like tea is 10,125 in company B, then what is the difference between the total number of males who like coffee in company B and the total number of males who like tea in company B?
    (a) 4895
    (b) 4925
    (c) 4975
    (d) 4750
    (e) None of these
34. In company A and company F, the total male employees who like coffee is 66,000 and 42,000 respectively, then what is the ratio between employees in both the companies?
    (a) 21 : 163
    (b) 24 : 147
    (c) 20 : 149
    (d) 20 : 147
    (e) None of these
35. The total employees of company D is 15,000. If the total number of employees who like coffee decreases by 5% next year, then what will be the total employees of those who like coffee in company D next year?
    (a) 3600
    (b) 4600
    (c) 2450
    (d) 3000
    (e) None of these

DIRECTIONS (Qs. 36-40): Study the following table and answer the questions given below.

Export of electronic goods from India (in ₹Crore)

Year	Total Exports	Electronic Goods
2011	5,143	552
2012	5,404	624
2013	5,426	717
2014	5,999	653

36. **Approximately** what percent of the total exports were electronic goods in 2013?
    (a) 13%
    (b) 19%
    (c) 21%
    (d) 23%
    (e) None of these
37. The fall in electronic goods exports in 2014 from 2013 was **nearly**
    (a) 20%
    (b) 15%
    (c) 9%
    (d) 12%
    (e) 16%
38. If the electronic goods are not exported in the year 2012, then what are the total exports of that year?
    (a) 4770
    (b) 4780
    (c) 4790
    (d) 4760
    (e) None of these
39. Percentage growth of electronic goods exports in the period of 2012 to 2013 exceeded the percentage growth of the total exports over the same period **approximately** by
    (a) 3.5
    (b) 12.5
    (c) 15.5
    (d) 11.5
    (e) 14.5
40. Over the 4-year period from 2011 to 2014, the electronic exports rose by **nearly**
    (a) 16.3%
    (b) 15.3%
    (c) 14.3%
    (d) 18.3%
    (e) 20.3%

REASONING ABILITY

DIRECTIONS (Qs. 41-45) : In each question below are two/three statements followed by two conclusions numbered I and II. You have to take the two/three given statements to be true even if they seem to be at variance from commonly known facts and then decide which of the given conclusions logically follows from the given statements disregarding commonly known facts.

Give answer (a) if **only** conclusion I follows.
Give answer (b) if **only** conclusion II follows.
Give answer (c) if **either** conclusion I or conclusion II follows.
Give answer (d) if **neither** conclusion I nor conclusion II follows.
Give answer (e) if **both** conclusion I and conclusion II follow.

41. **Statements** : All kites are birds. All aeroplanes are kites. No bird is a fish.
    Conclusions : I. No fish is a kite.
    II. All aeroplanes are birds.

42. **Statements** : Some wires are fires. All fires are tyres.
    Conclusions : I. Atleast some tyres are wires.
    II. Some fires are definitely not wires.

43. **Statements** : No clip is a pin. All badges are pins.
    Conclusions : I. No badge is a clip.
    II. All pins are badges.

44. **Statements** : No colour is a paint. No paint is a brush.
    Conclusions : I. No colour is a brush.
    II. All brushes are colours.

45. **Statements** : All stars are planets. All planets are galaxies.
    Conclusions : I. All galaxies are planets.
    II. All starts are galaxies.

DIRECTIONS (Qs. 46-50) : Study the following arrangement carefully and answer the questions given below :

B U B D C E D B D E U B **A D C B E** A C D A E
B A U A C D B C A C

46. How many such pairs of alphabets are there in the series of alphabets given in BOLD (A to E) in the above arrangement each of which has as many letters between them (in both forward and backward directions) as they have between them in the English alphabetical series ?
    (a) None (b) One
    (c) Two (d) Three
    (e) More than three

47. Which of the following is the eighth to the left of the twentieth from the left end of the above arrangement ?
    (a) C (b) E
    (c) U (d) B
    (e) A

48. How many meaningful words can be formed with the alphabets which are first, second, fifth and sixth from the left end of the above arrangement ?
    (a) None (b) One
    (c) Two (d) Three
    (e) More than three

49. How many such consonants are there in the above arrangement each of which is immediately preceded by a vowel and also immediately followed by a consonant ?
    (a) One (b) Two
    (c) Three (d) Four
    (e) More than Four

50. If all A are dropped from the above arrangement, which of the following will be eleventh from the right end of the above arrangement ?
    (a) E (b) C
    (c) D (d) U
    (e) None of these

DIRECTIONS (Qs. 51-55) : Study the following information to answer the given questions :

Eight people are sitting in two parallel rows containing four people each, in such a way that there is an equal distance between adjacent persons. In row-1 P, Q, R and S are seated (but not necessarily in the same order) and all of them are facing south. In row-2 A, B, C and D are seated (but not necessarily in the same order) and all of them are facing north. Therefore, in the given seating arrangement each member seated in a row faces another member of the other row.

R sits second to the right of P. A is an immediate neighbour of the person who faces R. Q sits second to left of the person who faces A. Only one person sits between B and C. C does not face P. C does not sit at any of the extreme ends of the line.

51. Four of the following five are alike in a certain way based on the given seating arrangement and thus form a group. Which is the one that does not belong to that group ?
    (a) A (b) P
    (c) R (d) B
    (e) S

52. Who amongst the following faces B ?
    (a) P (b) Q
    (c) R (d) S
    (e) Cannot be determined

53. Which of the following is true regarding S ?
    (a) S sits exactly between R and P
    (b) S sits second to left of Q
    (c) P is an immediate neighbour of S
    (d) D is an immediate neighbour of the person who faces S
    (e) None is true

54. Who amongst the following faces Q ?
    (a) A (b) B
    (c) C (d) D
    (e) Cannot be determined

55. Who amongst the following faces the person who sits exactly between B and C ?
    (a) P (b) Q
    (c) R (d) S
    (e) Cannot be determined

DIRECTIONS (Qs. 56-60): In each question below is given a group of letters followed by four combinations of digits/symbols numbered (a), (b), (c) and (d). You have to find out which of the combinations correctly represents the group of letters based on the coding system and the conditions given below and mark the number of that combination as your answer. If none of the combinations correctly represents the group of letters, mark (e) i.e. 'None of these' as your answer.

Letters	P	M	A	E	J	K	D	R	W	H	I	U	T	F
Digits/symbols Conditions	4	$	1	2	3	#	5	@	©	6	%	δ	7	9

(i) If the first letter is a consonant and the last letter is a vowel, the codes of both these are to be interchanged.

(ii) If both the first and the last letters are consonants both these are to be coded as per the code of the last letter.

(iii) If the first letter is vowel and the last letter is a consonant both these are to be coded as '★'
    Note: All the remaining letters are to be coded as per their original codes.

56. ERWHKA
    (a) 2@©6#1 (b) 1@©6#2
    (c) 1@©6#I (d) 2@©6#2
    (e) None of these

57. MPEKDU
- (a) $42#5δ
- (b) $42#5$
- (c) δ42#5δ
- (d) δ425#$
- (e) None of these

58. TMEIUF
- (a) 7$2%δ9
- (b) 7$2%δ7
- (c) 9$2%δ7
- (d) 9$2%δ9
- (e) None of these

59. JTAERI
- (a) % 712@3
- (b) 3712@3
- (c) 712@
- (d) %712@%
- (e) None of these

60. UKTMIH
- (a) #7$%6
- (b) 6#7$%δ
- (c) ★#7$%★
- (d) 7#$%6
- (e) None of these

61. Rasik walked 20 m towards north. Then he turned right and walks 30 m. Then he turns right and walks 35 m. Then he turns left and walks 15 m. Finally he turns left and walks 15 m. In which direction and how many metres is he from the starting position?
- (a) 15 m West
- (b) 30 m East
- (c) 30 m West
- (d) 45 m East
- (e) None of these

62. Sanmitra walks 4 kms. Towards north, turns right and walks 5 k.m. Then he turns towards south and walks 2 k.m. Again he takes a turn towards west walks 3 km and stops for a while. Then he further walks 2 km. What is the distance of Sanmitra from starting point ?
- (a) 16 k.m.
- (b) 2 k.m.
- (c) 4 k.m.
- (d) 3 k.m.
- (e) None of these

63. Pointing to a photograph of a boy Suresh said, "He is the son of the only son of my mother." How is Suresh related to that boy?
- (a) Brother
- (b) Uncle
- (c) Cousin
- (d) Father
- (e) None of these

64. If A + B means A is the mother of B; A - B means A is the brother B; A % B means A is the father of B and A × B means A is the sister of B, which of the following shows that P is the maternal uncle of Q?
- (a) Q – N + M × P
- (b) P + S × N – Q
- (c) P – M + N × Q
- (d) Q – S % P
- (e) None of these

65. A class of boys stands in a single line. One boy is nineteenth in order from both the ends. How many boys are there in the class?
- (a) 27
- (b) 37
- (c) 38
- (d) 39
- (e) None of these

DIRECTIONS (Qs. 66-70): Study the following information carefully and answer the given questions.

Eight colleagues, A, B, C, D, E, F, G and H, are sitting around a circular table facing the centre but not necessarily in the same order. Each one of them holds a different post–Manager, Company Secretary, Chairman, President, Vice President, Group Leader, Financial Advisor and Managing Director.

A sits third to the right of the Managing Director. Only two people sit between the Managing Director and H. The Vice President and the Company Secretary are immediate neighbours. Neither A nor H is a Vice President or a Company Secretary. The Vice President is not an immediate neighbour of the Managing Director. The Manager sits second to the left of E. E is not an immediate neighbour of H. The Manager is an immediate neighbour of both the Group Leader and the Financial Advisor. The Financial Advisor sits third to the -right of B. B is not the Vice President. C sits on the immediate right of the Chairman. A is not the Chairman. F is not an immediate neighbour of A. G is not an immediate neighbour of the Manager.

66. Who amongst the following sits third to the left of E?
- (a) Manager
- (b) G
- (c) A
- (d) Financial Advisor
- (e) B

67. Four of the following five are alike in a certain way based on the given arrangement and thus form a group. Which is the one that does not belong to that group?
- (a) F-Chairman
- (b) G-President
- (c) D-Manager
- (d) A-Financial Advisor
- (e) H-Managing Director

68. Who among the following is the President of the company?
- (a) A
- (b) C
- (c) H
- (d) G
- (e) D

69. Which of the following is true with respect to the given seating arrangement?
- (a) The Group Leader of the company is an immediate neighbour of the Vice President.
- (b) G sits second to the right of D.
- (c) The Group Leader and the Company Secretary are immediate neighbours.
- (d) The Chairman of the company sits to the immediate left of the Managing Director.
- (e) The Group Leader sits second to the left of D.

70. Which of the following posts does B hold in the company?
- (a) Chairman
- (b) Manager
- (c) Company Secretary
- (d) Vice President
- (e) Financial Advisor

DIRECTIONS (Qs. 71-75) : In the following questions, the symbols δ, %, $, # and @ are used with the following meaning as illustrated below:

'P $ Q' means 'P is not smaller than Q'.

'P @ Q' means 'P is not greater than Q'.

'P δ Q' means 'P is neither smaller than nor equal to Q'.

'P # Q' means 'P is neither greater than nor equal to Q'.

'P % Q' means 'P is neither smaller than nor greater than Q'.

Now in each of the following questions assuming the given statements to be true, find which of the two conclusions I and II given below them is/are **definitely true**?

Give answer
- (a) if only Conclusion I is true.
- (b) if only Conclusion II is true.
- (c) if either Conclusion I or II is true.
- (d) if neither Conclusion I nor II is true.
- (e) if both Conclusions I and II are true.

71. Statements: F @ N, N δ R, H @ R

    Conclusions:
    I. H δ N

    II. F # R

72. **Statements:** M # T, T @ K, K $ N
     Conclusions: I. M # N
                       II. K δ M
73. **Statements:** T % H, H $ W
     Conclusions: I. W # T
                       II. W % T
74. **Statements:** N δ K, K # D, D % M
     Conclusions: I. M δ K
                       II. D δ N
75. **Statements:** J $ B, B % R, R δ F
     Conclusions: I. F # B
                       II. R @ J

DIRECTIONS (Qs. 76-80) : Read the following information carefully and answer the questions following it.

Twelve persons are going for different movies. The persons are A, B, C, D, E, F, P, Q, R, S, T and U. The movies are the mask, Ironman, Superman, Avengers, Dark night rises and Unbreakable. There are some different colours. viz. blue, green, yellow, beige, pink and white. Each movie and each colour is liked by only two persons. A, B, Q, R, T and U are the only males in the group. Females' like the movie which names starts with consonant whereas males' like the movie which names starts with vowel. A and B likes same movie. C is not going with D. E does not like Unbreakable and likes yellow colour. The persons going for Ironman and Avengers does not like blue colour. The pink colour is liked by the person going to watch the movie name starts with consonant but it is not Superman. F likes Dark night rises and going with D. P's partner is not S. The person likes blue colour is going for movie which names starts with Vowel. R likes green colour whereas D likes white colour. S does not going to watch Superman. T's favorite colour is blue. the person who is going for Ironman does not like Green colour.

76. Who among the following is like pink colour?
     (a) E and S   (b) C and S
     (c) P and C   (d) Data inadequate
     (e) None of these

77. Who among the following are going to watch Superman?
     (a) P and C   (b) P and E
     (c) C and E   (d) Data inadequate
     (e) None of these

78. Which Movie watched by A and B?
     (a) Ironman   (b) Avengers
     (c) Unbreakable   (d) Data inadequate
     (e) None of these

79. Which of the following statements is/are definitely true?
     I.   U is the partner of T.
     II.   Q is the partner of T.
     III. R is the partner of Q.
     IV.   U is the partner of R.
     (a) Only I   (b) Only II
     (c) Only III   (d) Both I and III
     (e) None

80. Which of the following statements is/are definitely false?
     I.   A and B are likes Yellow colour.
     II.   Q is likes either blue or green colour.
     III. C is likes pink colour. IV. U is going to watch Ironman.
     (a) None   (b) Only IV
     (c) Only I and IV   (d) Only II and IV
     (e) All are true

HINTS & EXPLANATIONS

1. (a) $? = 40.83 \times 1.02 \times 1.2 = 49.97592$

2. (e) $? = 3\dfrac{1}{3} + 6\dfrac{3}{7} \times 1\dfrac{1}{2} \times \dfrac{22}{7}$

$= \dfrac{10}{3} + \dfrac{45}{7} \times \dfrac{3}{2} \times \dfrac{22}{7} = 2.44$

3. (d) $3978 + 112 \times 2 = ? \div 2$

$\therefore ? = (3978 + 224) \times 2 = 8404$

4. (e) $\left(10^{3.7} \times 10^{1.3}\right)^2 = 10^?$

$\Rightarrow \left(10^{3.7+1.3}\right)^2 = 10^? \quad [\because a^b \times a^c = a^{b+c}]$

$\therefore 10^? = \left(10^5\right)^2 = 10^{5\times2} \quad \left[\because \left(a^b\right)^c = a^{bc}\right] = 10^{10}$

5. (c) $25 \times 124 + 389 \times 15 = 3100 + 5835 = 8935$

6. (e) I. $8x^2 - 3y = 38$

$\Rightarrow 8x^2 - 3y - 38 = 0$

$\Rightarrow 8x^2 + 16x - 19x - 38 = 0$

$\Rightarrow 8x(x+2) - 19(x+2) = 0$

$\Rightarrow (8x - 19)(x+2) = 0$

$\Rightarrow x = \dfrac{19}{8}, -2$

II. $6y^2 + 34 = 29y$

$\Rightarrow 6y^2 - 29y + 34 = 0$

$\Rightarrow 6y^2 - 12y - 17y + 34 = 0$

$\Rightarrow 6y(y-2) - 17(y-2) = 0$

$\Rightarrow (6y - 17)(y-2) = 0$

$\Rightarrow y = \dfrac{17}{6}, 2$

$\therefore$ x = y or relationship is not established.

7. (c) I. $7x^2 + 15x - 18 = 0$

$\Rightarrow 7x^2 + 21x - 6x - 18 = 0$

$\Rightarrow 7x(x+3) - 6(x+3) = 0$

$\Rightarrow (7x - 6)(x+3) = 0$

$\Rightarrow x = \dfrac{6}{7}, -3$

II. $2y^2 - 13y + 21 = 0$

$\Rightarrow 2y^2 - 6y - 7y + 21 = 0$

$\Rightarrow 2y(y-3) - 7(y-3) = 0$

$\Rightarrow (2y - 7)(y-3) = 0$

$\Rightarrow y = \dfrac{7}{2}, 3$

Clearly, x < y

8. (a) I. $3x^2 - 15x + 18 = 0$

$\Rightarrow x^2 - 5x + 6 = 0$

$\Rightarrow x^2 - 2x - 3x + 6 = 0$

$\Rightarrow x(x-2) - 3(x-2) = 0$

$\Rightarrow (x-3)(x-2) = 0$

$\Rightarrow x = 3, 2$

II. $y^2 + 13y = -42$

$\Rightarrow y^2 + 13y + 42 = 0$

$\Rightarrow y^2 + 7y + 6y + 42 = 0$

$\Rightarrow y(y+7) + 6y(y+7) = 0$

$\Rightarrow (y+6)(y+7) = 0$

$\Rightarrow y = -6, -7$

Clearly, x > y

9. (c) $2x + 3y = 13 \qquad ....(i)$

$4x + y = 6 \qquad ....(ii)$

Now, equation (i) × 2 – equation (ii),

$\Rightarrow 4x + 6y - 4x - y = 26 - 6$

$\Rightarrow 5y = 20 \qquad \Rightarrow y = 4$

Put the value of y in equation (ii),

$4x + 4 = 6$

$\Rightarrow 4x = 2$

$\Rightarrow x = \dfrac{1}{2}$

clearly, x < y

10. (e) I. $x^2 = 529$

$\Rightarrow x = +23, -23$

II. $y^2 + 241 = 770$

$\Rightarrow y^2 = 770 - 241$

$\Rightarrow y^2 = 529$

$\Rightarrow y = +23, -23$

$\therefore$ x = y or relationship is not established.

11. (d) Let the total sales be 100x and total expenses by 100y

Then, profit of A = 20x – 10y.

B = 25x – 20y

C = 15x – 22y

D = 10x – 18y

E = 30x – 30y

Ratio of profit to expenses:

$A = \dfrac{20x - 10y}{10y} = \dfrac{20x}{10y} - 1$

$B = \dfrac{25x}{20y} - 1$

$C = \dfrac{15x}{22y} - 1$

$$D = \frac{10x}{18y} - 1$$

$$E = \frac{30x}{30y} - 1$$

The ratio of profit to expense will be least for D. So, the ratio of expense to profit will be the highest for D.

12. **(b)** Let the total sales be 100x and total expenses be 100y. According to the question.

$$\frac{100x - 100y}{100y} \times 100 = 50$$

$$\Rightarrow \quad \frac{(x - y)}{y} = \frac{1}{2}$$

$$\Rightarrow \quad 2x - 2y = y$$

$$\Rightarrow \quad 2x = 3y$$

$$\therefore \quad x = \frac{3}{2}y$$

Now, profit for :

$$A = 20 \times \frac{3}{2}y - 10y = 20y$$

$$B = 25 \times \frac{3}{2}y - 20y = \frac{35}{2}y$$

$$C = 15 \times \frac{3}{2}y - 22y = \frac{3}{2}y$$

$$D = 10 \times \frac{3}{2}y - 18y = -3y$$

$$E = 30 \times \frac{3}{2}y - 30y = 15y$$

Profit Percentage:

$$A = \left(\frac{20y}{10y} \times 100\right)\% = 200\%$$

$$B = \left(\frac{35y}{2 \times 20y} \times 100\right)\% = 87.5\%$$

$$C = \left(\frac{3y}{2 \times 22y} \times 100\right)\% = 6.81\%$$

$$D = \left(\frac{-3y}{18y} \times 100\right)\% = -16\frac{3}{3}\%$$

$$E = \left(\frac{15y}{30y} \times 100\right)\% = -50\%$$

Hence, only two companies have more than 60% profit.

13. **(d)** Total sales = 800 lakh

Let total expenses be E

Now, profit % = (profit/Expenses) × 100

$$\Rightarrow \quad 100 = \frac{800 - E}{E} \times 100$$

$$\Rightarrow \quad E = \text{Rs. } 400 \text{ lakh}$$

$$\therefore \quad \text{Expenses of company C} = \frac{400 \times 22}{100}$$

$$= ₹ 88 \text{ Lakh}$$

14. **(c)** Given that no company made a loss.

$$\therefore \quad \text{Value of sales} \geq \text{Value of expenses}$$

$$\therefore \quad \frac{\text{Sale}}{\text{Expenses}} \geq 1$$

Now, for company D, 10% of sales ≥ 18%

$$\therefore \quad \text{Least profit \%} = \left(\frac{8}{18} \times 100\right)\% = 44.44\% \approx 44\%$$

15. **(a)** Total sales of all companies together

$$\frac{594 \times 150}{100} = 891 \text{ lakh}$$

$$\therefore \quad \text{sales of company B} = \frac{891 \times 25}{100} = 222.75 \text{ lakh}$$

16. **(a)** $2^5 \times 9^2 = 32 \times 81 = 2592$.

$$\therefore \text{ Difference} = 2^5 \times 9^2 - 2592$$

$$= 2592 - 2592 = 0$$

Hence, the numerical difference is 0.

17. **(b)** Ratio of investment

$$= 3500 : 4500 : 5500 = 35 : 45 : 55 = 7 : 9 : 11$$

Since, Ratio of investment is same as ratio of profit.

$$\therefore \quad \text{Ratio of profit} = 7 : 9 : 11$$

Now, profit = ₹ 405

$$\therefore \quad \text{A's share} = \frac{7}{27} \times 405 = ₹ 105$$

18. **(d)** Part of the tank filled by the three pipes working simultaneously in one hour is $= \frac{1}{5} + \frac{1}{6} - \frac{1}{12} = \frac{17}{60}$

i.e. it takes $\frac{60}{17}$ hours to fill up the tank completely.

Now, $\frac{1}{2}$ of the tank is filled with all the pipes open, simultaneously together in $\frac{60}{17} \times \frac{1}{2} = 1\frac{13}{17}$ hours

19. **(a)** Volume of water left in the tank $= \ell \times b \times h$

$$= 20 \times 7 \times (10 - 2) = 1120 \text{ m}^3$$

20. **(c)** $\pi r^2 = 2 \times 11088$

$$\Rightarrow \quad \frac{22}{7} \times r^2 = 2 \times 11088$$

$$\Rightarrow \quad r^2 = \frac{2 \times 11088 \times 7}{22} = 7056$$

$$\therefore \quad r = \sqrt{7056} = 84 \text{ metre}$$

$$\therefore \quad \text{Circumference} = 2\pi r = 2 \times \frac{22}{7} \times 84 = 528 \text{ metre}$$

21. (a) $x + y = 8$

$$\frac{x - y = 8}{2x = 16}$$

$\Rightarrow \quad x = 8$

$\therefore \quad y = 0$

$\therefore \quad$ Two digit number $= 80$

22. (b) Required ratio
$= (4220 - 2420) : 2420$
$= 1800 : 2420$
$= 90 : 121$

23. (b) C.P. of 20 kg of rice

$$= ₹ \left(\frac{672}{14} \times 20 \right)$$

$$= ₹ 960$$

C.P. of 15 kg of wheat

$$= ₹ \left(\frac{432}{12} \times 15 \right)$$

$$= ₹ 540$$

C.P. of 16 kg of sugar

$$= ₹ \left(\frac{504}{18} \times 16 \right)$$

$$= ₹ 448$$

$\therefore \quad$ Total cost price
$= ₹ (960 + 540 + 448)$
$= ₹ 1948$

24. (e) Let the length and breadth of the original rectangle be 'L' m and 'B' m respectively.
After increasing the length by 20% and decreasing the breadth by 20% area is 192.
$(1.2 \, L) \times (0.8 \, B) = 192$
or $0.96 \, LB = 192$
$LB = 200$

25. (d) 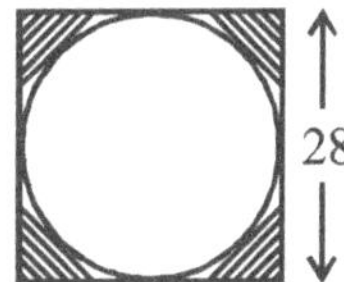

We have to calculate the area of the shaded region which is equal to area of square – Area of the circle

$$\text{Required answer} = (28)^2 - \frac{22}{7} \times 14 \times 14$$

$$= 784 - 616 = 168 \, \text{m}^2$$

26. (c) This is a series of prime number

27. (d) Let x = 8
then $15 = 2x - 1 = y$
$28 = 2y - 2 = z$
$53 = 2z - 3 = m$
Next term in the pattern should be $2m - 4 = 2 \times 53 - 4$
$$= 102$$

28. (b) The pattern of number series is:
$732 - 3 = 729 = 9^3$
$1244 - 732 = 512 = 8^3$
$1587 - 1244 = 343 = 7^3$
$1803 - 1587 = 216 = 6^3$
$1928 - 1803 = 125 = 5^3$
$\therefore \quad ? = 1928 + 4^3 = 1928 + 64 = \textbf{1992}$.

29. (d) The pattern of the number series is:
$16 \times 1.5 = 24$
$24 \times 2.5 = 60$
$60 \times 3.5 = 210$
$210 \times 4.5 = 945$

30. (d) The series exhibits the pattern of $n^2 + 1$, $n^2 - 1$, alternatively, n taking values 1, 2.............

31. (b) Total no. of employess in company B who like coffee

$$= \frac{11900}{7} \times 18 = 30, 600$$

$\therefore \quad$ Total no. of employees in company B

$$= \frac{30600}{10} \times 100 = 3, 06, 000$$

32. (a) Total no. of males in company C who like coffee

$$= 9200 \times \frac{8}{100} \times \frac{12}{23} = 384$$

Total no. of female in company C who like tea

$$9200 \times \frac{92}{100} \times \frac{13}{23} = 4784$$

$\therefore \quad$ Required difference $= 4784 - 384 = 4400$

33. (c) Total of employees in company B who like tea

$$= \frac{10125}{5} \times 8 = 16200$$

Total no. of males in company B who like coffee

$$= \frac{16200}{90} \times 10 \times \frac{11}{18} = 1100$$

and the total no. of male in company B who like tea
$= 16200 - 10125 = 6075$

$\therefore \quad$ Required difference $= 6075 - 1100 = 4975$

34. (d) Total no. of employees in company A

$$\frac{66000}{3} \times 5 \times \frac{100}{22} = 5, 00, 000$$

Total no. of employees in company F

$$\frac{42000}{4} \times 7 \times \frac{100}{2} = 36,75,000$$

$\therefore$ Required ratio $= 500000 : 3675000 = 20 : 147$.

35. (e) Total no. of employees in company D who like coffee

$$15000 \times \frac{20}{100} = 3000$$

$\therefore$ Total no. of employees in company D who like coffee

the next $3000 \times \dfrac{95}{100} = 2850$

36. (a) $\therefore$ Required % $= \dfrac{717}{5426} \times 100 = 13.21$

$\approx 13\%$ (Approx)

37. (c) Percentage fall in electronic goods exports in 2014 from 2013

$$= \frac{(717 - 653)}{717} \times 100 = 8.92\% \approx 9\%$$

38. (b) Required total exports of the year 2012
$= 5404 - 624 = 4780$

39. (e) Percentage growth of electronic goods exports in the period of 2012 to 2013

$$= \frac{717 - 624}{624} \times 100 = 14.90\%$$

$\Rightarrow$ % growth of total exports over the same period

$$= \frac{5426 - 5404}{5404} \times 100 = 0.40\%$$

$\therefore$ Difference $= 14.90 - 0.40$
$= 14.50\%$

40. (d) From 2011 to 2014, % rise in electronic exports

$$= \frac{(653 - 552)}{552} \times 100 = 18.29\%$$

$\approx 18.3\%$

41. (e)

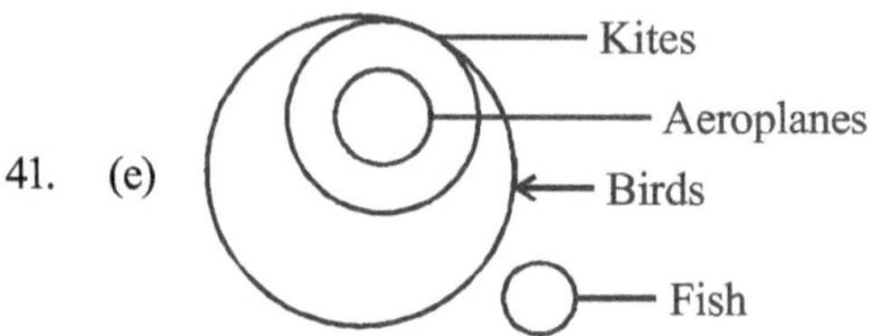

42. (a)

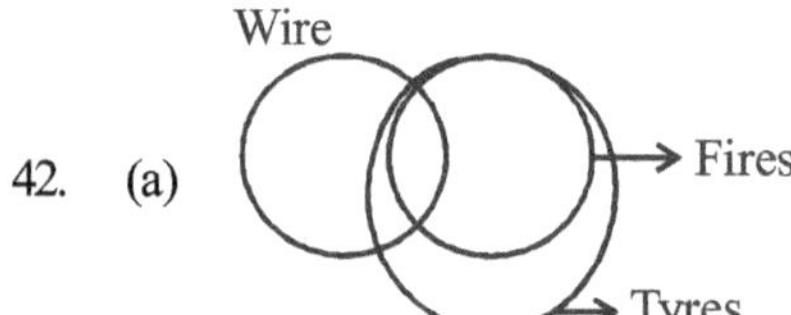

43. (a)

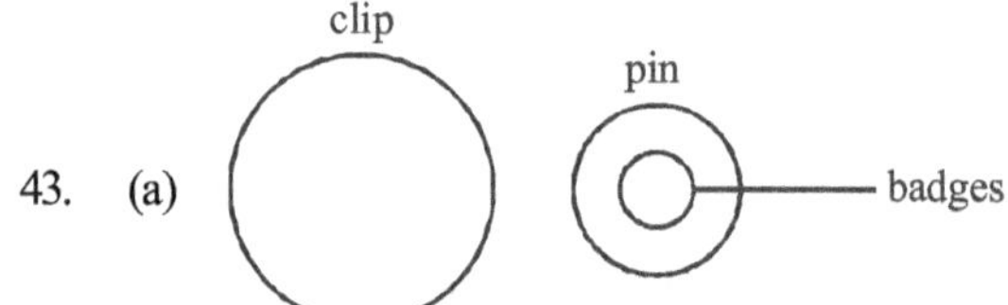

44. (c)

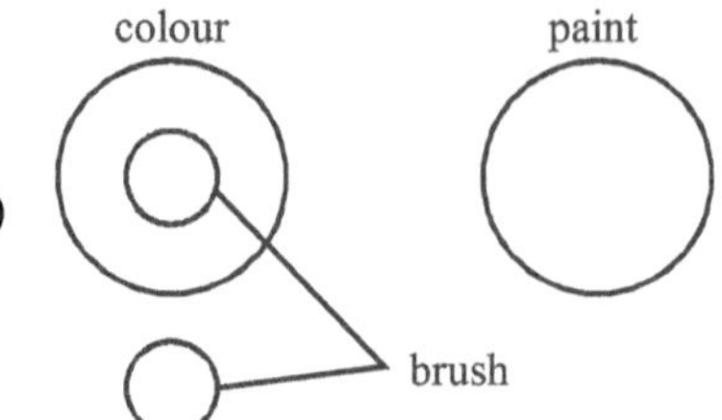

45. (b)

46. (e)

47. (d) The given arrangement is:

8th to the left of 20th

B U B D C E D B D E U (B) A D

C B E A C (D) A E B A U A C D

B C A C

20th from the left

48. (b) B U C E / CUBE

49. (e) U B D / E D B / A D C / A C D / A C D

50. (a) E

51-55.

S R   Q   P

A   C   D   B

51. (c) **52. (a)** **53. (e)** **54. (d)** **55. (b)**

56. (a)

Letter series	E	R	W	H	K	A
Code	2	@	©	6	#	1
without condition	2	@	©	6	#	1

57. (e) Letter series

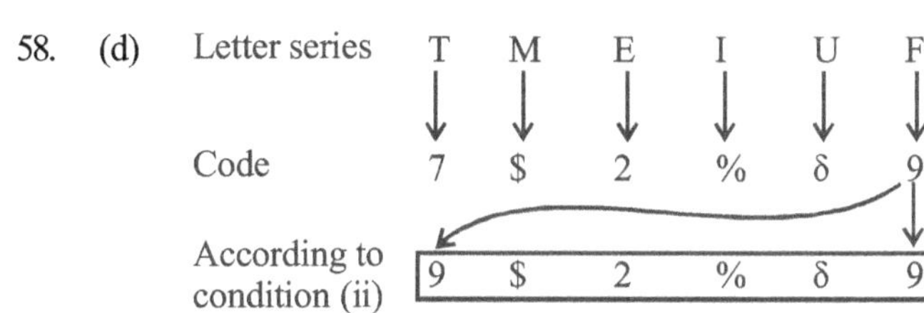

58. (d) Letter series

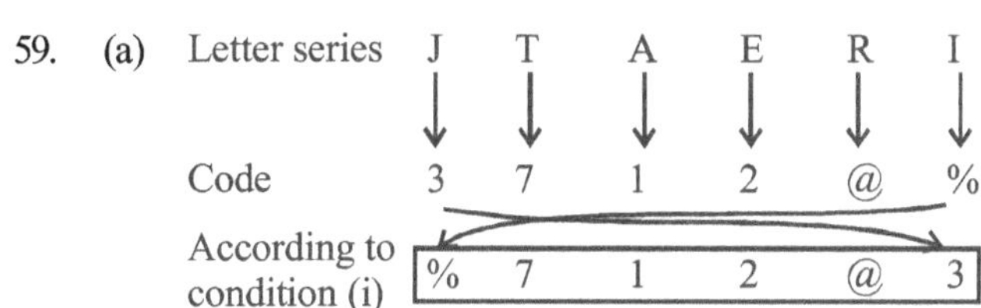

59. (a) Letter series

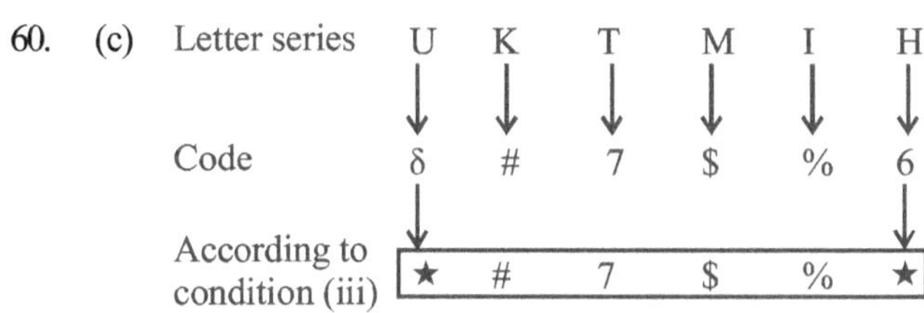

60. (c) Letter series

61. (d)

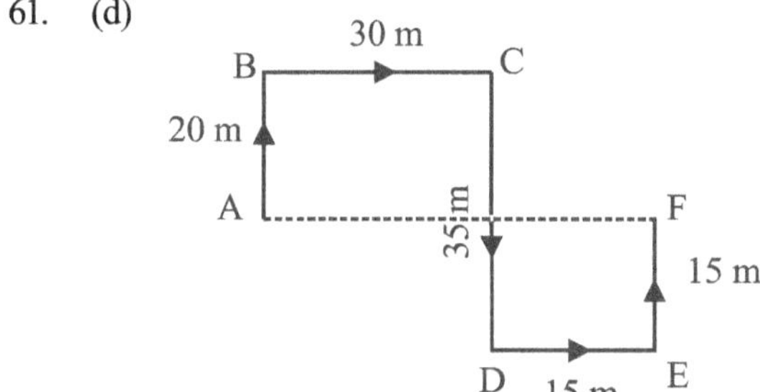

Required distance = AF = 30 + 15 = 45 m

From the above diagram, F is in East direction from A

Hence the required answer is '45' m East

62. (b)

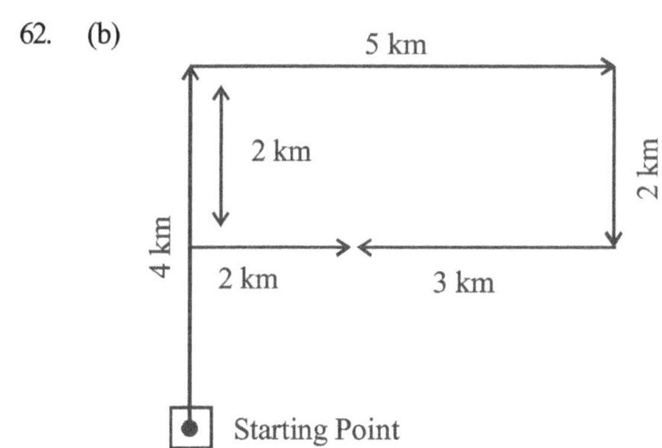

63. (d) The boy in the photograph is the only son of the son of Suresh's mother i.e., the son of Suresh. Hence, Suresh is the father of boy.

64. (c) P – M → P is the brother of M

M + N → M is the mother of N

N × Q → N is the sister of Q

Therefore, P is the maternal uncle of Q.

65. (b) Total number of persons in a row or class = (Rank of a person from upper end or left end) + (Rank of that person from lower or right end) – 1

Clearly, total number of boys in the row = 19 + 19 – 1 = 37.

(66-70) :

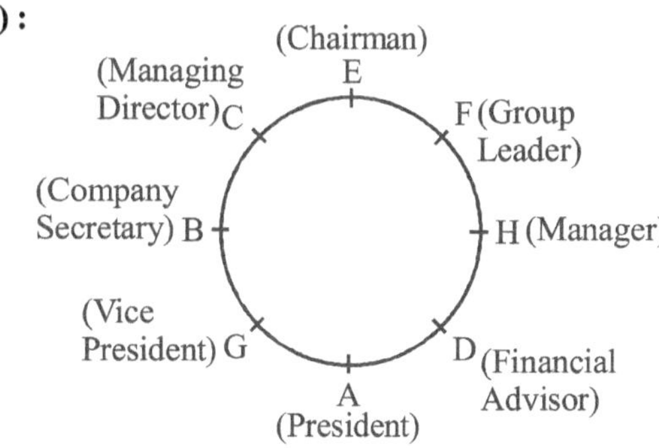

66. (d) **67.** (e) **68.** (a) **69.** (d) **70.** (c)

71. (d) Accordingly,

$$F @ N \Rightarrow F \le N$$
$$N \delta R \Rightarrow N > R$$
$$H @ R \Rightarrow H \le R$$
$$\therefore \quad F \le N > R \ge H$$

Conclusion : I. $H \delta N \Rightarrow H > N$ [not true]

II. $F \# R \Rightarrow F < R$ [not true]

If neither conclusion I nor II is true.

72. (b) Accordingly,

$$M \# T \Rightarrow M < T$$
$$T @ K \Rightarrow T \le K$$
$$K \$ N \Rightarrow K \ge N$$
$$\therefore \quad M < T \le K \ge N$$

Conclusion : I. $M \# N \Rightarrow M < N$ [not true]

II. $K \delta M \Rightarrow K > M$ [true]

Only conclusion II is true.

73. (c) Accordingly,

$$T \% H \Rightarrow T = H$$
$$H \$ W \Rightarrow H \ge W$$
$$\therefore \quad T = H \ge W$$

Conclusion : I. $W \# T \Rightarrow W < T$ [true]

II. $W \% T \Rightarrow W = T$ or

If either conclusion I or II is true. [true]

74. (a) Accordingly,

$$N \delta K \Rightarrow N > K$$
$$K \# D \Rightarrow K < D$$
$$D \% M \Rightarrow D = M$$
$$\therefore \quad N > K < D = M$$

Conclusion : I. $M \delta K \Rightarrow M > K$ [true]

         II. $D \delta N \Rightarrow D > N$ [not true]

Only conclusion I is true.

75. (e) Accordingly,

$$J \$ B \Rightarrow J \geq B$$
$$B \% R \Rightarrow B = R$$
$$R \delta F \Rightarrow R > F$$
$$\therefore \quad J \geq B = R > F$$

Conclusion : I. $F \# B \Rightarrow F < B$ [true]

         II. $R @ J \Rightarrow R \leq J$ [true]

Both conclusions I and II are true.

Solutions (76-80)

Movies	Person	Colour
The mask	C and S	Pink
Ironman	A and B	Beige
Superman	E and P	Yellow
Avengers	Q or U and R	Green
Dark night rises	F and D	White
Unbreakable	T and U or Q	Blue

76. (b)
77. (b)
78. (a)
79. (e)
80. (c)

PRACTICE SET   **11**

INSTRUCTIONS

- **This practice set consists of two sections. Quantitative Aptitude (Qs. 1-40) & Reasoning Ability (Qs. 41-80).**
- **All the questions are compulsory.**
- **Each question has five options, of which only one is correct. The candidates are advised to read all the options thoroughly.**
- **There is negative marking equivalent to $1/4^{th}$ of the mark allotted to the specific question for wrong answer.**

Time : 45 min.   **Max. Marks : 80**

QUANTITATIVE APTITUDE

DIRECTIONS (Qs. 1-5): What will come in place of the question mark (?) in the following questions ?

1. $\dfrac{5}{8}$ of $\dfrac{4}{9}$ of $\dfrac{3}{5}$ of $222 = ?$
   - (a) 42
   - (b) 43
   - (c) 39
   - (d) 37
   - (e) None of these

2. 56% of $450 + ? = 300$
   - (a) 52
   - (b) 48
   - (c) 42
   - (d) 56
   - (e) None of these

3. $27^{1.5} \times 27^{3.5} = 27^{?}$
   - (a) 5
   - (b) 7
   - (c) 3
   - (d) 2
   - (e) None of these

4. $27.06 \times 25 - ? = 600$
   - (a) 76.3
   - (b) 76.7
   - (c) 76.5
   - (d) 76.2
   - (e) None of these

5. $8^4 \times \dfrac{1}{8^3} \times 8^5 \div 8^2 = 8^{?}$
   - (a) 7
   - (b) 2
   - (c) 3
   - (d) 4
   - (e) None of these

DIRECTIONS (Qs. 6-10) : In each of these question, two equations (I) and (II) are given. You have to solve both the equations and give answer.
   - (a) If $x \geq y$
   - (b) If $x \leq y$
   - (c) If $x < y$
   - (d) If $x > y$
   - (e) If $x = y$, or relationship between x and y can't be established.

6.   I. $x^2 + 2x - 224 = 0$
     II. $y^2 + 4y - 437 = 0$

7.   I. $x^2 - 24x + 108 = 0$
     II. $y = \sqrt[3]{5832}$

8.   I. $6x + 16y = 16$
     II. $12x + 8y = 84$

9.   I. $6x^2 - 41x - 30 = 0$
     II. $5y^2 - 40y - 45 = 0$

10.   I. $6x^2 - 17x + 12 = 0$
      II. $6y^2 - 10y - 16 = 0$

11. A sum of money becomes eight times in 3 years if the rate is compounded annually. In how much time, the same amount at the same compound interest rate will become sixteen times?
    - (a) 6 years
    - (b) 4 years
    - (c) 8 years
    - (d) 5 years
    - (e) None of these

12. Two trains each of 120 m in length, run in opposite directions with a velocity of 40 m/s and 20 m/s respectively. How long will it take for the tail ends of the two trains to meet each other during the course of their journey ?
    - (a) 20 s
    - (b) 3 s
    - (c) 4 s
    - (d) 5 s
    - (e) None of these

13. Ramesh is twice as good a workman as Sunil and finishes a piece of work in 3 hours less than Sunil. In how many hours they together could finish the same piece of work ?
    - (a) $2\dfrac{1}{3}$
    - (b) 2
    - (c) $1\dfrac{2}{3}$
    - (d) 8
    - (e) None of these

14. The floor of a rectangular room is 15 m long and 12 m wide. The room is surrounded by a vrandah of width 2 m on all its sides. The area of the vrandah is :
    - (a) $124\,m^2$
    - (b) $120\,m^2$
    - (c) $108\,m^2$
    - (d) $58\,m^2$
    - (e) None of these

15. Pratul's monthly income is onefourth of Manoj's monthly income. Manoj's annual income is ₹ 2.16 lacs. What is Pratul's annual income? (In some cases monthly income and in some cases annual income are used.)
- (a) ₹54000
- (b) ₹ 5.4 thousand
- (c) ₹4500
- (d) ₹45000
- (e) None of these

16. The present ages of Trisha and Shalini are in the ratio of 7 : 6 respectively. After 8 years the ratio of their ages will be 9 : 8. What is the difference in their ages ?
- (a) 4 years
- (b) 8 years
- (c) 10 years
- (d) 12 years
- (e) None of these

17. Profit earned by an organisation is distributed among officers and clerks in the ratio of 5 : 3. If the number of officers is 45 and the number of clerks is 80 and the amount received by each officer is ₹25,000, what was the total amount of profit earned?
- (a) ₹ 22 lakh
- (b) ₹ 18.25 lakh
- (c) ₹ 18 lakh
- (d) ₹ 23.25 lakh
- (e) None of these

18. A shopkeeper labelled the price of his articles so as to earn a profit of 30% on the cost price. He, then sold the articles by offering a discount of 10% on the labelled price. What is the actual per cent profit earned in the deal?
- (a) 18%
- (b) 15%
- (c) 20%
- (d) Cannot be determined
- (e) None of these

19. Prema decided to donate 15% of her salary to an orphanage. On the day of donation she changed her mind and donated ₹ 1,896 which was 80% of what she had decided earlier. How much is Prerna's salary?
- (a) ₹ 18,500
- (b) ₹ 10,250
- (c) ₹ 15,800
- (d) Cannot be determined
- (e) None of these

20. Naresh purchased a TV set for ₹11,250 after getting discount of 10% on the labelled price. He spent ₹150 on transport and ₹800 on installation. At what price should it be sold so that the profit earned would be 15% if no discount was offered?
- (a) ₹12,937.50
- (b) ₹14,030
- (c) ₹ 13,450
- (d) ₹15,467.50
- (e) None of these

DIRECTIONS (Qs. 21-25) : Find the next term in the given series in each of the questions below.

---

21. 2, 4, ?, 16, 32
- (a) 6
- (b) 10
- (c) 8
- (d) 12
- (e) None of these

22. 0, 7, 26, ?, 124, 215
- (a) 37
- (b) 51
- (c) 63
- (d) 88
- (e) None of these

23. 4, 15, 16, ?, 36, 63, 64
- (a) 25
- (b) 30
- (c) 32
- (d) 35
- (e) None of these

24. 1, 8, 9, ?, 25, 216, 49
- (a) 60
- (b) 64
- (c) 70
- (d) 75
- (e) None of these

25. 336, 210, 120, ?, 24, 6, 0
- (a) 40
- (b) 50
- (c) 60
- (d) 70
- (e) None of these

DIRECTIONS (Qs. 26-30) : The given pie-chart shows the percentage distribution of employees among different departments of a Company and the line graph shows the percentage of graduate employees among them. Answer the following questions based on these graphs.

Total No. of employees = 18000

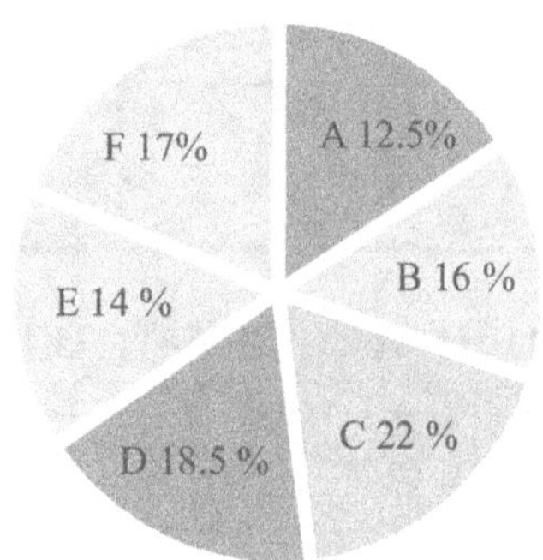

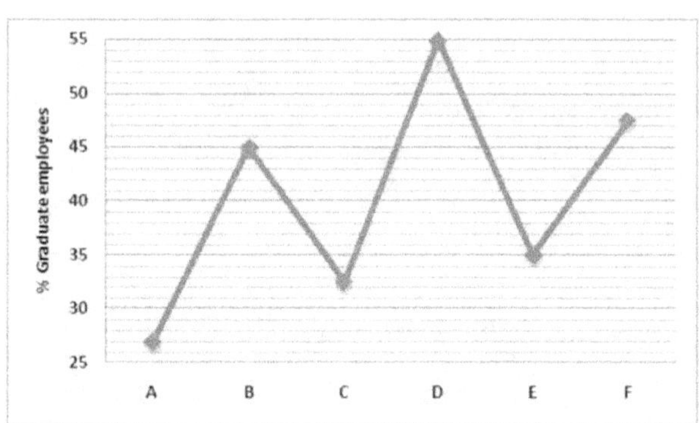

26. What is the total number of graduate employees working in Department A ?
- (a) 640
- (b) 608
- (c) 635
- (d) 1080
- (e) 740

27. What is the total number of employees working in the Company who are non-graduates?
- (a) 13780
- (b) 10940
- (c) 9360
- (d) 10642
- (e) 10730

28. The total number of graduate employees working in Department E is what percent of the total number of employees of the Company?
- (a) 7.2%
- (b) 6.4%
- (c) 4.9%
- (d) 4.3%
- (e) None of these

29. The Total number of graduate employees working in Department D is approximately what percent more or less than the total number of non-graduate employees working in that department?
    (a) 18% more
    (b) 22% more
    (c) 24% less
    (d) 27% less
    (e) 32% less

30. What is the average number of graduate employees working in the Company in all departments together?
    (a) 1435
    (b) 1227
    (c) 1555
    (d) 1565
    (e) 1375

DIRECTIONS (Qs. 31-35): Study of the following bar-graph carefully to answer the questions that follow. Earning (in rupees) of three different girls on four different days.

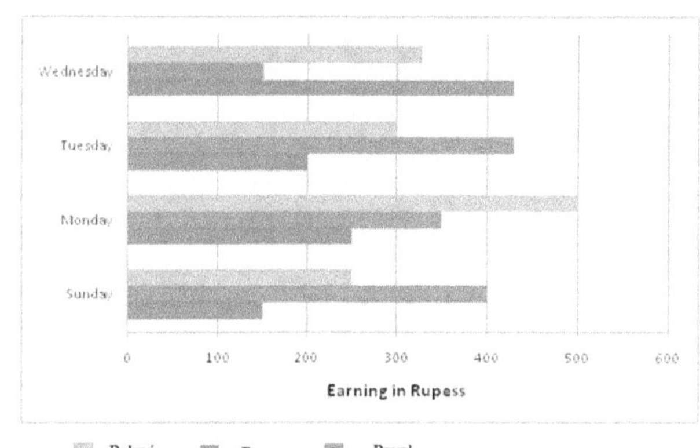

31. What is Palavi's average earning over all the days together?
    (a) 342.75
    (b) 348.75
    (c) 345.75
    (d) 343.75
    (e) 353.75

32. What is the total amount earned by Punam and Payal together on Monday and Wednesday together?
    (a) ₹1275
    (b) ₹1175
    (c) ₹1125
    (d) ₹1375
    (e) ₹1115

33. Punam donated her earnings of Wednesday to Payal. What was Payal's total earning on Wednesday after Punam donation?
    (a) ₹475
    (b) ₹525
    (c) ₹675
    (d) ₹575
    (e) None of these

34. What is the difference between Palavi's earning on Sunday and Payal's earning on Sunday?
    (a) ₹150
    (b) ₹180
    (c) ₹250
    (d) ₹170
    (e) None of these

35. What is the ratio of Payal's earning on Sunday, Tuesday and Wednesday?
    (a) 16 : 17 : 6
    (b) 15 : 17 : 6
    (c) 16 : 17 : 8
    (d) 16 : 19 : 6
    (e) None of these

DIRECTIONS (Qs. 36-40) : Study the data presented in the following graph to answer the questions :

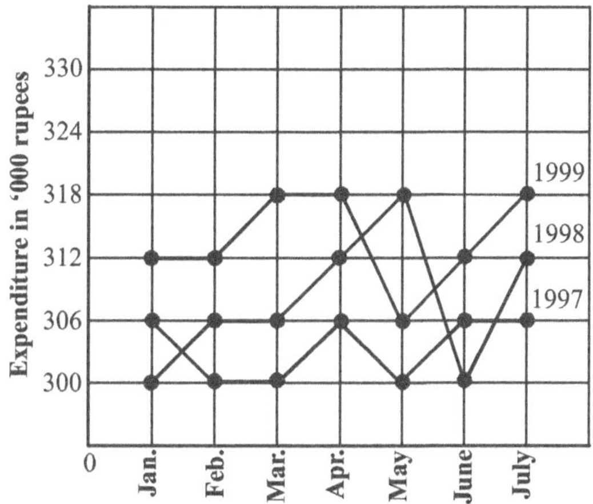

36. What is the total expenditure during the period under review (7 months) in 1997 ?
    (a) ₹21, 07, 000
    (b) ₹96, 07, 000
    (c) ₹21, 54, 000
    (d) ₹21, 24, 000
    (e) None of these

37. What total expenditure has been made during the year 1997 and 1998 in the period covered in the graph ?
    (a) ₹24, 87, 000
    (b) ₹2, 70, 000
    (c) ₹48, 27, 000
    (d) ₹42, 78, 000
    (e) None of these

38. What is the average monthly expenditure during the year 1999 covering the period shown in the graph ?
    (a) ₹2, 75, 000
    (b) ₹2, 70, 000
    (c) ₹3, 14, 000
    (d) ₹2, 47, 000
    (e) None of these

39. Which month has been the least expensive during 1999 ?
    (a) June
    (b) April
    (c) May
    (d) July
    (e) None of these

40. The expenditure in April 1999 was.....higher than that of corresponding period in 1998.
    (a) 1.5%
    (b) 2%
    (c) 2.5%
    (d) 0.94%
    (e) None of these

REASONING ABILITY

DIRECTIONS (Qs. 41-45): In the following questions, the symbols δ, %, $, # and @ are used with the following meaning as illustrated below:

'P $ Q' means 'P is not smaller than Q'.
'P @ Q' means 'P is not greater than Q'.
'P δ Q' means 'P is neither smaller than nor equal to Q'.
'P # Q' means 'P is neither greater than nor equal to Q'.
'P % Q' means 'P is neither smaller than nor greater than Q'.

Now in each of the following questions assuming the given statements to be true, find which of the two conclusions I and II given below them is/are **definitely true**?

Give answer

(a) if only Conclusion I is true.

(b) if only Conclusion II is true.

(c) if either Conclusion I or II is true.

(d) if neither Conclusion I nor II is true.

(e) if both Conclusions I and II are true.

41. Statements: F @ N, N δ R, H @ R

    Conclusions: I.   H δ N

                   II.   F # R

42. Statements: M # T, T @ K, K $ N

    Conclusions: I. M # N

                   II.   K δ M

43. Statements: T % H, H $ W

    Conclusions: I.   W # T

                   II.   W % T

44. Statements: N δ K, K # D, D % M

    Conclusions: I.   M δ K

                   II.   D δ N

45. Statements: J $ B, B % R, R δ F

    Conclusions: I.   F # B

                   II.   R @ J

DIRECTIONS (Qs.46-50) : Study the following information carefully and answer the questions given below :

A, B, C, D, E, F and G are sitting around a circle facing the centre, not necessarily in the same order. D is not second to the left of F but D is second to the right of A. C is third to the right of A and C is second to the left of G. B is not an immediate neighbour of G.

46. Who is to the immediate right of C?

(a) D   (b) G   (c) E   (d) B

(e) Data inadequate

47. Who is the only one person sitting between A and G?

(a) B   (b) D   (c) C   (d) E

(e) F

48. Who is to the immediate left of D ?

(a) B   (b) C   (c) A

(d) Data inadequate

(e) None of these

49. Who is second to the left of C?

(a) B   (b) G   (c) F

(d) Data inadequate

(e) None of these

50. What is E's position with respect to D?

(a) To the immediate right   (b) To the immediate left

(c) Third to the right   (d) Second to the right

(e) Third to the left

DIRECTIONS (Qs. 51-55) : Read the following information carefully and answer the questions that follow :

Eight friends P, Q, R, S, T, U, V and W are sitting around a circular table for lunch. Each person has a different birthplace, viz Noida, Jaipur, Patna, Mumbai, Punjab, Delhi, Goa and Madurai, but not necessarily in the same order.

The person born in Jaipur sits third to the right of V. R is an immediate neighbour of V. The person born in Mumbai sits second to the right of R. Q sits third to the right of W. W's birthplace is neither Jaipur nor Mumbai. Only one person sits between R and the person whose birthplace is Patna. P and U are immediate neighbours of each other. Neither P's nor U's birthplace is Jaipur. The person born in Madurai sits second to the right of P. Two persons sit between S and the person born in Punjab. S is not from Jaipur. The person born in Noida is not an immediate neighbour of the person born in Jaipur. The person born in Delhi sits second to the left of P.

51. Who among the following is from Goa?

(a) P   (b) W

(c) R   (d) U

(e) S

52. What is the position of U with respect to the person whose birthplace is Jaipur?

(a) Second to the left   (b) Second to the right

(c) Immediate right   (d) Immediate left

(e) None of these

53. Where is the birthplace of V?

(a) Goa   (b) Noida

(c) Delhi   (d) Patna

(e) Mumbai

54. Where is the birthplace of T?

(a) Goa   (b) Mumbai

(c) Delhi   (d) Jaipur

(e) Punjab

55. Who sits exactly between the persons whose birth places are Patna and Punjab?

(a) R and W

(b) R and Q

(c) Only Madurai-born person

(d) P and Q

(e) None of these

DIRECTIONS (Qs. 56-60): In each question below are two statements followed by two conclusions numbered I and II. You have to take the two given statements to be true even if they seem to be at variance from commonly known facts and then decide which of the given conclusions logically follows from the given statements disregarding commonly known facts. Give answer

(a) if only conclusion I follows.

(b) if only conclusion II follows.

(c) if either conclusion I or II follows.

(d) if neither conclusion I nor II follows.

(e) if both conclusions I and II follow.

56. Statements: No holiday is a vacation.

                    Some vacations are trips.

    Conclusions: I.   No trip is a holiday.

                   II.   Some holidays are definitely not trips.

57. Statements: Some kites are birds.

                    No kite is an aeroplane.

    Conclusions: I.   All aeroplanes are birds.

                   II.   Some birds are definitely not kites

58. **Statements:** All metals are plastics.
All plastics are fibres.
Conclusions: **I.** Atleast some fibres are metals.
II. Some metals are not fibres.

59. **Statements:** All roads are streets.
No street is a highway.
Conclusions: **I.** No highway is a road.
II. All streets are roads.

60. **Statements:** Some animals are plants.
All plants are rocks.
Conclusions: **I.** All plants are animals.
II. Atleast some rocks are animals.

DIRECTIONS (Qs. 61-67) : Study the information given below carefully and answer the questions that follow:

There are Eight homes namely P, Q, R, S, T, U, V and W. Q is 4 km West of R. V is 2 km West of W while S is 6 km East of V and U is 4 km North of V. T is just in Middle of W and S. Q is 2 km south of P and P is 4 km North of W.

61. Shortest Distance between T and U is?
(a) 8 km
(b) 4 km
(c) 3 km
(d) 2 km
(e) None of these

62. What is direction of R with respect to V?
(a) North East
(b) South East
(c) South West
(d) North West
(e) None of these

63. In a class of 35 children, Rohit's rank is sixth from the top. Amar is seven rank below Rohit. What is Amar's rank from the bottom?
(a) 22
(b) 20
(c) 19
(d) 23
(e) Cannot be determined

64. Town D is to the West of Town M. Town R is to the South of town D. Town K is to the east of town R. Town K is towards which direction of town D ?
(a) South
(b) East
(c) North-East
(d) South East
(e) None of these

65. D is brother of B. M is brother of B. K is Father of M. T is wife of K. How is B related to T?
(a) Son
(b) Daughter
(c) Mother
(d) Grand Mother
(e) None of these

66. If it is possible to make only one meaningful word with the first, the third, the fifth and the eight letters of the word **SHAREHOLDING,** which of the following will be the second letter of the word ? If no such word can be made, give 'X' as the answer and if more than one such word can be made, give 'Y' as the answer.
(a) L
(b) E
(c) S
(d) X
(e) Y

67. Denial walks 20m north from his house. Then, he turns to his west and covers 8m. Again, he turns south and covers 6m. Finally, turning to east, he covers 8m. How far is he from his house and in which direction?
(a) 12 metres, East
(b) 14 metres, North
(c) 20 metres, South
(d) 10 metres, West
(e) None of these

DIRECTIONS (Qs. 68-72) : Study the following information to answer the given questions

(a) Six plays are to be organized from Monday to Sunday-One play each day with one day when there is no play. 'No play' day is not Monday or Sunday.

(b) The plays are held in sets of 3 plays each in such a way that 3 plays are held without any break *ie*, 3 plays are held in such a way, that there is no 'No play' day between them but immediately before this set or immediately after this set it is 'No play' day.

(c) Play Z is held on 26th and play X was held on 31st of the same month.

(d) Play B was not held immediately after play A (but was held after A, not necessarily immediately) and play M was held immediately before Q.

(e) All the six plays were held in the same month.

68. Which play was organized on Monday?
(a) Z
(b) M
(c) Q
(d) Cannot be determined
(e) None of these

69. Which day was play Z organized?
(a) Tuesday
(b) Monday
(c) Wednesday
(d) Cannot be determined
(e) None of these

70. Which date was a 'No play' day?
(a) 26th
(b) 28th
(c) 29th
(d) Cannot be determined
(e) None of these

71. Which of the following is true?
(a) Play B is held immediately before play M
(b) Play Z is held after play B
(c) There was a gap after 2 plays and then 4 plays were organized
(d) First play was organized on the 25th
(e) Play B was held on Friday

72. Which day was play Q organized?
(a) Friday
(b) Wednesday
(c) Saturday
(d) Cannot be determined
(e) None of these

DIRECTIONS (73-77) : Study the following arrangement of consonants, vowels, numbers and symbols carefully and answer the questions given below:

H @ F ! 3 U 6 % G I T * P L 8 $ ∧ 9 S 2 7 & A M K + J © D 4 # 5 & E

73. Which of the following is ninth to the right of the twentieth from the right end of the above arrangement ?
(a) K
(b) M
(c) U
(d) A
(e) None of these

74. How many such consonants are there in the above arrangement, each of which is immediately preceded by a symbol and also immediately followed by a symbol ?
(a) None
(b) One
(c) Two
(d) Three
(e) More than three

75. If all the symbols are dropped from the arrangement, which of the following will be the twelfth from the left end ?
(a) 9   (b) 2   (c) S   (d) 7
(e) None of these

76. Four of the following five are alike in a certain way based on their positions in the above arrangement and so form a group. Which is the one that **does not** belong to the group?
(a) L\$8   (b) AKM
(c) @!F   (d) 6%G
(e) JD©

77. What should come in place of the question mark (?) in the following series based on the above arrangement.

F3U ,   %IT ,   L&^ ?

(a) 927   (b) 7&A
(c) 7AM   (d) 2&A
(e) 27&

DIRECTIONS (Q. 78-80) : Study the following information and answer the given questions. Q is the sister of M. P is wife of M. P has only one son R. S is mother of P. S is married to T. T has only one son and only one daughter.

78. If P is sister of J, how is J related to M?
(a) Sister-in-law   (b) Cannot be determined
(c) Brother   (d) Brother-in-law
(e) Uncle

79. As per the given information, how is M related to S?
(a) Son   (b) Son-in-law
(c) Niece   (d) Nephew
(e) Daughter-in-law

80. As per the given information, how is R related to Q?
(a) Nephew   (b) Cannot be determined
(c) Uncle   (d) Niece
(e) Aunt

HINTS & EXPLANATIONS

1. (d) $? = \dfrac{5}{8} \times \dfrac{4}{9} \times \dfrac{3}{5} \times 222 = 37$

2. (b) Let the number be x

$\therefore \dfrac{56}{100} \times 450 + x = 300$

or $x = 300 - 252 = 48$

3. (a) $(27)^{1.5} \times (21)^{3.5} = (27)^?$

$\therefore ? = 5 \left[\because a^x + a^y = a^{(x+y)} \right]$

4. (c) Let the number be x.

$\therefore 27.06 \times 25 - x = 600$

or, $x = 676.5 - 600 = 76.5$

5. (d) $8^4 \times \dfrac{1}{8^3} \times 8^5 \times \dfrac{1}{8^2} = 8^{4-3+5-2} = 8^4 \quad \therefore ? = 4$

6. (e) I. $x^2 + 2x - 224 = 0$
$(x - 14)(x + 16)$
$x = 14, -16$
II. $y^2 + 4y - 437 = 0$
$(y - 19)(y + 23)$
$y = 19, -23$
So relationship between x and y can't be established.

7. (b) I. $x^2 - 24x + 108 = 0$
$(x - 6)(x - 18)$
$x = 6, 18$
II. $y = \sqrt[3]{5832}$
$y = 18$
So $x \leq y$

8. (d) I. $6x + 16y = 16$
II. $12x + 8y = 84$
Equation (I) and (II)
$x = 152/3; y = -13/6$
So $x > y$

9. (e) I. $6x^2 - 41x - 30 = 0$
$(3x + 2)(2x - 15)$

$x = -\dfrac{2}{3}; \dfrac{15}{2},$

II. $5y^2 - 40y - 45 = 0$
$(y - 9)(5y + 5)$
$y = 9, -1$
So relationship between x and y can't be established.

10. (e) I. $6x^2 - 17x + 12 = 0$
$(3x - 4)(2x - 3)$

$x = \dfrac{4}{3}, \dfrac{3}{2},$

II. $6y^2 - 10y - 16 = 0$
$(2y + 2)(3y - 8)$

$y = \dfrac{8}{3}, -1$

So relationship between x and y can't be established.

11. (b) Let the sum of money be ₹ x.

Now, $8x = x\left(1 + \dfrac{r}{100}\right)^3$

or, $\left(1 + \dfrac{r}{100}\right)^3 = (2)^3$ or $1 + \dfrac{r}{100} = 2$

Again, let the sum becomes 16 times in n years. Then,

$16x = x\left(1 + \dfrac{r}{100}\right)^n$

$\Rightarrow 16 = 2^n$ or $2^4 = 2^n$ or $n = 4$

12. (c) Relative speed of the trains $= (40 + 20) = 60$ m/s
Distance $= (120 + 120) = 240$ m
Time taken by trains to cross each other completely

$$= \frac{240}{60} = 4s$$

∴ Larger the no. of cogs (tooth of wheel) of wheel, lesser will be that no. of revolution made by it.

13. (b) Let Sunil finishes the job in x hours.

Then, Ramesh will finish the job in $\frac{x}{2}$ hours.

We have, $x - \frac{x}{2} = 3 \Rightarrow x = 6$

Therefore, Sunil finishes the job in 6 hours and Ramesh in 3 hours.

Work done by both of them in 1 hour $= \frac{1}{6} + \frac{1}{3} = \frac{1}{2}$

They together finish the piece of work in 2 hours.

14. (a) Area of the outer rectangle $= 19 \times 16 = 304$ m^2

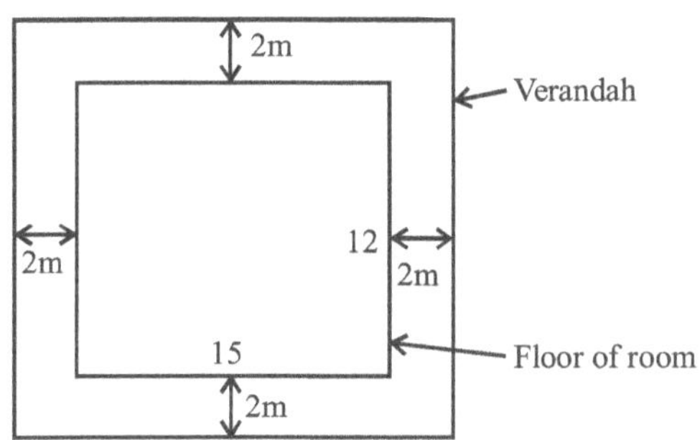

Area of the inner rectangle $= 15 \times 12 = 180$ m^2
∴ Required area $= (304 - 180) = 124$ m^2

15. (a) Manoj's monthly income

$$= \frac{2.16 \times 100000}{12} = ₹ 18000$$

∴ Pratul's monthly income

$$= 18000 \times \frac{1}{4} = ₹ 4500$$

∴ Pratul's annual income
$$= 12 \times 4500 = ₹ 54000$$

16. (a) Let Trisha's and Shalini's present ages be $7x$ and $6x$ years respectively.

After 8 years, $\frac{7x+8}{6x+8} = \frac{9}{8}$

$\Rightarrow$ $56x + 64 = 54x + 72$
$\Rightarrow$ $2x = 72 - 64 = 8$
$\Rightarrow$ $x = 4$
∴ Required difference $= 7x - 6x \Rightarrow x = 4$ years

17. (d) Amount received by all the officers
$$= 45 \times 25000 = 11,25,000$$

Amount received by each clerk $= \frac{3}{5} \times 25000 = 15000$

Amount received by all the clerks
$$= 80 \times 15000 = 12,00,000$$
Total amount of profit earned $= 11,25,000 + 12,00,000$
$$= ₹23.25 \text{ lakh.}$$

18. (e) Let the cost price of the articles be ₹100
Marked Price $= ₹130$
After giving a discount of 10% the selling price of the articles $= 0.9 \times 130 = 117$

So, actual profit per cent $= \frac{(117 - 100)}{100} \times 100 = 17\%$

19. (c) Let Prerna's salary be ₹ x
According to the question,
80% of 15% of $x = 1896$

$\Rightarrow$ $x \times \frac{15}{100} \times \frac{4}{5} = 1896$

∴ $x = \frac{1896 \times 5 \times 100}{15 \times 4} = ₹15800$

20. (d) Cost price of TV when discount is not offered

$$= 11250 \times \frac{100}{90} = ₹12500$$

Total cost of TV after transport and installation
$$= 12500 + 800 + 150 = 13450$$
To earn 15% profit, he must sell at

$$13450 \times \frac{115}{100} = ₹ 15467.50$$

21. (c) The terms exhibit the pattern $2^1, 2^2, 2^3$ and so on.
22. (c) Try the pattern $n^3 - 1, n = 1, 2, \ldots\ldots$
23. (d) Pattern is $2^2, 4^2 - 1, 4^2, 6^2 - 1, 6^2$ and so on.
24. (b) Can you see that the pattern is
$1^2, 2^3, 3^2, 4^3, 5^2, 6^3, 7^2$
25. (c) Note that
$0 = 1^3 - 1 \quad 6 = 2^3 - 2$
$24 = 3^3 - 3$

26. (b) Required answer $= \frac{12.5}{100} \times 18000 \times \frac{27}{100} = 608.$

27. (d) Total graduate $= \frac{18000}{100 \times 100} [12.5 \times 27 + 16 \times 45 + 22 \times$

$32.5 + 18.5 \times 55 + 14 \times 35 + 17 \times 47.5]$

Total graduate $= \frac{18000}{100 \times 100} (337.5 + 720 + 715 + 1017.5$

$+ 490 + 807.5) = 7358$
Total Non-graduate $= 18000 - 7358 = 10642$

28. (c) Required percentage $= \frac{14}{100} \times \frac{35}{100} \times \frac{18000}{18000} \times 100 = 4.9\%$

29. (b) Graduate $\% = 55\%$
Non-Graduate $= 45\%$

Req. % $= \frac{55 - 45}{45} \times 100 = 22.22$ (more)

30. (b) Total graduate employees working in the Company in all departments = 7358

Required Average = $\dfrac{7358}{6}$ = 1227

31. (d) Average earning of Palavi = (325 + 300 + 500 + 250)/4
= 1375/4 = 343.75

32. (b) Total amount earned by Punam and Payal together on Monday and Wednesday together
= (250 + 425 + 350 + 150) = ₹1175

33. (d) Punam's earning on Wednesday = 425
Total earning of Payal after Punam's donation
= 425 + 150 = ₹575

34. (a) Palavi's earning on Sunday = 250
Payal's earning on Sunday = 400
Required difference = (400 − 250) = ₹150

35. (a) Required ratio = 400 : 425 : 150 = 16 : 17 : 6

36. (d) Total expenditure
= 306 + 300 + 300 + 306 + 300 + 306 + 306
= ₹2124 thousands

37. (d) Total expenditure in the year 1998
= 300 + 306 + 306 + 312 + 318 + 300 + 312
= ₹2154 thousands
Total expenditure in 1997 and 1998
= 2124 + 2154 = 4278 thousands

38. (c) Average monthly expenditure in year 1999

$$= \dfrac{312 + 312 + 318 + 318 + 306 + 312 + 318}{7}$$

$$= \dfrac{2196}{7} = 313.714 \text{ thousands} \approx ₹3,14,000$$

39. (c) In the year 1999, the least expenses of ₹306 thousands is in the month of May.

40. (b) Expenditure in April 1998 = 312 thousands
Expenditure in April 1999 = 318 thousands

Required % = $\dfrac{6}{312} \times 100 = 1.92 \approx 2\%$

41. (d) Accordingly,

$$F @ N \Rightarrow F \leq N$$
$$N \delta R \Rightarrow N > R$$
$$H @ R \Rightarrow H \leq R$$
$$\therefore \quad F \leq N > R \geq H$$

Conclusion : I. $H \delta N \Rightarrow H > N$ [not true]
II. $F \# R \Rightarrow F < R$ [not true]

If neither conclusion I not II is true.

42. (b) Accordingly,

$$M \# T \Rightarrow M < T$$
$$T @ K \Rightarrow T \leq K$$
$$K \$ N \Rightarrow K \geq N$$
$$\therefore \quad M < T \leq K \geq N$$

Conclusion : I. $M \# N \Rightarrow M < N$ [not true]
II. $K \delta M \Rightarrow K > M$ [not true]

Only conclusion II is true.

43. (c) Accordingly,

$$T \% H \Rightarrow T = H$$
$$H \$ W \Rightarrow H \geq W$$
$$\therefore \quad T = H \geq W$$

Conclusion : I. $W \# T \Rightarrow W < T$ [true]
II. $W \% T \Rightarrow W = T$ or
If either conclusion I or II is true.   [true]

44. (a) Accordingly,

$$N \delta K \Rightarrow N > K$$
$$K \# D \Rightarrow K < D$$
$$D \% M \Rightarrow D = M$$
$$\therefore \quad N > K < D = M$$

Conclusion : I. $M \delta K \Rightarrow M > K$ [true]
II. $D \delta N \Rightarrow D > N$ [not true]

Only conclusion I is true.

45. (e) Accordingly,

$$J \$ B \Rightarrow J \geq B$$
$$B \% R \Rightarrow B = R$$
$$R \delta F \Rightarrow R > F$$
$$\therefore \quad J \geq B = R > F$$

Conclusion : I. $F \# B \Rightarrow F < B$ [true]
II. $R @ J \Rightarrow R \leq J$ [true]

Both conclusions I and II are true.

Solutions (46 - 50):

Sitting arrangement is as given below.

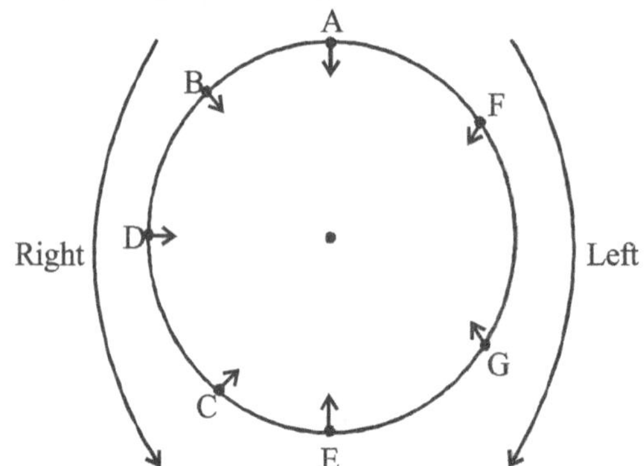

46. (c) E is to the immediate right of C
47. (e) F is sitting between A and G
48. (a) B is the immediate left of D
49. (a) Second to the left of C is B
50. (d) E is second to the right of D.

Solutions : (51-55)

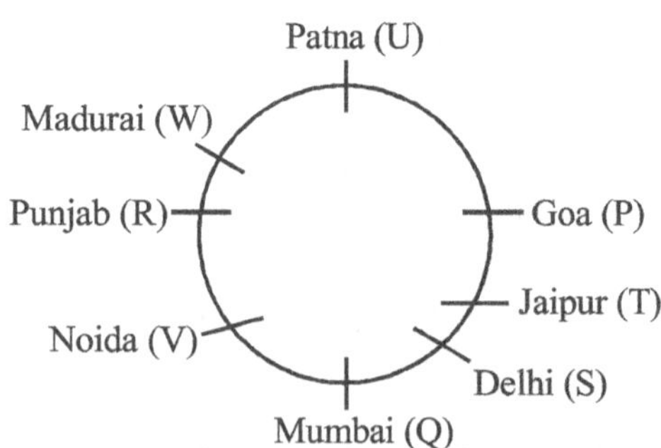

51. (a) 52. (b)
53. (b) 54. (d)
55. (c)
56. (d) According to statement

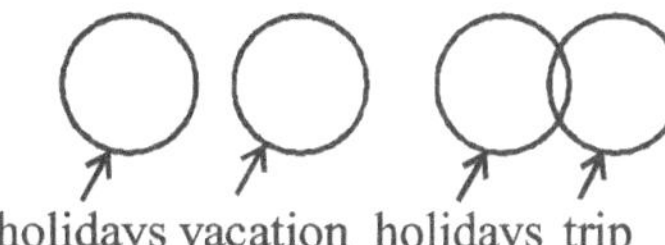

or,

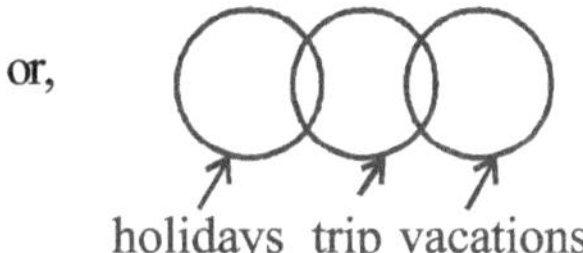

If neither conclusion I and nor II follow.

57. (d) According to statement

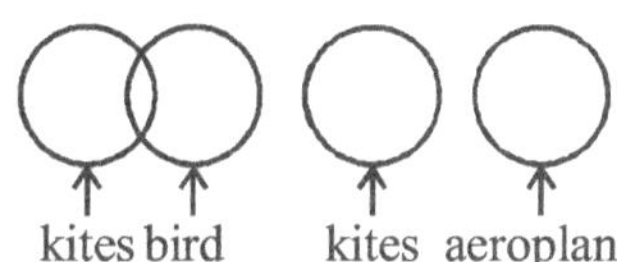

or

If neither conclusion I and II follows.

58. (a) According to statement

or,

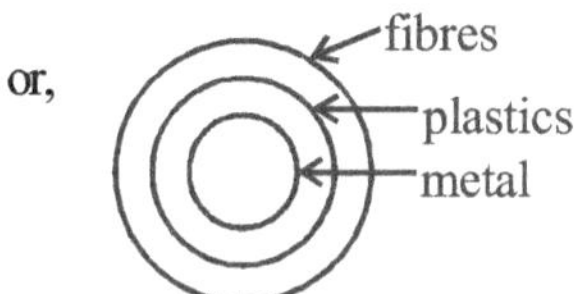

Only conclusion I follows.

59. (a) According to statement

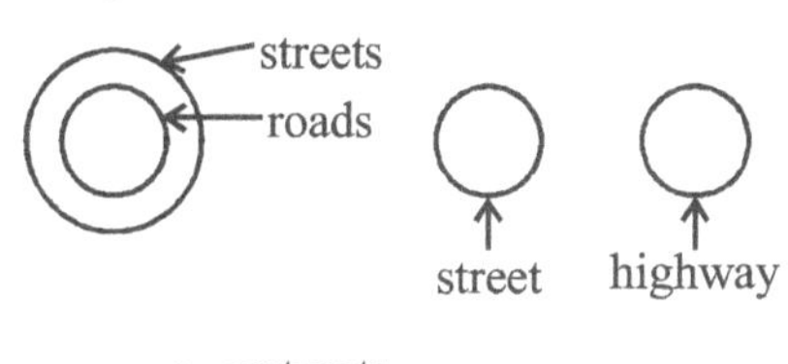

or,

Hence only conclusion I follows.

60. (b) According to statement I

or,

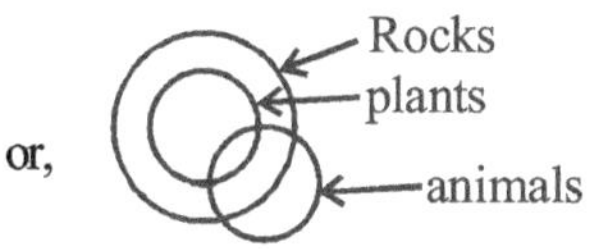

Hence, only conclusion II follows.

Solutions (61-62)

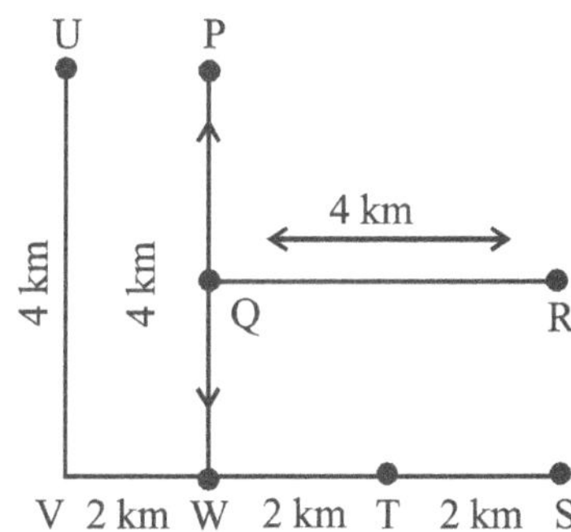

61. (e) 62. (a)
63. (d) Rohit's rank is 6th from the top.
Amar's rank Fram top is $(6 + 7) = 13$th
So, Amar's rank from bottom is $(35 - 13 + 1) = 23$th.

64. (d)

Town K is towards South-East direction of D.

65. (c)

So, B is son or daughter of T.

Solution (66-67)

66. (e) SALE, SEAL

67. (b)

Solution (68-72)

Given information can be represented as Follows:

DATE	25	26	27	28	29	30	31
DAY	MON	TUE	WED	THU	FRI	SAT	SUN
PLAY	A	Z	B	NO PLAY	M	Q	X

68. (e) Play A was organized on Monday.
69. (a)   70. (b)   71. (d)   72. (c)
73. (b) Ninth to the right of the 20th from the right means 11th from the right, i.e., M.

74. (a)

Symbol	Consonant	Symbol

Such combinations are :

| @ | F | ! | : | + | J | © |

75. (b) New arrangement

H F 3 U 6 G I T P L 8 \[9\] S 2 7 A M K ....

↑

12th from left

76. (d)

L $\xrightarrow{+2}$ S $\xrightarrow{-1}$ 8

A $\xrightarrow{+2}$ K $\xrightarrow{-1}$ M

@ $\xrightarrow{+2}$ I $\xrightarrow{-1}$ F

6 $\xrightarrow{+1}$ % $\xrightarrow{+1}$ G

J $\xrightarrow{+2}$ D $\xrightarrow{-1}$ ©

77. (c)

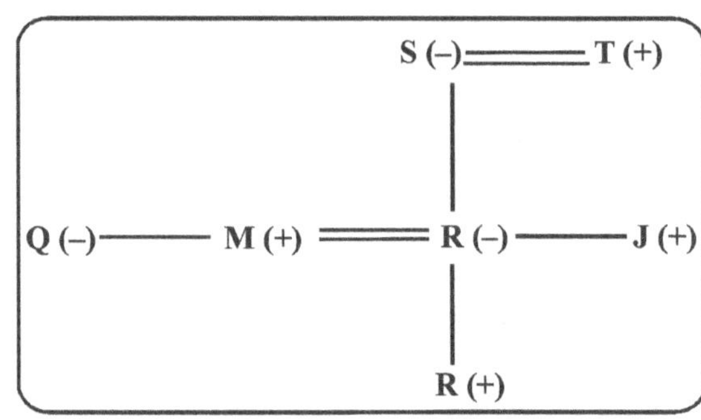

Solution (78-80)

78. (d)
79. (b)
80. (a)

PRACTICE SET 12

Time : 45 min. **Max. Marks : 80**

QUANTITATIVE APTITUDE

DIRECTIONS (Qs. 1-5): Study of the following graph carefully to answer the questions that follow.

Details about the distribution of employees and expenditure of an organization. (Distributed proportionately across the departments)

Annual expenditure on different items
Total Expenditure = 24 crores

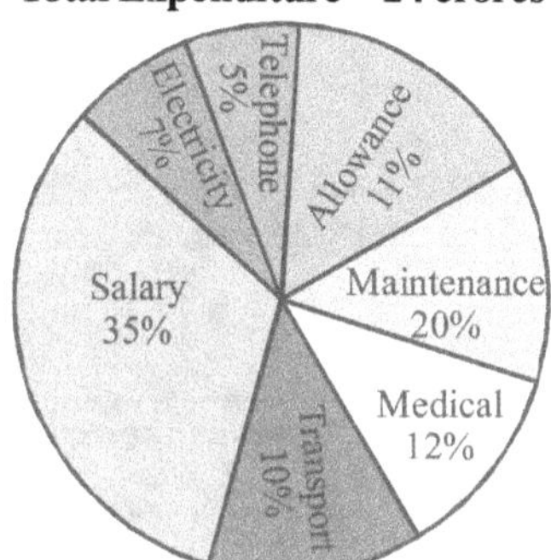

Department wise distrubition of employees:
Total number of employess = 2400

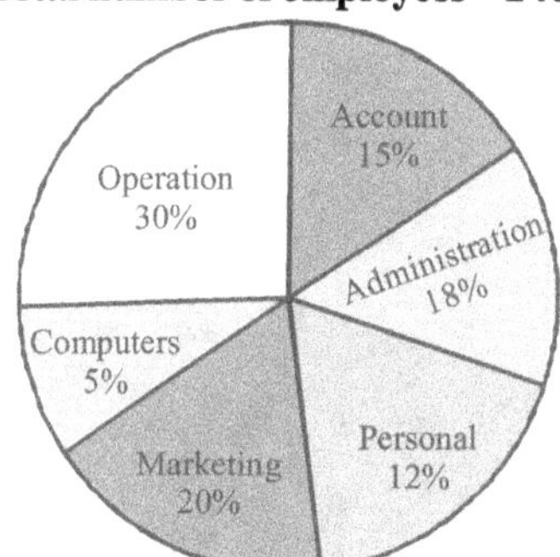

1. What was the total expenditure on Accounts department?
   - (a) ₹ 36 millions
   - (b) ₹ 26 millions
   - (c) ₹ 32.5 millions
   - (d) ₹ 34.5 millions
   - (e) ₹ 36.75 millions

2. What was per employee expenditure on medical?
   - (a) ₹12000
   - (b) ₹14000
   - (c) ₹12500
   - (d) ₹18000
   - (e) ₹13500

3. What was the total expenditure on salary of employees in marketing department?
   - (a) ₹ 16.40 millions
   - (b) ₹ 16.60 millions
   - (c) ₹ 16.50 millions
   - (d) ₹ 16.80 millions
   - (e) ₹ 17.80 millions

4. What was the amount spent on telephone?
   - (a) 13 millions
   - (b) 11.75 millions
   - (c) 11.5 millions
   - (d) 12.5 millions
   - (e) None of these

5. What was the expenditure on telephone for employees in computer department?
   - (a) 5.75 lakh
   - (b) 7.5 lakh
   - (c) 6.75 lakh
   - (d) 6.5 lakh
   - (e) None of these

DIRECTIONS (Qs. 6-10): Study of the following graph carefully to answer the questions that follow.

Total sales of English and Hindi Newspapers in five different districts of a State.

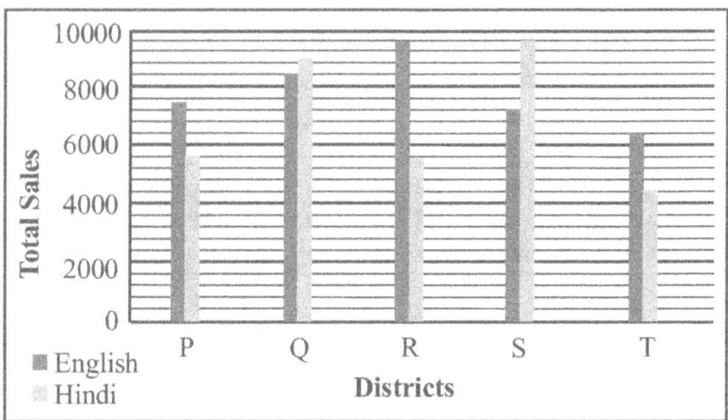

6. What is the difference between the total sale of English news papers and total sale of Hindi news papers in all the districts together?
   - (a) 4800
   - (b) 4650
   - (c) 5200
   - (d) 4950
   - (e) None of these

7. The sale of English newspapers in districts P is approximately what percent of the total sale of English newspapers in all the districts together?
   - (a) 24%
   - (b) 20%
   - (c) 28%
   - (d) 32%
   - (e) 25%

8. What is the ratio of the sale of Hindi news papers in district P to the sale of Hindi news papers in district S?
   - (a) 7:16
   - (b) 9:17
   - (c) 8:15
   - (d) 9:16
   - (e) 11:16

9. The sale of English newspapers in districts Q and S together is approximately what per cent of the sale of English newspapers in districts P, R and T together?
   - (a) 72%
   - (b) 68%
   - (c) 65%
   - (d) 78%
   - (e) None of these

10. What is the average sale of Hindi news papers in all the districts together?
    - (a) 6760
    - (b) 6890
    - (c) 7240
    - (d) 6450
    - (e) 3980

DIRECTIONS (Qs. 11-15) : What approximate value should come in the following questions at the questions places.

(You are not required to calculate the exact value)

11. $(13.001)^3 = ?$
    - (a) 1900
    - (b) 2200
    - (c) 2000
    - (d) 1800
    - (e) 2100

12. $55.003 \times 54.998 + 5.001 = ?$
    - (a) 3500
    - (b) 3630
    - (c) 2540
    - (d) 3030
    - (e) 2750

13. 50.001% of $99.99 \div 49.999 = ?$
    - (a) 1
    - (b) 0.1
    - (c) 0.01
    - (d) 0.02
    - (e) None of these

14. $999.0001 + 899.999 - 349.88 = ?$
    - (a) 1549
    - (b) 1560
    - (c) 1449
    - (d) 1460
    - (e) None of these

15. $(2.0001)^3 \times (1.999)^{-2} \div (3.999)^{-4} = ?$
    - (a) 32
    - (b) 16
    - (c) 64
    - (d) 256
    - (e) 512

DIRECTIONS (Qs. 16-20) : In the following questions, two equations numbered I and II are given. You have to solve both the equations and give answer

---

(a) if $x > y$
(b) if $x \geq y$
(c) if $x < y$
(d) if $x \leq y$
(e) if $x = y$ or the relationship cannot be established

16. I. $x^2 - 11x + 24 = 0$
    II. $2y^2 - 9y + 9 = 0$

17. I. $x^3 \times 13 - x^2 \times 247$
    II. $y^{1/3} \times 14 = 294 \div y^{2/3}$

18. I. $\dfrac{12 \times 4}{x^{4/7}} - \dfrac{3 \times 4}{x^{4/7}} = x^{10/7}$
    II. $y^3 + 783 = 999$

19. I. $\sqrt{500x} + \sqrt{402} = 0$
    II. $\sqrt{360}\, y + (200)^{1/2} = 0$

20. I. $(17)^2 + 114 \div 18 = x$
    II. $(26)^2 - 18 \times 21 = y$

21. 12 yr ago the ratio between the ages of A and B was 3 :4 respectively. The present age of A is $3\dfrac{3}{4}$ times of C's present age. If C's present age is 10 yr, then what is B's present age? (in years)
    - (a) 48
    - (b) 46
    - (c) 60
    - (d) 54
    - (e) 36

22. A certain number of capsules were purchased for ₹ 216, 15 more capsules could have been purchased in the same amount if each capsule was cheaper by ₹ 10. What was the number of capsules purchased?
    - (a) 6
    - (b) 14
    - (c) 8
    - (d) 12
    - (e) 9

23. M, N, O and P divided ₹ 44352 among themselves. M took $\dfrac{3}{8}$th of the money, N took $\dfrac{1}{6}$th of the remaining amount and rest was divided among O and P in the ratio of 3 : 4 respectively. How much did O get as his share?
    - (a) ₹9600
    - (b) ₹10600
    - (c) ₹10300
    - (d) ₹8700
    - (e) ₹9900

24. Pure milk costs ₹ 16 per litre. After adding water the milkman sells the mixture ₹ 15 per litre and thereby makes a profit of 25%. In what respective ratio does he mix milk with water?
    - (a) 3 : 1
    - (b) 4 : 3
    - (c) 3 : 2
    - (d) 5 : 3
    - (e) 4 : 1

25. 1/3rd the diagonal of a square is $3\sqrt{2}$ m. What is the measure of the side of the concerned square?
    - (a) 12 m
    - (b) 9 m
    - (c) 18 m
    - (d) 6 m
    - (e) 7 m

DIRECTIONS (Qs. 26-30) : What will come in place of question mark (?) in the given number series?

26.. 37, ?, 103, 169, 257, 367
    - (a) 61
    - (b) 59
    - (c) 67
    - (d) 55
    - (e) 71

27. 4, 6, 34, ?, 504, 1234
    - (a) 194
    - (b) 160
    - (c) 186
    - (d) 156
    - (e) 172

28. 3, ?, 14, 55, 274, 1643
    - (a) 11
    - (b) 5
    - (c) 6
    - (d) 8
    - (e) 7

29. 960, 839, 758, 709, ?, 675
    - (a) 696
    - (b) 700
    - (c) 688
    - (d) 678
    - (e) 684

30. 61, 72, ?, 73, 59, 74, 58
    - (a) 70
    - (b) 60
    - (c) 71
    - (d) 62
    - (e) 63

31. Two pipes can fill a tank in 10 h and 16 h respectively. A third pipe can empty the tank in 32 h. If all the three pipes function simultaneously, then in how much time the tank will be full? (in hours)

(a) $7\dfrac{11}{21}$ (b) $7\dfrac{13}{21}$

(c) $8\dfrac{4}{21}$ (d) $6\dfrac{5}{14}$

(e) $8\dfrac{9}{14}$

32. A merchant bought some goods worth ₹ 6000 and sold half of them at 12% profit. At what profit per cent should he sell the remaining goods to make and overall profit of 18%?

(a) 24   (b) 28
(c) 18   (d) 20
(e) 26

33. A and B are two numbers. 6 times of square of B is 540 more than the square of A. If the respective ratio between A and B is 3 : 2, what is the value of B?

(a) 10   (b) 12
(c) 16   (d) 8
(e) 14

34. The perimeter of a rectangle whose length is 6 m more than its breadth is 84 m. What would be the area of a triangle whose base is equal to the diagonal of the rectangle and whose height is equal to the length of the rectangle? (in m^2)

(a) 324   (b) 372
(c) 360   (d) 364
(e) 348

35. 56 workers can finish a piece of work in 14 days. If the work is to be completed in 8 days, then how many extra workers are required?

(a) 36   (b) 48
(c) 44   (d) 42
(e) 32

DIRECTIONS (Qs. 36-40) : Study the table carefully and answer the given questions.

Number of Pages Printed by 6 Printers in 5 Different Weeks

Week / Printer	A	B	C	D	E	F
1st	664	618	628	552	638	419
2nd	569	441	519	438	621	537
3rd	440	614	503	527	541	742
4th	256	563	347	651	412	321
5th	717	429	598	582	519	693

36. What is the respective ratio between the number of pages printed by Printer B in 2nd week and the number of pages printed by Printer F in 5th week?

(a) 4 : 9   (b) 11 : 13
(c) 9 : 13   (d) 7 : 11
(e) 9 : 11

37. What is the average number of pages printed by all the given printers in 4th week?

(a) 375   (b) 425
(c) 415   (d) 430
(e) 390

38. Which of the following printer printed maximum number of pages in all the given weeks together?

(a) Printer A   (b) Printer E
(c) Printer D   (d) Printer C
(e) Printer F

39. Number of pages printed by Printer A in 3rd week is what per cent of the total number of pages printed by Printed D in all the given weeks?

(a) 22   (b) 18   (c) 12   (d) 14
(e) 16

40. What is the difference between the total number of pages printed by Printer E in 1st, 2nd and 4th week together and total number of pages printed by Printer C in all the given weeks together?

(a) 952   (b) 878
(c) 924   (d) 934
(e) 918

REASONING ABILITY

DIRECTIONS (Qs. 41-45) : Study the following information carefully and answer the questions given below:

Seven representatives of a company - P, Q, R, S, T, U and V - travelled to three different countries i.e. South Africa, Australia and France. Each of them travelled on different days of the week (no two persons travelled on the same day), starting on Monday and ending on Sunday, Minimum two people travelled to each country and South Africa is the only country to which three people travelled. P travelled to South Africa on Monday. U travelled to Australia but neither on Tuesday nor on Saturday. V travelled on Sunday but not to France. The one who travelled to Australia travelled on Tuesday and the one who travelled to France travelled on Saturday. T travelled on Wednesday. R travelled to South Africa but not on Thursday. Q did not travel to France.

41. If everyone's trip is postponed by one day, who will be travelling on Wednesday?

(a) U   (b) R
(c) Q   (d) T
(e) None of these

42. Who amongst the seven representatives travelled on Saturday?

(a) S   (b) Q
(c) R   (d) Cannot be determined
(e) None of these

43. Which one of the following combinations is true according to the given information?

(a) U - Thursday - South Africa
(b) S - Wednesday - France
(c) V - Monday - South Africa
(d) R - Friday - Australia
(e) None of these

44. Who amongest the seven representatives travelled on friday?

(a) R   (b) S
(c) Q   (d) Can't be determined
(e) None of these

45. Who was the last one to travel?

(a) P   (b) R
(c) V   (d) S
(e) None of these

DIRECTIONS (Qs. 46-50) : Study the following information to answer the given questions :

Eight friends A, B, C, D, E, F, G and H are sitting around a circle facing the centre, not necessarily in the same order. F sits fourth to the left of B. A and H are immediate neighbours of F. C sits third to the left of A. G sits third to the right of E.

46. What is D's position with respect to B ?

(a) Immediate left   (b) Sixth to the right
(c) Second to the left   (d) Seventh to the left
(e) Fifth to the right

47. What are the immediate neighbours of G ?
    (a) F and H   (b) A and F
    (c) C and H   (d) A and B
    (e) B and C

48. If C is related to E in a certain way and similarly F is related B in the same way, to whom is A related to ?
    (a) H   (b) D
    (c) G   (d) C
    (e) None of these

49. Four of the following five are alike in a certain way based on their seating positions in the above arrangement and so form a group. Which is the one that **does not** belong to the group ?
    (a) FE   (b) HA
    (c) DG   (d) BE
    (e) CF

50. If all the eight friends are made to sit alphabetically in the clockwise direction starting from A, positions of how many will remain unchanged (excluding A) ?
    (a) None   (b) One
    (c) Two   (d) Three
    (e) Four

DIRECTIONS (Qs. 51-53) : In each question below are two statements followed by two conclusions numbered I and II. You have to take the two given statements to be true even if they seem to be at variance from commonly known facts and then decide which of the given conclusions logically follows from the given statements disregarding commonly known facts.

Give answer **(a)** if **only** conclusion 1 follows.
Give answer **(b)** if **only** conclusion II follows.
Give answer **(c)** if **either** conclusion I or conclusion II follows.
Give answer **(d)** if **neither** conclusion I nor conclusion II follows.
Give answer **(e)** if **both** conclusions I and II follow.

51. **Statements :**
    Some windows are grills.
    All glasses are grills.
    Conclusions :
    I.   All grills are windows.
    II.   At least some grills are glasses.

52. **Statements :**
    Some painters are artists. Some dancers are painters.
    Conclusions :
    I.   All artists are dancers.
    II.   All painters are dancers.

53. **Statements :**
    All cabins are rooms.
    All rooms are buildings.
    Conclusions:
    I.   All buildings are rooms.
    II.   All cabins are buildings.

DIRECTIONS (Qs. 54-55) : Study the following information carefully to answer these questions. Ashish starts running from point P and run 10 km towards North. It takes a right turn and runs 15 km. It now runs 6 km after taking a left turn. It takes a left turn, runs 15 km. Finally it takes right turn and run 5 km. andand stops at Ravi's house.

54. How far is Ravi's house with respect to point P?
    (a) 16km   (b) 25km
    (c) 4km   (d) 21km
    (e) None of these

55. Towards which direction was the Ashish running before it stopped at Ravi's house?
    (a) North   (b) East
    (c) South   (d) West
    (e) North - West

DIRECTIONS (Qs. 56-60) : Study the following information to answer the given questions :

Seven friends - L, M, N, O, P, Q and R are sitting in a straight line facing North, not necessarily in the same order. M sits fifth to the right of O. P sits third to the right of L. Both L and P do not sit at the extreme ends of the line. Q and R are immediate neighbours of each other. N sits third to the left of Q.

56. What is O's position with respect of R ?
    (a) Second to the right   (b) Third to the left
    (c) Second to the left   (d) Third to the right
    (e) None of these

57. Which of the following represents the friends sitting at the extreme ends of the line?
    (a) O, M   (b) Q, O
    (c) N, M   (d) Q, N
    (e) None of these

58. If all the seven friends are made to sit in alphabetical order from **left to right,** the positions of how many will remain unchanged ?
    (a) Four   (b) Three
    (c) One   (d) Two
    (e) None

59. Who sits exactly in the middle of the row ?
    (a) P   (b) L
    (c) Q   (d) R
    (e) None of these

60. Four of the following five are alike in a certain way based on their seating positions in the above arrangement and so form a group. Which is the one that **does not** belong to the group ?
    (a) MP   (b) RQ
    (c) ON   (d) LN
    (e) QL

DIRECTIONS (Qs. 61-63) : In each question below is given a group of numbers/symbols followed by five combinations of letter codes numbered (a), (b), (c), (d) and (e). You have to find out which of the combinations correctly represents the group of numbers/ symbols based on the following coding system and the conditions and mark the number of that combination as your answer.

Number/Symbols	9	4	&	5	%	3	#	7	6	@	8	+	2	$
Letter Codes	X	P	J	H	B	D	K	F	S	T	N	G	R	L

Conditions:
    (i)   If the first element is a symbol and the last element is a number, then the codes for both are to be interchanged.
    (ii) If both the first and last elements are symbols, then the last element is to be coded as the code for the first element.
    (iii) If the group of elements contains only one symbol, then that symbols is to be coded as A.

61. 28%956
    (a) RNBXHS   (b) RNAXSH
    (c) RNBXSH   (d) RNAXHS
    (e) RNASHX

62. @62+74
    (a) PSRGFT   (b) TSRFGP
    (c) PSRFGT   (d) PRSGFT
    (e) TSRGFP

63. +5963%
  (a) GHXSDG (b) GSHXDB
  (c) GHXDSG (d) GHSXDB
  (e) GXHSDG

DIRECTIONS (Qs. 64-67) : In these questions, relationships between different elements is shown in the statements. These statements are followed by two conclusions.

Give answer **(a)** if **only** conclusion I follows.
Give answer **(b)** if **only** conclusion II follows.
Give answer **(c)** if **either** conclusion I or conclusion II follows.
Give answer **(d)** if **neither** conclusion I nor conclusion II follows.
Give answer **(e)** if **both** conclusions I and II follow.

64. Statement : $A < L < T < R \le H > K$
  Conclusions : I. $H > L$
  II. $K > T$
65. Statement : $P = N > D \ge G < B = J$
  Conclusions : I. $G < P$
  II. $G < J$
66. Statement : $F \le C \ge V = Z < X = U$
  Conclusions : I. $V < U$
  II. $Z < F$
67. Statement : $Q \le E = I > N \ge R \ge S$
  Conclusions: I. $E = S$
  II. $S \le N$
68. Which of the following symbols should replace question mark (?) in the given expression in order to make the expressions 'A > D' and 'F ≥ C' definitely true?
  $A > B \ge C ? D \le E = F$
  (a) > (b) <
  (c) ≤ (d) =
  (e) Either = or ≥

DIRECTIONS (Qs. 69-70) : Some statements are given followed by some conclusions. You have to consider the statements to be true even if they seem to be at variance from commonly known facts. You have to decide which of the following conclusions if any, follow from the given statements:

69. **Statements:** All kings are royal
  No king is interesting
  Some kings are important
  No important is interesting
  Conclusion:
  (I) All important being royal is a possibility
  (II) All interesting being royal is a possibility
  (III) Some royal are not interesting
  (a) Only (I) and (III) follow
  (b) Only (III) follow
  (c) Only (I) and (II) follow
  (d) All follow
  (e) None of these
70. **Statements:** All chicken are muttons
  No Mutton is fish Some fishs are useless
  Some useless are chicken
  Conclusion:
  (I) All useless being mutton is a possibility
  (II) All useless being fishs is a possibility
  (III) Some useless are not fish
  (a) Only (I) and (III) follow
  (b) Only (III) follow
  (c) Only (I) and (II) follow
  (d) All follow
  (e) None of these

DIRECTIONS (Qs. 71-75) : Study the following information and answer the questions given.

In a certain code language "la na pa pu" means 'we provide study material',
"fa pa ma ju" means 'we score maximum selection',
"ma fa na ju " means "study score the selection"
and "ju bu sa fu" means "selection of the material". Then
71. What is the code of "score " in this code language?
  (a) ju (b) ma
  (c) fa (d) pa
  (e) Cannot be determined
72. What is the code of "provide " in this code language?
  (a) pu (b) bu
  (c) pa (d) na
  (e) Cannot be determined
73. What is the code of " provide of maximum"?
  (a) sa pu fu (b) fa pu sa
  (c) fu bu sa (d) pu fa ma
  (e) Cannot be determined
74. What is the code of "we the" in this code language?
  (a) pa fu (b) sa pu
  (c) pa sa (d) hu fu
  (e) Cannot be determined
75. What is the code of "material" in this code language?
  (a) hu (b) bu
  (c) sa (d) pa
  (e) Cannot be determined
76. Reena walks towards East, then towards North and tuning 45° right walks for a while and lastly turns towards left. In which direction is he walking now?
  (a) North (b) East
  (c) South East (d) North West
  (e) None of these
77. The positions of the first and the sixth letters of the word CARPET are interchanged; similarly, the positions of the second and fifth letters; and the third and fourth letters are interchanged. In the new arrangement thus formed, how many alphabets are there between the letter which is second from the right and the letter which is second from the left end, in the English alphabetical series?
  (a) None (b) One
  (c) Two (d) Three
  (e) More than three
78. Among A, B, C and D, A has to travel more than any other friend to reach the office. C travels a certain distance which is not as much as B but greater than D. Who amongst them travels the least distance to reach the office?
  (a) B (b) D
  (c) A (d) Cannot be determined
  (e) None of these
79. There are four students which are two girls and two boys are playing chess and are seated at North, East, South and West of a table. No girl is facing East. Students sitting opposite each other are not of the same gender. One boy is facing South. Which directions are the girls facing?
  (a) South and East (b) North and East
  (c) North and West (d) East and West
  (e) Data inadequate
80. Pointing to a girl, Mr. Arun said. "She is the daughter of my mother's only child". How is the girl related to Mr. Arun?
  (a) Sister (b) Mother
  (c) Cousin (d) Daughter
  (e) Cannot be determined

HINTS & EXPLANATIONS

Solutions (1-5):

Annual expenditure on different items:

Maintenance = Rs $(240000000 \times 20)/100 = 48000000$

Medical = Rs $(240000000 \times 12)/100 = 28800000$

Transport = Rs $(240000000 \times 10)/100 = 24000000$

Salary = Rs $(240000000 \times 35)/100 = 84000000$

Electricity = Rs $(240000000 \times 7)/100 = 16800000$

Telephone = Rs $(240000000 \times 5)/100 = 12000000$

Allowance = Rs $(240000000 \times 11)/100 = 26400000$

Department wise distribution of employees:

Number of employees in Account
$= (2400 \times 15)/100 = 360$

Number of employees in Administration
$= (2400 \times 18)/100 = 432$

Number of employees in Personnel
$= (2400 \times 12)/100 = 288$

Number of employees in Marketing
$= (2400 \times 20)/100 = 480$

Number of employees in Computer
$= (2400 \times 5)/100 = 120$

Number of employees in Operation
$= (2400 \times 30)/100 = 720$

1. (a) Total expenditure on accounts department
    $= (240000000 \times 360)/2400$
    $=$ Rs. 36 millions

2. (a) Per employee expenditure on medical
    $= 28800000/2400 =$ Rs.12000

3. (d) Total expenditure on salary of employees in marketing department
    $= (84000000/2400 \times 480) =$ Rs. 16.80 millions

4. (e) Amount spent on telephone
    $= 240000000 \times 5/100$
    $= 12000000 = 12$ millions

5. (e) Expenditure on telephone for employees in computer department
    $= 12000000/2400 \times 120 = 6$ lakh

Solutions (6-10):

6. (a) Total sale of English news papers in all the districts
    $= (7400+8400+9600+6800+6400) = 38600$
    Total sale of Hindi news papers in all the districts
    $(5400+9000+5400+9600+4400) = 33800$
    Required difference $= (38600-33800) = 4800$

7. (b) Total sale of English newspapers in districts P $= 7400$
    Total sale of English newspapers in all the districts together
    $= (7400+8400+9600+6800+6400) = 38600$
    Required percentage $= (7400 \times 100)/38600 = 20\%$

8. (d) Total sale of Hindi news papers in district P $= 5400$
    Total sale of Hindi news papers in district S $= 9600$
    Required ratio $= 5400/9600 = 9:16$

9. (c) Total sale of English newspapers in districts Q and S together
    $= (8400 + 6800) = 15200$
    Total sale of English newspapers in districts P, R and T together
    $= (7400 + 9600 + 6400) = 23400$
    Required percentage $= (15200 \times 100)/23400 = 65\%$

10. (a) Total sale of Hindi news papers in all the districts
    $(5400 + 9000 + 5400 + 9600 + 4400) = 33800$
    Required average $= 33800/5 = 6760$

11. (b) $? = (13.001)^3 = (13)^3$
    $= 2197 = 2200$

12. (d) $? = 55 \times 55 + 5$
    $= 3025 + 5 = 3030$

13. (a) $? = \dfrac{100 \times 50}{100} \div 50 = 1$

14. (a) $? = 999 + 900 - 350$
    $= 1549$

15. (e) $? = 2^3 \times (2)^{-2} \div (4)^{-4}$
    $= \dfrac{2}{(4)^{-4}} = 2 \times 2^8 = 2^9 = 512$

16. (b) I. $x^2 - 11x - 24 = 0$
    $x^2 - 8x - 3x - 24 = 0$
    $x(x-8) - 3(x-8) = 0$
    $(x-8)(x-3) = 0$
    $\therefore$ $x = 8$ or 3
    II. $2y^2 - 9y + 9 = 0$
    $2y^2 - 6y - 3y + 9 = 0$
    $2y(y-3) - 3(y-3) = 0$
    $(2y-3)(y-3) = 0$
    $\therefore$ $y = \dfrac{3}{2}$ or 3

    So $x \geq y$

17. (c) I. $x^3 \times 13 = x^2 \times 247$
    or $\dfrac{x^3}{x^2} = \dfrac{247}{13}$
    $x = 19$
    II. $y^{1/3} \times 14 = 294 \div y^{2/3}$
    or, $(y)^{1/3} \times (y)^{2/3} = \dfrac{294}{14}$
    or, $(y)^{\frac{1}{3}+\frac{2}{3}} = 21$ $\therefore y = 21$

    So $y > x$

18. (d) I. $\dfrac{12 \times 4}{(x)^{4/7}} - \dfrac{3 \times 4}{(x)^{4/7}} = (x)^{10/7}$
    or, $48 - 12 = (x)^{10/7} \times (x)^{4/7}$
    or, $36 = (x)^{\frac{10+4}{7}} = (x)^2$
    $x = \pm 6$

II. $y^3 + 783 = 999$
$$y^3 = 999 - 783$$
$$y^3 = 216$$
$$y = 6 \qquad \therefore y \geq x$$

19. (e) I. $\sqrt{500}\,x + \sqrt{402} = 0$

or, $\sqrt{500}\,x = -\sqrt{402}$

By squaring both sides, we get
$$500x^2 = 402$$
$$x = \sqrt{\frac{402}{500}} = \pm 0.897$$

II. $\sqrt{360}\,y + (200)^{\frac{1}{2}} = 0$

or, $(200)^{\frac{1}{2}} = -\sqrt{360}\,y$

By squaring both sides, we get
$$\left((200)^{\frac{1}{2}}\right)^2 = (-\sqrt{360}\,y)$$
$$200 = 360\,y^2$$
$$y = \sqrt{\frac{200}{360}} = \pm 0.75$$

Relationship cannot established.

20. (c) I. $(17)^2 + 144 + 18 = x$
$$289 + 8 = x$$
$$\therefore \quad x = 297$$

II. $(26)^2 - 18 \times 21 = y$
$$676 - 378 = y$$
$$\therefore \quad 298 = y$$

So, $y > x$.

21. (d) $\dfrac{A+12}{B+12} = \dfrac{3}{4}$

$$A = \frac{15}{4}C$$
$$A = \frac{15}{4} \times 10 = 37.5$$
$$\frac{37.5 + 12}{B + 12} = \frac{3}{4}$$
$$B = 54$$

22. (d) Let x be the price of one capsule
y be the total number of capsule.
$$xy = 216 \qquad \qquad ...(1)$$
$$(x - 10)(y + 15) = 216 \qquad ...(2)$$
From eqs (1) and (2)
$$\left(\frac{216}{y} - 10\right)(y + 15) = 216$$
$$(216 - 10y)(y + 15) = 216\,y$$
$$216y + 216 \times 15 - 10y^2 - 150y = 216\,y$$
$$216y + 3240 - 10y^2 - 150y = 216\,y$$
$$-10y^2 - 150y + 3240 = 0$$
$$y^2 + 15y - 324 = 0$$
$$y = 12$$

23. (e) M's share $= 44352 \times \dfrac{3}{8} = 16632$

Remaining after M's share $= 27720$

N's share $= 27720 \times \dfrac{1}{6} = 4620$

Remaining after M & N's share $= 23100$

$\dfrac{O}{P} = \dfrac{3}{4} \Rightarrow$ O's share $= 23100 \times \dfrac{3}{7} = 9900$

24. (a) $\because$ SP of the mixture $= ₹ 15$

$\therefore$ CP of the mixture $= 15 \times \dfrac{100}{125} = ₹ 12$

Now, by the rule of mixture,

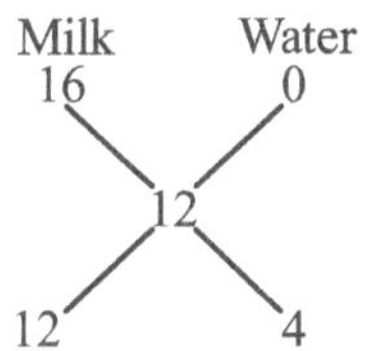

$\therefore$ Ratio of milk and water in the mixture
$= 12 : 4 = 3 : 1$

25. (b)

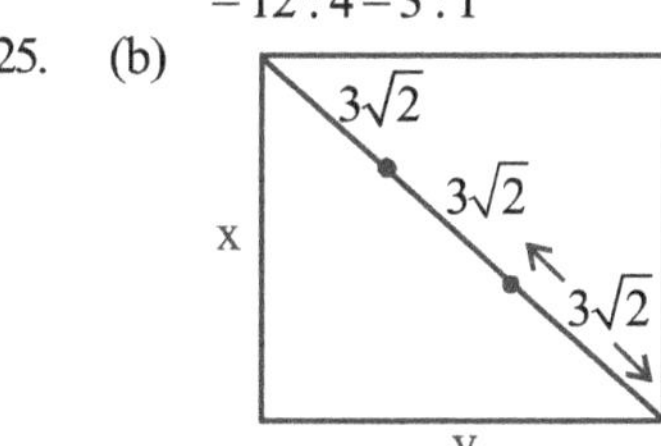

$$x^2 + y^2 = \left(9\sqrt{2}\right)^2$$
$$2x^2 = 81 \times 2$$
$$x = 9$$

26. (b)

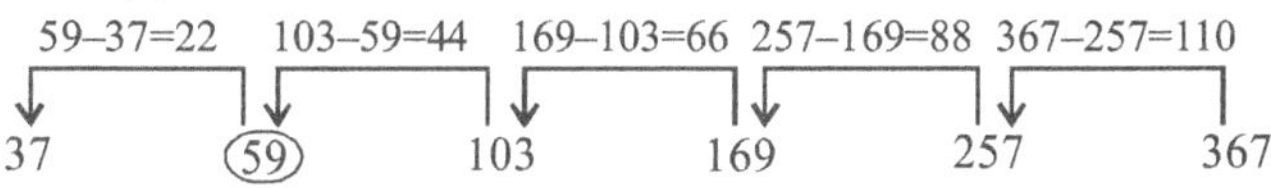

27. (b)

28. (b)

29. (e)
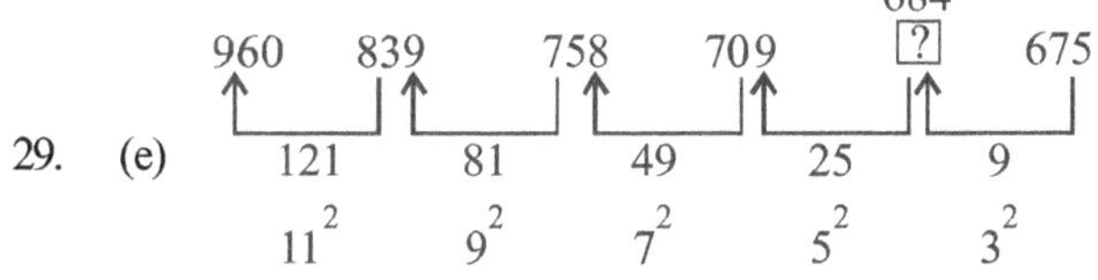

30. (b)

This is mixed series.

31. (b) 10 hr A pipe $\rightarrow$ 1
16 hr B pipe $\rightarrow$ 1
32 hr C pipe $\rightarrow$ 1

$$\frac{1}{10}+\frac{1}{16}-\frac{1}{32}=\frac{21}{160}$$

$$\frac{160}{21}=7\frac{13}{21}\text{ hr}$$

32. (a) Profit on all the goods = 18% of 6000 = ₹ 1080
Profit on half of the goods = 12% of 3000 = ₹ 360
∴ Profit on remaining half of the objects
= 1080 − 360 = ₹ 720

Hence, required profit percentage $=\dfrac{720}{3000}\times100\%$

= 24 %

33. (b) $6B^2 = A^2 + 540$

$$\frac{A}{B}=\frac{3}{2}$$

$$A=\frac{3B}{2}$$

$$6B^2=\frac{9B^2}{4}+540$$

$$3.75\,B^2=540$$

$$B=\sqrt{144}=12$$

34. (c) $x+x+x+6+x+6=84$
$4x + 12 = 84$
$x = 18\,m$

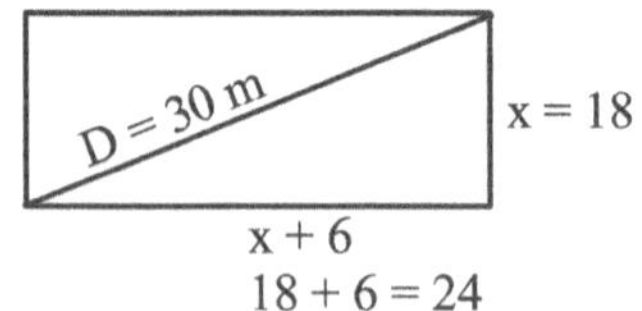

18 + 6 = 24
$D^2 = (x+6)^2 + x^2$

$D^2 = 24^2 + 18^2$
$D^2 = 576 + 324 = 900$
$D = 30\,m$
Base of triangle = 30 m
Height of triangle = x + 6 = 24 m

Area of triangle $=\dfrac{1}{2}\times30\times24=360\ m^2$

35. (d) Here, $M_1 = 56, D_1 = 14, M_2 = ?, D_2 = 8$
Using
$$M_1 D_1 = M_2 D_2,$$
$$56\times14=M_2\times8$$
$\Rightarrow M_2 = 98$
Hence, extra workers to be required
= 98 − 56 = 42

36. (d) Ratio

$=\dfrac{\text{number of pages printed by printer B in 2nd week}}{\text{number of pages printed by printer F in 5}^{th}\text{week}}$

$=\dfrac{441}{693}=\dfrac{7}{11}$

Required Ratio = 7 : 11

37. (b) Average number of pages printed by all the printer =

$$=\frac{256+563+347+651+412+321}{6}=425$$

38. (c)

Week \ Printer	A	B	C	D	E	F
1st	664	618	628	552	638	419
2nd	569	441	519	438	621	537
3rd	440	614	503	527	541	742
4th	256	263	347	651	412	321
5th	717	429	598	582	519	693
Total up to 5th week	2646	2365	2595	2750	2731	2712

Printer D printed maximum pages.

39. (e) Required percentage (%) =

$=\dfrac{\text{Pages printed by A in 3rd week}}{\text{Total page printed by D from 1st to 5th weeks}}\times100$

$=\dfrac{440}{2750}\times100=16\%$

40. (c) Required difference = Total no. of pages printed by printer C in all given weeks − Total no. of pages by E in 1st, 2nd, 4th week
= 2595 − (638 + 621 + 412) = 924

Solution(41-45)

Persons	Days	Countries
P	Monday	South Africa
Q	Tuesday	Australia
R	Friday	South Africa
S	Saturday	France
T	Wednesday	France
U	Thursday	Australia
V	Sunday	South Africa

41. (c)
42. (a)
43. (e)
44. (a)
45. (c)

Solution(46-50) :

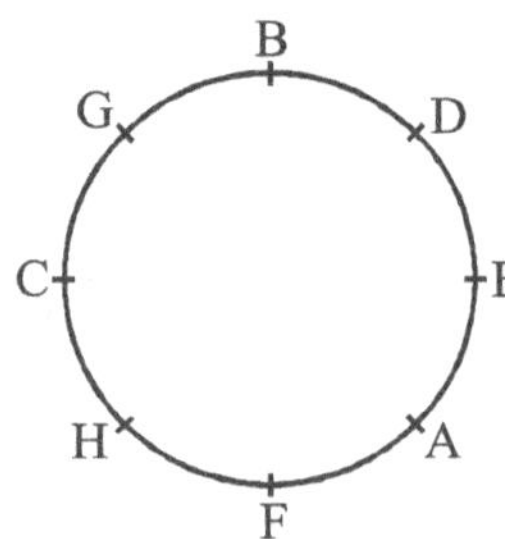

46. (a) D is to the immediate left of B.
47. (e) B and C are immediate neighbours of G.
48. (c) C is sitting just opposite to E. F is sitting just opposite to B. Similarly, A is sitting just opposite to G.
49. (d) Except in the pair BE, in all other pairs the first person is second to the left of the second person. B is second to the right of E.

50. (a) 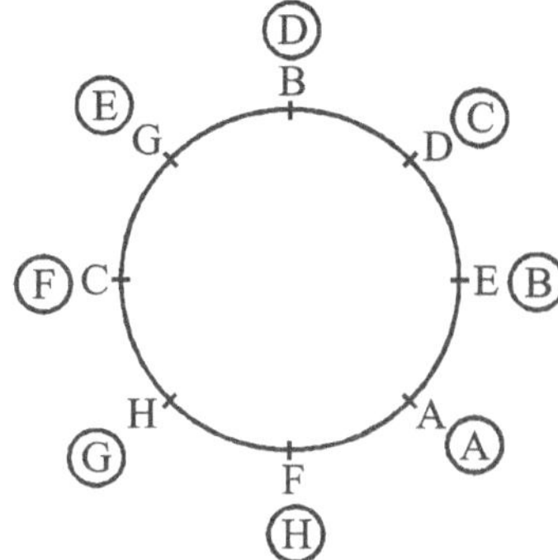

51. (b) 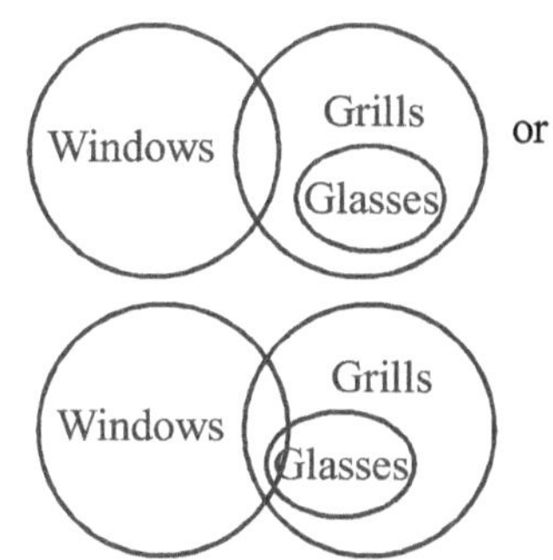
or

Conclusion: I. False
II. True

52. (d) 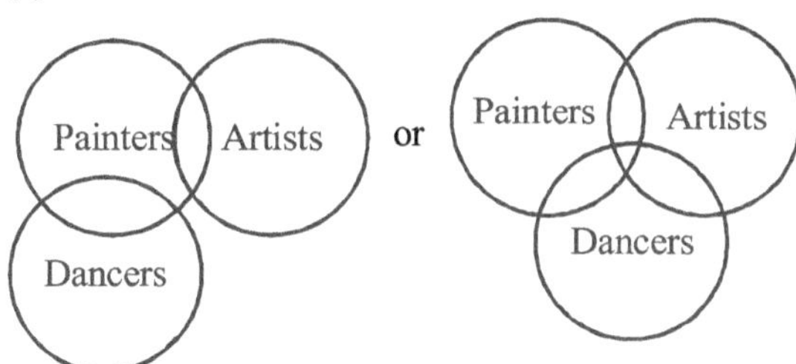
or

Conclusion: I. False
II. False

53. (b) 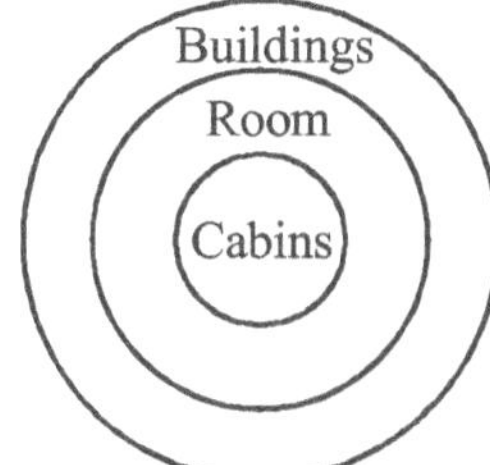

Conclusion: I. False
II. True

Solutions : (54-55)

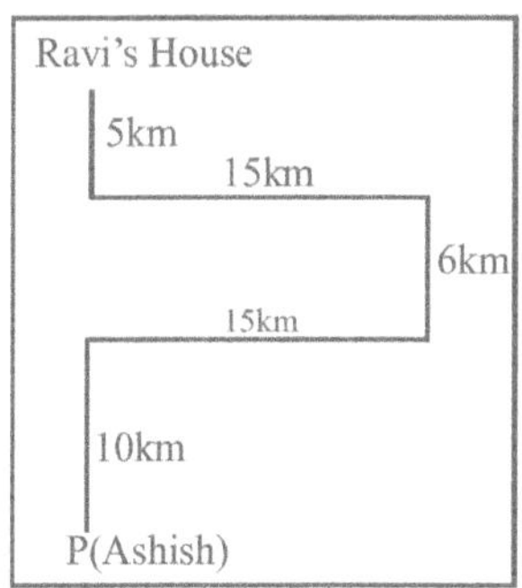

54. (d)   55. (a)

(56-60) :

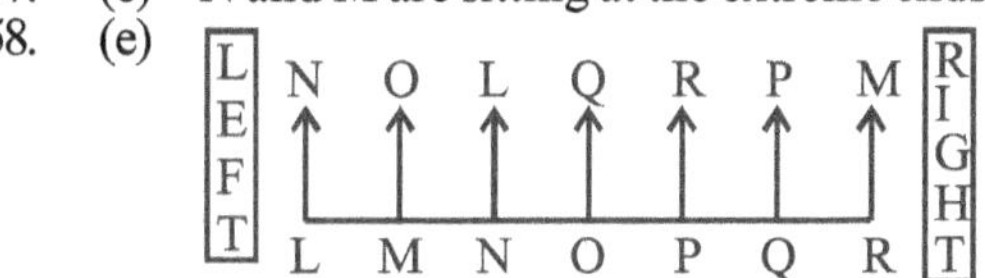

56. (b) O is third to the left of R.
57. (c) N and M are sitting at the extreme ends of the line.
58. (e)

59. (c) Q is sitting exactly in the middle of the row.
60. (d) Except LN, in all others the first person is to immediate right of the second person. L is second to the right of N.

61. (d)

2	8	%	9	5	6
↓	↓	↓	↓	↓	↓
R	N	A	X	H	S

Condition (iii) is applicable.

62. (a)

@	6	2	+	7	4
↓	↓	↓	↓	↓	↓
P	S	R	G	F	T

Condition (i) is applicable.

63. (a)

+	5	9	6	3	%
↓	↓	↓	↓	↓	↓
G	H	X	S	D	G

Condition (ii) is applicable.

64. (a) $H > K \geq R > T > L$
Conclusions: I. $H > L$: True
II. $K > T$: Not True

65. (e) $P = N > D \geq G < B = J$
Conclusions: I. $G < P$: True
II. $G < J$: True

66. (d) $F \leq C \geq V = Z > X = U$
Conclusions: I. $V < U$: Not True
II. $Z < F$: Not True

67. (b) $Q \leq E = 1 > N \geq R \geq S$
Conclusions : I. $E = S$: Not True
II. $S \leq N$: True

68. (d) In the expression $A > B \geq C \boxed{=} D \leq E = F$ to make $A > D$ true and $F \geq C$ true.

69. (d) 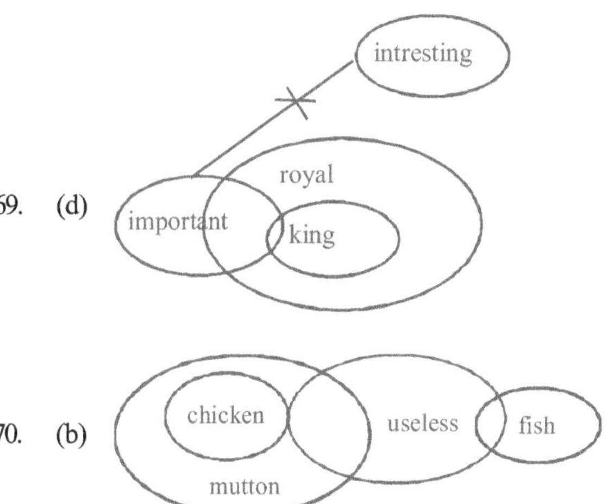

70. (b)

Solutions (71 - 75):

We → pa, Provide → pu, Study → na, Material → bu, Score → ma, Maximum → fa, Selection → ju, The → fu, of → sa

71. (b)   72. (a)   73. (b)   74. (a)   75. (b)

76. (d)

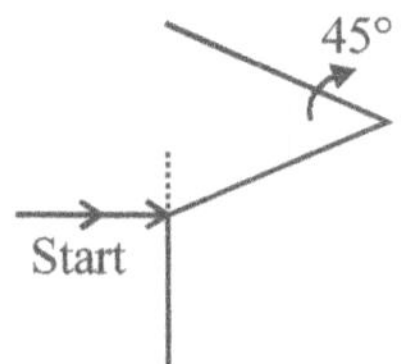

77. (d) 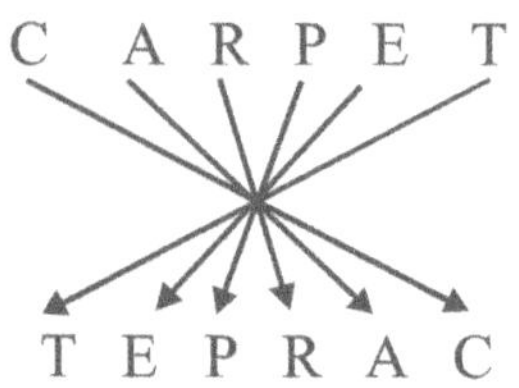

There are 3 letters between A and E.

78. (b) Order of distance travelled:
A > B > C > D

79. (c)

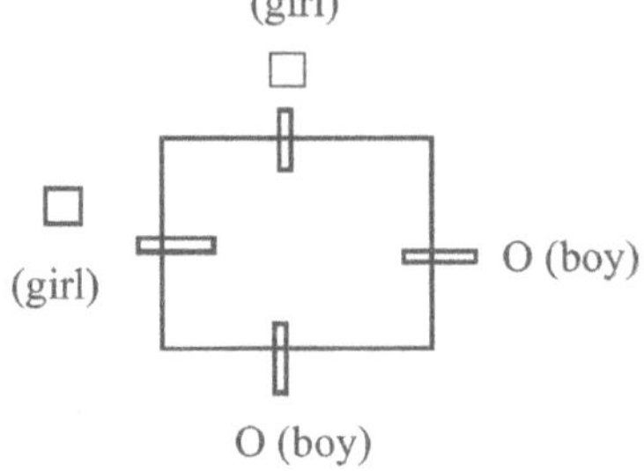

80. (d) Mother
↓ only child
Arun (Him Self)
↓
Daughter/she
Therefore, the girl is the daughter of Arun.

PRACTICE SET 13

Time : 45 min. **Max. Marks : 80**

QUANTITATIVE APTITUDE

DIRECTIONS (Qs. 1-5): What will come in place of the question mark(?) in the following questions?

1. $(3325 \div 25) \times (152 \div 16) = ?$
   - (a) 1269.4
   - (b) 1264.9
   - (c) 1265.3
   - (d) 1263.5
   - (e) None of these

2. $5\dfrac{1}{5} + 2\dfrac{2}{15} + 3\dfrac{2}{3} = ?$
   - (a) 15
   - (b) 13
   - (c) $\dfrac{11}{15}$
   - (d) 12
   - (e) None of these

3. $(2525 \times 0.25 \div 5) \times 7 = ?$
   - (a) 889.43
   - (b) 883.75
   - (c) 886.45
   - (d) 881.75
   - (e) None of these

4. 32% of $500 + 162\%$ of $50 = ?$
   - (a) 231
   - (b) 245
   - (c) 237
   - (d) 247
   - (e) None of these

5. $45316 + 52131 - 65229 = ? + 15151$
   - (a) 17063
   - (b) 17073
   - (c) 17076
   - (d) 17067
   - (e) None of these

DIRECTIONS (Qs. 6-10): Study of the following table carefully to answer the questions that follow.

Station	Arrival time	Departure time	Halt time(in minutes)	Distance travelled from origin(in km)	No. of passengers boarding the train at each station
Patna	Starting	12.15 am	-	0 km	435
Gaya	12:55 am	12.58 am	3 minutes	48 km	382
Ranchi	4:15 am	4.25 am	10 minutes	256 km	454
Dhanbad	6:15 am	6.20 am	5 minutes	382 km	238
Jamui	6.45 am	6.48 am	3 minutes	424 km	295
Koderma	7.05 am	7.08 am	3 minutes	445 km	135
Jhajha	8.00 am	8.25 am	25 minutes	492 km	315
Nawada	5.45 pm	Ending point	-	986 km	None

6. What is the distance travelled by the train Ranchi to Koderma junction?
   - (a) 189 km
   - (b) 178 km
   - (c) 182 km
   - (d) 186 km
   - (e) 199 km

7. How much time does the train take to reach Jhajha after departing from Jamui?
   - (a) 1 hr 10 minutes
   - (b) 1 hr 25 minutes
   - (c) 1 hr 20 minutes
   - (d) 1 hr 12 minutes
   - (e) 1 hr 14 minutes

8. What is the ratio of the number of passengers boarding from Patna to that from Jhajha in the train?
   - (a) 29:25
   - (b) 29:23
   - (c) 29:21
   - (d) 29:24
   - (e) 39:21

9. If the halt time (stopping time) of the train at Dhanbad is decreased by 2 minutes and increased by 25 minutes at Jhajha, at what time will the train reach Nawada?
   - (a) 6 : 08 pm
   - (b) 6 : 18 pm
   - (c) 6 : 06 pm
   - (d) 6 : 12 pm
   - (e) 6 : 05 pm

10. The distance between which two station is the second lowest?
   (a) Patna and Jhajha   (b) Jhajha and Gaya
   (c) Jamui and Dhanbad   (d) Ranchi and Gaya
   (e) None of these

DIRECTIONS (Qs. 11-15) : Study the following graphs which show the number of workers of different categories of a factory for two different years. The total number of workers in 2014 was 20000 and in 2015 was 24000.

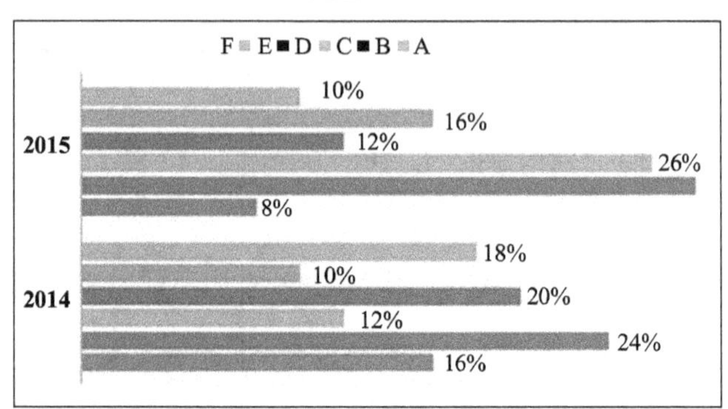

11. In which of the categories is the number of workers same in both the year?
   (a) F   (b) D   (c) C   (d) B
   (e) None of these

12. Find the percentage increased in the number of workers in categories E in 2015 from 2014.
   (a) 92%   (b) 33 1/3%   (c) 50%   (d) 66 1/3%
   (e) 80%

13. What is the total number of increased workers for the categories in which the number of workers has been increased?
   (a) 5680   (b) 7380   (c) 7400   (d) 7600
   (e) 5250

14. Which categories have shown decrease in the number of workers from 2014 to 2015?
   (a) F and D   (b) F, D and A
   (c) C and B   (d) F
   (e) D and A

15. Find the maximum difference between the number of workers of any two categories taken together for any one year and that of any two for the other year.
   (a) 8656   (b) 9416   (c) 8560   (d) 8392
   (e) 8450

DIRECTIONS (Qs. 16-20): Study the following pie-charts carefully and answer the questions.

The following graph represents percentage of number of employees in five departments of an organisation for two consecutive years.

Number of employees = 36000   Number of employees = 6000

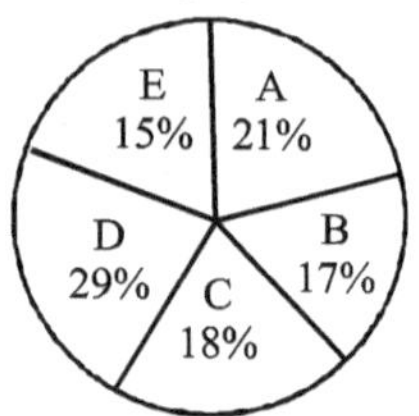

Year 2013

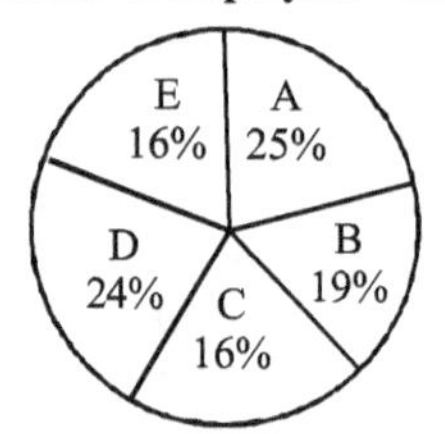

Year 2014

16. In terms of the number of the variation, in which of the following departments was minimum between 2013 and 2014?
   (a) C   (b) A
   (c) D   (d) B
   (e) E

17. If 2400 employees joined the department A in 2013, how many employees joined the department C in the same year?
   (a) 1100   (b) 1600
   (c) 1400   (d) 1200
   (e) Data inadequate

18. What was the approximate percentage increase in the number of employees in department C in 2014 as compared to the year 2013?
   (a) 55%   (b) 43%
   (c) 20%   (d) 48%
   (e) 58%

19. What was the difference between the number of employees in department D in 2013 and number of employees in department B in 2014?
   (a) 960   (b) 870
   (c) 820   (d) 1080
   (e) 920

20. If 1200 employees of department E left the organisation in 2013, how many more employees joined the organisation in department E in 2014 as compared to 2013?
   (a) 2800   (b) 5640
   (c) 5400   (d) 4800
   (e) 3000

21. Joel purchased 40 notebooks at the rate of ₹ 18 per notebook and 55 pencils at the rate of ₹ 8 per pencil. What is the total amount that he paid to the shopkeeper ?
   (a) ₹ 1,165   (b) ₹ 1,160
   (c) ₹ 1,166   (d) ₹ 1,161
   (e) None of these

22. The average of five numbers is 34.4. The average of the first and the second number is 46.5. The average of the fourth and the fifth number is 18. What is the third number ?
   (a) 45   (b) 46
   (c) 42   (d) 49
   (e) None of these

23. One of the angles of a parallelogram is 45°. What will be the sum of the larger angle and twice the smaller angle of the parallelogram ?
   (a) 228°   (b) 224°
   (c) 225°   (d) 222°
   (e) None of these

24. 9 women can complete a piece of work in 19 days. How many days will 18 women take to complete the same piece of work?
   (a) 12 days   (b) 6.5 days
   (c) 9 days   (d) 8.5 days
   (e) None of these

25. The ratio between Gloria's and Sara's present ages is 4 : 7 respectively. Two years ago the ratio between their ages was 1 : 2 respectively. What will be Sara's age three years hence ?
   (a) 17 years   (b) 14 years
   (c) 11 years   (d) 8 years
   (e) None of these

26. What is the difference between the simple and compound interest earned from a sum of ₹ 13,033 at a rate of 13 percent per annum for a period of 3 years (rounded off to 2 digits after decimal) ?
    (a) ₹ 5,082.87
    (b) ₹ 689.41
    (c) ₹ 5,772.28
    (d) ₹ 680.94
    (e) None of these

DIRECTIONS (Qs. 27-31) : In each of the following questions two equations I and II are given. Solve both the equations and give answer:

    (a) if x = y or relation can't be established between x and y
    (b) if x > y
    (c) if x < y
    (d) if x ≥ y
    (e) if x ≤ y

27. I. $x^2 + 2x - 195 = 0$
    II. $y^2 + 30y + 225 = 0$
28. I. $x^2 - 8x + 15 = 0$
    II. $y^2 - 5y + 6 = 0$
29. I. $4x^2 - 13x + 9 = 0$
    II. $y^2 + 3y + 2 = 0$
30. I. $36x^2 = 1$
    II. $4y^2 + 13y + 3 = 0$
31. I. $x^2 + 2x + 1 = 0$
    II. $y^2 = \pm 9$

DIRECTIONS (Qs. 32-34) : What should come in place of the question mark (?) in the following number series ?

32. 800   400   200   100   50   ?
    (a) 20
    (b) 30
    (c) 25
    (d) 35
    (e) None of these
33. 2   13   35   68   112   ?
    (a) 173
    (b) 178
    (c) 163
    (d) 167
    (e) None of these
34. 650   601   565   540   524   ?
    (a) 512
    (b) 514
    (c) 511
    (d) 515
    (e) None of these

DIRECTIONS (Qs. 35-36) : In the following number series only one number is wrong. Find out the wrong number.

35. 9050   5675   3478   2147   1418   1077   950
    (a) 3478
    (b) 1418
    (c) 5675
    (d) 2147
    (e) 1077
36. 8424   4212   2106   1051   526.5   263.25   131.625
    (a) 131.625
    (b) 1051
    (c) 4212
    (d) 8424
    (e) 263.25
37. Ramola's monthly income is three times Ravina's monthly income. Ravina's monthly income is fifteen percent more than Ruchira's monthly income. Ruchira's monthly income is ₹ 32,000. What is Ramola's annual income ?
    (a) ₹ 1,10,400
    (b) ₹ 13,24,800
    (c) ₹ 36,800
    (d) ₹ 52,200
    (e) None of these

38. In an Entrance Examination Ritu scored 56 percent marks, Smita scored 92 percent marks and Rina scored 634 marks. The maximum marks of the examination are 875. What are the average marks scored by all the three girls together?
    (a) 1929
    (b) 815
    (c) 690
    (d) 643
    (e) None of these

39. The respective ratio between the present age of Manisha and Deepali is 5 : X. Manisha is 9 years younger than Parineeta. Parineeta's age after 9 years will be 33 years. The difference between Deepali's and Manisha's age is same as the present age of Parineeta. What will come in place of X?
    (a) 23
    (b) 39
    (c) 15
    (d) Cannot be determined
    (e) None of these

40. Seema bought 20 pens, 8 packets of wax colours, 6 calculators and 7 pencil boxes. The price of one pen is ₹ 7, one packet of wax colour is ₹ 22, one calculator is ₹ 175 and one pencil box is ₹ 14 more than the combined price of one pen and one packet of wax colours. How much amount did Seema pay to the shopkeeper?
    (a) ₹ 1,491
    (b) ₹ 1,725
    (c) ₹ 1,667
    (d) ₹ 1,527
    (e) None of these

REASONING ABILITY

41. A school bus driver starts from the school, drives 2 km towards North, takes a left turn and drives for 5 km. He then takes a left turn and drives for 8 km before taking a left turn again and driving for 5 km. The driver finally takes a left turn and drives 1 km before stopping. How far and towards which direction should the driver drive to reach the school again?
    (a) 3 km towards North
    (b) 7 km towards East
    (c) 6 km towards South
    (d) 6 km towards West
    (e) 5 km towards North

DIRECTIONS (Qs. 42-44) : Study the following information and answer the given questions.

F and G are brothers of H. G is son of C and D. C is daughter of A. B is father-in-law of D. E is son of A

42. If J is brother of A, then how is J related to E?
    (a) Uncle
    (b) Nephew
    (c) Cannot be determined
    (d) Brother-in-law
    (e) Son-in-law
43. How is G related to B?
    (a) Nephew
    (b) Father
    (c) Brother-in-law
    (d) Grandson
    (e) Brother
44. How is H related to E?
    (a) Cannot be determined
    (b) Niece
    (c) Daughter
    (d) Nephew
    (e) Son-in-law

DIRECTIONS: (Qs. 45-47) Study the following information to answer the given question.

(I)   In a class of boys and girls, Sanjay ranks is 12th and Suman's rank is 8th.

(II)   Sanjay rank among the boys is 6th and Suman rank among girls is 3rd.

(III) In the class Suman rank is 52nd from the other end.

(IV)   From the other end, Sanjay rank among the boys is 26th.

45. How many girls are there in between Suman and Sanjay?
    (a) 1   (b) 2
    (c) 3   (d) Cannot be determined
    (e) None of these

46. How many boys are there in the class?
    (a) 31   (b) 28
    (c) 29   (d) Cannot be determined
    (e) None of these

47. How many boys are there before Suman?
    (a) 6   (b) 5
    (c) 7   (d) Cannot be determined
    (e) None of these

DIRECTIONS (Qs. 48-52) : In each question below are two/three statements followed by two conclusions numbered I and II. You have to take the two/three given statements to be true even if they seem to be at variance from commonly known facts and then decide which of the given conclusions logically follows from the given statements disregarding commonly known facts.

Give answer (a) if only conclusion I follows
Give answer (b) if only conclusion II follows.
Give answer (c) if either conclusion I or conclusion II follows.
Give answer (d) if neither conclusion I nor conclusion II follows.
Give answer (e) if both conclusion I and conclusion II follow.

(Qs. 48-50) :

Statements : All gliders are parachutes.
              No parachute is an airplane.
              All airplanes are helicopters.

46. Conclusions : I. No glider is an airplane.
                     II.All gliders being helicopters is a possibility.

47. Conclusions : I. No helicopter is a glider.
                     II. All parachutes being helicopters is a possibility.

50. Statements   : Some mails are chats.
                 All updates are chats.
    Conclusions : I. All mails being updates is a possibility.
                 II. No update is a mail.

(Qs. 51-52) :

Statements : No stone is metal.
              Some metals are papers.
              All papers are glass.

51. Conclusions : I. All stones being glass is a possibility.
                     II. No stone is a paper.

52. Conclusions : I. No glass is a metal.
                     II. Atleast some glass is metal.

DIRECTIONS (Qs. 53-57) : Study the following information to answer the given questions:

In a certain code, 'za la ka ga' is code for 'must obey traffic rules', 'za fa sa na ' is code for 'we obey the elders' , ' na la da sa' is a code for ' we must be elders' , and 'wa sa za da' is code for 'be elders obey younger'.

53. Which of the following is the code for 'must'?
    (a) sa   (b) da
    (c) la   (d) na
    (e) None of these

54. What does the code 'za' stand for ?
    (a) traffic   (b) must
    (c) be   (d) younger
    (e) obey

55. Which of the following is the code for 'elders'?
    (a) sa   (b) wa
    (c) za   (d) la
    (e) fa

56. How does 'rules of younger' coded in the code language?
    (a) ka da fa   (b) wa ka sa
    (c) ja da wa   (d) ka wa ya
    (e) Cannot be determined

57. Which of the following is the code for 'The'?
    (a) fa   (b) wa
    (c) za   (d) la
    (e) sa

DIRECTIONS (Qs 58- 62): Study the information below and answer questions based on it.

Twelve people are sitting in two parallel rows containing six people each, in such a way that there is an equal distance between adjacent persons .In rows 1 there are p , q , r , s , t , and v are seated and all of them are facing south .In row 2 there are a , b , c , d , e ,and f are seated and all of them are facing north. Therefore, in the given seating arrangement each member seated in a row faces another member of the other row.

1.   a, sits third to right of d

2.   Neither a nor d sits at the extremes ends

3.   't' faces 'd'

4.   v does not face a and v does not sit at any of the extreme ends.

5.   'v' is not an immediate neighbor of t

6.   'b' sit at on the extreme ends.

7.   Only two people sit between b and e

8.   'e' does not face v

9.   Two persons sit between r and q

10.   r is not the immediate neighbor of t

11.   c does not face v

12.   p is not an immediate neighbor of r

58. Who among the following sit at extreme ends of the rows?
    (a) b,c   (b) s,t
    (c) p,r   (d) b,f
    (e) None

59. Who among the following faces a?
    (a) r   (b) t
    (c) p   (d) q
    (e) s

60. How many persons are seated between t and s?

   (a) one   (b) two

   (c) three   (d) four

   (e) None

61. p is related to v in the same way as the c is related to f. To which of the following is e related to, following the same pattern:

   (a) b   (b) d

   (c) c   (d) a

   (e) None

62. Which of the following is true regarding f?

   (a) f sits second to the right of c

   (b) f is not an immediate neighbor of a

   (c) f sits third to the left of d

   (d) f sits at the one of the extreme ends of the line

   (e) f faces v

DIRECTIONS (Qs. 63 - 67) : Study the information below and answer questions based on it.

P, Q, R, S, T, V, Wand Z are travelling to three destinations Delhi, Chennai and hyderabad in three different vehicles-Honda City, Swift D'Zire and Ford Ikon. There are three females among them one in each car. There are at least two persons in each car. R is not travelling with Q and W. T, a male, is travelling with only Z and they are not travellingto Chennai. P is travelling in Honda City to Hyderabad. S is sister of P and travels by Ford Ikon. V and R travel together. W does not travel to Chennai.

63. Members travelling to Chennai are in the car:

   (a) Honda City   (b) Swift D'Zire

   (c) Ford Ikon

   (d) Either Swift D'Zire or Ford Ikon

   (e) None of these

64. In which car are four members travelling?

   (a) None   (b) Honda City

   (c) Swift D'Zire   (d) Ford Ikon

   (e) Honda City or Ford Ikon

65. Which of the following combinations represents the three female members?

   (a) QSZ   (b) WSZ

   (c) PSZ   (d) Cannot be determined

   (d) None of these

66. Who is travelling with W?

   (a) Only Q   (b) Only P

   (c) Both P and Q   (d) Cannot be determined

   (e) None of these

67. Members in which of the following combinations are travelling in Honda City?

   (a) PRS   (b) PQW

   (c) PWS   (d) Data inadequate

   (e) None of these

DIRECTIONS (Qs. 68-72) : In the following questions the symbols @, $\underline{@}$, =, © and $\underline{©}$ are used with the following meaning:

   P © Q means P is less than Q.

   P @ Q means P is greater than Q.

   P $\underline{@}$ Q means P is greater than or equal to Q.

   P = Q means P is equal to Q.

   P $\underline{©}$ Q means P is either smaller than or equal to Q.

Now in each of the following questions, assuming the given statements to be true, find which of the two conclusions I and II given below them is/are definitely true ? Give answer.

   (a) if only conclusion I is true.

   (b) if only conclusion II is true.

   (c) if either I or II is true.

   (d) if neither I nor II is true, and

   (e) if both I and II are true.

68. **Statements:** B @ V, K © C, C $\underline{©}$ B

   Conclusions : **I.** V @ C

                      II. B @ K

69. **Statements :** K @ T, S = K, T $\underline{©}$ R

   Conclusions : **I.** S @ R

                      II. T = R

70. **Statements :** U = M, P $\underline{@}$ U, M $\underline{@}$ B

   Conclusions : **I.** P = B

                      II. P @ B

71. **Statements:** L $\underline{@}$ N, J $\underline{©}$ P, P $\underline{@}$ L

   Conclusions : **I.** J = L

                      II. P = N

72. **Statements:** H $\underline{@}$ G, D @ E, H = E

   Conclusions : **I.** D @ H

                      II. G © D

DIRECTIONS (Qs. 73-77) : Study the following information carefully answer the given questions :

Twelve persons are sitting in two parallel rows containing six persons each, in such a way that there is an equal distance between adjacent persons. In row–1, A, B, C, D, E and F are seated (but not necessarily in the same order) and all of them are facing south. In row– 2, P, Q, R, S, T and V are seated (but not necessarily in the same order) and all of them are facing north. Therefore, in the given seating arrangement each person seated in a row faces another person of the other row.

A sits third to the left of E. The person facing A sits second to the left of T. Two persons are sitting between T and P. C and D are immediate neighbours. C and D do not sit at any of the extreme ends of the line. Only one person sits between B and C. The person facing D is an immediate neighbour of Q. V is not an immediate neighbour of P. S does not face A.

73. Who amongst the following sits seconds to the right of the person who faces R ?

   (a) C   (b) D

   (c) B   (d) E

   (e) Cannot be determined

74. Which of the following statements regarding B is true ?

    (a) B sits second to the left of C

    (b) A sits to immediate left of B

    (c) T faces B

    (d) D is an immediate neighbour of B

    (e) The person who faces B is an immediate neighbour of S

75. Who amongst the following faces P ?

    (a) A   (b) D

    (c) C   (d) E

    (e) Cannot be determined

76. Who amongst the following sits exactly between T and R ?

    (a) V   (b) Q

    (c) S   (d) P

    (e) Cannot be determined

77. Four of the following five are alike in a certain way based on the given seating arrangement and thus form a group. Which is the one that **does not** belong to the group ?

    (a) F   (b) Q

    (c) T   (d) C

    (e) E

78. Ranjan walks 60 m towards South, took a left turn and walked 30 m. He then took a right turn and walked 40m . He again took a right turn and walked 30 m . How far is he from the starting point .

    (a) 120 m   (b) 100m

    (c) 110 m   (d) Cannot be determined

    (e) None of these

79. In a raw of 25 children facing south R is 16th from the right ent and B is 18th from the left end. How many children are there between R and B ?

    (a) 2   (b) 3

    (c) 4   (d) Data indeqnate

    (e) None

80. If I stand on my head with my face pointing south wards in what direction will my right hand point ?

    (a) East   (b) West

    (c) North   (d) South

    (e) South-East

HINTS & EXPLANATIONS

1. (d) Given expression implies $? = \dfrac{3325}{25} \times \dfrac{152}{16}$

   $= 133 \times 9.5 = 1263.5$

2. (e) $? = 5 + \dfrac{1}{5} + 2 + \dfrac{2}{15} + 3 + \dfrac{2}{3}$

   $= 10 + \dfrac{1}{5} + \dfrac{2}{15} + \dfrac{2}{3}$

   $= 10 + \dfrac{3+2+10}{15} = 10 + \dfrac{15}{15}$

   $= 10 + 1 = 11$

3. (b) Given expression can be written as

   $? = \dfrac{2525 \times 0.25 \times 7}{5} = 883.75$

4. (e) $? = \dfrac{500 \times 32}{100} + \dfrac{50 \times 162}{100}$

   $= 160 + 81 = 241$

5. (d) $45316 + 52131 - 65229$

   $= ? + 15151$

   $\Rightarrow \quad 32218 = ? + 15151$

   $\therefore \quad ? = 32218 - 15151 = 17067$

6. (a) Total distance from Ranchi to Koderma Junction
   $= (445 - 256) = 189 \, km$

7. (d) Total time taken by the train from Jamui junction to Jhajha junction = 8:00 - 6:48 = 1 hr 12 minutes

8. (c) Required ratio = 435/315 = 29:21

9. (a) Arrival time of the train at Nawada = (5:45+0:25-0:2)
   = 6 : 08 pm

10. (c) According to question,
    We see in the graph that there is second lowest distance between Jamui and Dhanbad = 42 km

11. (e) According to graph no any categories is the number of workers same in both the year.

12. (a) Number of workers in 2014 = 20000 × 10/100 = 2000
    Number of workers in 2015 = 24000 × 16/100 = 3840
    Difference = 3840 – 2000 = 1840
    Increase % (1840/2000) ×100 = 92%

13. (d) In 2014, Number of workers in categories E
    = 20000×10/100 = 2000
    In 2015, Number of workers in categories E
    = 24000×16/100 = 3840
    Difference = (3840-2000) = 1840
    In 2014, Number of workers in categories C
    = 20000×12/100 = 2400
    In 2015, Number of workers in categories C
    = 24000×26/100 = 6240
    Difference = (6240-2400) = 3840
    In 2014, Number of workers in categories B

    = 20000×24/100 = 4800
    In 2015, Number of workers in categories B
    = 24000×28/100 = 6720
    Difference = (6720-4800) = 1920
    Total number of increased workers for the categories
    = 1840 + 3840 + 1920 = 7600

14. (b) For F in 2014 = 20000×18/100 = 3600
    For F in 2015 = 24000×10/100 = 2400
    For D in 2014 = 20000×20/100 = 4000
    For D in 2015 = 24000×12/100 = 2880
    For A in 2014 = 20000×16/100 = 3200
    For A in 2015 = 24000×8/100 = 1920
    So F, D and A categories have shown decrease in the number of workers from 2014 to 2015

15. (c) For C in 2015 = 24000×26/100 = 6240
    For B in 2015 = 24000×28/100 = 6720
    Total number = 12960
    For E in 2014 = 20000×10/100 = 2000
    For C in 2014 = 20000×12/100 = 2400
    Total number = 4400
    Required difference = (12960-4400) = 8560

16. (a) Total number of the variation in A departments between 2013 and 2014 = (60000×25/100) - (36000×21/100) = 7440
    Total number of the variation in B departments between 2013 and 2014 = (60000×19/100) - (36000×17/100) = 5280
    Total number of the variation in C departments between 2013 and 2014 = (60000×16/100) - (36000×18/100) = 3120
    Total number of the variation in D departments between 2013 and 2014 = (60000×24/100) - (36000×29/100) = 3960
    Total number of the variation in E departments between 2013 and 2014 = (60000×16/100) - (36000×15/100) = 4200
    So minimum variation in C departments

17. (e) Data is not sufficient for answer

18. (d) Total number of the employees in C departments in 2013
    = (36000×18/100) = 6480
    Total number of the employees in C departments in 2014
    = (60000×16/100) = 9600
    Increase % = (9600-6480)/6480×100 = 48%

19. (a) Total number of employees in department D in 2013
    = (36000×29/100) = 10440
    Total number of employees in department B in 2014
    = (60000×19/100) = 11400
    Required difference = 11400-10440 = 960

20. (c) Originally number of employees in department E in 2013
    = (36000×15/100) = 5400
    After 1200 employees of department E left the organisation in 2013
    Remaining employees = 5400-1200 = 4200
    Total number of employees in department E in 2014
    = (60000×16/100) = 9600
    Required employees = 9600-4200 = 5400

21. (b) Amount paid $= ₹(40 \times 18 + 55 \times 8) = ₹(720 + 440)$
$= ₹1160$

22. (e) Third number
$= 5 \times 34.4 - 2 \times 46.5 - 2 \times 18$
$= 172 - 93 - 36 = 43$

23. (c) Second angle of parallelogram $= 180° - 45° = 135°$
$\therefore$ Required value $= 135 + 2 \times 45 = 135 + 90 = 225°$

24. (e) $M_1 D_1 = M_2 D_2$
$\Rightarrow 9 \times 19 = 18 \times D_2$
$\Rightarrow D_2 = \dfrac{9 \times 19}{18} = 9.5$ days

25. (a) Let Gloria's and Sara's present ages be 4x and 7x years respectively.
Two years ago,
$$\frac{4x-2}{7x-2} = \frac{1}{2}$$
$\Rightarrow 8x - 4 = 7x - 2$
$\Rightarrow x = 2$
$\therefore$ Sara's age three years hence $= 7x + 3 = 17$ years

26. (b) S.I. $= \dfrac{13033 \times 13 \times 3}{100} = ₹5082.87$

C.I. $= 13033 \left[\left(1 + \dfrac{13}{100}\right)^3 - 1 \right] = 13033 \times 0.44 = ₹5772.28$

Difference $= 5772.28 - 5082.87 = ₹689.41$

27. (d)
I. $x^2 + 2x - 195 = 0$
$\Rightarrow (x+15)(x-13) = 0$
$\Rightarrow x = 13, -15$
II. $y^2 + 30y + 225 = 0$
$\Rightarrow (y+15)(y+15) = 0$
$\Rightarrow y = -15, -15$
So, $x \geq y$

28. (d)
I. $x^2 - 8x + 15 = 0$
$\Rightarrow (x-5)(x-3) = 0$
$\Rightarrow x = 3, 5$
II. $y^2 - 5y + 6 = 0$
$\Rightarrow (y-2)(y-3) = 0$
$\Rightarrow y = 2, 3$
So, $x \geq y$

29. (b)
I. $4x^2 - 13x + 9 = 0$
$\Rightarrow (x-1)(4x-9) = 0$
$\Rightarrow x = 1, 9/4$
II. $y^2 + 3y + 2 = 0$
$\Rightarrow (y+1)(y+2)$
$\Rightarrow y = -1, -2$
$x > y$

30. (b)
I. $36x^2 = 1$
$\Rightarrow x = -1/6, +1/6$

II. $4y^2 + 13y + 3 = 0$
$\Rightarrow (y+3)(4y+1)$
$\Rightarrow y = -3, -1/4$
So, $x > y$

31. (a)
I. $x^2 + 2x + 1 = 0$
$\Rightarrow (x+1)(x+1)$
$x = -1$
II. $y^2 = \pm 9$
$\Rightarrow y = -3, 3$
So no relation

32. (c) The pattern of the number series is :
$800 \div 2 = 400$
$400 \div 2 = 200$
$200 \div 2 = 100$
$100 \div 2 = 50$
$50 \div 2 = \boxed{25}$

33. (d) The pattern of the number series is :
$2 + 1 \times 11 = 2 + 11 = 13$
$13 + 2 \times 11 = 13 + 22 = 35$
$35 + 3 \times 11 = 35 + 33 = 68$
$68 + 4 \times 11 = 68 + 44 = 112$
$112 + 5 \times 11 = 112 + 55 = \boxed{167}$

34. (d) The pattern of the number series is :
$650 - 7^2 = 650 - 49 = 601$
$601 - 6^2 = 601 - 36 = 565$
$565 - 5^2 = 565 - 25 = 540$
$540 - 4^2 = 540 - 16 = 524$
$524 - 3^2 = 524 - 9 = \boxed{515}$

35. (e) The given number series is based on the following pattern:

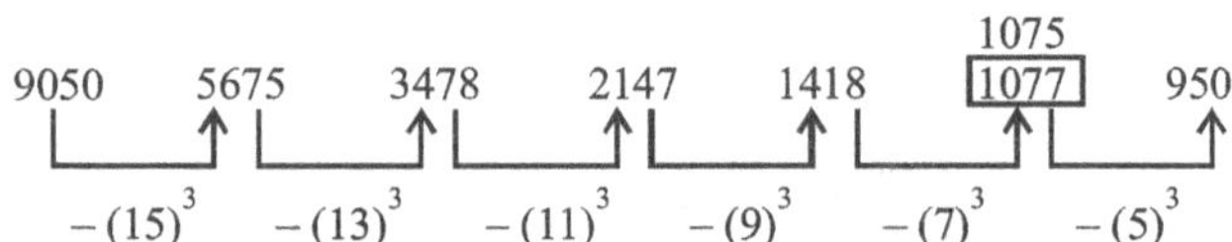

Hence, the number 1077 is wrong and it should be replaced by 1075.

36. (b) The given number series is based on the following pattern :

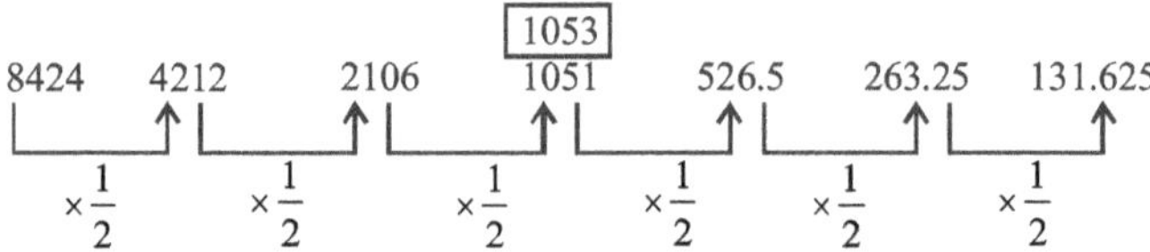

Hence, the number 1051 is wrong and it should be replaced by 1053.

37. (b) Ravina's monthly income
$$= 32000 \times \frac{100 + 15}{100} = 32000 \times \frac{115}{100} = ₹36800$$
$$= \text{Ramola's annual income} = 36800 \times 3 \times 12$$
$$= ₹1324800$$

38. (d) Marks scored by Ritu $= 875 \times \dfrac{56}{100} = 490$

    Marks scored by Smita $= 875 \times \dfrac{92}{100} = 805$

    ∴ Average marks scored by all the three together

    $= \dfrac{490 + 805 + 634}{3} = \dfrac{1929}{3} = 643$

39. (e) According to the question
    Present age of Parineeta $= 33 - 9 = 24$ years
    Present age of Manisha $= 24 - 9 = 15$ years
    Present age of Deepali $= 24 + 15 = 39$ years
    ∵ $5 : X = 15 : 39$

    ∴ $X = \dfrac{5 \times 39}{15} = 13$

40. (c) Cost of one pencil box $= 7 + 22 + 14 = ₹43$
    ∴ Required amount $= (20 \times 7) + (8 \times 22) + (6 \times 175) + (7 \times 43)$
    $= 140 + 176 + 1050 + 301 = ₹1667$

41. (e) According to questions.
    AB $= 2$ km
    BC $= 5$ km
    CD $= 8$ km
    DE $= 5$ km
    EF $= 1$ km
    BC $=$ DE $= 5$ km
    CD $=$ BE $= 8$ km
    BE $=$ EF $+$ AF $+$ AB
    ∴ AF $=$ BE $- ($EF $+$ AB$)$
    $= 8 - (1 + 2) = 8 - 3 = 5$ km

    ∴ Required distance $=$ AF $= 5$ km and required
    direction is North

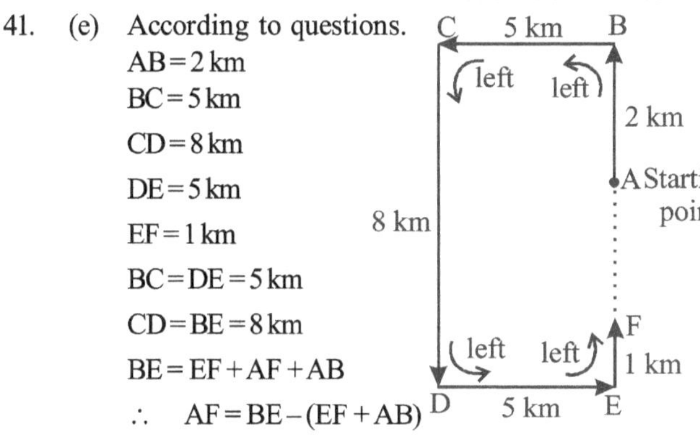

Solutions (42-44):

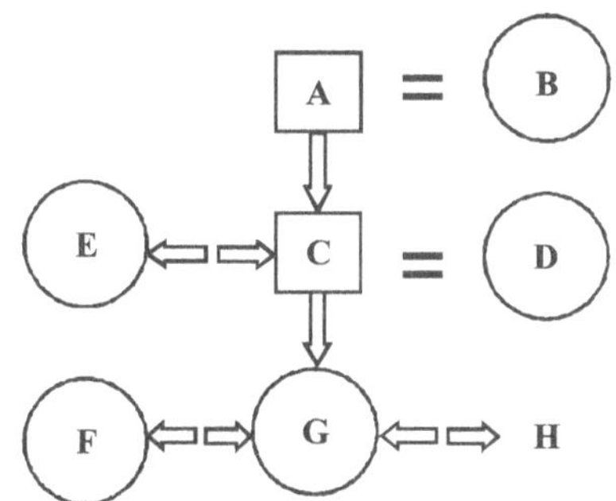

42. (a)
43. (d)
44. (a)

Solutions (45-47):
    Total No. of Students: $= 59$
    Total number of boys $= (6+26) -1 = 31$
    Now total number of girls $=$ Total number of students
    number of boys $= 59 - 31 = 28$

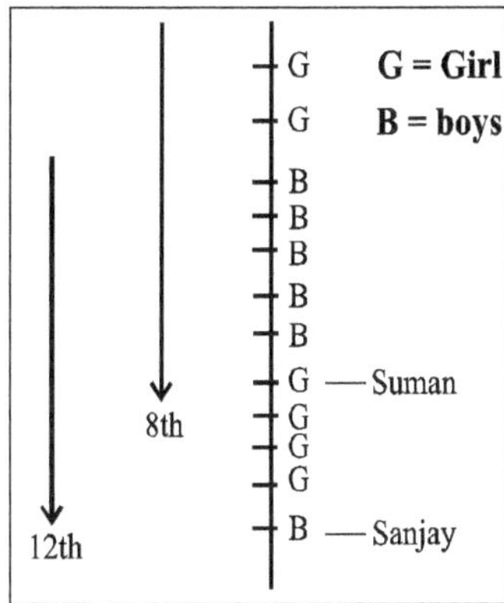

From the information (ii) and (iv), it is known that Sanjay's rank among boys from one end to another end is 6th and 26th respectively.
Therefore total number of boys $= (6+26) -1 = 31$
From the information above (i) and (ii) it is clear that Suman rank in the class is 8th from one end and 52nd from other end. Therefore total no. of students in the class $= (8+52) - = 59$.
Now total number of girls $=$ Total number of students - number of boys $= 59 - 31 = 28$
Suman rank from the other hand $= 28 - 3 + 1 - 26$

45. (c) There are 3 girls b/w Suman and Sanjay
46. (a) Total number of boys $= (6+26) -1 = 31$
47. (b) There are 5 boys before Suman as it is clear from figure.

For questions (48-49) :
    According to statements:

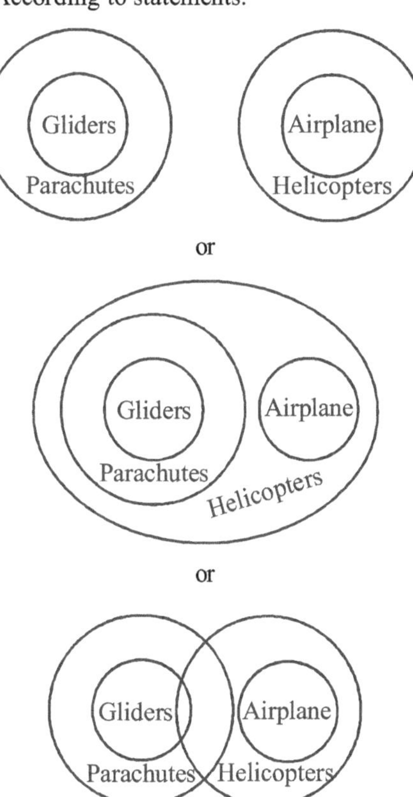

48. (e) Both conclusion I and couclution II follow
49. (b) Hence, conclusion II follows.
50. (d) According to statements.

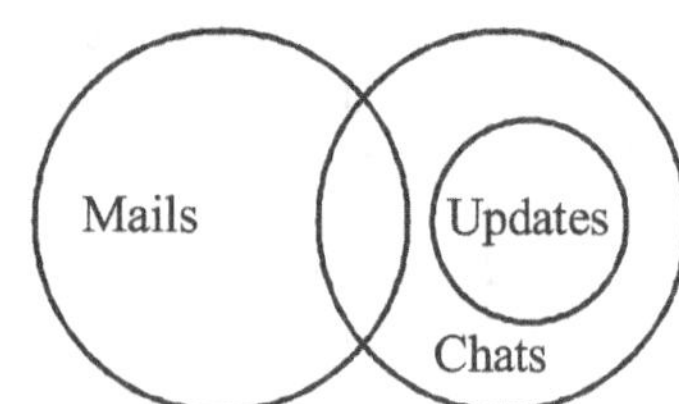

or

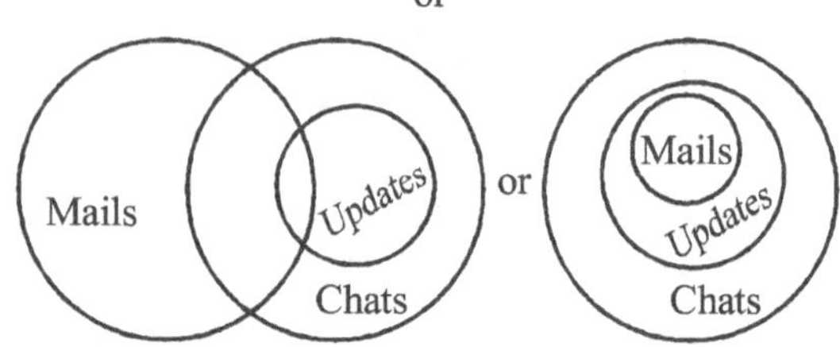

Hence, conclusion I follows.

Solutions (51-52) :

According to statements

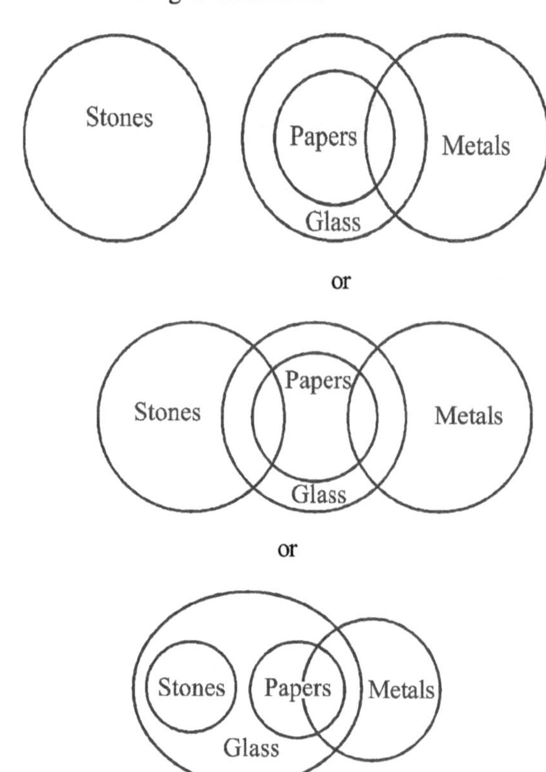

or

51. (a) Hence, conclusion I follows.
52. (b) Hence, only conclusion II follows.

Solutions (53-57) :

Sword	Obey	Must	Elders	We	Be	The	Younger	Traffic	rules
Code	za	la	sa	na	da	fa	wa	Ka/ga	ga/ka

53. (c)   54. (e)   55. (a)   56. (e)
57. (a)

Solutions: 58-62

From the given data we can come up with the following sequence:

Row 1   p   t   q   v   s   r

Row 2   c   d   e   f   a   b

58. (a)   59. (e)   60. (b)   61. (a)   62. (e)

Solutions: 63-67

The following table can be built to infer the answers:

Members	Car	Destination
TZ	Swift	Delhi
PQW	Honda city	Hyderabad
SVR	Ford Icon	Chennai

63. (c)   64. (a)   65. (d)   66. (c)
67. (b)
68. (b) $B > V$ ....(i) $K < C$ ...(ii); $C \leq B$ ...(iii)

No relationship can be find out between V and C.
Hence I does not follow.
From (ii) and (iii), $B > K$. Hence II follows.

69. (d) $K > T$ ...(i); $S = K$ ...(ii); $T \leq R$ ...(iii)
Neither relationship can be established .

70. (c) $U = M$ ...(i) $P \geq U$ ...(iii); $M \geq B$ ...(iii)
Combining, we get $P \geq U = M \geq B \Rightarrow P \geq B$
$\Rightarrow P = B$ or $P > B$

71. (d) $L \geq N$ ...(i); $J \leq P$ ...(ii); $P \geq L$ ...(iii)
Neither relationship can be established.

72. (e) $H \geq G$ ....(i); $D > E$ ...(ii); $H = E$ ...(iii)
Combining, we get $D > E = H \geq G$
$\Rightarrow D > H$ and $G < D$

Solutions (73-77):

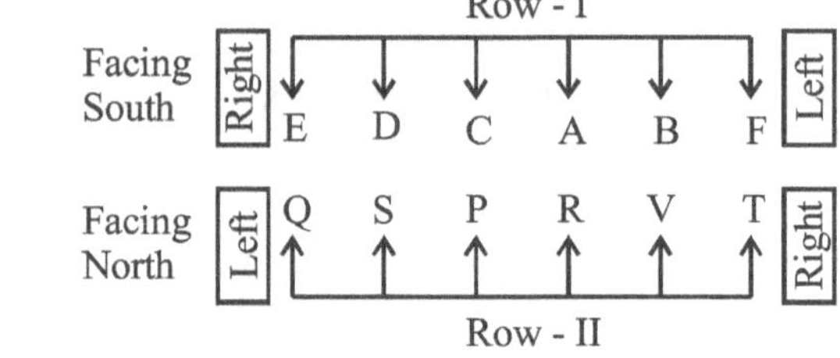

73. (b)   74. (a)   75. (c)   76. (a)
77. (d)
78. (b)

```
        60
            30
    40          40

        30
```

Total distance is 60 + 40 = 100

79. (e)

B is $(25 - 18 + 1)$ from the right end
so, there are seven children between R and B.

80. (a)

Eastward

PRACTICE SET ⬤ 14

Time : 45 Min. | **Max. Marks : 80**

QUANTITATIVE APTITUDE

DIRECTIONS (Qs. 1-5) : What should come in place of the question mark (?) in the following questions?

1. 16% of $450 \div ?\%$ of $250 = 4.8$
   - (a) 12
   - (b) 6
   - (c) 4
   - (d) 10
   - (e) None of these

2. $(5 \times 5 \times 5 \times 5 \times 5 \times 5)^4 \times (5 \times 5)^6 \div (5)^2 = (25)^?$
   - (a) 10
   - (b) 17
   - (c) 19
   - (d) 12
   - (e) None of these

3. $\dfrac{4}{5} \times 2\dfrac{3}{4} \div \dfrac{5}{8} = ?$
   - (a) $4\dfrac{12}{35}$
   - (b) $1\dfrac{12}{35}$
   - (c) $2\dfrac{11}{35}$
   - (d) $3\dfrac{13}{25}$
   - (e) None of these

4. $623.15 - 218.82 - 321.43 = ?$
   - (a) 89.2
   - (b) 82.2
   - (c) 89.9
   - (d) 79.2
   - (e) None of these

5. $5437 - 3153 + 2284 = ? \times 50$
   - (a) 96.66
   - (b) 91.36
   - (c) 96.13
   - (d) 93. 16
   - (e) None of these

DIRECTIONS (Qs. 6-10) : What should come in place of the question mark (?) in the following number series?

6. 2   16   112   672   3360   13440   ?
   - (a) 3430
   - (b) 3340
   - (c) 40320
   - (d) 43240
   - (e) None of these

7. 4   9   19   ?   79   159   319
   - (a) 59
   - (b) 39
   - (c) 49
   - (d) 29
   - (e) None of these

8. 4000   2000   1000   500   250   125   ?
   - (a) 80
   - (b) 65
   - (c) 62.5
   - (d) 83.5
   - (e) None of these

9. 588   563   540   519   ?   483   468
   - (a) 500
   - (b) 496
   - (c) 494
   - (d) 490
   - (e) None of these

10. 121   ?   81   64   49   36   25
   - (a) 92
   - (b) 114
   - (c) 98
   - (d) 100
   - (e) None of these

11. Vikram scored 72 per cent marks in five subjects together, viz; Hindi, Science, Maths, English and Sanskrit together, where in the maximum marks of each subject were 100. How many marks did Vikram score in Science if he scored 80 marks in Hindi, 70 marks in Sanskrit, 76 marks in Maths and 65 marks in English?
    (a) 72
    (b) 69
    (c) 59
    (d) 71
    (e) None of these

12. The respective ratio between Pooja's, Prarthana's and Falguni's monthly income is 53:70: 57. If Prarthana's annual income is ₹4,20,000, what is the sum of Pooja's and Falguni's annual incomes? (In some cases monthly income and in some cases annual income is used.)
    (a) ₹5,92,500
    (b) ₹6,83,500
    (c) ₹6,60,000
    (d) ₹7,79,200
    (e) None of these

13. What would be the simple interest accrued in 4 years on a principal of ₹16,500 at the rate of 16 p.c.p.a.?
    (a) ₹11,560
    (b) ₹10,250
    (c) ₹12,500
    (d) ₹9,980
    (e) None of these

14. A truck covers a distance of 360 km in 8 hours. A car covers the same distance in 6 hours. What is the respective ratio between the speed of the truck and the car?
    (a) 3 : 5
    (b) 3 : 4
    (c) 1 : 2
    (d) 4 : 5
    (e) None of these

15. In order to pass in an exam a student is required to get 975 marks out of the aggregate marks. Priya got 870 marks and was declared failed by 7 per cent. What are the maximum aggregate marks a student can get in the examination?
    (a) 1500
    (b) 1000
    (c) 1200
    (d) Cannot be determined
    (e) None of these

16. On children's day sweets were to be equally distributed amongst 200 children. But on that particular day 40 children remained absent; hence each child got 2 sweets extra. How many sweets were distributed?
    (a) 3000
    (b) 1500
    (c) 2000
    (d) 1600
    (e) Cannot be determined

17. The perimeter of a square is one-fourth the perimeter of a rectangle. If the perimeter of the square is 44 cm and the length of the rectangle is 51 cm, what is the difference between the breadth of the rectangle and the side of the square?
    (a) 30 cm
    (b) 18 cm
    (c) 26 cm
    (d) 32 cm
    (e) None of these

18. What is the difference between the compound interest and simple interest accrued on an amount of ₹12,000 at the end of three years at the rate of 12%?
    (a) ₹539.136
    (b) ₹602.242
    (c) ₹495.248
    (d) ₹488.322
    (e) None of these

19. The area of a rectangle is equal to the area of a circle with circumference equal to 220 metres. What is the length of the rectangle if its breadth is 50 metres?
    (a) 56 metres
    (b) 83 metres
    (c) 77 metres
    (d) 69 metres
    (e) None of these

20. Prashant incurred a loss of 75 per cent on selling an article for ₹ 6,800. What was the cost price of the article?
    (a) ₹ 27,700
    (b) ₹ 25,600
    (c) ₹ 21,250
    (d) ₹ 29,000
    (e) None of these

DIRECTIONS (Qs. 21-25): Study of the following table carefully to answer the questions that follow. Number of Candidates found Eligible and Number of Candidates Shortlisted for Mains Exam for a recent Recruitment Process for Six Posts from different States

Post	I		II		III		IV		V		VI	
State	E	S	E	S	E	S	E	S	E	S	E	S
Bihar	2800	68	7500	250	5200	85	4500	75	6200	120	4500	165
Jharkhand	3500	230	8500	450	8200	185	5600	52	4200	155	5500	145
Rajasthan	2500	320	5500	360	7200	180	3500	45	7200	140	6500	120
Punjab	3200	90	6400	200	2400	65	9400	60	8600	95	7500	110
Goa	2400	140	5200	260	3600	75	6800	75	9500	75	8500	85
Kerala	5200	350	6400	340	4500	240	5400	120	6600	65	9500	45
Tamilnadu	6800	650	8000	180	6500	340	4800	160	5200	45	3500	25

E - Eligible   S - Short listed

21. From Jharkhand state, which post had the highest percentage of candidates short listed for mains exam?
    (a) I
    (b) III
    (c) IV
    (d) V
    (e) None of these

22. What is the average number of candidates (approximately) found eligible for Post III from all states?
    (a) 5390
    (b) 5560
    (c) 5950
    (d) 6250
    (e) None of these

23. What is the overall percentage of candidates short listed over the total number of candidates eligible for Post I from all the States together?
    (a) 8%
    (b) 7%
    (c) 12%
    (d) 15%
    (e) None of these

24. What is the ratio of the number of candidates short listed for all the posts together from Goa state to that from Tamilnadu state?
    (a) 71 : 140
    (b) 71 : 145
    (c) 73 : 140
    (d) 71 : 30
    (e) None of these

25. What is the ratio of the total number of candidates short listed for post V to that for post VI from all states together?
    (a) 1 : 2
    (b) 3 : 2
    (c) 3 : 5
    (d) 3 : 7
    (e) None of these

DIRECTIONS (Qs. 26-30) : In the following bar diagram, the number of mobile phones and laptops (in thousands) sold by 6 different companies in a certain month has been given. Study the bar diagram carefully to answer the questions.

Number of mobile phones and laptops (in thousands) sold by 6 different companies in a month.

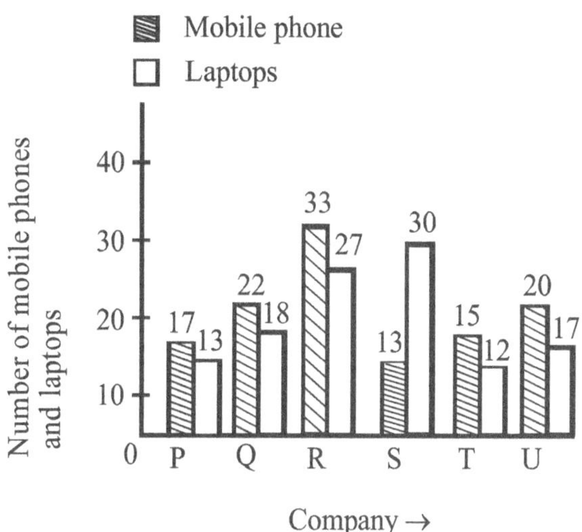

26. What is the average number of mobile phones sold by all companies taken together in a month ?
(a)   18 thousands
(b)   20 thousands
(c)   17 thousands
(d)   19 thousands
(e)   None of these

27. By what percent the number of mobile phones sold by company U is more than that of company T ?
(a) $33\dfrac{1}{3}\%$
(b)   22%
(c)   20%
(d) $23\dfrac{2}{3}\%$
(e)   None of these

28. What is the average of the number of laptops sold by companies P, R and T ?
(a)   17 thousands
(b)   17.3 thousands
(c)   18 thousands
(d)   16 thousands
(e)   None of these

29. What is the respective ratio between the number of mobile phones sold by company T and that of laptops sold by company Q ?
(a)   3 : 5
(b)   6 : 5
(c)   5 : 3
(d)   5 : 6
(e)   None of these

30. What is the respective ratio of the numbers of laptops sold by company Q and company R?
(a)   2 : 5
(b)   4 : 3
(c)   3 : 4
(d)   3 : 2
(e)   2 : 3

DIRECTIONS (Qs. 31-35): Study the following bar graph carefully and answer the following questions.

Earning (in Rs.) of three different persons on four different days.

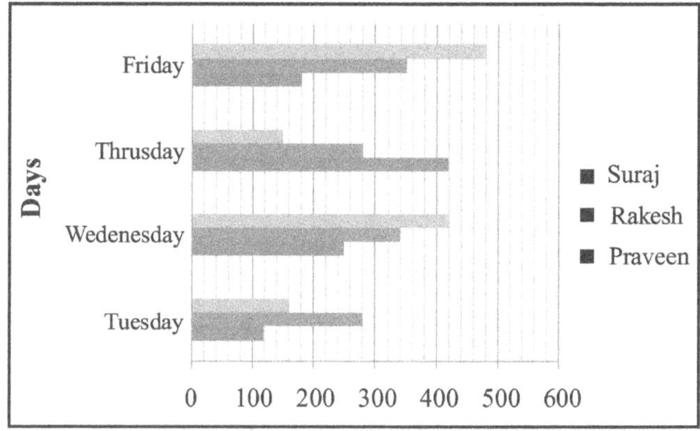

31. What is Suraj's average earnings over all the days together?
(a)   ₹ 285.5
(b)   ₹ 302.5
(c)   ₹ 320.5
(d)   ₹ 308.5
(e)   None of these

32. What is the total amount earned by Rakesh and Praveen together on Tuesday and Thursday together?
(a)   ₹ 1140
(b)   ₹ 1080
(c)   ₹ 1100
(d)   ₹ 1040
(e)   None of these

33. Suraj donated her earnings of Wednesday to Praveen. What was Praveen's total earnings on Wednesday after Suraj's donation?
(a)   ₹ 820
(b)   ₹ 750
(c)   ₹ 640
(d)   ₹ 670
(e)   None of these

34. What is the difference between Rakesh's earnings on Friday and Suraj's earnings on Tuesday?
(a)   ₹ 140
(b)   ₹ 120
(c)   ₹ 190
(d)   ₹ 130
(e)   None of these

35. What is the respective ratio between Praveen's earnings on Tuesday, Wednesday and Friday?
(a)   7 : 3 : 5
(b)   8 : 6 : 5
(c)   8 : 7 : 4
(d)   9 : 3 : 4
(e)   None of the above

DIRECTIONS (Qs.36-40) : In each of these questions, two equations are given. You have to solve these equations and find out the values of x and y and-

36. I. $3x^2-31x+78=0$
     II. $5y^2-43y+92=0$
(a)   If x > y
(b)   If x ≥ y
(c)   If x < y
(d)   If x ≤ y
(e)   If x = y or relationship cannot be established

37. I. $9x^2+16x+7=0$
     II. $27y^2-220y+217=0$
(a)   If x > y
(b)   If x ≥ y
(c)   If x < y
(d)   If x ≤ y
(e)   If x = y or relationship cannot be established

38. 　I.　$x - 752/x + 31 = 0$
　　II.　$y^2 - 31y - 816 = 0$
　(a)　If $x > y$　　　　(b)　If $x \geq y$
　(c)　If $x < y$　　　　(d)　If $x \leq y$
　(e)　If $x = y$ or relationship cannot be established

39. 　I.　$5x - 19y = 13$
　　II.　$13x - 17y = 5$
　(a)　If $x > y$　　　　(b)　If $x \geq y$
　(c)　If $x < y$　　　　(d)　If $x \leq y$
　(e)　If $x = y$ or relationship cannot be established

40. 　I.　$x^2 - 7x - 1628 = 0$
　　II.　$5y^2 - 176y - 333 = 0$
　(a)　If $x > y$　　　　(b)　If $x \geq y$
　(c)　If $x < y$　　　　(d)　If $x \leq y$
　(e)　If $x = y$ or relationship cannot be established

REASONING ABILITY

DIRECTIONS (Qs. 41-45) : Study the following information carefully to answer the questions given below.

Mark, Venn, Kevin, Shane, Kane and Starc are six friends studying in different specializations of engineering -Geo science, Telecommunication, Software, Mechanical, Electrical and Petroleum but not necessarily in the same order. Each likes a different game of hockey, cricket, swimming, football, badminton and tennis, but not in the same order. Shane does not study petroleum. Kane studies software and likes hockey. Kevin likes swimming and does not study petroleum. One who like football studies electrical. Starc studies mechanical and does not like tennis. One who likes badminton studies telecommunication. Mark and Venn do not like badminton. Mark does not like tennis.

41. Which specialization is Venn studying ?
　(a)　Geo science　　　(b)　Mechanical
　(c)　Petroleum　　　　(d)　Electrical
　(e)　None of these

42. Which game does Mark like ?
　(a)　Football　　　　(b)　Cricket
　(c)　Hockey　　　　(d)　Cannot be determined
　(e)　None of these

43. According to the given information which of the following combination of person and specialization is correct ?
　(a)　Shane-petroleum　　(b)　Venn-electrical
　(c)　Kevin-geo science　　(d)　Starc-software
　(e)　None is correct

44. Which game does Starc like ?
　(a)　Football　　　　(b)　Cricket
　(c)　Hockey　　　　(d)　Cannot be determined
　(e)　None of these

45. Which specialization is Shane studying ?
　(a)　Geo science　　　(b)　Mechanical
　(c)　Petroleum　　　　(d)　Electrical
　(e)　None of these

DIRECTIONS (Qs. 46-50) : Read the following information carefully and answers the questions given below.

Representatives of eight different banks, viz P, Q, R, S, T, U, V and W, are sitting around a circular table, facing the centre, but not necessarily in the same order. Each one of them is from a different bank, viz SBI Bank, Oriental Bank of Commerce, UBI Bank, Vijaya Bank, IOB Bank, Punjab National Bank, Bank of India and Indian Bank.

U sits second to the right of the representative of Vijaya Bank. The representative of Bank of India is an immediate neighbor of the representative of Vijaya Bank. Two persons sit between the representative of Bank of India and Q. R and T are immediate neighbours. Neither R nor T is an immediate neighbour of either Q or the representative of Vijaya Bank. The representative of UBI Bank sits second to the right of S. S is the representative of neighter Vijaya Bank nor Bank of India. V and the representative of SBI Bank are immediate neighbours. Q is not the representative of SBI Bank. Only one person sits between R and the representative of Oriental Bank of Commerce.

W sits third to the left of the representative of Indian Bank. The representative of Punjab National Bank sits second to the left of the representative of IOB Bank.

46. Four of the following five are alike in a certain way based on the given arrangement and thus form a group. Which is the one that does not belong to that group?
　(a)　W – SBI Bank　　　(b)　P – Vijaya Bank
　(c)　S – UBI Bank　　　(d)　T – IOB Bank
　(e)　U – Punjab National Bank

47. Which of the following is true with respect to the given seating arrangement?
　(a)　Q is the representative of UBI Bank.
　(b)　R sits second to the right of W.
　(c)　The representative of Indian Bank sits on 2nd the immediate left of the representative of SBI Bank.
　(d)　P sits second to the right of the representative of Bank of India.
　(e)　The representatives of UBI Bank and IOB Bank are immediate neighbours.

48. Who among the following sit exactly between Q and the representative of Bank of India?
　(a)　P and the representative of SBI Bank
　(b)　U and V
　(c)　W and the representative of UBI Bank
　(d)　W and V
　(e)　Representatives of IOB Bank of Oriental Bank of Commerce

49. Who among the following is the representative of Oriental Bank of Commerce?
　(a)　P　　　(b)　R　　　(c)　W　　　(d)　V
　(e)　S

50. Who amongst the following sits second to the left of Q?
　(a)　R　　　　　　　(b)　W
　(c)　The representative of Vijaya Bank
　(d)　The representative of Punjab National Bank
　(e)　V

DIRECTIONS (Qs. 51-55) : In each of the following questions there are three items. These three items may or may not be related with one another. Each group of items may fit into one of the diagrams (a), (b), (c), (d) and (e). You have to decide in which of the following diagrams and groups of items may fit. The number of that diagram is the answer.

Give answer (a) if only conclusion I follows.
Give answer (b) if only conclusion II follows.
Give answer (c) if either I or II follows.
Give answer (d) if neither I nor II follows.
Give answer (e) if both I and II follow.

51. Statements:
All leaders are good team workers.
All good team workers are good orators.
Conclusions:
I. Some good team workers are leaders.
II. All good orators are leaders.

52. Statements:
All terrorists are human.
All humans are bad.
Conclusions:
I. All terrorists are bad.
II. No human can be a terrorist.

53. Statements:
Some books are pens.
No pen is pencil.
Conclusions:
I. Some books are pencils.
II. No book is pencil.

54. Statements : All fans are lamps. Some lamps are tubes.
Conclusions:
I. Some tubes are fan.
II. All fan being tubes is a possibility.

55. Statements: Some pens are pencils. No pencil is sharpener.
Conclusions:
I. Some pens being sharpeners is a possibility
II. Some sharpeners are pencils

DIRECTIONS (Qs. 56-57) : Study the information given below and answer the questions following it:

Mohan is son of Arun's father's sister. Prakash is son of Reva, who is mother of Vikash and grandmother of Arun. Pranab is father of Neela and grandfather of Mohan. Reva is wife of Pranab.

56. How is Mohan related to Reva ?
(a) Grandson   (b) Son
(c) Nephew   (d) Data inadaequate
(e) None of these

57. How is Vikash's wife related to Neela ?
(a) Sister   (b) Niece
(c) Sister-in-law   (d) Data inadaequate
(e) None of these

DIRECTIONS (Qs. 58-62) : Read the following information carefully to answer the questions that follow.

There are six teachers A, B, C, D, E and F in a school. Each of the teachers teaches two subjects, one compulsory subject and the other optional subject. D's optional subject is History while three others have it as compulsory subject. E and F have Physics as one of their subjects. F's compulsory subject is Mathematics which is an optional subject of both C and E. History and English are A's subjects but in terms of compulsory and optional subjects, they are reverse of those of D's. Chemistry is an optional subject of any one of them. There is only one female teacher in the school who has English as her compulsory subject.

58. What is C's compulsory subject ?
(a) History   (b) Physics
(c) Chemistry   (d) English
(e) None of these

59. Who is a female member in the group ?
(a) A   (b) B
(c) C   (d) D
(e) None of these

60. Who among the following has same optional subjects as that of the compulsory subject of F ?
(a) D   (b) B
(c) A   (d) C
(e) None of these

61. Disregarding which is compulsory and which is the optional subject, who has the same two subjects combination as F ?
(a) A   (b) B
(c) E   (d) D
(e) None of these

62. Which of the following groups of teachers has History as the compulsory subject ?
(a) A, C and D   (b) B, C and D
(c) C and D   (d) A, B and C
(e) None of these

DIRECTIONS (Qs. 63-67) : In each of the questions below a group of letters are given followed by four groups of digits/symbol combinations numbered (a) (b), (c) and (d). Letters are to be coded as per the codes and conditions given below. You have to find out which of the combinations (a), (b) , (c) and (d) is correct and indicate your answer accordingly. If none of the four represents the correct code, mark (e) i.e. 'None of these' as your answer.

Letter	B	H	S	N	T	O	A	K	R	I	E	U	G
Digit/ Symbol Code	6	8	1	#	5	2	$	3	9	@	4	7	%

Conditions :
(i) If the first as well as last letter is vowel, both are to be coded as 'O'.
(ii) If the first letter is a vowel and the last letter is consonant, both are to be coded as 'Z'.
(iii) If the first letter is a consonant and the last letter is vowel, both are to be coded as '*'.

63. ONSIRT
(a) 2#1@95   (b) Z#@195
(c) Z#1@9Z   (d) Z#1@95
(e) None of these

64. KIUBSR
(a) O@76129   (b) O@7610
(c) 3@7691   (d) 3@6719
(e) None of these

65. BKAEUG
(a) 03$470   (b) 63$470
(c) 03$47%   (d) 63$47%
(e) None of these

66. STOKGA
(a) 1523%$ (b) 1523%*
(c) *523%*   (d) *523%$
(e) None of these

67. ORHSNU
(a) O98#17   (b) O981#O
(c) 298#10   (d) 2981#7
(e) None of these

DIRECTIONS (Qs. 68-72) : In the following questions, the symbols @, #, $, % and © are used with the following meaning as illustrated below :

'P $ Q' means 'P is not greater than Q'

'P @ Q' means 'P is neither smaller than nor equal to Q'.

'P % Q' means 'P is neither greater than nor equal to Q'.

'P © Q' means 'P is not smaller than Q'.

'P # Q' means 'P is neither greater than nor smaller than Q'.

Now in each of the following questions assuming the given statements to be true, find which of the three conclusions I, II and III given below them is/are definitely true.

68. **Statements :** M @ R, R © K, J % K

    Conclusions : I. M @ J

    II. J % R

    III. K % M

    (a) Only I follows   (b) Only I and II follow

    (c) Only II and III follow   (d) All follow

    (e) None of these

69. **Statements :** D © N, N # V, W $ V

    Conclusions : I. D # W

    II. W % D

    III. V # D

    (a) Only III follows

    (b) Only either I or II follows

    (c) Only either II or III follows

    (d) Only either I or III follows

    (e) None of these

70. **Statements :** H % B, M © B, K # M

    Conclusions : I. K @ H

    II. B # K

    III. K @ B

    (a) All follow

    (b) Only I follows

    (c) Only either II or III follows

    (d) Only either II or III and I follow

    (e) None of these

71. **Statement :** V © M, N $ V, J @ N

    Conclusions : I. J @ M

    II. M @ N

    III. V @ J

    (a) Only II follows

    (b) Only I follows

    (c) Only either I or II follows

    (d) Only III follows

    (e) None of these

72. **Statements :** A @ B, B © E, F % E

    Conclusions : I. A @ F

    II. F % B

    III. E % A

    (a) Only I follows

    (b) Only I and II follow

    (c) Only I and III follow

    (d) I, II and III follow

    (e) None of these

DIRECTIONS (Qs. 73-77): Study the following information carefully and answer the given questions.

In a certain code language- **'economics is not money'** is written as, **'ka la ho ga'** **'demand and supply economics'** is written as, **'mo ta pa ka'** money makes only part' is written as, **'zi la ne ki'** demand makes supply economics' is written as, **'zi mo ka ta'**

73. What is the code for 'money' in the given code language?

    (a) ga   (b) mo

    (c) pa   (d) ta

    (e) la

74. What is the code for 'supply' in the given code language?

    (a) only ta   (b) only mo

    (c) either pa or mo   (d) only pa

    (e) either mo or ta

75. What may be the possible code for 'demand only more' in the given code language?

    (a) xi ne mo   (b) mo zi ne

    (c) ki ne mo   (d) mo zi ki

    (e) xi ka ta

76. What may be the possible code for 'work and money' in the given code language?

    (a) pa ga la   (b) pa la tu

    (c) mo la pa   (d) tu la ga

    (e) pa la ne

77. What is the code for 'makes' in the given code language?

    (a) mo   (b) pa

    (c) ne   (d) zi

    (e) ho

78. Rajesh correctly remembers that his friend Sanjay started working after April but before September. Vinod correctly remembers that Sanjay did not have a job before May. Madan correctly remembers that the month Sanjay started working had 30 days. In which month of the year did Sanjay definitely start working?

    (a) July

    (b) August

    (c) September

    (d) Either August or September

    (e) June

79. A Policeman his left his police post and proceeded South 4km on hearing a loud sound from point A. On reaching the place, he heard another sound and proceeded 4km to his left to the point B. From B he proceeded left to reach another place C 4km away. In which direction, he has to go reach his police post?

    (a) North   (b) South

    (c) East   (d) West

    (e) None of these

80. In a class of 20 students, Mridul's rank is 12th from the top and Veena's rank is 17th from the bottom. If Rohan's rank is exactly between Mridul and Veena's rank, what is Rohan's rank from the top?

    (a) Ninth   (b) Eighth

    (c) Tenth   (d) Seventh

    (e) Cannot be determined

HINTS & EXPLANATIONS

1. (b) 16% of $450 \div ?\%$ of $250 = 4.8$

$$\Rightarrow \quad 450 \times \frac{16}{100} \div 250 \times \frac{?}{100} = 4.8$$

$$\Rightarrow \quad 72 \div 2.5 \times ? = 4.8$$

$$\Rightarrow \quad 2.5 \times ? = \frac{72}{4.8}$$

$$\therefore \quad ? = \frac{72}{4.8 \times 2.5} = 6$$

2. (b) $(25)^? = (5 \times 5 \times 5 \times 5 \times 5 \times 5)^4 \times (5 \times 5)^6 \div (5)^2$

$$= (25 \times 25 \times 25)^4 \times (25)^6 \div (25)^1$$

$$= (25^3)^4 \times (25)^6 \div 25^1 = (25)^{12} \times (25)^6 \div (25)^1$$

$$= (25)^{12+6-1} = (25)^{17}$$

$$\therefore \quad ? = 17$$

3. (d) $? = \dfrac{4}{5} \times 2\dfrac{3}{4} \div \dfrac{5}{8} = \dfrac{4}{5} \times \dfrac{11}{4} \div \dfrac{5}{8}$

$$= \frac{4}{5} \times \frac{11}{4} \times \frac{8}{5} = \frac{88}{25} = 3\frac{13}{25}$$

4. (e) $? = 623.15 - 218.82 - 321.43 = 623.15 - 540.25 = 82.9$

5. (b) $? \times 50 = 5437 - 3153 + 2284 = 7721 - 3153 = 4568$

$$\therefore \quad ? = \frac{4568}{50} = 91.36$$

6. (c) Given series

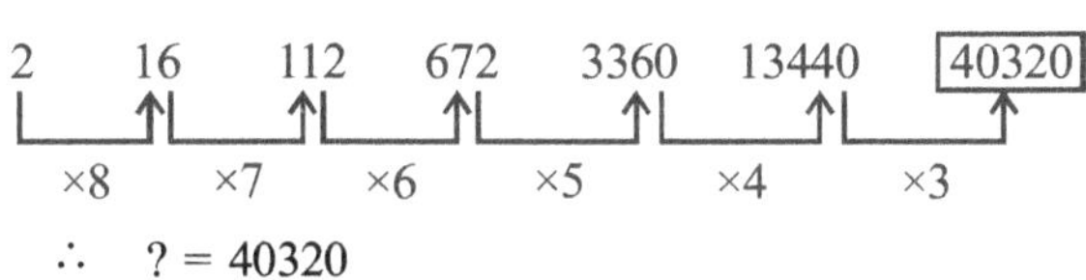

$$\therefore \quad ? = 40320$$

7. (b) Given series

$$\begin{array}{ccccccc} 4 & 9 & 19 & \boxed{39} & 79 & 159 & 319 \end{array}$$
$$\times 2+1 \quad \times 2+1 \quad \times 2+1 \quad \times 2+1 \quad \times 2+1 \quad \times 2+1$$

$$\therefore \quad ? = 39$$

8. (c) Given series

$$\begin{array}{ccccccc} 4000 & 2000 & 1000 & 500 & 250 & 125 & \boxed{62.5} \end{array}$$
$$\div 2 \quad \div 2 \quad \div 2 \quad \div 2 \quad \div 2 \quad \div 2$$

$$\therefore \quad ? = 62.5$$

9. (a) Given series

$$\begin{array}{ccccccc} 588 & 563 & 540 & 519 & \boxed{500} & 483 & 468 \end{array}$$
$$-25 \quad -23 \quad -21 \quad -19 \quad -17 \quad -15$$

$$\therefore \quad ? = 500$$

10. (d) Given series

$$\begin{array}{ccccccc} 121 & \boxed{100} & 81 & 64 & 49 & 36 & 25 \\ \uparrow & \uparrow & \uparrow & \uparrow & \uparrow & \uparrow & \uparrow \\ (11)^2 & (10)^2 & (9)^2 & (8)^2 & (7)^2 & (6)^2 & (5)^2 \end{array}$$

$$\therefore \quad ? = 100$$

11. (b) Total number obtained by Vikram

$$= (100 \times 5) \times \frac{72}{100} = 500 \times \frac{72}{100} = 360$$

$\therefore$ Number in science
$$= 360 - (80 + 70 + 76 + 65) = 360 - 291 = 69$$

12. (c) Monthly income of Prarthana's $= \dfrac{4,20,000}{12} = ₹\, 35,000$

Monthly income of Pooja and Falgunis

$$= 35,000 \times \frac{53+57}{70} = 35,000 \times \frac{110}{70} = ₹\, 55,000$$

$\therefore$ Annual income of Pooja and Falgunis
$$= 55,000 \times 12 = ₹\, 6,60,000$$

13. (e) Simple interest

$$= \frac{\text{principle} \times \text{time} \times \text{rate}}{100} = \frac{16500 \times 4 \times 16}{100} = ₹10560$$

14. (b) Speed of truck $= \dfrac{\text{distance}}{\text{time}} = \dfrac{360}{8} = 45\,\text{km/hr}$

Speed of car $= \dfrac{\text{distance}}{\text{time}} = \dfrac{360}{6} = 60\,\text{km/hr}$

$\therefore$ Ratio $= 45 : 60 = 3 : 4$

15. (a) Minimum marks to pass $= 975$
Priya failed by $975 - 870 = 105$ marks

$$\therefore \quad \text{Maximum mark} = \frac{105}{7} \times 100 = 1500$$

16. (d) Let x sweets is distributed to each children
According to question $(200 - 40) \times (x + 2) = 200 \times x$

$$\Rightarrow (160) \times (x + 2) = 200x \Rightarrow 160x + 320 = 200x$$

$$\Rightarrow 200x - 160x = 320 \Rightarrow 40x = 320$$

$$\therefore \quad x = \frac{320}{40} = 8$$

$\therefore$ Total no. of sweets $= 200 \times x = 200 \times 8 = 1600$

17. (c) One side of square $= \dfrac{\text{circumference}}{4} = \dfrac{44}{4} = 11\,\text{cm}$

Circumference of rectangle $= 4 \times$ perimeter of square
$$= 4 \times 44 = 176\,\text{cm}$$
width of rectangle

$$= \frac{\text{circumference of rectangle}}{2} - \text{length}$$

$$= \frac{176}{2} - 51 = 88 - 51 = 37\,\text{cm}.$$

$\therefore$ Required difference $=$ width $-$ side $= 37 - 11 = 26\,\text{cm}.$

18. (a) $S.I. = \dfrac{\text{principal} \times \text{time} \times \text{rate}}{100}$

$= \dfrac{12000 \times 3 \times 12}{100} = ₹\,4320$

$C.I. = P\left[\left(1 + \dfrac{\text{rate}}{100}\right)^{\text{time}} - 1\right]$

$= 12000\left[\left(1 + \dfrac{12}{100}\right)^3 - 1\right]$

$= 12000\left[\left(\dfrac{28}{25}\right)^3 - 1\right]$

$= 12000\left[\dfrac{21952}{15625} - 1\right] = 12000 \times \dfrac{6327}{15625}$

$= ₹\,4859.136$

$\therefore$ Required difference $= 4859.136 - 4320 = ₹\,539.136$

19. (c) Radius of circle (r) $= \dfrac{\text{circumference}}{2\pi} = \dfrac{220 \times 7}{2 \times 22} = 35$ m.

Area of circle $= \pi r^2 = \dfrac{22}{7} \times (35)^2 = \dfrac{22}{7} \times 35 \times 35$

$= 3850 \text{ m}^2 = $ area of rectangle

$\therefore$ Length of rectangle $= \dfrac{\text{area of rectangle}}{\text{width}}$

$= \dfrac{3850}{50} = 77$ m.

20. (e) CP of article

$= 6800 \times \dfrac{100}{100 - 75} = 6800 \times \dfrac{100}{25} = ₹\,27200$

Solutions (21-25)

21. (a) Percentage of candidates short listed for Post I = (230 × 100)/3500 = 6.57%

Percentage of candidates short listed for Post II = (450 × 100) / 8500 = 5.29%

Percentage of candidates short listed for Post III = (185 × 100)/8200 = 2.25%

Percentage of candidates short listed for Post IV = (52×100)/5600 = 0.92%

Percentage of candidates short listed for Post V = (155×100)/4200 = 3.69%

Percentage of candidates short listed for Post VI = (145×100)/5500 = 2.63%

So post I had the highest percentage of candidates short listed for mains exam.

22. (e) Required Average = (5200 + 8200 + 7200 + 2400 + 3600 + 4500 + 6500) = 37600/7 = 5370

23. (b) Number of candidates eligible for post I = (2800 + 3500 + 2500 + 3200 + 2400 + 5200 + 6800) = 26400

Number of candidates short listed for post I = (68 + 230 + 320 + 90 + 140 + 350 + 650) = 1848

Required Percentage $= \dfrac{1848}{26400} \times 100 = 7\%$

24. (a) Number of candidates shortlisted from Goa state for all the posts = (140 + 260 + 75 + 75 + 75 + 85) = 710

Number of candidates shortlisted from Tamilnadu state for all the posts = (650 + 180 + 340 + 160 + 45 + 25) = 1400

Required ratio = 710/1400 = 71/140 = 71:140

25. (e) Total candidates shortlisted post V = (120 + 155 + 140 + 95 + 75 + 65 + 45) = 695

Total candidates shortlisted post VI = (165 + 145 + 120 + 110 + 85 + 45 + 25) = 695

Required ratio = 695/695 = 1:1

26. (b) Required average $= \dfrac{17 + 22 + 33 + 13 + 15 + 20}{6}$

$= \dfrac{120}{6} = 20$ thousand

27. (a) Required per cent $= \dfrac{20 - 15}{15} \times 100 = \dfrac{100}{3} = 33\dfrac{1}{3}\%$

28. (b) Required average $= \dfrac{13 + 27 + 12}{3}$

$= \dfrac{52}{3} = 17.3$ thousands

29. (d) Required ratio = 15 : 18 = 5 : 6

30. (e) Required ratio = 18 : 27 = 2 : 3

31. (b) Suraj's average earnings over all the days = (160 + 420 + 150 + 480)/4 = 1210/4 = ₹302.5

32. (c) Required amount = (280 + 280 + 120 + 420) = ₹1100

33. (d) Praveen's total earnings on Wednesday after Suraj's donation = (420 + 250) = 670

34. (c) Required difference = (350 − 160) = 190

35. (e) Required ratio = 120 : 250 : 180 = 12 : 25 : 18

36. (e) $\Rightarrow$ x = 13/3, 6

$\Rightarrow$ y = 23/5, 4

No relationship can be established.

37. (c) $\Rightarrow$ x = −7/9, −1

$\Rightarrow$ y = 31/27, 7

So x < y

38. (e) $\Rightarrow$ x = −47, 16

$\Rightarrow$ y = 48, −17

No relationship can be established.

39. (a) $\Rightarrow$ x = −7/9,

$\Rightarrow$ y = −8/9,

So x > y

40. (e) $\Rightarrow$ x = 44, −37

$\Rightarrow$ y = 37, −9/5

No relationship can be established.

Solutions (41-45)

Person	Specializations	Games
Kane	Software	Hockey
Kevin	Geo Science	Swimming
Mark	Electrical	Football
Starc	Mechanical	Cricket
Shane	Telecommunication	Badminton
Venn	Petroleum	Tennis

41. (c)   42. (a)   43. (c)   44. (b)   45. (e)

Solutions (46-50)

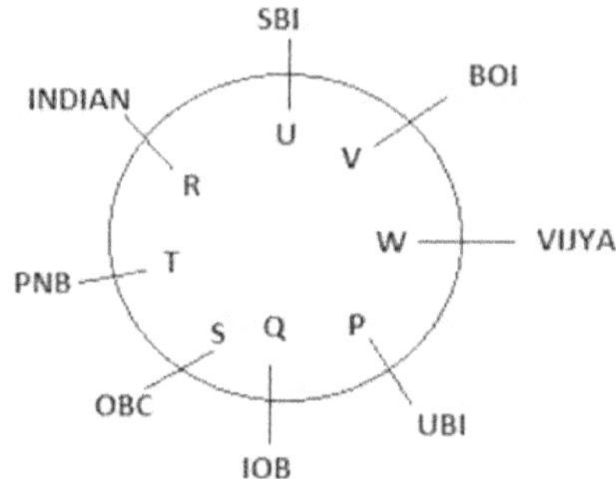

46. (b)   47. (e)   48. (c)   49. (e)   50. (d)

51. (a) Conclusion I is the conversion of first statement, hence I follows. But II does not follow because A + A = A i.e. All leaders are good orators but not *vice versa*.

52. (a) A + A = A; i.e. All terrorists are human.

53. (c)

54. (b) from the below diagrams, only (b) conclusion is true.

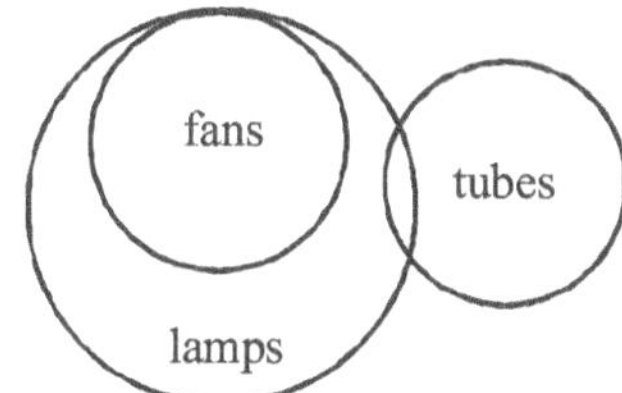

55. (a) from the diagrams below, only (a) conclusion follows.

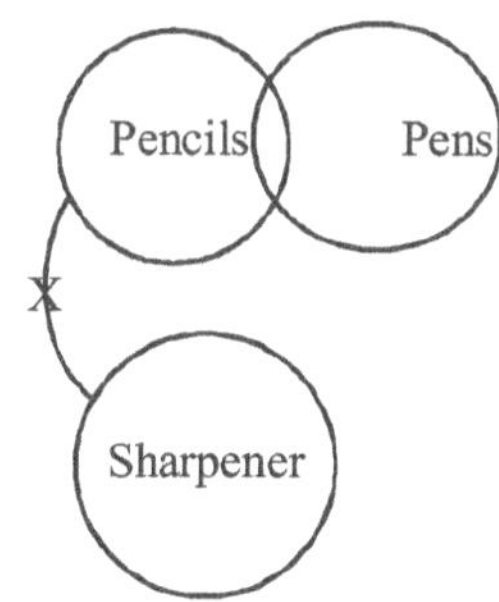

(56-57): Pranab   ⇔   Reva
    (+)   (−)
    ↓   ↓   ↓

Neela   Prakash Vikash
(−)   (+)
↓

Mohan   Arun
(+)

56. (a)   57. (c)

For (Qs. 58 to 62)

The given information is summarised in a table as follows :

Teachers	Subjects	
	Compulsory	Optional
A	History	English
B	History	Chemistry
C	History	Mathematics
D	(Female) English	History
E	Physics	Mathematics
F	Mathematics	Physics

58. (a) History is the compulsory subject of C.

59. (d) D is a female member in the group.

60. (d) The compulsory subject of F (Mathematics) is the optional subject of C.

61. (c) E has physics and Mathematics as his two subjects.

62. (d) A, B and C all have History as the compulsory subjects.

63. (c)

Letter	O	N	S	I	R	T
Code	Z	#	1	@	9	Z

Condition (ii) is applied.

64. (e)

Letter	K	I	U	B	S	R
Code	3	@	7	6	1	9

65. (d)

Letter	B	K	A	E	U	G
Code	6	3	$	4	7	%

66. (c)

Letter	S	T	O	K	G	A
Code	*	5	2	3	%	*

Condition (iii) is applied.

67. (b)

Letter	O	R	H	S	N	U
Code	O	9	8	1	#	O

Condition (i) is applied.

68. (d) $M > R$ ...(i)
$R \geq K$ ...(ii)
$J < K$ ...(iii)
Combining (i), (ii) and (iii), we get
$M > R \geq K > J \Rightarrow M > J$ (conclusion I)
$R > J$ (conclusion II)
$M > K$ (conclusion III)
Hence, conclusion I ($M > J$), conclusion II ($J < R$) and conclusion III ($K < M$) are true.

69. (b) $D \geq N$ ...(i)
$N = V$ ...(ii)
$W \leq V$ ...(iii)
Combining (i) and (ii), we get
$D \geq N = V \Rightarrow D \geq V$. Hence, conclusion III ($V = D$) is not necessary true.
Again, combining all (i), (ii) and (iii), we get
$D \geq N = V \geq W \Rightarrow D \geq W$. Hence, neither conclusion I ($D = W$) nor conclusion II ($W < D$) is true. But both conclusion I ($D = W$) and conclusion II ($W < D$) together make a complementary pair. Hence, either conclusion I or conclusion II is true.

70. (d) $H < B$ ...(i)
    $M \geq B$ ...(ii)
    $K = M$ ...(iii)
    Combining (ii) and (iii), we get

    $K = M \geq B \Rightarrow K \geq B$. Hence, neither conclusion II
    ($B = K$) nor conclusion III ($K > B$) is true. But, both
    conclusion I and conclusion II together make a
    complementary pair. Hence, either conclusion II
    ($B = K$) or conclusion III ($K > B$) is true.
    Again, combining all (i), (ii) and (iii), we get

    $K = M \geq B > H \Rightarrow K > H$ (conclusion I). Hence,

    conclusion I ($K > H$) is true.

71. (e) $V \geq M$ ...(i)
    $N < V$ ...(ii)
    $J > N$ ...(iii)
    From (i) and (ii), no specific relation between M and N
    can be established. Hence, conclusion II ($M > N$) is
    not necessarily true.
    Again, from all (i), (ii) and (iii), no specific relation
    between J and M can be established. Hence,
    conclusion I ($J > M$) is not necessarily true. Again,
    from (ii) and (iii), no specific relation between V and J
    can be established. Hence, conclusion III ($V > J$) is not
    necessarily true.

72. (d) $A > B$ ....(i)

    $B \geq E$ ....(ii)

    $F < E$ ....(iii)
    Combining (i), (ii) and (iii), we get

    $A > B \geq E > F$

    Hence, Conclusion I ($A > F$)
    Conclusion II ($F < B$)
    and Conclusion III ($E < A$) are true.

(73-77)
Economics is not money - ka la ho ga ....(i)
demand and supply economics - mo ta pa ka .... (ii)
money makes only part - zi la ne ki ...... (iii)
demand makes supply economics - zi mo ka ta ... (iv)
From (i) & (iii)
money → 'la'
From (iii) & (iv)
makes → 'zi'
From (i) & (iv)
economics – 'ka'
Also, and - 'pa'
demand - 'mo' or 'ta'
supply - 'mo' or 'ta'
only - 'ne' or 'ki'
part - 'ne' or 'ki'
is - 'ho' or 'ga'
not - 'ho' or 'ga;

73. (e) 74. (e) 75. (a) 76. (b) 77. (d)

78. (e) As per Rajesh $\Rightarrow$ May, Jun, Jul, Aug ... (i)
    As per Vinod $\Rightarrow$ May or after ... (ii)
    From (i) and (ii), we get May, Jun, Jul, Aug. Of these,
    only
    Jun has 30 days (Madan's criterion).

79. (d) West

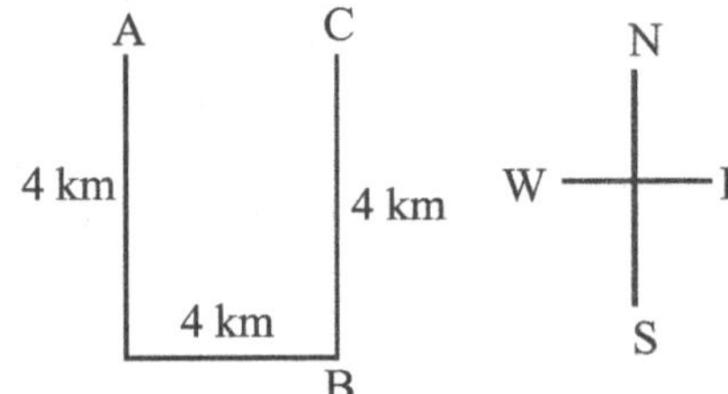

From C to reach A (starting point) policeman will have
to move in the West direction to reach his post.

80. (b) Veena's rank is 17th from the bottom means Veena's
    rank is 4th from the top. Rohan's rank is exactly
    between 4th and 12th, i.e. 8th.

PRACTICE SET

15

Time : 45 Min. **Max. Marks : 80**

QUANTITATIVE APTITUDE

DIRECTIONS (Qs. 1-5) : What will come in place of question mark (?) in the following questions ?

1. 48% of $525 + ?\%$ of $350 = 399$
   (a) 42 (b) 46 (c) 28
   (d) 26 (e) None of these

2. $\dfrac{3}{7}$ of $\dfrac{4}{5}$ of $\dfrac{5}{8}$ of $490 = ?$
   (a) 115 (b) 105 (c) 108
   (d) 116 (e) None of these

3. 125% of $560 + 22\%$ of $450 = ?$
   (a) 799 (b) 700 (c) 782
   (d) 749 (e) None of these

4. $18.76 + 222.24 + 3242.15 = ?$
   (a) 3384.15 (b) 3483.15 (c) 3283.25
   (d) 3383.25 (e) None of these

5. 1.05% of $2500 + 2.5\%$ of $440 = ?$
   (a) 37.50 (b) 37.25 (c) 370.25
   (d) 372.50 (e) None of these

DIRECTIONS (Qs.6-10):In each of these questions two equations are given. You have to solve these equations and give answer.

   (a) If $x < y$
   (b) If $x > y$
   (c) If $x = y$, or relation cannot be established
   (d) If $x \geq y$
   (e) If $x \leq y$

6. I. $3x^2 + 13x + 14 = 0$
   II. $3y^2 + 11y + 10 = 0$

7. I. $49x^2 - 84x + 36 = 0$
   II. $25y^2 - 30y + 9 = 0$

8. I. $3x + 4y = 49$
   II. $5x + 8y = 91$

9. I. $x + 1/x = 17/4$
   II. $4y^2 + 4 + 17y = 0$

10. I. $x^2 - 9x + 18 = 0$
    II. $2y^2 - 5y = 3$

11. What is the compound interest accrued on an amount of ₹ 8500 in two years @ interest 10% per annum?
    (a) ₹ 1875 (b) ₹ 1885 (c) ₹ 1775
    (d) ₹ 1765 (e) None of these

12. The ratio of the ages of A and B seven years ago was 3 : 4 respectively. The ratio of their ages nine years from now will be 7 : 8 respectively. What is B's age at present ?
    (a) 16 years (b) 19 years (c) 28 years
    (d) 23 years (e) None of these

13. The perimeter of a square is thrice the perimeter of a rectangle. If the perimeter of the square is 84 cm and the length of the rectangle is 8 cm, what is the difference between the breadth of the rectangle and the side of the square?
    (a) 15 cm (b) 19 cm (c) 10 cm
    (d) 8 cm (e) None of these

14. The area of a circle is equal to the area of a rectangle with perimeter equal to 42 m and breadth equal to 8.5 m. What is the area of the circle?
    (a) 116.25 sq m (b) 104.25 sq m (c) 146.25 sq m
    (d) 128.25 sq m (e) None of these

15. 4 women and 12 children together take four days to complete a piece of work. How many days will four children alone take to complete the piece of work if two women alone can complete the piece of work in 16 days?
    (a) 32 (b) 24 (c) 16
    (d) 12 (e) None of these

16. A man riding a bicycle completes one lap of a square field along its perimeter at the speed of 43.2 km/hr in 1 minute 20 seconds. What is the area of the field?
    (a) 52900 sq m   (b) 57600 sq m   (c) 48400 sq m
    (d) Can't be determined
    (e) None of these

17. On Teacher's Day, 4800 sweets were to be equally distributed among a certain number of children. But on that particular day 100 children were absent. Hence, each child got four sweets extra. How many children were originally supposed to be there?
    (a) 300   (b) 400   (c) 540
    (d) 500   (e) Can't be determined.

18. The ratio of the monthly incomes of Sneha, Tina and Akruti is 95:110:116. If Sneha's annual income is ₹3,42,000, what is Akruits annual income?
    (a) ₹3,96,900   (b) ₹5,63,500   (c) ₹4,17,600
    (d) ₹3,88,000   (e) None of these

19. A truck covers a distance of 256 km at the speed of 32 km/hr. What is the average speed of a car which travels a distance of 160 km more than the truck in the same time?
    (a) $46\,\text{kmh}^{-1}$ (b) $52\,\text{kmh}^{-1}$ (c) $49\,\text{kmh}^{-1}$
    (d) $64\,\text{kmh}^{-1}$ (e) None of these

20. In an examination, the maximum aggregate marks is 1020. In order to pass the exam a student is required to obtain 663 marks out of the aggregate marks. Shreya obtained 612 marks. By what per cent did Shreya fail the exam?
    (a) 5%   (b) 8%   (c) 7%
    (d) Can't be determined
    (e) None of these

DIRECTIONS (Qs. 21-25): The following chart shows Classification of 200 Students based on the Marks Obtained by them in Accounts and Mathematics in an Examination.

Subject	Marks out of 100				
	>80	>60	>40	>20	>0
Accounts	18	64	160	184	200
Maths	8	42	132	162	200
Average	14	54	146	174	200

21. What is the difference between the number of students passed with 60 as cut-off marks in Math's and those passed with 60 as cut-off marks in aggregate?
    (a) 13   (b) 14
    (c) 15   (d) 12
    (e) None of these

22. If at least 60% marks in Accounts are required for pursuing higher studies in Accounts, how many students will be eligible to pursue higher studies in Accounts?
    (a) 57   (b) 64
    (c) 68   (d) 48
    (e) None of these

23. The percentage of number of students getting at least 60% marks in Math's over those getting at least 40% marks aggregate, is approximately?
    (a) 21%   (b) 27%
    (c) 29%   (d) 31%
    (e) None of these

24. The number of students scoring less than 40% marks aggregate is?
    (a) 13   (b) 19
    (c) 20   (d) 54
    (e) None of these

25. If it is known that at least 46 students were eligible for a symposium on Math's, then the minimum qualifying marks in Math's for eligibility to symposium would lie in the range?
    (a) 40-45   (b) 30-40
    (c) 40-60   (d) below 20
    (e) None of these

DIRECTIONS (Qs. 26 - 30) : The following pie-chart shows the sources of funds (in crores) to be collected by a company. Study the pie-chart and answers the question that follow.

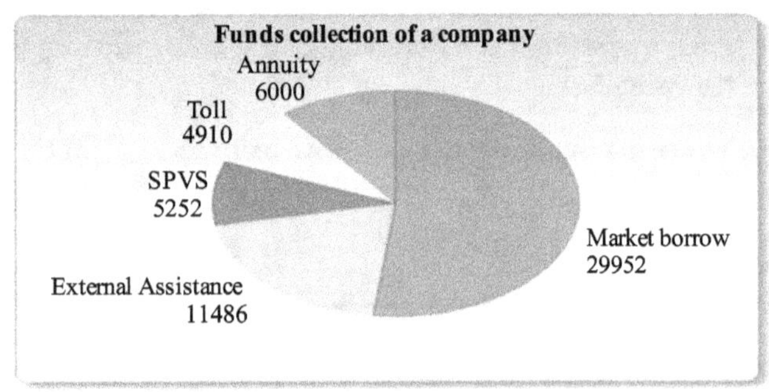

26. If company could receive a total of Rs. 9695 crores as External Assistance, by what percent (approximately) should it increase the Market Borrowing to arrange for the shortage of funds?
    (a) 4 %   (b) 6%
    (c) 8%   (d) 10%
    (e) None of these

27. Near about 20% of the funds are to be arranged through ?
    (a) SPVS   (b) Annuity
    (c) External Assistance   (d) Market borrowing
    (e) None of these

28. The central angle corresponding to Market Borrowing is ?
    (a) 187.2 degree   (b) 183.2 degree
    (c) 181.2 degree   (d) 180.2 degree
    (e) None of these

29. If the toll is to be collected through an outsourced agency by allowing a maximum 10% commission, how much amount should be permitted to be collected by the outsourced agency, so that the project is supported with Rs. 4,910 crores?
    (a) Rs. 5401 crore   (b) Rs. 5301 crore
    (c) Rs. 5201 crore   (d) Rs. 5101 crore
    (e) None of these

30. The approximate ratio of the funds to be arranged through Toll and that through Market Borrowing is ?
    (a) 1 : 6   (b) 2 : 5
    (c) 3 : 7   (d) 6 : 7
    (e) None of these

DIRECTIONS (Qs. 31-35) : What should come in place of question mark (?) in the following number series?

31. 8 52 ? 1287 4504.5 11261.25 16891.875
    (a) 462   (b) 286   (c) 194
    (d) 328   (e) None of these
32. 3 42 504 ? 40320 241920 967680
    (a) 6048   (b) 5544   (c) 4536
    (d) 5040   (e) None of these
33. 403 400 394 382 358 310 ?
    (a) 244   (b) 210   (c) 214
    (d) 256   (e) None of these
34. 7 8 4 13 –3 22 ?
    (a) –7   (b) –10   (c) –12
    (d) –14   (e) None of these
35. 250000 62500 12500 3125 625 ? 31.25
    (a) 156.25   (b) 172.25   (c) 125
    (d) 150   (e) None of these

DIRECTIONS (Qs. 36-40) : Study the following graph carefully to answer the questions that follow:

Number of Students Enrolled in Three Different Disciplines in Five Different Colleges

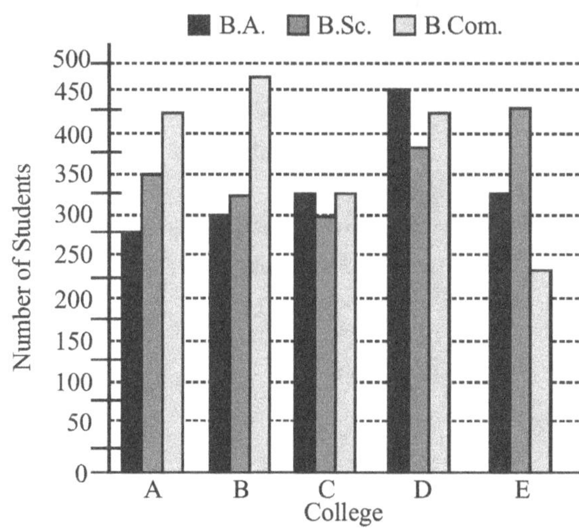

36. What is the total number of students studying B.Sc in all Colleges together?
    (a) 1825   (b) 1975
    (c) 1650   (d) 1775
    (e) None of these
37. What is the respective ratio of total number of students studying B.Sc. in the colleges C and E together to those studying B.A. in the Colleges A and B together?
    (a) 24 : 23   (b) 25 : 27
    (c) 29 : 23   (d) 29 : 27
    (e) None of these
38. What is the respective ratio of total number of students studying B.Sc., B.A. and B.Com. in all the Colleges together?
    (a) 71 : 67 : 75   (b) 67 : 71 : 75
    (c) 71 : 68 : 75   (d) 75 : 71 : 68
    (e) None of these

39. Number of students studying B.Com. in College C forms **approximately** what percent of the total number of students studying B.Com. in all Colleges together?
    (a) 39   (b) 21
    (c) 44   (d) 33
    (e) 17
40. Number of students studying B.A in College B forms what percent of total number of students studying all the disciplines together in that College? (rounded off two digits after decimal)
    (a) 26.86   (b) 27.27
    (c) 29.84   (d) 32.51
    (e) None of these

REASONING ABILITY

DIRECTIONS (Qs. 41-45) : Study the following information carefully and answer the questions carefully

Five experts on Nino-technology involved in an international Research Project hold a Quarterly Review Meeting in Singapore. There are certain limitations on their language skills. Expert R1 knows only Japanese and Hindi; R2 is good at Japanese and English; R3 is good at English and Hindi; R4 knows French and Japanese quite well, and R5, an Indian, knows Hindi, English, and French.

41. Besides R5, which of the following can converse with R4 without an interpreter?
    (a) Only R1   (b) Only R2
    (c) Only R3   (d) Both R1 and R2
    (e) None of these
42. Which of the following cannot converse without an interpreter?
    (a) R2 and R5   (b) R1 and R2
    (c) R1 and R3   (d) R3 and R4
    (e) None of these
43. Choose the language that is least commonly used at the meeting.
    (a) English   (b) French
    (c) Japanese   (d) Hindi
    (e) None of these
44. Which of the following can act as an interpreter when R3 and R4 wish to discuss?
    (a) Only R1   (b) Only R2
    (c) Only R5   (d) All of the above
    (e) None of these
45. Suppose a sixth Expert R6 joins the session. Which are the languages that he should know so that a maximum number of original experts are able to understand him?
    (a) English and French
    (b) Japanese and Hindi
    (c) English and Hindi
    (d) French and Japanese
    (e) None of these

DIRECTIONS (Qs. 46-49): Study the following information to answer the given questions.

In a certain code, 'ze lo ka gi' is a code for 'must save some money', 'fe ka so ni' is a code for 'he made good money', 'ni lo da so' is a code for 'he must be good' and 'we so ze da' is a code for 'be good save grace'.

46. Which of the following is the code for 'must'?
   (a) so
   (b) da
   (c) lo
   (d) ni
   (e) Cannot be determined

47. What does the code 'ze' stand for?
   (a) some
   (b) must
   (c) be
   (d) grace
   (e) save

48. Which of the following is the code for 'good'?
   (a) so
   (b) we
   (c) ze
   (d) lo
   (e) fe

49. 'grace of money' may be coded as
   (a) ka da fe
   (b) we ka so
   (c) ja da we
   (d) ka we yo
   (e) ja ka ze

DIRECTIONS (Qs. 50-54): Study the following information carefully and answer the questions carefully.

In a Public Sector Undertaking Township, there are five executives - Ambrish, Amit, Rohit, Manu and Tarun and they stay in five different flats, numbered 1 to 5.

1. Two of them play Cricket while the other three play different games viz. Football, Tennis and Chess.
2. One Cricket player and a Chess player stay in the third flat, whereas the other three stay in different flats, i.e. 2nd, 4th and 5th.
3. Two of these five players are mechanical engineers while the other three are quality inspector, design engineer, and power engineer respectively.
4. The chess player is the oldest in age while one of the cricket players, who plays at the national level, is the youngest in age.
5. The age of the other cricket player, who plays at the regional level, lies between the football player and the chess player.
6. Manu is a regional level player and stays in the 3rd flat while Tarun is a quality inspector and stays in the 5th flat.
7. The football player is a design engineer and stays in the 2nd Flat.
8. Amit is a power engineer and plays Chess while Ambrish is the mechanical engineer and plays Cricket at the national level.

50. Who stays in the 4th flat?
   (a) Ambrish
   (b) Amit
   (c) Rohit
   (d) Manu
   (e) None of these

51. Which sport does Tarun play?
   (a) Chess
   (b) Football
   (c) Cricket
   (d) Tennis
   (e) None of these

52. Who plays football?
   (a) Ambrish
   (b) Amit
   (c) Rohit
   (d) Manu
   (e) None of these

53. Who stay in the same flat?
   (a) Ambrish and Amit
   (b) Maim and Tarun
   (c) Amit and Manu
   (d) Rohit and Tarun
   (e) None of these

54. The Chess player is a:
   (a) Power engineer
   (b) Mechanical Engineer
   (c) Design engineer
   (d) Quality inspector
   (e) None of these

DIRECTIONS (Qs. 55-57) : Study the information given below carefully to answer the following questions.

In a certain code language the following lines written as:
'lop eop aop fop' means 'Traders are above laws'
'fop cop bop gop' means 'Developers were above profitable'
'aop bop uop qop' means 'Developers stopped following traders'
'cop jop eop uop' means 'Following maps were laws'

55. 'Developers are following laws' would be correctly written as
   (a) 'bop cop uop eop'
   (b) 'lop bop eop uop'
   (c) 'oup cop lop aop'
   (d) 'gop cop uop qop'
   (e) None of these

56. 'qop gop cop eop' would correctly mean
   (a) profitable laws were stopped
   (b) developers stopped following laws
   (c) traders were above profitable
   (d) were laws profitable traders
   (e) None of the above

57. 'aop qop bop' would correctly mean
   (a) following were above
   (b) traders stopped developers
   (c) developers are laws
   (d) traders above stopped
   (e) laws are stopped

DIRECTIONS (Qs. 58-62) : In each of the questions below are given four statements followed by three conclusions numbered I, II and III. You have to take the given statements to be true even if they seem to be at variance from commonly known facts. Read all the conclusions and then decide which of the given conclusions logically follows from the given statements disregarding commonly known facts.

58. Statements: All petals are flowers. Some flowers are buds. Some buds are leaves. All leaves are plants.
   Conclusions: I. Some petals are not buds.
   II. Some flowers are plants.
   III. No flower is plant.
   (a) Only I follows
   (b) Either II or III follows
   (c) I and II follow
   (d) Only III follows
   (e) None of the above

59. Statements: Some pens are keys. Some keys are locks. All locks are cards. No card is paper

Conclusions:

I. No lock is paper.

II. Some cards are keys.

III. Some keys are not paper.

(a) I and II follow   (b) Only I follows

(c) Only II follows   (d) All follow

(e) None follows

60. Statements: Some pearls are gems. All gems are diamonds. No diamond is stone. Some stones are corals.

Conclusions:

I. Some stones are pearls.

II. Some corals being diamond is a possibility.

III. No stone is pearl.

(a) Only I follows   (b) Only II follows

(c) Either I or III follows   (d) I and II follow

(e) None of these

61. Statements: Some apartments are flats. Some flats are buildings. All buildings are bungalows. All bungalows are gardens.

Conclusions:

I. All apartments being building is a possibility

II. All bungalows are not buildings.

III. No flat is garden.

(a) None follows   (b) Only I follows

(c) Either I or III follows   (d) II and III follow

(e) Only II follows

62. Statements: All chairs are tables. All tables are bottles. Some bottles are jars. No jar is bucket.

Conclusions:

I. Some tables being jar is a possibility.

II. Some bottles are chairs.

III. Some bottles are not bucket.

(a) Only I follows   (b) I and II follow

(c) All follow   (d) Only II follows

(e) None of these

DIRECTIONS (Qs. 63-67) : In these questions the symbols @, #, \$, % and ★ are used with different meanings as follow.

'A @ B' means 'A is not smaller then B'.

'A # B' means 'A is neither smaller than nor equal to B'.

'A \$ B' means 'A is neither greater than nor smaller than B'.

'A % B' means 'A is not greater than B'.

'A ★ B' means 'A is neither greater than nor equal to B'.

In each questions, four statements showing relationships have been given, which are followed by three conclusions I, II and III. Assuming that the given statements are true, find out which conclusion (s) is/are definitely true?

63. **Statements:** V \$ Y, Y @ Z, Z % X, X # T

Conclusions:

I. T # Z   II. X # Y

III. Z ★ Y

(a) None follows   (b) Only I follows

(c) II and III follow   (d) I and III follow

(e) Only III follows

64. **Statements:** R @ J, J % F, F ★ E, E % M

Conclusions:

I. M # J   II. F % M

III. M ★ R

(a) Only I follows   (b) Only II follows

(c) Only III follows   (d) I and II follow

(e) All follow

65. **Statements:** H#R, R@L, L ★ W, W%F

Conclusions:

I. H # J   II. F # L

III. H \$ F

(a) Only I follows   (b) I and II follow

(c) II and III follow   (d) Either I or II follows

(e) All follow

66. **Statements:** M # K, M \$ F, F % Q, Q ★ H

Conclusions:

I. H # K   II. Q # K

III. Q @ M

(a) I and II follow   (b) Either I or II follows

(c) All follow   (d) II and III follow

(e) None of the above

67. **Statements:** D ★ Q, Q \$ L, L#T, T % H

Conclusions:

I. D ★ L

II. L @ H

III. H # L

(a) Only I follows   (b) I and II follow

(c) Either II or III follows   (d) All follow

(e) None follow

68. Introducing a boy, a girl said, "He is the only son of my mother's mother". How is the girl related to the boy?

(a) Mother   (b) Aunt

(c) Sister   (d) Niece

(e) None of these

69. Daksh is toller than maick but not as tak as Rohan. Somegh is shorter than Daksh but toller than Farhan. Who among them is the shortest ?

(a) Daksh   (b) Maick

(c) Farhan   (d) Cannot be determined

(e) None of these

70. D said "A's father is the only brother of my sister's son. How is A's Father related to D ?

(a) Uncle   (b) Nephew

(c) Brother in law   (d) Brother

(e) Cousin

71. 40 persons are sitting in a raw. Haw many person are sitting between 31st person from left and 25th person from right ?

(a) 18   (b) 14

(c) 29   (d) 9

(e) Cannot be determined

DIRECTIONS (72-73) Read the following infromation carefully and answer the question given below-

Amit goes to the house of his sister seema who is the neighbour of gunjan. Gunjan has a daughter Meena. Meena studies in the First year of college. Anshu is the Father of Amit and is married to arti and has a sister who is Gunjan.

72. How is Gunjan related to Amit ?
  - (a) Anut
  - (b) Mother
  - (c) Cousin
  - (d) Sister
  - (e) None of these

73. How is Meena related to Amit ?
  - (a) Niece
  - (b) Cousin
  - (c) Uncle
  - (d) Brother
  - (e) None of these

74. From a point, Rajesh started walking towards east and walked 35m. Then he turned towards his right and walked 10m and he again turned right and walked 35m. Finally he turned to his left and walked 10m and he reached his destination. Now, how far is he from his starting point ?
  - (a) 50m
  - (b) 55m
  - (c) 10m
  - (d) 20m
  - (e) None of these

DIRECTIONS (Qs. 75-78) : Read the following passage carefully and answer the Question given below it.

Six friends Abhishek, Deepak, Mridul, Pritam, Ranjan and Salil married within a year in the months of February, April, July, September, November and December and in the cities of Ahmedabad, Bengaluru, Chennai, Delhi, Mumbai and Kolkata, but not necessarily following the above order. The brides' names were Geetika, Jasmine, Hema, Brinda, Ipsita and Veena, once again not following any order. The following are some facts about their weddings.

(i) Mridul's wedding took place in Chennai, however he was not married to Geetika or Veena

(ii) Abhishek's wedding took place in Ahmedabad and Ranjan's in Delhi; however neither of them was married to Jasmine or Brinda

(iii) The wedding in Kolkata took place in February

(iv) Hema's wedding took place in April, but not in Ahmedabad

(v) Geetika and Ipsita got married in February and November and in Chennai and Kolkata but not following the above order

(vi) Pritam visited Bengaluru and Kolkata only after his marriage in December

(vi) Salil was married to Jasmine to September

75. Hema's husband is
  - (a) Abhishek
  - (b) Deepak
  - (c) Ranjan
  - (d) Pritam
  - (e) Mridul

76. Deepak's wedding took place in
  - (a) Bengaluru
  - (b) Mumbai
  - (c) Kolkata
  - (d) Delhi
  - (e) Chennai

77. In Mumbai, the wedding of one of the friends took place in the month of
  - (a) April
  - (b) September
  - (c) November
  - (d) December
  - (e) July

78. Salil's wedding was held in
  - (a) Bengaluru
  - (b) Chennai
  - (c) Kolkata
  - (d) Delhi
  - (e) Mumbai

DIRECTIONS (Qs. 79-80): Read the following information carefully and answer the questions given below it –

A + B means 'A is father of B'
A ÷ B means 'B is brother of A'
A × B means 'A is husband of B'
A – B means 'A is sister of B'

79. In the expression A +B ×C – D÷E, how is D related to B?
  - (a) Brother - in - law
  - (b) Sister -in- law
  - (c) Nephew
  - (d) Brother
  - (e) Can't be determined

80. Which of the following expressions shows that "R is sister of Q" ?
  - (a) P + Q – R + Z
  - (b) T × Q + Z – R
  - (c) P + Q – R × Z
  - (d) None of these
  - (e) Can't be determined.

HINTS & EXPLANATIONS

1. (a) 48% of $525 + ?\%$ of $350 = 399$

$\Rightarrow \quad \dfrac{48}{100} \times 525 + \dfrac{?}{100} \times 350 = 399$

$\Rightarrow \quad 25200 + ? \times 350 = 399 \times 100$

$\Rightarrow \quad ? \times 350 = 39900 - 25200 = 14700$

$\Rightarrow \quad ? = \dfrac{14700}{350} = 42$

2. (b) $? = \dfrac{3}{7}$ of $\dfrac{4}{5}$ of $\dfrac{5}{8}$ of 490

$\Rightarrow \quad ? = \dfrac{3}{7} \times \dfrac{4}{5} \times \dfrac{5}{8} \times 490$

$\Rightarrow \quad ? = 35 \times 3 = 105$

3. (a) $? = 125\%$ of $560 + 22\%$ of 450

$\Rightarrow \quad ? = \dfrac{125}{100} \times 560 + \dfrac{22}{100} \times 450$

$\Rightarrow \quad ? = 700 + 99 = 799$

4. (b) $? = 18.76 + 222.24 + 3242.15$

$\Rightarrow \quad ? = 3483.15$

5. (b) $? = 1.05\%$ of $2500 + 2.5\%$ of 440

$\Rightarrow \quad ? = \dfrac{1.05}{100} \times 2500 + \dfrac{2.5}{100} \times 440$

$\Rightarrow \quad ? = \dfrac{2625}{100} + \dfrac{1100}{100}$

$\Rightarrow \quad ? = \dfrac{3725}{100} = 37.25$

6. (e) I. $3x^2 + 13x + 14 = 0$

$\Rightarrow \quad (3x + 7)(x + 2) = 0$

$\Rightarrow \quad x = -7/3, -2$

II. $3y^2 + 11y + 10 = 0$

$\Rightarrow \quad (y + 2)(3y + 5)$

$\Rightarrow \quad y = -2, -5/3 = 0$

So $x \le y$

7. (b) I. $49x^2 - 84x + 36 = 0$

$\Rightarrow \quad (7x - 6)(7x - 6) = 0$

$\Rightarrow \quad x = 6/7, 6/7$

II. $25y^2 - 30y + 9 = 0$

$\Rightarrow \quad (5y - 3)(5y - 3) = 0$

$\Rightarrow \quad y = 3/5, 3/5$

So $x > y$

8. (c) I. $3x + 4y = 49$ $\qquad \dots\dots(i)$

II. $5x + 8y = 91$ $\qquad \dots\dots(ii)$

From (I) and (II)

We get $x = 7$ and $y = 7$

So relation cannot be established.

9. (b) I. $x + 1/x = 17/4$

$\Rightarrow \quad (x - 4)(4x - 1) = 0$

$\Rightarrow \quad x = 4, 1/4$

II. $4y^2 + 4 + 17y = 0$

$\Rightarrow \quad (y + 4)(4y + 1) = 0$

$\Rightarrow \quad y = -4, -1/4$

So $x > y$

10. (d) I. $x^2 - 9x + 18 = 0$

$\Rightarrow \quad (x - 6)(x - 3) = 0$

$\Rightarrow \quad x = 6, 3$

II. $2y^2 - 5y = 3$

$\Rightarrow \quad (y - 3)(2y + 1) = 0$

$\Rightarrow \quad y = 3, -1/2$

So $x \ge y$

11. (e) Compound Interest after two years

$= 8500\left(1 + \dfrac{10}{100}\right)^2 - 8500$

$= 10285 - 8500 = ₹ 1785$

12. (d) Let the present age of $A = x$ and $B = y$ years

According to first condition

$\dfrac{x - 7}{y - 7} = \dfrac{3}{4} \Rightarrow 4x - 28 = 3y - 21 \Rightarrow 4x - 3y = 7 \quad \dots\dots (i)$

According to second condition

$\dfrac{x + 9}{y + 9} = \dfrac{7}{8} \Rightarrow 8x + 72 = 7y + 63$

$\Rightarrow 7y - 8x = 9 \quad \dots\dots (ii)$

$8x - 6y = 14$

$\dfrac{7y - 8x = 9}{y = 23 \text{ years.}}$

13. (a) Perimeter of the square $= 84$ cm

Perimeter of the rectangle $= 28$ cm

Perimeter of the rectangle $= 2(1 + b)$

or, $2(8 + b) = 28$ cm

or, $b = 14 - 8 = 6$ cm.

$\therefore$ Breadth of the rectangle $= 6$ cm

Side of the square $= \dfrac{84}{4} = 21$ cm

Difference $= 21 - 6 = 15$ cm.

14. (e) Perimeter of the rectangle $= 42$ m

$2(l + b) = 42$ m

or, $l + 8.5 = 21$ m

or, $l = 12.5$ m.

Area of the rectangle $= 12.5 \times 8.5 = 106.25$ sq.m.

$\therefore$ Area of the circle. $= 106.25$ sq.m.

15. (b) Two women alone can complete a piece of work in 16 days.

$\therefore$ Four women can complete the same work in 8 days.

Since 12 children can complete the work in

$\dfrac{4 \times 8}{8 - 4} = \dfrac{4 \times 8}{4} = 8$ days.

$\therefore$ Four children can complete the work in $\dfrac{12 \times 8}{4}$

$= 24$ days.

16. (b) 43.2 km/hr $= 43.2 \times \dfrac{5}{18} = 12$ m/s

Total distance covered $= 12 \times 80 = 960$ m.

Perimeter of the square $= 960$ m.

Side of the square $= 240$ m.

Area $= (240)^2 = 57600$ sqm.

154

17. (b) Let the number of children be x.
Now, according to the question

$$\left(\frac{4800}{x} - 100\right)(x + 4) = 4800$$

or, $\left(\frac{48}{x} - 1\right)(x + 4) = 48$

or, $(x + 16)(x - 12) = 0$

∴ x = 12 sweets

Number of students = $\frac{4800}{12} = 400$.

18. (c) Sneha's monthly income = $\frac{342000}{12} = 28500$

∴ Akruti's monthly income = $\frac{28500}{95} \times 116 = 34800$

Akruti's annual income = 417600.

19. (b) Time taken by the truck = $\frac{256}{32} = 8$ hr.

Distance covered by the car = (256 + 160) = 416 km.
Time = 8 hr.

∴ Speed of the car = $\frac{416}{8} = 52$ km / hr.

20. (a) Required percentage = $\frac{663 - 612}{1020} \times 100 = 5\%$.

21. (d) Required difference = 54 - 42 = 12.

22. (b) 60 % of 100 = 60/100 × 100 = 60
So required no = 64

23. (c) Required percentage = (42/146) x 100 = 28.76% = 29%.

24. (d) 40% of 100 = 40/100 x 100 = 40.
Required number = 200 - 146 = 54.

25. (c) Since 32 students get 40 and above marks in Maths and out of these 42 students get 60 and above marks, therefore to select top 46 students in maths, the qualifying marks should lie in the range 40-60.

26. (b) New funds = 11486 - 9695 = Rs. 1791 crores
Increase in requirement of market borrowing is 1791 crore
Now, 1791 crore is what percent of Market Borrowing
= [(1791)/(29952)]?100% = 5.98% = 6% (approx)

27. (c) Total funds are = 29952+11486+5252+4910+6000
= 57600 crore
Now 20% of 57600 = 20/100 × 576000 = 11520 crore
Which is approximately equal to External Assistance

28. (a) Central angle corresponding to Market Borrowing
[(29952/57600)] ×360 = 187.2 degree

29. (a) Amount required = (Funds required from toll) + (10% of these funds) = 4910 + 10% of (4910) = 4910 + (10/100) ×4910 = 4910 + 491 = 5401 crore

30. (a) Required Ratio = 4910/29952 = 1/6.1 = 1 : 6

31. (b) 8 × 6.5 = 52

52 × 5.5 = $\boxed{286}$

286 × 4.5 = 1287.

32. (d) 3 × 14 = 42
42 × 12 = 504

504 × 10 = $\boxed{5040}$

5040 × 8 = 40320.

33. (c) 403 − 3 = 400
400 − 6 = 394
394 − 12 = 382
382 − 24 = 358
358 − 48 = 310

310 − 96 = $\boxed{214}$.

34. (d)

$$\begin{array}{ccccccc} & & +5 & & +9 & & \\ 7 & 8 & 4 & 13 & -3 & 22 & -14 \\ & -3 & & -7 & & -11 & \end{array}$$

35. (a) 250000 ÷ 4 = 62500
62500 ÷ 5 = 12500
12500 ÷ 4 = 3125
3125 ÷ 5 = 625

625 ÷ 4 = $\boxed{156.25}$
156.25 ÷ 5 = 31.25.

36. (d) Total number of students studying B.Sc. in all the colleges together
= 350 + 325 + 300 + 375 + 425 = 1775

37. (c) Total number of students studying B.Sc. in colleges C and E
= 300 + 425 = 725
Total number of students studying B.A. in colleges A and B
= 275 + 300 = 575
∴ Required ratio = 725 : 575 = 29 : 23

38. (a) Total number of students studying in different streams in all the colleges:
B.Sc. → 1775
B.A. → 275 + 300 + 325 + 450 + 325 = 1675
B.Com. → 425 + 475 + 325 + 425 + 225 = 1875
∴ Required ratio = 1775 : 1675 : 1875 = 71 : 67 : 75

39. (e) Number of students studying B. Com. in college C = 325
Total number of students studying B. Com = 1875

∴ Required percentage = $\frac{325}{1875} \times 100 \approx 17$

40. (b) Total number of students in college
B = 300 + 325 + 475 = 1100
Number of students studying B.A. in college B = 300

∴ Required percentage = $\frac{300}{1100} \times 100 = 27.27$

Sol. (41-45) :
From the given information, following table can be build:

	Japanese	Hindi	English	French
R1	yes	yes	no	no
R2	yes	no	yes	no
R3	no	yes	yes	no
R4	yes	no	no	yes
R5	no	yes	yes	yes

41. (d) 42. (d) 43. (b) 44. (d) 45. (b)

Solution (46- 49):
ze lo ka gi = must save some money ... (i)
fe ka so ni = he made good money ... (ii)
ni lo da so = he must be good ... (iii)
we so ze da = be good save grace ... (iv)
From (i) and (iii), lo = must ... (v)
From (i) and (iv), ze = save ... (vi)
From (ii), (iii) and (iv), so = good ... (vii)
From (i) and (ii), ka = money ... (viii)
From (i), (v), (vi) and (viii), gi = some ... (ix)
From (ii), (iii) and (vii), ni = he ... (x)

From (ii), (vii), (viii) and (x), fe = made ... (xi)
From (iii), (v), (vii) and (x), da = be ... (xii)
From (iv), (vi), (vii) and (xii), we = grace ... (xiii)
46. (c)   47. (e)   48. (a)   49. (d)
Sol. (50 – 54) :

Game	Profession	Name	Flat number
Tenis	Quality Inspector	Tarun	5
Cricketer (National)	Mechanical Engg	Ambrish	4
Chess	Power Engg.	Amit	3
Cricket (regional)	Mechanical Engg.	Manu	3
Football	Design Engg.	Rohit	2

50. (a)   51. (d)   52. (c)   53. (c)   54. (a)
Sol. (55-57):
lop eop aop fop - Traders are above laws → (i)
fop cop bop gop - Developers were above profitable → (ii)
aop bop uop qop - Developers stopped following traders → (iii)
cop job cop uop - Following maps were laws → (iv)
From (i) and (ii), fop - above
From (i) and (iii), aop - traders
From (ii) and (iii), bop - developers
From (ii) and (iv), cop - were
From (iii) and (iv), uop - following
From (i) and (iv), eop - laws
Therefore, remaining codes are
lop - are   [from (i)]
gop - profitable   [from (ii)]
qop - stopped   [from (iii)]
jop - maps   [from (iv)]
55. (b)   56. (a)   57. (b)
58. (b) According to question,

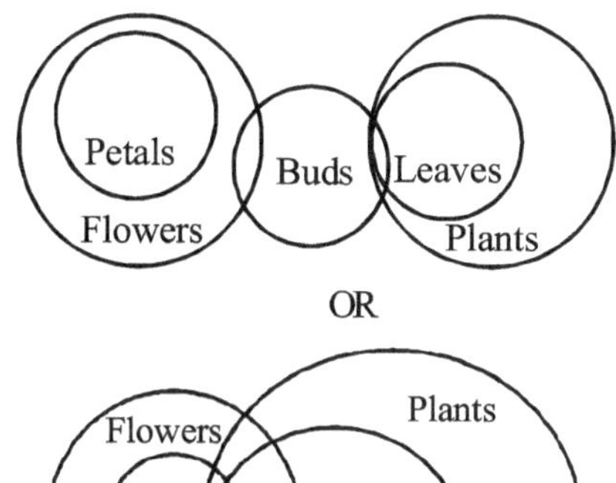

OR

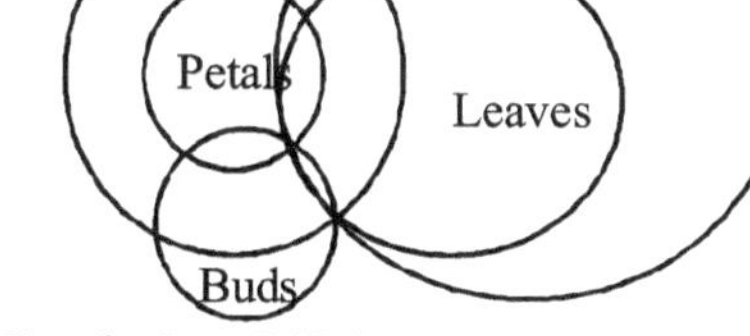

Conclusions I. False
II. False ⎤ or
III. False ⎦

Hence, only either II or III follows.
59. (d) According to question

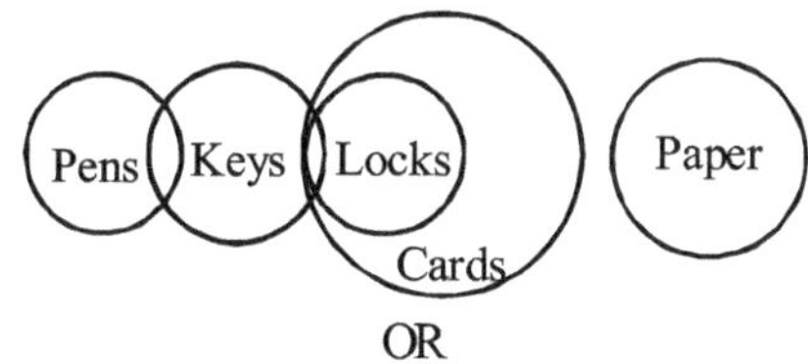

OR

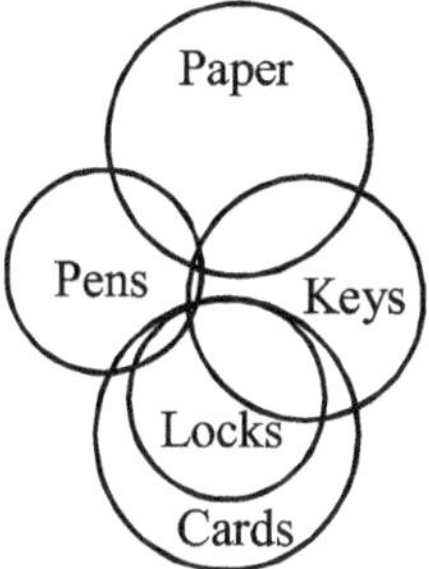

Conclusions I. True
II. True
III. True
Hence, All conclusions follow.
60. (e) According to question,

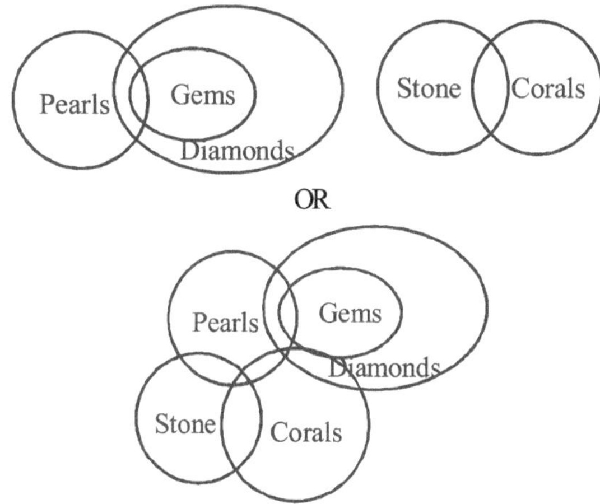

I. False ⎤
Conclusion II. True ⎬ or
III. False ⎦

Hence, only conclusions II and either I or III follow.
61. (a) According to question,

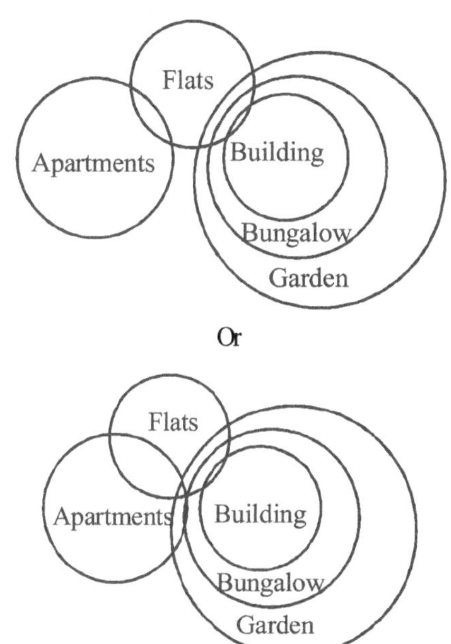

Conclusions I. True, II. False, III. False
Hence, only conclusion I follows.

62. (c) According to question,

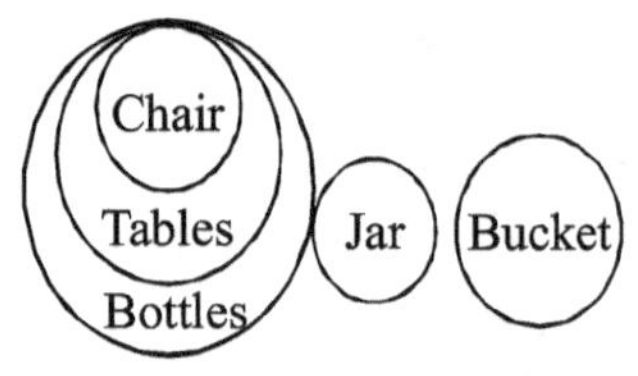

OR

Conclusions, I. True, II. True, III. True.
Hence, All I, II and III follow.

(63-67) :

$\star \Rightarrow <$	$\# \Rightarrow >$	$@ \Rightarrow \geq$
$\% \Rightarrow \leq$	$\$ \Rightarrow =$	

63. (a) $V \$ Y \Rightarrow V = Y$

$Y @ Z \Rightarrow Y \geq Z$

$Z \% X \Rightarrow Z \leq X$

$X \# T \Rightarrow X > T$

From all above statements,

$V = Y \geq Z \leq X > T$

Conclusions I. $T \# Z \Rightarrow T > Z$ (False)

II. $X \# Y \Rightarrow X > Y$ (False)

III. $Z \star Y \Rightarrow Z < Y$ (False)

64. (a) $R @ J \Rightarrow R \geq J$

$J \% F \Rightarrow J \leq F$

$F \star E \Rightarrow F < M$

$E \% M \Rightarrow E \leq M$

From all above statements, $R \geq J \leq F < E \leq M$

Conclusions I: $M \# J \Rightarrow M > J$ (True)

II. $F \% M \Rightarrow F \leq M$ (False)

III. $M \star R \Rightarrow M < R$ (False)

65. (b) $H \# R \Rightarrow H > R$

$R @ L \Rightarrow R \geq L$

$L \star W \Rightarrow L < W$

$W \% F \Rightarrow W \leq F$

From all above statements, $H > R \geq L < W \leq F$

Conclusions I. $H \# L \Rightarrow H > L$ (True)

II. $F \# L \Rightarrow F > L$ (True)

III. $H \$ F \Rightarrow H = F$ (False)

66. (e) $M \# J \Rightarrow M > F$

$M \$ F \Rightarrow M = K$

$F \% Q \Rightarrow F \leq Q$

$Q \star H \Rightarrow Q < H$

From all above statements,

$K < M = F \leq Q < H$

Conclusions. I. $H \# K \Rightarrow H > K$ (True)

II. $Q \# K \Rightarrow Q > K$ (True)

III. $Q @ M \Rightarrow Q \geq M$ (True)

67. (e) $D \star Q \Rightarrow D < Q$

$Q \$ L \Rightarrow Q = L$

$L \# T \Rightarrow L > T$

$T \% H \Rightarrow T \leq H$

From all above statemens,

$D < Q = L > T \leq H$

Conclusions. I. $D \star L \Rightarrow D < L$ (True)

II. $L @ H \Rightarrow L \geq H$ (False)

III. $H \# L \Rightarrow H > L$ (False)

68. (d)

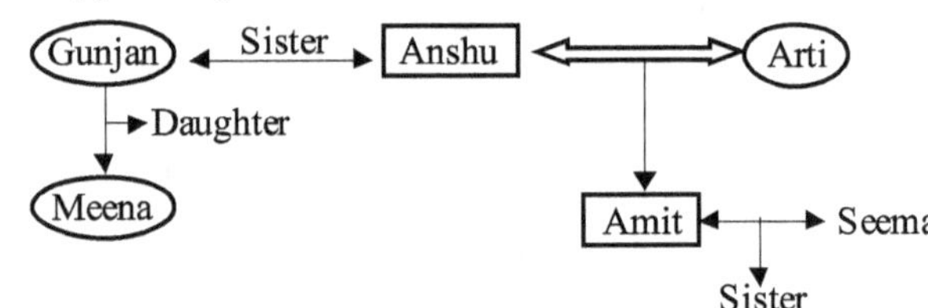

69. (d) Rohan > Daksh > Maick   .....(i)
Daksh > Somegh > Farhan   ....(ii)
So, either Maick or Farhan is shortest

70. (b) Only brother of my sister's son is nephew. So, A's father is the nephew of D.

71. (b) 31st position from left = 10th position from right
25th positon from left = 16th from right
So, required no. of person = $[40 - (10 + 16)] = 14$

72. (a) Gunjan is the Aunt of Amit

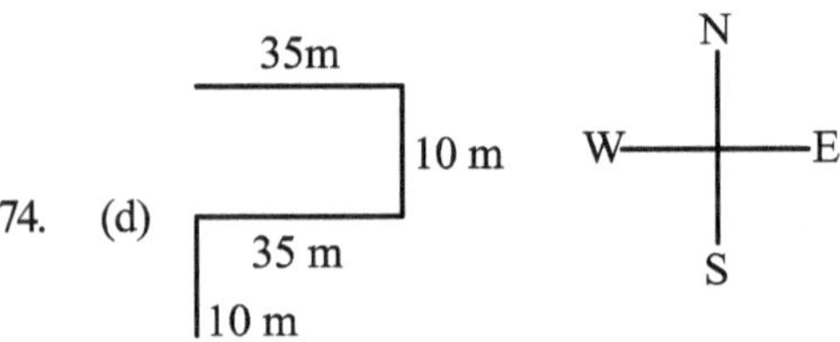

73. (b) Meena is the cousin of Amit.

74. (d)

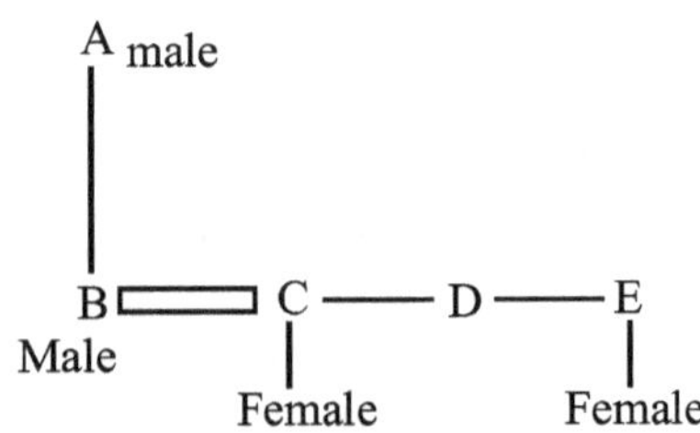

Solution (75 –78):

	Mridul	Abhishek	Ranjan	Salil	Deepak	Pritam
Place	Chennai	Ahmedabad	Delhi	Bengaluru	Kolkata	Mumbai
Month	November	July	April	September	February	December
Brides	Ipsita	Veena	Hema	Jasmine	Geetika	Brinda

75. (c)   76. (c)   77. (d)   78. (a)

Solution (79 –80):

79. (e)

A male

B — C — D — E
Male   Female   Female

Hence D may be either male or female. Thus, we cant'determined the relation between D and B because D many be either brother- in- law or sister- in- law of B.

80. (d) None of these

PRACTICE SET 16

INSTRUCTIONS

- This practice set consists of two sections. Quantitative Aptitude (Qs. 1-40) & Reasoning Ability (Qs. 41-80).
- All the questions are compulsory.
- Each question has five options, of which only one is correct. The candidates are advised to read all the options thoroughly.
- There is negative marking equivalent to $1/4^{th}$ of the mark allotted to the specific question for wrong answer.

Time : 45 Min.   **Max. Marks : 80**

QUANTITATIVE APTITUDE

DIRECTIONS (Qs. 1-5): Study the table carefully to answer the questions that follow :

Yearly fees (in ₹ thousands) of five different courses in five different years :

Years	Courses				
	B.A.	**B.Sc.**	**B.E.**	**MBA**	**MCA**
2008	1.3	1.8	4.4	4.2	4.5
2009	2.4	2.8	5.6	5.4	5.4
2010	3.6	4.2	6.4	6.8	6.6
2011	4.8	5.6	8.2	7.6	7.2
2012	6.2	7.4	9.6	8.8	9.4

1. If 30% of the yearly fees were reduced for B.E course in the year 2011, what was the rectified yearly fees for B.E course in the year 2011 ?
(a) ₹ 2460   (b) ₹ 5740
(c) ₹ 6260   (d) ₹ 3230
(e) None of these

2. Total yearly fees for MBA course overall the years together was what percentage of total yearly fees of MCA course in the year 2010, 2011 and 2012 together.?
(a) 70.73%   (b) 104.46%
(c) 87.26%   (d) 141.38%
(e) None of these

3. What was the percentage increase in yearly fees of B. A in the year 2009 as compared to the previous year.?
(a) $84\frac{8}{13}\%$ (b) $45\frac{7}{24}\%$
(c) $61\frac{5}{24}\%$ (d) $26\frac{2}{13}\%$
(e) None of these

4. What was the difference between the total yearly fees for all the courses together in the year 2012 and the yearly fees of B.Sc course in the year 2010 ? (in ₹)
(a) 34240   (b) 28300
(c) 37200   (d) 25350
(e) None of these

5. What was the average yearly fees of MCA course overall the years together ?
(a) ₹ 7120   (b) ₹ 6620
(c) ₹ 5940   (d) ₹ 6460
(e) None of these

6. Ram had ₹ 2 lakh, part of which he lent at 15% per annum and rest at 12% per annum. Yearly interest accured was ₹ 27600. How much did he lent at 15%?
(a) ₹ 120000   (b) ₹ 100000
(c) ₹ 80000   (d) ₹ 60000
(e) None of these

7. A and B can do a piece of work in 8 days, B and C can do the same work in 12 days. If A,B and C can complete the same work in 6 days, in how many days can A and C complete the same work?
(a) 8 days   (b) 10 days
(c) 12 days   (d) 16 days
(e) None of these

8. Two trains each 200 m long move towards each other on parallel lines with velocities 20 km/h and 30 km/h, respectively. What is the time that elapses when they first meet until they have cleared each other ?
(a) 20 s   (b) 24.8 s
(c) 28.8 s   (d) 30 s
(e) None of these

9. Ravi's brother is 3 years elder to him. His father was 28 years of age when his sister was born while his mother was 26 years of age when he was born. If his sister was 4 years of age when his brother was born, the ages of Ravi's father and mother, respectively when his brother was born were

   (a) 32 years and 23 years
   (b) 32 years and 29 years
   (c) 35 years and 29 years
   (d) 35 years and 33 years
   (e) None of these

10. Three unbiased coins are tossed. What is the probability of getting at least 2 heads?

   (a) $\dfrac{1}{4}$
   (b) $\dfrac{1}{2}$
   (c) $\dfrac{1}{6}$
   (d) $\dfrac{1}{8}$
   (e) None of these

11. If the sum of a few numbers is 450 and their mean is 50 and if another number 100 is included, the mean would become

   (a) 55
   (b) 60
   (c) 75
   (d) 150
   (e) None of these

12. In a mixture of 60 litres, the ratio of milk and water is 2 : 1. What amount of water must be added to make the ratio of milk and water as 1 : 2 ?

   (a) 42 Litres
   (b) 56 Litres
   (c) 60 Litres
   (d) 77 Litres
   (e) None of these

13. The average weight of 5 men is increased by 2 Kg when one of the men whose weight is 60 Kg is replaced by a new man. The weight of the new man is

   (a) 50 Kg
   (b) 65 Kg
   (c) 68 Kg
   (d) 70 Kg
   (e) None of these

14. Two-third of a consignment was sold at a profit of 5% and the remainder at a loss of 2% if the total profit was ₹400, what was the value of the consignment ?

   (a) ₹13,000/-
   (b) ₹17,000/-
   (c) ₹15,000/-
   (d) ₹40,000/-
   (e) None of these

15. The sum of the number of boys and girls in a school is 150. If the number of boys is x, then the number of girls becomes x% of the total number of students. How many boys are there in the school ?

   (a) 51
   (b) 65
   (c) 60
   (d) 95
   (e) None of these

DIRECTIONS (Qs. 16-20): What approximate value should come in place of question mark (?) in the following questions?

You are not expected to calculate the exact value

16. 32.05% of 259.99 = ?

   (a) 92
   (b) 88
   (c) 78
   (d) 90
   (e) 83

17. $\dfrac{1}{8}$ of $\dfrac{2}{3}$ of $\dfrac{3}{5}$ of 1715 = ?

   (a) 80
   (b) 85
   (c) 90
   (d) 95
   (e) 75

18. $25.05 \times 123.95 + 388.999 \times 15.001 = ?$

   (a) 900
   (b) 8950
   (c) 8935
   (d) 8975
   (e) 8995

19. $561 \div 35.05 \times 19.99 = ?$

   (a) 320
   (b) 330
   (c) 315
   (d) 325
   (e) 335

20. $(15.01)^2 \times \sqrt{730} = ?$

   (a) 6125
   (b) 6225
   (c) 6200
   (d) 6075
   (e) 6250

DIRECTIONS (Qs. 21-25): In each of these questions, a number series is given. In each series, only one number is wrong. Find out the wrong number.

21. 3601 3602 1803 604 154 36 12

   (a) 3602
   (b) 1803
   (c) 604
   (d) 154
   (e) 36

22. 4 12 42 196 1005 6066 42511

   (a) 12
   (b) 42
   (c) 1005
   (d) 196
   (e) 6066

23. 2 8 12 20 30 42 56

   (a) 8
   (b) 42
   (c) 30
   (d) 20
   (e) 12

24. 32 16 24 65 210 945 5197.5

   (a) 945
   (b) 16
   (c) 24
   (d) 210
   (e) 65

25. 7 13 25 49 97 194 385

   (a) 13
   (b) 49
   (c) 97
   (d) 194
   (e) 25

DIRECTIONS (Qs. 26-30) : In the following questions two equations numbered I and II are given. You have to solve both equations and Give answer if

   (a) $x > y$ (b) $x \geq y$

   (c) $x < y$ (d) $x \leq y$

   (e) $x = y$ or the relationship cannot be established

26. I. $x^2 - 7x + 10 = 0$

     II. $y^2 + 11y + 10 = 0$

27. I. $x^2 + 28x + 192 = 0$

     II. $y^2 + 16y + 48 = 0$

28. I. $2x - 3y = -3.5$

     II. $3x - 2y = -6.5$

29. I. $x^2 + 8x + 15 = 0$

     II. $y^2 + 11y + 30 = 0$

30. I. $x = \sqrt{3136}$

     II. $y^2 = 3136$

DIRECTIONS (Qs. 31-35): Study the following graph and table carefully and answer the questions given below them.

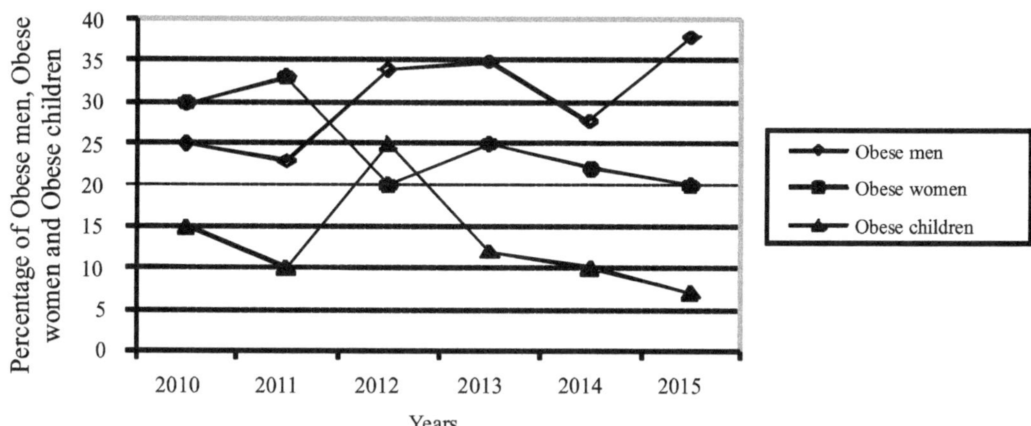

Total Number of Men, Women and Children in the state over the years

Years	Men	Women	Children
2010	54,000	38,000	15,000
2011	75,000	64,000	21,000
2012	63,000	60,000	12,000
2013	66,000	54,000	16,000
2014	70,000	68,000	20,000
2015	78,000	75,000	45,000

31. What was the **approximate** average of obese men, obese women and obese children in 2013?

   (a) 12,683   (b) 12,795

   (c) 12,867   (d) 12,843

   (e) 12,787

32. The number of obese men in the year 2015 was what per cent of the men not suffering from obesity in the same year?

   (a) 55   (b) 60

   (c) 50.5   (d) 65.5

   (e) None of these

33. What was the ratio of the obese women in the year 2014 to the obese men in the year 2014?

   (a) 716 : 798   (b) 621 : 656

   (c) 815 : 733   (d) 765 : 952

   (e) None of these

34. What is the difference between the number of obese women and obese children together in the year 2012 and the number of obese men in the same year?

   (a) 5,475   (b) 5,745

   (c) 4,530   (d) 31,650

   (e) None of these

35. What was the total number of children not suffering from obesity in the year 2010 and 2011 together?

   (a) 4,350   (b) 31,560

   (c) 4,530   (d) 31,650

   (e) None of these

DIRECTIONS (Qs. 36-40) : Following bar-graph shows the percentage of passed girls with respect to total passed students of two schools A and B.

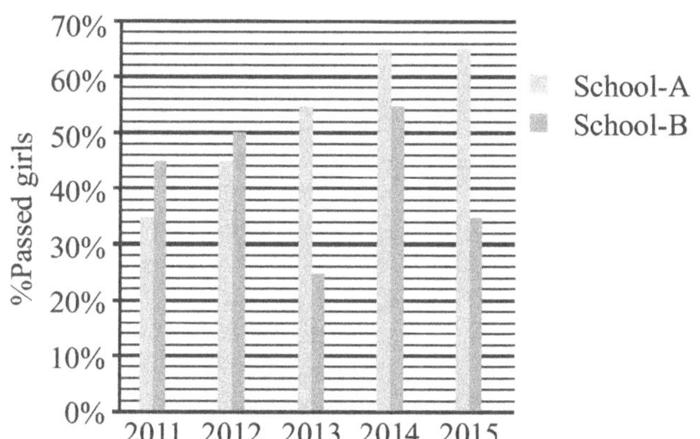

36. If the number of boys passed from School A and School B is 520 and 660 respectively in the year 2011, then what is the difference between number of girls passed from A and B in year 2011?

  (a) 275   (b) 280
  (c) 295   (d) 240
  (e) None of these

37. If the number of girls passed from School A and School B in year 2012 is equal to 360, then what is the sum of total number of passed students of School A and School B in the same year?

  (a) 845   (b) 615
  (c) 480   (d) 760
  (e) None of these

38. If the number of girls passed from School A in year 2014 is equal to the number of boys passed from School B in year 2012 and it is 195, then what is the difference to total number of students passed from School A in 2014 and School B in year 2012?

  (a) 90   (b) 120
  (c) 135   (d) 80
  (e) None of these

39. If total number of students passed from School A and School B in year 2015 is 1200 and 1600 respectively, then number of girls passed from School B is how much percent more than the number of girls passed from School A in the same year?

  (a) 35%   (b) 45%
  (c) 40%   (d) 48%
  (e) 38%

40. If the number of girls passed from School A and School B in year 2013 is 800 and 960 respectively, then number of boys passed from School B is what percent of number of boys passed from School A in same year?

  (a) 80%   (b) 110%
  (c) 120%   (d) 124%
  (e) None of these

REASONING ABILITY

DIRECTIONS (Qs. 41-45): In each question below are given two/ three statements followed by two conclusions numbered I and II. You have to take the given statements to be true even if they seem to be at variance with commonly known facts. Read all the conclusions and then decide which of the given conclusions logically follows from the given statements, disregarding commonly known facts. Give answer

  (a) if only conclusion I follows.
  (b) if only conclusion II follows.
  (c) if either conclusion I or conclusion II follows.
  (d) if neither conclusion I nor conclusion II follows.
  (e) if both conclusions I and conclusion II follow.

41. Statements : No house is an apartment.
                 Some bungalows are apartments.
  Conclusions : **I.** No house is a bungalow.
                 II. All bungalows are houses.

42. Statements : Some gases are liquids.
                 All liquids are water.
  Conclusions : **I.** All gases being water is a possibility.
                 II. All such gases which are not water can never be liquids.

43. Statements : All minutes are seconds.
                 All seconds are hours.
                 No second is a day.
  Conclusions : **I.** No day is an hour.
                 II. At least some hours are minutes.

(44-45): Statements : Some teachers are professors.
                 Some lecturers are teachers.

44. Conclusions : **I.** All teachers as well as professors being lecturers is a possibility.
                 II. All those teachers who are lecturers are also professors.

45. Conclusions : **I.** No professor is a lecturer.
                 II. All lecturers being professors is a possibility.

DIRECTIONS (Qs. 46-50) : Study the following information carefully and answer the given questions :

A, B, C, D, E, F, G and H are sitting around a circle facing the centre but not necessarily in the same order.

- B sits second to left of H's husband. No female is an immediate neighbour of B.
- D's daughter sits second to right of F. F is the sister of G. F is not an immediate neighbour of H's husband.
- Only one person sits between A and F. A is the father of G. H's brother D sits to the immediate left of H's mother. Only one person sits between H's mother and E.
- Only one person sits between H and G. G is the mother of C. G is not an immediate neighbour of E.

46. What is position of A with respect to his mother-in-law ?
  (a) Immediate left   (b) Third to the right
  (c) Third to the left   (d) Second to the right
  (e) Fourth to the left

47. Who amongst the following is D's daughter ?
  (a) B   (b) C
  (c) E   (d) G
  (e) H

48. What is the position of A with respect to his grandchild ?
  (a) Immediate right   (b) Third to the right
  (c) Third to the left   (d) Second to the left
  (e) Fourth to the left

49. How many people sit between G and her uncle ?
  (a) One   (b) Two
  (c) Three   (d) Four
  (e) More than four

50. Four of the following five are alike in a certain way based on the given information and so form a group. Which is the one that does not belong to that group ?
  (a) F   (b) C
  (c) E   (d) H
  (e) G

DIRECTIONS (Qs. 51) :Study the following information carefully and answer the questions given below :

There are five statues - L, M, N, O and P - each of them having different height. Statue L is smaller than only statue M. Statue O is smaller than statue N. Statue O is longer than statue P. The height of the tallest statue is 20 feet. The height of the second smallest statue is 11 feet.

51. What will be the height of statue P?
    (a) 13 feet   (b) 15 feet
    (c) 9 feet   (d) 12 feet
    (e) 14 feet

DIRECTIONS (Qs. 52-55) : Study the following information to answer the given questions:

In a certain code, 'ze lo ka gi' is a code for 'must save some money', 'fe ka so ni' is a code for 'he made good money', 'ni lo da so' is a code for 'he must be good' and 'we so ze da' is a code for 'be good save grace'.

52. Which of the following is the code of 'must'?
    (a) s o   (b) da
    (c) lo   (d) ni
    (e) Cannot be determined

53. What does the code 'ze' stand for?
    (a) some   (b) most
    (c) be   (d) grace
    (e) save

54. Which of the following is the code of 'good'?
    (a) s o   (b) we
    (c) ze   (d) lo
    (e) fe

55. 'grace of money' may be coded as
    (a) ka da fe   (b) we ka so
    (c) ja da we   (d) ka we yo
    (e) ja ka ze

DIRECTIONS (Qs. 56-60) : In the following questions, the symbols δ, $\star$, %, # and @ are used with the following meaning as illustrated below.

'P % Q' means 'P is neither greater than nor equal to Q'.

'P δ Q' means 'P is neither smaller than nor equal to Q'.

'P @ Q' means 'P is not greater than Q'.

'P $\star$ Q' means 'P is not smaller than Q'.

'P # Q' means 'P is neither greater than nor smaller than Q'.

Now, in each of the follwoing questions assuming the given statements to be true, find which of the four conclusions I, II, III and IV given below them is/are definitely true and give your answer.

56. **Statement:** R $\star$ T, T δ M, M % K, K @ V
    Conclusions
    I. V δ M   II. V δ T
    III. M % R   IV. K δ R
    (a) I and II are true   (b) I and III are true
    (c) II and IV are true   (d) I, III and IV are true
    (e) None of these

57. **Statement:** H δ J, J # N, N @ R, R δ W
    Conclusions
    I. W % N   II. W % H
    III. R # J   IV. R δ J
    (a) Only I is true   (b) Only II is true
    (c) Only III is true   (d) Only IV is true
    (e) Either III or IV is true

58. **Statement:** B @ D, D δ F, F % M, M $\star$ N.
    Conclusions
    I. B % F   II. M δ D
    III. N % F   IV. N % F
    (a) None is true   (b) Only I is true
    (c) Only II is true   (d) Only III is true
    (e) Only IV is true

59. **Statement:** F # Z, Z @ H, H % N, N δ B
    Conclusions
    I. F @ H   II. N % Z
    III. B % H   IV. B % Z
    (a) I and III are true   (b) II, III and IV are true
    (c) I and II are true   (d) I, II and III are true
    (e) None of the above

60. **Statement :** M % K, K $\star$ W, W δ V, V @ N
    Conclusions
    I. N $\star$ K   II. M % W
    III. K δ V   IV. V % M
    (a) None is true   (b) Only I is true
    (c) Only II is true   (d) Only III is true
    (e) Only IV is true

DIRECTIONS (Qs. 61-65): Following questions are based on the five three-digit numbers given below.

519   328   746   495   837

61. If half of the second highest number is subtracted from the third highest number, what will be the value ?
    (a) 156   (b) 146
    (c) 213   (d) 314
    (e) None of these

62. If the positions of the first and the third digits in each of the numbers are interchanged, which of the following will be the second digit of the lowest number?
    (a) 1   (b) 2
    (c) 4   (d) 9
    (e) 3

63. If in each number the third digit becomes the first digit, the first digit becomes the second digit and the second digit becomes the third digit, which of the following will be the first digit of the second highest number?
    (a) 9   (b) 6
    (c) 5   (d) 7
    (e) 8

64. Which of the following represents the difference between the first and the second digits of the second highest number?
    (a) 4   (b) 1
    (c) 3   (d) 5
    (e) None of these

65. If '1' is subtracted from eh third digit of each number and '1' is added to the first digit of each number, which of the following will be the sum of the second and third digits of the second lowest number?
    (a) 13   (b) 9
    (c) 8   (d) 6
    (e) None of these

DIRECTIONS (Qs. 66-70): Study the following information to answer the given questions:

Twelve people are sitting in two parallel rows containing six people each such that they are equidistant from each other. In row 1: P, Q, R, S, T and V are seated and all of them are facing South. In row 2: A, B, C, D, E and F are seated and all of them are facing North. Therefore, in the given seating arrangement, each member seated in a row faces another member of the other row.

S sits third to the right of Q. Either S or Q sits at an extreme end of the line. The one who faces Q sits second to the right of E. Two people sit between B and F. Neither B nor F sits at an extreme end of the line. The immediate neighbour of B faces the person who sits third to the left of P. R and T are immediate neighbours. C sits second to the left of A. T does not face the immediate neighbour of D.

66. Who amongst the following sit at the extreme ends of the rows?
(a) S, D
(b) Q, A
(c) V, C
(d) P, D
(e) Q, F

67. Who amongst the following faces S?
(a) A
(b) B
(c) C
(d) D
(e) F

68. How many persons are seated between V and R?
(a) One
(b) Two
(c) Three
(d) Four
(e) None of these

69. P is related to A in the same way as S is related to B based on the given arrangement. Which of the following is T related to, following the same pattern?
(a) C
(b) D
(c) E
(d) F
(e) Cannot be determined

70. Which of the following is true regarding T?
(a) F faces T.
(b) V is an immediate neighbour of T.
(c) F faces the one who is second to the right of T.
(d) T sits at one of the extreme ends of the line.
(e) Q sits second to the right of T.

DIRECTIONS (Qs. 71-72): Read the following information carefully and answr the questions which follow.

If 'P ★ Q' means 'P is the mother of Q'.
If 'P × Q' means 'P is the father of Q'.
If 'P + Q' menas ' P is the sister of Q'.
If 'P – Q' menas 'P is the brother of Q'.
If 'P > Q' menas 'P is the son of Q'.
If 'P < Q' menas 'P is the daughter of Q'.

71. Which of the following means P is the father of S?
(a) P × Q > R ★ S
(b) R × P < Q – S
(c) R + S > Q + P
(d) S + Q – R ★ P
(e) Cannot be determined

72. Which of the following means D is the aunt of C?
(a) D > B ★ A ★ C
(b) D + B – C ★ A
(c) D – B – A × C
(d) D + B × A × C
(e) None of these

DIRECTIONS (Qs. 73-74): Study the following information to anwer the given questions.

Point A is 5 m towards the West of point B. Point C is 2 m towards the North of point B. Point D is 3 m towards the East of point C. Point E is 2 m towards the South of point D.

73. If a person walks 2 m towards the north from point A, takes a right turn and continues to walk, which of the following points would he reach the first?
(a) D
(b) B
(c) E
(d) C
(e) Cannot be determined

74. Which of the following points are in a straight line?
(a) ABE
(b) DCA
(c) CED
(d) BDA
(e) ACE

DIRECTIONS (Qs. 75-77) : Study the following information carefully and answer the questions which follow-

'P - Q' means 'P is father of Q'
'P ÷ Q' means 'P is sister of Q'
'P × Q' means 'P is mother of Q'
'P + Q' means 'P is brother of Q'

75. Which of the following means 'A is nephew of B'?
(a) A + C - B × K
(b) B ÷ H - A + D
(c) B ÷ G - A ÷ R
(d) B + T × A ÷ E
(e) None of these

76. Which of the following means 'P is grandfather of J'?
(a) J ÷ W - U - P
(b) P × G + J ÷ A
(c) P - B ÷ J ÷ R
(d) P - T - J ÷ S
(e) None of these

77. How is R related to B in the expression 'B ÷ C - S + R'?
(a) nephew or niece
(b) niece
(c) nephew
(d) None of these
(e) Cannot be determined

78. Two cars start from the opposite places of a main road, 150 km apart. First car runs for 25 km and takes a right turn and then runs 15 km. It then turns left and then runs for another 25 km and then takes the direction back to reach the main road. In the mean time, due to minor break down the other car has run only 35 km along the main road. What would be the distance between two cars at this point?
(a) 65 km
(b) 75 km
(c) 80 km
(d) 85 km
(e) None of these

79. Among P, T, J, F and L who scored the highest?
I. P scored less than J and F.
II. T scored more than F but less than L.
III. J has not scored the highest.
(a) Only I and II
(b) Only I and III
(c) Only II and either I or III
(d) Only I and either II or III
(e) All I, II and III

80. Anil ranked seventeenth from the top and thirty seventh from the bottom in a class. How many students are there in the class?
(a) 53
(b) 45
(c) 54
(d) 52
(e) None of these

HINTS & EXPLANATIONS

1. (b) Required Fee $= 8200 \times 70/100 = ₹\,5740$

2. (d) $(4.2 + 5.4 + 6.8 + 7.6 + 8.8)/(6.6 + 7.2 + 9.4) \times 100$
$= 32.8/23.2 \times 100 = 141.38\%$

3. (a) $= (2.4 - 1.3)/1.3 \times 100 = 1.1/1.3 \times 100 = 84\frac{8}{13}\%$

4. (c) $= \{(6.2 + 7.4 + 9.6 + 8.8 + 9.4) - (4.2)\} = 37.2$
So, $₹\,37200$

5. (b) $= (4.5 + 5.4 + 6.6 + 7.2 + 9.4)/5 = 6.62$
So, $₹\,6620$

6. (a) Let first part be $₹\,x$, then second part be $₹\,(200000 - x)$
According to question,

$$\frac{x \times 1 \times 15}{100} + \frac{(200000 - x) \times 1 \times 12}{100} = 27600$$

$\Rightarrow\quad 15x - 12x + 2400000 = 2760000$
$\Rightarrow\quad 3x = 2760000 - 2400000$
$\Rightarrow\quad 3x = 360000$
$\therefore\quad x = 120000$
Therefore he lent $₹\,120000$ at 15%.

7. (a) $A's$ and $B's$ one day work $= \dfrac{1}{8}$

$B's$ and $C's$ one day work $= \dfrac{1}{12}$

$A's$, $B's$ and $C's$ one day work $= \dfrac{1}{6}$

$B's$ one day work $= \dfrac{1}{8} + \dfrac{1}{12} - \dfrac{1}{6} = \dfrac{1}{24}$

$A's$ and $C's$ one day work $= \dfrac{1}{6} - \dfrac{1}{24} = \dfrac{3}{24} = \dfrac{1}{8}$

A and C can do the work in 8 days.

8. (c) Relative speed of trains $= (20 + 30)$ km/h

$= 50\,\text{km/h} = 50 \times \dfrac{5}{18}$ m/s
Total relative distance $= 200 + 200 = 400$ m

$\therefore$ Required time $= \dfrac{400 \times 18}{50 \times 5} = 28.8$ s

9. (a) Mother's age when Ravi was born
$= 26$ years ... (i)
Father's age when his sister was born
$= 28$ years ... (ii)
Sister's age when his brother was born
$= 4$ years ... (iii)
Ravi's brother is 3 years elder to him ... (iv)
From (i) and (iv),
Mother's age when brother was born
$= 26 - 3 = 23$ years
From (ii) and (iii),
Father's age when brother was born
$= 28 + 4 = 32$ years

10. (b) Here $S = \{TTT, TTH, THT, HTT, THH, HTH, HHT, HHH\}$.
Let E = event of getting at least two heads
$= \{THH, HTH, HHT, HHH\}$.

$\therefore P(E) = \dfrac{n(E)}{n(S)} = \dfrac{4}{8} = \dfrac{1}{2}$.

11. (a) $50 = \dfrac{\text{Sum of all numbers}}{\text{number of observations}}$

$50 = \dfrac{450}{\text{Number of observations}}$

Number of observations $= \dfrac{450}{50} = 9$

New mean $= \dfrac{450 + 100}{10} = \dfrac{550}{10} = 55$

12. (c) Milk $= \dfrac{2}{3} \cdot 60 = 40l$

Water $= \dfrac{1}{3} \times 60 = 20l$

Let 'x' be the amount to be added to milk and water.
$\dfrac{40 + x}{20 + x} = \dfrac{1}{2}$
$80 + 2x = 20 + x$
$60 = x$

13. (d) Let total weight of 5 men be x kg and weight of new man y kg.

$\dfrac{x - 60 + y}{5} = \dfrac{x}{5} + 2$

$\Rightarrow \dfrac{x}{5} - 12 + \dfrac{y}{5} = \dfrac{x}{5} + 2$

$\Rightarrow y = 70\,\text{kg}$
weight of new man $= 70$ kg

14. (c) Let value of consignment was $₹\,x$

$\left(\dfrac{2}{3}\right)^{rd}$ consignment costs $\dfrac{2x}{3}$

Selling price of $\left(\dfrac{2}{3}\right)^{rd}$ consignment

$= \dfrac{2x}{3} + \dfrac{5}{100} \times \dfrac{2x}{3} = \dfrac{7}{10}x$

S.P of $\left(\dfrac{1}{3}\right)^{rd}$ consignment $= \dfrac{x}{3} - \dfrac{2}{100} \times \dfrac{x}{3} = \dfrac{49}{150}x$

Total S.P $= \dfrac{49x}{150} + \dfrac{7x}{10} = \dfrac{49x + 105x}{150} = \dfrac{154x}{150}$

Profit $=$ S.P $-$ C.P

$400 = \dfrac{154x}{150} - x = \dfrac{4x}{150}$

$x = \dfrac{400 \times 150}{4} = 15000$

Value of consignment was $₹\,15,000$

15. (c) If number of boys is x, then number of girls is $(150-x)$
$(150-x) = x\%$ of 150

$$150 - x = \frac{x}{100} \times 150 = \frac{3x}{2}$$

$$\Rightarrow \frac{5x}{2} = 150$$

$$\Rightarrow x = \frac{150 \times 2}{5} = 60$$

Number of boys is 60

16. (e) $\dfrac{32}{100} \times 260 = 83.2 \approx 83$

17. (b) $\dfrac{1}{8} \times \dfrac{2}{3} \times \dfrac{3}{5} \times 1715 = 85.75 \approx 85$

18. (c) $25 \times 124 + 389 \times 15 = 3100 + 5835 = 8935$

19. (a) $\dfrac{561}{35} \times 20 = 320.5 \approx 320$

20. (d) $(15)^2 \times \sqrt{730} = 225 \times 27 = 6075$

21. (d)

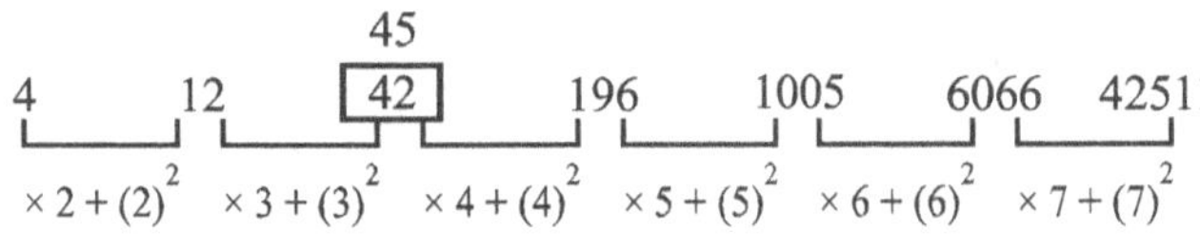

154 is written in place of 155.

22. (a)

42 is written in place of 45.

23. (a)

8 is written in place of 6.

24. (e)

65 is written in place of 60.

25. (d)

194 is written in place of 193.

26. (a) I. $x^2 - 7x + 10 = 0$
$\Rightarrow x^2 - 5x - 2x + 10 = 0$
$\Rightarrow x(x-5) - 2(x-5) = 0$
$\Rightarrow (x-2)(x-5) = 0$
$\Rightarrow x = 2$ or 5
II. $y^2 + 11y + 10 = 0$
$\Rightarrow y^2 + 10y + y + 10 = 0$
$\Rightarrow y(y+10) + 1(y+10) = 0$

$\Rightarrow (y+1)(y+10) = 0$
$\Rightarrow y = -1$ or -10
Clearly, $x > y$

27. (d) I. $x^2 + 28x + 192 = 0$
$\Rightarrow x^2 + 16x + 12x + 192 = 0$
$\Rightarrow x(x+16) + 12(x+16) = 0$
$\Rightarrow (x+12)(x+16) = 0$
$\Rightarrow x = -12$ or -16
II. $y^2 + 16y + 48 = 0$
$\Rightarrow y^2 + 12y + 4y + 48 = 0$
$\Rightarrow y(y+12) + 4(y+12) = 0$
$\Rightarrow (y+12)(y+4) = 0$
$\Rightarrow y = -12$ or -4
Clearly, $x \leq y$

28. (c)

29. (b) I. $x^2 + 8x + 15 = 0$
$\Rightarrow x^2 + 5x + 3x + 15 = 0$
$\Rightarrow x(x+5) + 3(x+5) = 0$
$\Rightarrow (x+5)(x+3) = 0$
$\Rightarrow x = -5$ or -3
II. $y^2 + 11y + 30 = 0$
$\Rightarrow y^2 + 6y + 5y + 30 = 0$
$\Rightarrow y(y+6) + 5(y+6) = 0$
$\Rightarrow (y+5)(y+6) = 0$
$\Rightarrow y = -5$ or -6
Clearly, $x \geq y$

30. (b) $x = \sqrt{3136} = 56$
$y^2 = 3136$

$\Rightarrow y = \sqrt{3136} = \pm 56$
Clearly, $x \geq y$

31. (c) Total number of obese men in 2013
$= 66000 \times 35\% = 23100$
Total number of obese women in 2013
$= 54000 \times 25\% = 13500$
Total number of obese children in 2013
$= 16000 \times 12.5\% = 2000$
Required average $= (32100 + 13500 + 2000) \div 3$
$= 38600 \div 3 = 12867$

32. (b) Required percentage
$$\frac{78000 \times 37.5\%}{78000 \times 62.5\%} \times 100 = 60\%$$

33. (d) Required ratio
$$= \frac{68000 \times 22.5\%}{70000 \times 27.5\%} = 765 : 952$$

34. (a) No, of obese women in 2012
$= 20\%$ of $60000 = 12000$
Number of obese children in 2012
$= 25\%$ of $12000 = 3000$
Number of obese men in 2012 $= 32.5\%$ of $63000 = 20475$
Required difference $= 20475 - (12000 + 3000)$
$= 20475 - 15000 = 5475$

35. (d) Number of children not suffering from obesity in 2011 and 2010 $= 90\%$ of $21000 + 85\%$ of 15000
$= 18900 + 12750$
Total of these two equals of 31650.

36. (d) Total number of passed students of School A
    = (520× 100)/65 = 800
    Number of girls passed = 35% of 800 = 280
    Total number of passed students of School B
    = (660× 100)/55 = 1200
    Number of girls passed = 45% of 1200 = 540
    Required Difference = 540 - 280 = 260

37. (d) For School A,
    45% of girls = 180
    Total student = (180× 100)/45 = 400
    For School B,
    50% of girls = 180
    Total student = (180× 100)/50 = 360
    Sum = 400 + 360 = 760

38. (a) Total students passed of School A in 2014
    = (195× 100)/65 = 300
    Total students passed of School B in 2012 = (195× 100)/50 = 390
    Required Difference = 390 - 300 = 90

39. (C) Number of girls passed of School A
    = (1200× 65)/100 = 780
    Number of girls passed of School B
    = (1600× 35)/100 = 560
    % difference = (780-560)/560× 100 = 40%

40. (d) Number of girls passed from School A in 2013 = 770
    Number of students passed from School A in 2013
    = (770× 100)/55 = 1400
    Number of boys passed from School A = (1400× 45)/100 = 630
    Number of girls passed from School B in 2013 = 770
    Number of students passed from School B in 2013
    = (420× 100)/35 = 1200
    Number of boys passed from School B = (1200× 65)/100 = 780
    Required percentage = (780× 100)/630 = 124%

41. (d) 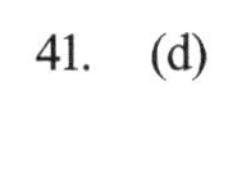 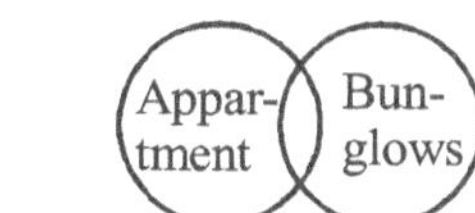

    OR

    Conclusion I : False
    Conclusion II : False

42. (a) 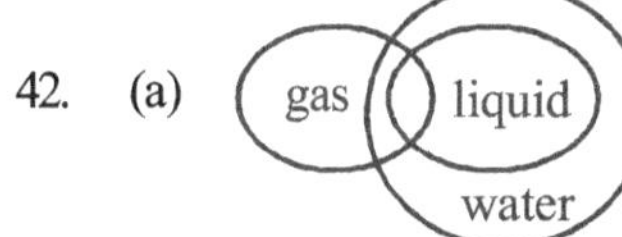

43. (b) 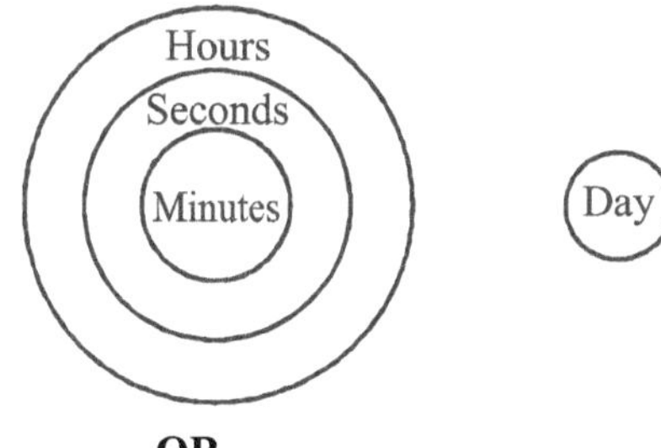

    OR

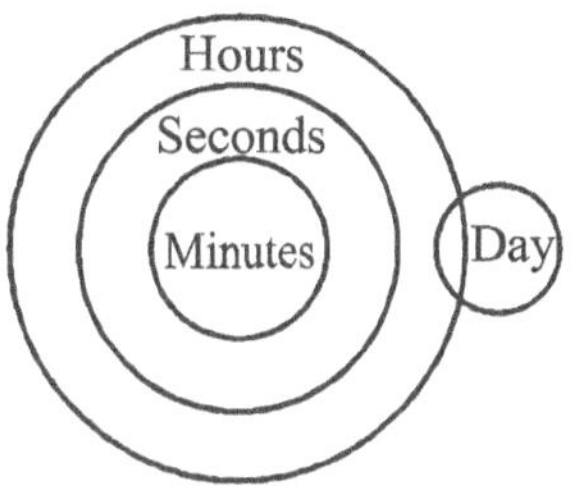

Conclusion I : False
Conclusion II : True

(44-45) :

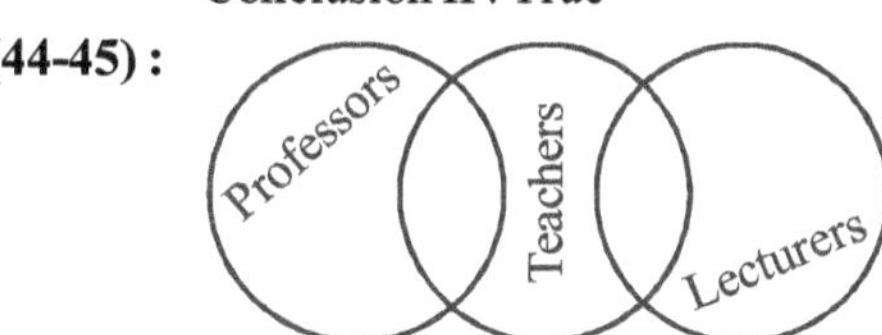

44. (a) Conclusion I : True
        Conclusion II : False
45. (b) Conclusion I : False
        Conclusion II : True.

(46-50) :

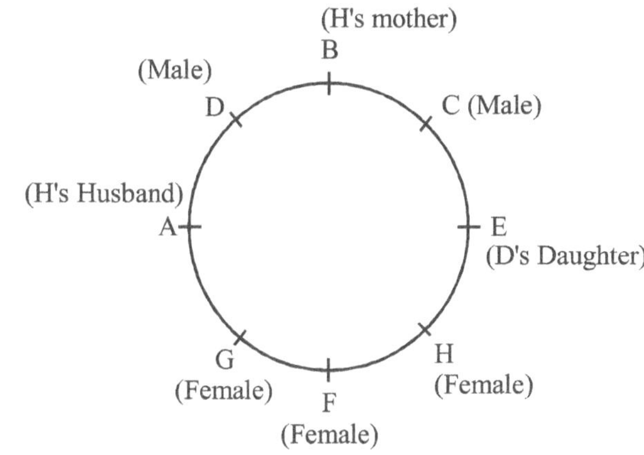

46. (d)   47. (c)   48. (b)
49. (a)   50. (b)   51. (c)

(52-55):

    ze ko ka gi → must save some money   ... (i)
    fe ka so ni → he made good money   ... (ii)
    ni lo da so → he must be good   ...(iii)
    we so ze da → he good save grace   ...(iv)

52. (c) From eqs. (i) and (ii), the code of must is 'lo'.
53. (e) From eqs. (i) and (iv), ze is 'save'.
54. (a) From eqs. (i) and (ii), the code of good is 'so'.
55. (d)

(56-60):

    $P \% Q \Rightarrow P < Q$
    $P \delta Q \Rightarrow P > Q$
    $P @ Q \Rightarrow P \leq Q$
    $P \bigstar Q \Rightarrow P \geq Q$
    $P \# Q \Rightarrow P = Q$

56. (e) $R \bigstar T \Rightarrow R \geq T; T \delta M \Rightarrow T > M; M \% K \Rightarrow M < K; K @ V \Rightarrow K \leq V$
    So, $R \geq T > M < K \geq V$
    Conclusions
    I. $V \delta M \Rightarrow V > M$ (False)
    II. $V \delta T \Rightarrow V > T$ (False)
    III. $M \% R \Rightarrow M < R$ (True)
    IV. $K \delta R \Rightarrow K > R$ (False)

57. (e) H δ J ⇒ H > J; J # N ⇒ J = N; N @ R ⇒ N ≤ R; R δ W ⇒ R > W
So, H > J = N ≤ R > W
Conclusions
I. W % N ⇒ W < N (False)
II. W % H ⇒ W < H (False)
III. R # J ⇒ R = J (True)
IV. R δ J ⇒ R > J (True)
Only either III or IV is true.

58. (a) B @ D ⇒ B ≤ D; D δ F ⇒ D > F; F % M ⇒ F < M, M ✱ N ⇒ M ≥ N
So, B ≤ D > F < M ≥ N
Conclusions
I. B % F ⇒ B < F (False)
II. M δ D ⇒ M > D (False)
III. N % F ⇒ N < F (False)
IV. D δ N ⇒ D > N (False)
So, none of the given conclusions is correct.

59. (c) F # Z ⇒ F = Z; Z @ H ⇒ Z ≤ H; H % N ⇒ H < N; N δ B ⇒ N > B
So, F = Z ≤ H < N > B
Conclusions
I. F @ H ⇒ F ≤ H (True)
II. N % Z ⇒ N > Z (True)
III. B % H ⇒ B < H (False)
IV. B % Z ⇒ B < Z (False)
Only I and II are true.

60. (d) M % K ⇒ M < K; K ✱ W ⇒ K ≥ W; W δ V ⇒ W > V, V @ N ⇒ V ≤ N
So, M < K ≥ W > V ≤ N
Conclusions
I. N ✱ K ⇒ N ≥ K (False)
II. M % W ⇒ M < W (False)
III. K δ V ⇒ K > V (True)
IV. V % M ⇒ V < M (False)
Only III is true.

61. (b) $519 - \dfrac{746}{2} = 146$

62. (d) 915 823 647 495 837
Smallest number = 594 and 2nd digit = 9

63. (e) 951 832 674 549 783
Second largest number = 832
and their first digit = 8

64. (c) Second hightest number = 746
7 − 4 = 3

65. (a)
$$\begin{array}{ccc}
5\ 1\ 9 & 3\ 2\ 6 & 7\ 4\ 6 \\
{}_{+1}\quad {}_{-1} & {}_{+1}\quad {}_{-1} & {}_{+1}\quad {}_{-1} \\
\hline
6\ 1\ 8 & 4\ 2\ 7 & 8\ 4\ 5
\end{array}
\qquad
\begin{array}{c}
4\ 9\ 4 \\
{}_{+1}\quad {}_{-1} \\
\hline
5\ 9\ 4
\end{array}$$
$$\begin{array}{c}
8\ 3\ 7 \\
{}_{+1}\quad {}_{-1} \\
\hline
9\ 3\ 6
\end{array}$$
Second samllest number = 594 and 9 + 4 = 13

(66-70):
Row 1. ↓ P V S T R Q
Row 2. ↑ C F A E B D
66. (d)   67. (a)   68. (b)
69. (b)   70. (c)
71. (a) Hence, P × Q > R ✶ S shows that P is father of S.

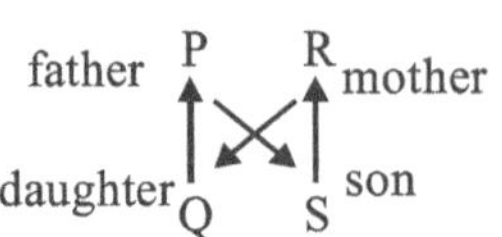

72. (e) None of these

(73-74):

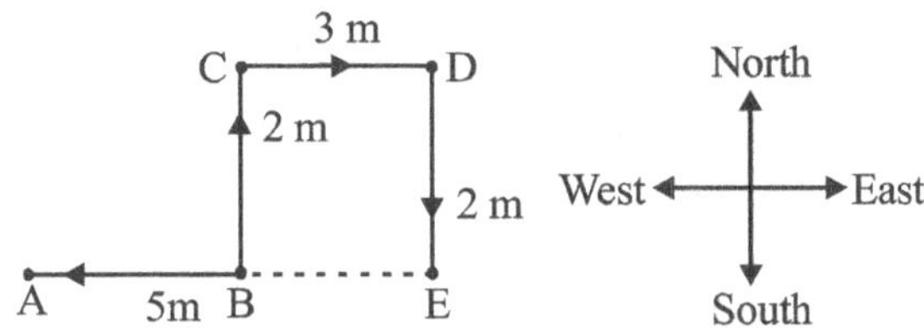

73. (c)
74. (a) ABE

75. (b)
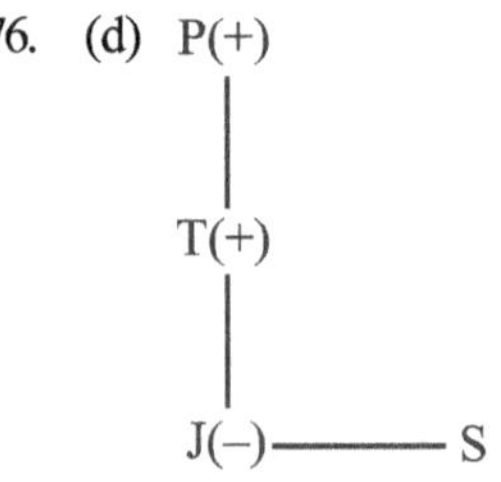

76. (d)
P(+)
│
T(+)
│
J(−) ——— S

77. (e)
B(-) ——— C(+)
│
R ——— S(+)

78. (a)
A —25 km→ B
15 km
C —25 km→ D   F ←35 km— E
X |←— 150 km —→| Y

Required distance = DF
= 150 − (25 + 25 + 35) = 150 − 85 = 65 m

79. (e) All I, II and III are necessary to answer the question.
L > T > F > P and it is given that J has not scored the highest. So, L scored the highest.

80. (a) Required answer = 16 + 1 + 36 = 53 students

PRACTICE SET · 17

Time : 45 Min. **Max. Marks : 80**

QUANTITATIVE APTITUDE

1. A trader mixes 26 kg of rice at ₹ 20 per kg with 30 kg rice of another variety costing ₹ 36 per kg. If he sells the mixture at ₹ 30 per kg his profit will be-
   (a) 7% (b) 5%
   (c) 8% (d) 10%
   (e) None of these

2. A towel was 50 cm broad and 100 cm long. When bleached, it was found to have lost 20% of its length and 10% of its breadth. Find the percentage of decrease in area ?
   (a) 32% (b) 28%
   (c) 33% (d) 24%
   (e) None of these

3. In an examination 75% of the total students passed in English and 65% passed in Mathematics, while 15% failed in English as well as Mathematics. If a total of 495 candidates who passed in both exams. Find the total number of students who appeared in the exam.
   (a) 850 (b) 900
   (c) 1000 (d) 1050
   (e) None of these

4. A man deposited a total sum of ₹ 88400/- in the name of his two sons aged 19 and 17 years so that at the age of 21, both will get equal amounts. If the money is invested at the rate of 10% compound interest per annum what are the shares of his two sons ?
   (a) ₹48200/- (b) ₹48400
   (c) ₹42600/- (d) ₹44200
   (e) None of these

5. The price of sugar increases by 20% due to the festive season. By what percentage should a family reduce the consumption of sugar so that there is no change in the expenditure ?
   (a) 20% (b) $18\dfrac{1}{3}\%$
   (c) $16\dfrac{2}{3}\%$ (d) $16\dfrac{1}{3}\%$
   (e) None of these

6. How many words can be formed from the letters of the word 'SIGNATURE' so that the vowels always come together ?
   (a) 720 (b) 1440
   (c) 2880 (d) 3600
   (e) 17280

7. The distance between two points (A and B) is 110 km. X starts running from point A at a speed of 60 km/h and Y starts running from point B at a speed of 40 km/h at the same time. They meet at a point C, somewhere on the line AB. What is the ratio of AC to BC ?
   (a) 3 : 2 (b) 2 : 3
   (c) 3 : 4 (d) 4 : 3
   (e) 3 : 1

8. Two vessels are full of milk with milk-water ratio 1 : 3 and 3 : 5 respectively. If both are mixed in the ratio 3 : 2, what is the ratio of milk and water in the new mixture ?
   (a) 4 : 15 (b) 3 : 7
   (c) 6 : 7 (d) 4 : 8
   (e) None of these

9. Two person Ravi and Shyam can do a work in 60 days and 40 days respectively. They began the work together but Ravi left after some time and Shyam finished the remaining work in 10 days. After how many days did Ravi leave?
   (a) 8 days (b) 12 days
   (c) 15 days (d) 18 days
   (e) 20 days

10. The respective ratio of the present ages of a mother and daughter is 7 : 1. Four years ago the respective ratio of their ages was 19 : 1. What will be the mother's age four years from now?
    (a) 42 years (b) 38 years
    (c) 46 years (d) 36 years
    (e) None of these

DIRECTIONS (Qs. 11-15) : Study the following line graphs which show the production (in, 0000 units) and percentage exported of scooters, motorbikes and car respectively over the years.

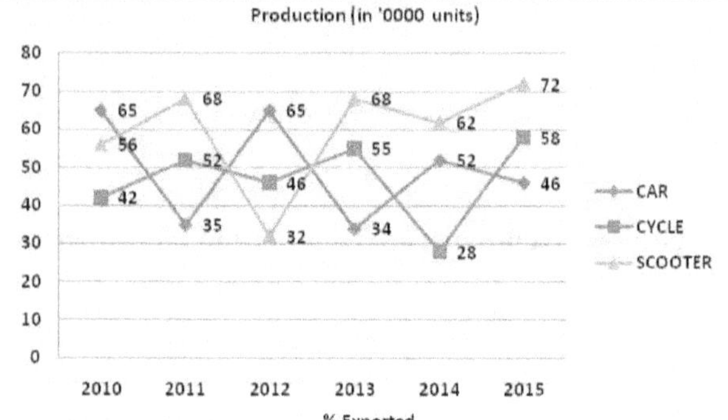

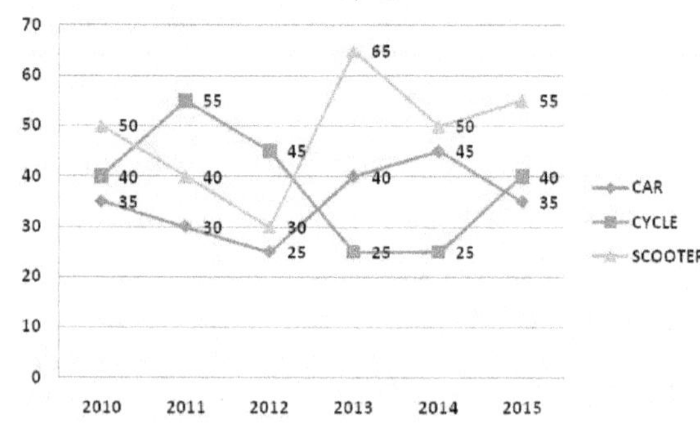

11. Find the total number cars exported in the year 2011, 2013 and 2015?
    (a) 402000 (b) 420010
    (c) 419980 (d) 409960
    (e) None of these

12. Find the total number of automobiles exported in the year 2011.
    (a) 643500 (b) 653000
    (c) 663000 (d) 683000
    (e) None of these

13. Find the ratio of cars, scooters and motorbikes exported in 2012.
    (a) 325:316:419 (b) 325:192:414
    (c) 319:216:425 (d) 256:355:135
    (e) None of these

14. If the ratio of export prices of cars, scooter and motorbike was 2 : 1 : 1.5 in 2014, what was the proportion of their export earnings?
    (a) 454 : 232 : 213 (b) 476 : 210 : 213
    (c) 468 : 310 : 105 (d) cannot be determined
    (e) None of these

15. In which of the following years was the production of motorbikes exactly 40% of the total production of automobiles in that year?
    (a) 2011 (b) 2012
    (c) 2015 (d) 2014
    (e) None of these

DIRECTIONS (Qs. 16-20) : What will come in place of the question mark (?) in the following questions ?

16. $\sqrt{11449} \times \sqrt{6241} - (54)^2 = \sqrt{?} + (74)^2$
    (a) 384 (b) 3721
    (c) 381 (d) 3638
    (e) None of these

17. $\left[\left(3\sqrt{8} + \sqrt{8}\right) \times \left(8\sqrt{8} + 7\sqrt{8}\right)\right] - 98 = ?$
    (a) $2\sqrt{8}$ (b) $8\sqrt{8}$
    (c) 382 (d) 386
    (e) None of these

18. $3463 \times 295 - 18611 = ? + 5883$
    (a) 997091 (b) 997071
    (c) 997090 (d) 999070
    (e) None of these

19. $\dfrac{28}{65} \times \dfrac{195}{308} \div \dfrac{39}{44} + \dfrac{5}{26} = ?$
    (a) $\dfrac{1}{3}$ (b) 0.75
    (c) $1\dfrac{1}{2}$ (d) $\dfrac{1}{2}$
    (e) None of these

20. $(23.1)^2 + (48.6)^2 - (39.8)^2 = ? + 1147.69$
    (a) $(13.6)^2$ (b) $\sqrt{12.8}$
    (c) 163.84 (d) 12.8
    (e) None of these

DIRECTIONS (Qs. 21–25) : In the following number series only one number is wrong. Find out the wrong number.

21. 9050 5675 3478 2147 1418 1077 950
    (a) 3478 (b) 1418
    (c) 5675 (d) 2147
    (e) 1077

22. 7 12 40 222 1742 17390 208608
    (a) 7 (b) 12
    (c) 40 (d) 1742
    (e) 208608

23. 6 91 584 2935 11756 35277 70558
    (a) 91 (b) 70558
    (c) 584 (d) 2935
    (e) 35277

24. 1 4 25 256 3125 46656 823543
    (a) 3125 (b) 823543
    (c) 46656 (d) 25
    (e) 256

25. 8424 4212 2106 1051 526.5 263.25 131.625
    (a) 131.625 (b) 1051
    (c) 4212 (d) 8424
    (e) 263.25

DIRECTIONS (Qs. 26-30) : In the following questions two equations numbered I and II are given.

You have to solve both the equations and Give answer If

  (a)   X > Y   (b)   X ≥ Y
  (c)   X < Y   (d)   X ≤ Y
  (e)   X = Y or the relationship cannot be established

26.   I. $\dfrac{45}{x^3} - \dfrac{15}{x^2} - \dfrac{10}{x^3} = 0$

     II. $\sqrt{5^3 - 5^2} = y^2$

27.   I. $5.0002x + 3.0002 = 33.541$

     II. $2.912y - 3.142 = 45.526$

28.   I. $3375 = x^3$

     II. $y = 12^2 - 5^3$

29.   I. $4x + 6y = 18$

     II. $8x - 2y = 22$

30.   I. $x^2 - \sqrt{36}x + \sqrt[3]{512} = 0$

     II. $y^2 - \sqrt[3]{125} + 4 = 0$

DIRECTIONS (Qs. 31-35) : Study the following pie chart carefully to answer the questions.

Degree Wise Break-up of Employees Working in Various Departments of an Organization and the ratio of Men to Women

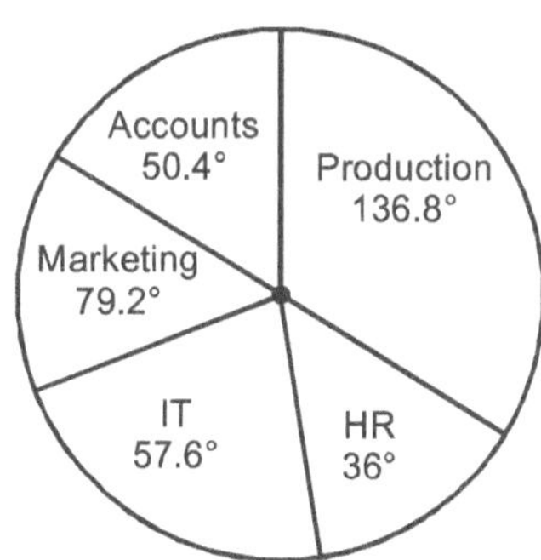

Total number of employees = 3250
Respective Ratio of Men to Women in each Department

Department	Men	Women
Production	4	1
HR	12	13
IT	7	3
Marketing	3	2
Accounts	6	7

31. What is the number of men working in the Marketing department?
  (a)   462   (b)   454
  (c)   418   (d)   424
  (e)   None of these

32. What is the respective ratio of the number of women working in the HR department to the number of men working in the IT department?
  (a)   11:12   (b)   17:29
  (c)   13:28   (d)   12:35
  (e)   None of these

33. The number of men working in the production department of the organisation forms what per cent of the total number of employees working in that department?
  (a)   88%   (b)   90%
  (c)   75%   (d)   65%
  (e)   None of these

34. The number of women working in the IT department of the organization forms what per cent of the total number of employees in the organization from all departments together?
  (a)   3.2%   (b)   4.8%
  (c)   6.3%   (d)   5.6%
  (e)   None of these

35. What is the total number of men working in the organization?
  (a)   2198   (b)   2149
  (c)   2073   (d)   2236
  (e)   None of these

DIRECTIONS (Qs.36-40): Study the following table carefully to answer the questions.

Rate of interest (P.C.P.A.) offered by five companies on deposits under different schemes

Company → Scheme ↓	A	B	C	D	E
I	8.5	9.0	8.0	8.5	9.0
II	9.5	8.5	9.0	9.0	8.5
III	8.0	8.0	7.5	8.5	8.5
IV	10.0	9.5	10.5	9.5	10.0

36. Mr X. deposited an amount in Scheme II with Company C for two years. After that he withdrew the amount and reinvested only the principal amount in Scheme IV of Company B for two years. Total amount of simple interest accrued from the two schemes is ₹ 14,800. What was the principal amount?
  (a)   ₹48,000   (b)   ₹42,000
  (c)   ₹40,000   (d)   Cannot be determined
  (e)   None of these

37. Company E offers compound interest under Scheme I and Company A offers simple interest under Scheme IV. What will be the difference between the interest earned under Scheme I of Company E and Scheme IV of Company A respectively in two years on an amount of ₹ 1.2 lakhs?
  (a)   ₹1,428   (b)   ₹1,328
  (c)   ₹1,528   (d)   ₹1,548
  (e)   None of these

38. Company D offers compound interest under Scheme II simple interest under Scheme IV. Abhijit invested ₹ 25,000 with this company under Scheme IV and after one year switched to Scheme II along with the interest for one more year. What is the total amount he will get at the end of two years?
  (a)   ₹28,939.25   (b)   ₹29,838.75
  (c)   ₹31,748.25   (d)   ₹31,738.75
  (e)   None of these

39. Abhishek invested an amount of ₹ 45,000 for two years with Company B under Scheme III, which offers compound interest, and Jeevan invested an equal amount for two years with Company C under Scheme IV, which offers simple interest. Who earned more interest and how much?
  (a)   Abhishek, ₹1,875   (b)   Jeevan, ₹1,875
  (c)   Abhishek, ₹1,962   (d)   Jeevan, ₹1,962
  (e)   None of these

40. Mr. Lal invested ₹ 30,000 in Company A under Scheme II, which offers compound interest and ₹ 48,000 in Company D under Scheme II, which offers compound interest. What will be the total amount of interest earned by Mr. Lal in two years?
    - (a) ₹14,928.80
    - (b) ₹17,428.50
    - (c) ₹14,827.70
    - (d) ₹16,728.20
    - (e) None of these

REASONING ABILITY

DIRECTIONS (Qs. 41-45) : In each of the questions below are given four statements followed by three conclusions numbered I, II and III. You have to take the given statements to be true even if they seem to be at variance from commonly known facts. Read all the conclusions and then decide which of the given conclusions logically follows from the given statements disregarding commonly known facts.

41. Statements: All petals are flowers. Some flowers are buds. Some buds are leaves. All leaves are plants.
    Conclusions: I. Some petals are not buds.
    II.   Some flowers are plants.
    III. No flower is plant.
    - (a) Only I follows
    - (b) Either II or III follows
    - (c) I and II follow
    - (d) Only III follows
    - (e) None of the above
42. Statements: Some pens are keys. Some keys are locks. All locks are cards. No card is paper
    Conclusions:
    I.   No lock is paper.
    II. Some cards are keys.
    III. Some keys are not paper.
    - (a) I and II follow
    - (b) Only I follows
    - (c) Only II follows
    - (d) All follow
    - (e) None follows
43. Statements: Some pearls are gems. All gems are diamonds. No diamond is stone. Some stones are corals.
    Conclusions:
    I.   Some stones are pearls.
    II. Some corals being diamond is a possibility.
    III. No stone is pearl.
    - (a) Only I follows
    - (b) Only II follows
    - (c) Either I or III follows
    - (d) I and II follow
    - (e) None of these
44. Statements: Some apartments are flats. Some flats are buildings. All buildings are bungalows. All bungalows are gardens.
    Conclusions:
    I.   All apartments being building is a possibility
    II. All bungalows are not buildings.
    III. No flat is garden.
    - (a) None follows
    - (b) Only I follows
    - (c) Either I or III follows
    - (d) II and III follow
    - (e) Only II follows
45. Statements: All chairs are tables. All tables are bottles. Some bottles are jars. No jar is bucket.
    Conclusions:
    I.   Some tables being jar is a possibility.
    II. Some bottles are chairs.
    III. Some bottles are not bucket.
    - (a) Only I follows
    - (b) I and II follow
    - (c) All follow
    - (d) Only II follows
    - (e) None of these

DIRECTIONS (Qs. 46-50): Study the following information carefully and answer the given questions.

Nine friends A, B, C, D, E, F, G, H and K are sitting around a circle facing the centre. A sits second to left of D. K sits third to right of F. Neither K nor F is an immediate neighbour of A or D. G and H are immediate neighbours of each other. E sits third to right of H. B is not an immediate neighbor of F.

46. What is the position of F with respect to the position of B ?
    - (a) Second to the right
    - (b) Third to the left
    - (c) Second to the left
    - (d) Third to the right
    - (e) Sixth to the right
47. Who amongst the following is an immediate neighbour of H ?
    - (a) C
    - (b) B
    - (c) K
    - (d) F
    - (e) A
48. Starting from A, if all the friends are made to sit in the alphabetical order in clockwise direction, the positions of how many (except A) will remain unchanged ?
    - (a) None
    - (b) One
    - (c) Two
    - (d) Three
    - (e) Four
49. H is related to C and B is related to E in a certain way. To whom amongst the following is G related following the same pattern ?
    - (a) F
    - (b) H
    - (c) C
    - (d) A
    - (e) D
50. What will come in place of the question mark ?
    DC DB DF DA?
    - (a) DG
    - (b) DE
    - (c) DH
    - (d) DK
    - (e) Either DK or DE

DIRECTIONS (Qs. 51-55): Study the following arrangement carefully and answer the questions given below :

P 1 % T R A 5 # D M 7 K ★ E G 2 8 $ H 3 I 4 V U 6 F ⊕ 9 Z

51. How many such symbols are there in the above arrangement, each of which is immediately preceded by a consonant and also immediately followed by a consonant?
    - (a) None
    - (b) One
    - (c) Two
    - (d) Three
    - (e) More than three
52. Four of the following five are alike in a certain way based on their position in the above arrangement. Which is the one that **does not** belong to that group?
    - (a) VIF
    - (b) EK8
    - (c) R%#
    - (d) 6V9
    - (e) $G3
53. How many such vowels are there in the above arrangement, each of which is immediately preceded by a digit and immediately followed by a consonant?
    - (a) None
    - (b) One
    - (c) Two
    - (d) Three
    - (e) More than three
54. Which of the following is exactly in the middle between the fifth element from the left end and the seventh element from the right end?
    - (a) G
    - (b) 2
    - (c) E
    - (d) ★
    - (e) None of these

55. If the positions of last twelve elements in the above arrangement are reversed, which of the following will be the eight element to the right of the eleventh element from the left ?

(a) H   (b) I
(c) ⊕   (d) 9
(e) None of these

DIRECTIONS (Qs. 56-60): In the following questions, the symbols ⋆, δ, %, @ and © are used with the following meaning illustrated below:

'P%Q' means 'P is not smaller than Q'.

'P©Q' means 'P is neither smaller than nor equal to Q'.

'P⋆Q' means 'P is neither greater than nor equal to Q'.

'PδQ' means 'P is not greater than Q'.

'P @ Q' means 'P is neither greater than nor smaller than Q'.

Now, in each of the following questions, assuming the given statements to be true, find which of the three conclusions I, II and III given below them is/are definitely true and give your answer accordingly.

56. **Statements:**   R δ K,   K ⋆ M,   M @ J
    Conclusions: I. J © K
                  II. M © R
                  III. R ⋆ J
(a) Only I and II are true
(b) Only II and III are true
(c) Only I and III are true
(d) All I, II and III are true
(e) None of these

57. **Statements:**   Z @ M,   M © K,   K ⋆ F
    Conclusions: I. F © Z
                  II. K ⋆ Z
                  III. F © M
(a) None is true   (b) Only I is true
(c) Only II is true   (d) Only III is true
(e) Only II and III are true

58. **Statements:**   B ⋆ J,   J % W,   W © M
    Conclusions: I. M ⋆ J
                  II. W ⋆ B
                  III. B © M
(a) None is true   (b) Only I is true
(c) Only II is true   (d) Only III is true
(e) Only I and III are true

59. **Statements:**   V % H,   H @ F,   F δ E
    Conclusions: I. F @ V
                  II. F ⋆ V
                  III. E % H
(a) Only either I or II is true
(b) Only III is true
(c) Only I and II are true
(d) All I, II and III are true
(e) Only either I or II and III are true

60. **Statements:**   W © T,   T δ N,   N % D
    Conclusions: I. D ⋆ T
                  II. W © N
                  III. D @ T
(a) None is true   (b) Only I is true
(c) Only II is true   (d) Only III is true
(e) Only I and II are true

DIRECTIONS (Qs. 61-65) : Use the information given below to answer.

(i)   There is a group of 5 persons A, B, C, D and E
(ii)   In the group there is one badminton player, one chess player and one tennis player
(iii) A and D are unmarried ladies and do not play any games
(iv)   No lady is a chess player or a badminton player
(v)   There is a married couple in the group of which E is the husband
(vi)   B is the brother of C and is neither a chess player nor a tennis player

61. Which of the group has only ladies?
(a) ABC   (b) BCD
(c) CDE   (d) CDA
(e) None of these

62. Who is the tennis player?
(a) B   (b) C
(c) D   (d) E
(e) None of these

63. Who is the wife of E?
(a) A   (b) B
(c) D   (d) C
(e) None of these

64. Who is Badminton player?
(a) A   (b) D
(c) E   (d) B
(e) C

65. Who is sister of B ?
(a) C   (b) A
(c) D   (d) E
(e) None of these

66. Consider the following statements and answer the question. M, N, O and P are all different individuals
M is the daughter of N.
N is the son of O.
O is the father of P.
Which among the following statements is contradictory to the above premises?
(a) P is the father of M.
(b) O has three children.
(c) M has one brother.
(d) M is the granddaughter of O.
(e) None of these

67. A man starts walking in south and walks for 7 km, then turns left and walks for 2 km, Then, once again turns left and walks for 12 km, turns left one more time and walks for 2 km. How much distance he has to cover to reach the starting point?
(a) 7 km   (b) 12 km
(c) 4 km   (d) 5 km
(e) None of these

68. Pointing to a boy, Mamta said, "he is the only son of my father-in-law's only child." How is the boy related to Mamta?
(a) Brother   (b) Daughter
(c) Son   (d) Husband
(e) None of these

69. If A is to the South of B and C is to the East of B, in what direction is A with respect to?
(a) North-East   (b) North-West
(c) South-East   (d) South-West
(e) None of these

70. Read the following information carefully to answer the following question:
    A * B means A is the sister of B
    A ÷ B means A is the brother of B
    A + B means A is the father of B
    A - B means A is the mother of B
    What is the relation between Q and S in 'P + Q ÷ R - S'?
    (a) Q is the aunt of S
    (b) Q is the uncle of S
    (c) Q is the mother of S
    (d) Q is the father of S
    (e) None of these

DIRECITONS(Qs 71-75) : Study the following information carefully to answer the given questions.

Eight people M, N, O, P, Q, R, S and T are sitting in a straight line with equal distances between each other,but not necessarily in the same order. Some of them are facing North and some of them are facing south.

- M sits at one of the extreme ends of the line. Only three people sit between M and S. Q sits exactly between M and S.
- T sits third to the right of Q. N is an immediate neighbour of T and faces south. O sits second to the right of R. O is not an immediate neighbour of S.
- Immediate neighbour of S face opposite directions(i.e. if one neighbour faces North then the other neighbour faces south and Vice-Versa)
- M and P face the same direction as Q(i.e if Q faces north then M and P also face North and Vice-Versa). Both the immediate neighbours of Q face south.

71. In the given arrangement, if two people come and sit to the immediate left of Q, how many people will sit between R and O?
    (a) Two
    (b) Three
    (c) Four
    (d) More than four
    (e) One

72. Who amongst the following sits third to the right of R?
    (a) M
    (b) Q
    (c) Other than those given as options
    (d) N
    (e) S

73. How many people face North as per the given arrangement?
    (a) Two
    (b) Three
    (c) Four
    (d) More than four
    (e) One

74. Four of the following five are alike in a certain way based upon their seating arrangement and so form a group. Which of the following does not belong to the group?
    (a) QO
    (b) MR
    (c) NR
    (d) OS
    (e) PS

75. Who amongst the following sits at extreme right end of row?
    (a) O
    (b) R
    (c) T
    (d) P
    (e) M

76. Reshma and pratima are ranked ninth and thirteenth from the top in a class of 57 students. What will be their respective ranks from the bottom of the class?
    (a) 48, 44
    (b) 49, 45
    (c) 45, 49
    (d) 47, 43
    (e) None of these

77. Starting from the point X, Jayant walked 15 m towards west. He turned left and walked 20 m. He then turned left and walked 15 m. After this he turned to his right and walked 12 m. How far and in which directions is now Jayant from X?
    (a) 32 m, South
    (b) 47 m, East
    (c) 42 m, North
    (d) 27 m, South
    (e) None of these

DIRECITONS(Qs 78-80) : Study the following information carefully to answer the given questions.

- T is the sister of D. D is married to P. P is the son of M.
- T is the mother of J. Y is the father of U.
- Y has only one son and only one daughter.
- U is the daughter of T. Q is the son of D.

78. How is P related to T ?
    (a) Brother
    (b) cannot be determined
    (c) Brother-in-law
    (d) Cousin brother
    (e) Uncle

79. How is J related to D ?
    (a) Son
    (b) Niece
    (c) Son-in-law
    (d) Nephew
    (e) Daughter

80. If M is wife of W then how is Q related to W ?
    (a) Son-in-law
    (b) Grandson
    (c) Nephew
    (d) Cousin
    (e) None of these

HINTS & EXPLANATIONS

1. (b) C. P. of 56 kg rice $= (26 \times 20 + 30 \times 36)$
$= ₹(520 + 1080) = ₹1600$
S. P. of 56 kg rice $= 56 \times 30 = ₹1680$

Profit % $= \dfrac{80}{1600} \times 100 = 5\%$

2. (b) Area of towel $= l \times b = 100 \text{ cm} \times 50 \text{ cm} = 5000 \text{ cm}^2$
Now, length decreased by 20% and breadth decreased by 10%
$l' = 100 - 20\% \text{ of } 100 = 80 \text{cm}$
$b' = 50 - 10\% \text{ of } 50 = 45 \text{cm}$
New area $= l' \times b' = 80 \text{cm} \times 45 \text{cm} = 3600 \text{cm}^2$
Change in area $= (5000 - 3600) \text{ cm}^2 = 1400 \text{ cm}^2$

% change in area $= \dfrac{1400}{5000} \times 100 = 28\%$

3. (b) Let A and B represent the sets of students who passed in English and Mathematics respectively.
If 15% of candidates failed in both, then 85% passed at least one of the exams.
Then, the total number of students passed in one or both subjects

$= (A \cup B) = n(A) + n(B) = n(A \cap B)$

$0.85 = 0.75 + 0.65 - n(A \cap B)$

$n(A \cap B) = 1.40 - 0.85 = 0.55$
0.55% of number of students = 495

$\therefore$ Number of students $= \dfrac{495}{55} \times 100 = 900$

4. (b) Let son aged 19 years getting $₹x$ and son aged 17 years getting $(88400 - x)$.
At the age of 21, both will get equal amount

$x\left(1 + \dfrac{10}{100}\right)^2 = (88400 - x)\left(1 + \dfrac{10}{100}\right)^4$

$\Rightarrow \dfrac{121x}{100} = (88400 - x) \times \dfrac{121}{100} \times \dfrac{121}{100}$

$\Rightarrow 100x = 88400 \times 121 - 121x$
$\Rightarrow 221x = 88400 \times 121$

$\Rightarrow x = \dfrac{88400 \times 121}{221} = 48400$
$x = ₹48400$

5. (c) Let x and y be the rate of sugar per Kg and quantity of sugar.

$xy = \left(x + \dfrac{20}{100} \times x\right)y'$

$xy = \dfrac{6x}{5}y'$

$y' = \dfrac{5}{6}y = y - \dfrac{y}{6}$

Reduction in consumption $= \dfrac{100}{6} = 16\dfrac{2}{3}\%$

6. (e) The word 'SIGNATURE' contains 9 different letters. When that vowels IAUE are taken together, they can be supposed to form an entity, treated as one letter.

Then, the letters to be arranged are SGNTR (IAUE)
These 6 letters can be arranged in $^6P_6 = 6! = 720$ ways.
The vowels in the group (IAUE) can be arranged themselves in $^4P_4 = 4! = 24$ ways.
$\therefore$ Required number of words $= (720 \times 24) = 17280$.

7. (a) Distance between two points = 110 km
Relative speed $= 60 + 40 = 100$ km/h
Time after which they meet

$= \dfrac{\text{Total distance}}{\text{Relative speed}} = \dfrac{110}{100} = 1.10 \text{ h}$

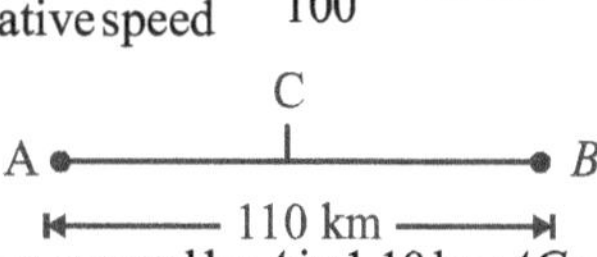

Distance covered by A in 1.10 h $= AC = 60 \times 1.10 = 66$ km
Remaining distance $= BC = 110 - 66 = 44$ km
Required ratio $= AC : BC = 66 : 44 = 3 : 2$

8. (e) By alligation method,

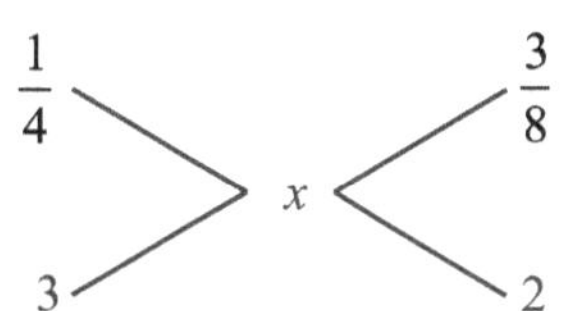

$\therefore \dfrac{\dfrac{3}{8} - x}{x - \dfrac{1}{4}} = \dfrac{3}{2}$

$\Rightarrow \dfrac{3}{4} - 2x = 3x - \dfrac{3}{4}$

$\Rightarrow 5x = \dfrac{6}{4} = \dfrac{3}{2}$

$\therefore x = \dfrac{3}{10}$

9. (d) Shyam alone worked 10 days. So work done by him

$= \dfrac{10}{40} = \dfrac{1}{4}$

$\therefore$ (Ravi + Shyam) have done

$1 - \dfrac{1}{4} = \dfrac{3}{4}$ of the work.

(Ravi + Shyam) do $\dfrac{3}{4}$ of the work in $24 \times \dfrac{3}{4} = 18$ days

10. (c) Let the ages of the mother and daughter be 7x and x years respectively.

$\therefore$ Four years ago, $\dfrac{7x - 4}{x - 4} = \dfrac{19}{1}$

$\Rightarrow 19x - 76 = 7x - 4$
$\Rightarrow 12x = 72 \Rightarrow x = 6$
$\therefore$ Mother's age after four years
$= 7x + 4 = 7 \times 6 + 4 = 46$ years

11. (a) Total number cars exported in the year 2011, 2013 and 2015
Required number of cars $= (350000 \times 30/100 + 340000 \times 40/100 + 460000 \times 35/100)$
$= (105000 + 136000 + 161000) = 402000$

12. (c) Total number of automobiles exported in 2011
$(680000\times40/100 + 520000\times55/100 + 350000\times30/100)$
$= 272000 + 286000 + 105000 = 663000$

13. (b) Ratio of cars, scooters and motorbikes exported in 2012
$(650000\times25/100 : 320000\times30/100 : 460000\times45/100)$
$= 162500 : 96000 : 207000$
Required ratio $= 325 : 192 : 414$

14. (c) Ratio of export earnings is given by multiplying by export prices.
For 2014 figures are 45% of $52\times2 : 50\%$ of $62\times1 : 25\%$ of $28\times1.5 = 468 : 310 : 105$

15. (e) No any years was the production of motorbikes exactly 40% of the total production of automobiles in that year

16. (b) $\sqrt{11449} \times \sqrt{6241} - (54)^2 = \sqrt{?} + (74)^2$
$\Rightarrow \quad \sqrt{?} = 107 \times 79 - 2916 - 5476$
$= 8453 - 2916 - 5476 = 61$
$\therefore \quad ? = (61)^2 = 3721$

17. (c) $? = \left[\left(3\sqrt{8} + \sqrt{8}\right) \times \left(8\sqrt{8} + 7\sqrt{8}\right)\right] - 98$
$= \left(4\sqrt{8} \times 15\sqrt{8}\right) - 98 = \left(60 \times 8\right) - 98 = 480 - 98 = 382$

18. (a) $3463 \times 295 - 18611 = ? + 5883$
$\therefore \quad ? = 1021585 - 18611 - 5883 = 997091$

19. (d) $? = \dfrac{28}{65} \times \dfrac{195}{308} \div \dfrac{39}{44} + \dfrac{5}{26} = \dfrac{28}{65} \times \dfrac{195}{308} \times \dfrac{44}{39} + \dfrac{5}{26}$
$= \dfrac{4}{13} + \dfrac{5}{26} = \dfrac{8+5}{26} = \dfrac{13}{26} = \dfrac{1}{2}$

20. (c) $? + 1147.69 = (23.1)^2 + (48.6)^2 - (39.8)^2$
$\therefore \quad ? = 533.61 + 2361.96 - 1584.04 - 1147.69 = 163.84$

21. (e) The given number series is based on the following pattern:

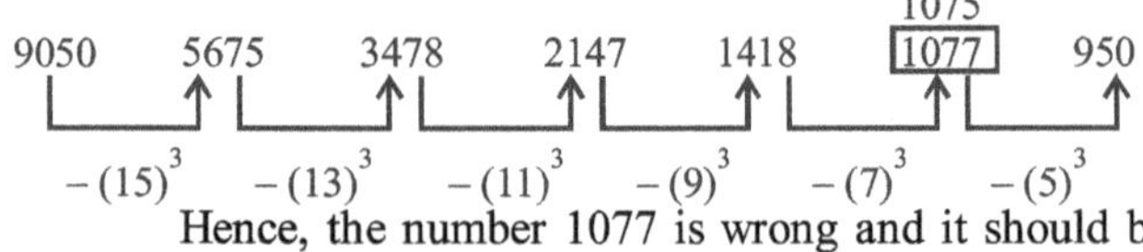

Hence, the number 1077 is wrong and it should be replaced by 1075.

22. (d) The given number series is based on the following pattern :

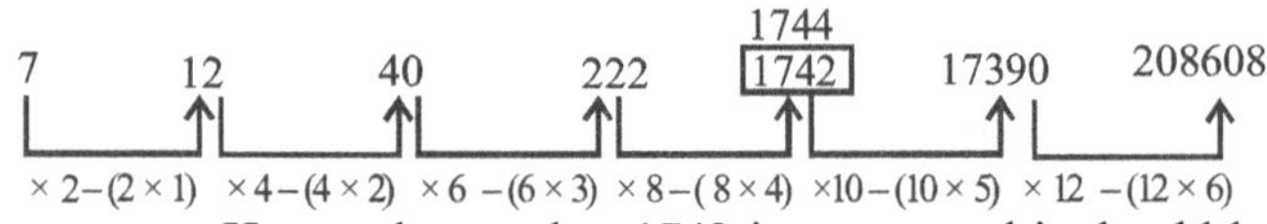

Hence, the number 1742 is wrong and it should be replaced by 1744.

23. (c) The given number series is based on the following pattern:

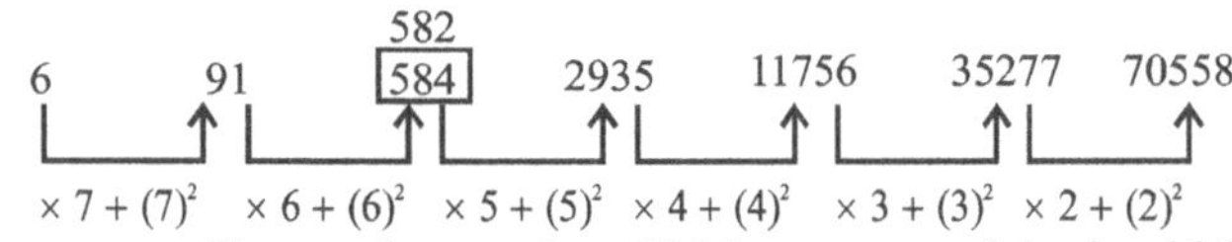

Hence, the number 584 is wrong and it should be replaced by 582.

24. (d) The given number series is based on the following pattern.

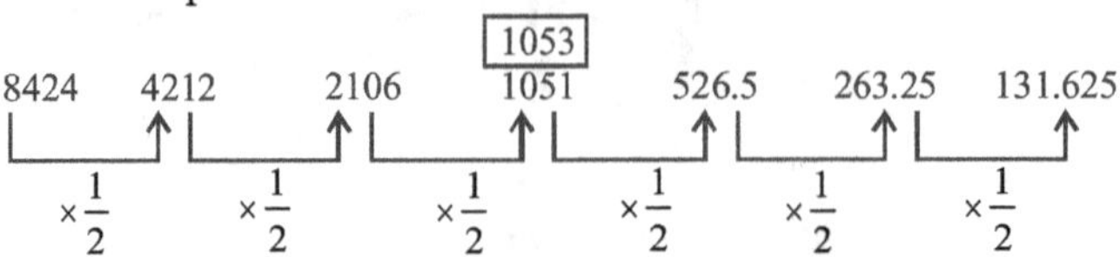

Hence, the number 25 is wrong and it should be replaced by 27.

25. (b) The given number series is based on the following pattern :

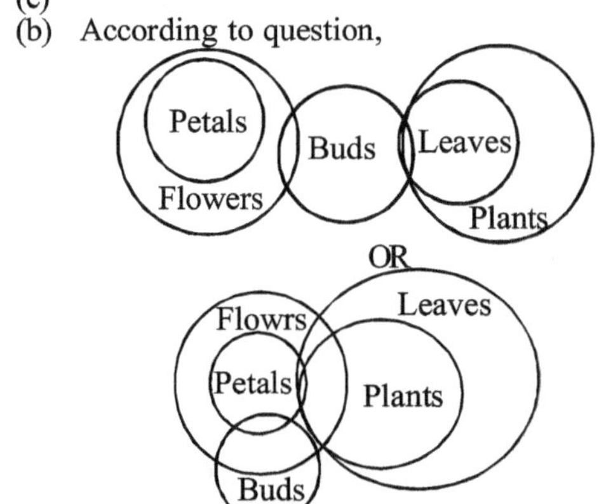

Hence, the number 1051 is wrong and it should be replaced by 1053.

26. (e) I. $\dfrac{45}{x^3} - \dfrac{15}{x^2} - \dfrac{10}{x^3} = 0$
$\Rightarrow \quad x = \dfrac{7}{3}$
II. $\sqrt{5^3 - 5^2} = y^2$
$\Rightarrow \quad y = \pm 10$
So the relationship cannot be established

27. (c) I. $5.0002x + 3.0002 = 33.541$
$\Rightarrow \quad 5.0002x = 30.5408$
$\Rightarrow \quad x = 6.10$
II. $2.912y - 3.142 = 45.526$
$\Rightarrow \quad 2.912y = 48.668$
$\Rightarrow \quad y = 16.71$
So $y > x$

28. (c) I. $3375 = x^3$
$\Rightarrow \quad x = 15$
II. $y = 12^2 - 5^3$
$\Rightarrow \quad y = 19$
So $y > x$

29. (a) I. $4x + 6y = 18$
II. $8x - 2y = 22$
$\Rightarrow \quad x = 3, y = 1$
So $x > y$

30. (a) I. $x^2 - \sqrt{36}x + \sqrt[3]{512} = 0$
$\Rightarrow \quad (x-2)(x-4) \Rightarrow x = 2, 4$
II. $y^2 - \sqrt[3]{125} + 4 = 0$
$\Rightarrow \quad y = \pm 1$
So $x > y$

31. (e) 32. (c) 33. (e) 34. (b) 35. (e)

36. (c) Amount $= \dfrac{14800}{0.18 + 0.19} = 40,000$

37. (a) Required difference
$= 1.2\left\{\left(1 + \dfrac{9}{100}\right)^2 - 1\right\} - \dfrac{1.2\times10\times2}{100} = ₹1428$

38. (e) Required sum
$= (25000 + 2375 \times 2)(1.09)(1.09) = ₹35345.97$

39. (d) Required difference $=$ SI $-$ CI
$= ₹9450 - ₹7488 = 1962$

40. (e)

41. (b) According to question,

Conclusions I. false
 II. false ⎤
 III. false ⎦ or
Hence, only either II or III follows.

42. (d) According to question

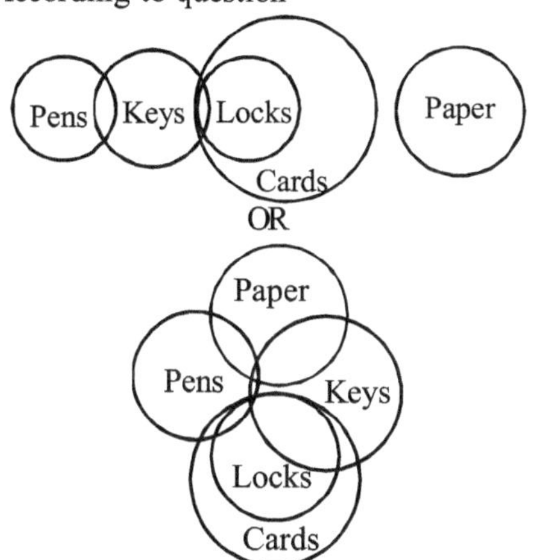

Conclusions I. True   II. True   III. True
Hence, All conclusions follow.

43. (e) According to question,

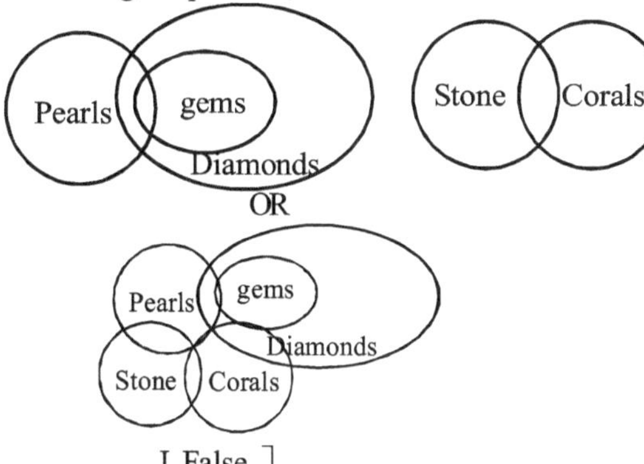

 I. False ⎤
Conclusion II. True ⎥ or
 III. False ⎦

Hence, only conclusions II and either I or III follow.

44. (b) According to question,

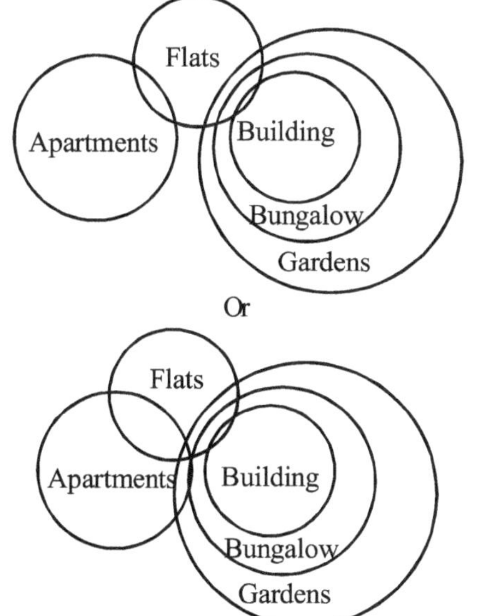

Conclusions I. ✓, II. X, III. X
Hence, only conclusion I follows.

45. (c) According to question,

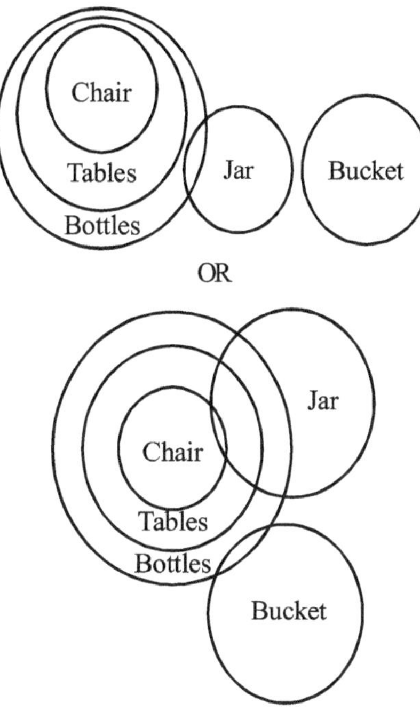

Conclusions, I. ✓, II. ✓, III. ✓
Hence, All I, II and III follow.

Solutions (46-50) :

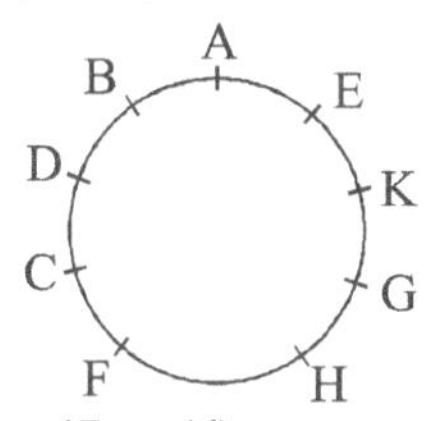

46. (d)   47. (d)

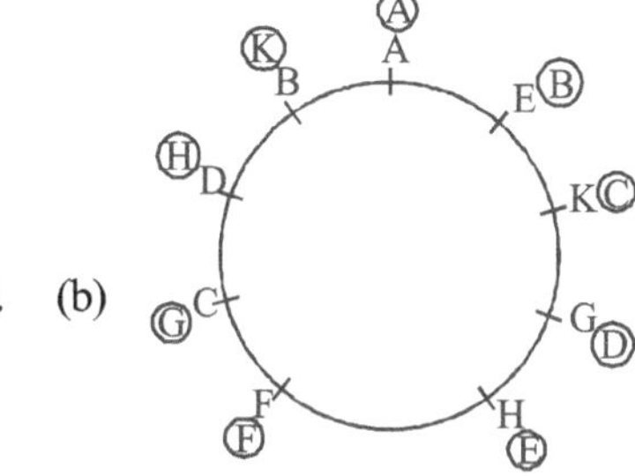

48. (b)

49. (a) H is second to the right of C.
 B is second to the right of E.
 G is second to the right of F.

50. (c) DC, DB ⇒ Immediate neighbours of D.
 DF, DA ⇒ F is second to the right of D.
 A is second to the right of D.
 Therefore, ? = DH
 H is third to the right of D.

51. (a) P1%TRA5#DM7K★EG28$H314VU6F⊕9Z
 In the above series there is no consonant symbol-consonant sequence.

52. (e) Except it in each choice second and third elements are second to the left of first elements and third to the right of first element respectively.

53. (a) We have to look for digit-vowel-consonant sequence in the following series.
 P1%TRA5#DM7K★EG28$H314VU6F⊕9Z
 There is no such sequence.

54. (d)
55. (d) After changing the series becomes as follows:
P1%TR A 5#DM7K ★ EG28Z9 ⊕ F6UV413H$
Now, eigth element to the right of eleventh from the left, i.e., 9.
56. (d) R ≤ K ... (i); K < M ... (ii); M = J ... (iii) Combining these, we get R ≤ K < M = J
Hence J > K and I follows.
Also, M > R and II follows.
Again, R < J and III follows.
57. (c) Z = M ... (i); M > K ... (ii); K < F ... (iii)
Combining these, we get Z = M > K < F
From this F and Z can't be compared. Neither can F and M.
Hence, I and III do not follow. But K < Z and II follows.
58. (b) B < J ... (i); J ≥ W ... (ii); W > M ... (iii)
Combining these, we get B < J ≥ W > M.
Hence M < J and I follows.
But W and B can't be compared. Neither can B and M.
Hence II and III do not follow.
59. (e) V ≥ H ... (i); H = F ... (ii); F ≤ E ... (iii)
Combining these, we get.
V ≥ H = F ≤ E. Hence V ≥ F.
Which means either I (F = V) or II (F < V) follows.
Again, E ≥ H. Hence III follows.
60. (a) W > T ... (i); T ≤ N ... (ii); N ≥ D ... (iii)
No comparisons can be made.

(61-65):

	Badminton	Chess	Tennis	Gender	Marriage status	Relation
A	×	×	×	F	Unmarried	
B	✓	×	×	M		Brother of C
C	×	×	✓	F	Married with E	
D	×	×	×	F	Unmarried	
E		✓		M		Husband C + E

61. (d) ACD is the group of ladies.
62. (b) It is clear from above table.
63. (d) It is clear from above table.
64. (d) B is the Badminton player.
65. (a) It is clear from the above table that C is the sister of B.

66. (a) 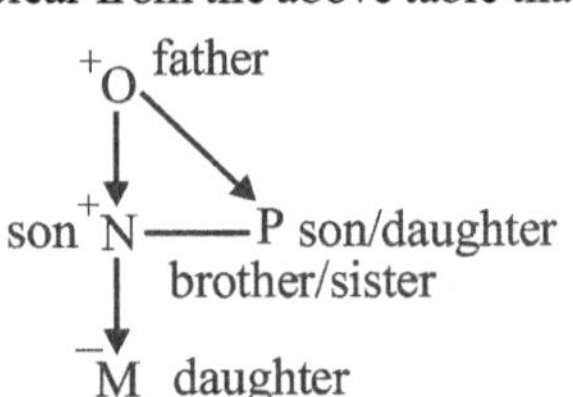

From above relation diagram, P is the sibling of M's father.
67. (d) Aman has taken a rectangular path as is clear from the diagram below.

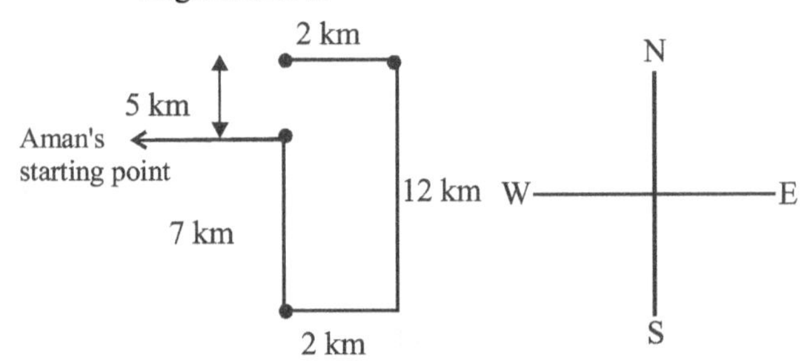

68. (c) 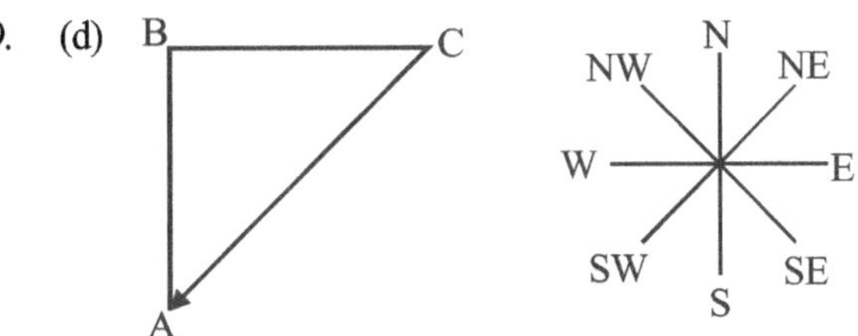

Mamta's father-in-law's only child is Mamta's husband and only child's only son is her husband's only son i.e. Mamta's son.

69. (d) 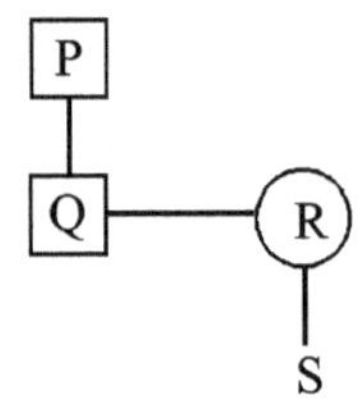

Hence, A is to south west of C.

70. (b) Q is the uncle of S
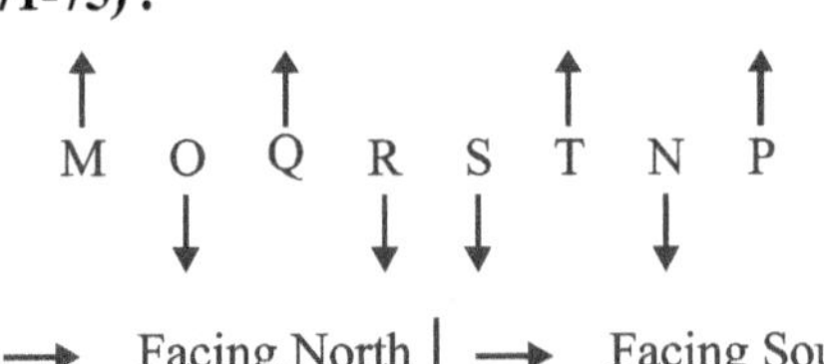

Solutions (71-75) :
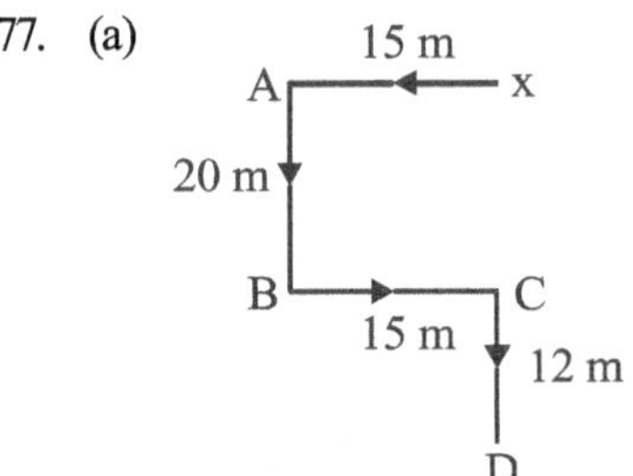

71. (b) 72. (a) 73. (c) 74. (a) 75. (d)
76. (b) Reshma rank = 57 - 9 = 48, Reshma 49th from the bottom.
Pratima rank = 57 - 13 = 44, Pratima 45th from the bottom.

77. (a) 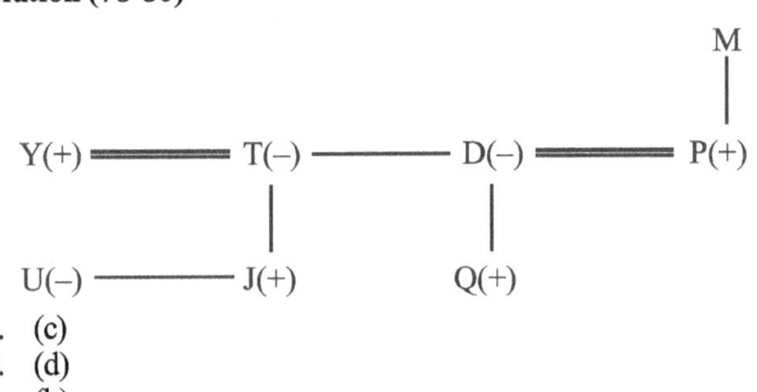

Required distance = 20 + 12 = 32 m in South

Solution (78-80)

78. (c)
79. (d)
80. (b)

PRACTICE SET  18

Time : 120 Min.   **Max. Marks : 200**

QUANTITATIVE APTITUDE

DIRECTIONS (Qs. 1–5) : Study the graphs carefully to answer the questions that follow :

Total number of children in 6 different schools and the percentage of girls in them

Number of Children

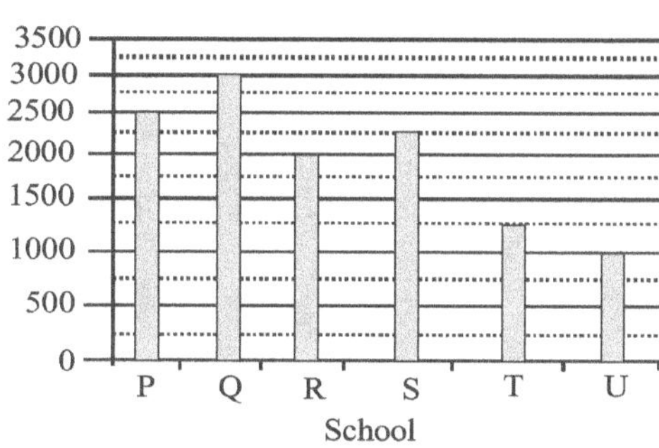

Percentage of Girls

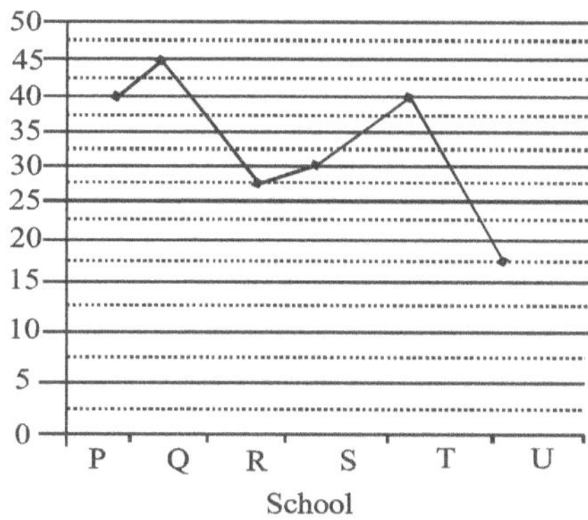

1. What is the total percentage of boys in schools R and U together (rounded off to two digits after decimal)
(a) 78.55   (b) 72.45   (c) 76.28
(d) 75.83   (e) None of these

2. What is the total number of boys in School T ?
(a) 500   (b) 600   (c) 750
(d) 850   (e) None of these

3. The total number of students in school R, is **approximately** what percent of the total number of students in school S ?
(a) 89   (b) 75   (c) 78
(d) 82   (e) 94

4. What is the average number of boys in schools P and Q together ?
(a) 1425   (b) 1575   (c) 1450
(d) 1625   (e) None of these

5. What is the respective ratio of the number of girls in school P to the number of girls in school Q ?
(a) 27 : 20   (b) 17 : 21   (c) 20 : 27
(d) 21 : 17   (e) None of these

DIRECTIONS (Qs. 6-10): Study the information carefully to answer the following questions.

There are 7200 students in an engineering college. The ratio of boys of girls is 7:5, respectively. All the students are enrolled in six different specialization viz., B.Tech. (electronics), B.Tech. (Computer science), B.Tech. (Mechanical), B. Tech. (Aerospace), B.Tech. (nano technology), B.Tech. (civil). 22% of the total students are in B. Tech. (nano technology). 16% of the girls are in B.Tech. (computer science). 18% of boys are in B.Tech. (Mechanical). Girls in B.Tech. (civil) are 30% of the girls in B. Tech. (computer science). 15% of boys are in B. Tech. (electronics). Boys in B. Teach (Computer Science) are 50% of the girls in the same 15% of girls are in B. Tech. (aerospace). The ratio of boys to girls in B.Tech. (civil) is 3:1 respectively. 24% of the total numbers of students are in B.Tech. (electronics). The ratio of boys to girls in B.Tech. (aerospace) is 12:5, respectively.

6. What is the total number of students enrolled in B.Tech. (mechanical)?
(a) 1062   (b) 1530   (c) 1584
(d) 1728   (e) 1800

7. Number of girls enrolled in B.Tech. (electronics) forms approximately. What per cent of total number of students in the college?
(a) 7%   (b) 13%   (c) 15%
(d) 22%   (e) 24%

8. What is the total number of girls enrolled in B.Tech. (nano technology)?
(a) 144   (b) 306   (c) 365
(d) 480   (e) 522

9. Number of boys enrolled in B. Tech. (aerospace) forms, what per cent of the total number of girls enrolled in B.Tech. (computer science)?
(a) 187.5%   (b) 200%   (c) 212.5%
(d) 225%   (e) 232.5%

10. What is the total number of boys enrolled in B. Tech. (civil)?
(a) 240   (b) 432   (c) 630
(d) 756   (e) 810

11. When the price of a radio was reduced by 20%, its sale increased by 80%. What was the net effect on the sale?
(a) 44% increase   (b) 44% decrease
(c) 66% increase   (d) 75% increase
(e) None of these

DIRECTIONS (Qs. 12-16): For the two given equations I and II.

Give answer (a) if p is greater than q.
Give answer (b) if p is smaller than q.
Give answer (c) if p is equal q.
Give answer (d) if p is either equal to or greater than q.
Give answer (e) if p is either equal or smaller than q.

12. I. $p^2 + 5p + 6 = 0$ II. $q^2 + 3q + 2 = 0$
13. I. $p^2 = 4$ II. $q^2 + 4q = -4$
14. I. $p^2 + p = 56$ II. $q^2 - 17q + 72 = 0$
15. I. $3p + 2q - 58 = 0$ II. $4q + 4p = 92$
16. I. $3p^2 + 17p + 10 = 0$ II. $10q^2 + 9q + 2 = 0$

17. A tap can fill a tank in 16 hours whereas another tap can empty the tank it in 8 hours. If in a three fourth filled tank both the taps are opened, then how long will it take to empty the tank in this scenario?
    (a) 6 hours (b) 8 hours (c) 10 hours
    (d) 12 hours (e) 14 hours

18. Raman adds 12% of his salary in PPF. 3/8th of the remaining amount is spent on clothes and the difference between PPF and clothes expenses is Rs 21000. Remaining amount is spent on house rent and other expenses. If house rent expenses is Rs 3000 less than other expenses, then what is the house rent expenses?
    (a) ₹ 32000 (b) ₹ 30000 (c) ₹ 26000
    (d) ₹ 28000 (e) None of these

19. Box A contains wheat worth ` 30 per kg and box B contains wheat worth ` 40 per kg. If both A and B are mixed in the the ratio 4:7 then the price of mixture per kg is
    (a) 36.36 (b) 35.80 (c) 42.50
    (d) 31.30 (e) None of these

DIRECTIONS (Qs. 20-24): Study the following graph carefully and answer the questions that follow:

Percentage of employees in different departments of a company Total No. of employees = 4500

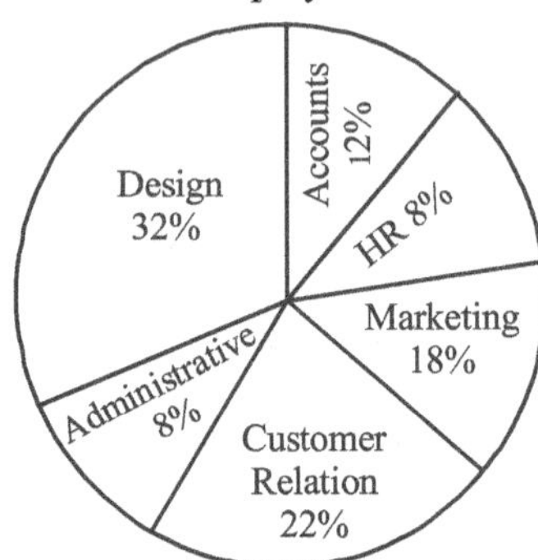

Percentage of females in each department in the same company Total No. of females in the organisation = 2000

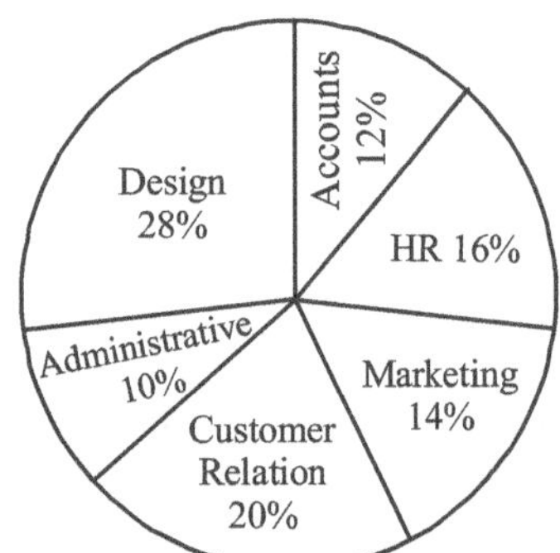

20. What is the total number of males from Design, Customer Relation and HR departments together ?
    (a) 1550 (b) 1510 (c) 1540
    (d) 1580 (e) None of these

21. What is the ratio of number of males in HR department to the number of males in Accounts department respectively ?
    (a) 3 : 17 (b) 4 : 15 (c) 2 : 15
    (d) 2 : 13 (e) None of these

22. The number of females in the Marketing department are **approximately** what per cent of the total employees in Marketing and Customer Relation Departments together?
    (a) 26 (b) 36 (c) 6
    (d) 46 (e) 16

23. What is the respective ratio of number of employees in Administrative department to the number of males in the same department ?
    (a) 9 : 4 (b) 8 : 3 (c) 7 : 2
    (d) 8 : 5 (e) None of these

24. The total number of females are what per cent of the total number of males in the organisation ?
    (a) 90 (b) 70 (c) 80
    (d) 60 (e) None of these

25. The respective ratio between the present ages of son, mother, father and grandfather is 2 : 7 : 8 : 12. The average age of son and mother is 27 yr. What will be mother's age after 7 yr?
    (a) 40 yr (b) 41 yr (c) 48 yr
    (d) 49 yr (e) None of these

26. In how many different ways can the letters of the word 'TROUBLE' be arranged ?
    (a) 840 (b) 5040 (c) 1260
    (d) 2520 (e) None of these

DIRECTIONS (Qs. 27-31) : Each of the questions below consists of a question and two statements numbered I and II given below it. You have to decide whether the data provided in the statements are sufficient to answer the question. Read the question and both the statements and -

Give answer (a) if the data in **statement I alone are sufficient** to answer the question, while the data in **statement II alone are not sufficient** to answer the question.
Give answer (b) if the data in **statement II alone are sufficient** to answer the question, while the data in **statement I alone are not sufficient** to answer the question.
Give answer (c) if the data **either in statement I alone or in statement II alone are sufficient** to answer the question.
Give answer (d) if the data even in both the **statements I and II together are not sufficient** to answer the question.
Give answer (e) if the data in both the statements I and II together are necessary to answer the question.

27. Train 'A' running at a certain speed crosses another train 'B' running at a certain speed in the opposite direction in 12 seconds. What is the length of train 'B'?
    I. The length of both the trains together is 450 metres.
    II. Train 'A' is slower than train 'B'.

28. Area of a rectangle is equal to the area of a right angled triangle. What is the length of the rectangle ?
    I. The base of the triangle is 40 cms.
    II. The height of the triangle is 50 cms.

29. What was the total compound interest on a sum after three years ?
    I. The interest after one year was ₹ 100/- and the sum was ₹ 1,000/-.
    II. The difference between simple and compound interest on a sum of ₹1,000/- at the end of two years was ₹10/-.

30. What is the two digit number where the digit at the unit place is smaller ?
I. The difference between the two digits is 5.
II. The sum of the two digits is 7.

31. What is the speed of the boat in still water ?
I. It takes 2 hours to cover distance between A and B downstream.
II. It takes 4 hours to cover distance between A and B upstreams.

32. An ice-cream company makes a popular brand of ice-cream in rectangular shaped bar 6 cm long, 5 cm wide and 2 cm thick. To cut the cost, the company has decided to reduce the volume of the bar by 20%, the thickness remaining the same, but the length and width will be decreased by the same percentage amount. The new length L will satisfy :
(a) $5.5 < L < 6$ (b) $5 < L < 5.5$ (c) $4.5 < L < 5$
(d) $4 < L < 4.5$ (e) None of these

DIRECTIONS (Qs. 33-37) : Study the following table carefully and answer the questions that follow: .

Number of employees from six different banks located in different cities
M = Males, F = Females

City	Agra		Delhi		Mumbai		Chennai		Patna		Kolkata	
Name of Bank	M	F	M	F	M	F	M	F	M	F	M	F
A	553	224	254	456	457	388	114	378	234	120	353	325
B	673	116	346	256	346	456	124	235	241	156	348	174
C	443	500	366	345	124	456	235	388	350	234	399	439
D	534	454	478	285	235	235	255	175	124	165	358	234
E	256	235	256	166	574	599	324	198	124	334	125	235
F	556	357	346	287	589	190	189	256	155	181	278	192

33. What is the ratio of the number of males to the number of females respectively in Patna from Bank A. Bank C and Bank E together ?
(a) $175:173$ (b) $177:173$ (c) $177:172$
(d) $175:172$ (e) None of these

34. What is the ratio of the number of males to the number of females respectively in Bank D from all the cities together ?
(a) $496:387$ (b) $487:356$ (c) $422:385$
(d) $486:397$ (e) None of these

35. The number of females in all the banks together in Delhi are **approximately** what per cent of the number of males from all the banks together in the same city ?
(a) 88   (b) 98   (c) 78
(d) 68   (e) 58

36. The number of females in Bank B from Agra is what per cent of the females in Bank C from the same city?
(a) 33.2   (b) 23.2   (c) 13.2
(d) 28.2   (e) None of these

37. What is the **approximate** average of the number of males working in all the banks together in Kolkata ?
(a) 350   (b) 310   (c) 340
(d) 380   (e) 360

38. 8 men and 4 women together can complete a piece of work in 6 days. The work done by a man in one day is double the work done by a woman in one day. If 8 men and 4 women started working and after 2 days 4 men left and 4 new women joined, in how many more days will the work be completed?
(a) 5 days   (b) 8 days   (c) 6 days
(d) 4 days(e) 9 days

39. Out of five girls and three boys, four children are to be randomly selected for a quiz contest. What is the probability that all the selected children are girls?
(a) $\dfrac{1}{14}$ (b) $\dfrac{1}{7}$ (c) $\dfrac{5}{17}$

(d) $\dfrac{2}{17}$ (e) None of these

40. Total distance between A and B is d kms. If the distance travelled along the stream is three time of the total distance and the distance travelled against the stream is two times of the total distance. If the time taken to cover the distance along the stream is 10% less then the time taken to cover the distance against the stream. If a person cover a distance of 21 km in 1 hr 24 min along the stream, then find the rate of current ?
(a) 2 km/hr   (b) 3 km/hr   (c) 1 km/hr
(d) 4 km/hr   (e) None of these

REASONING ABILITY

DIRECTIONS (Qs. 41-45): In each question below is given a statement followed by two assumptions numbered I and II. An assumption is something supposed or taken for granted. You have to consider the statement and the following assumptions and decide which of the assumptions is implicit in the statement.

Give answer (a) if only Assumption I is implicit.
Give answer (b) if only Assumption II is implicit.
Give answer (c) if either I or II is implicit.
Give answer (d) if neither I nor II is implicit.
Give answer (e) if both I and II are implicit.

41. **Statement** : A nationalised bank issued an advertisement in the national dailies asking the eligible candidates for applying for 100 posts of chartered accountants.
Assumptions :
I. The eligible chartered accountants may respond to the advertisement
II. There may be adequate number of eligible chartered accountants who may want to join a nationalized bank.

42. **Statement** : The municipal authority announced before the onset of monsoon that the roads within the city will be free of potholes during monsoon.
Assumptions:
I. The roads were repaired so well that potholes may not reappear.
II. People may not complain even if the potholes reappear.

43. **Statement :** "Our Europe Holiday Package costs less than some of the holiday Packages within the country" - An advertisement by an Indian travel company.

Assumptions:

I. People may prefer to travel to foreign destinations than to the places within the country at comparable cost.

II. People generally take their travel decisions after getting information from such advertisements.

44. **Statement :** The retail vegetable vendors increased the prices of vegetables by about 20 percent due to non availability of vegetables at lower prices at the wholesale market.

Assumptions:

I. The customers may totally stop buying vegetables at higher prices.

II. The customers may still buy vegetables from the retail vendors.

45. **Statement :** A large number of students and parents stood in the queue to collect forms for admission to various undergraduate courses in the college.

Assumptons :

I. The college authority may be able to admit all those who stood in the queue.

II. The college authority may have adequate number of forms for all those standing in the queue.

DIRECTIONS (Qs. 46-50): Study the following information carefully and answer the given questions.

When a word and number arrangement machine is given an input line of words and numbers, it arranges them following a particular rule. The following is an illustration of input and rearrangement:

(All the numbers are two digit numbers)

Input : 40 made butter 23 37 cookies salt extra 52 86 92 fell now 19

Step I : butter 19 40 made 23 37 cookies salt extra 52 86 92 fell now

Step II : cookies 23 butter 19 40 made 37 salt extra 52 86 92 fell now

Step III : extra 37 cookies 23 butter 19 40 made salt 52 86 92 fell now

Step IV : fell 40 extra 37 cookies 23 butter 19 made salt 52 86 92 now

Step V : made 52 fell 40 extra 37 cookies 23 butter 19 salt 86 92 now

Step VI : now 86 made 52 fell 40 extra 37 cookies 23 butter 19 salt 92

Step VII : salt 92 now 86 made 52 fell 40 extra 37 cookies 23 butter 19

Step VII : is the last step of the above arrangement as the intended arrangement is obtained.

As per the rules followed in the given steps, find out the appropriate steps for the given input.

Input: 32 proud girl beautiful 48 55 97 rich family 61 72 17 nice life

46. How many steps will be required to complete the given input?
(a) Five   (b) Six   (c) Seven
(d) Eight   (e) Nine

47. Which of the following is the third element from the left end of step VI?
(a) beautiful   (b) life   (c) 61
(d) nice   (e) 17

48. Which of the following is step III of the given input?
(a) Proud 72 girl 48 family 32 beautiful 17 55 97 rich 61 nice life
(b) life 55 girl 48 family 32 beautiful A proud 97 rich 61 72 nice.

(c) girl 48 family 32 beautiful 17 proud 55 97 rich 61 72 nice life
(d) family 32 beautiful 17 proud girl 48 55 97 rich 61 72 nice life
(e) girl 48 life 55 family 32 beautiful 17 proud 97 rich 61 72 nice

49. What is the position of 'nice' from the left end in the final step?
(a) Fifth   (b) Sixth   (c) Seventh
(d) Eighth   (e) Ninth

50. Which element is third to the right of 'family' in Step V?
(a) beautiful   (b) 17   (c) proud
(b)` 97   (e) 32

DIRECTIONS (Qs. 51-55) : Each of the questions below consists of a question and two statements numbered I and II given below it. You have to decide whether the data provided in the statements are sufficient to answer the question. Read both the statements and and answer the questions.

Give answer (a) if the data in statement I alone is sufficient to answer the question, while the data in statement II alone are not sufficient to answer the question.

Give answer (b) if the data in statement II alone are sufficient to answer the question, while the data in statement I alone are not sufficient to answer the question.

Give answer (c) if the data either in statement I alone or in statement II alone are sufficient to answer the question; and

Give answer (d) if the data given in both the statements I and II together are not sufficient to answer the question; and

Give answer (e) if the data in both the statements I and II together are necessary to answer the question.

51. How is J related to K?
I. J's father P is the brother of N. N is K's wife.
II. J is the son of P. P is the brother of N. N is K's wife.

52. On which floor of the building does G stay? (the building has five floor 1, 2, 3, 4, 5.)
I. Only the even-numbered floors are occupied and G does not stay on the second floor.
II. G does not stay on an odd-numbered floor.

53. How many days did Raju take to complete his assignment?
I. Mohit correctly remembers that Raju took more than 3 days less than 9 days to complete his assignment.
II. Mina correctly remembers that Raju took more than 7 days less than 11 days to complete his assignment.

54. How is the word 'GATES' coded in the code language?
I. 'BRICK' is coded as 'LDJSC' and 'PIN' is coded as 'OJQ'
II. 'WATER' is coded as 'SFUBX' and 'DISH' is coded as 'ITJE'

55. Among A, B, C and D, which school has the highest number of students.
I. School A has fewer students than school D.
II. School C has fewer students than school D.

DIRECTIONS (Qs. 56-60): Study the following information carefully and answer the questions which follow–

Five boys J, K, L, M and N are working in five different banks- Bank of India (BOI), Punjab national Bank (PNB), Indian overseas Bank (IOB), Bank of Maharashtra (BOM) and SBI Bank. Five girls P, Q, R, S and T are working in five different banks- Bank of Baroda (BOB), Oriental Bank of Commerce (OBC), Union Bank of India (UBI), Central Bank of India (CBI) and Industrial Development Bank of India (IDBI). These five boys are married to these five girls but not necessary in that order. S is either working in BOB or IDBI but does not married to one who works in PNB. J does not work in PNB or BOI but married to one who works in IDBI. The one who works in UBI is married to N. The boy who works in BOI is either married to S or T. N is not married to P, who works either in UBI or CBI. M does not work in IOB or SBI Bank but married to one who works in OBC. L is married to R but does not work with SBI Bank or PNB. R does not married to one who works in PNB. Q is married to one who works in IOB.

56. Who is married to S?
    (a) J   (b) K   (c) L
    (d) M   (e) N

57. Who is employee of Bank of Maharashtra?
    (a) J   (b) K   (c) L
    (d) M   (e) N

58. In which of the following bank the wife of N is working?
    (a) UBI   (b) IDBI   (c) BOB
    (d) OBC   (e) CBI

59. Who works with Oriental Bank of Commerce?
    (a) Wife of L (b) P   (c) Q
    (d) T   (e) Wife of one who works in PNB

60. Who is married to one who works with SBI Bank?
    (a) The one who works with CBI
    (b) The one who works with BOB
    (c) The one who works with UBI
    (d) The one who works with IDBI
    (e) Cannot be determined

DIRECTIONS (Qs. 61-65): Study the following information Carefully to answer the given questions

P, Q, R, S, T, U, V, W and X are sitting in a straight line, facing North. Three of them are not males. Two females sit adjacent to each other. Q is fourth to the left of V, who is second to the right of R, who is not the immediate neighbour of P.

· U is fourth to the right of R and is second to the left of X. S is not an immediate neighbour of either X or Q.

· S is not male. One of the persons sitting on the extreme ends is a female. T is not an immediate neighbour of either V or U.

· No female is an immediate neighbour of U. W does not sit second to the left of P. The immediate neighbour of S are male

61. Which of the following is a group of females ?
    (a) QTS   (b) TXP   (c) SVR
    (d) UWX   (e) None of these

62. Who is sitting to the immediate left of S ?
    (a) V   (b) Q   (c) W
    (d) R   (e) None of these

63. In which of the following combinations is the third person sitting between the first and the second person ?
    (a) PWU   (b) QTR   (c) RST
    (d) WUP   (e) None of these

64. If Q and R, V and U interchange their position then how many persons are sitting between R and V ?
    (a) Four   (b) Five   (c) Six
    (d) Two   (e) None of these

65. Who among the following sits third to the left of P ?
    (a) W   (b) V   (c) R
    (d) X   (e) None of these

DIRECTIONS (Qs. 66-71) : Study the following information carefully and answer the given questions :

Eight people - A. B, C, D, E, F, G and H are sitting around a circular table facing towards the centre, but not necessarily in the same order. All of them are at equidistant. Each one of them teaches different subjects viz., English, Hindi, Mathematics, Biology, Psychology, Physics, Chemistry and Accounts, but not necessarily in the same order.

The person who teaches Accounts, sits third to the right of G. C is an immediate neighbour of G. The person who teaches Mathematics sits second to the left of C. B sits third to the right of H. H teaches neither Accounts nor Mathematics. Only two persons sit between C and the person who teaches Physics. A and F are immediate neighbours of each other. Neither A nor F teaches Accounts. The person who teaches English sits second to the right of A. Two persons sit between D and the person who teaches Hindi. D does not teach Accounts. The person who teaches Psychology is an immediate neighbour of the person who teaches Accounts. The person who teaches Physics sits second to the left of A. One of the immediate neighbours of G teaches Chemistry.

66. Who among the following teaches Chemistry?
    (a) A   (b) H   (c) D
    (d) G   (e) None of these

67. What is the position of B with respect to the person who teaches Psychology?
    (a) Second to the left   (b) Third to the right
    (c) Third to the left   (d) Second to the right
    (e) None of these

68. Who among the following sits exactly between the person who teaches Biology and the person who teaches Physics?
    (a) The person who teaches Mathematics
    (b) E
    (c) The person who teaches Accounts
    (d) Cannot be determined
    (e) There is no such person

69. Which of the following subjects does E teach?
    (a) Chemistry (b) Hindi   (c) Accounts
    (d) English   (e) None of these

70. Which of the following statements is true with regard to the given sitting arrangement?
    (a) The person who teaches Hindi is an immediate neighbour of both H and D.
    (b) One of the immediate neighbours of F teaches Biology
    (c) E is sitting exactly between B and the person who teaches Mathematics
    (d) The person who teaches Chemistry is second to the right of E
    (e) All are true

71. Four of the following five are alike in a certain way based on the given sitting arrangement and hence form a group. Which is the one that does not belong to the group?
    (a) CF   (b) GA   (c) BD
    (d) EH   (e) BA

72. Pole P is 13 km towards the East of Pole Q. Siddharth, starts from Pole Q, travels 8 km towards West and takes a right turn. After taking the right turn, he travels 5 km and reaches Pole B. From Pole B , Siddharth takes a right turn again, travels 21 km and reaches Pole C. How far and towards which direction must the Siddharth travel to reach Pole P?
    (a) 5 km towards South   (b) 5 km towards West
    (c) 21 km towards South (d) 13 km towards South
    (e) None of these

73. Mohan walked 30 metres towards South, took a left turn and walked 15 metres. He then took a right turn and walked 20 metres. He again took a right turn and walked 15 metres. How far is he from the starting point?
    (a) 95 metres   (b) 50 metres
    (c) 70 metres   (d) Cannot be determined
    (e) None of these

74. If 'P $ Q', means 'P is father of Q'; 'P # Q' means 'P is mother of Q'; 'P * Q' means 'P is sister of Q', then how is D related to N in N # A $ B * D?
(a) Nephew
(b) Grandson
(c) Granddaughter
(d) Cannot be determined
(e) None of these

DIRECTIONS (Qs. 75-76) : Study the information below and answer the following question:-

---

In a certain code language,
'Arrive today eagles later' is written as 21×R,6$A, 14$O, 25×A
'Begin work faster table' is written as 14$A, 17%O, 26×A, 22$E
'Length error arrow burn' is written as 6×E, 25$R, 22%U, 21$R
'Trial better than wisdom' is written as 14$R, 14%H, 22×E, 17×I

75. The code for the word ' Table'
(a) 26×A
(b) 17%O
(c) 14$A
(d) 22$E
(e) None of these

76. The code word 6$A for the word
(a) Later
(b) Arrive
(c) Earlier
(d) Today
(e) Either 1 or 3

77. Ashok started walking towards South. After walking 50 metres he took a right turn and walked 30 metres. He then took a right turn and walked 100 metres. He again took a right turn and walked 30 metres and stopped. How far and in which direction was he from the starting point ?
(a) 50 metres South
(b) 150 metres North
(c) 180 metres East
(d) 50 metres North
(e) None of these

78. Vikas walked 10 metres towards North, took a left turn and walked 15 metres and again took a left turn and walked 10 metres and stopped walking. Towards which direction was he facing when he stopped walking ?
(a) South
(b) South-West
(c) South-East
(d) Cannot be determined
(e) None of these

79. There has been a considerable drop in sales of four wheelers during the past six months when compared to the number of four wheelers sold during this period last year.
Which of the following can the probable cause of the above phenomenon?
(A) The govt. has imposed higher excise duty on four wheelers at the beginning of this year.
(B) The petrol prices have risen considerably during the past eight months.
(C) The rate of interest on home and car loans have been rising for the past seven months.
(a) All (A), (B) and (C)
(b) (A) and (C) Only
(c) (B) and (C) Only
(d) (B) Only
(e) (A) Only

80. There is an alarming trend of skewed sex ratio against women in India during the past decade and situation may get out of hand if adequate steps are not taken to stop female foeticide.
Which of the following can be an effective step to reverse the trend?
(A) The Govt. should immediately completely ban the use of scanners / sonography on expectant mothers at all health centres.
(B) The Govt. should announce a substantial incentive scheme for couples who have at least one girl child.
(C) The Govt. should launch a nationwide campaign to create awareness against female foeticide.

(a) (A) only
(b) (A) and (B) Only
(c) (B) and (C) Only
(d) All (A), (B) and (C)
(e) None of these

GENERAL KNOWLEDGE

81. Which of the following company had signed a Statement of Intent (SOI) with NITI Aayog's Atal Innovation Mission (AIM) to collectively drive the charter of developing creative skills and spreading digital literacy across all Atal Tinkering Labs in India?
(a) Microsoft
(b) Adobe
(c) CTS
(d) TCS
(e) None of these

82. Name the Scheme launched by Union HRD Ministry, with an aim to provide industry apprenticeship opportunities to the general graduates?
(a) Sarva Shiksha Abhiyan (SSA)
(b) Scheme for Higher Education Youth in Apprenticeship and Skills (SHREYAS)
(c) Strengthening for providing quality Education in Madrassas (SPQEM)
(d) Rashtriya Madhyamik Shiksha Abhiyan
(e) None of these

83. With which of the following country India had signed MoU to cooperate in the field of Anti-microbial drugs?
(a) Swedan
(b) Russia
(c) Germany
(d) Japan
(e) None of these

84. To collaborate in the area of food and agriculture, Indian Council of Agricultural Research (ICAR) had signed MoU with which of the following organization?
(a) Food and Agriculture Organization
(b) Federation of Indian Chambers of Commerce and Industry
(c) Council of Scientific and Industrial Research (CSIR)
(d) Australian International Food Security Centre
(e) None of these

85. Where d Union Railway Minister Piyush Goyal did launch a new Railway zone?
(a) Andhra Pradesh
(b) Telangana
(c) Kerala
(d) New Delhi
(e) None of these

86. Which of the following Bank had signed a bancassurance agreement with Life Insurance Corporation of India (LIC) to lend LIC's insurance products?
(a) IDBI Bank
(b) State Bank of India
(c) Yes Bank
(d) ICICI Bank
(e) None of these

87. The currency of Afghanistan is :
(a) Afghani
(b) Rupee
(c) Dinar
(d) Ruble
(e) None of these

88. The currency of Algeria is :
(a) Franc
(b) Dollar
(c) Dinar
(d) Suham
(e) None of these

89. Who presented the Union Budget of India and it is presented in which house/houses of the parliament?
(a) Finance Minister of India; Lok Sabha
(b) Prime Minister of India; Rajya Sabha
(c) Cabinet Secretary; Both Lok Sabha and Rajya Sabha
(d) President of India; in joint session of Parliament
(e) None of these

90. Who among the following presented Union Budget maximum number of times?
(a) P. Chidambaram
(b) Pranav Mukherjee
(c) R K Shanmukham Chetty
(d) Morarji Desa
(e) None of these

91. What is the cost of credit expressed as a percentage on a yearly basis called?
(a) APR   (b) APY   (c) WPI
(d) NPI   (e) None of these

92. What is the percentage rate reflecting the total amount of interest paid on a deposit account called?
(a) APR   (b) APY   (c) WPI
(d) CRP   (e) None of these

93. Who works as RBI's agent at places where it has no office of its own?
(a) State Bank of India
(b) Ministry of Finance
(c) Government of India
(d) International Monetary Fund
(e) None of these

94. Which among the following is incorrect?
(a) RBI is the Bank of Issue
(b) RBI acts as Banker to the Government
(c) RBI is Banker's Bank
(d) RBI does not regulate the flow of credit—
(e) None of these

95. Who wrote the famous book - 'We the people'?
(a) T.N.Kaul   (b) J.R.D. Tata
(c) Khushwant Singh   (d) Nani Palkhivala
(e) None of these

96. Who is the author of the book 'Nineteen Eighty Four'?
(a) Thomas Hardy   (b) Emile Zola
(c) George Orwell   (d) Walter Scott
(e) None of these

97. A person pay a tax on whom the tax is incident is known as,–
(a) Direct tax   (b) state tax
(c) Indirect tax   (d) Goods and Service Tax
(e) none of the above

98. How does the rate of growth of an economy is measured?
(a) In terms of per capita
(b) in terms of poverty line
(c) in terms of industrial development
(d) in terms of national income.
(e) None of these

99. what does Reserve Repo Mean?
(a) Rate RBI charges on funds lent to banks
(b) Rate offered to Blue chip companies
(c) A rate equal to Bank rate
(d) All of these
(e) None of these

100. RRBs are refinanced at
(a) 2 % below the bank rate
(b) 1 % below the bank rate
(c) 2 % below the repo rate
(d) 1 % below the repo rate
(e) None of these

101. Which of the following bank has launched 'iwatch' Banking project?
(a) SBI   (b) ICICI   (c) HDFC
(d) PNB   (e) None of these

102. Which of the following term is not related to banking sector?
(a) BASEL III
(b) Forex Reserve
(c) Statutory Liquidity Ratio
(d) Marginal Standing Facility
(e) None of these

103. Which of the following organisation led the foundation towards the formation of the International society nations?
(a) League of Nations
(b) United Nations
(c) International UN Federation
(d) International Institution
(e) None of these

104. Which organisation is termed as "a Child of War"?
(a) UN   (b) League of Nations
(c) SAARC   (d) WHO

105. Which organisation is termed as "a Child of War"?
(a) UN   (b) League of Nations
(c) SAARC   (d) WHO
(e) None of these

106. Better products, Better value, Better living" is the mission statement of which company:
(a) VICCO   (b) HUL
(c) P&G   (d) NIRMA
(e) None of these

107. The FIFA World Cup 2026 will be hosted in
(a) China
(b) France and Germany
(c) Brazil and Argentina
(d) Canada, Mexico, and United States
(E) None of these

108. The Nobel Peace Prize 2018 was awarded to
(a) Denis Mukwege
(b) Nadia Murad
(c) Denis Mukwege and Nadia Murad
(d) International Atomic Energy Agency (IAEA)
(e) None of these

109. The Turkish government accused that the faction of the army that tried to imposed Martial Law was linked to
(a) Opposition Parties   (b) Kurds Forces
(c) Syria   (d) Fethullah Gulen
(e) None of these

110. Fathullah Gulen is a religious and political leader lives in self-imposed exile in the
(a) United States   (b) United Kingdom
(c) Saudi Arabia   (d) Egypt
(e) None of these

111. The 2020 Olympics will be held in ________.
(a) London   (b) Doha
(c) Tokyo   (d) Beijing
(e) None of these

112. The opening match in FIFA World Cup 2018 was between Russia and
(a) Argentina   (b) Germany
(c) Qatar   (d) Saudi Arabia
(e) None of these

113. Which sector is the backbone of Indian economy?
(a) Service Sector   (b) Financial Sector
(c) Tourism Sector   (d) Agriculture Sector
(e) None of these

114. Which among the following is not a cereal?
(a) Rice   (b) Wheat   (c) Gram
(d) Maize   (e) None of these

115. Which among the following does not belong to welfare schemes for the farmers?
(a) Kisan Credit Card Scheme
(b) SHG Bank Linkage Programme
(c) National Agricultural Insurance Scheme
(d) Employee Referral Scheme
(e) None of these

116. When did the Government present Kisan Credit Card Scheme?
(a) April 1853   (b) August 1998
(c) July 1991   (d) November 1995
(e) None of these

117. In which year, SBI was given control of 8 state associated banks under the State Bank of India (Subsidary Banks) Act, 1959:

(a) 1955   (b) 1960
(c) 1965   (d) 1970
(e) None of these

118. Reserve Bank of India was established under which among the following act:

(a) Reserve Bank of India Act 1930
(b) Reserve Bank of India Act 1921
(c) Reserve Bank of India Act 1934
(d) Reserve Bank of India Act 1947
(e) None of these

119. Who can issue Rupee Denominated Bonds Overseas?

(a) REITs   (b) Indian Banks
(c) InvITs   (d) All of these
(e) None of these

120. The minimum maturity period for Masala Bonds raised up to USD 50 million equivalent in INR per financial year should be _____ years

(a) 2 years   (b) 4 years
(c) 3 years   (d) 5 years
(e) None of these

ENGLISH LANGUAGE

DIRECTIONS (Qs. 121-130) : Read the following passage carefully and answer the questions given below it. Certain words are given in bold to help you locate them while answering some of the questions.

Nearly **6000** years ago, man took a giant step forward in his evolution on this earth when, giving up a nomadic type of life, he took to agriculture. This memorable event happened in certain river valleys of India, China, Mesopotamia (modern Iraq) and Egypt. The reason was that the conditions in these areas were favourable for the cultivation of grains like wheat, rice etc because of plenty of rich soil and water. Consequently, the farmer was able to produce more grains than he required for his needs. This helped in the development of settled cooperative living and villages appeared where some people could make a living using some specialised skills or take up other jobs useful to the society instead of tilling the soil.

As time passed more and more families started living together for the sake of security against barbarians and wild animals. They built big buildings and cities sprang up. Such developments took place in many parts of the world where conditions were suitable for agriculture, trade and commerce. Since it was not hard to make a good living, men had **spare** time for the development of arts and crafts and engage in other activities which characterise a cultured life.

The ancient civilizations, though quite far removed from each other, did not develop in complete **isolation**. There was some trade and commerce accompanied at times by sharing of knowledge. It was not uncommon to have from time to time small or big wars and mass **exodus** of people for greener pastures. By **1000** BC, with considerable **intermingling** of races, several well-developed and prosperous civilisations had come into existence. Their borders of course were not well defined but kept on shifting due to wars. Here we shall be concerned essentially with some of the fundamental contributions of the ancient Indian and Greek civilisations to human knowledge. One may like to know why these two could make more important and enduring contributions than other civilisations. The answer briefly is that by and large both in India and Greece conditions for free, **sober** and intelligent thought were an integral part of the social structure. Furthermore, the philosophers were highly respected and they could without a care

Follow knowledge like a sinking star
Beyond the utmost bound of human thought.

To begin with, the philosophical developments in the two civilisations started along similar lines, with attempts to answer some basic questions like : Who am I? How was the world created? Is there life after death? And so on. This is not surprising since the forefathers of the Indo-Aryans and the Greeks lived together in Central Asia before mass migration. But in due course, around 500 BC, the effects of different environments and some intermixing with other races began to have their effect and change in emphasis in the pursuit of knowledge was noticeable. The Greeks, because of their rugged surrounding and contacts with other seafaring people in trade and commerce, had to be practical. They turned more and more to the study and understanding of the 'outer world'. So successful were they in their endeavour and so basic were their contributions that it is now quite generally accepted that the entire modern intellectual education of the West, both philosophical and scientific, originates from the Greeks. The Indo-Aryans, on the other hand, once they had settled down comfortably in different parts of India did not have to face many challenges from the outside world. Consequently, they turned more and more towards religion and the study of man's 'inner world'. The degree of success and the mastery they achieved is best summed up by Schopenhauer, a German philosopher. Commenting about Upanishidic knowledge, he remarked, "Thinking was finished on the banks of river Ganges."

121. Which step of man marks the end of his life as wanderers on this earth?

(a) his taking up of jobs which were useful to the society
(b) his shift towards agricultural activities
(c) development of the sense of brotherhood
(d) evolution of trade and commerce
(e) None of these

122. What led to the development of farming in India, China, Mesopotamia and Iraq?

(a) curiosity for producing grains among the people in these areas
(b) early knowledge of agriculture among the people in these areas
(c) proper climate for agriculture
(d) vast area was available
(e) None of these

123. Development of villages became easy because

(a) people gave up agriculture and took to alternate jobs.
(b) a sense of security led people to live in units like villages.
(c) people were fed up of nomadic lifestyle.
(d) people got easy lifestyle in such a condition
(e) None of these

124. Which of the following is true in the context of the passage?

(a) Agriculture, trade and commerce marked the development of the society.
(b) Living together made people brave enough to kill the wild animals.
(c) Man's nomadic lifestyle gave birth to agriculture
(d) Man took up to nomadic lifestyle nearly **6000** years from now.
(e) None of these

125. Which of the following is false in the context of the passage.

(a) Concern for security was one of the reasons which made families live together.
(b) Fertile lands supported agriculture in India, China, Mesopotamia and Egypt.
(c) Ancient civilisations developed without having any support from one another.
(d) Trade and commerce supported the cause of development.
(e) None of these

126. Why did the established civilisations have no fixed places or properly demarcated borders?
(a) because several civilisations established themselves close to each other
(b) because of the changing nature of the civilisations
(c) because of the merging of smaller civilisations into bigger ones
(d) because of wars and migration of people to different areas
(e) None of these

127. What led the Greeks to expand their knowledge of the 'outer world'?
(a) their conquest of various countries
(b) their access to the other countries of the world via sea route
(c) their social recognition in foreign countries
(d) their constant fighting with other countries
(e) None of these

128. The Indo-Aryans with a religious bent of mind turned to the study of man's inner world because
(a) they were at peace in their home and having little interference from the outside world
(b) they never reflected aggression even if challenged by other countries
(c) the study of the outer world was assigned to the Greeks.
(d) they had no idea of the outer world.
(e) None of these

129. Which of the following is most similar in meaning toward 'Exodus' as used in the passage?
(a) departure   (b) trial
(c) awareness   (d) sensitivity
(e) fleet

130. Which of the following is most opposite in meaning to word 'Rugged' as used in the passage?
(a) smooth   (b) straight
(c) furnished   (d) polished
(e) curved

DIRECTIONS (Qs. 131-138) : Read each sentence to find out whether there is any error in it. The error, if any, will be in one part of the sentence. The letter of that part is the answer. If there is no error, the answer is (e). (Ignore errors of punctuation, if any.)

131. The ongoing merger among /the two companies will/
        (a)   (b)
have an adverse/impact on consumers. No error
    (c)   (d)   (e)

132. It is evident that/the banking sector has underwent/
        (a)   (b)
tremendous changes during/the past two decades. No error
                                      (e)

133. According to the consultant/a more detail analysis of/
          (a)   (b)
customer needs / and product pricing is required. No error
      (c)   (d)   (e)

134. Over the next five years / the government needs to invest/
        (a)   (b)
at less 350 billion dollars/in rural infrastructure. No error
        (c)   (d)   (e)

135. The lack of no funds / has resulted in several / delays in
        (a)   (b)
launching our / new product in India. No error
    (c)   (d)   (e)

136. In the first two months of this fiscal, tractor sales has seen (a)/a drop of about five percent (b)/ however, the industry is waiting for the monsoon (c)/ to really arrive at a firm conclusion about growth prospects for the current year. (d)/ No error (e)

137. Dolphins are truly out of the ordinary because of their intelligence. (a) / And among the many creatures that share the earth form (b)/they come closest to humankind in terms of (c)/familial traits, emotions and learning. (d)/ No error (e)

138. Corruption indulged in by the high and mighty adversely impacts (a)/ our nation and in the coming months (b) / we may see revival of efforts (c)/ to tackle such large scale corruption. (d)/ No error (e).

DIRECTIONS (Qs. 139-145): In the following passage there are blanks, each of which has been numbered. These numbers are printed below the passage and against each, five words/phrases are suggested, one of which fits the blank appropriately. Find out the appropriate word/phrase in each case.

There is a considerable amount of research about the factors that make a company innovate. So is it possible to create an environment **(139)** to innovation? This is a particularly pertinent **(140)** for India today. Massive problems in health, education etc. **(141)** be solved using a conventional approach but **(142)** creative and innovative solutions that can ensure radical change and **(143)**. There are several factors in India's **(144)**. Few countries have the rich diversity that India or its large, young population **(145)**.

139. (a) stimuli   (b) conducive
(c) incentive   (d) facilitated
(e) impetus

140. (a) objective   (b) controversy
(c) doubt   (d) question
(e) inference

141. (a) cannot   (b) possibly
(c) should   (d) never
(e) must

142. (a) necessary   (b) apply
(c) need   (d) consider
(e) requires

143. (a) quantity   (b) advantages
(c) increase   (d) chaos
(e) growth

144. (a) challenges   (b) praises
(c) favour   (d) leverage
(e) esteem

145. (a) blessed   (b) enjoys
(c) endows   (d) prevails
(e) occurs

DIRECTIONS (Qs. 146-150): Rearrange the following six sentences (A), (B), (C), (D) and (F) in the proper sequence to form a meaningful paragraph, then answer the questions given below them.

(A) The group desired to enhance the learning experience in schools with an interactive digital medium that could be used within and outside the class-room

(B) Then the teacher can act on the downloaded data rather than collect it from each and every student and thereby save his time and effort.

(C) Eductor, decided the group of engineers, all alumni of the Indain Institute of technology, when the founded Edutor Technologies in August 2009.

(D) They can even take tests and submit them digitally using the same tablets and the teachers in turn can download the tests using the company's cloud services.

(E) With this desire they created a solution that digitzes school textbooks and other learning materials so that students no longer need to carry as many books to school and back as before, but can access their study material on their touch-screen tablets.

(F) A mechanic works on motors and an accountant has his computer. Likewise, if a student has to work on a machine or device, what should it be called?

146. Which of the following sentences should be the **FIRST** after rearrangement?

(a) F   (b) D   (c) A
(d) C   (e) E

147. Which of the following sentences should be the **THIRD** after rearrangement?

(a) A   (b) B   (c) D
(d) E   (e) F

148. Which of the following sentences should be the **SIXTH (LAST)** after rearrangement?

(a) A   (b) F   (c) E
(d) B   (e) D

149. Which of the following sentences should be the **FOURTH** after rearrangement?

(a) A   (b) F   (c) E
(d) B   (e) D

150. Which of the following sentences should be the **FIFTH** after rearrangement?

(a) A   (b) D   (c) C
(d) E   (e) F

DIRECTIONS (Qs. 151-155): In question given below there are two statements, each statement consists of two blanks. You have to choose the option which provides the correct set of words that fits both the blanks in both the statements appropriately and in the same order making them meaningful and grammatically correct.

---

151. (1) Despite the fact that cancerous ovarian stem cells are ______________ to chemoresistance, they are the ______________ targets for therapy.

(2) How quickly the __________ branch of Homo heidelbergensis turned into something that could be called Homo sapiens was therefore __________.

(a) Feigned, indeterminate   (b) Pertinent, inane
(c) Relevant, obscure   (d) affiliated, fatuous
(e) analogous, insignificant

152. (1) The molecular targeting of CSCs may improve the __________ of current chemotherapeutic __________ needed for the management of this disease.

(2) __________ and safety of once-daily __________ in the treatment of HIV infection is currently under inspection.

(a) Germaneness, medication
(b) Efficacy, regimens
(c) Emasculation, nutriments
(d) Potency, sustenance
(e) Sufficiency, subsistence

153. (1) The six-day war was the last unalloyed military victory for Israel, and the start of a ____________ from existential wars against Arab states, which it always won, to ______________ campaigns against non-state militias which it could never wipe out.

(2) He sees these dualities as having been maintained through the ________________ by a deliberate and ______________ general amnesia.

(a) Transition, enervating
(b) Progression, invigorating
(c) Concatenation, exhilarating
(d) Juncture, frivolous
(e) Movement, enfeeble

154. (1) The obvious ____________ between China's level of participation and other Asian states' requires some ____________.

(2) For years there has been talk Aldo's lazy performances had more to do with a brutal weight cut than any skill ____________. That's always been a pretty probable __________, given the number of horrendous weight cuts MMA sees.

(a) Deviation, delineation
(b) Discrepancy, explanation
(c) Incongruity, cogitation
(d) contrast, contemplation
(e) Contrariety, rumination

155. (1) Polish environment minister to ____________ over COP24 conference, the choice was made ________ ______ by the climate-change committee of the United Nations.

(2) The Labour Party is led by two Marxists: Mr Corbyn and John McDonnell, his shadow chancellor, who believe in the materialist interpretation of history. Yet they now ____________ over a coalition of voters defined ____________ by their shared values.

(a) Debate, diligently
(b) Concoct, congruently
(c) Supervise, perspicaciously
(d) Conduct, unanimously
(e) Preside, overwhelmingly

DIRECTIONS (Qs. 156-160) : In each of the following questions four words are given of which two words are most nearly the same or opposite in meaning. Find the two words which are most nearly the same or opposite in meaning and find the number of the correct letter combination, that is your answer.

---

156. (A) consent   (B) nascent
       (C) emerging   (D) insecure
(a) A - C   (b) B - D   (c) B - C
(d) A - D   (e) A - B

157. (A) elated   (B) eccentric
       (C) explicit   (D) abnormal
(a) A - B   (b) B - D   (c) A - C
(d) A - D   (e) D - C

158. (A) abundance   (B) incomparable
       (C) projection   (D) plethora
(a) A - C   (b) A - B   (c) C - D
(d) B - D   (e) A - D

159. (A) purposefully (B) inaccurately
       (C) inadvertently (D) unchangeably
(a) A - C   (b) A - B   (c) B - C
(d) B - D   (e) A - D

160. (A) germane　　(B) generate
　　　(C) reliable　　(D) irrelevant
　　　(a) B - D　　(b) B - C　　(c) A - B
　　　(d) C - D　　(e) A - D

HINDI LANGUAGE

निर्देश (प्र.सं.121-130): नीचे दिए गए गद्यांश को ध्यानपूर्वक पढ़िए और उस पर आधारित प्रश्नों के उत्तर दीजिए। कुछ शब्दों को मोटे अक्षरों में मुद्रित किया गया है, जिससे आपको कुछ प्रश्नों के उत्तर देने में सहायता मिलेगी।

तत्त्ववेता शिक्षाविदों के अनुसार विद्या दो प्रकार की होती है। प्रथम वह, जो हमें जीवन-यापन के लिए अर्जन करना सिखाती है और द्वितीय वह, जो हमें जीना सिखलाती है। इनमें से एक का अभाव भी जीवन को निरर्थक बना देता है। बिना कमाए जीवन-निर्वाह सम्भव नहीं। कोई भी नहीं चाहेगा कि वह परावलम्बी हो, माता-पिता, परिवार के किसी सदस्य, जाति या समाज पर आश्रित रहे। ऐसी विद्या से विहीन व्यक्ति का जीवन दूभर हो जाता है। वह दूसरों के लिए भार बन जाता है। साथ ही दूसरी विद्या के बिना सार्थक जीवन नहीं जिया जा सकता। बहुत अर्जित कर लेने वाले व्यक्ति का जीवन यदि सुचारू रूप से नहीं चल रहा, उसमें यदि वह जीवन शक्ति नहीं है, जो उसके अपने जीवन को तो सत्पथ पर अग्रसर करती ही है, साथ ही वह अपने समाज, जाति एवं राष्ट्र के लिए भी मार्गदर्शन करती है, तो उसका जीवन भी मानव जीवन का अभिधान नहीं पा सकता। वह भारवाही गर्दभ बन जाता है या पूँछ-सींग-विहीन पशु कहा जाता है। वर्तमान भारत में पहली विद्या का प्रायः अभाव दिखाई देता है, परन्तु दूसरी विद्या का रूप भी विकृत ही है, क्योंकि न तो स्कूलों-कॉलेजों में शिक्षा प्राप्त करके निकला छात्र जीविकोपार्जन के योग्य बन पाता है और न ही वह उन संस्कारों से युक्त हो पाता है, जिन्हें 'जीने की कला' की संज्ञा दी जाती है, जिनसे व्यक्ति 'कु' से 'सु' बनता है, सुशिक्षित, सुसभ्य और सुसंस्कृत कहलाने का अधिकारी होता है।

वर्तमान शिक्षा पद्धति के अन्तर्गत हम जो विद्या प्राप्त कर रहे हैं, उसकी विशेषताओं को सर्वथा नकारा भी नहीं जा सकता है। यह शिक्षा कुछ सीमा तक हमारे दृष्टिकोण को विकसित भी करती है, हमारी मनीषा को प्रबष्टी बनाती है तथा भावनाओं को चेतन करती है, किन्तु कला, शिल्प, प्रौद्योगिकी आदि की शिक्षा नाम मात्र की होने के फलस्वरूप इस देश के स्नातक के लिए जीविकार्जन ढेढ़ी खीर बन जाता है और बृहस्पति बना युवक नौकरी की तलाश में अर्जियाँ लिखने में ही अपने जीवन का बहुमूल्य समय बर्बाद कर देता है। जीवन के सर्वांगीण विकास को ध्यान में रखते हुए यदि शिक्षा के क्रमिक सोपानों पर विचार किया जाए तो भारतीय विद्यार्थी को सर्वप्रथम इस प्रकार की शिक्षा दी जानी चाहिए जो आवश्यक हो, दूसरी जो उपयोगी हो, और तीसरी जो हमारे जीवन को परिष्कृत एवं अलंकृत करती हो, ये तीनों सीढ़ियाँ एक के बाद एक आती हैं। इनमें व्यतिक्रम नहीं होना चाहिए। इस क्रम में व्याघात आ जाने से मानव-जीवन का चारू-प्रासाद खड़ा करना असम्भव है। वह तो भवन की छत बनाकर नींव बनाने के सर्द है। वर्तमान भारत में शिक्षा की अवस्था देखकर ऐसा ही प्रतीत होता है। प्राचीन भारतीय दार्शनिकों ने 'अन्न' से 'आनन्द' की ओर बढ़ने को जो 'विद्या का सार' कहा था, वह सर्वथा समीचीन ही था।

121. मानव की संज्ञा के लिए निम्नांकित विद्या अभीष्ट है-
　　(a) अर्जनकारी विद्या
　　(b) शिल्प और प्रौद्योगिकी विद्या
　　(c) जीवन-यापन के लिए उपयोगी विद्या
　　(d) जीना सिखलाने वाली विद्या
　　(e) इनमें से कोई नहीं

122. शिक्षा के सोपानों का क्रम इस प्रकार होना चाहिए-
　　(a) परिष्कार, उपयोगिता एवं आवश्यकता
　　(b) आवश्यकता, आविष्कार एवं उपयोगिता
　　(c) आवश्यकता, उपयोगिता एवं परिष्कार
　　(d) उपयोगिता, आवश्यकता एवं परिष्कार
　　(e) इनमें से कोई नहीं

123. अर्जनकारी विद्या इसलिए महत्वपूर्ण है क्योंकि वह व्यक्ति को सिखाती है-
　　(a) धनार्जन के साधन　　(b) जीवन-यापन की विधि
　　(c) जीवन-उत्कर्ष की विधि　　(d) ज्ञानार्जन के ढंग
　　(e) इनमें से कोई नहीं

124. प्रत्येक व्यक्ति जीवन-यापन के लिए स्वावलम्बी होना पसन्द करता है क्योंकि-
　　(a) वह जीने की कला सीखना चाहता है
　　(b) वह अपने जीवन को दूभर नहीं बनाना चाहता
　　(c) वह अपने सामाजिक ऋण से मुक्त होना चाहता है
　　(d) वह अपने परिवार के प्रति कृतज्ञ होता है
　　(e) इनमें से कोई नहीं

125. 'कु' से 'सु' बनने में यह आशय सन्निहित है-
　　(a) दुर्जन से सुजन बनना　　(b) दुष्कर से सुकर बनना
　　(c) दुर्लभ से सुलभ बनना　　(d) दुर्गम से सुगम बनना
　　(e) इनमें से कोई नहीं

126. मानव-जीवन की सर्वतोमुखी उन्नति का लक्ष्य क्या है?
　　(a) मनुष्य की भौतिक साधन सम्पन्नता
　　(b) मानव-जीवन की सम्पन्नता एवं परिष्कार
　　(c) सहज सुख-सुविधा सम्पन्न जीवन
　　(d) मनुष्य का स्वावलम्बन
　　(e) इनमें से कोई नहीं

127. 'भारवाही गर्दभ' पदबन्ध से अभिप्रेत क्या है?
　　(a) धनार्जन में अक्षम पुरूष　　(b) अध्ययन में प्रवृत्त विद्यार्थी
　　(c) बोझा ढोने वाला श्रमिक　　(d) जीने की कला से रहित साक्षर
　　(e) इनमें से कोई नहीं

128. उपर्युक्त अनुच्छेद का सर्वाधिक उपयुक्त शीर्षक निम्नलिखित में कौन-सा है?
　　(a) वर्तमान भारतीय शिक्षा　　(b) शिक्षा के सोपान
　　(c) जीने की कला　　(d) मानव जीवन की सार्थकता
　　(e) इनमें से कोई नहीं

129. 'अन्न' से 'आनन्द' की ओर बढ़ने में 'विद्या का सार' इसलिए निहित है क्योंकि ऐसी विद्या मनुष्य का-
　　(a) आध्यात्मिक विकास करती है
　　(b) सर्वांगीण विकास करती है
　　(c) भौतिक विकास करती है
　　(d) सामाजिक विकास करती है
　　(e) इनमें से कोई नहीं

130. 'जीने के लिए अर्जन करना सिखाने वाली' और 'जीना सिखलाने वाली' विद्याओं के पारस्परिक सम्बन्ध में निम्नांकित तथ्य सर्वाधिक उपयुक्त है-
　　(a) ये दोनों एक ही सिक्के के पहलू हैं
　　(b) ये दोनों विरोधी विधाएँ हैं
　　(c) इन दोनों में पूर्वापर सम्बन्ध हैं
　　(d) इन दोनों में अन्योन्याश्रित संबंध हैं
　　(e) इनमें से कोई नहीं

निर्देश (प्र.सं.131-135) नीचे दिए गए प्रत्येक प्रश्न में (5) शब्द दिए गए हैं जिनमें से (4) समानार्थी हैं। जो समानार्थी नहीं है वही आपका उत्तर है।

131. (a) स्तेन　　(b) खनक　　(c) धूसर
　　　(d) साहसिक　　(e) तस्कर

132. (a) छद्म　　(b) तट　　(c) तीर
　　　(d) कूल　　(e) रोध

133. (a) गेह　　(b) निकेतन　　(c) निलय
　　　(d) आलय　　(e) नचक

134. (a) मसलश　　(b) अरूक्ष　　(c) नरम
　　　(d) परूष　　(e) मष्टु

135. (a) किस्सा　　(b) शोणित　　(c) गाथा
　　　(d) कथा　　(e) वार्ता

निर्देश (प्र.सं.136-140) नीचे दिए गए प्रत्येक प्रश्न में एक रिक्त स्थान छूटा हुआ है और उसके नीचे पाँच शब्द सुझाए गए हैं। इनमें से कोई एक उस रिक्त स्थान पर रख देने से वह वाक्य एक अर्थपूर्ण वाक्य बन जाता है। सही शब्द ज्ञात कर उसको उत्तर के रूप में अंकित कीजिए। दिए गए शब्द ज्ञात कर उसको उत्तर के रूप में अंकित कीजिए। दिए गए शब्दों में से सर्वाधिक उपयुक्त का चयन करना है।

136. प्रकृति में वायु-प्रदूषण को कम करने वाली ..... स्वत: होती रहती है।

   (a) प्रतिक्रिया   (b) क्रिया   (c) प्रक्रिया

   (d) विक्रिया   (e) इनमें से कोई नहीं

137. लोकसभा चुनाव क्षेत्रों का पुन: .... किया जाना चाहिए।

   (a) परीक्षण   (b) परिगणन   (c) परिक्षालन

   (d) परिसीमन   (e) इनमें से कोई नहीं

138. तुम्हें बड़ों से बात करने का .... सीखना चाहिए।

   (a) सदाचार   (b) आचरण   (c) शिष्टाचार

   (d) भलमनसाहत   (e) इनमें से कोई नहीं

139. महात्मा गाँधी चाहते थे कि आर्थिक .... के लिए घरेलू-उद्योग धंधों पर बल दिया जाना चाहिए।

   (a) विकास   (b) स्वावलंबन   (c) समषद्धि

   (d) सुधार   (e) इनमें से कोई नहीं

140. इस समय हमारे देश पर कई प्रकार के अन्तर्राष्ट्रीय .... है।

   (a) ऋण   (b) प्रवाद   (c) दबाव

   (d) आक्रमण   (e) इनमें से कोई नहीं

निर्देश (प्र.सं.141-145): नीचे दिया गया हरेक वाक्य चार भागों में बांटा गया है और जिन्हें **(a), (b), (c)** और **(d)** क्रमांक दिए गए हैं। आपको यह देखना है कि वाक्य के किसी भाग में व्याकरण, भाषा, वर्तनी, शब्दों के गलत प्रयोग या इसी तरह की कोई त्रुटि तो नहीं है। त्रुटि अगर होगी तो वाक्य के किसी एक भाग में ही होगी। उस भाग का क्रमांक ही आपका उत्तर है। अगर वाक्य त्रुटिरहित है तो उत्तर **(e)** दीजिए।

141. दहेज-प्रथा के कारण (a)/ महिलाओं को (b)/ उत्पीड़न एवं कठोर दण्ड का (c)/ भोगी बनना पड़ता है (d)/ त्रुटिरहित (e)

142. मैं यह निस्संकोचपूर्वक (a)/ नहीं कह सकता हूँ कि (b)/ हम दिन-प्रतिदिन जरूरतों के (c)/ गुलाम होते जा रहें हैं (d)/ त्रुटिरहित (e)

143. विद्या समाप्त करके (a)/ मैं व्यापार करूंगा (b)/ यह कह कर छात्र ने सिर नीचा कर लिया (c)/ और विनम्र भाव से खड़ा रहा (d)/ त्रुटिरहित (e)

144. दानवीर दयालु व्यक्ति को (a)/ महादानी कहते हैं (b)/ क्योंकि वह अकेला (c)/ दीन-दुखियों की रक्षा करता है (d)/ त्रुटिरहित (e)

145. जवाहरलाल नेहरू ने (a)/ अपनी आत्मकथा में (b)/ स्वातन्त्र्य संघर्ष का (c)/ जीवन्त अंकन किया है (d)/ त्रुटिरहित (e)

निर्देश (146-150): नीचे कुछ वाक्यांश या शब्द दिए गए हैं और उसके बाद चार शब्द दिए गए हैं जो एक ही शब्द में इस वाक्यांश या शब्द-समूह का अर्थ प्रकट करता है। आपको यह पता लगाना है कि वह शब्द कौन-सा है जो वाक्यांश या शब्द समूह का सही अर्थ प्रकट करता है। उस विकल्प का क्रमांक ही आपका उत्तर है। यदि कोई शब्द अर्थ नहीं प्रकट करता है तो उत्तर **(e)** अर्थात् 'इनमें से कोई नहीं' दीजिए।

146. जो गहरी नींद में सो रहा हो

   (a) निद्रा मग्न   (b) बेसुध   (c) विक्षिप्त

   (d) सुगुप्त   (e) इनमें से कोई नहीं

147. निर्धनों को निशुल्क भोजन

   (a) सदाव्रत   (b) दातव्य   (c) धर्मदा

   (d) धर्मशाला   (e) इनमें से कोई नहीं

148. बालकों को सुलाने के लिए गाया जाने वाला गीत

   (a) बालगीत   (b) गीतिका   (c) लोरी

   (d) लोहड़ी   (e) इनमें से कोई नहीं

149. जिसको सिद्ध करने के लिए प्रमाण की आवश्यकता न हो

   (a) स्वयंसिद्ध   (b) अप्रमाणित   (c) प्रमाणित

   (d) प्रस्तावित   (e) इनमें से कोई नहीं

150. जिसको देश से निकाल दिया गया हो

   (a) प्रवासित   (b) निर्वासित   (c) दण्डित

   (d) विदेशी   (e) इनमें से कोई नहीं

निर्देश (प्र.सं.151-160): नीचे दिए गए परिच्छेद मे कुछ रिक्त स्थान छोड़ दिए गए हैं तथा उन्हें प्रश्न संख्या में दर्शाया गया है। ये संख्याएँ परिच्छेद के नीचे मुद्रित हैं, और प्रत्येक के सामने **(a), (b), (c), (d)** और **(e)** विकल्प दिए गए हैं। इन पाँचों में से कोई एक इस रिक्त स्थान को पूरे परिच्छेद के संदर्भ में उपयुक्त ढंग से पूरा कर देता है। आपको वह विकल्प ज्ञात करना है, और इसका क्रमांक ही उत्तर के रूप में दर्शाना है। दिए गए विकल्पों में से उचित विकल्प चुनिए और उसके अनुसार सही उत्तर दीजिए।

यह बहुत पुरानी बात है। मैं उत्तर प्रदेश के एटा जिले की तहसील कासगंज के एक हाई स्कूल में सातवीं कक्षा में पढ़ता था। पढ़ता क्या था, छठीं पास करने के बाद सातवीं में .... (31)....... ही था। जुलाई का महीना था। गरमी की छुट्टियों के बाद .... (32)....... खुल गया था। मेरे लिए नयी . ... (33)....... की किताबें आ गयी थीं। नयी छपी हुई किताबों का गंध, जो पता नहीं, नये कागज की होती थी या उस पर की गयी .... (34). ...... में इस्तेमाल हुई स्याही की, या जिल्दसाजी में .... (35)....... चीजों की, या बरसात के मौसम में कागज में आयी हल्की-सी ...... (36)....... की, मुझे बहुत अच्छी लगती थी। ज्यों ही मेरे लिए ....(37)....... आतीं, मैं सबसे पहले अपनी हिंदी की पाठ्य-पुस्तक पढ़ डालता, सो एक दिन स्कूल से लौटकर मैं अपनी हिन्दी की पाठ्य-पुस्तक .... (38)....... रहा था, जिसमें एक पाठ था 'बड़े भाई साहब'। पुस्तक में अवश्य ही लिखा रहा होगा कि यह एक .... (39)....... है और इसके लेखक हैं प्रेमचंद। लेकिन इस सबसे मुझे क्या! मैं तो 'बड़े भाई साहब' .... (40)....... देखकर ही उसे पढ़ने लगा।

151. (a) पढ़ता   (b) आया   (c) घुसा

   (d) पढ़ा   (e) उठा

152. (a) रास्ता   (b) मौसम   (c) कॉलेज

   (d) स्कूल   (e) शरीर

153. (a) नवीन   (b) पढ़ाई   (c) कक्षा

   (d) छपाई   (e) पुरानी

154. (a) छपाई   (b) नक्काशी   (c) सजावट

   (d) कसीदाकारी   (e) छिड़काई

155. (a) फंसी   (b) दबी   (c) जड़ी

   (d) लगी   (e) उभरी

156. (a) पीलाई   (b) सफेदी   (c) बूंदों

   (d) नीलाई   (e) सीलन

157. (a) कॉपियाँ   (b) साइकिलें   (c) किताबें

   (d) पेंसिलें   (e) पढ़ाइयाँ

158. (a) पढ़   (b) खोल   (c) घोट

   (d) रट   (e) दिखा

159. (a) कविता   (b) कहानी   (c) उपन्यास

   (d) लोककथा   (e) नसीहत

160. (a) को   (b) की तरफ   (c) को सामने

   (d) को बोल   (e) शीर्षक

COMPUTER KNOWLEDGE

161. The index register in a digital computer is used for?
    (a) Pointing to the stack address
    (b) Indirect addressing
    (c) Keeping track of number of times a loop is executed
    (d) Address modification
    (e) None of these

162. In 8085 the overflow flag is set when
    (a) The sum is more than 16 bits
    (b) Signed numbers go out their range after an arithmetic operation
    (c) Carry and sign flags are set
    (d) During subtraction
    (e) None of these

163. The drawbacks of the binary tree sort are remedied by the
    (a) Linear sort   (b) Quick Sort
    (c) Heap Sort   (d) Insertion Sort
    (e) None of these

164. The number of binary trees with 3 nodes which when traversed in post order gives the sequence A, B, C is?
    (a) 3   (b) 9
    (c) 7   (d) 5
    (e) None of these

165. Relocation bits used by relocating loader are specified (generated) by
    (a) Relocating loader itself
    (b) Linker
    (c) Assembler or translator
    (d) Macro processor
    (e) None of these

166. Regular expression (0, 1) is equivalent to
    (a) 0 U 1   (b) 0/1
    (c) 0 + 1   (d) All of the above
    (e) None of these

167. Which of the following function is performed by the loader?
    (a) Conversion   (b) Relocation
    (c) Binding   (d) All of the above
    (e) None of these

168. The mechanical diskette drive in which you insert your diskette is connected to the computer's—bus
    (a) Data   (b) Communication
    (c) Address   (d) Parallel
    (e) None of these

169. An important application of cryptography, used in computerized commercial and financial transaction —
    (a) Data mining   (b) Data warehousing
    (c) Digital signature   (d) Media convergence
    (e) None of these

170. Which uses a Pre-Shared Key that is more than 7 and less than 64 characters in length?
    (a) WPA-PSK   (b) TKIP
    (c) AES   (d) All of the above
    (e) None of these

171. Which of the following is a service not supported by the operating system?
    (a) Protection   (b) Accounting
    (c) Compilation   (d) I/O operation
    (e) None of these

172. Multilevel feedback queue scheduling
    (a) allows to select a process and load it to memory for execution
    (b) allows to select a process, that are ready to execute and allows CPU to one of them.
    (c) does not allow a process to move between queues
    (d) allows processes which are permanently assigned to a queue on the entry to the system.
    (e) None of these

173. Which of the following is correct?
    (a) An SQL query automatically eliminates duplicates
    (b) An SQL query will not work if there are no indexes on the relations
    (c) SQL permits attribute names to be repeated in the same relation
    (d) None of these
    (e) All of the above

174. Which of the following statement manages the changes made by DML statements?
    (a) SELECT   (b) UPDATE
    (c) DELETE   (d) COMMIT
    (e) None of these

175. The design tool used to illustrate the logic of a new computer software logic diagram that uses symbols to represent program elements is called a (n)
    (a) data logic chart   (b) dataflow diagram
    (c) software logic diagram (d) system flowchart
    (e) entity relationship illustration

176. The UML designation for a public class member is
    (a) the symbol @   (b) the symbol #
    (c) the minus symbol (–) (d) the plus symbol (+)
    (e) the word public

177. Which of the following statements mentioning the name of the array begins DOES NOT yield the base address?
    1. When array name is used with the sizeof operator.
    2. When array name is operand of the & operator.
    3. When array name is passed to scanf() function.
    4. When array name is passed to printf() function.
    (a) 1   (b) 1, 2
    (c) 2   (d) 2, 4
    (e) 1, 2, 3, 4

178. What is the output of the following 'C' fragment? for (i = 1 , j = 10; i<6; i++, - - j)
printf ("%d%d", i.j);
    (a) 11 0 29 38 47 56   (b) 12 345 109876
    (c) 11 11 199999   (d) All of the above
    (e) None of these

179. Which circuit is generated from D-flipflop due to addition of an inverter by causing reduction in the number of inputs?
    (a) Gated JK- latch   (b) Gated SR- latch
    (c) Gated T- latch   (d) Gated D- latch
    (e) None of these

180. An IC contains 50 gates each of which consists of 6 components. Its belongs to
    (a) VLSI   (b) LSI
    (c) MSI   (d) SSI
    (e) None of these

181. Which are not used in case of applet?
    (a) Read/write   (b) Internet
    (c) Search engine   (d) All of the above
    (e) None of these

182. Which one of the following objects is passed to a JavaBean when one of its properties is set via a JSP action?
(a) ServletRequest   (b) HttpServletRequest
(c) ServeletResponse   (d) HttpServeletResponse
(e) None of these

183. Each array declaration need not give, implicitly or explicitly, the information about
(a) the name of array
(b) the data type of array
(c) the first data from the set to be stored
(d) the index set of the array
(e) None of these

184. The indirect change of the values of a variable in one module by another module is called
(a) internal change   (b) inter-module change
(c) side effect   (d) side-module update
(e) None of these

185. In which of the following sorting algorithm, the number of comparison needed is the minimum if the items are initially in reverse order and is the maximum if the times are in order?
(a) Straight insertion sort (b) Binary insertion sort
(c) Heap sort   (d) Bubble sort
(e) None of these

186. This _____ data mining technique derives rules from real world case examples.
(a) Waterfall model   (b) RAD
(c) White Box   (d) Spiral model
(e) Case based reasoning

187. From what location are the 1st computer instructions available on boot up ?
(a) ROM BIOS   (b) CPU
(c) Boot.ini   (d) CONFIG.SYS
(e) None of these

188. In Internet protocol stack, when data is sent from device A to device B, the 5th layer to receive data at B is
(a) Application layer   (b) Transport layer
(c) Link layer   (d) Session layer
(e) None of these

189. An implementation of a queue Q, using two stacks S1 and S2 is given below
```
void insert (Q, x) { push (S1, x);}
void delete (Q) {if (stack-empty (S2)) then
if (stack-empty (S1)) then {print ("Q is empty");
return;}
else while (! (stack-empty (S1)))
{x = pop (S1); push (S2, x);}
x = pop (S2);}
```
Let n insert and m($£$ n) delete operations be performed in an arbitrary order on an empty queue Q. Let x and y be the number of push and pop operations performed respectively in the process. Which one of the following is true for all m and n?

(a) $n + m \leq x < 2n$ and $2m \leq y \leq n + m$

(b) $n + m \leq x \leq 2n$ and $2m \leq y \leq 2n$

(c) $2m \leq x < 2n$ and $2m \leq y \leq n + m$

(d) $2m \leq x < 2n$ and $2m \leq y \leq 2n$

(e) None of these

190. In what kind of storage structure for strings, one can easily insert, delete, concatenate and rearrange substrings?
(a) Fixed length storage structure
(b) Variable length storage with fixed maximum
(c) Linked list storage
(d) Array type storage
(e) None of these

191. Ethernet uses how many bit/byte physical address, that is imprinted on the network interface card?
(a) 64 bit   (b) 64 byte   (c) 6 bit
(d) 6 byte   (e) 32 bit

192. Which class of IP address provides a maximum of only 254 host addresses per network ID?
(a) A Class   (b) B Class   (c) C Class
(d) D Class   (e) E Class

193. Which of the following is the process of splitting a message into multiple packets at transport layer?
(a) Fragmentation   (b) Segmentation
(c) Synchronization   (d) Defragmentation
(e) Framing

194. In which type of SQL join returns all the rows from left table combine with the matching rows of the right table?
(a) Inner join   (b) Left outer join
(c) Right outer join   (d) Full join
(e) Self join

195. By which of the following statements, we can undo all the updates performed on the transaction?
(a) Undo   (b) Commit
(c) Rollback   (d) Replace
(e) Reverse

196. Which feature in Object Oriented Programming allows reusing code?
(a) Polymorphism   (b) Inheritance
(c) Encapsulation   (d) Data hiding
(e) Recursion

197. Amazon Web Services is which type of cloud computing distribution model?
(a) Software as a service
(b) Platform as a service
(c) Infrastructure as a service
(d) Communication as a service
(e) None of these

198. Which level of testing is evaluating the software/system compatibly with the business requirements?
(a) Integration testing   (b) System testing
(c) Acceptance testing   (d) Unit Testing
(e) Evaluation Testing

199. A direct Memory Access (DMA) transfer implies:
(a) Direct transfer of data between memory and accumulator
(b) Direct transfer of data between memory and I/O device without the use of microprocessor
(c) Transfer of data exclusively within microprocessor registers
(d) A fast transfer of data between microprocessor and I/O devices
(e) None of these

200. Banker's Algorithm is used for:
(a) Deadlock Detection   (b) Deadlock Prevention
(c) Deadlock Avoidance   (d) Page Scheduling
(e) CPU Scheduling

HINTS & EXPLANATIONS

1. (d)

School	Number of Girls	Number of Boys
P	1000	1500
Q	1350	1650
R	550	1450
S	675	1575
T	500	750
U	175	825

Number of boys in schools R and U together
$= (1450 + 825) = 2275$

$\therefore$ Required percentage $= \dfrac{2275}{3000} \times 100 = 75.83$

2. (c) Number of boys in school T = 750

3. (a) Required percentage $= \dfrac{2000}{2250} \times 100 = 89$

4. (b) Required average $= \dfrac{1}{2}(1500 + 1650) = 1575$

5. (c) Required ratio $= 20 : 27$

(6-10):

Number of students in the college = 7200

Number of boys $= \dfrac{7}{12} \times 7200 = 4200$

Number of girls $= \dfrac{5}{12} \times 7200 = 3000$

Number of student in B. Tech. (nano technology)
$= 22\%$ of $7200 = 1584$

Number of girls in B. Tech. (computer science)
$= 16\%$ of $3000 = 480$

Number of boys in B.Tech. (mechanical) $= 18\%$ of $4200 = 756$

Number of girls in B.Tech. (civil) $= 30\%$ of $480 = 144$

Number of boys in B.Tech. (electronics) $= 15\%$ of $4200 = 630$

Number of boys in B.Tech. (computer science) $= 50\%$ of $480 = 240$

Number of girls in B.Tech. (aerospace) $= 15\%$ of $3000 = 4500$

Number of boys in B.Tech. (civil) $= \dfrac{3}{1} \times 144 = 432$

Number of students in B.Tech (electronics) $= 24\%$ of $7200 = 1728$

$\therefore$ Number of girls in B.Tech. (electronics) $= 1728 - 630 = 1098$

Number of boys in B.Tech. (aerospace) $= \dfrac{12}{5} \times 450 = 1080$

Number of boys in B.Tech. (nano technology) = Remaining
Number of boys $= 4200 - (756 + 630 + 240 + 432 + 1080)$
$= 4200 - 3138 = 1062$

$\therefore$ Number of girls in B.Tech. (nano technology)
$= 1584 - 1062 = 522$

Number of girls in B.Tech. (mechanical) = Remaining
Number of girls $= 3000 - (480 + 144 + 450 + 1098 + 522) = 3000 - 2694 = 306$
Tabular form of above information is shown below.

Subjects	Number of boys	Number of girls
B.Tech. (computer science)	240	480
B.Tech. (mechanical)	756	306
B.Tech. (civil)	432	144
B.Tech. (electronics)	630	1098
B.Tech. (aerospace)	1080	450
B.Tech. (nano technology)	1062	522
Total	4200	3000

6. (a) From the table, it is clear that total number of students enrolled in B.Tech. (meachanical)

7. (c) Number of girls enrolled in B.Tech. (electronics) = 1098

$\therefore$ Required percentage $= \dfrac{1098}{7200} \times 100\%$

$= 15.25\% \simeq 15\%$

8. (e) Number of girls enrolled in B.Tech. (nano technology) $= 522$

9. (d) Number of boys enrolled in B.Tech. (aerospace) = 1080
Number of girls enrolled in B.Tech. (computer science) $= 480$

$\therefore$ Required percentage $= \dfrac{1080}{480} \times 100\% = 225\%$

10. (b) Total number of boys enrolled in B.Tech. (civil) = 432

11. (a) Net effect $= x + y + \dfrac{xy}{100} = -20 + 80 + \dfrac{(-20 \times 80)}{100}$
$= 60 - 16 = 44\%$ increase

12. (e) I. $\Rightarrow p^2 + 3p + 2p + 6 = 0$
$\Rightarrow p(p+3) + 2(p+3) = 0$
$\Rightarrow (p+3)(p+2) = 0$
$\Rightarrow p = -2 \text{ or } -3$
II. $\Rightarrow q^2 + q + 2q + 2 = 0$
$\Rightarrow q(q+1) + 2(q+1) = 0$
$\Rightarrow (q+1) + (q+2) = 0$
$\Rightarrow q = -1 \text{ or } -2$
Obviously $p \le q$

13. (d) I. $\Rightarrow p = \pm 2$
II. $\Rightarrow q^2 + 2q + 2q + 4 = 0$
$\Rightarrow q(q+2) + 2(q+2) = 0$
$\Rightarrow (q+2) + (q+2) = 0$
$\Rightarrow q = -2$
Obviously $p \ge q$

14. (b) I. $p^2 + p - 56 = 0$
$\Rightarrow p^2 + 8p - 7p - 56 = 0$
$\Rightarrow p(p+8) - 7(p+8) = 0$
$\Rightarrow (p+8)(p-7) = 0$
$\Rightarrow p = 7 \text{ or } -8$
II. $q^2 - 8q - 9q + 72 = 0$
$\Rightarrow q(q-8) - 9(q-8) = 0$
$\Rightarrow (q-8)(q-9) = 0$
$\Rightarrow q = 8 \text{ or } 9$

Obviously $p < q$

15. (a) We have,

$3p + 2q = 58$ ...(i)

$4p + 4q = 92$

$\Rightarrow 2p + 2q = 46$ ...(ii)

By (i), (ii) we get $p = 12$

From (i), $3 \times 12 + 2q = 58$

$\Rightarrow 2q = 58 - 36 = 22$

$\Rightarrow q = 11$

Hence, $p > q$

16. (b) I. $\Rightarrow 3p^2 + 15p + 2p + 10 = 0$

$\Rightarrow 3p(p + 5) + 2(p + 5) = 0$

$\Rightarrow (p + 5)(3p + 2) = 0$

$p = -5 \text{ or } -\dfrac{2}{3}$

II. $\Rightarrow 10q^2 + 5q + 4q + 2 = 0$

$\Rightarrow 5q(2q + 1) + 2(2q + 1) = 0$

$\Rightarrow (2q + 1)(5q + 2) = 0$

$\Rightarrow q = -\dfrac{1}{2} \text{ or } -\dfrac{2}{5}$

Hence, $p < q$

17. (d) Let the capacity of the tank be C

Speed of inlet tap = C/16

Speed of outlet tap = C/8

Difference in speed = C/8 – C/16 = C/16 hours

Time to empty 3/4$^\text{th}$ of the tank = (3C/4) / C/16 = 3C/4 × 16/C = 12 hours

18. (c) According to question,

12% of the salary is add in PPF.

Remaining part = (100 – 12) = 88%

Amount spent on clothes = $\dfrac{3}{8} \times 88 = 33\%$

Difference between PPF and cloth expanses

= (33 – 12) = 21%

$\because$ 21% of salary = 21,000

$\therefore$ Total salary = 100000

Other expanses = House rent expanses + 3000.

House rent expanses + other expanses

= (100 – 33 – 12)% = 55%

$\therefore$ 55% of salary = 55000

House rent expanses + House expanses + 3000

= 55000

2 × House rent expanses = 55,000 – 3000 = 52,000

$\therefore$ House rent expanses = $\dfrac{52,000}{2} = 26,000$

19. (a)

30   40

x

40–x   x–30

(40 – x) / (x – 30) = 4/7

280 – 7x = 4x – 120

$11x = 400 \Rightarrow x = 36.36$

20. (b) Number of employees in design, customer relation and HR departments together

$4500 \times (32 + 22 + 8)\%$

$= \dfrac{4500 \times 62}{100} = 2790$

Number of women employees in these departments

$= 2000 \times (28 + 20 + 16)\%$

$= \dfrac{2000 \times 64}{100} = 1280$

$\therefore$ Required number of males

= 2790 – 1280 = 1510

21. (c) Number of employees in HR department

$= \dfrac{4500 \times 8}{100} = 360$

$\therefore$ Number of males

$= 360 - \dfrac{2000 \times 16}{100} = 360 - 320 = 40$

Number of employeess in Accounts department

$= \dfrac{4500 \times 12}{100} = 540$

$\therefore$ Number of males

$= 540 - \dfrac{2000 \times 12}{100} = 540 - 240 = 300$

$\therefore$ Required ratio = 40 : 300 = 2 : 15

22. (e) Number of employees in marketing and customer relation departments

$= \dfrac{4500 \times 40}{100} = 1800$

Number of females in the marketing department

$= \dfrac{2000 \times 14}{100} = 280$

$\therefore$ Required percentage = $\dfrac{280}{1800} \times 100 \approx 16$

23. (a) Total number of employees in administrative department $= \dfrac{4500 \times 8}{100} = 360$

Number of males in the same department

= 360 – 200 = 160

$\therefore$ Required ratio = 360 : 160 = 9 : 4

24. (c) Required percentage $= \dfrac{2000}{2500} \times 100 = 80$

25. (d) Total age of son and mother

$2x + 7x = 2 \times 27$

$9x = 54$

$x = 6$

$\therefore$ Mother's age after 7 yr = 7x + 7 = 7 × 6 + 7 = 49 yr

26. (b) Required ways = 7! = 7 × 6 × 5 × 3 × 2 × 1 = 5040

27. (d) Let S_1 and S_2 be the speed of train A and B respectively Time taken by both the trains in crossing each other.

$$\frac{450}{S_1+S_2}=12,\ S_1+S_2=37.5$$

S_1 and S_2 can have so many values. Both statement I and II are not sufficient to find speed of train B.

28. (d) Area of rectangle = Area of triangle.
From the information given in both the statements, we can find area of triangle or area of rectangle. For finding length, breadth is required, which is not known.

29. (c) From the statement I.

$$r=\frac{100\times100}{1000}=10\%$$

Thus we have,
$P=\text{₹ }1000,\ r=10\%,\ t=3\ \text{years}$
Hence, C.I. can be determined
From the statement II.

$$\text{S.I.}=\frac{1000\times r\times2}{100}=20r$$

$$\text{C.I.}=1000\left[\left(1+\frac{r}{100}\right)^2-1\right]$$

$\therefore$ C.I. $-$ S.I.

$$=1000\left[\frac{200r+r^2}{10000}\right]-20r$$

$\Rightarrow\ 2000r+r^2-200r=100$
$\Rightarrow\ r=10$
Hence, C.I. can be determined

30. (e) Let the unit's digit be x and ten's digit be y and $x<y$.
$\therefore$ Number $=10y+x$
From statement I,
$y-x=5$ ... (i)
From statement II,
$y+x=7$ ... (ii)
From (i) and (ii), x, y can be calculated and two digit number can be found.

31. (d) Let the distance between A and B be z km.
Again, let speed of boat in still water be x kmph and that of stream be y kmph.
$\therefore$ Rate downstream $=(x+y)$ kmph
Rate upstream $=(x-y)$ kmph
From statement I,

$$\frac{z}{x+y}=2$$ ... (i)

From statement II,

$$\frac{z}{x-y}=4$$ ... (ii)

we have two equations and three variables, therefore both equations are not sufficient.

32. (b) $L\times B\times2=48$
$\Rightarrow L\times B=24$
Now, $6-6\times10\%=5.4,$
$5-5\times10\%=4.5$ and
Therefore, $5.4\times4.5=24.3$
Clearly, $5<L<5.5$

33. (c) Required ratio
$=(234+350+124):(120+234+334)$
$=708:688=177:172$

34. (a) Number of males in bank D from all the cities together
$=534+478+235+255+124+358=1984$
Number of females in the same bank
$=454+285+235+175+165+234=1548$
$\therefore$ Required ratio $=1984:1548=496:387$

35. (a) Number of males in all banks in Delhi
$=254+346+366+478+256+346=2046$
Number of females in the same city
$=456+256+345+285+166+287=1795$
$\therefore$ Required percentage

$$=\frac{1795}{2046}\times100\approx\frac{1800}{2000}\times100\approx90$$

$\therefore$ Required answer $=88$

36. (b) Required percentage $=\dfrac{116}{500}\times100=23.2$

37. (b) Required average

$$=\frac{353+348+399+358+125+278}{6}$$

$$=\frac{1861}{6}\approx310$$

38. (a) $1M=2W$
$(8M+4W)\times(6\ \text{days}-2\ \text{days})=(4M+8W)\times x\ \text{days}$
$(8\times2W+4W)\times(6-2)\ \text{days}$
$\qquad=(4\times2W+8W)\times x\ \text{days}$
$(16+4)W\times4\ \text{days}=16W\times x\ \text{days}$

$$\therefore\ \ x=\frac{20\times4}{16}=5\ \text{days}\ [M_1D_1=M_2D_2]$$

39. (a) Total number of ways of selecting 4 children out of 8

$$={}^8C_4=\frac{8\times7\times6\times5}{1\times2\times3\times4}=70$$

Number of ways of selecting 4 girls out of $5={}^5C_4=5$

Required probability $=\dfrac{5}{70}=\dfrac{1}{14}$

40. (b) Distance covered along the stream = 3d
Distance covered against the stream = 2d
Let speed of boat in still water = x km/hr
Let speed of current = y km/hr

$$\therefore\quad \frac{21}{x+y}=\frac{7}{5}$$

$x+y=15$ ...(i)

$$\text{And}\ \frac{3d}{(x+y)}=\frac{90}{100}\times\frac{2d}{x-y}$$

$x-y=9$ ....(ii)
$\therefore x=12$
$y=3$
$\therefore$ Rate of current = 3 km/hr

41. (e) Both the assumptions are implicit because daily newspapers provide instant reach. Again 100 vacancies of Chartered Accountants were announced assuming sufficient eligible candidates may join the nationalised bank."

42. (a) Only assumption I is implicit because repairing of roads is carried out so efficiently to leave potholes. Assumption II is not implicit because it is people's right to complain against any pothole.

43. (e) Both the assumption are implicit because main consideration for people is cost factor. People would prefer foreign destination at competitive prices. Advertisement provides sufficient information on this.

44. (b) Only assumption II is implicit because customers prefer to buy vegetables from retail vondors as there is a lot of innovation in retail sector.

45. (b) Only assumption II is implicit because college authority cannot admit all those standing in the queue.

Sol. (46-50):

Input	32	proud	girl	beautiful	48	55	97	rich	family	61	72	17	nice	life
Step I	beautiful	17	32	proud	girl	48	55	97	rich	family	61	72	nice	life
Step II	family	32	beautiful	17	proud	girl	48	55	97	rich	61	72	nice	life
Step III	girl	48	family	32	beautiful	17	proud	55	97	rich	61	72	nice	life
Step IV	life	55	girl	48	family	32	beautiful	17	proud	97	rich	61	72	nice
Step V	nice	61	life	55	girl	48	family	32	beautiful	17	proud	97	rich	72
Step VI	proud	72	nice	61	life	55	girl	48	family	32	beautiful	17	97	rich
Step VII	rich	97	proud	72	nice	61	life	55	girl	48	family	32	beautiful	17

46. (c) 47. (d) 48. (c) 49. (a) 50. (b)

51. (b) I. $P \leftrightarrow N \rightleftharpoons K^+$
     (+) (−) J

Using I only, we cannot determine if J is the nephew or niece of K.

II. $P \leftrightarrow N \rightleftharpoons K^+$
     (+) (−) J (+)

J is the nephew of K.

52. (a) I. Using I only, we can determine that G stays on 4th floor.

53. (e) I. Raju can take 4 to 8 days to complete the work.
II. Raju can take 8 to 10 days to complete the work.
Using both the statements together we can determine that Raju took 8 days to complete the work.

54. (c)

55. (d) Even by using both the statements together we cannot determine whether B has highest number of student or D.

Sol. (56-60) :

Boys	Bank	Married to	Girls	Bank	Married to
J	SBI	S	P	CBI	K
K	PNB	P	Q	UBI	N
L	BOM	R	R	BOB	L
M	BOI	T	S	IDBI	J
N	IOB	Q	T	OBC	M

56. (a) 57. (c) 58. (a) 59. (d) 60. (d)

Sol. (61-65) :

Q(−) T(−) R(+) S(−) V(+) P(+) U(+) W(+) X(+)

61. (a) 62. (d) 63. (a) 64. (b) 65. (c)

Sol. (66-71) :

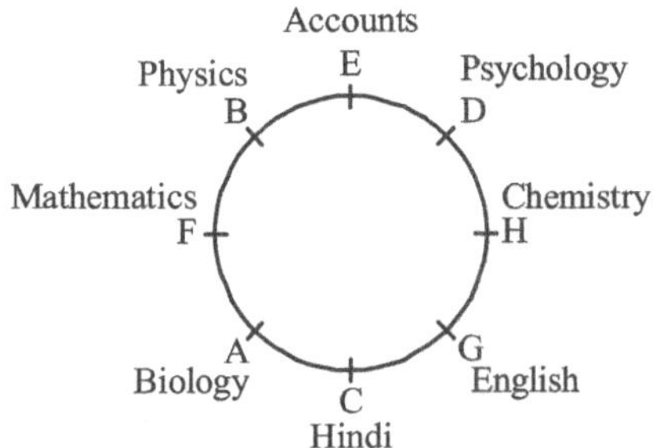

66. (b) H teaches Chemistry.

67. (d) D teaches Psychology. B is second to the right of D.

68. (a) A teaches Biology and B teaches Physics. F, who teaches Mathematics is exactly between A and B.

69. (c) E teaches Accounts.

70. (b) The person who teaches Hindi is C and C is an immediate neighbour of A and G.
Immediate neighbours of F are A and B. A teaches Biology.
E is sitting exactly between B and D, who teaches Accounts.
H teaches Chemistry and H is second to the left of E.

71. (e) Except in the pair BA, in all others the first person is second to the right of the second person. In BA, the first person is second to the left of the second person.

72. (a)

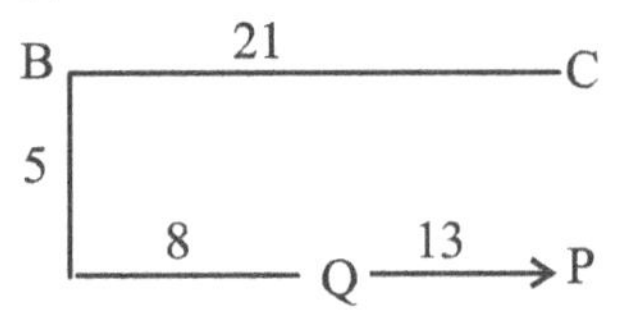

Sidharth travels 5 km towards South to reach Pole P.

73. (b)

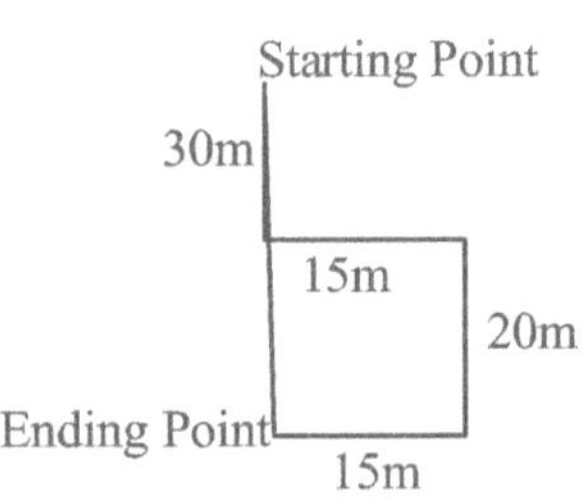

74. (d)

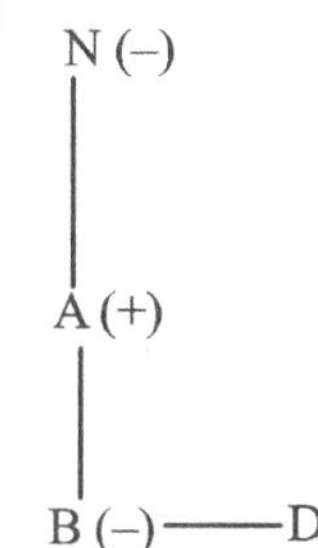

Data is not sufficient. So can't be determined.

75. (c)　76. (a)

77. (d)

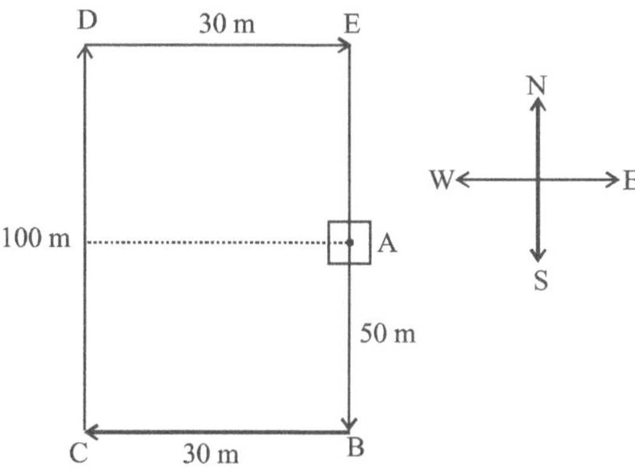

Required distance = (BE – AB) = (100 – 50) m = 50 m
Direction ⇒ North

78. (a)

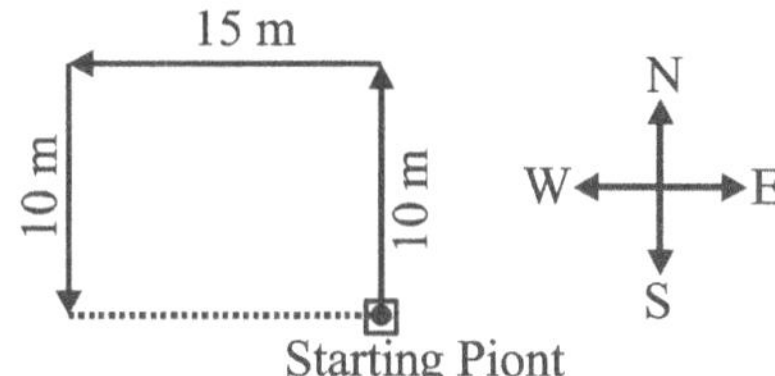

79. (a)　All the three causes will effect the sales of four wheelers.

80. (c)　(A) would not be effective step as it will create a lots of problems to others. Steps (B) and (C) will encourage in favour of the girl child.

81. (b)　82. (b)　83. (a)　84. (c)　85. (a)　86. (b)
87. (a)　88. (c)　89. (a)　90. (d)　91. (a)　92. (b)
93. (a)　The State Bank of India works as RBI's agent at places where it has no office of its own.

94. (d)　The Reserve Bank of India, as the central bank of the country, regulates the flow of credit.

95. (d)　96. (c)　97. (a)　98. (d)　99. (a)　100. (a)
101. (c)　iwatch' is a mobile app; available on the apple watch launched by the HDFC bank in April 2015.

102. (b)　Explanation: Forex Reserve is the short form of Foreign Exchange Reserve which is the collection of foreign currency.

103. (a)　104. (b)　105. (c)　106. (d)　107. (d)　108. (c)
109. (d)　110. (a)　111. (c)　112. (d)
113. (d)　Agriculture is the pillar of the Indian economy because of its high share in employment and livelihood creation.

114. (c)　Food grains consist of cereals and pulses. Rice, wheat, jowar, bajra, maize, etc. are included among the cereals whereas gram, moong, masur, arhar, etc. are included among the pulses.

115. (d)　To encourage employees to refer friends and relatives for employment in the organization, employee referral scheme is implemented in several companies.

116. (b)　KCC scheme was introduced in the Banks in August 1998. The aim of Kisan Credit Card Scheme (KCC) is to provide adequate and timely support from the banking system to the farmers for their short-term credit needs during their cultivation for purchase of inputs etc., during the cropping season.

117. (b)　118. (c)
119. (d)　Any corporate (entity registered as a company under the Companies Act, 1956/ 2013) or body corporate (entity specially created out of a specific act of the Parliament) and Indian banks are eligible to issue Rupee denominated bonds overseas. Real Estate Investment Trusts (REITs) and Infrastructure Investment Trusts (InvITs) coming under the regulatory jurisdiction of the Securities and Exchange Board of India (SEBI) are also eligible.

120. (c)　The minimum maturity period for Masala Bonds raised up to USD 50 million equivalent in INR per financial year should be 3 years.

ENGLISH LANGUAGE

121. (b)　Man gave up his nomadic type of life after he took to agriculture.

122. (e)　plenty of fertile land and water

123. (e)　There was boost in agriculture production which helped generate other jobs useful to the society.

124. (a)　125. (c)　126. (d)　127. (b)　128. (a)　129. (a)
130. (a)
131. (a)　Substitute 'between' for 'among'
132. (b)　Substitute 'undergone' for 'underwent'
133. (b)　Substitute 'detailed' for 'detail'
134. (c)　Substitute 'at least' for 'at less'
135. (a)　Remove 'no'.
136. (a)　Here subject (tractor sales) is plural. Hence, ... tractor sales **have** seen .... should be used.
137. (b)　Delete 'form'
138. (c)　See **a** revival.
139. (b)　conducive ; the other words do not fit in correctly
140. (d)　question
141. (a)　cannot fits correctly
142. (c)　need
143. (e)　growth
144. (c)　favour
145. (b)　enjoys
146. (a)　Sentence F is first (correct sequence- F,C,A,E,D,B)
147. (a)　A is the third sentence
148. (d)　Sentence B will be the correct answer.
149. (c)　150. (b)
151. (c)　'Relevant, obscure' fits the two blank most appropriately.
Relevant means closely connected or appropriate to what is being done or considered while **obscure** means not discovered or known about; uncertain.

152. (b) 'Efficacy, regimens' fits the two blank most appropriately.

Efficacy means the ability to produce a desired or intended result.

Regimen means a prescribed course of medical treatment, diet, or exercise for the promotion or restoration of health.

153. (a) 'Transition, enervating' fits the two blank most appropriately.

Transition means the process or a period of changing from one state or condition to another.

Enervating means make (someone) feel drained of energy or vitality.

154. (b) 'Discrepancy, explanation' fits the two blank most appropriately.

Discrepancy means an illogical or surprising lack of compatibility or similarity between two or more facts

155. (e) 'preside, overwhelmingly' fits the two blank most appropriately. **Preside** means be in the position of authority in a meeting or other gathering. **Overwhelmingly** means to a very great degree or with a great majority.

156. (c) The word **Nascent (Adjective)** means: beginning to exist; not yet fully developed.

The word **nascent** and **emerging** are synonymous.

157. (a) The word **Eccentric (Adjective)** means: considered by other people to be strange or unusual.

The word **eccentric** and **abnormal** are synonymous.

158. (e) The word **Plethora (Noun)** means: an amount that is greater than is needed; excess.

The word **Abundance (Noun)** means: a large quantity that is more than enough.

159. (a) The word **Inadvertently (Adverb)** means: unintentionally; without intending to; by accident.

The word **purposefully** and **inadvertently** are antonymous.

160. The word **Germane (Adjective)** means: connected with something in an important or appropriate ways; relevant.

The word **germane** and **irrelevant** are antonymous.

HINDI LANGUAGE

121. (d)	122. (c)	123 (d)	124. (b)	125. (a)	126. (b)
127. (d)	128. (b)	129. (b)	130. (a)	131. (c)	132. (a)
133. (e)	134. (d)	135. (b)	136. (c)	137. (d)	138. (c)
139. (d)	140. (c)				

141. (d) भोगी के स्थान पर 'भागी' होगा।

142. (a) 'निस्संकोचपूर्वक' के स्थान पर 'दावे के साथ' होगा।

143. (a) 'समाप्त' के स्थान पर 'सम्पन्न' होगा।

144. (a) 'दयालु' का प्रयोग अनावश्यक है।

145. (b) 'अपनी' का प्रयोग अनावश्यक है।

146. (d)	147. (a)	148. (c)	149. (a)	150. (b)	151. (b)
152. (d)	153. (c)	154. (a)	155. (d)	156. (e)	157. (c)
158. (a)	159. (b)	160. (e)			
161. (d)	162. (b)	163. (c)	164. (d)	165. (b)	166. (d)
167. (b)	168. (b)	169. (c)	170. (d)	171. (c)	172. (d)
173. (d)	174. (d)	175. (d)	176. (d)	177. (b)	178. (b)
179. (c)	180. (c)	181. (a)	182. (b)	183. (c)	184. (c)
185. (b)	186. (e)	187. (a)	188. (a)	189. (a)	190. (c)
191. (d)	192. (c)	193. (b)	194. (b)	195. (c)	196. (b)
197. (c)	198. (c)	199. (b)	200. (c)		

PRACTICE SET 19

Time : 120 Min.   Max. Marks : 200

QUANTITATIVE APTITUDE

DIRECTIONS (Qs. 1-4): In the given questions, two equations numbered I and /I are given. Solve both the equations and mark the appropriate answer.

(a) $x > y$ (b) $x \geq y$ (c) $x < Y$
(d)   Relationship between x and y cannot be determined
(e) $x \leq y$

1.   I. $6x^2 + 25x + 24 = 0$ II. $12y^2 + 13y + 3 = 0$
2.   I. $12x^2 - x - 1 = 0$ II. $20y^2 - 41y + 20 = 0$
3.   I. $10x^2 + 33x + 27 = 0$ II. $5y^2 + 19y + 18 = 0$
4.   I. $15x^2 - 29x - 14 = 0$ II. $6y^2 - 5y - 25 = 0$
5.   I. $3x^2 - 22x + 7 = 0$ II. $y^2 - 20y + 91 = 0$

6.   The sum of the ages of 4 members of a family 5 years ago was 94 years. Today, when the daughter has been married off and replaced by a daughter-in-law, the sum of their ages is 92. Assuming that there has been no other change in the family structure and all the people are alive, what is the difference in the age of the daughter and the daughter-in-law ?

    (a)   22 years   (b)   11 years   (c)   25 years
    (d)   19 years   (e)   15 years

7.   A started with an investment of ₹ 28000. After 2 months, B joins with ₹ 20000 and after another two months C joins with ₹ 18000. At the end of 10th month from start of the business, if B withdraws ₹ 2000 and C withdraws ₹ 2000 what is the respective ratio in which profit should be distributed among A, B and C at the end of the year?

    (a) $12 : 7 : 5$ (b) $12 : 9 : 5$ (c) $12 : 6 : 3$
    (d) $14 : 7 : 5$ (e) $11 : 9 : 7$

DIRECTIONS (8-12): The following information is about the production of cars by 3 different companies from Monday to Friday in a specific week. Read the information carefully and answer the following question:

The total production by 3 companies on Monday was 540 out of which 100/3% cars were produced by Tata. The number of cars produced by Renault on Monday is less than the cars produced by Tata on Monday by the same extent as the number of cars produced by Maruti on Monday is more than the cars produced by Tata on Monday. The difference between cars produced by Renault and Maruti on Monday is 40. 150 cars are produced by Tata on Tuesday, which is 100 less than the cars produced by the same company on Wednesday. A total of 910 cars were produced by Tata from Monday to Friday. The ratio between cars produced by Tata on Thursday to cars produced by the same company on Friday is 5 : 6. 220 cars were produced by Renault on Tuesday, which is 80 less than the cars produced by Maruti on Wednesday. A total of 570 cars were produced on Tuesday, which is 76% of the total cars produced on Wednesday. The number of cars produced by Maruti on Thursday is 200/3% more than cars produced by Tata on the same day. Total 580 cars were produced on Thursday. The number of cars produced by Maruti on Friday is same as that on Monday. 140 cars were produced by Renault on Friday.

8.   Find the ratio between total cars produced on Monday to that on Wednesday.
    (a) $18 : 29$ (b) $18 : 25$ (c) $18 : 31$
    (d) $3 : 5$ (e)   None of these

9.   Find the total number of cars produced by Renault from Monday to Friday.
    (a)   900   (b)   980   (c)   950
    (d)   960   (e)   None of these

10.   Find the average number of cars produced per day by Maruti from Monday to Friday. (approximate)
    (a)   250   (b)   220   (c)   270
    (d)   240   (e)   230

11.   On which pair of days out of the following, the number of cars produced by Tata is the same?
    (a)   Tuesday and Wednesday
    (b)   Wednesday and Thursday
    (c)   Tuesday and Thursday
    (d)   Monday and Wednesday
    (e)   Monday and Tuesday

12.   On which day the total number of cars produced was the maximum?
    (a)   Monday   (b)   Tuesday   (c)   Wednesday
    (d)   Thursday   (e)   Friday

13.   A person lent out a certain sum on simple interest and the same sum on compound interest at certain rate of interest per annum. He noticed that the ratio between the difference of compound interest and simple interest of 3 years and that of 2 years is 25 : 8. The rate of interest per annum is:
    (a)   10%   (b)   11%   (c)   12%
    (d) $12\frac{1}{2}\%$ (e)   None of these

14.   **Quantity I:** Value of 'a' if 's' is an acute angle and PR || QT.

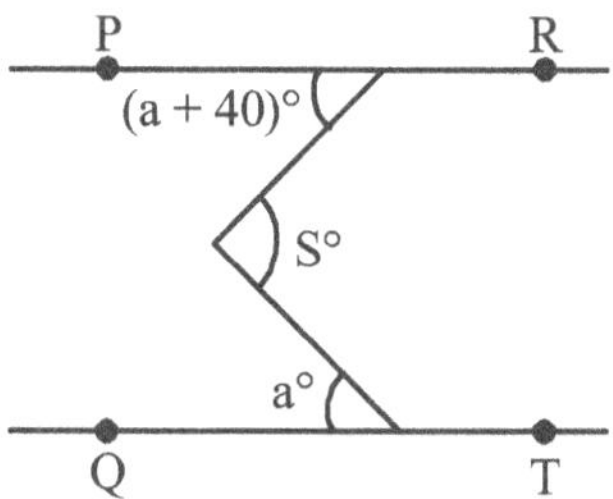

Quantity II : 25°
    (a)   Quantity I > Quantity II   (b)   Quantity I < Quantity II
    (c)   Quantity I ≥ Quantity II   (d)   Quantity I ≤ Quantity II
    (e)   Quantity I = Quantity II or No relation

15. There are 63 cards in a box numbered from 1 to 63. Every card is numbered with only 1 number.

Quantity I : Probability of picking up a card whose digits, if interchanged, result in a number which is 36 more than the number picked up.

Quantity II : Probability of picking up a card, the number printed on which is a multiple of 8 but not that of 16.

(a) Quantity I > Quantity II (b) Quantity I < Quantity II
(c) Quantity I = Quantity II (d) Quantity I = Quantity II
(e) Quantity I = Quantity II or No relation

DIRECTION (Q. 16) : In the following questions consists of 3 statements A, B and C. You have to determine that which of the following statement/statements are necessary to answer the questions:

16. If m and n are integers then is n completely divisible by 10?

A. The value of $\left(\dfrac{m}{10}+\dfrac{n}{10}\right)$ is an integer value.

B. The value of $\left(\dfrac{m}{7}+\dfrac{n}{10}\right)$ is an integer value.

C. value of n is greater than m.

(a) Any two of them
(b) A and B together
(c) Any of them
(d) All statements are required
(e) Data is not sufficient and it requires more information to answer the given question.

17. Quantity I: Area of quadrilateral BFDE, given ABCD is a rectangle having AB = 10 cm & BC = 12 cm.

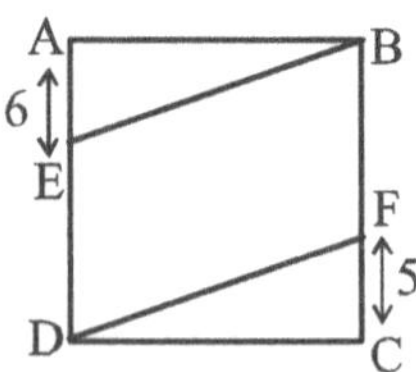

Quantity II : 15cm²

(a) Quantity I > Quantity II (b) Quantity I < Quantity II
(c) Quantity I ≥ Quantity II (d) Quantity I ≤ Quantity II
(e) Quantity I = Quantity II or No relation

18. A, B and C entered into a partnership. A invested ₹ 3000 at the start. B invested $33\dfrac{1}{3}\%$ more than that invested by A and C invested the average of the investment made by A and B. After 4 months, A withdrew 40% of his amount, B doubled his amount and C increased his amount by 20%. After another 5 months, B got away from partnership and A doubled his amount while C maintained his amount. Profit at the end of year was ₹ 677000 and profit was shared in the ratio of their investment and time.

Quantity I: Profit earned by C.

Quantity II: Average of profit earned by A, B and C together.

(a) Quantity I > Quantity II
(b) Quantity I < Quantity II
(c) Quantity I ≥ Quantity II
(d) Quantity I ≤ Quantity II
(e) Quantity I = Quantity II or No relation

19. The metal to be used for covering a cylinder having external radius 5 cm, height 21 cm and thickness 1 cm is to be cast from a cylinder. What should be the height of the cylinder of radius 3 cm from which this casting can be done?
(a) 12 cm   (b) 39 cm   (c) 21 cm
(d) 20 cm   (e) 18 cm

20. An article is marked up 40% higher than CP but it was sold x% on discount. The shopkeeper thus gains 12%. What would be the S.P. of the article with C.P. ₹ 120 and sold on x % profit ?
(a) ₹ 134.50   (b) ₹ 144   (c) ₹ 128
(d) ₹ 148   (e) None of these

21. In how many different ways can the letters of the word 'THERAPY' be arranged so that the vowels never come together ?
(a) 720   (b) 1440   (c) 5040
(d) 3600   (e) 4800

DIRECTIONS (Qs.22-26) : Study the table carefully to answer the questions that follow:

Station Name	Arrival time	Departure time	Halt time (in minutes)	Distance travelled from origin (in km)	No. of Passengers boarding the train at each station
Dadar	Starting point	12.05 am	-	0 km	437
Vasai Road	12.53 am	12.56 am	3 minutes	42 km	378
Surat	4.15 am	4.20 am	5 minutes	257 km	458
Vadodara	6.05 am	6.10 am	5 minutes	386 km	239
Anand Jn.	6.43 am	6.45 am	2 minutes	422 km	290
Nadiad Jn.	7.01 am	7.03 am	2 minutes	440km	132
Ahmedabad	8.00 am	8.20 am	20 minutes	486 km	306
Bhuj	5.40 pm	Ending point	–	977 km	None

22. What is the distance travelled by the train from Surat to Nadiad Jn.?
(a) 176 km   (b) 188 km   (c) 183 km
(d) 193 km   (e) 159 km

23. How much time does the train take to reach Ahmedabad after departing from Anand Jn. (including the halt time)?
(a) 1 hr. 59 min   (b) 1 hr. 17 min.   (c) 1 hr. 47 min.
(d) 1 hr. 45 min.   (e) 1 hr. 15 min.

24. What is the respective ratio between the number of passengers boarding from Vasai Road and from Ahmedabad in the train?
(a) 21 : 17   (b) 13 : 9   (c) 21 : 19
(d) 15 : 13   (e) 13 : 15

25. If halt time (stopping time) of the train at Vadodara is decreased by 2 minutes and increased by 23 minutes at Ahmedabad. At what time will the train reach Bhuj?
(a) 6.10 am   (b) 6.01 pm   (c) 6.05 am
(d) 6.50 pm   (e) 6.07 pm

26. Distance between which two stations is second lowest?
(a) Nadiad Jn. to Ahmedabad
(b) Anand Jn. to Nadiad Jn.
(c) Dadar to Vasai Road
(d) Anand Jn. to Vadodara
(e) Vasai Road to Surat

27. Two pipes A and B can fill a tank in 15 hours and 20 hours respectively while a third pipe C can empty the full tank in 25 hours. All the three pipes are opened in the beginning. After 10 hours, C is closed. Now how much time more is required to fill the tank?
(a) 2 hrs (b) 3 hrs (c) 6 hrs
(d) 1 hr (e) None of these

28. A man is 40% more efficient than a woman, and a child is 40% less efficient than a woman. 3 men, 5 women, and 4 children work for 7 days to complete a job. How many days will 2 men, 7 women and 3 children take to complete the same job?
(a) 4.5 days (b) 5.5 days (c) 6.5 days
(d) 7 days (e) None of the above

DIRECTIONS (Qs. 29-33) : In the following bar diagram the number of engineers employed in various companies has been given. Study the bar diagram carefully to answer the questions.

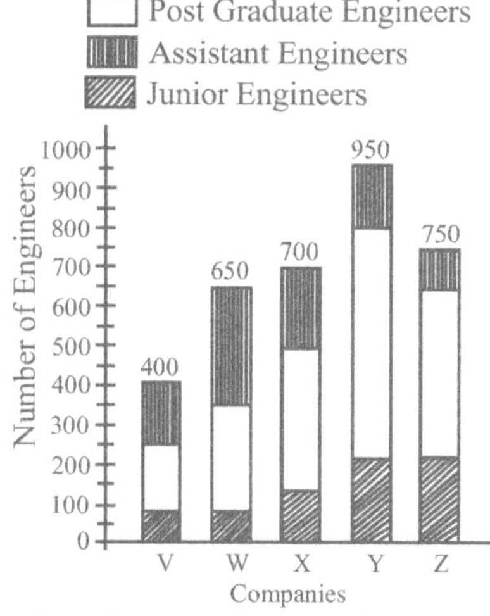

29. The number of post graduate engineers employed in the company W is what per cent of the total engineers employed in that company ?
(a) $33\frac{1}{3}\%$ (b) $30\frac{1}{3}\%$ (c) $25\frac{1}{3}\%$
(d) $36\frac{1}{3}\%$ (e) None of these

30. What is the average number of junior engineers employed in all the companies?
(a) 150 (b) 170 (c) 160
(d) 180 (e) 190

31. What is the difference between the average number of junior engineers and assistant engineers taking all the companies together?
(a) 18 (b) 15 (c) 10
(d) 22 (e) 25

32. If the number of assistant engineers employed in all the companies be increased by 37% and the number of post graduate engineers employed in all the companies b decreased by 20%, by what percent will the number of assistant engineers be less than that of post graduate engineers?

(a) 5.6% (b) 7.8% (c) 8%
(d) 9.3% (e) None of these

33. If the numbers of all the engineers in the company V, company X and company Y be increased by 30%, 35% and 40% respectively, what will be the overall percentage increase in the number of all engineers of all the companies taken together?
(a) 20% (b) 22% (c) 24%
(d) 25% (e) None of these

34. A bag contains 13 white and 7 black balls. Two balls are drawn at random. What is the probability that they are of the same colour ?
(a) $\dfrac{41}{190}$ (b) $\dfrac{21}{190}$ (c) $\dfrac{59}{190}$
(d) $\dfrac{99}{190}$ (e) $\dfrac{77}{190}$

35. Two cities A and B are at a distance of 60 km from each other. Two persons P and Q start from First city at a speed of 10km/hr and 5km/hr respectively. P reached the second city B and returns back and meets Q at Y. Find the distance between A and Y.
(a) 30 km (b) 40 km (c) 50 km
(d) 55 km (e) 53 Km

36. Rakesh adds 12% of his salary in PPF. 3/8 of the remaining salary is spent in clothes. Difference between PPF and clothes expenses is Rs 10500. Remaining in house rent and others. If house rent expenses ins Rs 1500 less than expenses in others, then what is the house rent expense?
(a) 17000 (b) 10000 (c) 9000
(d) 13000 (e) None of these

DIRECTIONS (Qs. 37-40): Study the pie charts given below and answer the following questions.

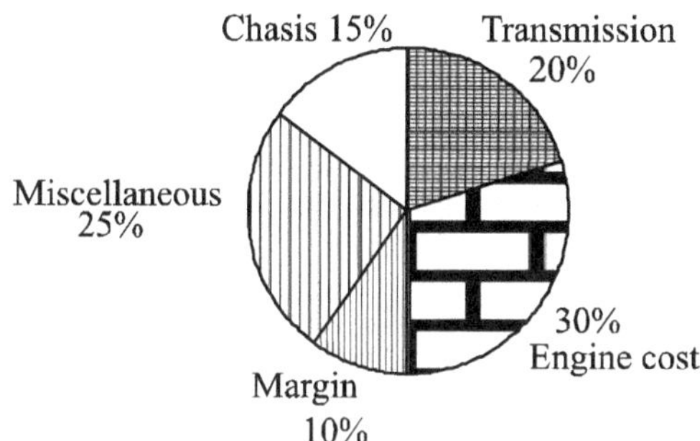

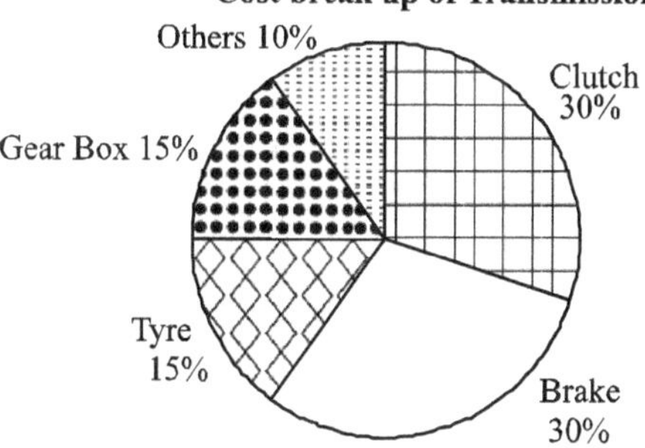

Price of Car = ₹1, 00, 000

37. What is the cost of Gear Box?
(a) ₹9000 (b) ₹6000 (c) ₹3000
(d) ₹15,000 (e) None of these

38. What percentage of total cost is contributed by the brake?
    (a) 5.5%   (b) 6.6%   (c) 6%
    (d) 5.4%   (e) None of these
39. If the price of tyres goes up by 25%, by what amount should be the sale price be increased to maintain the amount of profit?
    (a) ₹750   (b) ₹2250   (c) ₹3750
    (d) ₹375   (e) None of these
40. If transmission cost increases by 20%, by what amount is the profit reduced (total price of car remains same)?
    (a) ₹3000   (b) ₹4000   (c) ₹6000
    (d) Cannot be determined
    (e) None of these

REASONING ABILITY

DIRECTIONS (Qs. 41-45): Read the following statements carefully and answer the questions which follow.

41. The ministry of sports has been advised by a committee to take the highest award in the field of sports back from two players who were allegedly-involved in match fixing.
    Which of the following statements would **weaken** the argument put forward by the committee to the sports ministry?
    (a) A good conduct in the past and a lack of evidence against the players make the case against them very weak.
    (b) The ministry of sports has never declined the recommendations made by the committee earlier.
    (c) Taking the award back from the players would set a good example to other players for avoiding such actions in the future.
    (d) There have been past cases where the award had to be taken back from the players owing to some misconduct later on.
    (e) The committee is constituted of some of the most respected from the fields of sports and politics.
42. Many organizations have been resorting to recruitment based upon performance at graduate post-graduate level exams rather than conducting exams for the same purpose. Which of the following statements would **strengthen** the argument given in the above statement?
    (a) A recent study shows no link of past performance with the performance in recruitment exams.
    (b) The graduate/post-graduate exams are considered to be severely deficient in training in job related environment
    (c) Organisations which had undertaken recruitment on the basis of graduate / post-graduate exams report a significant drop in the quality of the recruited employees.
    (d) Such policies would add to unemployment amongst students having below average performance in graduation or post-graduation.
    (e) Such policies could save time, money and resources of the organisation which are wasted in the conduct of recruitment examinations.
43. According to a recent government directive, all bank branches in rural areas should be computerized.
    Which of the following statements would **weaken** the government's argument?
    (a) Computerisation of bank branches in urban areas has helped in making their performance more efficient and fast.
    (b) Lack of skilled and qualified manpower has been suitably substituted by computers in banks.
    (c) Non-computerised bank branches in the rural areas have been proved to be as efficient as their computerized counterparts.
    (d) The government has introduced a special test for computer knowledge in all recruitment exams for banks.
    (e) Unemployment in the rural areas could be controlled by training more and more professionals in computers.
44. Nations do not complete with each other in the way corporations do.
    Which of the following most favours the weakness of the argument?
    (a) Trade deficit is a sign of national strength, profits are a sign of corporate strength.
    (b) Increase in human development index improves national standing, increase in market share improves corporate standing.
    (c) Climate change negotiations lead to global improvement; CSR initiatives lead to image improvement.
    (d) Nations go to war to capture territory, corporates contend against each other to capture market share.
    (e) None of the above.
45. Civilization has taught us to be friendlier towards one another
    Which of the following most favours the strengthens of the argument?
    (a) Cats are loyal to their children, whereas men are loyal to their communities
    (b) Elephants move in a herd, whereas men live in nuclear families
    (c) Lions protect their own territories, whereas men capture other men's territories
    (d) Nilgai and Cheetal stay together, whereas men of one race dominate another
    (e) None of the above

DIRECTIONS (Qs. 46-50): Study the following information carefully and answer the given question:

A word and number arrangement machine when given an input line of words and numbers rearrange them following a particular rule in each step. The following is an illustration of input and rearrangement. (All the numbers are two-digit numbers).

Input : gate 20 86 just not 71 for 67 38 bake sun 55
Step I : bake gate 20 just not 71 for 67 38 sun 55 86
Step II : for bake gate 20 just not 67 38 sun 55 86 71
Step III : gate for bake 20 just not 38 sun 55 86 71 67
Step IV : just gate for bake 20 not 38 sun 55 86 71 67
Step V : not just gate for bake 20 sun 86 71 67 55 38
Step VI : sun not just gate for bake 86 71 67 55 38 20
Steps VI is the last step of the arrangement the above input.
As per the rule followed in the above steps, find out in each of the following questions the appropriate step for the given input.
Input: 31 rise gem 15 92 47 aim big 25 does 56 not 85 63 with moon
46. How many steps will be required to complete the rearrangement?
    (a) Eight   (b) Six   (c) Seven
    (d) Five   (e) None of these
47. Which words numbers would be at 7th position from the left in step IV?
    (a) rise   (b) aim   (c) big
    (d) 15   (e) 47
48. Which step number is the following output?
    rise not moon gem does big aim 15 with 92 85 63 56 47 31 25
    (a) Step V   (b) Step VII   (c) Step IV
    (d) Step VIII   (e) There is no such step
49. Which of the following represents the position of '92' in step VI?
    (a) Ninth from the left   (b) Fifth from the right
    (c) Sixth from the right   (d) Ninth from the right
    (e) Seventh from the left

50. Which words numbers would be at 5th position from the right in the last step?

   (a) gem   (b) 63   (c) 56
   (d) 85   (e) does

DIRECTIONS (Qs. 51-55): Study the following information carefully and answer the questions given below:

Six friends - Arun, Sathish, Yogesh, Ganesh, Peter and Hemanth are studying six different specialisations of engineering which are - metallurgy, telecommunication, software, mechanical, electrical and hardware not necessarily in the same order. Each one likes a different sport - hockey, cricket, swimming, football, badminton and tennis again not in the same order.
Ganesh is not studying hardware. Peter is studying software and likes hockey. Yogesh likes swimming and is not studying hardware. The one who likes football is studying electrical. Hemanth is studying mechanical and does not like tennis. The one who likes badminton is studying telecommunication. Arun and Sathish do not like badminton. Arun doesnot like tennis.

51. Which specialisation is Sathish studying?

   (a) Metallurgy   (b) Mechanical
   (c) Hardware   (d) Electrical
   (e) None of these

52. Which sport does Arun like?

   (a) Football   (b) Cricket
   (c) Hockey   (d) Cannot be determined
   (d) None of these

53. Which of the following person-specialization combination is correct according to the given information?

   (a) Ganesh-Hardware   (b) Sathish-Electrical
   (c) Yogesh-Metallurgy   (d) Hemanth-Software
   (e) None is correct

54. If all six friends are asked to sit in a straight line, facing north, in an alphabetical order (according to their names), from left to right, then who will be to the immediate left of the one studying electrical?

   (a) The one who likes badminton
   (b) The one who is studying telecommunication
   (c) The one who is studying hardware
   (d) The one who likes hockey
   (e) None of these

55. If all six friends are asked to sit in a straight line, facing north, in an alphabetical order (according to their names), from left to right, then which of the following combinations will represent the favourite sport ofthe immediate neighbours of Peter?

   (a) Badminton - Football   (b) Cricket-Tennis
   (c) Cricket-Football   (d) Tennis - Football
   (e) Cricket - Badminton

DIRECTIONS (Qs.56–60): Each of the questions below consists of a question and two statements numbered I and II given below it. You have to decide whether the data provided in the statements are sufficient to answer the question. Read both the statements and—

Give answer (a) if the data in Statement I alone are sufficient to answer the question, while the data in Statement II alone are not sufficient to answer the question.
Give answer (b) if the data in Statement II alone are sufficient to answer the question, while the data in Statement I alone are not sufficient to answer the question.
Give answer (c) if the data either in Statement I alone or in Statement II alone are sufficient to answer the question.
Give answer (d) if the data even in both Statements I and II together are not sufficient to answer the question.
Give answer (e) if the data in both Statements I and II together are necessary to answer the question.

56. What is the code of 'shine' in a certain code language ?
   I. In that code language 'shine was peeled off' is written as '& # @ 9' and 'no paint but shine' is written as '7 5 # 8'.
   II. In that code language 'try the new shine' is written as '13 # 0' and 'we try the new' is written as '6013'.

57. How C is related to H?
   I. N is son of H. J is mother of Z. N and Z are cousins. C is husband of J.
   II. L is father of C. A is mother of D. L is married to A. H is wife of D. J is wife of C.

58. In which direction point 'A' is located with respect to point 'B'?
   I. A man starts walking from point 'A' towards east and after walking 3 metres reaches point 'N', he turns right and walks 7 metres to reach point 'M'. Then he turns right and walks 6 metres to reach point 'O'. He again turns right and walks 7 metres to reach point 'P'. He, then, turns left and walks 2 metres to reach point 'B'.
   II. A man starts walking from point 'A' towards east and after walking 3 metres reaches point 'N'. From point 'N' he walks 7 metres towards south and reaches point 'M'. From point 'M' he walks 6 metres towards west and reaches Point 'O'. From point 'O' he walks 7 metres towards north and reaches point 'P'. From point 'P' he walks towards west and reaches point 'B'. The distance between points A and B is 8 metres.

59. How many students scored more than B in a class of 25 students?
   I. More than four but less than ten students scored more than that of B. B's rank is an odd number. Seventeen students scored less than D.
   II. The rank of C is 16th from the last. B got more marks than C. Only two students are there between B and C.

60. Five persons - A, B, C, D and E - are sitting around a circular table. Some of them are facing towards centre while others are facing outside.
Who is sitting second to the left of A?
   I. B is facing outside. C is to the immediate left of B. D is second to the right of C. A is to the immediate left of E.
   II. D is to the immediate right of A. Both D and A are facing towards the centre. D and B are immediate neighbours of each other.

DIRECTIONS (Qs. 61-65): Study the following information carefully and answer the questions which follow–

There are 10 persons in an award function J, K, L, M, N, O, P, Q, R and S. they are standing in a row facing north. These persons play 7 different instruments i.e., piano, Drum, Flute, Trumpet, Guitar, Struck and String. One person plays only one instrument but there are two players each of Drum, String and Struck.

   I. Out of the two persons who are standing in the middle of the row, one of them is P and another one is a player of Struck, which is not played by Q or O.
   II. O is to the immediate left of M, who is near the player of Struck.
   III. R plays Guitar and seated third to the left of P. Two players of a same game are not standing together.
   IV. The player of piano is fifth to the right of the player of String, who is second to the left of Q.

V.   Trumpet player and piano player neither stand together nor at the end of the row but one of them is L, who is second to the left of S.

VI.   There are only two persons between the player of String and R. There are four persons between N and the player of Guitar.

VII. J is the player of Flute but not near to K.

VIII. The person who plays Drum is seated between String players.

61. Who are standing at the end of the row?
(a) K and Q   (b) O and J
(c) L and R   (d) J and K
(e) M and S

62. Which of the following statement/s is/are true about the given arrangement?
(I)   There are only two persons between the player of Trumpet and Drum.
(II)   M is a player of String and third from the left end.
(III) S is neither player of Flute nor of String and not stand on extreme end.
(IV)   Player of Piano is only near the player of Drum.
(V)   M is on third place from K and N plays Drum.
(a) Only I, II and V   (b) Only I, III and IV
(c) Only III and V   (d) Only I, II, III
(e) None of these

63. Which of the following statement is true with respect to the given information?
(a) K plays Struck while O plays Flute
(b) The piano player is on sixth place from the String player
(c) The String player and Trumpet player are standing on the extreme end of the row
(d) The Flute player is on third place from the piano player
(e) None of the above

64. Which of the following pair is correct?
(a) O – String   (b) M – Flute
(c) K – Flute   (d) J – Struck
(e) S – Trumpet

65. What is the position of the piano player with respect to Drum player?
(a) Immediate right   (b) Second to the right
(c) Fourth to the left   (d) Sixth to the left
(e) Third to the right

DIRECTIONS (Qs. 66-69): Study the following information carefully and answer the given questions.

(i)   A, B, C, D, E, F, G and H are sitting around a circle facing the centre but not necessarily in the same order.

(ii)   B sits second to left of H's husband. No female is an immediate neighbour of B.

(iii) D's daughter sits second to right of F, F is the sister of G. F is not an immediate neightbour of H's husband.

(iv)   Only one person sits between A and F. A is the father of G. H's brother D sits to the immediate left of H's mother. Only one person sits between H's mother and E.

(v)   Only one person sits between H and G. G is the mother of C. G is not an immediate neighbour of E.

66. What is position of A with respect of his mother-in-law?
(a) Immediate left   (b) Third to the right
(c) Third to the left   (d) Second to the right
(e) Fourth to the left

67. What is the position of A with respect to his mother-in-grandchild?

(a) Immediate Right   (b) Third to the right
(c) Third to the left   (d) Second to the right
(e) Fourth to the left

68. Four of the following five are alike in a certain way based on the given information and so form a group. Which is the one that **does not** belong to that group?
(a) F   (b) C   (c) E
(d) H   (e) G

69. Which of the following is true with respect to the given seating arrangement?
(a) C is the cousin of E
(b) H and H's husband are immediate neighbours of each other
(c) No female is an immediate neighbour of C
(d) H sits third to left of her daughter
(e) B is the mother of H

DIRECTIONS (Qs. 70-71): Study the following information to answer the given questions :

Point P is 5 m towards the South of Point M. Point Q is 3 m towards the East of Point P. Point O is 3 m towards the East of Point M. Point N is 2 m towards the South of Point Q.

70. A person, facing North, takes a left turn from point M, walks 4m and stops. He then takes another left turn, walks 5 m and stops at point R. Which of the following points, including R, fall in a straight line ?
(a) M, O, R   (b) N, R, P   (c) R, O, Q
(d) R, Q, N   (e) Q, P, R

71. How far and towards which direction is Point O from Point N ?
(a) 5 m towards South   (b) 7 m towards North
(c) 8 m towards West   (d) 7 m towards West
(e) 5 m towards North

72. If 'A $ B' means 'A is father of B', 'A # B' means 'A is daughter of B', 'A @ B' means 'A is sister of B', then how is K related to M in H @ K $ L # M ?
(a) Husband   (b) Uncle
(c) Father   (d) Cannot be determined
(e) None of these

DIRECTIONS (Qs. 73-74): Study the following information and answer the questions that follow:

In a certain code language, 'hope to see you' is coded as 're so na di', 'please come to see the party' is coded as 'fi ge na di ke zo', 'hope to come' is coded as 'di so ge' and 'see you the party' is coded as 're fi zo na'.

73. How is 'party' coded in the given code language ?
(a) Either 're' or 'fi'   (b) Either 'zo' of 'na'
(c) Either 'zo' of 'fi'   (d) Either 'zo' or 'ge'
(e) 'Either 'ke' or 'fi'

74. Which one of the following will be coded as 'so di re' in the given code language ?
(a) you see hope   (b) hope you please
(c) hope you come   (d) the hope to
(e) you hope to

75. Vijay started walking towards South. After walking 15m, he turned to the left and walked 15 m. He again turned to his left and walked 15 m. How far is he from his original position and in which direction?
(a) 15 m, North   (b) 15 m, South
(c) 30 m, East   (d) 15 m, West
(e) None of these

76. A river flows West to East and on the way turns left and goes in a semi-circle round a hillock and then turns left at right angles. In which direction is the river finally flowing?
(a) East
(b) West
(c) North
(d) South
(e) None of these

77. If it is possible to make only one meaningful word from the first, the fifth, the seventh, the eighth and the eleventh letters of the word DEPARTMENTAL, first letter of the word is your answer. If more than one such word can be formed, your answer is 'X' and if no such word can be formed, your answer is 'Y'
(a) A
(b) D
(c) R
(d) X
(e) Y

78. **Cause:** Govt has recently decided to hike the procurement price of paddy for the rabi crops.
Which of the following will be a possible effect of the above cause?
(a) The farmers may be encouraged to cultivate paddy for the rabi season.
(b) The farmers may switch over to other cash crops in their paddy fields.
(c) There was a drop in production of paddy during Kharif season
(d) Govt may not increase the procurement price of paddy during the next Kharif season.
(e) Govt. will buy paddy from the open market during next few months.

79. **Cause :** A severe cyclonic storm swept away most part of the state during the last two days.
Which of the following cannot be a possible effect of the above cause ?
(a) Heavy rainfall was reported in most part of the state during the last two days.
(b) Many people were rendered homeless as their houses were flown away.
(c) The communication system of the state was severely affected and continues to be out of gear.
(d) Government has ordered that all the offices and schools should be kept open.
(e) All are possible effects.

80. A few travellers were severely beaten up by villagers recently in a remote rural part of the state as the villagers found the movement of the travellers suspicious. The district authority has sent a police team to nab the culprits. Which of the following inferences can be drawn from the above statement?
(An inference is something which is not directly stated but can be inferred from the given facts)
(a) The villagers dislike presence of strangers in their vicinity.
(b) Villagers are generally suspicious in nature.
(c) Travellers prefer to visit countryside.
(d) The Govt. generally provides protection to travellers across the country.
(e) None of these

GENERAL KNOWLEDGE

81. Name the platform that had partnered with ICICI Lombard to provide the insurance cover of ICICI to lenders and borrowers?
(a) Sureify.in
(b) AnyTimeLoan.in
(c) Ladder.in
(d) Bima.in
(e) None of these

82. To mark the 150th birth anniversary of Mahatma Gandhi,_______________ based company will release 12 bank notes of zero value which is the first ever limited edition commemorative series?
(a) Germany
(b) US
(c) India
(d) UAE
(e) None of these

83. Which of the following State received the first prize in the National Water Awards ceremony under the category best state in resource management?
(a) Gujarat
(b) Maharashtra
(c) Punjab
(d) Haryana
(e) None of these

84. Name the first Indian-origin woman to be honoured with a Blue Plaque at 4 Taviton Street in Bloomsbury, London?
(a) Brinda Karat
(b) Noor Inayat
(c) Lilly Singh
(d) Amelia Rajput
(e) None of these

85. Name the person who became the First Indian to join top 10 richest billionaire list of Hurun Research?
(a) Mukesh Ambani
(b) Azim Premji
(c) Pallonji Mistry
(d) Lakshmi Mittal
(e) None of these

86. Which of the following company has unveiled India's first indigenous 4G/5G semiconductor chips?
(a) DCM Data Systems Ltd.
(b) SIGNALCHIP
(c) CMOS Chips
(d) HCL Technologies India Pvt.
(e) None of these

87. The rate which the income tax is imposed in India is called....
(a) Digressive rate
(b) Progressive rate
(c) Regressive rate
(d) Proportionate rate
(e) None of these

88. How much cess is imposed currently by the Central Government?
(a) 4%
(b) 3.5%
(c) 3%
(d) 0.5%
(e) None of these

89. In which type of banking, electronic financial transactions are done?
(a) E-Banking
(b) Internet Banking
(c) M-Banking
(d) Universal Banking
(e) None of these

90. Which one of the following helps the consumers protect their credit identities and recover from identity theft?
(a) FACTA
(b) FCRA
(c) FDCPA
(d) FOIA
(e) None of these

91. Which one of the following is a financial ratio that gives a measure of a company's ability to meet its financial losses?
(a) Cash Reverse Ratio
(b) Leverage Ratio
(c) Statutory Liquidity Ratio
(d) Loan-to-Value Ratio
(e) None of these

92. When did the Reserve Bank of India notify the draft regulations relating to the Credit Information Companies (Regulation) Act, 2005?
(a) April 5, 2006
(b) May 26, 2006
(c) June 29, 2007
(d) September 30, 2005
(e) None of these

93. When did the draft guidelines for building grievance redressal mechanism within NBFCs (Non-Banking Financial Companies) publish?
(a) April 5, 2006   (b) May 26, 2006
(c) June 29, 2007   (d) September 30, 2005
(e) None of these

94. The Gir National Park and wild life sanctuary is located at
(a) Madhya Pradesh   (b) Gujarat
(c) Rajasthan   (d) Uttar Pradesh
(e) None of these

95. In which year wildlife protection act was implemented in India?
(a) 1952   (b) 1962
(c) 1972   (d) 1982
(e) None of these

96. In which of the following states is Dachigam wildlife sanctuary located?
(a) Jammu & Kashmir   (b) Himanchal Pradesh
(c) Uttrakhand   (d) Uttar Pradesh
(e) None of these

97. AMCs are entities, authorised by the RBI under _______ of the Foreign Exchange Management Act, 1999.
(a) Section 10   (b) Section 12
(c) Section 16   (d) Section 14
(e) Section 11

98. I" in IBBI stands for_______
(a) Institute   (b) Indian
(c) Information   (d) Insolvency
(e) None of these

99. The Central Government has constituted National Company Law Tribunal (NCLT) under _______ of the Companies Act, 2013.
(a) Section 108   (b) Section 408
(c) Section 308   (d) Section 208
(e) None of these

100. Permanent Account Number (PAN) is used to identify the Indian nationals and regular Income Tax payer under the_____________.
(a) Indian Income Tax Act, 1981
(b) Indian Income Tax Act, 1961
(c) Indian Income Tax Act, 1971
(d) Indian Income Tax Act, 1996
(e) None of these

101. Society for Worldwide Interbank Financial Telecommunication (SWIFT) is 8 to 11 __________.
(a) digit code
(b) Alphabetic code
(c) Alpha numeric code
(d) Alpha numeric and upper case code
(e) None of these

102. What does the last character represent in PAN CARD?
(a) type of holder   (b) Surname of holder
(c) Check digit   (d) State of holder
(e) .None of these

103. International Securities Identification Number(ISIN) is a 12 alphanumeric code. What do the first two characters represent?
(a) Branch code   (b) Country code
(c) State code   (d) City code
(e) None of these

104. What is the theme of World Milk Day?
(a) Drink Milk Be Strong   (b) Drink More Be Strong
(c) Drink Many Be Strong (d) Drink Move Be Strong
(e) none of these.

105. In which city The First biannual Indian Air Force Commanders' Conference was inaugurated by Defence Minister Nirmala Sitharaman?
(a) New Delhi   (b) Bangalore
(c) Mumbai   (d) Chennai
(e) None of these

106. Who has become the face of Central Railways` antitrespassing campaign?
(a) Kailash Satyarthi   (b) Thomas Antony
(c) Vijay Goel   (d) Amitabh Bachchan
(e) None of these

107. Name the state which launched the health insurance scheme for journalists?
(a) Odisha   (b) Telangana
(c) Uttar Pradesh   (d) Uttarakhand
(e) None of these

108. Under which person's chairpersonship, an executive committee is constituted to celebrate 150th birth anniversary of Mahatma Gandhi?
(a) Narendra Modi   (b) Arvind Kejriwal
(c) Raj Nath Singh   (d) Narendra Singh Tomar
(e) None of these

109. What is the theme of World Environment Day?
(a) Beat Smoke Pollution   (b) Beat Pollution Smoke
(c) Beat Plastic Pollution   (d) Beat Air Pollution
(e) None of these

110. Which state has launched 'Rythu Bandhu' investment support scheme for farmers?
(a) Kerala   (b) Tamil Nadu
(c) Karnataka   (d) Andhra Pradesh
(e) None of these

111. Who has become the first visually-challenged woman IAS officer in India?
(a) Beno Zephine   (b) Priya Jhingan
(c) Shaya Ram   (d) Pranjal Patil
(e) None of these

112. Which bank Best Expectation Management (Mid Cap)' award for 2017-18?
(a) Canara Bank   (b) Cooperative Bank
(c) Corporation Bank   (d) Karnataka Vikas Bank
(e) None of these

113. What is the theme of World Ocean Day?
(a) Preventing Air pollution and encouraging solutions for a healthy ocean
(b) Preventing plastic pollution and enrich solutions for a healthy ocean
(c) Prevent plastic pollution and enrich solutions for a healthy ocean
(d) Preventing plastic pollution and encouraging solutions for a healthy ocean
(e) Preventing plastic and encouraging solutions for a healthy ocean

114. Who will be heading the ARC panel for stressed assets?
(a) Sunil Mehta   (b) Anil Mehta
(c) Rajiv Mehta   (d) Aravind Mehta
(e) None of these

115. Manoj Kumar Panday who was the recipient of Param Vir Chakra belongs to which of the following military regiment or rifles?
(a) Rajputana Rifles   (b) 1/11 Gorkha Rifles
(c) 18 Grenadiers   (d) 13 JAK Rifles
(e) None of these

116. B. C. Roy Award is given in the field of
(a) Music   (b) Journalism
(c) Medicine   (d) Environment
(e) None of these

117. The prestigious Ramon Magsaysay Award was conferred was conferred upon Ms. Kiran Bedi for her excellent contribution to which of the following fields?
  (a) Literature   (b) Community Welfare
  (c) Government Service (d) Journalism
  (e) None of these

118. he goals of monetary policy do NOT include the promotion of __________
  (a) Maximum employment
  (b) Low Taxes
  (c) Stable Prices
  (d) Moderate long-term interest rates
  (e) None of these

119. Monetary policy refers to what the Federal Reserve does to influence the amount of __________ and __________ in the U.S. economy.
  (a) Currency and gold reserves
  (b) Money and credit
  (c) Taxes and revenue
  (d) Interest and debt
  (e) None of these

120. Which of the following is not the function of the RBI?
  (a) Banker's Bank
  (b) Controller of credit
  (c) Custodian of Foreign Exchange Reserve
  (d) Allotting money directly to farmers for agricultural development
  (e) None of these

ENGLISH LANGUAGE

DIRECTIONS (Qs. 121–130): Read the following passage carefully and answer the question given below it. Certain words have been printed in bold to help you locate them while answering some of the questions.

Agriculture has always been celebrated as the primary sector in India. Thanks to the Green Revolution, India is now self-sufficient in food production. Indian agriculture has been making technological advancement as well. Does that mean everything is looking **bright** for Indian agriculture? A **superficial** analysis of the above points would tempt one to say yes, but the truth is far from it. The reality is that Indian farmers have to face extreme poverty and financial crisis, which is driving them to suicides. What are the **grave** adversities that drive the farmers to commit suicide, at a time when Indian economy is supposed to be gearing up to take on the world?

Indian agriculture is predominantly dependent on nature. Irrigation facilities that are currently available, do not cover the entire cultivable land. If the farmers are at the mercy of monsoons for timely water for their crops, they are at the mercy of the government for alternative irrigation facilities. Any failure of nature, directly affects the fortunes of the farmers. Secondly, Indian agriculture is largely an unorganised sector, there is no systematic planning in cultivation, farmers work on lands of uneconomical sizes, institutional finances are not available and minimum purchase prices of the government do not in reality reach the poorest farmer. Added to this, the cost of agricultural inputs have been steadily rising over the years, farmers' margins of profits have been **narrowing** because the price rise in inputs is not complemented by an increase in the purchase price of the agricultural produce. Even today, in several parts of the country, agriculture is a seasonal occupation. In many districts, farmers get only one crop per year and for the remaining part of the year, they find it difficult to make both ends meet.

The farmers normally resort to borrowing from money lenders, in the absence of institutionalized finance. Where institutional finance is available, the ordinary farmer does not have a chance of availing it because of the **"procedures"** involved in disbursing the finance. This calls for removing the elaborate formalities for obtaining the loans. The institutional finance, where available is mostly availed by the medium or large land owners, the small farmers do not even have the awareness of the existence of such facilities. The money lender is the only source of finance to the farmers. Should the crops fail, the farmers fall into a debt trap and crop failures piled up over the years give them no other option than ending their lives.

Another disturbing trend has been observed where farmers commit suicide or deliberately kill a family member in order to avail relief and benefits announced by the government to support the families of those who have committed suicide so that their families could atleast benefit from the Government's relief programmes. What then needs to be done to prevent this sad state of affairs? There cannot be one single solution to end the woes of farmers.

Temporary measures through monetary relief would not be the solution. The governmental efforts should be targeted at improving the entire structure of the small where in the relief is not given on a drought to drought basis, rather they are taught to overcome their difficulties through their own skills and capabilities. Social responsibility also goes a long way to help the farmers. General public, NGOs, Corporate and other organisations too can play a part in helping farmers by adopting drought affected villages and families and helping them to rehabilitate.

The nation has to realise that farmers' suicides are not minor issues happening in remote parts a few states, it is a reflection of the true state of the basis of our economy.

121. What does the author mean by "procedures" when he says that 'farmers do not get a chance of availing institutional finance because of procedures involved in it'?
  (a) He refers to the government guideline of disbursing finance only to medium and large land owners?
  (b) Refers to the strict government rule of providing loans to only such farmers who can guarantee a default–free–tenure
  (c) The formalities to avail these facilities are enormous and too difficult for an ordinary farmer to understand
  (d) Refers to the danger farmers must face from the local money-lenders they availed the loan from government instead
  (e) None of these

122. Why have many farmers resorted to killing family members?
  (A) It is difficult for the farmers to sustain their family's livelihood.
  (B) So that the killed family member may get rid of the persistent adversities.
  (C) To avail relief package announced by the government to support the family of those who commit suicide.
  (a) Only A   (b) Only B
  (c) Only B and C   (d) Only A and B
  (e) None of these

123. According to the author why does the situation of agricultural sector remain grim even after making several technological advances ?
  (a) Indian farmers continue to face adversities from nature as well as the government.
  (b) India has failed to match the technological advances taking place in the rest of the world
  (c) Natural calamities have been very frequent in India
  (d) Banks have failed to provide adequate loans to the farmers
  (e) None of these

124. Which of the following is **not true** in context of the passage?
   (a) Many farmers struggle to sustain themselves after reaping one crop in a year
   (b) The government has relieved the farmers from any elaborate formalities while availing the loans
   (c) India was made self–sufficient in food production because of green revolution
   (d) Some farmers commit suicide in order to avail relief package from the government
   (e) None of these

125. What does the author suggest as opposed to providing temporary monetary relief to the farmers ?
   (A) To improve the entire agricultural setup in India instead of providing relief in the face of adversities.
   (B) Providing the local money lender with large amount of money so that small farmers can easily obtain loans from them.
   (C) Empowering the farmers so that they can sustain a livelihood throughout life without having to face the desperation that adversity drives them to.
   (a) Only A   (b) Only A and B
   (c) Only B   (d) Only A and C
   (e) None of these

126. What are the adversities faced by Indian farmers according to the passage?
   (a) Lack of adequate irrigation facilities
   (b) Ownership of only a small piece of land by a majority of farmers, which fails to generate any profit
   (c) Lack of financial help to the farmers
   (d) All of these
   (e) None of these

127. According to the passage why don't farmers avail the institutional finance facilities?
   (a) Banks are not willing to provide loans to the farmers because of high risk associated with it
   (b) Many NGOs and corporate organisations provide them the loans in a hassle free manner
   (c) Most of the farmers do not need finance in large scale since they work on small size lands
   (d) The local money-lenders charge lower interest rates as compared to such financial facilities
   (e) None of these

128. According to the passage, how can general public lend a helping hand to the struggling farmers ?
   (a) By adopting the affected families and helping them to rehabilitate
   (b) By acting as a relief worker in the drought hit areas
   (c) To provide help for building dams and better irrigation facilities
   (d) Not specified in the passage
   (e) None of these

129. Why is the profit margin of farmers narrowing even after increasing the minimum purchase price?
   (A) The minimum purchase price of the government is too low to make any profit.
   (B) The quality of the inputs such as seeds and fertilizers is very poor.
   (C) There has been a continuous rise in the price of agricultural inputs which adversely affects the profit.
   (a) Only A   (b) Only B
   (c) Only C   (d) Only A and C
   (e) None of these

130. What is the author's main objective in writing the passage?
   (a) Criticising the policy of providing relief packages to the family of farmers who commit suicide

   (b) To appeal to the non institutional money lenders for providing loans to farmers in a hassle-free manner
   (c) To applaud the dauntless spirit of the farmers
   (d) To highlight the drawbacks in the agriculture sector
   (e) None of these

DIRECTIONS (Qs. 131-138): Read each sentence to find out whether there is any grammatical error in it. The error, if any, will be in one part of the sentence, the letter of that part is the answer. If there is no error, then the answer is (e). (Ignore the errors of punctuation, if any)

131. It is notable and welcome that the ministry of (a)/ environmental and forests is to issue approvals online (b)/ in a time bound manner, with clear timelines (c)/in place for the various sub-steps along the way. (d)/No error (e)

132. To portray (a)/ what a fairness cream does without (b)/ any sort of comparison or visual (c)/ references are very difficult. (d)/ No error (e)

133. Our housing society comprises (a)/six block and thirty flats (b)/in an area of (c)/about thousand square metres. (d)/No error (e)

134. Still remaining in the ancient castle (a)/are the Duke's collection of early Dutch paintings (b)/ which will be (c)/ donated to a museum. (d)/No error (e)

135. He picked up (a)/the books (b)/and put it (c)/on the table. (d)/ No error (e)

136. Everyone knows (a)/that the tiger (b)/ is faster (c)/of all animals. (d)/No error (e)

137. When he (a)/had got what (b)/ he wanted (c)/he has gone home. (d)/No error (e)

138. Governments and businesses must reduce (a)/ its own energy use (b)/ and promote conservation (c)/ to their citizens and employees. (d)/ No error (e)

DIRECTIONS (Qs. 139 -145): In the following passage there are blanks, each of which has been numbered. These numbers are printed below the passage and against each, five words are suggested, one of which fits the blank appropriately. Find out the appropriate word in each case.

(**139**) a country needs money for a development project, what can it do? It can (**140**) to the World Bank or Asian Development Bank for aid. A country with a foreign currency problem can ask the International Monetary Fund for (**141**). However, (**142**) there is no way out for a country which has shortage of food. The country cannot (**143**) import the food if it is rare like pulses which are grown only by a few countries in such cases the problem is more (**144**). This situation has led experts to suggest the (**145**) of establishing a World Agricultural Bank.

139. (a) Though   (b) Supposed   (c) Unless
   (d) That   (e) When
140. (a) appeals   (b) go   (c) approach
   (d) solicit   (e) requests
141. (a) backing   (b) helping   (c) solution
   (d) assistants   (e) relieve
142. (a) simply   (b) during   (c) fact
   (d) presently   (e) while
143. (a) attempt   (b) yet   (c) even
   (d) try   (e) start
144. (a) address   (b) acute   (c) declined
   (d) achievable   (e) prohibited
145. (a) object   (b) implementation (c) knowledge
   (d) advice   (e) idea

DIRECTIONS (Qs. 146-150): The sentences given in each question, when properly sequenced, form a coherent paragraph. Each sentence is labelled with a letter. Choose the most logical order of the sentences from amongst the given choices so as to form a coherent paragraph.

146. P : In the past, the customised tailoring units were localised to the township or city and catered exclusively to domestic demand.
   Q : Traditionally, Indians preferred custom-made clothing and the concept of ready-to-wear is a relatively recent one.
   R : Consumer awareness of styling issues and the convenience afforded by ready-to-wear helped RMG industry make small inroads into the domestic market in the 1980s.
   S : The customised tailoring outfits have always been a major source of clothing for domestic market.
   (a) Q R S P   (b) Q S P R   (c) R S Q P .
   (d) S Q P R   (e) None of these

147. P : Such a system will help to identify and groom executives for positions of strategists.
   Q : Evaluation of performance is more often than not done for the purpose of reward or punishment for past performance.
   R : They must become an integral part of the executive system' .
   S : Even where the evaluation system is for one's promotion to assume higher responsibilities, it rarely includes terms that are a key for playing the role of strategist effectively, e.g., the skills of playing the role of change agent and creative problem solving.
   (a) S Q P R   (b) S R Q P   (c) R S Q P
   (d) Q S R P   (e) None of these

148. P : Participation involves more than the formal sharing of decisions.
   Q : Through anticipation individuals or organisations consider trends and make plans, shielding institutions from trauma of learning by shock.
   R : Innovative learning involves both anticipation and participation.
   S : It is an attitude characterised by the cooperation, dialogue and empathy.
   (a) Q R S P   (b) P Q R S   (c) R Q P S
   (d) S P Q R   (e) None of these

149. P : Almost a century ago, when the father of the modem automobile industry, Henry Ford, sold the first Model T car, he decided that only the best would do for his customers.
   Q : Today, it is committed to delivering the' finest quality with over six million vehicles a year in over 200 countries across the world.
   R : And for over 90 years, this philosophy has endured in the Ford Motor company.
   S : Thus a vehicle is ready for the customers only, if it passes the Ford 'Zero Defect Programme'.
   (a) P Q R S   (b) P R Q S   (c) R S P Q
   (d) P R S Q   (e) None of these

150. P: Finish specialists recommended a chewing gum containing xylitol-a natural sweetener present in birch, maple, corn and straw-to be used several times a day by young children.
   Q : Chewing gum is a new solution that "may work for parents whose children suffer from chronic ear infections.
   R : An experiment was conducted involving three hundred and six children between two and six years.
   S : After Finish studies showed that xylitol is effective in preventing cavities, a team of researchers decided to investigate its effects on a very similar type of bacteria which causes ear infections.
   (a) Q R S P   (b) P Q R S   (c) R Q P S
   (d) Q P S R   (e) None of these

DIRECTIONS (Qs. 151-155): In each of the questions given below, an incomplete sentence which must be filled/completed with one of the sentences given below. Choose the correct option and complete the given sentences.

151. The body was taken into custody and police stations of nearby districts .... her identity
   (a) were commanded to reveal
   (b) were commanded to conceal
   (c) were forced to hide
   (d) were ordered to trace
   (e) were reluctant to know

152. We need data so that various government schemes for different categories .... smoothly.
   (a) can be implemented   (b) can be debarred
   (c) can be executed   (d) can be resolved
   (e) can be entered into

153. A question on the form asks whether parents of the applicant .... occupation
   (a) are involved in a disguised
   (b) are indulged in the illegal
   (c) are engaged in a clean
   (d) are absorbed in the self created
   (e) are engaged in an unclean

154. She added that too much information was being sought in the form and the school could not ....
   (a) find that the students are doing well or not
   (b) understand the purpose behind it
   (c) discover the reason of mismanagement
   (d) understand the politics behind it
   (e) analyse the reason of doing so

155. The focus has been on finishing the syllabus instead of concentrating on whether the student ....
   (a) is being able to understand what is being taught
   (b) is being able to understand what is not taught
   (c) is being able to judge whether the school is reducing the fees or not
   (d) is being able to know whether the school is organising the fest or not
   (e) is being able to perform well or not

DIRECTIONS (Qs. 156-160) : In each of the following questions four words are given, of which two are most nearly the same or opposite in meaning. Find the two words which are most nearly the same or opposite in meaning and mark the number of the correct letter combination as your answer.

156. (A) Discomfit   (B) Baffle
   (C) Epicure   (D) Enumerate
   (a) A-B   (b) A-C   (c) A-D
   (d) B-C   (e) B-D

157. (A) Testimony   (B) Aura
   (C) Augment   (D) Decrease
   (a) A-B   (b) B-C   (c) C-D
   (d) A-D   (e) B-D

158. (A) Unkempt   (B) Unremitting
   (C) Slackening   (D) Distasteful
   (a) A-B   (b) B-C   (c) C-D
   (d) A-D   (e) B-D

159. (A) Gregarious   (B) Quixotic
    (C) Sociable   (D) Discernible
    (a) A-B   (b) B-C   (c) C-D
    (d) A-C   (e) B-D
160. (A) Apathetic   (B) Wrath
    (C) Whirl   (D) Twirl
    (a) A-B   (b) A-C   (c) A-D
    (d) B-C   (e) C-D

HINDI LANGUAGE

निर्देश (प्र.सं.121-125): नीचे दिये गए प्रत्येक प्रश्न में एक रिक्त स्थान छूटा हुआ है और उसके नीचे पाँच शब्द सुझाए गए हैं। इनमें से कोई एक उस रिक्त स्थान पर रख देने से वह वाक्य अर्थपूर्ण वाक्य बन जाता है। सही शब्द को ज्ञात कर उसको उत्तर के रूप में अंकित कीजिए। दिए गए शब्दों में से सर्वाधिक उपयुक्त शब्द का चयन करना है।

121. अपराध रोकने में पुलिस की अक्षमता को देखकर अब जनसाधारण ने .... का रास्ता अपनाना शुरू कर दिया है।
    (a) पलायन   (b) आत्मरक्षा   (c) छिप जाने
    (d) फौजी मदद   (e) इनमें से कोई नहीं
122. रवीन्द्रनाथ टैगोर का जन्म सांस्कृतिक एवं .... जगत में सदा अविस्मरणीय रहेगा।
    (a) चित्रकला   (b) साहित्य   (c) संगीत
    (d) दार्शनिक   (e) इनमें से कोई नहीं
123. देवानन्द की काम के प्रति लगन और निष्ठा .... है।
    (a) शोभनीय   (b) साहित्य   (c) हास्यास्पद
    (d) अनुकरणीय   (e) इनमें से कोई नहीं
124. न्यायविदों के बीच तंदूर कांड पर .... में बहस होगी।
    (a) वकालत   (b) अदालत   (c) संसद
    (d) खिलाफत   (e) इनमें से कोई नहीं
125. वेद गुरु परम्परा के कारण .... सुरक्षित रह सके।
    (a) अनुचर   (b) दीर्घ   (c) शिष्य
    (d) लघु   (e) इनमें से कोई नहीं

निर्देश (प्र.सं.126-130): नीचे दिये गए प्रत्येक प्रश्नों के विकल्प में शुद्ध वर्तनी का चयन करें।

126. (a) मृत्युजय   (b) म्रित्युन्जय   (c) मृत्युजय
    (d) मृत्युन्जय   (e) इनमें से कोई नहीं
127. (a) निर्दिशन   (b) निदर्शन   (c) निर्दशन
    (d) निदर्शन   (e) इनमें से कोई नहीं
128. (a) अस्प्रस्यता   (b) अस्पृश्यता   (c) अस्प्रशयता
    (d) अस्पृष्यता   (e) इनमें से कोई नहीं
129. (a) कलेष   (b) किलेस   (c) कलेस
    (d) क्लेश   (e) इनमें से कोई नहीं
130. (a) चिहन्   (b) चिह्न   (c) चिंह
    (d) चिन्ह   (e) इनमें से कोई नहीं

निर्देश (प्र.सं.131-135): निम्नलिखित पाँच में से चार समानार्थी शब्द हैं। जिस क्रमांक में इनसे भिन्न शब्द दिया गया है, वही आपका उत्तर है।

131. (a) भायों   (b) दारा   (c) कलत्र
    (d) शरीरी   (e) वल्लभा
132. (a) अश्म   (b) पाषाण   (c) प्रस्तर
    (d) इषु   (e) उपल
133. (a) चंचला   (b) चपला   (c) दामिनी
    (d) सौदामिनी   (e) ज्योति
134. (a) अभ्र   (b) जलधर   (c) हलधर
    (d) धाराधर   (e) जीमूत
135. (a) पुहुप   (b) कुसुम   (c) सुमन
    (d) प्रसून   (e) राग

निर्देश (प्र.सं.136-140): नीचे दिया गया प्रत्येक वाक्य चार भागों में बाँटा है और इन्हें **(a)**, **(b)**, **(c)** और **(d)** क्रमांक दिए गए है। आपको यह देखना है कि वाक्य के किसी भाग में व्याकरण, भाषा वर्तनी शब्दों के गलत प्रयोग या इसी तरह की कोई त्रुटि तो नहीं है। त्रुटि अगर होगी तो वाक्य के किसी एक भाग में ही होगी। उस भाग का क्रमांक ही आपका उत्तर है। अगर वाक्य त्रुटिरहित है तो उत्तर **(e)** दीजिए।

136. भारतीय किसान आजीवन-भर (a)/ पूरी मेहनत करता है (b)/ पर साहुकारों के चंगुल से (c)/ नहीं निकल पाता (d)/ कोई त्रुटि नहीं (e)
137. साहित्यकार का दायित्व (a)/ बल्कि उनके कारणों का (b)/ विवेचन करते हुए श्रेयस मार्ग की ओर ले जाना है (c)/वस्तुस्थिति का यथातथ्य चित्रण मात्र प्रस्तुत कर देना ही नहीं (d)/ कोई त्रुटि नहीं (e)
138. जनसंख्या में (a)/ हम अपने जीवन को (b)/ सुखी और संतुष्ट नहीं बना सके (c)/ असाधारण वृद्धि के कारण (d)/ कोई त्रुटि नहीं (e)
139. स्वार्थ के वशीभूत होकर (a)/ मानव हर बात को (b)/ अपने मनोनुकूल (c)/ देखना चाहता है (d)/ कोई त्रुटि नहीं (e)
140. समाज-सुधारकों के (a)/ दहेज प्रथा ने (b)/ प्रयत्नों के बावजूद (c)/ अत्यन्त विकट रूप धारण कर लिया है (d)/ कोई त्रुटि नहीं (e)

निर्देश (प्र.सं.141-145): नीचे कुछ वाक्यांश या शब्द दिए गए हैं और उसके बाद चार शब्द दिए गए हैं जो एक ही शब्द में इस वाक्यांश या शब्द-समूह का अर्थ प्रकट करता है। आपको यह पता लगाना है कि वह शब्द कौन-सा है जो वाक्यांश या शब्द समूह का सही अर्थ प्रकट करता है। उस विकल्प का क्रमांक ही आपका उत्तर है। यदि कोई शब्द अर्थ नहीं प्रकट करता है तो उत्तर   (e) अर्थात् 'इनमें से कोई नहीं' दीजिए।

141. जिसके द्वारा अभियोग लगाया गया हो
    (a) अधियुक्त   (b) अभियुक्त   (c) अधियोक्ता
    (d) अभियोक्ता   (e) इनमें से कोई नहीं
142. सेना की किसी छोटी टुकड़ी या समूह का नेता
    (a) अध्यक्ष   (b) पृथप   (c) क्षत्रप
    (d) स्वामी   (e) इनमें से कोई नहीं
143. खाद्य सामग्री जो यात्रा के समय राह में उपभोग के लिए रखी जाती है
    (a) स्वल्पाहार   (b) पाथेय   (c) उपाहार
    (d) पथ्य   (e) इनमें से कोई नहीं
144. पीढ़ी दर पीढ़ी चला आने वाला
    (a) क्रमागत   (b) अन्वयागत   (c) परागत
    (d) तथागत   (e) इनमें से कोई नहीं
145. जिसे जीता न जा सके
    (a) अजित   (b) अज्ञेय   (c) अपराजेय
    (d) दुर्जेय   (e) इनमें से कोई नहीं

निर्देश (प्र.सं.146-150): नीचे दिए गए गद्यांश को ध्यानपूर्वक पढ़िए और उस पर आधारित प्रश्नों के उत्तर दीजिए। कुछ शब्दों को मोटे अक्षरों में मुद्रित किया गया है, जिससे आपको कुछ प्रश्नों के उत्तर देने में सहायता मिलेगी।

ब्रिटेन के आधिपत्य ने भारत में शांति की स्थापना की और मुगल साम्राज्य के पतन के बाद जो अशांति और विपत्तियाँ आई, उनमें भारत को निश्चित रूप से शांति की आवश्यकता थी। शांति एक बहुमूल्य वस्तु है, जो किसी भी तरक्की के लिए आवश्यक है और जब यह हमें मिली, तो इसका स्वागत हुआ, परन्तु शांति को बहुत बड़ी कीमत पर खरीदा जा सकता है, हम कब्र की पूर्ण शांति प्राप्त कर सकते हैं और पिंजड़े या कारागार की पूर्ण सुरक्षा भी। शांति उन लोगों की आकस्मिक निराशा का भी परिणाम हो सकती है,

जो अपनी हालत सुधारने में असमर्थ हैं जो शांति विदेशी विजेताओं द्वारा थोपी जाती है, उसमें असली शांति, सुख और संतोष प्रदान करने वाले गुण नहीं होते। युद्ध एक भयंकर चीज होती है, जिससे बचना चाहिए, परंतु फिर भी इससे कुछ सद्गुणों को बढ़ावा मिलता है, जो सुप्रसिद्ध मनोवैज्ञानिक विलियम जेम्स के अनुसार इस प्रकार हैं– निष्ठा, संबद्धता, दृढ़ता, वीरता, विवेक, शिक्षा, आविष्कारशील, मितव्ययता, शारीरिक स्वास्थ्य तथा बल। इसी कारण से जेम्स युद्ध का नैतिक-पर्याय खोजना चाहता था, जो युद्ध की विभीषिकाओं के बिना ही समाज में इन सद्गुणों को प्रोत्साहित कर सके। शायद उसे यदि असहयोग और सविनय अवज्ञा के बारे में पता चल गया होता, तो उसे अपनी मनपसंद चीज मिल गई होती, जो युद्ध का एक नैतिक तथा शांतिपूर्ण पर्याय है।

146. इस परिच्छेद का सबसे उपयुक्त शीर्ष क्या होगा?
- (a) भारत में मुगल साम्राज्य का पतन
- (b) युद्ध का एक नैतिक तथा शांतिपूर्ण पर्याय
- (c) युद्ध और शांति
- (d) भारत में ब्रिटेन का आधिपत्य
- (e) इनमें से कोई नहीं

147. परिच्छेद से यह निष्कर्ष निकाला जा सकता है कि-
- (a) भारत में ब्रिटिश-आधिपत्य से जो शांति स्थापित हुई, वह भारत की जनता के हित में नहीं थी
- (b) भारत के लिए किसी भी कीमत पर शांति आवश्यक थी
- (c) लोगों में कुछ सद्गुणों के विकास के लिए शांति आवश्यक है
- (d) लोगों में कुछ सद्गुणों के विकास के लिए युद्ध आवश्यक है
- (e) इनमें से कोई नहीं

148. परिच्छेद के अनुसार युद्ध-
- (a) मुख्यत: एक भयंकर चीज है
- (b) मुख्यत: एक सद्गुण है
- (c) कभी भयंकर है, तो कभी सद्गुण है
- (d) एक ऐसी चीज है, जो अश्वयम्भावी है, चाहे अच्छी हो या बुरी
- (e) इनमें से कोई नहीं

149. लेखक इस बात पर बल देना चाहता है कि-
- (a) असहयोग एवं सविनय अवज्ञा के तरीकों से वही लाभ है, जो युद्ध के हैं
- (b) विलियम जेम्स एक महान् मनोवैज्ञानिक था
- (c) भारत में यदि ब्रिटिश शासन नहीं आया होता, तो अशांति और विपत्तिया जारी रहती
- (d) ब्रिटेनवासी यदि भारत में आकर शासन नहीं करते, तो मुगल साम्राज्य जारी रहता
- (e) इनमें से कोई नहीं

150. सविनय अवज्ञा एवं असहयोग को लेखक क्या मनता है?
- (a) समाज का सद्गुण
- (b) युद्ध जीतने के साधन
- (c) शांति, संतोष और सुख प्रदान करने वाले हथियार
- (d) युद्ध का शांतिपूर्ण एवं नैतिक पर्याय
- (e) इनमें से कोई नहीं

निर्देश (प्र.सं.151-160): नीचे दिए गए परिच्छेद में कुछ रिक्त स्थान छोड़ दिए गए हैं तथा उन्हें प्रश्न संख्या में दर्शाया गया है। ये संख्याएँ परिच्छेद के नीचे मुद्रित हैं, और प्रत्येक के सामने (a), (b), (c), (d) और (e) विकल्प दिए गए हैं। इन पाँचों में से कोई एक इस रिक्त स्थान को पूरे परिच्छेद के संदर्भ में उपयुक्त ढंग से पूरा कर देता है। आपको वह विकल्प ज्ञात करना है, और इसका क्रमांक ही उत्तर के रूप में दर्शाना है। दिए गए विकल्पों में से उपयुक्त विकल्प का चयन करना है।

दुनिया के अनेक दोषों की तरह हमारे .....(151).... का भी दुर्भाग्य है कि आम, केला, सेब, अंगूर, अनन्नास, अनार, पपीता सरिखे लोकप्रिय और प्रचुर मात्रा में ....(152)...... होने वाले फलों के सामने बेर, करोंदा, जामुन,

बेल, खिरनी, फालसा, आंवला, अंजीर, कोकम, बड़हल, शरीफा जैसे फल कम मात्रा में पैदा होते हैं और बाजार में आसानी से उपलब्ध नहीं होते हैं इसलिए लोग इनका (153) भूलते जा रहे हैं। अनुपलब्धता की व्यावसायिक वजह यही बताई जाती है कि (154) कम या नहीं के बराबर होने के कारण थोक व्यापारी इनमें रुचि नहीं लेता। इसी तरह आम का उदाहरण लें। सुदूर दक्षिण से लेकर उत्तर पूर्व तक फैले (155) भूभाग में इसकी लगभग एक हजार प्रजातियाँ उगाई जाती रही हैं जिनके रंग, रूप, गंध और स्वाद एक दूसरे से (156) रहें हैं। पर आज की तरीख में दशहरी, लंगड़ा, अल्फांजो जैसी भारी मांग वाली प्रजातियों ने इतने (157) ढंग से बाजार को अपनी गिरफ्त में ले लिया है कि अन्य (158) कुछ सालों बाद हाथ में दिया लेकर ढूंढ़ने पर भी नही मिलेगी। कहते हैं कि पुरी के भगवान् जगन्नाथ को साल के तीन सौ पैंसठ दिन तीन सौ पैंसठ प्रजातियों के भात का (159) लगाया जाता था ताकि साल में किसी किस्म के भात की पुनरावृत्ति न हो, पर आज तो यह किसी परी कथा जैसा (160) लगता है।

151. (a) देश (b) बाजार (c) व्यापार (d) करोबार (e) विज्ञान

152. (a) उगे (b) सजे (c) पैदा (d) बिके (e) मिलते

153. (a) याद (b) स्वाद (c) कायदा (d) रंग (e) सुगंध

154. (a) कम (b) संगठन (c) लदाई (d) आकर्षण (e) मांग

155. (a) भारी (b) बर्फीलें (c) वनीय (d) विशाल (e) महान

156. (a) करीब (b) अलग (c) विपरीत (d) खट्टे (e) बढ़कर

157. (a) आक्रामक (b) जांबाज (c) उछाल (d) अच्छे (e) आदर्श

158. (a) बाड़ियाँ (b) मंडियाँ (c) प्रजातियाँ (d) सहजातियाँ (e) उपजातियाँ

159. (a) थाल (b) सजाया (c) चढ़ाया (d) भोग (e) तिलक

160. (a) व्यवहार (b) उपन्यास (c) कल्पना (d) काव्य (e) किस्सा

COMPUTER KNOWLEDGE

161. The tracks on a disk which can be accused without repositioning the R/W heads is
- (a) Surface
- (b) Cylinder
- (c) Cluster
- (d) All of the above
- (e) None of these

162. The TRAP is one of the interrupts available its INTEL 8085 Which one statement is true of TRAP?
- (a) It is level triggered
- (b) It is negative edge triggered It is positive edge triggered
- (c) It is positive edge triggered
- (d) It is both positive edge triggered and level triggered
- (e) None of these

163. Method of graph traversal?
- (a) Depth first search
- (b) Breadth first search
- (c) Both (a) and (b)
- (d) Length first search
- (e) None of these

164. The following sequence of operations is performed one a stack; PUSH(10), PUSH(20). POP, PUSH(10), PUSH(20), POP, POP, POP PUSH(20), POP The sequence of values popped out is
- (a) 20, 10, 20,10, 20
- (b) 20, 20 ,10, 10, 20
- (c) 10, 20, 20, 10, 20
- (d) 20, 20, 10, 20, 20
- (e) None of these

165. Which of the following is most general phase-structured grammer?
    (a) Regular
    (b) Context-sensitive
    (c) Context-free
    (d) All of the above
    (e) None of these

166. The language which are having many types, but the type of every name and expression must be calculable at compile time is called
    (a) strongly typed
    (b) weakly typed
    (c) dynamic typed
    (d) boldly typed
    (e) None of these

167. Modem is a ____ that modulates and demodulate signals

    (a) DCE (Data circuit-terminating equipment)
    (b) DTE (Data terminal equipment)
    (c) DTE-DCE
    (d) Both (a) and (b)
    (e) None of these

168. Which is the general network standard for the data link layer in the OSI Reference Model?
    (a) IEEE 802.1
    (b) IEEE 802.2
    (c) IEEE 802.3
    (d) IEEE 802.4
    (e) IEEE 802.6

169. ________ is primarily used for mapping host names and e-mail destinations to IP address but can also be used for other purposes.
    (a) TCP(transfer control protocol)
    (b) DNS(Domain Name System)
    (c) SHA (Secure Hash Algorithm)
    (d) Simple Network Management Protocol (SNMP)
    (e) None of these

170. In UNIX, cached disk blocks are managed by the kernel and referred to as-
    (a) Cache
    (b) Super cache
    (c) Buffer cache
    (d) All of the above
    (e) None of these

171. Match the following :

List-I	List - II
(a) Threads	(1) Operating system
(b) Scheduling	(2) First come first served
(c) Process switch	(3) Light weight process with reduced state
(d) Non preemptive	(4) Mode switch

    Codes :

	A	B	C	D
(a)	1	2	3	4
(b)	3	1	4	2
(c)	4	3	1	2
(d)	3	4	2	1

    (e) None of these

172. Which of the following are placeholders for literal values in a SQL query being sent to the database
    (a) reduction and resolution variables
    (b) resolution variables
    (c) reduction variables
    (d) assimilation variables
    (e) bind variables

173. Which of the following is used to create and delete views and relations within tables?
    (a) SQL Data Identification Language
    (b) SQL Data Identification and Manipulation Languages
    (c) SQL Data Relational Language
    (d) SQL Data Definition Language
    (e) SQL Data Manipulation Language

174. ________ is a set design steps that allows a DFD with transform flow characteristics to be mapped into a predefined template for program structure.
    (a) Transaction flow
    (b) Contributor
    (c) Transform mapping
    (d) Design evaluation
    (e) None of these

175. Which type of software is used for development of solution for problem ?
    (a) most reliable and cost effective
    (b) cost effective not most reliable
    (c) reliable but not cost effective
    (d) All of the above
    (e) None of these

176. What is the output of the following C program main

```
0
{
int i = 32, j = 0×20, k,I,m;
K=i/j;
1=i&j
m=k^I;
print f("%d%d%d%d%d", i,j,k,l,m);
```
    (a) 32 32 32 32 0
    (b) 0 0 0 0 0
    (c) 32 32 32 32 32
    (d) 32 0 32 0 32
    (e) None of these

177. What is printed by the print statements in the program P1 assuming call by reference parameter passing?

```
Program P1()
{
    x = 10;
    y = 3 ;
    funcl (y, x, x);
    print x;
    print y;
}
funcl (x, y, z)
{
    y = y + 4;
    z = x + y + z;
}
is
```
    (a) 10, 3
    (b) 31, 3
    (c) 27, 7
    (d) All of the above
    (e) None of these

178. A counter is fundamentally a ________ sequential circuit that proceeds through the predetermined sequence of states only when input pulses are applied to it.
    (a) register
    (b) memory unit
    (c) flipflop
    (d) arithmatic logic unit
    (e) None of these

179. What is the maximum possible range of bit-count specifically in n-bit binary counter consisting of 'n' number of flipflops?
    (a) 0 to 2^n
    (b) 0 to 2^{n-1}
    (c) 0 to 2^{n+1}
    (d) 0 to $2^{n+1/2}$
    (e) None of these

180. Which of the following is not a WebApp Interface mechanism?
    (a) Links
    (b) Cookies
    (c) Browser
    (d) Cookies and Links
    (e) Forms

181. Character encoding is
    (a) method used to represent numbers in a character
    (b) method used to represent character in a number
    (c) a system that consists of a code which pairs each character with a pattern, sequence of natural numbers or electrical pulse in order to transmit the data
    (d) All of the above
    (e) None of these

182. A linker is given object modules for a set of programs that were compiled separately. What information need not be included in an object module?
(a) Object code
(b) Relocation bits
(c) Names and locations of all external symbols defined in the object module
(d) Absolute addresses of internal symbols
(e) None of these

183. The reason the data outputs of most ROM ICs are tri-state outputs is to:
(a) allow for three separate data input lines.
(b) allow the bidirectional flow of data between the bus lines and the ROM registers.
(c) permit the connection of many ROM chips to a common data bus.
(d) isolate the registers from the data bus during read operations.
(e) None of these

184. ________ data type can store unstructured data
(a) RAW   (b) CHAR
(c) NUMERIC   (d) VARCHAR
(e) None of these

185. If the programmer does not explicitly provide a destructor, then which of the following creates an empty destructor?
(a) Preprocessor   (b) Compiler
(c) Linker   (d) main() function
(e) None of these

186. The decimal value 0.5 in IEEE single precision floating point representation has
(a) fractions bits of 000 .... 000 and exponent value of 0
(b) fractions bits of 000 .... 000 and exponent value of -1
(c) fractions bits of 100 .... 000 and exponent value of 0
(d) no exact representation
(e) None of these

187. Define the connective * for the Boolean variables X and Y as X*Y = XY + X'Y'. Let Z = X*Y. Consider the following expressions P, Q and R"
$P : X = Y * Z$ $Q : Y = X * Z$
$R : X * Y * Z = 1$
Which of the following is true?
(a) P and Q are valid   (b) Q and R are valid
(c) P and R are valid   (d) All P, Q, R are valid
(e) None of these

188. The correct matching for the following pairs is
A. All pairs shortest paths
B. Quick Sort
C. Minimum weight spanning tree
D. Connected Components
1. Greedy
2. Detph-First search
3. Dynamic Programming
4. Divide and Conquer
(a) A-2, B-4, C-1, D-3   (b) A-3, B-4, C-1, D-2
(c) A-3, B-4, C-2, D-1   (d) A-4, B-1, C-2, D-3
(e) None of these

189. The space factor when determining the efficiency of algorithm is measured by
(a) Counting the maximum memory needed by the algorithm
(b) Counting the minimum memory needed by the algorithm
(c) Counting the average memory needed by the algorithm
(d) Counting the maximum disk space needed by the algorithm
(e) None of these

190. In which of the following sorting algorithm the number of comparisons needed is the minimum if the items are initially in reverse order and is the maximum if the items are in order?
(a) Straight insertion sort   (b) binary insertion sort
(c) Heap sort   (d) Bubble sort
(e) None of these

191. Which type of network consists set of switches connected by physical links?
(a) Circuit Switched Network
(b) Datagram Network
(c) Virtual Circuit Network
(d) All of these
(e) None of these

192. Bridge work at which layer of OSI Model?
(a) network layer   (b) Data link layer
(c) Physical layer   (d) application layer
(e) Transport layer

193. An accountant office has four employees. They have four computers and two printers. What kind of network would you suggest they install?
(a) Client server network   (b) Peer-to peer network
(c) Intranet   (d) MAN
(e) None of the above

194. In E-R Diagram, total participation in entities is represented by which of the following shape?
(a) Double Rectangle   (b) Eclipse
(c) Diamond   (d) Double line
(e) Double eclipse

195. Which of the following concepts is applicable with respect of 2 NF?
(a) Full functional dependency
(b) Partial dependency
(c) Transitive dependency
(d) None- transitive dependency
(e) None of these

196. By which statement you can force immediate termination of a loop, by passing the conditional expression and any remaining code in the body of the loop.
(a) Break   (b) Continue
(c) Terminate   (d) Loop Close
(e) Return

197. Which of the following phase produce intermediate representations of the source program in compiler design?
(a) Lexical Analyzer
(b) Syntax Analyzer
(c) Semantic Analyzer
(d) Intermediate code generator
(e) Machine Independent code optimizer

198. What is UML (Uniform Modeling Language)?
(a) Designing technique
(b) Testing technique
(c) Maintenance technique
(d) Delivery Technique
(e) Debugging Technique

199. Which of the following is the time interval between the submission and completion of job?
(a) Waiting time   (b) Turnaround time
(c) Throughput   (d) Response time
(e) Seek time

200. Which of the following is the process of taking control over an existing session between a client and a server?
(a) IP spoofing   (b) Replay attack
(c) Session hijacking   (d) WarDriving
(e) Backdoor

HINTS & EXPLANATIONS

1. (c) I. $6x^2 + 25x + 24 = 0$

$$D = \sqrt{b^2 - 4ac}$$
$$D = \sqrt{625 - 4 \times 24 \times 6}$$
$$= \sqrt{49} = 7$$
$$x_1 = \frac{-b+7}{12} = \frac{-25+7}{12} = \frac{-18}{12} = -\frac{3}{2}$$
$$x_2 = \frac{-b-7}{12} = \frac{-25-7}{12} = \frac{-32}{12} = -\frac{8}{3}$$
$$x = \frac{-3}{2}, \frac{-8}{3}$$

II. $12y^2 + 13y + 3 = 0$

$$y_1 = \frac{-13 + \sqrt{169 - 144}}{24}$$
$$= \frac{-13 + 5}{24} = \frac{-8}{24} = \frac{-1}{3}$$
$$y_2 = \frac{-13 - \sqrt{169 - 144}}{24} = \frac{-18}{24} = \frac{-3}{4}$$
$$y = \frac{-1}{3}, \frac{-3}{4} \Rightarrow x < y$$

2. (c) I. $12x^2 - x - 1 = 0$

$$x_1 = \frac{-b + \sqrt{D}}{2a} = \frac{1 + \sqrt{1 - 4 \times 12 \times -1}}{24}$$
$$= \frac{1 + 7}{24} = \frac{8}{24} = \frac{1}{3}$$
$$x_2 = \frac{-b - \sqrt{D}}{2a}$$
$$x_2 = \frac{1 - 7}{24} = \frac{-6}{24} = \frac{-1}{4}$$
$$x = \frac{1}{3}, -\frac{1}{4}$$

II $20y^2 - 41y + 20$

$$y_1 = \frac{41 - \sqrt{1681 - 1600}}{40}$$
$$y_2 = \frac{41 - \sqrt{1681 - 1600}}{40}$$
$$y_1 = \frac{41 + 9}{40} = \frac{50}{40}, y_2 = \frac{32}{40}$$
$$y = \frac{5}{4}, \frac{4}{5} \Rightarrow x < y$$

3. (b) I. $10x^2 + 33x + 27 = 0$

$$x_1 = \frac{-33 + \sqrt{b^2 - 4ac}}{2a} = \frac{-33 + \sqrt{1089 - 4 \times 10 \times 27}}{20}$$
$$x_2 = \frac{-33 - \sqrt{b^2 - 4ac}}{2a}$$
$$x_2 = \frac{-33 - \sqrt{1089 - 1080}}{20}$$

$$x_1 = \frac{-33 + 3}{20}, x_2 = \frac{-33 - 3}{20}$$
$$x_1 = \frac{-30}{20}, x_2 = \frac{-36}{20} = \frac{-9}{5}, x = \frac{-3}{2}, \frac{-9}{5}$$

II. $5y^2 + 19y + 18 = 0$

$$y_1 = \frac{-19 - \sqrt{361 - 4 \times 18 \times 5}}{10}$$
$$y_2 = \frac{-19 - \sqrt{361 - 360}}{10}$$
$$y_1 = \frac{-19 + 1}{10}$$
$$y_2 = \frac{-19 - 1}{10} = \frac{-18}{10} = \frac{-9}{5} = \frac{-20}{10} = -2$$
$$y = \frac{-9}{5}, -2 \Rightarrow x \geq y$$

4. (d) I. $15x^2 - 29x - 14 = 0$

$$x_1 = \frac{29 + \sqrt{841 + 60 \times 14}}{30}$$
$$= \frac{29 + 41}{30} = \frac{70}{30}$$
$$x_2 = \frac{29 - \sqrt{1681}}{30}$$
$$x_2 = \frac{29 - 41}{30} = \frac{-12}{30}$$
$$x = \frac{7}{3}, \frac{-2}{5}$$

II. $6y^2 - 5y - 25 = 0$

$$y_1 = \frac{5 + \sqrt{25 - 4 \times 6 \times -25}}{12} = \frac{5 + \sqrt{625}}{12} = \frac{30}{12}$$
$$y_2 = \frac{5 - \sqrt{25 - 4 \times 6 \times -25}}{12} \Rightarrow y_2 = \frac{5 - \sqrt{625}}{12} = \frac{-20}{12}$$
$$y = \frac{5}{2}, \frac{-5}{3}$$

So, relationship between x and y can't be determined.

5. (b) I. $3x^2 - 22x + 7 = 0$
$$3x^2 - 21x - x + 7 = 0$$
$$x(3x - 1) - 7(3x - 1) = 0$$
$$(3x - 1)(x - 7) = 0$$
$$x = \frac{1}{3}, 7$$

II. $y^2 - 20y + 91 = 0$
$$y^2 - 13y - 7y + 91 = 0$$
$$y(y - 7) - 13(y - 7) = 0$$
$$(y - 13)(y - 7) = 0$$
$$y = 13, 7 \Rightarrow y \geq x$$

6. (a)   Let the 4 members are x_1, x_2, x_3, daughter
Sum of 4 members five years ago
$= x_1 + x_2 + x_3 +$ daughter $= 94$
After 5 years,
$x_1 + x_2 + x_3 +$ daughter $= 114$ ...(1)

daughter + daughter in law = 92
Daughter = 92 – daughter in law
Put this eqn. ...(1)
$x_1 + x_2 + x_3 + 92$ – Daughter in law = 114
$x_1 + x_2 + x_3 = 22$ + Daughter in law
So, the required difference is 22 years.

7. (a)

A	B	C
28000 × 12	20000 × 8 +	18000 × 6 +
28 × 12	18000 × 2 196	16000 × 2 140
12	7	5

Ratio : 12 : 7 : 5

Sol. (8 -12):

	Monday	Tuesday	Wednesday	Thursday	Friday
Tata	180	150	250	150	180
Renault	160	220	200	180	140
Maruti	200	200	300	250	200
	540	570	750	580	520

8. (b) Required ratio $= \dfrac{540}{750} = 18 : 25$

9. (a) Total number of cars produced by Renault from monday to Friday = 900

10. (e) Required average $= \dfrac{1150}{5} = 230$

11. (c) No. of cars produced on Tuesday and Thursday is same i.e. 150.

12. (c) Maximum number of cars produced = 750, on Wednesday.

13. (d) Let the principal be ₹ P and rate of interest be R% per annum.
Differecne of C.I. and S.I. for 3 years

$$= \left[P \times \left(1 + \frac{R}{100}\right)^3 - P \right] - \left(\frac{P \times R \times 3}{100} \right) = \frac{PR^2}{10^4}\left(\frac{300 + R}{100} \right).$$

Difference of C.I. and S.I. for 2 years $= P\left(\dfrac{R}{100} \right)^2$

$$\therefore \quad \frac{\dfrac{PR^2}{10^4}\left(\dfrac{300 + R}{100} \right)}{\dfrac{PR^2}{10^4}} = \frac{25}{8} \Rightarrow \left(\frac{300 + R}{100} \right) = \frac{25}{8}$$

$$\Rightarrow R = \frac{100}{8} = 12\frac{1}{2}\%.$$

14. (b) For quantity I →
Since S is an acute angle means < 90°
∴ (a + 40) + a < 90
(2a + 40) < 90
2a < 50
a < 25°
For quantity II → 25°
∴ Quantity I < Quantity II

15. (a) For Quantity I →
Let required no. = 10x + y
∴ 10y + x = 10x + y + 36
9y – 9x = 36
y – x = 4
∴ unit digit of the no. should be 4 more than the ten's digit of the number.

∴ such possible numbers from 1 to 63 are
= 04, 15, 26, 37, 48, 59

∴ Required probability $= \dfrac{6}{63}$

For quantity II →
Possible numbers from 1 to 63 = 8, 24, 40, 56

Required probability $= \dfrac{4}{63}$

∴ Quantity I > Quantity II

16. (b) From A → m + n = 10 × k (let k is an integer value)
From B → 10m + 7n = 70 × 1 (Let ℓ is an integer value)
From C → n > m
From A and B

$$\begin{aligned} 10m + 10n &= 100k \\ 10m + 7n &= 70\ell \\ \hline 10n - 7n &= 100k - 70\ell \\ 3n &= 100k - 70\ell \end{aligned}$$

3n = 10(10k–71) : Hence n is divisible by 10. Thus option A and B together are needed to solve the question.

17. (a) Area of quadrilateral BFDE = Area of rectangle ABCD – Area of ∆ABE – Area of ∆DCF
= 120 – 30 – 25 = 65

18. (a) Ratio of Investment of A, B and C
(3000 × 4 + 1800 × 5 + 3600 × 3)
: (4000 × 4 + 8000 × 5)
: (14000 + 33600)
31800 : 56000 : 47600
159 : 280 : 238

Profit of C $= \dfrac{238}{677} \times 6770000 = 238000$

Average of profit earned by (A + B + C) ≈ 225666

19. (c) Volume of metal to be casted = (22/7) × [(5)² – (4)²] × 21
So (22/7) × 3² × h = (22/7) × [(5)² – (4)²] × 21
Solve, h = 21

20. (b) Let C. P. = 100
∴ M.P. = 140

And S.P. $= \dfrac{100 - x}{100} \times 140$

Also, S.P. $= \dfrac{112}{100} \times 100 = 112$

$\therefore \quad \dfrac{100 - x}{100} \times 140 = 112 \quad \Rightarrow \quad x = 20$

Now, C.P. = 120, Profit = x% i.e. 20%

$\therefore$ S.P. $= \dfrac{120}{100} \times 120 = ₹144$

21. (d) No. of vowels in the word THERAPY
= 2 i.e. E and A
In such cases we treat the group of two vowels as one entity or one letter because they are supposed to always come together. Thus, the problem reduces to arranging 6 letters i.e. T, H, R, P, Y and $\boxed{EA}$ in 6 vacant places.
No. of ways 6 letters can be arranged in 6 places = 6!
= 6 × 5 × 4 × 3 × 2 × 1 = 720
But the vowels can be arranged themselves in 2

different ways by interchanging their position. Hence, each of the above 720 arrangements can be written in 2 ways.

∴ Required no. of total arrangements when two vowels are together = $720 \times 2 = 1440$

Total no. of arrangements of THERAPY = 7!

$= 7 \times 6 \times 5 \times 4 \times 3 \times 2 \times 1 = 5040$

No. of arrangement when vowels do not come together $= 5040 - 1440 = 3600$

22. (c) Distance travelled by train from Surat to Nadiad Jn.
$= 440 - 257 = 183$ kms

23. (b) Time taken to reach Ahmedabad
$= 8 : 00\,Am - 6 : 43\,Am = 1$ hour 17 min.

24. (a) Ratio between No. of passengers boarding from Vasai Road and from Ahmedabad
$= 378 : 306 = 21 : 17$

25. (b) Total time increase $= 23 - 2 = 21$ min.
∴ Train will reach Bhuj at $= 5{:}40PM + 21$ min $= 6{:}01$ PM

26. (d) Distance between Anand Jn. to Vadodara is second lowest.

27. (a) Let the required time be T hours. Now part filled by A in $(10 + T)$ hours + part filled by B in $(10 + T)$ hours + part empty by C in 10 hours = 1

$$\Rightarrow \frac{T+10}{15} + \frac{T+10}{20} - \frac{10}{25} = 1 \Rightarrow T = 2 \text{hrs}$$

28. (d) Let us suppose Women give 10 units a day
Therefore, a man gives $1.4 \times 10 = 14$ units a day
Similarly, a child gives $0.6 \times 10 = 6$ units a day
Total job (units) = (7 days × per day contribution)
$= 7 \times (3 \times 14 + 5 \times 10 + 4 \times 6) = 812$ units
New combination $= 2\,M + 7\,W + 3\,C$
Contribution per day $= 2 \times 14 + 7 \times 10 + 3 \times 6 = 116$ units
Days required to complete the job = 812/116 = 7 days

29. (a) Post graduate engineers employed in company W = 200

$$\therefore \quad \text{Required percentage} = \frac{200}{600} \times 100$$

$$= \frac{100}{3} = 33\frac{1}{3}\%$$

30. (b) Average number of junior engineers

$$= \frac{100 + 100 + 150 + 250 + 250}{5} = \frac{850}{5} = 170$$

31. (c) Average number of assistant engineers

$$= \frac{150 + 300 + 200 + 150 + 100}{5} = \frac{900}{5} = 180$$

Required difference $= 180 - 170 = 10$

32. (d) In all companies:
Assistant engineers $= 150 + 300 + 200 + 150 + 100 = 900$

$$\text{Number after 37\% increase} = \frac{900 \times 137}{100} = 1233$$

Postgraduate engineers $= 100 + 250 + 400 + 550 + 400 = 1700$

$$\text{Number after 20\% decrease} = \frac{1700 \times 80}{100} = 1360$$

∴ Required percentage

$$= \frac{1360 - 1233}{1360} \times 100 = \frac{127}{1360} \times 100 = 9.3$$

33. (b) Increase in the number of engineers:

$$\text{Company V} \Rightarrow \frac{400 \times 130}{100} = 520$$

$$\text{Company X} \Rightarrow \frac{700 \times 135}{100} = 945$$

$$\text{Company Y} \Rightarrow \frac{950 \times 140}{100} = 1330$$

Total engineers $= 520 + 945 + 1330 + 650 + 750$
$= 4195$
Total original number of engineers $= 400 + 650 + 700 + 950 + 750 = 3450$
Percentage increase

$$= \frac{4195 - 3450}{3450} \times 100 = 21.59\%$$

$$\simeq 22\%$$

34. (d) No. of ways of getting 2 white balls $= {}^{13}C_2$
No. of ways of getting 2 black balls $= {}^{7}C_2$
Probability of getting 2 same colour ball

$$= \frac{\text{Probability of 2 white balls or Probability of 2 Black balls}}{\text{Total number of balls drawn}}$$

$$\Rightarrow \frac{{}^{13}C_2 + {}^{7}C_2}{{}^{20}C_2} \Rightarrow \frac{\dfrac{13!}{2! \times 11!} + \dfrac{7!}{2! \times 5!}}{\dfrac{20!}{18! \times 2!}}$$

$$\Rightarrow \frac{\dfrac{13 \times 12 \times 11!}{2! \times 11!} + \dfrac{7 \times 6 \times 5!}{2! \times 5!}}{\dfrac{20 \times 19 \times 18!}{18! \times 2!}} = \frac{13 \times 12 + 7 \times 6}{20 \times 19}$$

$$\Rightarrow \frac{198}{380} = \frac{99}{190}$$

35. (b) Time taken by P to reach city B is 6hr. In 6 hr, distance covered by Q is 30km. Now at some x distance they will meet. So

$$\frac{x}{5} = \frac{(30 - x)}{10} ; X = 10.$$

So distance between A and Y is $30 + 10 = 40$ km

36. (d) Let Rakesh's salary be '100x'
Salary spent in PPF = 12x
Remaining Salary = 88x
So, Salary spent on clothes = 3/8 of 88x = 33x
As per the question,
$33x - 12x = 10500$
$21x = 10500$
i.e. $x = 500$
So, Rakesh's Salary = ₹50000
Amount spent on Remaining expenses = 50000
$- ((12 \times 500) + (33 \times 500))$
$= 50000 - (6000 + 16500) = 50000 - 22500 = 27500.$
Now, let House rent be 'a'
Other expenses $= a + 1500$
ATQ
$a + (a + 1500) = 27500$
$2a = 26000$
$a = ₹ 13000$

37. (c) Cost of gear box $= 20 \times \dfrac{1,00,000}{100} \times \dfrac{15}{100} = 3000$

38. (c) Cost of brake $= \dfrac{20 \times 1,00,000}{100} \times \dfrac{30}{100} = 6000$

$$\therefore \text{ Required percentage} = \frac{6000}{1,00,000} \times 100 = 6.0\%$$

39. (a) Price of tyres $= \dfrac{20 \times 1,00,000}{100} \times \dfrac{15}{100} = 3000$

Increased price of tyres $= 3000 \times \dfrac{125}{100} = 3750$

$\therefore$ Price should be increased $= 3750 - 3000 = ₹750$

40. (b) Increased transmission cost $= 20,000 \times \dfrac{120}{100} = 24000$

$\therefore$ increase in transmission cost $= 24000 - 20000 = ₹4000$
Here, this increase will reduce the profit by 4000.

41. (a) Option (a) would weaken the argument put forward by the committee to the sports ministry.
42. (e) Option (e) would strengthen the argument.
43. (c) Option (c) would strengthen the argument of government.
44. (d) This option says that aggressiveness is a common way for both.
45. (a) Cultivation taught us the moral duties regarding the children and relatives.

Sol. (46-50) : After careful analysis of the given input and various steps of rearrangement it is evident that in each step one word and one number are rearranged.

The word are rearranged from left in alphabetical order and the numbers are rearranged from the right in descending order but in the final step the word get rearranged in alphabetical order in reserves manner and number appear in descending order.

Input : 31 rise gem 15 92 47 aim big 25 does 56 not 85 63 with moon
Step I : aim 31 rise gem 15 47 big 25 does 56 not 85 63 with moon 92
Step II : big aim 31 rise gem 15 47 25 does 56 not 63 with moon 92 85
Step III : does big aim 31 rise gem 15 47 25 56 not with moon 92 85 63
Step IV : gem does big aim 31 rise 15 47 25 not with moon 92 85 63 56
Step V : moon gem does big aim 31 rise 15 25 not with 92 85 63 56 47
Step VI : not moon gem does big aim rise 15 25 with 92 85 63 56 47 31
Step VII : rise not moon gem does big aim 15 with 92 85 63 56 47 31 25
Step VIII : with rise not moon gem does big aim 92 85 63 56 47 31 25 15

46. (a) 47. (d) 48. (b) 49. (c) 50. (c)

Sol. (51-55):

Friend	Specialisation	Sport
Arun	Electrical	Football
Sathish	Hardware	Tennis
Yogesh	Metallurgy	Swimming
Ganesh	Telecommunication	Badminton
Peter	Software	Hockey
Hemanth	Mechanical	Cricket

51. (c) Hardware
52. (a) Football
53. (c) Yogesh-Metallurgy
54. (e) None of these
55. (b) Cricket-Tennis
56. (c) **From Statement I :**

shine was peeled off $\Rightarrow$ & # @ 9

no paint but shine $\Rightarrow$ 7 5 # 8
The code for shine is #
From Statement II :

try the new shine $\Rightarrow$ 13 # 0

we try the new $\Rightarrow$ 6 0 1 3
The code for shine is #

57. (c)
58. (c) From statement I

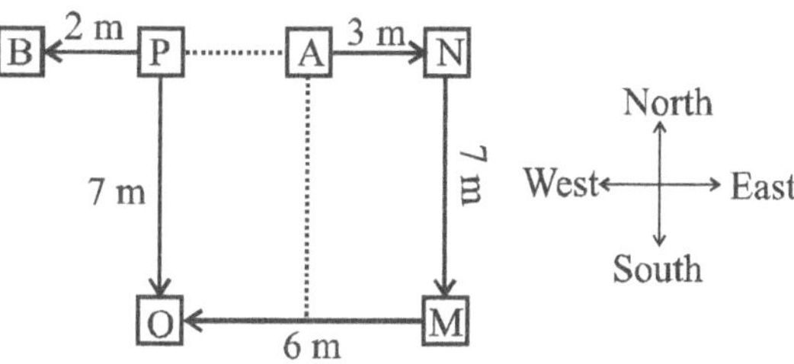

It is clear from the diagram that Point A is to the east of Point B.
From statement II
From the information given in statement II, we get the same diagram given above.

59. (b) From statement I
Five to nine students scored more than that of B. The rank of D is 8th from the top.
From statement II
Rank of C from the beginning
$= 25 - 16 + 1 = 10$th

7th $\longleftarrow$ 10th
B ☐ ☐ E

Thus, six students scored more than that of B.

60. (e)

Sol. (61-65) :

0	M	R	Q	K	P	L	N	S	J
1	2	3	4	5	6	7	8	9	10
Struck	String	Guitar	Drum	Struck	String	Piano	Drum	Trumpet	Flute

61. (b) 62. (c) 63. (d) 64. (e) 65. (e)

Sol. (66-69) :
Eight persons sitting arrangements areas as follows.

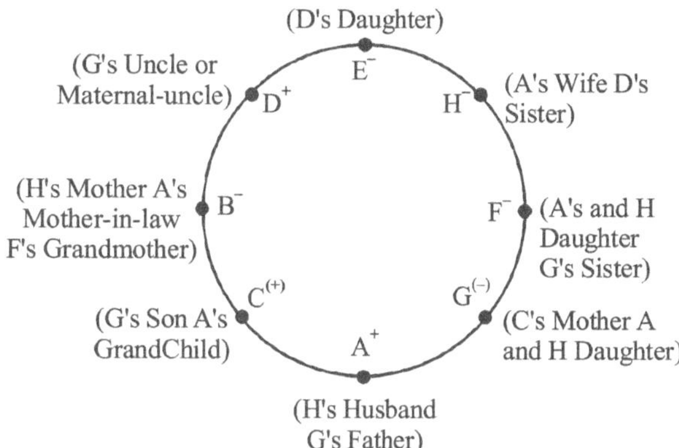

66. (d) A's mother-in-law is B and A is second to the right of B.
67. (a) A's grandchild is C and A is immediate right of C.
68. (c) Except C all others are women.
69. (e) B is the mother of H which is true with respect to the given sitting arrangement.

70. (e)
71. (b) Points O is 7 metres towards North of Point N.
72. (a)

Sol. (73-74) :
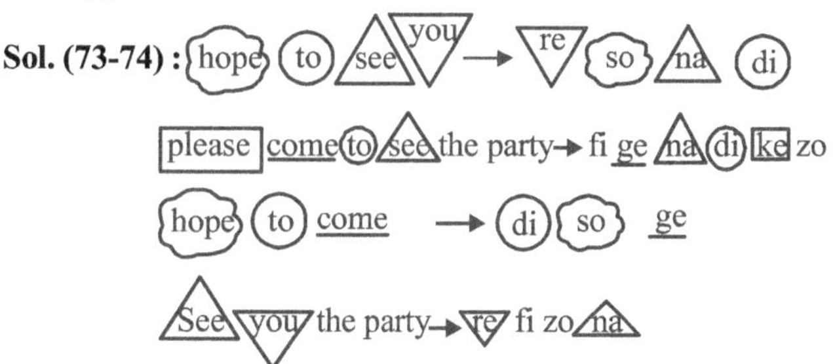

Codes are :

hope ⇒   so   please ⇒ ke
to ⇒   di   come ⇒ ge
see ⇒   na   the ⇒ fi or zo
you ⇒   re   party ⇒ fi or zo

73. (c) party ⇒ fi/zo
74. (e) so ⇒ hope; di ⇒ to: re ⇒ you
75. (e) Follow the given movements,

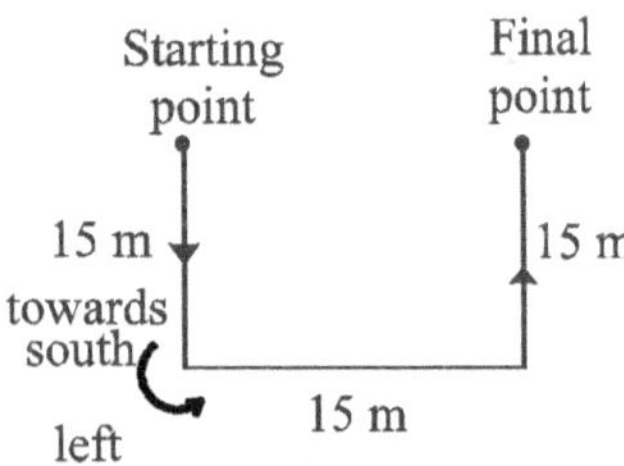

Hence, he is 15 m to the East from the starting point.

76. (a) 77. (b)
78. (a) The very purpose of hiking the procurement price of a crop is encouraging the farmers to cultivate it.
79. (e) All 4 are possible effects because heavy rainfall after cyclonic storm is obvious and next 3 statements are the natural after affects of cyclonic storm.
80. (d) From given fact it can be inferred that the government generally provides protection to travellers accross the country.

81.	(b)	82.	(d)	83.	(b)	84.	(b)	85.	(a)
86.	(b)	87.	(a)	88.	(a)	89.	(a)	90.	(a)
91.	(d)	92.	(a)	93	(b)	94.	(b)	95.	(c)
96.	(a)	97.	(a)	98.	(c)	99.	(b)	100.	(b)
101.	(b)	102.	(c)	103.	(b)	104.	(d)	105.	(a)
106.	(d)	107.	(a)	108.	(a)	109.	(c)	110.	(e)
111.	(d)	112.	(b)	113.	(d)	114.	(e)	115.	(b)
116.	(c)	117.	(c)	118.	(b)	119.	(b)	120.	(d)

ENGLISH LANGUAGE

121. (c)
122. (c) It is mentioned in the last few lines of the third paragraph nad the first few lines of the fourth paragraph.
123. (a) It can be inferred from the entire passage.
124. (b) It is mentioned in the third paragrpah how the lenghty procedures make it difficult for the needy farmers to avail loans. Nowhere in the passage is it mentioned that the government has relieved the farmers of the loans.
125. (d) It is mentioned in the last paragraph.
126. (d) 127. (e)
128. (a) It is mentioned in the last line of the fifth paragraph
129. (c) It is mentioned in the second paragraph
130. (d)
131. (b) Preposition 'of' should be followed by noun object; 'environmental' is an adjective. 'environment' and forests.
132. (d) Here, the clause 'To portray what ..... refer is the singular subject. Hence, singular verb 'is' should be used instead of 'are'.
133. (b) Change 'block' to 'blocks'
134. (b) Use 'is' in place of 'are' as the noun 'collection' is singular.
135. (c) Use 'them' in place of 'it' as 'the books' are plural.
136. (d) Change 'of all animals' to 'than any other animal'
     Alternatively,
     (c) Change 'is faster' to 'is **the fastest**'.
137. (d) Change 'has gone' to 'went'.
138. (b) Change 'its' to 'their'.
139. (e) 140. (b) 141. (a) 142. (d) 143. (c)
144. (b) 145. (e)

146. (b) Q is the opening sentence, it defines the status quo, followed by S, because S illustrates about customised tailoring outfit, a subject mentioned in Q 'custom made clothing'. Thus will be followed by P, since P explains further customised tailoring industry.
147. (d) Q is the opening sentence as it introduces the subject of evaluation followed by S, which is linked with Q because, it gives conditions attached with the subject of Q.
148. (c) R is the opening sentence as it has the subject. There may be a confusion between P and R, but the subject of P- participation, is an object in R, Thus R will be the just sentence, followed Q and then P, as Q and P explain the objects of R.
149. (b) P is the opening sentence, followed by R because the 'this' in R refers to the idea stated in the opening sentence and works as a link between them. This will be followed by Q, because the pronoun subject 'it' refers to Ford Motor company.
150. (d) Q is the opening sentence, it introduces the subject. This will be followed by P which has a link with Q-Chewing gum, then will be S which has a link with P-Finish.
151. (d) 'were ordered to trace'- it is obvious that the police stations were ordered to trace the identity as the body mentioned in the statement is a dead body which is taken into custody.
152. (a) 'can be implemented'- as the schemes can only be implemented.
153. (e) 'are engaged in an unclean'- the form mentioned in the given sentence simply reflects that it has asked about whether the parents are involved in that unclean occupation
154. (b) 'understand the purpose behind it'- as there is a 'form' mentioned in the context of the statement through which some sort of information has been sought, so, the school, in return, could not understand the purpose behind it of doing so.
155. (a) 'is being able to understand what is being taught'- as the focus is not on the quality of the education but on the quantity of what is being taught.
156. (a) 157. (c) 158. (b) 159. (d) 160. (e)

HINDI LANGUAGE

121.	(b)	122.	(b)	123.	(b)	124.	(b)	125.	(c)
126.	(c)	127.	(b)	128.	(b)	129.	(d)	130.	(d)
131.	(d)	132.	(d)	133.	(e)	134.	(c)	135.	(e)

136. (a) 'आजीवन–भर' के स्थान पर केवल 'आजीवन' का प्रयोग होगा।
137. (d) खण्ड (d) का प्रयोग खण्ड (a) को पूरा करने के लिए दायित्व के साथ होना चाहिए।
138. (d) खण्ड (d) का प्रयोग खण्ड (a) को पूरा करने के लिए जनसंख्या में के साथ होना चाहिए।
139. (c) मनोनुकूल पर्याप्त है। अपने शब्द का प्रयोग अनावश्यक है।
140. (b) 'दहेज प्रथा ने' का प्रयोग, खण्ड (c) के बाद होना चाहिए। वाक्य इस प्रकार होगा – समाज सुधारकों के प्रयत्नों के बावजूद 'दहेज प्रथा ने अत्यन्त विकट रूप धारण कर लिया है'

141.	(d)	142.	(b)	143.	(b)	144.	(b)	145.	(b)
146.	(b)	147.	(a)	148.	(a)	149.	(a)	150.	(c)
151.	(a)	152.	(c)	153.	(b)	154.	(e)	155.	(d)
156.	(b)	157.	(d)	158.	(c)	159.	(d)	160.	(e)
161.	(b)	162.	(d)	163.	(c)	164.	(b)	165.	(b)
166.	(a)	167.	(a)	168.	(b)	169.	(b)	170.	(c)
171.	(b)	172.	(e)	173.	(d)	174.	(c)	175.	(a)
176.	(a)	177.	(b)	178.	(a)	179.	(b)	180.	(c)
181.	(c)	182.	(c)	183.	(c)	184.	(b)	185.	(a)
186.	(b)	187.	(d)	188.	(b)	189.	(a)	190.	(b)
191.	(a)	192.	(b)	193.	(b)	194.	(d)	195.	(a)
196.	(a)	197.	(d)	198.	(a)	199.	(b)	200.	(c)